FORTRESSES
OF THE
BIG TRIANGLE FIRST

FORTRESSES
OF THE
BIG TRIANGLE FIRST

A HISTORY OF THE AIRCRAFT ASSIGNED TO THE

FIRST BOMBARDMENT WING AND FIRST BOMBARDMENT DIVISION

OF THE

EIGHTH AIR FORCE

FROM

AUGUST 1942 to 31st MARCH 1944

CLIFF T BISHOP

AIRCRAFT CRASH RESEARCH BY STANLEY D BISHOP

PUBLISHED BY

EAST ANGLIA
BOOKS

Copyright © Cliff Bishop

First impression 1986

First published in the United Kingdom in 1986 by
East Anglia Books
Station Road, Elsenham,
Bishops Stortford, England

ISBN 1 869987 00 4

Typeset by D P Media Ltd,
Hitchin, Hertfordshire

Printed in the United Kingdom by
Biddles Limited, Guildford, Surrey

Selected Bibliography

Airfields of the Eighth–Then and Now: After the Battle
Air Force Combat Units of World War Two: Maurer Maurer
Army Air Forces in World War Two: Craven and Cate
Aviation in Northamptonshire: Michael L Gibson
Combat Squadrons of the Air Force in World War Two: Maurer Maurer
First Over Germany: Russell A Strong
Mighty Eighth: Roger Freeman
Mighty Eighth War Diary: Roger Freeman
Target Berlin: Jeffrey Ethell and Alfred Price
The 351st Bomb Group: Peter Harris and Ken Harbour
The Eighth Air Force Yearbook: Lt Col John C H Woolnough

Research Sources

Air Force Inspection and Safety Center Norton Air Force Base, CA
The Albert F Simpson Historical Research Center Maxwell Air Force Base, AL
Defense Audiovisual Agency Washington, DC
Imperial War Museum, London
National Air and Space Museum, Smithsonian Institution, Washington DC
National Archives, Washington DC
Public Record Office, London
Royal Air Force Museum, Hendon

CONTENTS

ACKNOWLEDGEMENTS

This book has over 2000 entries covering the histories of aircraft which served in sixteen United States Army Air Force Units. Such a wide and detailed record could never have been acquired without the help so gladly given by many individuals who have devoted their efforts over many years to researching the histories of the units that made up the Eighth Air Force. In particular, many of the photographs used to illustrate this book, have been contributed by these individuals.

It is impossible to name all who assisted but I would like to give thanks to: Paul Andrews, Mike Bailey, Bernard Bains, Brian Collins, Alan Dann, G Darnell, Dick Dennison, Stuart Evans, Steve Gotts, Edmund Hicks, Ed Huntzinger, Roger Freeman, Joost Klootwyk, Vic Maslen, Michael Gibson, Ron McKay, Ian McLachlan, Barry Railton, Gordon and Connie Richards, Ben Smith, Russell Strong, the late Doug Vincent, Geoff Ward, John Ward and the Boeing and Douglas Airplane Companies.

My brother Stanley contributed by making his extensive knowledge of Eighth Air Force aircraft accidents available and in researching the names of crews of crashed and missing aircraft.

Special thanks are due to the staff at the Albert F Simpson Historical Research Center, Maxwell, for all the help given so generously during the week I spent there in 1984. To the staff of the Air Force Inspection and Safety Center at Norton, the National Air and Space Museum and the National Archives in Washington and the Royal Air Force Museum at Hendon.

Even after the task of collecting the material together had been accomplished, there was the equally daunting prospect of putting it together into a book. With no previous experience to draw on, I had to rely heavily on others with more expert knowledge to bring this to a conclusion. First thanks in this are due to those who assisted with the typing of the draft; Shirley Crouchman, Susan Stringer, Catherine Smith and my daughter Marilyn. My sons also helped; Kevan undertook the copying of the photographs and Adrian assisted with the indexing. A special thanks must go to Alan Melton and the staff of D P Media who have so ably done the typesetting and who have made many helpful suggestions to improve my own mediocre attempts at page layouts.

Finally, thanks are due to all those who supported the idea of this book over the years. Their constant enquiries to ask when it would be finished has probably been the biggest incentive to keep going, when at times it seemed that the task was impossible and could never be complete. Now that it is finished I must thank you all and ask for forbearance with me in any omissions and inadequacies in my efforts.

Cliff Bishop
Elsenham
Bishops Stortford
England

Six Fortresses, safely back over their base, peel off to land in a stormy evening sky. During the period covered by this book, '831 did not come back', official records list them as 'Missing in Action'. At the end of an operational day, they were dropped from their holding unit's records and soon replaced with a new serial number. Over 200 more B-17s were destroyed in accidents or salvaged after returning to England. *US Air Force*

INTRODUCTION

The idea for this book had its beginnings almost before the colourfully painted Fortresses had departed from Suffolk in 1945. How is it that this project has taken so long to come to fruition? and why is it that an idea born amid the 'Big Square' Fourth Wing/Third Bombardment Division county of Suffolk, the most Easterly area occupied by the 'Mighty Eighth', has resulted in a book about the 'Big Triangle' Fortresses that graced the airfields much farther inland?

It was many years before time and the release of official records allowed detailed research to be undertaken. In the intervening period there had been a considerable output of books dealing with the Eighth Air Force and with so many historians concentrating on the Eighth and its aircraft it seemed that those other Fortresses operated in lesser numbers in more far-off fields were being neglected and so the idea was born that a full chronological history of all B-17s built would afford a more challenging project.

To start with, a full list of B-17 serial numbers was compiled; there were 12 731 of them produced between the Model 299 of 1935 and B-17G-110-VE 44-85841 in May 1945. This production record, for such a large aircraft, was exceeded only by the B-24 Liberator.

Next a study of where they served and a big surprise resulted. B-17s had served on every major war front between 1941 and 1945 and they had served in a variety of roles since the end of hostilities. It was a record that few types of aircraft could equal. This presented problems and also highlighted the enormity of the task which had been embarked on. A full history of each aircraft in chronological order would entail a study of the records covering every theatre in which the American Air Force participated plus some Royal Air Force and other operations. It soon became obvious that such a project would be impossible within practical time and cost scales.

Over a period it became apparent that a new approach would have to be taken and the idea of concentrating on those aircraft which served in a particular theatre emerged as being the only practical solution. Once a decision had been made that this was the way to go, then it did not take much thought to decide that the B-17s of the Eighth Air Force would have to be first choice. They had after all been the original reason for undertaking the project and the information acquired over the years had leaned heavily in favour of the aircraft operated by this Air Force.

Once the decision had been made to concentrate solely on the B-17s operated by the Eighth Air Force and serious work had started it very soon became obvious that even this was too big a task to tackle all at once and it had to be narrowed to more manageable proportions. It was then decided to concentrate on one Bombardment Wing/Division only. Since chronologically the First Wing fitted in better and previous research had resulted in more information on this unit's aircraft being available, it was

the natural choice, and this is how an idea born over forty years ago when watching the Third Division's aircraft over Suffolk has now emerged as a book dealing with the aircraft operated by the First Bombardment Wing/Division. One more major change was made, when it was decided to narrow down the time scale covered, and to stop at 31st March 1944.

As far as can be ascertained this book lists every aircraft assigned to the Groups in the First Wing or First Division up to 31st March 1944. If there are any omissions then they will be in the early months of the First Wing's existence in England, a period for which records are not very complete.

During the period covered by this book 1938 B-17s are recorded as being assigned into the First Wing or Division. Of these, 678 were still assigned on 31st March 1944. Of the 1260 aircraft recorded as leaving the units, 831 had been lost 'Missing in Action' and a further 219 had been destroyed or salvaged due to crashes, accidents or battle damage. This represents a total loss of 1050 aircraft or about 8¼ per cent of all the B-17s built.

Just how much of the total history of the B-17 this volume represents is difficult to ascertain. Perhaps it covers a quarter of the aircraft that served in the Eighth Air Force. Even for the aircraft listed here the full story has not been told. Every plane that served in the Eighth Air Force in England had already aged by a few weeks at the time it was assigned to a Bomb Group. Each aircraft had been to a Depot or Modification centre in the USA and had then flown across the Atlantic and been to a Depot in England before joining a tactical unit. At the end of their operational life with the Eighth Air Force, some of the aircraft listed had gone on to serve in the Twelfth and Fifteenth Air Forces, others were returned to the USA where they served in a variety of roles. Some of those retired from the First Wing or Division had been assigned to other duties within the Eighth Air Force. Even those that failed to return from their last operational flights and were posted as 'Missing in Action', have a history beyond that detailed in this book; where and how were they lost, how were the remains disposed of and what happened to their gallant crews?

It is hoped that this volume can be followed by a second which will continue the story up to the end of the European conflict in May 1945. Fortunately, records for the period March 1944 to May 1945 are more comprehensive and much of the ground work has already been done. However, there remains much detail work to be covered before such a final volume can appear in print. This will also depend on the reception accorded this present volume.

Any information, suggestions, photographs etc, which would assist in compiling this second book would be welcomed by the publishers.

Cliff Bishop

One of the Third Bombardment Division airfields visited by the author in 1944 was Framlingham, Suffolk, the most easterly of all the Eighth Air Force B-17 bases. Being near the coast, Framlingham was a favourite haven for returning First Division B-17s, short of fuel, damaged, or with wounded on board. Sometimes, as on 30th July 1943, these force landings ended in tragedy. Photograph shows B-17s of the resident 390th Bomb Group displaying the Square 'J', preparing to take off. *US Air Force*

NOTES

Aircraft Names: The names of aircraft, where known, are given in the serial listings in Part Three with an alphabetical listing in the appendices at the back of the book. As a general rule, only named aircraft with known serial numbers are included.

Dates Gained: The date an aircraft was assigned to a unit as given in this book, is the date the aircraft was added to the unit's inventory and first appeared on the unit's statistical returns. Note that these are not necessarily the dates on which the aircraft arrived on the unit's home station. In the interests of brevity, the word 'assigned' has been dropped from the dates assigned in the serial listings in Part Three; eg 'Assigned to 306BG' will read 'To 306BG'.

Dates Lost: Aircraft were removed from unit inventories for four major reasons: (1) Missing in Action, (2) Destroyed or damaged beyond economical repair in an accident or in combat, (3) Transferred permanently out to another unit or organisation, (4) Temporarily dropped while undergoing major overhaul, repair or on temporary duty with another unit or organisation.

(1) Aircraft 'Missing in Action' were nearly always struck off the inventory on the day they were lost. Occasionally mistakes were made or some doubt existed as to the aircraft's fate, where these occur and are known, they are noted in the serial listings in Part Three.

(2) Aircraft destroyed or badly damaged in accidents, were normally struck off on the same day or the day following the accident. Aircraft involved in more minor incidents where surveys were needed to establish if repair or salvage was to be the aircraft's fate, were frequently retained on the holding unit's inventory for some time after the incident. Surveys were normally carried out by Air Depot personnel and if the aircraft was not on the holding unit's home station then it would be carried as assigned but not on hand during this period. Where an aircraft was salvaged and its date of being removed from its holding unit's inventory was different to the date of the incident causing the salvage, then in the listings in Part Two and Part Three the date of the incident is given, followed by the struck off date in brackets.

(3) Transfers out to other units or organisations could be for a variety of reasons. The major reasons affecting such transfers of the aircraft listed in this book were: 'The Tokyo tank' installation, the introduction of 'Natural Metal Finish' (Silver) aircraft and the policy of returning older aircraft to the United States for training duties. These are covered in detail in other sections of this book.

(4) Aircraft were temporarily dropped from unit inventories when it was estimated that they would be out of service for some time. Although one document quotes fifteen days as being the maximum time that an aircraft should be away from its holding unit and still be retained as assigned, there does not in practice appear to have been any hard and fast rules governing this. Some aircraft were dropped from assignment after a few days while others were held for much longer periods. Aircraft loaned to other units were not always dropped from assignment. Frequently they were classified as being on 'Detached Service' (DS) and were carried as assigned but not on hand.

Group and Squadron Markings: These have been covered in an abundance of publications and are not repeated here. The reader wishing to acquire more information on this is recommended to Roger Freeman's 'Mighty Eighth' series.

Order of Serial Numbers: All tabulated listings of B-17 serial numbers in this book are in the numerical sequence shown in the serial number block table on page 12.

Pilots' Names: The names of pilots in command of aircraft that were Missing in Action or involved in accidents is given in the serial number listings in Part Three. An alphabetical listing is included in the appendices.

Reporting of Aircraft: The Eighth Air Force had a system of three letter codes for security in reporting aircraft statistics. These do not appear to have been widely used in unit reports. The only unit noted to have used them during research for this book, being the 379th Bomb Group. The usual method was to report the aircraft as B-17E, B-17F, B-17G etc.

Salvaged Aircraft: There were two classes of salvage. Operational and Non operational (see Explanation of Terminology, page 9). All operational accidents not directly attributable to enemy action and all non operational accidents were reported on War Department A.A.F. Form 14. No Form 14 was raised when an aircraft was salvaged due to direct enemy action. In Part One, maps are included showing all salvaged aircraft each month. Operational salvage being denoted by ● and non operational salvage by ▲. Where details of the cause of salvage are not known then 'Unknown' is quoted.

This photograph breaks the general rule followed in this book that only aircraft with known serial numbers and histories are included. Nothing is known about '**MARYLAND MY MARYLAND**. It is believed to have belonged to the 306th Bomb Group. *Imperial War Museum*

EXPLANATION OF TERMINOLOGY

Accepted   Out of assembly aircraft for which property responsibility has been assumed by the Air Force.

Activate   To bring a constituted unit into physical existence by assigning personnel.

Assignment   The allotment of an aircraft by serial number to a legally authorised recipient for the use of that recipient in the accomplishment of his mission.

BOLERO   Code for Build up of American Forces in the United Kingdom.

Constitute   To designate a unit and place it on the inactive list. This makes it available for activation.

Delivered   Accepted aircraft which have been signed for by an authorised representative or for a designated recipient.

Dropped   Used in loss and gain reports to indicate the removal of an aircraft from a reporting unit's inventory. See 'PICKED UP'.

FIS   Code for YB-40. Used in transmission of Eighth Air Force reports.

Gained   The addition by assignment of an aircraft to a reporting unit's inventory.

GEM   Code for B-17E. Used in transmission of Eighth Air Force reports.

GUP   Code for B-17G. Used in transmission of Eighth Air Force reports.

Lost   The removal of an aircraft from the inventory of a reporting unit, for any reason.

Missing in action   An aircraft failing to return to friendly territory after taking off on an operational flight.

Non operational flight   All flights not classed as operational.

Non operational loss   An aircraft lost while on a non operational flight or salvaged as a result of damage incurred while on a non operational flight.

Not on hand   An aircraft assigned to a reporting unit which is not on the unit's home station.

On hand   An aircraft on the home station of a reporting unit. Can be assigned to the reporting unit or to another unit.

Operational aircraft   An aircraft which is capable of performing a tactical mission.

Operational flight   A flight in which the crew have been briefed to take part in an operational mission. The flight lasts from the time the crew enter the aircraft until they vacate it at the end of the mission.

Operational loss   An aircraft lost while on an operational flight or salvaged as a result of damage incurred while on an operational flight.

Original aircraft   An operational aircraft, assigned to a unit to bring that unit's inventory up to authorised level at the time the unit finishes training and is placed on operational status.

Out of assembly   An assembled aircraft, identified by a serial number, which has not yet been inspected.

Picked up   Used in Loss and Gain reports to add an aircraft to a reporting unit's inventory. Note: 'PICKED UP' and 'DROPPED' were often used to correct errors or to retrospectively update overlooked changes to an inventory; they were also used to make changes of status within the inventory: e.g. an operational aircraft could be 'DROPPED' to War Weary status. The terms used for normal day to day changes as they occurred were 'LOST' and 'GAINED'.

PRO   Code for B-17F. Used in transmission of Eighth Air Force reports.

Replacement aircraft   An operational aircraft assigned to a unit to replace an aircraft which had been lost.

Salvage   The disposal of aircraft which have been damaged beyond economical repair.

Scrap   Complete loss, nothing salvaged except sale of residue as junk.

Slow time   A test flight after repair or replacement of an engine. Normally of one hour's duration, the first 50 minutes being at reduced power on the new or repaired engine.

SOXO   Shipping designator for cargo to be received in the United Kingdom zone One. Comprising that area north of a line drawn through London and Banbury, excluding Northern Ireland. Instituted 1943 and was the most commonly used shipping designator for Eighth Air Force B-17 deliveries.

Status   The state of an aircraft such as Assigned, Operational, Storage etc.

Tokyo tanks   Fuel cells in the outer wings of a B-17. Derived from similar tanks installed in the wings of the Mitchells used in the Doolittle Tokyo raid.

TORCH   Code for plan for Allied landings in North and Northwest Africa November 1942.

Transition flight   A class of non operational flight.

UGLY   Shipping designator for cargo to be received anywhere in United Kingdom regardless of Zone. Instituted 1943 and sometimes used for Eighth Air Force B-17 deliveries.

War weary   Aircraft in a combat area which are unfit to perform a tactical mission, but which can be restored to full operational or training status by the expenditure of a limited number of man hours.

WILDFLOWER   Code for Great Britain. Used for B-17 deliveries in 1942.

Wrecked   An aircraft damaged beyond economical repair.

'DINAH MITE' 42-30704. A veteran of six months. One of eleven B-17Fs still operational with the 305th Bomb Group on 31st March 1944. *Mike Gibson*

ABBREVIATIONS

AAC	Army Air Corps
AAD	Advanced Air Depot
AAF	Army Air Force
AAFFSCC	Army Air Force Foreign Service Concentration Command
Act	Aircraft
Acc	Accident
AF	Air Force
Afd	Airfield
AFSC	Air Force Service Command
Ant Sub Gp	Anti Submarine Group
Arr	Arrive/Arrived
ASR	Air Sea Rescue
Ass	Assigned
ATC	Air Transport Command
BAD	Base Air Depot
BAT	Blind Approach Training
BD	Bombardment Division
BG	Bomb Group
Brig	Brigadier
BS	Bomb Squadron
BW	Bombardment Wing
BW 1	Bluie West 1, Narsarssuak, Greenland
BW 8	Bluie West 8, Sondre Stromfjord, Greenland
Bwd	Burtonwood
Capt	Captain
CCRC	Combat Crew Replacement Centre
Col	Colonel
Coll	Collision
Com Cnd	Composite Command
Cr	Crashed
CW	Combat Wing
Dam	Damaged
Del	Delivered
Dep	Departed
Desp	Despatched
Dest	Destroyed
DS	Detached Service
ETO	European Theatre of Operations
FG	Fighter Group
FO	Flight Officer
FRN	Further Research Needed
GB	Glide Bomb
Gen	General
Gp	Group
HSL	High Speed Launch
Hq	Headquarters
IFF	Identification Friend or Foe
Inj	Injured
Int	Interned
IP	Initial Point
KIA	Killed in Action
Kld	Killed
Ld	Landed/landing
LG	Landing Gear
LH	Left Hand
L Ldg	Langford Lodge
Lt	Lieutenant
Lt Stn	Little Staughton
Main	Maintenance
Maj	Major
MIA	Missing in Action
Miss	Mission
Mod	Modification
Mrk	Marrakesh
MRU	Mobile Repair Unit
MTO	Mediterranean Theatre of Operations
MU	Maintenance Unit
NMF	Natural Metal Finish
Nth Fy Rt	Northern Ferry Route
On Hd	On Hand
Op	Operational
Orig	Original
PBCW	Provisional Bombardment Combat Wing
PFC	Private First Class
POW	Prisoner of War
Pwk	Prestwick
RAF	Royal Air Force
Rec	Received
Rep	Repair
Repd	Repaired

RN	Royal Navy
Rpt	Replacement
Ret	Return(ed)
RH	Right Hand
Rwy	Runway
SAD	Strategic Air Depot
Sal	Salvage
SBA	Standard Beam Approach
Ser	Serial
Sgt	Sergeant
Sqdn	Squadron
Sqdn Ldr	Squadron Leader
Sta	Station
SS	Staff Sergeant
Sth Fy Rt	Southern Ferry Route
Sub	Submarine
Sur	Survived
Tgt	Target
Tgt Op	Target of Opportunity
TO	Take off
Trans	Transferred
TRE	The Radar Establishment
T Sgt	Technical Sergeant
TT	Target Tug
UK	United Kingdom
USAAF	United States Army Air Force
VHF	Very High Frequency
WW	War Weary

B-17 Crew Positions

B	Bombardier
BTG	Ball Turret Gunner
CP	Co Pilot
LWG	Left Waist Gunner
N	Navigator
P	Pilot
TG	Tail Gunner
RO	Radio Operator
RWG	Right Waist Gunner
TTG	Top Turret Gunner
WG	Waist Gunner
X	Passenger

'GOIN DOG' takes off for Berlin 6th March 1944. *Mike Gibson*

FURTHER RESEARCH NEEDED

The research for this book has been deep and extended. Even so there are many areas where for various reasons it has not been possible to follow up every line of research to an ultimate conclusion. This has led in many cases to items where only part of the story can be told and where further research is needed to complete the narrative.

It is hoped that some of those reading this book will have first hand experience of the events described and will be able to add information which will fill some of the omissions, or that there will be others who will be encouraged to undertake further research into some of the unknown areas.

Following is listed some of the items where the author would appreciate hearing from any persons having information. This list is by no means conclusive.

1. Confirmation of the serial number of the 92BG B-17E MIA on 6th September 1942. Was it 41-9026?
2. Did Lt William J Crumm and crew fly B-17E 41-9112 back to the USA in February 1943?
3. The 2nd and 99th BGs were scheduled to join the Eighth Air Force in early 1943. Advanced elements of the 2nd arrived in the UK and the 99th was briefed to fly to England from North Africa but was re-directed to join the Twelfth Air Force almost on the day it was due to fly to England. In spite of this there is no record of airfields being assigned or of any other preparations to receive these two Groups in England. The Eighth Air Force's 91st and 303rd BGs were assigned to the Twelfth Air Force in early 1943 but continued to operate with the Eighth Air Force. Details of these assignments would be welcome.
4. How did YB-40 42-5732 leave Stornoway after crash landing in May 1943 and what happened to it after it left?
5. Confirmation that 306th BG's 42-3127 was being flown by a 94th BG crew when it went MIA on 21st May 1943. No missing aircrew report can be found for this aircraft.
6. B-17F 42-29944 of 303BG went on a secret mission 16th to 23rd August 1943. What was this mission?

7. B-17F 42-30018 of 305BG landed at St Just on 16th September 1943. How was this accomplished on a non operational airfield rendered unusable by obstacles and how did the aircraft leave?
8. B-17G 42-31052 was assigned to the 303BG from October 1943 to March 1944. It does not appear to have flown on any operations after November 1943, any information on this aircraft or its fate?
9. Did B-17F 42-29705 of 379BG land at Foulsham on return from the mission of 26th November 1943 and was it salvaged after this mission? Any other information on its fate?
10. Was B-17G 42-37828 of 384BG salvaged as a result of damage following an accident with a truck on 29th November 1943, or was it repaired and then suffered another accident resulting in its salvage on 3rd January 1944?
11. 303BG's 'HELLS ANGELS' was assigned to the RAF in January 1944 but the assignment was cancelled, any information concerning this assignment and its cancellation.
12. Why was 306BG's B-17G 42-31715 at Drem on 3rd February 1944 and how did an RAF and Royal Naval person come to be on board when it crashed on the 4th February?
13. Some of the Pathfinder aircraft assigned to the 305th and 482nd BGs were natural metal finished and were painted olive drab after arrival in England. Where and when was this done?
14. The 303BG had a B-24D 42-40748 on loan/assigned in February/March 1944. Was this aircraft on hand at Molesworth and for what purpose was it used?
15. Information regarding the structural changes needed to install the Tokyo tanks in the B-17F and how were these introduced on the production lines?
16. Any information regarding the salvage of the following B-17s: 41-24475 of 306BG on 5th December 1942, 41-24461 of 306BG on 27th February 1943, 41-24482 of 91st BG on 27th February 1943, 42-29819 of 305th BG on 18th May 1943, 42-29793 of 91st BG on 5th October 1943, 42-37757 of 303BG on 13th December 1943, 42-37928 of 92nd BG on 6th January 1944 and 42-39797 of 381st BG on 4th February 1944.

Two long serving B-17Fs that were still assigned on 31st March 1944.

Above: 42-5264 'YANKEE DOODLE DANDY' which had joined the 303rd Bomb Group in February 1943. It was retired from the Group on 3rd April 1944 and returned to the USA. *Mike Bailey*

Below: 42-29815 'MIAMI CLIPPER' was assigned to the 306th Bomb Group on 20th April 1943 and transferred to the 91st Bomb Group on 14th September 1943. It would be one of three veteran B-17Fs leaving the 91st on 6th April 1944 to be returned to the USA. *Mike Bailey*

B-17 SERIAL NUMBERS

Listed below are the serial number blocks of all B-17Es, B-17Fs and B-17Gs produced up to approximately 31st March 1944.

MODEL	SERIAL NUMBERS	TOTAL NUMBER IN BLOCK	APPROX DATES OF DELIVERY	NUMBER SERVING IN FIRST BW/BD UP TO 31 MARCH 1944
B-17E-BO	41-2393 to 41-2417	277	1941 to March 42	4
B-17E-BO	41-9011 to 41-9245	235	March 42 to May 42	37
B-17F-**-BO	41-24340 to 41-24639	300	30 May 42 to 31 August 42	207
B-17F-**-DL	42-2964 to 42-3482	519	9 June 42 to 3 July 43	152
B-17G-**-DL	42-3483 to 42-3563	81	5 July 43 to 10 August 43	41
B-17F-**-BO	42-5050 to 42-5484	435	31 August 42 to 11 December 42	77
B-17F-**-VE	42-5705 to 42-5731	27	17 June 42 to 20 October 42	9
YB-40	42-5732 to 42-5744	13	29 October 42 to 18 November 42	12
B-17F-**-VE	42-5745 to 42-6204	460	21 November 42 to 20 August 43	67
B-17F-**-BO	42-29462 to 42-31031	1569	16 December 42 to 2 September 43	456
B-17G-**-BO	42-31032 to 42-32116	1085	4 September 43 to 25 January 44	370
B-17G-**-DL	42-37714 to 42-38213	500	3 August 43 to 17 January 44	203
B-17G-**-VE	42-39758 to 42-40057	300	21 August 43 to 16 November 43	136
B-17G-**-BO	42-97058 to 42-97407	350	24 January 44 to 27 February 44	66
B-17G-**-VE	42-97436 to 42-98035	600	From 16 November 44	87
B-17G-**-BO	42-102379 to 42-102978	600	From 1 March 44	None
B-17G-**-DL	42-106984 to 42-107233	250	From 18 January 44	24

** These are Block Numbers -1, -5, -10, -15 etc denoting changes in equipment or structural alterations. These are not listed in this book as they have been well covered in many previous publications.

These blocks numbers never appeared in tactical unit reports. They were important to the organisations responsible for the maintenance of the aircraft's equipment and for the provisioning of spares.

Many of the aircraft assigned during the winter of 1943/44 became 100-plus missions veterans. One was 42-31333 **'WEE WILLIE'** assigned to the 91st Bomb Group on 20th December 1943. It was to be one of the last of the Group's aircraft to go, 'Missing in Action'. *US Air Force*

LAST THREE DIGITS OF SERIAL NUMBER

Many records only quote the last three digits of the aircraft's serial number. The serious researcher wishing to establish the full serial number, is presented with a number of problems. There could be as many as ten B-17s with the same last three digits in the serial number and a Group could have two of these on assignment at the same time. The serial number block chart on the opposite page has been designed to assist in the conversion of last three serials to full numbers; it works like this.

Suppose the known last three digits of a B-17 serial are 175. By placing the edge of a rule at 175 on the last three numbers scale at top of chart and at right angles to the serial block bars, it can easily be read off that there are nine possible serials with 175 as the last three. They are: B-17E 41-9175, B-17Fs 42-3175, 42-5175, 42-6175, 42-30175 and B-17Gs 42-31175, 42-38175, 42-97175 and 42-107175. By now checking the serial number listings in Part Three it can be ascertained which of these aircraft served in the Wing or Division. These are found to be, B-17E 41-9175, B-17Fs 42-3175, 42-5175 and 42-30175 and B-17G 42-31175. Reference to the serial number listings will also give details of the units the aircraft served in and the dates between which they were assigned. The researcher will normally have other information available and by applying this, it is often possible to establish the full serial number or at least to narrow down the possibilities to two or three aircraft.

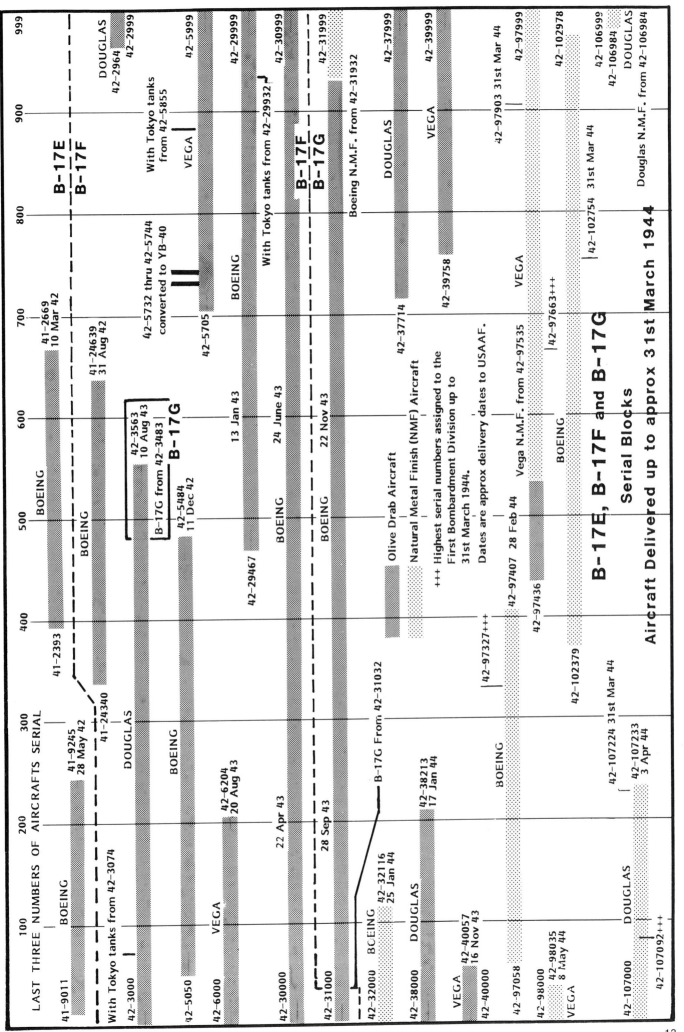

LAST THREE NUMBERS OF AIRCRAFTS SERIAL

B-17E, B-17F and B-17G

Serial Blocks

Aircraft Delivered up to approx 31st March 1944

Olive Drab Aircraft

Natural Metal Finish (NMF) Aircraft

+++ Highest serial numbers assigned to the First Bombardment Division up to 31st March 1944.

Dates are approx delivery dates to USAAF.

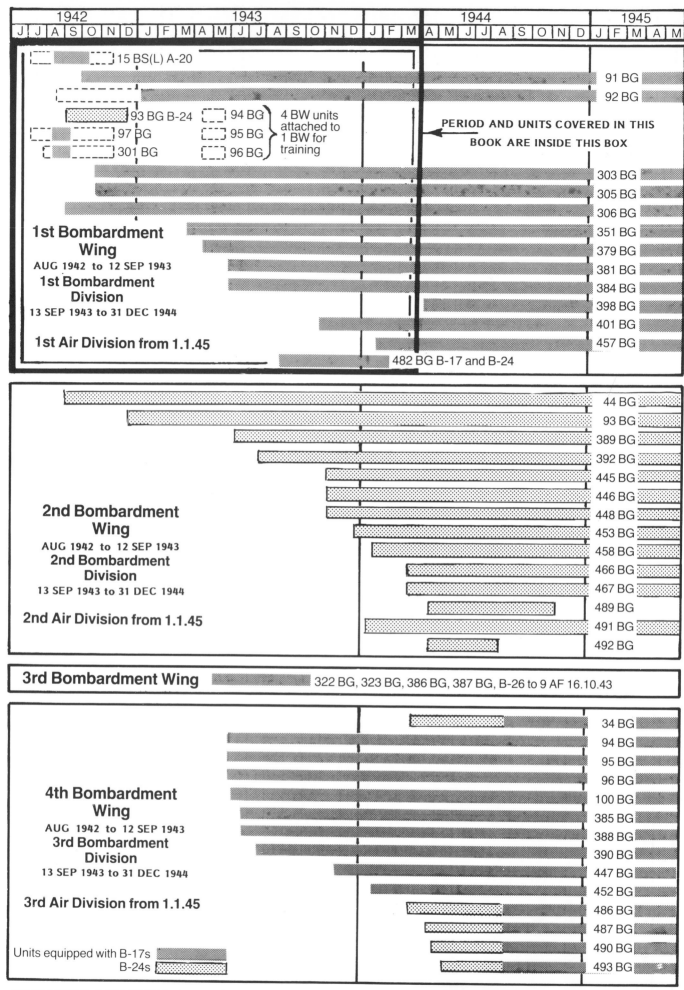

EIGHTH AIR FORCE BOMBARDMENT WINGS/DIVISIONS 1942–1945

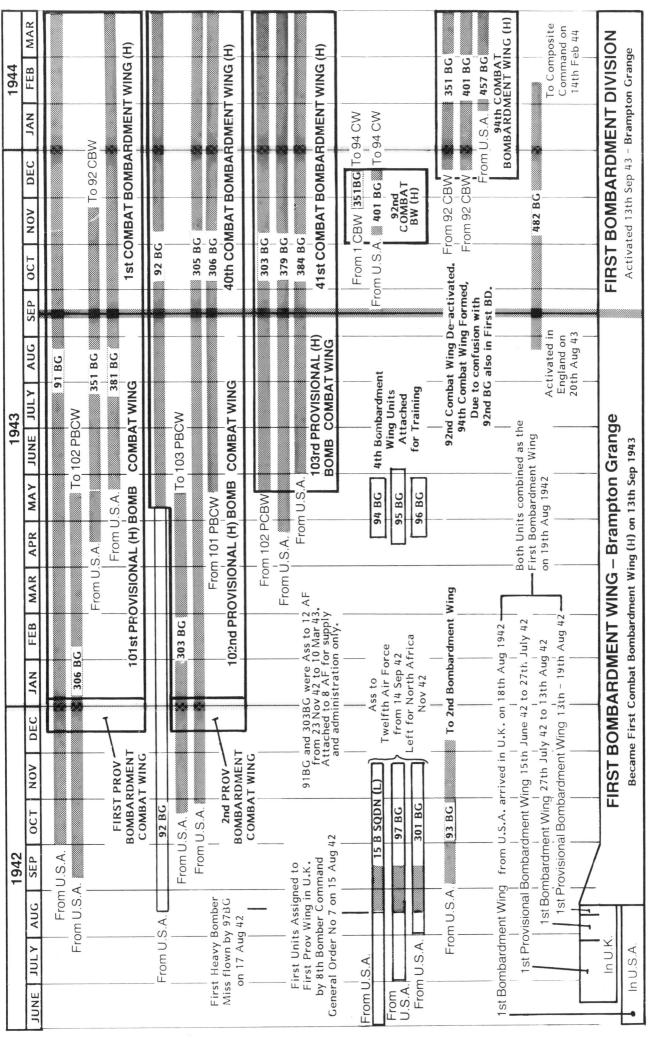

ORGANISATION OF FIRST BOMBARDMENT WING/DIVISION JUNE 1942 – MARCH 1944

15

41-24388. One of the original B-17Fs of the 92nd Bomb Group that was re-assigned to the 97th Bomb Group in England in exchange for the B-17Es. It was damaged on the mission of 6th September 1942 but made it back to England. One of six B-17Fs detailed to carry Allied Commanders for the TORCH operation to Gibraltar on 5th November 1942. Carrying Generals Doolittle and Lemnitzer as passengers, a brake failure when taxiing out at Hurn delayed its departure until 6th November. On the flight it was attacked over the Bay of Biscay by Junkers 88s but arrived safely at Gibraltar where this photograph was taken. The aircraft's life in the Twelfth Air Force was short as in January 1943 it was damaged on the ground by German bombing and salvaged. *Imperial War Museum*

FORTRESSES OF THE BIG TRIANGLE FIRST

PART ONE

THE FIRST BOMBARDMENT WING/DIVISION

HISTORY UP TO 15th August 1942

OPERATIONAL HISTORIES

15th to 31st August 1942

September 1942

October 1942

November 1942

December 1942

January 1943

February 1943

March 1943

April 1943

May 1943

June 1943

July 1943

August 1943

September 1943

October 1943

November 1943

December 1943

January 1944

February 1944

March 1944

FIRST BOMBARDMENT WING
HISTORY TO 15th AUGUST 1942

The First Bombardment Wing had a history dating back to the First World War when it served in France. Between the wars there were numerous changes in designation and role assignment. By the outbreak of the Second World War the Wing had ceased to exist as an active unit. The function of Wings had been taken over by Commands in 1939 and Wings were disbanded; but for some reason of policy or administration, the First Wing did not go out of existence and it still remained on paper with Brig Gen Frank D Lackland in command and a Table of Organisation of one sergeant.

In June 1942, the War Department decided to equip the First Bombardment Wing as an active unit and send its personnel overseas. Brig Gen Lackland had retired on 30th June, due to disabilities and, on 11th July, Maj Woodrow W Dunlop was assigned as Commanding Officer. The Second Air Force was made responsible for bringing the Wing up to strength for shipment overseas.

At this time, it would appear that the existence of a First Bombardment Wing in the USA was unknown to the Eighth Bomber Command in England, as, on 15th June, General Order No 3 brought the First Provisional Bombardment Wing into being with Headquarters at Brampton Grange, Huntingdonshire. First Commanding Officer was Col Claude E Duncan.

This was not the first time a First Provisional Bombardment Wing had been formed within the Eighth Air Force, for on 20th May 1942, Headquarters Eighth Air Force Bolling Field had issued General Order No 5, activating a First Provisional Bomber Wing to be stationed at Grenier Field, New Hampshire, for movement to overseas station, and having assigned to it the 97th Bomb Group and its attached units. It is not known if this order was co-ordinated with the Eighth Air Force, then in England, but First Wing records make no mention of this US organised Provisional Bombardment Wing, the only reference to it being in the records for the BOLERO movement and it is probable that it was a local administrative arrangement to bring the 97th Bomb Group and attached units under one controlling unit for the ferry flight to England.

Meanwhile, the organisation and build-up of the official First Wing in the USA was progressing at Davis Monthan Field, Tucson, Arizona, where the 32nd Base Headquarters and Air Base Squadron, also based at Tucson, provided a few key enlisted personnel in the latter part of June. With the complement being filled by the arrival, on 9th July, of 72 enlisted men, mostly privates from the replacement pool at Salt Lake City, Utah. At the time of their arrival, 1st Lt Francis J Bennett was temporarily in command, pending the arrival of Maj Dunlop. The only other officer attached to the Wing at this time was 2nd Lt Donald S McCure. Additional officers soon drifted in: Maj Dunlop arrived to take command; Maj Manvel H Davis – a First World War flyer; Maj James L Travis – an operations officer; Maj Arthur L Streeter – Base Surgeon at Davis Monthan, and Maj James V Laird were added to the list.

Special Order No 197–Davis Monthan Field, dated 17th July 1942, started the officers and 90 enlisted men constituting the First Bombardment Wing (H) on the four day rail journey to the staging area at Fort Dix, New Jersey. The movement orders, dated 9th July 1942, were forwarded to the First Bombardment Wing Headquarters at Tucson, from the Office of the Commanding Officer, Fort Dix, New Jersey, designating the shipment under the Code No 5164K. The journey from Davis Monthan was started on the evening of Friday, 17th July, and they arrived at Fort Dix just after midnight on the 22nd July 1942.

The days at Fort Dix were busy with all the necessary preparations for a troop movement overseas and the procurement of last minute supplies. Indoctrination lectures on security and their duties as American soldiers abroad and here, for the first time in many cases, the men took a gun into their hands. The complement of the Wing was filled here with a total strength of 29 officers and 90 enlisted men.

The staff were organised at Fort Dix. Maj Travis was made executive and other staff positions were assigned as follows: Maj Gay was made S–1, Capt George Cronin was made S–2, Maj Edwin R Debrill was made S–3, and Capt Edward S Dodge was made S–4. Three days later, Maj Travis replaced Maj Debrill as S–3, retaining his duties as executive, while Maj Manvil Davis succeeded Capt Cronin as S–2.

On the evening of the 4th August 1942, the Wing left Fort Dix for embarkation at Staten Island, New York. The journey was made by ferry from the railroad terminus on the New Jersey side of the Hudson River. At Staten Island, they boarded the former luxury liner, *Uruquay*. Also boarding the *Uruquay* was the ground echelon of the 301st Bombardment Group (H), which had come from Richmond, Virginia. Also sailing with the ten ship convoy was the USS *West Point* on which the ground echelon of the 92nd Bombardment Group (H), which had travelled from Sarasota in Florida, was embarked. These two units were also being shipped under the code No 5164, along with many other units destined for England.

The *Uruquay*, owned and operated by the United States Maritime Commission. It was this converted former luxury liner that brought the First Wing across the Atlantic in August 1942. Also embarked was the ground echelon of the 301st Bomb Group. *National Maritime Museum, London*

The first US operated B-17 to be salvaged in the UK was B-17E 41-9024 **'KING CONDOR'** of 97th Bomb Group which overran the runway at Grafton Underwood when landing on 1st August 1942. The crew were not injured but the number four engine struck a British lorry whose driver was killed. *US Air Force*

Early on the morning of the 6th August the convoy left the harbour, picked up an escort of a battleship, a heavy cruiser and 19 destroyers, and moved slowly up the Atlantic coast. The following morning, the convoy was assembled in the harbour off Halifax, Nova Scotia, where Canadian ships were added. From Halifax, the convoy moved out into the Atlantic, and, after an uneventful crossing, the *Uruquay* docked at Swansea, Wales, on the 18th August. By nightfall on the 19th, the First Bomb Wing had joined the First Provisional Bomb Wing at Brampton Park and were spending their first night in England in tents. The First Provisional Bomb Wing was disbanded immediately and the combined units became the First Bombardment Wing.

While the official First Bombardment Wing had been building up strength in the USA and preparing to embark for England, the new First Bombardment Wing, established by Eighth Bomber Command in England, had not been idle. Two changes in designation had taken place. The first on 27th July, by General Order No 5, had changed the designation to First Bombardment Wing and then on 13th August, presumably because the existence of the official First Wing now on its way across the Atlantic had become known, General Order No 3 was issued, reverting the designation back to the First Provisional Bombardment Wing. The Wing had already been given the task of receiving and organising the first heavy bombers assigned to American Air Forces in the European Theatre of Operations. By the end of July, a nucleus staff of officers and enlisted men had been gathered at Brampton Grange, from various units of Eighth Bomber Command, to carry on the work of preparing the 15th Bombardment Squadron (Light) and the 97th Bombardment Group (Heavy) for combat.

On 28th July, an order was published assigning personnel to the positions to which they were most suitable. Additional work involved making arrangements for the reception, housing, messing and transportation of new units (which were scheduled to arrive in the First Bombardment Wing), as well as all the other administrative tasks involved in getting the Wing and subordinate units organised and established.

All of this preliminary work up to 15th August was carried on without any official assignment of units, or airfields, to the First Provisional Bombardment Wing. On 15th August, Eighth Bomber Command General Order No 7 was issued, and this assigned the following units to the Wing.

Units Assigned to the First Provisional Wing by 8th Bomber Command General Order No 7 15th August 1942

Unit	Station
HQ and HQ Squadron 37th Service Group	Molesworth
689th Quartermaster Platoon (LM)	Molesworth
168th Quartermaster Platoon Service Group	Chelveston
689th Quartermaster Platoon (LM)	Brusche Hall
Detachment, 176th Quartermaster Company Service AVN	Molesworth
38th Signal Platoon, Air Base	Brampton Grange
One Platoon, 684th Ordnance Company	Molesworth
33rd Signal Platoon	Molesworth
726th Ordnance Company (AVN)	Molesworth
731st Ordnance Company (AVN)	Thurleigh
50th Service Squadron	Molesworth
303rd Dispensary	Molesworth
304th Dispensary	Polebrook
309th Dispensary	Chelveston
97th Bombardment Group (H)	Polebrook
92nd Bombardment Group (H)	Bovingdon
301st Bombardment Group (H)	Chelveston
15th Bombardment Squadron (L) Separate	Molesworth
HQ and HQ Squadron 1st Provisional Bombardment Wing	Brampton Grange

No airfields were officially assigned to the First Bombardment Wing until September 1942. The task of procuring airfields from which the bombers would operate had been carried out by the Eighth Air Force, in conjunction with the British Air Ministry, during the spring and summer of 1942, and when the first heavy bombers arrived in July the bases from which they would operate and the organisation to service these airfields was established. These airfields were in the East Midlands and had been under construction since 1941. Originally intended for the Royal Air Force Eight Group, they were selected because of their advanced stage of construction. They had been built with a communications network centred on Brampton Grange, hence the choice of this location for the Headquarters of the First Bombardment Wing.

It can be seen that the unified Provisional and First Bombardment Wings faced considerable problems. Both had their own Commanding Officer and their own staffs. It would be assumed that the actual organisation coming in from the US would get preference in appointing staff positions, and the officers who came in with the Wing did expect to retain

HISTORY TO 15th AUGUST 1942

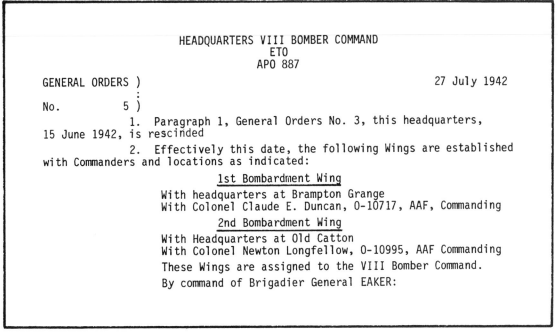

```
                    HEADQUARTERS VIII BOMBER COMMAND
                                   ETO
                                APO 887

   GENERAL ORDERS )                                    27 July 1942
                  :
   No.        5 )
                    1.  Paragraph 1, General Orders No. 3, this headquarters,
   15 June 1942, is rescinded
                    2.  Effectively this date, the following Wings are established
   with Commanders and locations as indicated:
                            1st Bombardment Wing
                    With headquarters at Brampton Grange
                    With Colonel Claude E. Duncan, O-10717, AAF, Commanding
                            2nd Bombardment Wing
                    With Headquarters at Old Catton
                    With Colonel Newton Longfellow, O-10995, AAF Commanding
                    These Wings are assigned to the VIII Bomber Command.
                    By command of Brigadier General EAKER:
```

The order of 27th July 1942 establishing the First Bombardment Wing with headquarters at Brampton Grange. This order had been preceded by order No 3 on 15th June establishing the First Provisional Bombardment Wing and was followed by another order on 13th August re-designating the Wing once more into a provisional unit.

their assigned job. The organisation in England had been working under actual field conditions and had their jobs very well in hand. Therefore, in almost every case, the men holding positions in the Provisional Wing retained their jobs, whilst the new men coming in from the United States were given other positions in the Headquarters.

Of the 19 units assigned by the order of 15th August, only four – the 92nd, 97th and 301st Bomb Groups (H) and the 15th Bomb Squadron (L) – were tactical units which had aircraft assigned and are relevant to this history. It must, however, go to emphasise the often overlooked fact, that behind each operational unit there were many more service units looking after the supply of items: from rivets, nuts and bolts to whole aircraft; the maintenance of these items; the welfare and processing of personnel; and a multitude of other tasks without which the operational units could never have functioned.

The 97th Bomb Group was at this time fully operational with 35 B-17Es and was ready to launch the first US heavy bomber mission against German occupied Europe. Two squadrons, the 340th and 341st, were based at Polebrook, and the 342nd and 414th were at Grafton Underwood.

Since arriving from the USA during July, the Group had been in continual training and during the period up to 15th August had lost three more B-17Es in accidents. The first loss had occurred on 1st August, when 41-9024 of the 414th Bomb Squadron had a brake failure on landing at Grafton Underwood and overshot the runway, hitting a British lorry. The crew escaped injury but the aircraft was damaged beyond repair, and so became the first US operated B-17 to be salvaged in the UK. It was also the first loss of an aircraft the 414th Bomb Squadron had suffered.

The second loss had occurred on 11th August, and this time the crew were not so fortunate, the aircraft, 41-9098, crashed in the mountains at Llanrhawdr, Wales, and all on board were killed.

The third loss came on the 14th when 41-9115 crashed at Elvedon, Suffolk. This brought the losses of B-17Es, since the original 49 were assembled in the USA ready for the ferry flight across the Atlantic, to 11. The losses in the 97th had been made up by some of the aircraft which had been assigned to the weather squadrons. These had been modified to combat standard since arrival in England.

The first B-17Fs of the 301st Bomb Group had arrived in late July, and by 15th August, there were 20 on hand, but none were ready for operations. One, 41-24347, had been lost on 9th August, when it made a wheels up landing at Church Lawford, whilst on a flight from Bovingdon to Chelveston. This was the first loss of a US operated B-17F in the UK.

The first B-17Fs of the 92nd Bomb Group were on their way across the Atlantic and would arrive at Prestwick the day after the order assigning the units to the First Wing was made. Although this Group was one of those assigned to the First Wing, by the order of 15th August, it had already been decided that it would become a training unit on arrival in England and would be stationed at Bovingdon, where it would come under the

control of Eighth Bomber Command. It would be January 1943 before it moved into the First Wing.

The only unit to have seen operational service among those assigned was the 15th BS (Light), then stationed at Molesworth and equipped with DB-7Bs. The squadron had carried out the first Eighth Air Force operation against occupied Europe on 4th July, and had mounted another operation on 12th July.

For these operations, the squadron had used Bostons, borrowed from 226 Squadron RAF, and had then been stood down pending the arrival of its own aircraft.

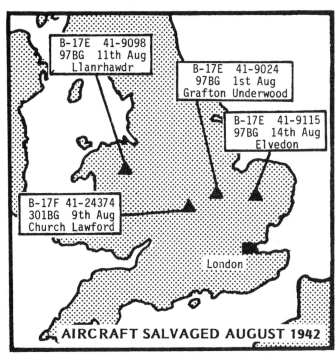

Aircraft salvaged in UK prior to 15th August 1942. Note: These aircraft were lost before their holding units were officially assigned to the First Bombardment Wing. For the purposes of this history however they are included in the First Wing's statistics. At the time of their loss it is evident that no organisation existed for dealing with such losses and these aircraft were carried on hand for some considerable time after being lost.

	Status of Aircraft and Crews at 15th August 1942 when Units First Assigned to First Provisional Bombardment Wing
97BG	35 B-17E – Operational. Of 47 combat crews, 24 were ready for operations
301BG	20 B-17F – None operational
	3 B-17E – Not operational, location and assignment not known
TOTAL	58 B-17s on hand – 35 operational
15BS (L)	17 DB-7Bs on hand – 9 operational – 8 of 9 crews ready for operations

The first US operated B-17F to be salvaged in the UK was 41-24347 **'STORK'** of the 301st Bomb Group which crash landed at RAF Church Lawford on 9th August 1942 after developing engine trouble on a flight from Bovingdon to Chelveston. *US Air Force*

OPERATIONAL HISTORY 15th TO 31st AUGUST 1942

Two days after the official assignment of units to the First Provisional Bombardment Wing, the first heavy bomber mission was carried out against a target in German occupied France. The 12 B-17Es and crews participating in the historic 17th August mission were drawn from the 97th Bomb Group, the only one then operational. The detailed story of this first mission has already been well documented, notably in Roger Freeman's 'Mighty Eighth' series.

By the end of August, 16 Combat Orders had been issued by the Commanding General, Eighth Bomber Command, to the Commanding Officer, First Bombardment Wing, at Brampton Grange. Eight missions had resulted from these Combat Orders. No aircraft were lost to enemy action during these eight missions, but several had been damaged in combat. The first combat fatality occurred on the mission of 21st August, when B-17E 41-9089 was attacked by FW-190s and the co-pilot 2nd Lt Donald A Walter was killed and the pilot 2nd Lt Richard F Starks wounded. The aircraft made it back to Horsham St Faith.

On the 24th, three aircraft were damaged so seriously that they were reported as being out of action for at least 15 days. One of these, 41-9175 of the 340th Bomb Squadron, landed at Manston with five wounded crew and so became the first US operated B-17 to land at this Kent airfield. Many more were to follow during the next 33 months. B-17E 41-2629 was sent to Manston to pick up the uninjured crew members and 9175 was repaired and survived until late 1944.

The remainder of the 301st Bomb Group's B-17Fs came in during the latter half of August, except Lt Sylvester's 41-24348 which had been damaged in Greenland and was delayed until September. The Group continued intensive training during this period, but did not take part in any of the August operations.

The first aircraft belonging to the 92nd Bomb Group arrived at Prestwick on 16th August and flew on to Bovingdon where the Group had already been earmarked as a training unit. Starting on 24th August, the 92nd carried out an exchange of its B-17Fs with the B-17Es assigned to the 97th Bomb Group. Like the 301st Group, the 92nd did not make any contribution to the operations of August.

The 15th Bomb Squadron had not participated in any operations since being assigned to the First Bombardment Wing; the squadron's last operation had been on 12th July using the Bostons borrowed from the RAF and since this date had been re-equipped with more ex-RAF Boston IIIs or DB-7Bs as they were called by their new owners.

On 19th August Col Duncan left the Wing. His place at Brampton as Commanding Officer First Bombardment Wing was taken by Col Newton Longfellow, who was appointed on 21st August.

Three factories on the US West Coast were now engaged in the production of B-17Fs. This was the result of a call made by President Roosevelt in 1941, requesting the Air Corps to initiate a programme to build 500 heavy bombers a month. It had been realised that no individual manufacturer could hope to achieve this level of output singlehanded, and that a joint production effort would be necessary.

Only the B-17 and B-24 Liberator were available and sufficiently developed and both were selected for mass production. For the B-17, Douglas and Lockheed were persuaded to enter the joint endeavour with Boeing and this led in May 1941 to the formation of the joint production organisation known as the BDV committee (Boeing, Douglas and Vega, the three companies that were going to work on the joint B-17 project). Vega was the subsidiary of Lockheed that would undertake that company's share of the programme.

An early Douglas built B-17F being prepared for test flight at Long Beach. Note that this aircraft has no astro dome fitted in the roof of the nose compartment. This was not fitted until the forty-first Aircraft. *Douglas*

AUGUST 1942

A unique contractual relationship existed between the three companies. Although Boeing had designed and developed the B-17, and was required by contract to provide the other two participants with all the necessary drawings and engineering data, these companies did not assume the role of subcontractors to Boeing. Instead, both Douglas and Lockheed held prime contracts from the government calling for the B-17 in production quantities. Boeing was designated the design prime contractor, while the other two were called participating prime contractors.

The first B-17F was delivered from the Boeing factory at Seattle on 30th May 1942, following closely was the first from the Douglas factory at Long

Beach which was delivered on 9th June, and the first from the Vega factory at Burbank, which was delivered on the 17th June. By the end of August, Boeing had delivered some 300 B-17Fs from its Seattle factory, and production at this plant was running at 110 aircraft a month. All the B-17Fs arriving in England with the 92nd and 301st Bomb Groups were Boeing built. The third off the line, 41-24342, was one of those arriving with the 92nd Bomb Group and was to be the earliest built B-17F to serve in the Eighth Air Force. Production at Douglas and Vega was building up slowly but it would be several weeks before aircraft from these two manufacturers would arrive in the European Theatre.

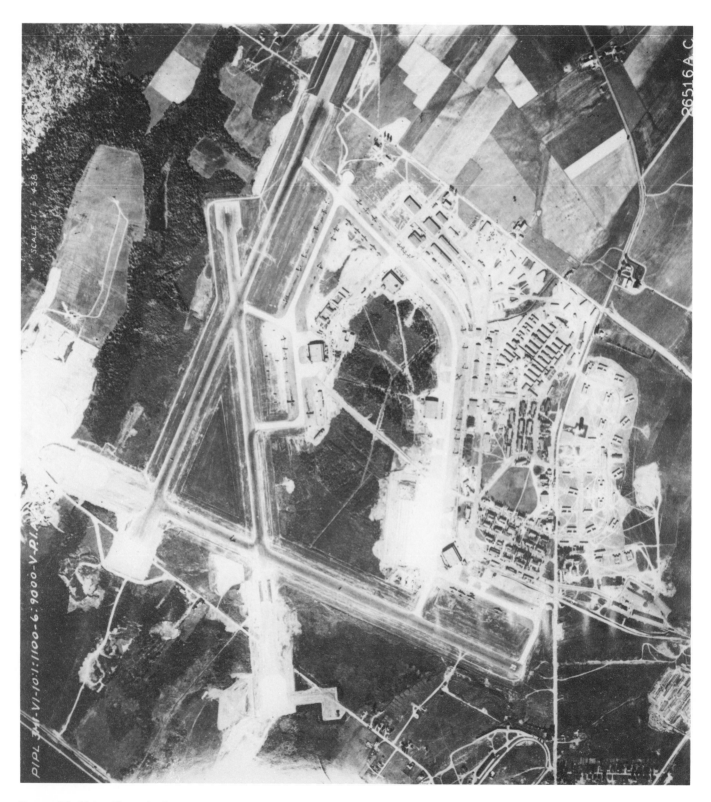

Presque Isle, Maine. The major departure airfield for B-17s leaving the USA for the North Atlantic crossing. Above is the airfield and opposite the control tower and hangar. *US Air Force*

AUGUST 1942

OPERATIONAL DIARY: AUGUST 1942							
COMBAT ORDER No	8AF MISS No	DAY	TARGET	No OF AIRCRAFT			
				DESP	BOMB	LOST	
						MIA	OTHER
2	1	17th	Rouen, Marshalling Yards	12	12	0	0
			Diversion	6	0	0	0
4	2	19th	Abbeville Drucat, Airfield	24	22	0	0
5	3	20th	Amiens, Marshalling Yards	12	11	0	0
6	4	21st	Rotterdam, Shipyards	12	0	0	0
9	5	24th	Le Trait, Shipyards	12	12	0	0
13	6	27th	Rotterdam, Shipyards	9	7	0	0
14	7	28th	Meaulte, Industrial	14	11	0	0
16	8	29th	Courtrai/Wevelgham, Airfield	13	12	0	0
				114	87	0	0

No aircraft were lost in action or to salvage in the period 15th to 31st August 1942

After the rather concentrated operations rate of August, when the 97th Bomb Group flew eight combat operations in the last fifteen days of the month, there was a slowing down in September. Only four missions were flown, three of these on consecutive days early in the month and a final large, but abortive one, on the 26th.

The 92nd and 301st Bomb Groups were making their first contributions to the bombing effort and the number of aircraft despatched rose from 120 in August, to 195 in September, but the recall of the large force despatched on the 26th kept the numbers bombing only just above the August figures. On the 1st of the month there were 101 B-17s on hand of which 42 were available for operations.

On the 2nd September the first airfields were officially assigned to the First Bombardment Wing, with the issue of Eighth Bomber Command General Order No 11 which read as follows:

The following airdromes assigned to Eighth Bomber Command by General Order No 17, Headquarters Eighth Air Force 21st August 1942, are further assigned to the First Bombardment Wing.

Thurleigh	Bedfordshire
Little Staughton	Huntingdonshire
Kimbolton	Huntingdonshire
Podington	Bedfordshire
Chelveston	Northamptonshire
Molesworth	Huntingdonshire
Alconbury	Huntingdonshire
Polebrook	Northamptonshire
Grafton Underwood	Northamptonshire

The Wing Commander is charged with the administration and tactical control of all airdromes and stations under this command. He will designate for each airdrome or station, a Station Commander who will have command of all installations and troops on his station.

The first B-24s to join the Eighth Air Force arrived at Alconbury in early September. Assigned to the 93rd Bomb Group they joined the B-17s already in the First Bombardment Wing and very soon became familiar sights in the skies in the Huntingdon area. Above, one of the 93rd's B-24Ds reposes on one of Alconbury's frying pan hardstands.
Below: 41-23754 'TEGGIE ANN' which would lead the first B-24 mission. Assigned initially to the 409th Bomb Squadron it later transferred to the 329th and remained in England when the 93rd went to North Africa in December 1942. *Mike Bailey*

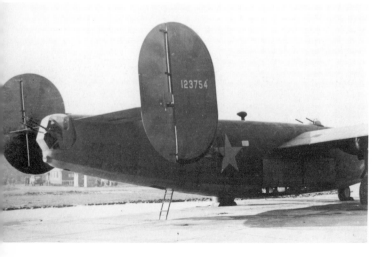

This assignment of airfields to the First Bombardment Wing, would remain unchanged until the spring of 1943, except for Little Staughton, which was transferred to Eighth Air Force Service Command on 18th December 1942, and Bassingbourn, which would be assigned to the First Bombardment Wing on 28th January 1942. It had already been a base for a First Bombardment Wing Group since October 1942.

All these airfields, except Little Staughton, were eventually occupied by First Bombardment Wing units. Originally it was planned to use Little Staughton as a temporary advanced supply and repair depot for the Wing.

A mission was scheduled for the 3rd, and some aircraft were airborne when it was cancelled. One, from 342nd Bomb Squadron, landed at Syerston after the weather had closed in.

On the 5th, the 301st Bomb Group made its first combat mission by contributing five aircraft from the 352nd and seven from the 419th Bomb Squadrons for an attack on the Rouen-Sottville marshalling yards. The 97th despatched 25 aircraft, its largest number to date. Also taking part in the day's operations was the 15th Bomb Squadron, which despatched 12 DB-7Bs, 11 of which attacked the Le Havre port area. This was the first operation for the Squadron since it was assigned to the First Bombardment Wing. There were no losses from the day's operations.

The next day, the 92nd Bomb Group, on its first mission flying the B-17Es acquired from the 97th Bomb Group, contributed 14 to a force of 54 B-17s despatched to bomb airfields and aviation repair facilities in France. A fateful day for the Eighth Air Force, as the first losses of heavy bombers to enemy action were sustained. Two B-17s failed to return; the first, a B-17F from the 97th Bomb Group, and the second, a B-17E from the 92nd Bomb Group. Two others from the 97th Bomb Group, 41-24388 Lt Lee, and 41-24412 Lt Summers, both from 340th Bomb Squadron, were damaged but returned to base. The 15th Bomb Squadron sent 12 DB-7Bs to bomb the airfield at Abbeville-Drucat, all returning safely.

On the 7th, a small force from 97th and 301st Bomb Groups were despatched to Rotterdam shipyards. Only nine aircraft of this force were able to bomb; two of these on a target of opportunity. One of the 340th Bomb Squadron aircraft participating was a B-17E, 41-9074, and this aircraft was severely damaged, with the ball turret gunner killed and two other crew members severely wounded. This aircraft was salvaged on its return to England and so became the first Eighth Air Force B-17 to be salvaged as a result of damage received in combat.

After this mission there was a break in operations. The Eighth Air Force had been allotted the task of organising and equipping the Twelfth Air Force, which was to be prepared for the forthcoming TORCH operation in North Africa. This task had been allotted priority over the Eighth's commitment to strategic daylight bombing and, on the 14th September, the 97th and 301st Bombardment Groups, together with the 15th Bomb Squadron (L), were transferred to the new Twelfth Air Force. So important was the need to keep these units up to strength and fully equipped for this new assignment that orders were issued to the Eighth Bomber Command to cease operations and to concentrate on training and preparations in aid of the forthcoming invasion of North Africa.

These instructions were soon rescinded, and the 97th and 301st Groups were able to continue operating under First Bombardment Wing control until just before their departure for North Africa in November. Even so, it was the 26th before another operation was attempted, and with 75 aircraft airborne it was by far the largest force despatched to date. The 92nd despatched 30 B-17Es on a diversionary sweep; quite a feat considering there were no more than 37 of these remaining in the Eighth Air Force, and the struggle being experienced with obtaining spares and personnel to keep the aircraft on hand in operational condition. At this time the full effects of the efforts to build up and sustain the Twelfth Air Force had not been felt. This must have been the biggest formation of B-17Es ever assembled for one operation in a combat area.

The mission itself did not go well as deteriorating weather forced a recall with no bombs being dropped. The 97th Bomb Group had flown over the Bay of Biscay, and on return some of their aircraft landed at Hurn and Exeter, thus giving many residents of the South and South-West areas their first glimpse of US operated B-17s. In the months ahead these were to become familiar sights in the skies and on the airfields in these areas, as they lay on the route to and from the Atlantic coast of France and the submarine bases thereon which would be the First Wing's priority targets during the remainder of 1942 and early 1943.

On 5th September, the 93rd Bomb Group, equipped with B-24D Liberators, began arriving in England, was assigned to the First Bombardment Wing and moved into Alconbury. These were the first Liberators to join the Eighth Air Force in England. One B-24D and its crew, had been lost over the Atlantic on the flight from the USA.

Three days later, the first B-17F of the 306th Bomb Group arrived at Thurleigh and all were in by the 13th. One plane and crew had been lost over the Atlantic, and another ditched in the Irish Sea but the crew had been rescued. Like the 92nd and 301st Groups, all the aircraft assigned to the 306th were of Boeing manufacture.

SEPTEMBER 1942

The 93rd and 306th Groups did not take part in combat operations during September, but engaged in intensive training flights over the Midlands and eastern England, adding to the growing numbers of RAF and USAAF aircraft to be seen by day and heard at night in skies that had now become the most crowded in the world.

```
AIRCRAFT MISSING IN ACTION:   SEPTEMBER  1942

     6th  B-17E  41-9026*   92BG
     6th  B-17F  41-24445   97BG
     * Serial No not confirmed
```

```
B-17E  41-9074
97BG  7th Sep
Polebrook

London
```

AIRCRAFT SALVAGED: SEPTEMBER 1942

OPERATIONAL DIARY: SEPTEMBER 1942

COMBAT ORDER No	8AF MISS No	DAY	TARGET	No OF AIRCRAFT			
				DESP	BOMB	LOST	
						MIA	OTHER
21	9	5th	Le Havre, Port Area (15th Bomb Squadron)	12	11	0	0
			Rouen-Sotteville, Marshalling Yards	37	31	0	0
22	10	6th	Abbeville/Drucat, Airfield (15th Bomb Squadron)	12	12	0	0
			Meaulte, Industrial Aviation	41	30	2	0
			St Omer/Longuenesse, Airfield	13	11	0	0
			St Omer/Ft Rouge, Airfield	0	2	0	0
23	11	7th	Rotterdam, Shipyard	29	7	0	1
			Utrecht, Target of Opportunity	0	2	0	0
	12	26th	Cherbourg/Maupertuis, Airfield	26	0	0	0
			Morlaix/Poujean, Airfield	19	0	0	0
			Diversionary Sweep	30	0	0	0
				219	106	2	1

Control Tower at Little Staughton. Although B-17s were never despatched on operations from here, the presence of the repair facilities of the Air Depot made it a favourite crash landing field and provided plenty of drama. At least five First Wing B-17s were salvaged here as a result of these crash landings. Photograph taken in 1985. *Kevan Bishop*

Little Staughton: one of nine airfields assigned to the First Bombardment Wing in September 1942. Never used operationally by the Wing, it was transferred to the Eighth Air Force Service Command and housed the Second Strategic Air Depot which performed major maintenance and repair work on First Wing's B-17s. Photograph taken in August 1945, RAF Lancasters and Mosquitos can be seen on dispersals. *Crown Copyright*

OCTOBER 1942

Only three missions this month, but this does not imply there was lack of action. The 97th and 301st Bomb Groups went to Meaulte on the 2nd, the same target that had cost the Eighth Air Force the first losses of B-17s on the 6th September. Both Groups were engaged by the Luftwaffe and although no aircraft were lost in the ensuing air battle, there was some costing to be done after the bombers had returned to England. 41-24416, piloted by Lt Schwarzenbeck of the 342nd Bomb Squadron, was badly damaged and landed at Oakington with three crew wounded. Out for repairs, the aircraft never rejoined the 97th Group and was left in the UK when the Group left for Africa in November. 41-24397, 'PHYLLIS' of the 301st Group, was also badly damaged by FW-190s and was put down on its belly at Gatwick, where the nose was cut off to facilitate the removal of the injured top turret gunner. The aircraft was salvaged.

Flying their third and last mission with the First Bombardment Wing on the 2nd, was the 15th Bomb Squadron which despatched 12 DB-7Bs to bomb a ship in the docks at Le Havre. One aircraft aborted and eleven made a successful attack and returned without loss.

The second mission of the month, that to Lille on the 9th, became the high point of the operations carried out by the First Bombardment Wing during 1942. It would be April, 1943, before a force of equivalent numbers could be despatched again. This mission was also the first for the 306th and 93rd Bomb Groups, the latter flying the B-24s which were making their first operation over Europe and one of which failed to return, being the first Eighth Air Force B-24 lost in action and the only one lost to the First Bombardment Wing/Division up to March 1944.

For the 306th, the first of the four pioneer Groups, it was a hard initiation into combat over German occupied Europe. One of its B-17s failed to return and another, 41-24487, was badly damaged and landed at Manston on return. Subsequently repaired at the Advanced Air Depot at Honington, it would be the end of December before she returned to the Group. By 31st March 1944, this aircraft would be the sole surviving example from the original B-17Fs assigned at Westover, still serving with the Group, albeit in a training role.

The 301st Bomb Group also had reason to remember the Lille mission. The only operational loss suffered by the Group during its operations from England occurred on this day when 41-24362 ditched about a mile from North Foreland. The crew were fortunate in that the ditching had been observed by a passing Spitfire which radioed their position to Air Sea Rescue who then picked up all ten crew within an hour of the ditching. This

in itself made a new record by being the first successful ditching of a US operated B-17 and the rescue of its crew in the European Theatre. Another 301st aircraft, 41-24352, landed at Earls Colne on return, with three wounded crew members.

The fourth B-17 Group taking part in the 9th October Lille operation, was the 92nd, flying the B-17Es. The Group did not escape the ferocious onslaught of the Luftwaffe and one of the B-17Es was lost; the second and last of these to be lost on an operational mission. The Group also made another record on this day, fortunately this one with a happy ending, but many similar occurrences in the months and years ahead would have much more disastrous consequences. This was the first mid-air collision between two B-17s of the Eighth Air Force. With so many aircraft being flown in close formation, and often in marginal weather conditions, it was inevitable that this had to occur before long and on this day, two of the B-17Es collided over the Channel causing major damage to both. 41-9051 made an emergency landing at Detling, where the crew immediately alerted the Air Sea Rescue Services, as they had seen the other aircraft, 41-9021, losing altitude with a large part of its vertical stabiliser missing and thought it had gone down in the Channel. They were later surprised to find it had returned safely to its base. Another 92nd B-17E, 41-2626, was damaged and made an emergency landing at Gatwick where it was salvaged and taken to Burtonwood for use as spares.

The third and last mission of the month was made to Lorient on the 21st. On the previous day the Commanding General European Theatre of Operations had issued a directive making the submarine bases on the French Atlantic coast first priority for attack, and the raid on Lorient was the first as a result of this directive. This was the 15th and last operation flown by the 97th Bomb Group whilst operating from England with the First Bombardment Wing. This Group was used to going it alone, it had done so on its first eight missions and did so on its final one. Heavy cloud over the target made the 301st, 306th and 92nd Bombardment Groups turn back without bombing, but the 97th, using its hard earned experience, pressed on and fifteen aircraft bombed the target. The order had changed and no longer could so small a force expect to challenge the Luftwaffe over so heavily a defended target. For its perseverence, the Group lost three aircraft, a record loss for a single Group up to this date. Two more, 41-24400 and 41-24411, were damaged and subsequently salvaged, and 41-24417 was out of commission for repairs and would be left in England when the Group departed for North Africa in November.

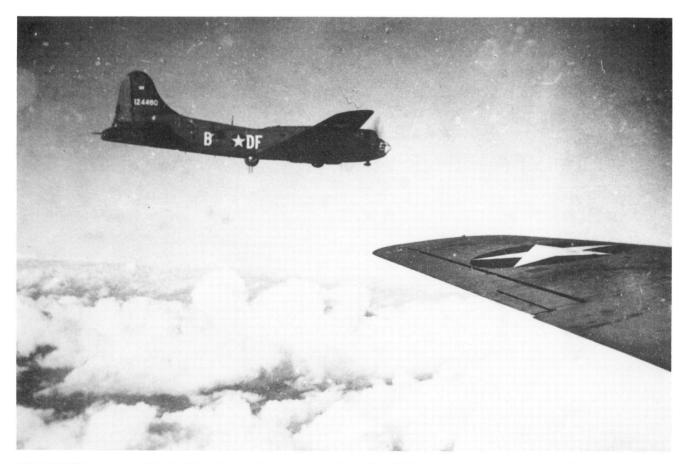

'BAD PENNY', an original of the 91st Bomb Group, displays the curvy lines of the B-17 above a carpet of cumulus clouds. This aircraft was later assigned to the Eighth Air Force Service Command. *US Air Force*

While the amount of operational flying during October was limited to the three completed missions, training flights continued as often as weather conditions allowed and this often proved just as harrowing for the crews and as expensive in planes expended as did the early combat missions. This point was proved by the 306th Bomb Group which lost two planes on training flights during the month. The first was on the 2nd, when 41-24492, on a flight near Spalding, became the first Group aircraft to be lost in England when it broke up in the air after being overstressed in an attempt to dive to a lower altitude following a crew member experiencing oxygen trouble. Six crew lost their lives in this crash.

On the 27th, 41-24508 was on a two plane low level formation flight when it struck some trees causing damage to the nose and controls. The pilot, 1st Lt R J Check, managed to keep the aircraft airborne and made an emergency landing at RAF Graveley, where it was salvaged. Five of the eleven crew and passengers received minor injuries.

A third B-17 lost during training flights was 41-24398 of the 301st Bomb Group which experienced trouble with its landing gear and crash landed at RAF Newmarket on 3rd October. The first Eighth Air Force B-24 lost in a crash in England occurred on the 27th, when the 93rd's 41-23712 crashed at Porlock Bay while on a routine flight. Eleven crew were killed and only one survived.

The month had started with 134 B-17s on hand of which 105 were operational, a number which would not be available for operations again until April 1943.

During October, three new Groups arrived from the USA. The first aircraft of the 91st Bomb Group had arrived at Prestwick on 30th September, and flew down to their base at Kimbolton on 1st October; with most of the Group being in by 7th October. One aircraft was lost in a crash in Northern Ireland at the end of the flight from Gander. The 91st was, like the Groups arriving earlier, equipped with an all Boeing built complement of aircraft.

On the 14th, the 91st Group moved to Bassingbourn. This move placed the Group on a station more accessible than were those occupied by the other Groups. It was also the only Group to occupy a pre-war RAF station with all the comforts afforded by permanent brick-built quarters. Factors contributing in the months to come in making the Group the most well known and publicised Eighth Air Force Bomb Group. Not to be envied however, was the Group's final record in losing more B-17s than any other Group in the US Air Forces.

The official order for the 91st's move from Kimbolton to Bassingbourn was dated 19th October, five days after the move was made. It is well known that Col Stanley Wray, the Group Commander, had moved fast in

---

```
                                                    :By authority    :
                                                    :of CG, VIII BC  :
                    HEADQUARTERS VIII BOMBER COMMAND :Initials        :
                            ETO                      :Date            :
                          APO 634                                  (G)


GENERAL ORDERS )                                    19 October 1942
               :
No.        26 )


        1.   The VOCG on 15 October 1942 as follows
             "The following-named organisations will move on or about
16 October 1942 by rail, air and/or motor transportation to the places in-
dicated for a permanent change of station:

     UNIT                        FROM                     TO
91st Bomb Gp (H)               Kimbolton               Bassingbourn
17th Bomb Gp (M)               Bassingbourne           Kimbolton


        All organisational property and equipment will accompany
these units.


        The provisions of paragraph 18, AR 345-800, 1 July 1942
are to be complied with by these organisations

        QMNT TDN.   FD 33 P99 A 0425-23."


        are hereby confirmed and made a matter of record.


        By command of Major General EAKER;


                                         CHAS. B. B. BUBB,
                                         Colonel, G. S. C.
                                         Chief of Staff.

OFFICIAL:

EDWARD B. TORO,
Major, A. G. D.
Adjutant General.


DISTRIBUTION: "C" plus (5) CG, ETO.
```

The Order for 91st Bomb Group's move from Kimbolton to Bassingbourn

getting the Group into Bassingbourn following an inspection and discovery of its potential comforts by himself and senior Group officers.

The second Group to arrive in October, the 303rd, started coming in to Molesworth on the 21st. Later known as the 'Hells Angels' Group. Some of the B-17s arriving would stay with the Group into 1944, and carried names which would become some of the most famous in the Eighth Air Force – **'HELLS ANGELS'**, **'KNOCK OUT DROPPER'** and **'DUTCHESS'** were among them. Also assigned to the 303rd, were 42-2966 and 42-2967; the third and fourth B-17Fs to come off the Douglas production line at Long Beach and the first from this manufacturer to be assigned to the Eighth Air Force in England.

Finally, the 305th Bomb Group's B-17Fs came into Grafton Underwood. The first touching down at 1116 hours on 27th October. Twenty-six were in by 1700 hours on that date but some were delayed into November by bad weather over the ferry route. One B-17F, had been wrecked in an accident on take off at Gander, and another was landed in the sea off Nova Scotia after fourteen hours in the air. Assigned to the 305th was 42-5713, the ninth B-17F to come off the Vega assembly lines at Burbank and the first from this manufacturer to arrive in the Eighth Air Force in England. It was closely followed by 42-5715, also built by Vega, which left Gander on the 27th, this was a replacement aircraft. Both were assigned to the 97th Bomb Group on their arrival in England.

Also arriving in England, on 1st October, were four B-17Fs, 41-24433, 24434, 24438 and 24440 – belonging to the 15th Mapping Squadron which was assigned to the Twelfth Air Force while in England, but made use of Eighth Air Force facilities.

Even before the 97th had flown its final mission on the 21st October, it had started flying in support of the complicated TORCH operation which would provide it with a new base on another continent. On the 19th, **'RED GREMLIN'** flown by Maj Paul Tibbets and **'BOOMERANG'**, flown by Lt Wayne Connors, left Polebrook for Gibraltar. Masked in secrecy, their arrival on Gibraltar was recorded as 'Two B-17s of USAAF training flight arrived from UK'. The two aircraft were the first USAAF B-17s to be seen on the Rock and carried Gen Mark Clark, Eisenhower's deputy, and other senior allied officers who had arranged a secret meeting with the French Commander in Algiers, Gen Charles Emmanuel Mast. The party left Gibraltar by submarine for a secret rendezvous with the French on the coast, 60 miles west of Algiers, returned to Gibraltar after the meeting was concluded and were flown back to Polebrook in the two B-17s on 24th October.

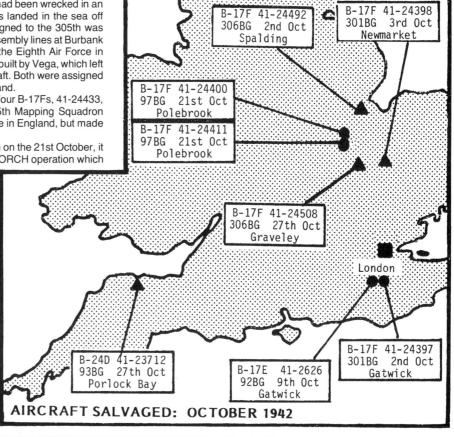

AIRCRAFT SALVAGED: OCTOBER 1942

```
AIRCRAFT MISSING IN ACTION
        OCTOBER  1942

9th   B-17E  41-9018    92BG
      B-17F  41-24362  301BG
      B-17F  41-24510  306BG
      B-24D  41-23678   93BG

21st  B-17F  41-24344   97BG
      B-17F  41-24441   97BG
      B-17F  41-24443   97BG
```

OPERATIONAL DIARY: OCTOBER 1942

COMBAT ORDER No	8AF MISS	DAY	TARGET	No OF AIRCRAFT			
						LOST	
				DESP	BOMB	MIA	OTHER
28	13	2nd	Meaulte, Aircraft Factory	43	30	0	1
			St Omer, Longuenesse Airfield	6	6	0	0
			Armed Raider in Le Havre Docks, (15th Bomb Squadron)	12	11	0	0
			Diversionary Sweep along Coast	13	0	0	0
32	14	9th	Lille	84	59	3	0
			B-24	24	10	1	0
			Courtrai/Wevelghem, Airfield	2	2	0	0
			Roubaix, Target of Opportunity	2	2	0	0
			Diversionary Sweep	7	0	0	0
35	15	21st	Lorient, U-Boat Base	66	15	3	2
			B-24	24	0	0	0
			Diversion-Cherbourg/Maupertuis Airfield	17	8	0	0
				300	149	7	4

NOVEMBER 1942

For the leaders of the Eighth who had worked so hard over the months and were dedicated to the expansion of the daylight precision bombing campaign, this must have been a depressing month. It had taken four months to build up a sizeable B-17 force, there were 209 on hand in the Theatre on the 1st of the month, but only 73 were available for combat operations. A much smaller number than were available at the beginning of October.

During October, 93 new B-17s had arrived in the UK the highest number for any month in 1942. Most of these were with the three new Groups that had arrived and were not operational on the 1st November. The 97th Group had ceased operations after the mission of 21st October, and was preparing to depart for North Africa. This required the Group to be brought up to a strength of 35 B-17Fs. It had lost six aircraft from its inventory on its final mission with the Eighth. These losses had to be made good from the other Groups or from new replacements. The newly arrived 305th Group lost five of its originals to the 97th. The 301st Group would complete the first two November missions and it too would then start preparing for departure to North Africa. Since arriving in the Theatre, the Group had lost one aircraft Missing in Action, three in crash landings and one had left for reasons unknown. None of these losses had been made up prior to November and five replacements were assigned early in the month.

Eight missions were flown during November, seven were to U-Boat bases on the French Atlantic coast. The first was to Brest on the 7th, when 14 B-17s of the 91st Group making their first mission joined those of the 301st and 306th Groups. There were no losses. Also this day, the 44th Bomb Group flew its B-24s on a diversion, the first mission for this Group and the first for the Second Bombardment Wing to which the 44th was assigned.

The next day, 53 aircraft were despatched to Lille and the airfield at Abbeville/Drucat. The 301st Group sent 18 aircraft on this, its last mission with the Eighth Air Force. One B-17F from the 306th Group failed to return. A 91st plane, 41-24484, landed at Hunsdon on return.

On the 9th, the third successive days mission was flown with St Nazaire the target, the first of several visits this city, which would become one of the most heavily defended outside of Germany, would receive from the Eighth in November. Thirty-three B-17s were despatched by the 91st and

306th Groups. These were joined by 14 B-24s from the 44th and 93rd Groups. Thirty-one B-17s and 12 B-24s bombed the target. Three 306th aircraft failed to return and several others were damaged. The Group landed at Portreath on return where one of the damaged aircraft, 41-24494, was salvaged. Some planes from the 91st Group landed at Exeter. One was 'QUITCHURBITCHIN' which had been badly damaged on the mission.

On the 14th, La Pallice was the briefed target for the 21 B-17s and 13 B-24s despatched by the 91st, 306th and 93rd Groups. As the target was covered in cloud, St Nazaire, the secondary was bombed by the 13 B-17s and nine B-24s that completed the mission. There were no losses this day.

It was back to St Nazaire on the 17th – the 73 B-17s and B-24s despatched included 16 from the 303rd Bomb Group which was making its first mission. They failed to locate the target and brought their bombs back. The 305th Bomb Group also flew its first mission this day when ten of its B-17s carried out a diversionary sweep. No aircraft were lost but 41-24496, of the 306th Group, was badly damaged and put down at Exeter. It never flew again.

Next day, the largest force of the month set out for the La Pallice U-Boat yards. Of the 65 B-17s and B-24s despatched, only 21 B-17s of the 91st and 306th Bomb Groups bombed the briefed target. The 303rd mistook St Nazaire as La Pallice and 19 of its aircraft bombed this target. The B-24s of the 93rd bombed Lorient. Once again the 305th sent 20 aircraft on a diversion. The only loss in action was a 306th Bomb Group aircraft. A B-24D, 41-23745 'KATY BUG', of the 93rd Bomb Group crashed near Alconbury on return, killing four of the crew. A mid air collision had occurred over England between two 91st Bomb Group B-17s, resulting in 41-24499 landing at Turweston, where it was salvaged and 41-24453 landing at Yeovilton, where it was repaired and put back into service. There were no injuries to the crews involved in this, the second, mid air collision to occur on a combat mission since the Eighth had started operations.

U-Boat bases were the targets again on the 22nd. This time Lorient, with most of the 76 aircraft despatched finding 10/10 cloud and returning with their bombs. The exception being the 303rd which found a gap in the clouds and 11 of their aircraft were able to bomb. For the 305th, it should

Out on test flight, 42-2997 displays the Douglas production number on nose below side gun. This was later moved to the decking aft of the cockpit. Missing is the familiar B-17 astro dome in roof of nose section. This aircraft was delivered on 11th November 1942 and did not see service outside the USA. In early 1943 it was based at Pueblo, Colorado, where many Eighth Air Force crews received part of their training. *Douglas*

'**DELTA REBEL No 2**' 42-5077, made famous due to its association with Clark Gable, one of the first replacements received by the 91st Bomb Group. Exact date of assignment is unknown, but it flew with the Group on the abortive mission of 22nd November. *US Air Force*

have been the first real bombing mission but they brought their bombs back to base. There were no losses.

Next day, the 23rd, St Nazaire was again the target. Fifty B-17s and eight B-24s were despatched, with 28 B-17s and eight B-24s bombing the target. A record four B-17s failed to return; two of these from the 91st and one from the 303rd, being the first operational losses these Groups had incurred. The fourth was from the 306th, the seventh aircraft this Group had lost in action, giving the Group the highest loss rate in Eighth Bomber Command. Another, 91st B-17F, 41-24506, crashed at Leavesden when returning to Bassingbourn, killing two crew and injuring eight. This was the last time that the B-24s of 93rd Bomb Group flew in combat as part of the First Bombardment Wing, they would shortly be leaving Alconbury to join the Second Bombardment Wing in Norfolk.

So operations for November came to an end. During the month's eight missions nine B-17s had been lost in action, equalling the losses during the first three months of operations. Six more had been lost in accidents or salvaged due to battle damage, and others were out of commission following damage sustained on operations. One of the aircraft salvaged due to battle damage, was the 91st's 41-24570 '**PANHANDLE DOGY**'. Records give the salvage date as 27th November; the last mission the plane participated on was that to Abbeville on 8th November, and it would seem that the damage, causing the plane to be salvaged, was incurred on this date.

Added to the demands of the Twelfth Air Force, the losses had made the task of the four operational Bomb Groups to keep a sizeable number of aircraft ready for combat operations very difficult. The efficient supply of spare parts for the planes had not yet been organised, and the only way aircraft were kept in commission was by the establishment of 'Hangar Queens' (ships that had been damaged on missions, or in crashes, that were taken off flying status and stripped for replacement parts for other ships).

The ground crews developed a real art in stripping clean any plane that might become disabled at a base. This enthusiasm was not always shared by the Air Force Service Command whose responsibility it was, to decide if damaged planes were beyond economical repair and to carry out salvage or repairs as appropriate.

A typical case was the 303rd Bomb Group's 41-24563, which was damaged in a landing accident at Luton on 11th November. It sustained damage to one wing and Air Force Service Command inspectors who viewed it following the accident estimated it would take 100 man hours to put it into flying condition. It was inspected again on 1st December, and found to have been completely cannibalised in such a way that it was considered to be beyond economical repair. This plane was practically new, with less than 100 flying hours. The Air Force Service Command sent a complaining letter to the Commanding General Eighth Air Force and an investigation followed. In spite of this and other similar incidents, the practice of Groups robbing spares from disabled planes assigned to the Group continued, and interestingly, an almost identical incident occurred as late as May 1943, when a 94th Bomb Group B-17F, which had crash landed at North Weald, was wrecked in a similar way.

The 97th's '**RED GREMLIN**' and '**BOOMERANG**' made their second visit to Gibraltar on 5th November. Flying from Hurn, '**RED GREMLIN**' piloted again by Maj Paul Tibbets, carried Gen Eisenhower, and '**BOOMERANG**' flown by Lt Wayne Connors, carried Gen Mark Clark. There were six B-17s in this airlift carrying the American and British Commanders for the opening of the North African operation. Taxiing out for take off at Hurn, 41-24388, flown by John C Summers, had a hydraulic failure, causing a loss of brakes; this resulted in the plane being delayed until 6th November. On the flight to Gibraltar, this aircraft, which carried Generals Doolittle and Lemnitzer, was attacked by Junkers 88s and damaged but made it safely to Gibraltar. Three of these aircraft returned to Predannack on the 9th from where they later made their final departure for North Africa.

Following later in the month were the remainder of the 97th and 301st Bomb Groups and the four B-17Fs assigned to the 15th Photo Mapping Squadron, as well as the 13 DB-7Bs belonging to the 15th Bomb Squadron (L).

In all, 74 B-17Fs were despatched to the Twelfth Air Force. Not all the aircraft that departed had served in the First Bombardment Wing. Some of the late additions were assigned directly to the departing groups before they had been added to the strength of the Eighth Air Force. Two that joined the 301st Group, 42-5082 and 42-5085, had been ferried directly from Prestwick, to the Group, by two minimum crews who had been despatched by train to pick them up.

The aircraft flown by Maj John Knox, the 341st Bomb Squadron's Commander, which left Predannack on the 17th, caught fire and crashed in the Channel with the loss of all on board; flying as a passenger on this aircraft was Brig Gen Duncan. This plane, 42-2969, had been one of the originals, assigned to the 305th Bomb Group, which had been transferred to the 97th Group on arrival in England. It was the first loss of a Douglas built B-17 in the European Theatre.

Most of the 97th and 301st's aircraft transferring to Africa had started operations with the Eighth Air Force. Those which survived in the Twelfth Air Force until November 1943, would be transferred to the Fifteenth Air Force, where they were re-assigned to the Second Bomb Group which was equipped with non Tokyo Tank B-17s. For the aircraft that had started out with the 92nd Group they had then served in three different Groups in three separate Air Forces.

Twenty-three new B-17s arrived via the North Atlantic ferry route during the month. Some were weather-bound stragglers from the 305th Group and others were new replacements. Ten aircraft had been required to bring the 97th and 301st Groups up to strength. Losses in the four active

Bomb Groups remaining in the First Bombardment Wing had been 15; so even without allowances for those planes out of action for battle damage repairs there were not enough replacements to make up the losses.

During November, the B-17Es of the 92nd Bomb Group found a new and important task assigned them. To assist the TORCH operation and to carry VIPs and urgent freight, a courier service was established between Britain and North Africa. The responsibility for operating this service was given to Eighth Fighter Command. Eighth Bomber Command was ordered to make three B-17 type aircraft available complete with crews, which were to be replaced as necessary to ensure that three were always available in operating condition. The despatch of the courier flights was controlled by the Eighth Fighter Command Control Centre at Gloucester, using initially Predannack and later Portreath, as the UK terminal airfields.

Serial	Group	Sqdn	Date	Airfield of Departure
41-24342	97	414	20th Nov	Hurn
41-24343	97	343	22nd Nov	Hurn
41-42345	97	342	20th Nov	Hurn
41-24346	301	419	24th Nov	Hurn
41-24348	301	353	24th Nov	Hurn
41-24350	301		24th Nov	Hurn
41-24351	301	352	24th Nov	Hurn
41-24352	301	352	24th Nov	Hurn
41-24360	301	419	24th Nov	Hurn
41-24361	301		24th Nov	Hurn
41-24363	301		24th Nov	Hurn
41-24364	301	353	24th Nov	Hurn
41-24366	301	353	24th Nov	Hurn
41-24367	301	419	25th Nov	Hurn
41-24368	301	352	24th Nov	Hurn
41-24369	301		24th Nov	Hurn
41-24370	97	342	20th Nov	Hurn
41-24371	301	353	24th Nov	Hurn
41-24372	301	352	24th Nov	Hurn
41-24373	97	341	17th Nov	Predannack
41-24374	301		24th Nov	Hurn
41-24376	97	341	15th Nov	Predannack
41-24377	97	342	5th Nov	Hurn
41-24378	97	342	20th Nov	Hurn
41-24379	97	341	17th Nov	Predannack
41-24380	97	340	10th Nov	Predannack
41-24382	97	341	17th Nov	Predannack
41-24385	97	340	10th Nov	Predannack
41-24386	301	353	24th Nov	Predannack
41-24388	97	340	6th Nov	Hurn
41-24390	301	419	23rd Nov	Portreath
41-24392	97	414	20th Nov	Hurn
41-24393	301	419	28th Nov	Hurn
41-24394	301	419	24th Nov	Hurn
41-24395	301	419	24th Nov	Hurn
41-24396	301	419	24th Nov	Hurn
41-24404	301	352	24th Nov	Hurn
41-24405	301	353	24th Nov	Hurn
41-24406	97	414	20th Nov	Hurn
41-24407	301	352	24th Nov	Hurn
41-24408	301		24th Nov	Hurn
41-24409	301		24th Nov	Hurn
41-24412	97	340	10th Nov	Predannack
41-24413	97	414	20th Nov	Hurn
41-24414	97	342	20th Nov	Hurn
41-24415	97	414	20th Nov	Hurn
41-24418	301	352	24th Nov	Hurn
41-24419	97	341	17th Nov	Predannack
41-24421	97	341	17th Nov	Predannack
41-24422	301	352	24th Nov	Hurn
41-24423	301	353	24th Nov	Hurn
41-24433	*3	+15	18th Nov	Hurn
41-24434	*3	+15	18th Nov	Hurn
41-24435	97	340	11th Nov	Predannack
41-24437	97	341	17th Nov	Predannack
41-24438	*3	+15	18th Nov	Hurn
41-24440	*3	+15	19th Nov	Hurn
41-24442	97	342	20th Nov	Hurn
41-24444	97	340	5th Nov	Hurn
41-24473	97	414	20th Nov	Hurn
41-24477	97	340	10th Nov	Predannack
41-24532	97	414	20th Nov	Hurn
41-24572	97	414	20th Nov	Hurn
41-24576	97	341	17th Nov	Predannack
41-24618	301		24th Nov	Hurn
42-2969	97	341	17th Nov	Predannack
42-5087	97	340	11th Nov	Predannack
42-5061	301	353	24th Nov	Hurn
42-5082	301	419	28th Nov	Hurn
42-5085	301		24th Nov	Hurn
42-5090	97	414	20th Nov	Hurn
42-5131	301		24th Nov	Hurn
42-5713	97	342	20th Nov	Hurn
42-5715	97	342	20th Nov	Hurn

* 3rd Reconnaissance Group   + 15th Photo Mapping Squadron

The six aircraft that carried General Eisenhower and other Commanders to Gibralter were; 41-24377, 24385, 24435, 24437 and 24444 which left Hurn on 5th November and 41-24388 which left Hurn on 6th November. 41-24385, 24435 and 24437 returned to Predannack on 9th November and then made their final departure as detailed above. 42-2969 crashed in the sea with the loss of all on board

B-17Fs Transferred to the 12th Air Force November 1942

NOVEMBER 1942

COMBAT ORDER No	8AF MISS No	DAY	TARGET		No OF AIRCRAFT			
					DESP	BOMB	LOST	
							MIA	OTHER
44	16	7th	Brest, U-Boat Base		56	23	0	0
				B-24	12	11	0	1
46	17	8th	Lille		38	30	1	0
			Abbeville/Drucat Airfield		15	11	0	0
47	18	9th	St. Nazaire, U-Boat Base		33	31	3	1
				B-24	9	7	0	0
50	19	14th	St. Nazaire, U-Boat Base		21	15	0	0
				B-24	13	9	0	0
51	20	17th	St. Nazaire, U-Boat Base		59	23	0	1
				B-24	14	12	0	0
			Diversionary Sweep		10	0	0	0
52	21	18th	La Pallice, U-Boat Yard		31	19	1	1
			Lorient, U-Boat Base	B-24	13	13	0	1
			St. Nazaire, U-Boat Base		21	19	0	0
			Diversionary Sweep		20	0	0	0
55	22	22nd	Lorient, U-Boat Base		68	11	0	0
				B-24	8	0	0	0
56	23	23rd	St.Nazaire, U-Boat Base		50	28	4	1
				B-24	8	8	0	0
					489	270	9	6

OPERATIONAL DIARY: NOVEMBER 1942

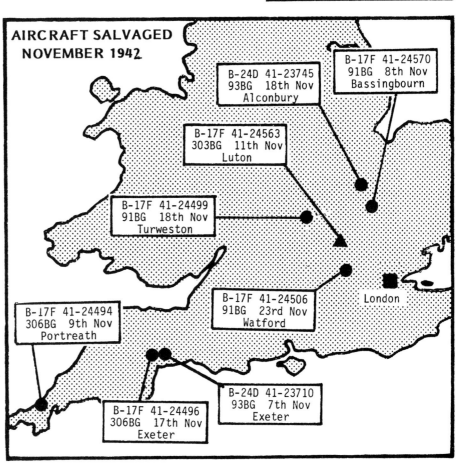

AIRCRAFT MISSING IN ACTION NOVEMBER 1942

8th	B-17F	41-24472	306BG
9th	B-17F	41-24486	306BG
	B-17F	41-24491	306BG
	B-17F	41-24509	306BG
18th	B-17F	41-24474	306BG
23rd	B-17F	41-24478	306BG
	B-17F	41-24479	91BG
	B-17F	41-24503	91BG
	B-17F	41-24568	303BG

DB-7Bs of 15th Bomb Squadron
to 12th Air Force. All left from Predannack on 15th November 1942

AL372	AL445	AL495
AL429	AL486	AL497
AL436	AL489	AL498
AL442	AL492	AL499
	AL494	

AIRCRAFT SALVAGED NOVEMBER 1942

B-24D 41-23745
93BG 18th Nov
Alconbury

B-17F 41-24570
91BG 8th Nov
Bassingbourn

B-17F 41-24563
303BG 11th Nov
Luton

B-17F 41-24499
91BG 18th Nov
Turweston

B-17F 41-24494
306BG 9th Nov
Portreath

B-17F 41-24506
91BG 23rd Nov
Watford

London

B-17F 41-24496
306BG 17th Nov
Exeter

B-24D 41-23710
93BG 7th Nov
Exeter

December the 7th was the first anniversary of the Japanese attack on Pearl Harbor. Not only had this precipitated the United States into the Second World War, it had also marked the entry into combat in the US Army Air Force of the B-17. Since that date, B-17s had seen service on every front. They had engaged the Japanese from that first day of action in Hawaii and the Philippines, through Borneo and the Dutch East Indies, the Solomons, New Guinea and Australia. They had been in action in the Aleutian Islands and the Battle of Midway and had fought over the jungles of Burma. They had engaged the Germans and Italians in the Eastern Mediterranean, helping to smash the supply routes to Rommel's armies which threatened the Suez Canal. They had flown anti-submarine patrols from the Panama Canal zone and seen service with RAF Coastal Command.

Now, with the establishment of the Twelfth Air Force in Northwest Africa, which included the two B-17 Groups transferred from England, the area of action was widened still further, although more thinly spread. No other allied aircraft had seen such wide and varied service. It was a record which only the B-24 Liberator would surpass in the years to come.

Numerically, the efforts of the Eighth Air Force had exceeded all others. With the loss of the 97th and 301st Bomb Groups, December started with a depleted inventory and the months of attrition had begun. Even so, the Eighth Air Force was still the major user of the B-17 and would remain so until the end of hostilities in 1945. On 1st December, there were 149 B-17s on hand in the UK. There were four operational Bomb Groups, who between them, had 95 aircraft available for combat. The most experienced of these was the 306th at Thurleigh, which had been operational since early October.

On 1st December, two Vega built B-17Fs, 42-5714 and 42-5717, were assigned to the 306th Bomb Group. Both had arrived in the UK as replacements at the end of November and were the first Vega built B-17Fs to see action with the Eighth Air Force. Two Vega built aircraft had arrived in October but had been assigned to the 97th Bomb Group on their arrival, and had left for North Africa in November, without serving operationally in the First Bombardment Wing.

The month's operations started on the 6th, when the greater part of the operational B-17 force was despatched to Lille. The Second Bomb Wing sent its B-24s to Abbeville/Drucat airfield, making it the third occasion on which the Eighth Bomber Command had despatched over one hundred aircraft. Only 37 from the First Wing were able to bomb the target, losing one plane, this from the 305th, the Group's first operational loss.

On the 12th, 78 aircraft were despatched to the Romilly Air Depot, but cloud conditions were bad and the secondary target at Rouen was attacked. The 305th Group could not bomb because of cloud and only 17 aircraft from the other three groups were able to bomb. The two planes lost came from the 303rd Group which was harassed by enemy fighters.

The most costly mission of 1942, in terms of aircraft and crews lost, was that on 20th December, to Romilly-sur-Seine Air Depot. Eighty B-17s of the First Wing were despatched with 21 B-24s from the Second Wing making it the second time in December that over 100 planes were despatched. Sixty B-17s bombed the target giving a 75 per cent effective rate, which from this standpoint, also made it one of the most successful missions carried out in 1942. Missing in Action were two planes from 91st Bomb Group, one from 303rd Bomb Group, and three from 306th Bomb Group. On return, 91st Group's 41-24439 **'CHIEF SLY'** crashed at Parsonage Farm, Fletching, all the crew were safe, and 41-24581 **'THE 8 BALL'** from 303rd Group belly landed at Bovingdon after eight of the crew had baled out. This brought the losses for the day's operation to eight B-17s.

The last mission of the month, and of 1942, came on the 30th, when 77 aircraft were despatched to Lorient U-Boat base. The 306th Group, with the exception of one aircraft which joined the 305th Bomb Group formation, abandoned the mission. This single aircraft was the only one from 306th Group to be credited with a sortie. It did not return as shortly after leaving the target, it was shot down by enemy fighters, becoming the eleventh of the Group's aircraft to go missing in action. It was also the first Douglas built B-17 to be lost while serving in the Eighth Air Force. The 91st and 305th Bomb Groups also lost one aircraft each this day.

Twelve B-17s had been lost in action during the month. Three had been salvaged in England. These were the two that crashed on return on the 20th December and the third was the 306th's 41-24475 that was salvaged on the 5th. The reason is not known but it was probably due to damage received on one of the November missions.

Since the first B-17E of the 97th Bomb Group had touched down at Prestwick on 1st July, seven B-17Es, 44 B-17Fs and four B-20Ds had been lost, either missing in action or salvaged for various reasons. All the B-17s, apart from the single Douglas built plane, lost on the 30th December, had come from the Boeing Seattle factory.

After five months of operations the First Wing had by December, gained considerable experience in the handling and execution of complex missions involving formations of heavy bombers. Although the numbers involved up to this time had been small compared with what was to come in the next two years; it was the experience gained on these early missions that saw the birth of the techniques that would allow the take off and assembly into combat formations of up to 2,000 heavy bombers in the next two years.

One of the most important lessons learned, was that a single group did not possess sufficient fire power to provide adequate protection against a determined attack by Luftwaffe fighters. Despite the fact that the Bible (Field Manual No 1–10) specified that the group was the largest unit which would be flown in formation, some method had to be devised to provide the necessary concentration of defensive fire power in order to keep the losses from enemy fighters within tolerable limits.

The 303rd Bomb Group received two of the first Douglas built B-17Fs as part of its original equipment and was the first Group to use them in combat. An early replacement was the tenth Douglas built, 42-2973 **'IZA VAILABLE'**. It joined the Group on 14th December and served for over 15 months before being withdrawn for return to the USA. *Roger Freeman*

AIRCRAFT STATUS		
5th December 1942		
UNIT	TYPE	ASS
91BG	B-17F	29
303BG	B-17F	33
305BG	B-17F	36
306BG	B-17F	33
1 BW	B-17F	131
92BG	B-17E	30
93BG	B-24D	38

DECEMBER 1942

Existing ground facilities, the length of time needed to taxi, take off and land, and the number of aircraft which could be handled in a single traffic pattern, were the limiting factors affecting the number of aircraft which could be despatched on a mission from a single airfield. To offset these limitations to the use of a single airfield for despatch of the required number of aeroplanes, a plan for formation of Combat Wings was evolved in the First Bombardment Wing.

Under this plan, the four heavy bombardment Groups then in the First Bombardment Wing, were to be formed into two Combat Wings, with two groups in each. The Senior Group Commander of each Combat Wing was to be designated Combat Wing Commander and was given clear and unquestioned command and authority over both Groups when planning missions, and when in the air, but in no other field and on no other subject. Thus the primary purpose of the Combat Wings was to facilitate the preparation and execution of Combat missions and to co-ordinate their performance. The Combat Wings were to be tactical rather than administrative organisations. As a further step to facilitate and expedite the preparations for missions, arrangements were to be made for the Eighth Bomber Command to transmit its field orders direct to the Combat Wing simultaneously with transmittal to Bombardment Wing Headquarters. As soon as the field order began coming to the Combat Wing, the Group Commanders would be notified and would assemble with necessary Staff Officers at Combat Wing Headquarters to discuss, plan and brief for the mission.

This plan was submitted to Headquarters Eighth Bomber Command by Headquarters First Bombardment Wing on 6th December 1942 and it was approved.

The first steps towards implementation of the plan were taken on 13th December, when the First and Second Provisional Bombardment Combat Wings (H) were designated. The 91st and 306th Bomb Groups (H) comprised the First Provisional Bomb Combat Wing (H) with the 303rd and 305th Bomb Groups (H) in the Second Provisional Bomb Combat Wing (H).

On the 3rd January 1943, the designation of these Combat Wings were changed to 101st and 102nd Provisional Bomb Combat Wings (H) respectively. These Provisional Combat Wings functioned on an informal basis. They had no tables of organisation and were not constituted legal organisations within the Air Force. General Armstrong, of the 306th Group, was the Combat Wing Commander of the First Provisional Bomb Combat Wing and Col Le May, of the 305th Group, was the Combat Wing Commander of the Second Provisional Bomb Combat Wing.

The first changes in airfield assignment since the initial allocation of airfields to the First Bombardment Wing came on 18th December, when Little Staughton was transferred from Eighth Bomber Command to Eighth Air Force Service Command. On 9th December in a ceremony at Thurleigh, the airfield had been formally handed over to the control of the USAAF, the first airfield to be transferred from RAF to USAAF control. Also at Thurleigh a temporary Advanced Supply Depot had been set up to stock B-17 parts pending completion of the Second Advanced Depot at Little Staughton.

On 5th December, the 93rd Bomb Group was ordered to proceed immediately to North Africa. Twenty-four B-24Ds from the 328th, 330th and 409th Bomb Squadrons left Alconbury at approximately 0900 hours on 6th December, the 328th and 409th proceeding via Portreath and the 330th Bomb Squadron via Exeter. One aircraft, 41-23707 of the 329th Bomb Squadron, crashed into a mountain on arrival in Africa killing all fourteen occupants. The 329th Bomb Squadron remained at Alconbury and during the next few weeks this squadron and the other personnel at Alconbury moved to Hardwick in Norfolk where they were assigned to the Second Bombardment Wing.

While with the First Bombardment Wing, the 93rd Bomb Group had taken part in nine operational missions, had despatched 125 B-24Ds, of which 70 had been given credit sorties. One B-24D had been lost in action, and a further three had been lost in accidents. Two of the Group's squadrons had been detached to Holmesley South and St Eval during October–November, to operate in conjunction with the RAF Coastal Command. With the departure of the 93rd Bomb Group, the First Wing was now solely equipped with B-17s.

AIRCRAFT STATUS		
29th December 1942		
UNIT	TYPE	ASS
91BG	B-17F	27
306BG	B-17F	27
1 PBW	B-17F	54
303BG	B-17F	32
305BG	B-17F	35
2 PBW	B-17F	67
1 BW	B-17F	121
92BG	B-17E	29

Three 306th Bomb Group aircraft on runway, await signal to take off. RD-B was one of five replacements assigned on 28th November, the first the Group had received since arriving in England. RD-F was one of two Vega built aircraft assigned on 1st December, the first from this manufacturer to fly on operations. RD-F was also the first Vega built B-17F to go missing in action. RD-A at the rear was a Group original. It later served in the 482nd Bomb Group and in March 1944 was assigned to the First Bomb Division Special Purpose Flight at Kimbolton and was at that time the oldest B-17F serving in the Eighth Air Force. *306th BG Historical Association*

DECEMBER 1942

OPERATIONAL DIARY: DECEMBER 1942

COMBAT ORDER No	8AF MISS No	DAY	TARGET	No OF AIRCRFT			
				DESP	BOMB	LOST	
						MIA	OTHER
	24	6th	Lille	66	37	1	0
			Diversion	16	0	0	0
	25	12th	Rouen-Sotteville, Marshalling Yard	78	17	2	0
	26	20th	Romilly-Sur-Seine, Airfield	80	60	6	2
	27	30th	Lorient, U-Boat Base	77	40	3	0
				317	154	12	2

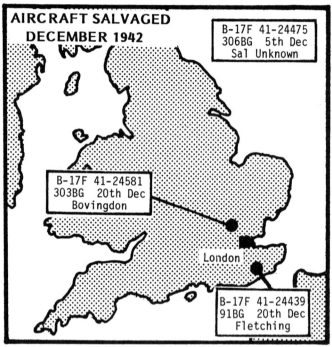

AIRCRAFT SALVAGED DECEMBER 1942

B-17F 41-24475
306BG 5th Dec
Sal Unknown

B-17F 41-24581
303BG 20th Dec
Bovingdon

London

B-17F 41-24439
91BG 20th Dec
Fletching

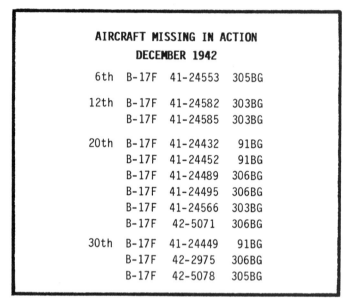

AIRCRAFT MISSING IN ACTION
DECEMBER 1942

6th	B-17F	41-24553	305BG
12th	B-17F	41-24582	303BG
	B-17F	41-24585	303BG
20th	B-17F	41-24432	91BG
	B-17F	41-24452	91BG
	B-17F	41-24489	306BG
	B-17F	41-24495	306BG
	B-17F	41-24566	303BG
	B-17F	42-5071	306BG
30th	B-17F	41-24449	91BG
	B-17F	42-2975	306BG
	B-17F	42-5078	305BG

One of the B-17Es contributed by the 301st Bomb Group to the BOLERO weather detachment was 41-9082. Later serving in the 97th and 92nd Bomb Groups, the latter using it for at least one courier flight to North Africa in December 1942. It later transferred to the 12th Air Force and was used by Maj Gen Bernard Montgomery. Photograph shows it in North Africa with a P-40 of 13 Squadron RAF in the background. *Imperial War Museum*

JANUARY 1943

Four combat operations were completed this month, all directed at targets concerned with U-Boat operations. Historically the most important was the last one of the month when, for the first time, the Eighth Air Force heavy bombers attacked a target on German soil.

Starting the month with 144 B-17s on hand and 83 operational, 72 of these were despatched on the 3rd to St Nazaire. Living up to its name of 'Flak City' the opposition was intense, and seven B-17s failed to return – a record loss to date. Four were from the 303rd – a record loss for a single Group up to this time.

The 306th lost two more aircraft and on return, landed at St Eval. Bad weather kept the Group there until the 6th, when with the forecast of clear weather over Thurleigh, they departed only to find the promised clearance at their base had not materialised and they had to return to St Eval. During this return, 41-24469, flown by Lt Robert E Brandon, became lost and despite extensive searches, no trace of aircraft or crew were found. It was 8th January before the Group finally made it back to Thurleigh.

On the 13th, 72 aircraft were despatched to Lille with 64 bombing and three failing to return. Two from 306th Bomb Group had collided in mid air north of Lille. This was the first recorded occasion when two Eighth Air Force B-17s were missing in action for this reason.

Every Group had during its period of operations, one or more missions which stood out above the others, perhaps due to intense opposition, heavy losses or good bombing results. For the 303rd, the operation of 23rd January became one of these. Twenty-one aircraft were despatched from Molesworth to Lorient port area and 14 bombed the target. The only Group to lose aircraft Missing in Action this day, the five failing to return set a new high for losses to a single Group on one day; the second time the 303rd had achieved this unenviable record this month. A sixth Group loss this day was 41-24579, which made a belly landing at Lulsgate Bottom on return and was salvaged. Another loss to the Group was 41-24606, which only just managed to regain the Devon coast when engine failure caused Lt Oxrider to give the bale out order and he executed a skilful landing in the grounds of a mental hospital at Dawlish. Although repaired and flown out on an improvised runway, 'WEREWOLF' never rejoined the Group.

Finally, on 27th January, came the first mission to Germany. The U-Boat yards at Wilhelmshaven were the target and 64 B-17s were despatched, of which 55 bombed the target. Opposition was much less than expected. Flak was encountered over Germany and the Frisian Islands causing slight damage to some of the bombers. The fighters encountered seemed much less experienced than those that had been met over France. One B-17F, from 305th Group was lost. The Second Bomb Wing had contributed 27 B-24s to the force, but due to weather and problems with navigation, none of these dropped bombs. Two B-24s were lost, the first occasion when losses of B-24s exceeded those of B-17s.

The month's losses of 16 B-17s were the highest in any month to date – nine had come from the 303rd Bomb Group. All the losses this month had been Boeing built aircraft.

With the new year came changes, which, while having no immediate affect on the month's operations, would establish the foundations for the expansion of the Wing in the months to follow. The first came on the 3rd, when with the issue of General Order No 2 from Headquarters First Bomb Wing, the two Provisional Bomb Combat Wings were re-numbered. The First became the 101st Provisional Bombardment Combat Wing (H) and the Second became the 102nd Provisional, Bombardment Combat Wing (H).

Next, on the 6th January, the first steps in returning the 92nd Bomb Group to operational status took place when the Group moved from Bovingdon to Alconbury, taking 12 B-17Es with them. The 326th Bomb Squadron remained at Bovingdon with fifteen B-17Es. This squadron, supplemented by personnel from the Headquarters and Headquarters Squadrons of Eighth Bomber and Fighter Commands, operated the Combat Crew Replacement Centre, an arrangement made necessary due to the fact that no Table of Organisation had been authorised for a Combat Crew Replacement Unit.

The 92nd's hopes for an early return to combat operations were raised, when, on the 22nd, two B-17Fs were assigned to the 327th Bomb Squadron, but these hopes were soon dampened when the two aircraft were transferred out to another Group.

The flow of replacement B-17Fs resumed this month. With the North Atlantic ferry route closed for the winter these came via the much longer South Atlantic ferry route. The first had left the USA in late December and were delivered initially to the Twelfth Air Force in North Africa from where they were despatched to the UK. Marrakesh in French Morocco was the despatch point in North Africa, with St Eval in Cornwall the designated terminal in England. Portreath and Chivenor were used as emergency alternates.

The first B-17s delivered by the southern route arrived in the UK about 5th January, and 29 were received during the month. Most went to the four operational Bomb Groups. It was about a week from the date of their arrival to the date of assignment to their new owners.

One badly needed new aircraft the Group did not get was 42-5250. Piloted by 1st Lt A F Burch, it was one of four, which departed from Marrakesh shortly after midnight on 12th January. Radio communications were very poor and proper contact with the four aircraft was never established, but three landed safely at St Eval, one and a half hours after their estimated time of arrival. 42-5250 was reported circling the Brest peninsula for over an hour and a half at altitudes as low as 500 feet and was fired on by the Germans whenever it came below the overcast. At 1215 hours it crash landed out of fuel, one and a half miles from Brixham, without serious injury to the crew, after having been airborne for approximately 12 hours.

Another of the B-17Es, 41-9045, was lost on the 15th, when it crash landed at Athenry in Ireland when returning from a courier flight to North Africa, having overshot its destination at Portreath. On board were four Generals and several other high ranking officers who were driven over the border into Northern Ireland. The aircraft was dismantled and taken to Langford Lodge.

During the month, the Casablanca Conference took place with British Prime Minister Winston Churchill and US President Roosevelt attending. During this conference, the question of the Eighth Bomber Command's performance to date and its future role in the strategic bombing campaign came up for critical review. A cable from General Eisenhower, dated 13th January, summoned General Eaker, Commander of the Eighth Air Force to Casablanca, to answer questions and to put the case for high altitude daylight bombing before the conference. General Eaker left on the 15th, in B-17F 41-24611 'BOOMERANG', of the 305th Group, piloted by Captain Pyle. They returned with the VIP passenger on 24th January and were escorted into Eglinton, Northern Ireland, by Spitfires of 501 Squadron, leaving later for Langford Lodge.

The first replacement B-17Fs to reach England via the Southern Ferry Route arrived at Portreath on 5th January. Three arrived on this day, one being 42-5404. It went to the 306th Bomb Group and then to the 384th Group and put in over a year's service before being lost on 30th January 1944. *306 BG Historical Association*

Left: 303rd Bomb Group's **'WEREWOLF'** where it stopped in the grounds of a hospital after force landing at Dawlish on return from Lorient, 23rd January. *Doug Vincent*

Below: What a sight this would be today; **'WEREWOLF'** unsticks at the point where a hedge has been removed to make a temporary runway. Many locals turned out to see her depart. She never returned to Molesworth, but spent a short time assigned to the 91st Bomb Group before going to the 1st Combat Crew Replacement Centre at Bovingdon. *US Air Force – National Air and Space Museum*

OPERATIONAL DIARY: JANUARY 1943

COMBAT ORDER No	8AF MISS No	DAY	TARGET	No OF AIRCRAFT			
				DESP	BOMB	LOST	
						MIA	OTHER
	28	3rd	St. Nazaire, U-Boat Base	72	60	7	0
	29	13th	Lille, Industrial Transport	72	64	3	0
	30	23rd	Lorient, Port Area	51	36	5	1
			Brest, U-Boat Base	22	18	0	0
	31	27th	Wilhelmshaven, U-Boat Base	64	53	1	0
			Emden, U-Boat Yards		2	0	0
				281	233	16	1

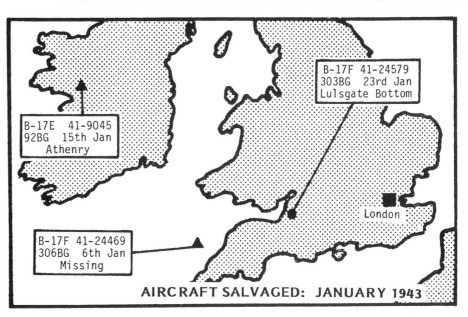

Back at Molesworth from the Eighth's first raid on Germany on 27th January is 41-24635 'THE 8 BALL', and her crew. This aircraft was a replacement for the original '8 Ball' which was lost in a belly landing at Bovingdon in December 1942. Holding the propeller is 2nd Lt Jack W Mathis, Bombardier who seven weeks later was awarded a posthumous Medal of Honour for his actions in 'THE DUCHESS'. The pilot 1st Lt Harold L Stouse is on extreme right. *Roger Freeman*

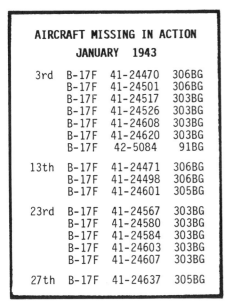

AIRCRAFT MISSING IN ACTION
JANUARY 1943

3rd	B-17F	41-24470	306BG
	B-17F	41-24501	306BG
	B-17F	41-24517	303BG
	B-17F	41-24526	303BG
	B-17F	41-24608	303BG
	B-17F	41-24620	303BG
	B-17F	42-5084	91BG
13th	B-17F	41-24471	306BG
	B-17F	41-24498	306BG
	B-17F	41-24601	305BG
23rd	B-17F	41-24567	303BG
	B-17F	41-24580	303BG
	B-17F	41-24584	303BG
	B-17F	41-24603	303BG
	B-17F	41-24607	303BG
27th	B-17F	41-24637	305BG

B-17E 41-9045 92BG 15th Jan Athenry

B-17F 41-24579 303BG 23rd Jan Lulsgate Bottom

London

B-17F 41-24469 306BG 6th Jan Missing

AIRCRAFT SALVAGED: JANUARY 1943

'THE UNCOUTH BASTARD'. A B-17F of 305th Bomb Group. Serial not known. *Mike Gibson*

FEBRUARY 1943

February started with 102 B-17s on hand and 90 operational in the four Bomb Groups. This was the lowest point reached since September 1942.

The situation regarding combat crews was even worse and beginning this month, availability of full combat crews would generally govern the number of bombers that could be despatched on any day, a situation that would continue through most of 1943.

Neither was it a good month operationally, with fewer than 50 per cent of the B-17s despatched, bombing the target.

On the 6th, 61 B-17s were despatched to the Hamm marshalling yards on what should have been the second mission to Germany. All returned without bombing due to bad weather over the North Sea.

On the 4th, 65 aircraft were sent to Emden, but only 39 were able to claim effective sorties, while five were missing in action. For the second time this month, the First Wing despatched aircraft to the Hamm marshalling yards on the 14th – an all B-17 force this day, as the Second Bomb Wing stayed at home. Once again the weather upset carefully made plans and all 74 planes returned without bombing. The next day it was the turn of the B-17s to rest from operations, while for the first time, the Liberators flew on their own to Dunkirk, but the Fortresses were back to business on the 16th, when St Nazaire was the target and 59 out of 71 despatched aircraft were able to bomb the target, losing six, the highest loss for the month. One of the missing planes, the 306th Bomb Group's 42-5717, was a Vega built aircraft, the first to be lost in the Eighth Air Force. This gave the 306th the distinction of having lost the first Douglas and Vega built B-17s from the Eighth Air Force.

Three missions, for which Eighth Bomber Command issued field orders, on the 19th, 20th and 25th were scrubbed and it was the 26th before another operation took place – this time to Wilhelmshaven. This second visit to the U-Boat yards met with much stronger fighter opposition than that which was encountered on 27th January, and five B-17s were lost.

Continuing the campaign against the U-Boats on the French Atlantic coast had now taken second place to industrial targets in Germany but these targets still received attention, often when weather conditions prevented operations over Germany itself. The U-Boat yards at Brest were attacked on the 27th. This, the last operation of the month, was the first time since 22nd November 1942 when planes went over the target and came away with no losses.

Flying with the 91st to Emden on the 4th was Lt William J Crumm and his crew. Their Fortress was '**JACK THE RIPPER**' and this was their eleventh and last mission, as they had been selected to fly back to the States, the first Eighth Air Force crew to be returned. It has been assumed in some reports that '**JACK THE RIPPER**' returned with them, but this is not the case as this aircraft continued in service in the 91st for over another year and was the last of the Group's original aircraft to go Missing in Action. In fact, it seems almost certain that they took with them B-17E 41-9112, which departed for North Africa on the first leg of its flight back to the USA on 14th February, being the first Eighth Air Force B-17 to return to the USA.

The 92nd lost another B-17E when 41-9044 developed engine trouble soon after leaving Portreath for Gibraltar in the early hours of 11th February. Unable to get back in to Portreath due to bad weather, it was diverted to Chivenor, where, on the first attempt to land, the aircraft struck something in the darkness and had to overshoot. It managed to land at the next attempt but the landing gear was intentionally retracted resulting in the loss of the plane but all on board were uninjured. One bonus gained from this accident was that 1st Lt Davis and two mechanics from Bovingdon flew down to Chivenor to procure parts necessary for getting some of the B-17Es at Bovingdon, which were grounded for spares, in the air again.

The 91st lost one of their original aircraft, 41-24431 on the 12th, when it was taxiing out to take off for Honington, a strong wind lifted the tail, causing the nose to strike the ground. Two more aircraft taken off the inventory in February, were 41-24461 of 306th Bomb Group and 41-24482 of 91st Bomb Group. Both were reported as salvaged on the 27th, and no reason is known for their salvage. They were most likely damaged on earlier missions and had been robbed of parts to keep other aircraft airworthy and were then deemed to be beyond economical repair.

Two more Bomb Groups had been scheduled to join the Eighth in February – the 99th and 2nd. Both were diverted to the Twelfth Air Force in North Africa. The 99th had arrived at Marrakesh and had been readied to fly to England when the orders came through for it to proceed to the Twelfth Air Force. An advance party from the 2nd Bomb Group had

AIRCRAFT and CREW STATUS at 2000 Hours on 28th February 1943

| UNIT | OPERATIONAL AIRCRAFT | | | | COMBAT CREWS |
	TYPE	ASS	ON HAND	OP	
91BG	B-17F	30		16	16
306BG	B-17F	30		21	14
101PBW	B-17F	60		37	30
303BG	B-17F	28		20	17
305BG	B-17F	29		13	14
102PBW	B-17F	57		33	31
1 BW	B-17F	117		70	61
92BG	B-17E	11			

OPERATIONAL DIARY: FEBRUARY 1943

| COMBAT ORDER No | 8AF MISS No | DAY | TARGET | No OF AIRCRAFT | | LOST | |
				DESP	BOMB	MIA	OTHER
94	32	2nd	Hamm, Marshalling Yards	61	0	0	0
95	33	4th	Emden, Industrial Area	65	39	5	0
99	34	14th	Hamm, Marshalling Yards	74	0	0	0
	35	15th	Second Bombardment Wing B-24 Mission	-	-	-	-
100	36	16th	St. Nazaire, U-Boat Yards	71	59	6	0
105	37	26th	Wilhelmshaven, U-Boat Yard	76	59	5	0
106	38	27th	Brest, U-Boat Yards	63	46	0	0
				410	203	16	0

FEBRUARY 1943

arrived in England and was distributed between the Bomb Groups of the First Wing to gain operational experience, but were then ordered to proceed to North Africa.

Only 14 replacement B-17s reached England during the month, the lowest monthly number since deliveries started in July 1942. All came via the southern route.

One which made it to England but not to its intended destination was 42-5258 which left Marrakesh on 10th February. On arrival over England, bad visibility prevented a landing at St Eval and it was diverted to try Chivenor where conditions were found to be no better. It was then asked to go to Lyneham, but the pilot, 2nd Lt Edwin G Pipp, considered he did not have enough fuel to do this and he flew around trying to get below the weather and into St Eval. Finally, with fuel running low, a forced landing became inevitable, and was successfully accomplished in a field at Cardingham near Bodmin. It seems that the crew were unsure of their position as they destroyed the bomb sight, blew up the IFF and burned all wireless papers, charts and books.

Another B-17F, 42-5723, which also left Marrakesh on the 10th, nearly suffered the same fate as Lt Pipp's aircraft. Finding zero visibility over St Eval, it was diverted to Lyneham, where there was no improvement and it flew around for some two hours trying to get DF stations to give it a bearing. Getting low on fuel, the pilot had selected a large field in which to put the plane down, and was circling to land when Hurricanes sighted it and led it safely into Yeovilton.

The first Eighth Air Force B-17 (above) and the first crew (below) to return to the USA. 41-9112 left via the Southern Ferry Route on 14th February. While in the US it went to Wright Field and was extensively modified as photograph shows. It returned to the United Kingdom in October 1943. The crew was that of Lt William J Crumm who flew their last mission on 4th February. Their plane, 41-24490 '**JACK THE RIPPER**' of 91st Bomb Group carried on for another twelve months before going Missing in Action. It is thought that Crumm's was the crew that returned 41-9112 to the USA but no proof has been found. Details of the story and modifications to 41-9112 can be found in *The Mighty Eighth War Manual. US Air Force – National Air and Space Museum* and *Stan Bishop*

B-17E, 41-9044 of 92nd Bomb Group, took off from Portreath at 0200 hours on 11th February with a load of freight, mail and passengers bound for Gibraltar. About 30 minutes after take off, number four engine gave trouble and was shut down but the propeller would not feather. On returning to Portreath several unsuccessful attempts to land were made and the aircraft was then instructed to proceed to Chivenor where on the first attempt to land the aircraft touched down too far down the runway and a three-engine take off was made. With its heavy load, climb was slow and something was struck in flight which removed the right elevator (lower photograph), but flight round the traffic pattern was continued and a landing made. After touchdown the landing gear was intentionally retracted and the aircraft slid to a stop just short of the end of the runway. In upper photograph the propeller on number four engine which caused the trouble can be seen still 'un-feathered'. *US Air Force*

FEBRUARY 1943

AIRCRAFT MISSING IN ACTION FEBRUARY 1943			
4th	B-17F	41-24544	91BG
	B-17F	41-24569	303BG
	B-17F	41-24589	91BG
	B-17F	41-24593	305BG
	B-17F	42-5060	305BG
16th	B-17F	41-24541	303BG
	B-17F	41-24611	305BG
	B-17F	42-2967	303BG
	B-17F	42-5058	305BG
	B-17F	42-5175	306BG
	B-17F	42-5717	306BG
26th	B-17F	41-24447	91BG
	B-17F	41-24604	305BG
	B-17F	41-24623	305BG
	B-17F	42-5056	305BG
	B-17F	42-5362	91BG

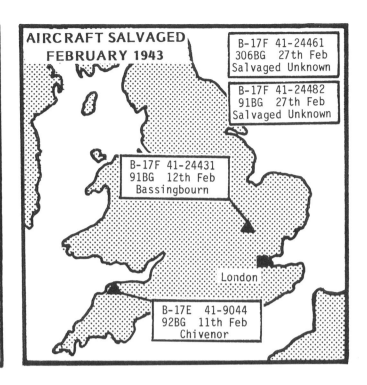

AIRCRAFT SALVAGED FEBRUARY 1943

B-17F 41-24461 306BG 27th Feb Salvaged Unknown

B-17F 41-24482 91BG 27th Feb Salvaged Unknown

B-17F 41-24431 91BG 12th Feb Bassingbourn

London

B-17E 41-9044 92BG 11th Feb Chivenor

Left, 'FIGHTING PAPPY' 42-5407, joined 306th Bomb Group on 25th February, also served in 91st and 379th Bomb Groups before being lost on 9th October 1943. *306th BG Memorial Association*

Right: 'WINDY CITY CHALLENGER' 42-3049, one of four new replacements assigned to the 305th Group on 25th March. It would be the sole 305th aircraft Missing in Action on 14th July 1943. Crew on photograph not identified. *Mike Gibson*

Above: 'OOOLD SOLJER' 41-24559, and below, 'TWO BEAUTS' 42-29573. The two 303rd Bomb Group aircraft involved in the Eighth's first fatal mid air collision while forming for the mission of 31st March. *Ben Smith*

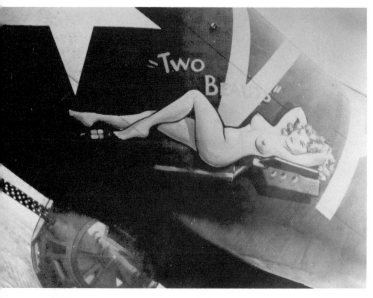

A good month operationally. Number of aircraft bombing was more than double the previous best of January, and losses were the lowest since December 1942. Ten missions were scheduled, of which nine were completed, the tenth was recalled, when bad weather prevented the escort fighters taking off.

There were 117 B-17s on hand at the start of the month, with 70 available for operations. An increasing number of aircraft were arriving via the southern route, but the numbers operational, would stay below 100 for most of the month.

On the first day of the month, there was a mid air collision which took out another original from the 306th Bomb Group when 41-24476 hit 42-5251 during a local flight. Both were extensively damaged, 476 belly landed at Chelveston, where it was salvaged, 251 survived but was out for repairs until 9th April.

Twice in February, the B-17s had set out for Hamm, and on both occasions the weather had prevented any bombing. On 4th March, another force of 71 aircraft set out for this important marshalling yard. Once again, the weather prevented most of the force from attacking. The 306th Group returned to base without bombing, and the 303rd and 305th Groups attacked the secondary target, Rotterdam shipyards. Only the 91st, which had found itself in clear weather and on its own, pressed on and bombed Hamm. Coming out from the target, this Group was attacked by some 50 enemy fighters. These attacks were well co-ordinated, many being made from between ten and two o'clock. Four of the Group's B-17s were shot down, one carrying a 92nd Group crew. For its actions this day, the 91st received a Distinguished Unit Citation. A fifth aircraft lost, came from the 306th Group. It was the heaviest day's loss of the month.

On the 6th, 71 bombers were despatched to Lorient port area. Sixty-five bombed, for the loss of three. On return, most of the aircraft were scattered around Devon and Cornwall. The 91st had eleven land at Davidstowe Moor and one at St Eval. The 306th had ten at Exeter, eight at Chivenor and one at Davidstowe Moor. Fourteen 303rd planes were at Portreath, two at Predannack and one at Harrowbeer. The 305th had 16 land at advanced bases. Most of the aircraft returned to their home stations on the 7th, but 41-24529 of the 305th, which was at Portreath, did not return until 28th March.

On 8th March, 67 aircraft set out for the marshalling yards at Rennes, where 54 bombed, losing two Missing in Action. Two more attacks on targets in France, on 12th and 13th March, were carried out without losses. These relatively short penetrations into occupied territory, could be provided with fighter escort, and it was the inability of this fighter escort to take off, due to bad weather, that caused the 78 aircraft despatched to Rouen-Sotteville on 17th March, to be recalled before they had departed the English coast.

It was back to Germany on the 18th, when the U-Boat yards at Vegesack were the target for 73 B-17s of the First Wing and 24 B-24s of the Second Wing. This was one of the most successful bombing missions of this period, and gave Eighth Air Force Commanders considerable optimism about the ability of the bombers to defend themselves against the Luftwaffe, once the forces engaged could be increased to 300 or more which was the number originally conceived for such operations. On this day, the German fighters had engaged the bombers in a running battle from Heligoland to the target area, and then out on the return trip, as far as sixty miles beyond the coastline, yet only one B-17 and one B-24 were lost. Considering that it provided an example of accurate and apparently effective bombing, it was a reassuring mission.

The 303rd Group scored a triple distinction on the Vegesack mission. The sole First Wing aircraft missing, came from this Group although it was manned by a crew on detachment from the 92nd Group. Another 303rd aircraft, 42-5723, was lost when it was skilfully landed in a field three miles south-west of Molesworth on return from the mission, and the Group provided the Eighth's first Medal of Honour winner when 1st Lt Jack Mathies flying in the 'DUTCHESS' was hit by shrapnel from exploding flak and mortally wounded. He continued to man his bomb sight and dropped the bombs on the target.

A return was made to Wilhelmshaven U-Boat yards on the 22nd. Sixty-nine B-17s out of 76 despatched, were able to bomb with the loss of one aircraft from the 91st Group. The ill fated aircraft had been assigned to the Group for only one week, and carried a 92nd Bomb Group crew.

Twelve new aircraft joined the 303rd Bomb Group during March. One was 42-5483 'RED ASS', shown here with Capt Brinkley's crew. None of the twelve survived into 1944. 'RED ASS' went Missing in Action on 29th November 1943 leaving 42-29664 'JERSEY BOUNCE Jr' as the only survivor of the twelve remaining in the Group. *Ben Smith*

Next day, the 91st lost another aircraft in totally different circumstances. This time, it was one of the originals, 41-24545 'MATSIE', it had its interior burned out at Bassingbourn when a mechanic lit a cigarette during repairs to the oxygen system. 'MATSIE' became the first Eighth Air Force B-17 to be salvaged due to an accident on the ground when an air crew were not in control of the aircraft.

Two more short trips to occupied territory rounded off the month. Rouen-Sotteville marshalling yards on the 28th where another 91st Group plane was lost, and Rotterdam shipyards on the 31st, the third mission of the month when there were no losses in action. This last mission of the month, provided the first fatal mid-air collision between two Eighth Air Force B-17s over England, when two 303rd Bomb Group aircraft collided during assembly and crashed at Mears Ashby. Eight were killed in 41-24559 'OOOLD SOLJER' one of the Group's original aircraft and seven were killed in 42-29573 'TWO BEAUTS', a comparatively new aircraft which had joined the Group on 6th March. On return from this mission, the 305th Group's 41-24617 'SOUTHERN COMFORT' crashed at Wickam Bishops, after the crew had baled out.

The 92nd Bomb Group was still without operational aircraft. At the start of the month it had eleven B-17Es assigned and two of these were transferred on detached service to the Provisional Blind Approach Training Flight at Bassingbourn on 30th March. Two or three of the B-17Es were away on detached service with Eighth Air Force Service Command acting as navigational lead aircraft for fighters ferrying to the Twelfth Air Force in North Africa.

During March, replacement aircraft for the First Wing Groups, were sent to Alconbury for distributing and this gave rise to optimism among the 92nd's personnel that they were at last receiving new aircraft, but then hopes were dashed as the aircraft soon left for the other Groups.

Several crews from the 92nd were on detached service to the 91st and 303rd Bomb Groups during the month. Three of these crews were Missing in Action. In fact, the Group had lost more crews on operations during March, than had the 303rd and 305th Bomb Groups.

During the winter months, weather had been the cause of many cancelled missions. The English and European weather would plague the Eighth to the bitter end, and sometimes caused more losses than the enemy. For really successful precision daylight bombing, good clear weather was needed, both over the bases in eastern England and the targets in western Europe. Such combinations were rare, and by March 1943 this matter was appreciated, and began to receive the attention of Eighth Air Force leaders.

Each bombing mission had four critical phases. One! Take off. Two! Assembly. Three! The Bomb Run. Four! Landing. The disruption by the weather of any of these phases, could wreck much careful and detailed planning and on occasions caused heavy losses of aircraft and crews.

Take off could be accomplished in near blind conditions, by skilled co-ordination between the pilot and co-pilot and was often done when only a few lights were visible on either side of the runway. However, the margin for error was small, and with a heavily loaded aircraft on a relatively short runway often proved too small with disastrous consequences. An additional hazard was that, should any problems develop after take off, it was impossible to land in such conditions, although poor visibility at take off was often localised, and other airfields not too far away were often in clearer weather.

The assembly of large formations of heavily loaded four engined bombers, even in clear weather was no easy task, and no other Air Force developed this with more skill and precision than the Eighth. During 1943, with increasing experience, larger formations were assembled and it was during this period that the Buncher and Splasher Beacons came into use which allowed the assembly of many missions which would otherwise have been cancelled.

It was during March that real efforts began to be made to develop Blind Bombing and Blind Landing Techniques in the Eighth Air Force. The First Bombardment Wing Provisional BAT (Blind Approach Training) Flight had been set up at Bassingbourn and during the month, 30 officers completed training at this flight. On the 30th March, B-17Es 41-9023 and 41-9103 were transferred from the 92nd Bomb Group to Bassingbourn for the use of the flight.

During February, Eighth Bomber Command sent six men to the Radar Establishment at Great Malvern to study the British System 9000 (OBOE) and in March, two officers and four mechanics went to Great Malvern to study the British ARS5153 (H2S).

On 3rd March, 305th Bomb Group's B-17F 42-5745 was sent on detached service to RAF Wyton where, helped by the men who had been at TRE, the Eighth's first installation of OBOE was carried out. A second installation was carried out on 41-24359 which positioned at Wyton on 23rd March.

On 10th March, the 91st and 303rd Bomb Groups were relieved from assignment to the Twelfth Air Force. This assignment had started on 23rd November 1942 but the two Groups had continued to operate with the Eighth Air Force, to which they were attached for supply and administration.

During the month, 64 B-17s were despatched to the Eighth from North Africa, the greatest number to reach the UK in any month since October 1942. Many were assigned to the active Bomb Groups direct from St Eval, some on the day following their arrival in England.

Prior to 1st March, each of the four operational Groups had acquired a DB-7B for training. The one assigned the 91st Bomb Group, AL441, was wrecked in a taxiing accident at Bassingbourn on 4th March when the landing gear was raised instead of the flaps.

UNIT	\multicolumn{4}{}{OPERATIONAL AIRCRAFT}	COMBAT CREWS	NON OPERATIONAL AIRCRAFT ASSIGNED

UNIT	TYPE	ASS	ON HAND	OP	COMBAT CREWS	NON OPERATIONAL AIRCRAFT ASSIGNED
91BG	B-17F	37		24	20	2 B-17E
306BG	B-17F	39		33	21	1 DB-7B
101PBW	B-17F	76		57	41	
303BG	B-17F	36		29	18	1 DB-7B
305BG	B-17F	42		25	20	1 DB-7B
102PBW	B-17F	78		54	38	
1 BW	B-17F	154		111	79	
92BG	B-17E	9		5	2	1 DB-7B

AIRCRAFT and CREW STATUS at 2000 Hours on 31st March 1943

COMBAT ORDER No	8AF MISS No	DAY	TARGET	DESP	BOMB	LOST MIA	LOST OTHER
			OPERATIONAL DIARY: MARCH 1943		**No OF AIRCRAFT**		
108	39	4th	Hamm, Marshalling Yards	71	14	5	0
			Rotterdam, Shipyards		28	0	0
109	40	6th	Lorient, Port Area	71	65	3	0
110	41	8th	Rennes, Marshalling Yards	67	54	2	0
113	42	12th	Rouen Sotteville, Marshalling Yards	72	63	0	0
114	43	13th	Amiens-Longueau, Marshalling Yards	80	44	0	0
			Abbeville/Drucat, Airfield		8	0	0
			Romescamps, Target of opportunity		21	0	0
			Crevecoeur, Target of opportunity		1	0	0
116	44	17th	Rouen-Sotteville, Marshalling Yards	78	0	0	0
117	45	18th	Vegesack, U-Boat Yards	76	73	1	1
120	46	22nd	Wilhelmshaven, U-Boat Yards	76	69	1	0
123	47	28th	Rouen-Sotteville, Marshalling Yards	79	70	1	0
124	48	31st	Rotterdam, Shipyards	78	33	0	3
				748	543	13	4

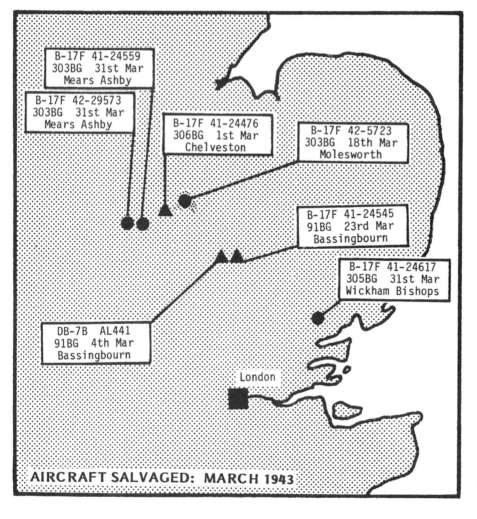

AIRCRAFT SALVAGED: MARCH 1943

B-17F 41-24559
303BG 31st Mar
Mears Ashby

B-17F 42-29573
303BG 31st Mar
Mears Ashby

B-17F 41-24476
306BG 1st Mar
Chelveston

B-17F 42-5723
303BG 18th Mar
Molesworth

B-17F 41-24545
91BG 23rd Mar
Bassingbourn

B-17F 41-24617
305BG 31st Mar
Wickham Bishops

DB-7B AL441
91BG 4th Mar
Bassingbourn

London

AIRCRAFT MISSING IN ACTION
MARCH 1943

4th	B-17F	41-24464	91BG
	B-17F	41-24512	91BG
	B-17F	41-24549	91BG
	B-17F	42-5129	306BG
	B-17F	42-5370	91BG
6th	B-17F	42-5130	306BG
	B-17F	42-5262	303BG
	B-17F	42-5378	306BG
8th	B-17F	41-24514	306BG
	B-17F	41-24588	305BG
18th	B-17F	41-24558	303BG
22nd	B-17F	42-29659	91BG
28th	B-17F	42-29537	91BG

APRIL 1943

The last full month when the four pioneer groups would go it alone. The months of attrition were now over and changes were taking place, although the effect of these on operations would not be felt until the middle of May.

Operationally, it was a bad month, with only four operational missions being completed. Increasingly fierce opposition from enemy fighters was encountered during the month. The first three missions, to Paris on the 4th, to Antwerp on the 5th and to Lorient on the 16th, had strong RAF support after leaving the target but no escort over the target itself and it was while the bombers were thus unprotected that the heaviest fighter attacks occurred. During these three operations the bombers defended themselves well and losses were no higher than on previous occasions.

It was a different story on the 17th, when Bremen was the target, the only one in Germany during the month. An all B-17 force participated and despatched 115 aircraft which equalled the previous best of 9th October 1942. A record 107 bombed the target, the first time the Eighth had had over 100 bombers over a target. This force also suffered a record loss when sixteen aircraft failed to return. Forty-six more were damaged. Never had such sustained and well co-ordinated defences been encountered before.

It was the leading 101st Provisional Wing which sustained all the losses, the 91st losing six and the 306th ten. A measure of the disaster that had befallen the 306th was that the previous highest loss incurred by a Group on a mission had been the 303rd's five on 23rd January.

Such losses of planes could now be made up more quickly than in the past, the 91st received six and the 306th four new aircraft on the 19th, and a further eight were assigned to the 306th on the 20th. The lost combat crews were much more difficult to replace, however, many replacement crews were received by the 306th during the last week of April and on the 30th, the Group had twenty-seven full crews available for combat operations, a figure exceeded only by the 305th Bomb Group.

For the 92nd Bomb Group, the month provided the first real proof that at last the group was to go back to combat operations. On the 20th, the first two B-17Fs, 42-5745 and 41-24359, arrived. These were the two aircraft which had served in the 305th Bomb Group and had been sent to RAF Wyton in March to have OBOE fitted. A third arrived on the 23rd. Eight on the 24th, and eight on the 25th, giving the Group 19 by the end of the month. Several of these were the newest B-17Fs assigned to the Eighth, barely one month old and equipped with the new Tokyo tanks in the outer wings. These aircraft were assigned to the 325th and 407th Bomb Squadrons. The 326th Bomb Squadron was still at Bovingdon and the 327th had more exotic equipment to come in May. The group still had nine B-17Es assigned, three were away on detached service, being used as navigational escorts for fighter aircraft ferrying to North Africa.

Several 92nd Bomb Group combat crews spent the month on detached service with the 91st Bomb Group and on that fateful 17th April mission, when the 91st lost six aircraft, one of them carried a 92nd Bomb Group crew, the fourth crew the Group had lost while on detached service.

FIELD ORDER No	8AF MISS No	DAY	TARGET	No OF AIRCRAFT			
				DESP	BOMB	LOST	
						MIA	OTHER
125	49	4th	Billancourt, Paris, Industrial	97	85	4	0
126	50	5th	Antwerp, Industrial	79	64	4	0
129	51	16th	Lorient, Port Area	83	59	1	0
130	52	17th	Brement, Industrial Area	115	106	16	0
			Target of opportunity		1	0	0
				374	315	25	0

OPERATIONAL DIARY: APRIL 1943

'TAINT A BIRD' 42-3090, in open country at Clonakilty, Ireland, after landing on 7th April. Flown out on 2nd May, it went to the 4th Wing before joining the 351st Bomb Group on 17th June. Later served in No 2 Combat Crew Replacement Unit. *Stan Bishop*

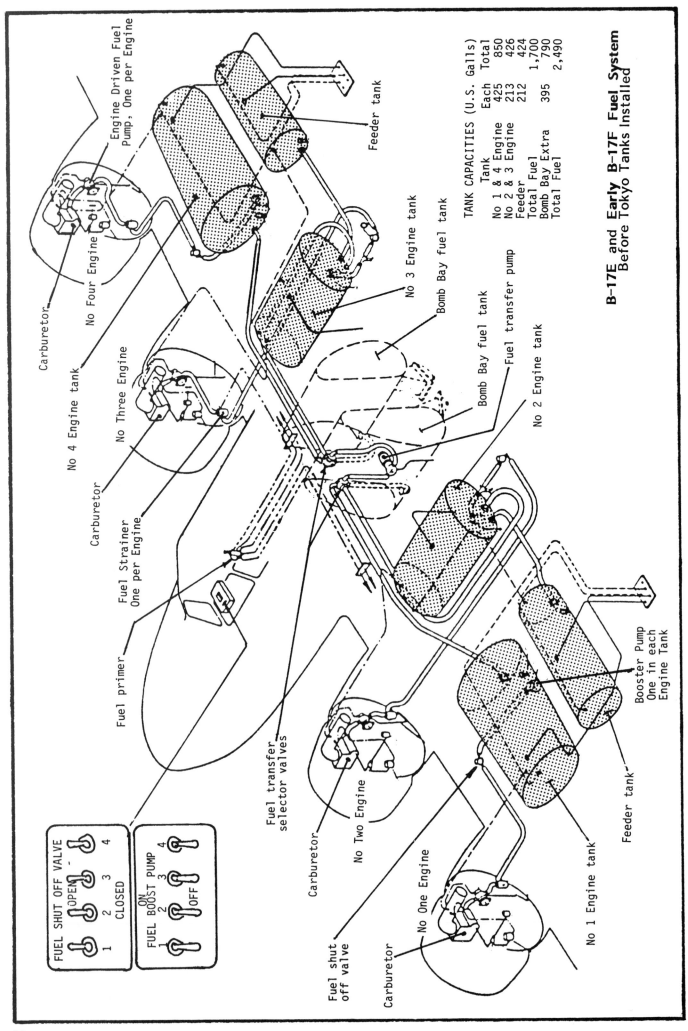

B-17E and Early B-17F Fuel System
Before Tokyo Tanks Installed

TANK CAPACITIES (U.S. Galls)		
Tank	Each	Total
No 1 & 4 Engine	425	850
No 2 & 3 Engine	213	426
Feeder	212	424
Total Fuel		1,700
Bomb Bay Extra	395	790
Total Fuel		2,490

Engine Driven Fuel Pump, One per Engine

Carburetor

No Four Engine

Feeder tank

No 4 Engine tank

No Three Engine

No 3 Engine tank

Carburetor

Bomb Bay fuel tank

Bomb Bay fuel tank

Fuel transfer pump

No 2 Engine tank

Fuel Strainer One per Engine

Fuel primer

Fuel transfer selector valves

Carburetor

No Two Engine

Fuel shut off valve

Carburetor

No One Engine

No 1 Engine tank

Booster Pump One in each Engine Tank

Feeder tank

FUEL SHUT OFF VALVE
OPEN
CLOSED
1 2 3 4

FUEL BOOST PUMP
ON
OFF
2 3 4

50

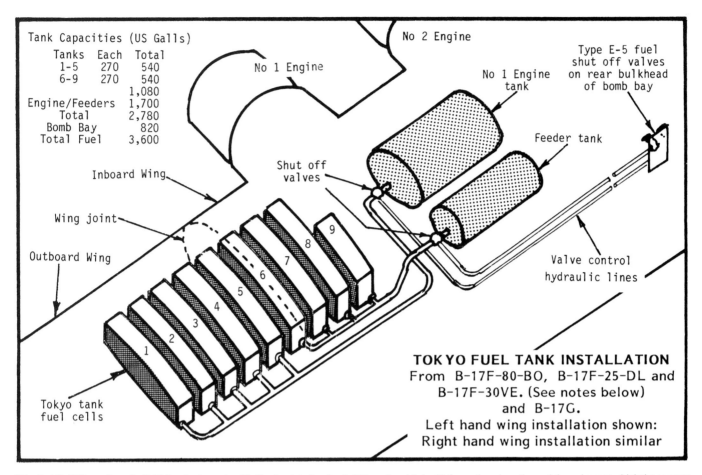

Tank Capacities (US Galls)

Tanks	Each	Total
1-5	270	540
6-9	270	540
		1,080
Engine/Feeders		1,700
Total		2,780
Bomb Bay		820
Total Fuel		3,600

No 2 Engine

No 1 Engine

Type E-5 fuel shut off valves on rear bulkhead of bomb bay

No 1 Engine tank

Feeder tank

Inboard Wing

Wing joint

Outboard Wing

Shut off valves

Valve control hydraulic lines

Tokyo tank fuel cells

TOKYO FUEL TANK INSTALLATION
From B-17F-80-BO, B-17F-25-DL and B-17F-30VE. (See notes below) and B-17G.
Left hand wing installation shown:
Right hand wing installation similar

The first B-17Fs equipped with Tokyo tanks arrived in England during April. Although published information gives the serial numbers at which these were first installed as: Boeing 42-29932, Douglas 42-3074 and Vega 42-5855, it is not possible to establish which were the first Tokyo tank planes to arrive as there appears to be some variance from these serial numbers.

The installation of these tanks caused more re-assignments of aircraft between Groups than did any other reason. The first movement occurring during June/July 1943 after it had been decided that the Fourth Bombardment Wing would be equipped entirely with aircraft having Tokyo tanks fitted. This resulted in several planes being swapped between First and Fourth Bombardment Wing Groups.

It was due to this exchange that the variance in serial numbers becomes apparent as many of the aircraft leaving the Fourth Wing due to them not having the Tokyo tanks fitted had serial numbers well past those normally quoted.

Since the fitting of these tanks was a major engineering change, involving alterations to the inboard and outboard wings, as well as the installation of the cells and fuel lines, it would be logical that it was done progressively on the production lines and therefore some planes arrived with the changes only partially complete. The fact that the Base Air Depots had personnel at Fourth Bombardment Wing stations helping to install these tanks would seem to confirm this theory.

The second movement of aircraft between Groups occurred in September 1943 when the First Division concentrated the remaining Tokyo tank aircraft into the 41st Combat Wing. The final changes came in March 1944 when it was decided to withdraw 100 non-Tokyo tank planes and return them to the United States where they would be used for training purposes.

The Tokyo tanks consisted of nine leakproof cells in each wing. Cells one to five being in the outboard wing and cells seven, eight and nine being in the inboard wing with cell number six being in the space at the wing joint. The five outboard cells (1–5) were connected to the outboard engine tank and the four inboard cells (6–9) were connected to the inboard engine feeder tank. To remove the cells it was first necessary to remove the outboard wing panel. There was no means of indicating the fuel quantity in the tanks. Control was by hydraulic means from valves located on the rear bulkhead of the bomb bay and was accomplished by pulling the 'TEE' handle out, hence the term often used by combat crews 'to pull the Tokyo's'. When the valves were opened the fuel drained by gravity into the engine or feeder tank. In the event of damage to the hydraulic lines, spring pressure automatically opened the valves.

This month, for the first time since December 1942, the North Atlantic ferry route was used for deliveries of aircraft from the USA. A record 289 B-17s made the crossing, 261 of these by the northern route. Many of them were assigned to the five new groups which arrived in the Theatre during the month. They were spearheaded by eight B-17Fs of the 95th Bomb Group which arrived at Alconbury on the 9th. On the 18th, seven aircraft of the 94th Bomb Group arrived at Bassingbourn, and the next day, 20 belonging to the 96th and 14 from the 351st Bomb Groups, arrived at Polebrook. By the 27th, 28 B-17Fs assigned to the 379th Bomb Group, had arrived at Bovingdon.

The 94th, 95th and 96th Bomb Groups were scheduled to join the Fourth Bombardment Wing but would spend most of May on First Bombardment Wing airfields and would fly their first three missions on Field Orders issued by the First Bombardment Wing Headquarters. The 351st and 379th Bomb Groups were assigned to the First Bombardment Wing on their arrival in England.

The three factories producing B-17s had between them produced over 300 B-17Fs during April. The aircraft now coming off the production lines were equipped with additional fuel tanks (Tokyo tanks) in the wings outboard of the Nos 1 and 4 engines. Some of these 'Tokyo tank' aircraft were assigned as replacements to the four active groups in the First Bombardment Wing.

UNIT	OPERATIONAL AIRCRAFT				COMBAT CREWS	NON OPERATIONAL AIRCRAFT ASSIGNED
	TYPE	ASS	ON HAND	OP		
91BG	B-17F	42		34	24	2 SBA B-17E, 1 SBA B-17F, 1 DB-7B
306BG	B-17F	38		33	27	1 SBA B-17F, 1 DB-7B
101PBW	B-17F	80		67	51	
303BG	B-17F	41		27	19	1 SBA B-17F, 1 DB-7B
305BG	B-17F	45		34	29	1 SBA B-17F 1 DB-7B
102PBW	B-17F	86		61	48	
1 BW	B-17F	166		128	99	
92BG	B-17E	9		0	0	1 DB-7B, 2 L-4B
92BG	B-17F	18		0	0	
94BG	B-17F	17		0	0	At Bassingbourn
94BG	B-17F	17		0	0	At Thurliegh
95BG	B-17F	33		0	0	
96BG	B-17F	34		0	0	
351BG	B-17F	39		0	0	
379BG	B-17F	29		0	0	

Table title: AIRCRAFT and CREW STATUS at 2000 Hours on 30th April 1943

AIRCRAFT MISSING IN ACTION
APRIL 1943

4th	B-17F	41-24609	303BG
	B-17F	42-5146	305BG
	B-17F	42-5232	305BG
	B-17F	42-5253	305BG
5th	B-17F	41-24465	306BG
	B-17F	42-5072	306BG
	B-17F	42-5431	306BG
	B-17F	42-29660	306BG
16th	B-17F	42-5220	305BG
17th	B-17F	41-24459	91BG
	B-17F	41-24467	306BG
	B-17F	41-24488	306BG
	B-17F	42-3034	306BG
	B-17F	42-5070	91BG
	B-17F	42-5171	306BG
	B-17F	42-5172	91BG
	B-17F	42-5251	306BG
	B-17F	42-5337	91BG
	B-17F	42-5391	91BG
	B-17F	42-5394	306BG
	B-17F	42-29574	91BG
	B-17F	42-29625	306BG
	B-17F	42-29631	306BG
	B-17F	42-29643	306BG
	B-17F	42-29658	306BG

Note: There were no losses to Salvage during April.

'STELLA' 42-29651 being worked by a mobile repair unit in a field at Lytchett Minster, where it landed on arrival from Marrakesh on 7th April. After repair it was flown out and joined the 384th Bomb Group on 27th June, surviving to return to the USA in 1944. *US Air Force*

Two B-17Fs being ferried from Marrakesh were lost on arrival in England. These were 42-3062 which crashed at Hayle on the 5th and 42-29505 which overshot St Eval and crashed in the mountains at Foel Cwm in Wales on the 11th. Two others made emergency landings in fields where they were repaired and flown out to depots before joining operational Groups. These were 42-3090 which landed at Clonakilty in Ireland on the 7th and was flown out on the 2nd May and the second was 42-29651 which landed at Lytchet Minster and was repaired and flown out.

Two L-4B-Pl Piper Cubs, the smallest aircraft to serve in the Eighth Air Force, were assigned to the 92nd Bomb Group on 8th April and on the 17th, DB-7B, AL397 joined the 91st Bomb Group as a replacement for AL441 which had been wrecked on 4th March.

MAY 1943

A month almost as significant as August 1942 when the Eighth had first started operations against German occupied Europe.

Five new Groups would start combat operations during the month and the 92nd Bomb Group would resume operations. For the first time, over 1,000 aircraft were despatched during a month. The Eighth still had a long way to go to match its nocturnal partner, RAF Bomber Command, which had despatched 1,000 aircraft on a single night, twelve months before.

At the beginning of the month, only the four pioneer Groups with 128 B-17s were available for combat and they would fly two more missions alone. The first on May-Day to St Nazaire was the only mission flown by these four Groups together when they all lost aircraft Missing in Action. For the 306th, which lost three, it was particularly disastrous, coming so soon after the Group's loss of ten over Bremen on the 17th April. The battered remnants of the Group put down at Predannack, here the badly damaged 42-29649, piloted by Lt Lewis P Johnson, crumpled to a standstill, its final flight completed. For his actions in this plane this day Sgt Maynard Smith received the Medal of Honour.

The final go it alone mission came on 4th May, when 79-B-17s were despatched to Antwerp. For the first time P-47s provided high cover and withdrawal support. Only three Groups provided B-17s for this attack, the 306th put up 20 aircraft which joined 13 B-24s from the 2nd Bomb Wing on a diversion. Thanks to this diversion and to the excellent fighter cover provided, the main force encountered only 20 to 30 enemy fighters and no bombers were lost.

Since the start of operations in August 1942 the First Bombardment Wing had despatched 3,286 B-17s and 125 B-24s on operational flights. Two B-17Es, 103 B-17Fs and one B-24 had been lost, Missing in Action. The highest losses had been incurred by the 306th Group which had lost 37 aircraft. The 91st had lost 23, the 303rd 21, and the 305th, 17.

On 13th May the newly arrived 94th, 95th and 96th Bomb Groups assigned to the Fourth Bombardment Wing commenced operations and the 351st Bomb Group, the newest Group to join the First Bombardment Wing was ready and operational. This day also saw the opening of the Eighth's most intensive period of operations to date. The First Wing despatching aircraft on six days out of nine.

Objectives on 13th May, were Luftwaffe airfields in France. The four experienced Groups despatching 97 planes to the airfield at Meaulte, where 88 bombed. The three Fourth Wing Groups and the 351st Bomb Group were briefed to attack airfields at St Omer. For the 96th Bomb Group, things went wrong early in the day when a waist gun was accidently fired inside 42-29752 during take off, injuring two gunners and damaging the tailplane. Unable to land the aircraft, the pilot ordered the crew, except the co-pilot, to bale out over land and then took the aircraft out over the Wash where the two pilots baled out. The co-pilot survived but the pilot was lost. This aircraft was officially listed as Missing in Action. The Group had abandoned the mission in mid-Channel and had therefore achieved the dubious distinction of having lost its first aircraft in action without ever having crossed the enemy coast or having been fired on by hostile forces. The 351st had also abandoned the mission in mid-Channel and only the 94th and 95th Groups had carried on to their assigned targets.

The next day the First Wing despatched 115 aircraft to bomb Kiel, the most distant target attempted so far by the Eighth. The force included seven from the 92nd Bomb Group making its re-appearance in combat after months of inactivity. One hundred and nine aircraft bombed for the loss of three, one coming from the 92nd Group. The 351st joined the 96th in an attack on Courtrai Air Depot making this its first mission when bombs were dropped and losing two Missing in Action. Also taking part in operations for the first time this day were B-26 Marauders of the 322nd Bomb Group (M) assigned to the Third Bombardment Wing.

The 14th May had been the first occasion when the Eighth had despatched over 200 bombers in one day; 196 were B-17s. On the 15th, Wilhelmshaven should have been the target but weather caused targets of opportunity on Heligoland, Dunne and Wangerooge Islands to be bombed. The 351st flew with the Fourth Wing to Emden. Six B-17s from the First Wing were Missing in Action, including three from the 306th

305th Bomb Group marshals at end of Chelveston's runway '06' awaiting the take off signal. J type hangar on right and new loop type dispersal being constructed at left foreground. *US Air Force – National Air and Space Museum*

42-5382 'THE WITCHES TIT' had joined the 303rd Bomb Group in February 1943. It spent most of May with the Air Force Service Command. On the 31st, it was assigned to the 379th Bomb Group and on 2nd June the 379th reported it as on DS at Little Staughton. On 7th June it was assigned once more to the 303rd Bomb Group (from Langford Lodge via Little Staughton). How did it come to be assigned to the 379th Bomb Group and then return to the 303rd? Was it ever on hand with the 379th at Kimbolton? There are many questions like this that the records can not answer. More un-answered questions lie in the 'PROJ MK 86' stencilled under the aircraft's data panel. Aircraft crossing by the Southern Route seem to have had this style of two or three letter project number, while those crossing by the Northern Route carried un-prefixed five figure numbers. Additionally the records show this aircraft as being allocated to PROJ MK 103 and not 86 as shown on this photograph. *Ben Smith*

Group. The 92nd lost an aircraft which was not reported in the loss listings and it has taken considerable research to establish its identity. One plane which did return, but never flew again, was the 305th's 42-29673 'OLD BILL', it had come through a most severe encounter with enemy fighters. A 20mm burst had shattered the nose, instantly killing the navigator and wounding the bombardier, subsequent attacks had injured the pilot, co-pilot, radio operator, top turret gunner, waist gunner and a photographer who was on board.

After a day's rest, the U-Boat base at Lorient was visited on the 17th. For the first time, the Fourth Wing was briefed for the same target as the First Wing. For the first time too the Fourth Wing issued its own Field Order, the Wing's first three missions having been flown on Field Orders issued by the First Wing. The 351st Bomb Group did not participate on this days operations. Four First Wing aircraft were lost, all coming from the 305th Bomb Group.

On the 19th, the U-Boat yards at Kiel were the target, for the first time the 351st Bomb Group flew with the First Wing. The 305th Group led the Wing and again suffered heavily, four of the six aircraft missing coming from this Group. Three were originals brought to England by the Group in October 1942.

AIRCRAFT and CREW STATUS at 2000 Hours on 31st May 1943						
UNIT	OPERATIONAL AIRCRAFT				COMBAT CREWS	NON OPERATIONAL AIRCRAFT ASSIGNED
	TYPE	ASS	ON HAND	OP		
91BG	B-17F	36	36	28	20	2 B-17E, 1 DB-7B, 4 Oxford
351BG	B-17F	45	42	9	23	1 B-17E
101PBW	B-17F	81	78	37	43	
92BG	B-17F	20	19	13	25	8 B-17E, 1 DB-7B, 3 L-4B
305BG	B-17F	41	41	20	18	1 B-17E, 1 B-17F
306BG	B-17F	41	41	37	24	1 B-17E, 1 B-17F
102PBW	B-17F	102	101	70	67	
303BG	B-17F	41	41	23	17	14 B-17F, 1 B-17E, 1 DB-7B
379BG	B-17F	38	37	14	21	1 B-17E
384BG	B-17F	25	25	0	0	
103PBW	B-17F	104	103	37	38	
1 BW	B-17F	287	282	144	148	
92BG	YB-40	11	11	3	11	

MAY 1943

There were no operations on the 20th but a plane which had been with the 306th Group a month, 42-29786, was wrecked when it struck the ground at Dunsby when low flying on return from a practice bombing mission to the Wash.

Wilhelmshaven U-Boat yards were the target for the 98 B-17s despatched on the 21st. The 92nd Group had been briefed to accompany the Fourth Wing to Emden but the six planes that took off were unable to find the other Group formations and returned without bombing. At Wilhelmshaven, 77 planes bombed the target. The Luftwaffe put up a determined resistance and four planes from 91st and three from 306th Groups were missing. One of the 306th's aircraft lost was piloted by 1st Lt M V Judas who had been flying the aircraft which had crashed at Dunsby the previous day.

A fourth 306th aircraft, 42-3127, was Missing in Action this day. This aircraft was not one of those scheduled to fly the mission with the 306th Group and it is thought that it was flying with the Fourth Bomb Wing's 94th Group and was carrying a 94th Group crew.

It was a week before the final mission of the month was flown. It came on the 29th, when the Wing despatched 169 aircraft, the largest force to date, to the old favourite, St Nazaire U-Boat base. One hundred and forty-seven planes bombed the target, losing eight. Three came from 379th Bomb Group, which had despatched 24 on this its first bombing operation. A hard initiation into combat for the Group.

One of the first replacement aircraft received by the 379th Group was 42-5859 which had been with the Group nine days when it flew the 29th May mission. On return it was crash landed at Little Staughton finishing its brief career with the 379th. Its pilot, Maj Carson had also been at the controls of 42-29942 when it was wrecked at Prestwick at the end of the ferry flight from the USA and it seems that 42-5859 had been assigned to replace this aircraft. Although out of the 379th, 42-5859 still had an eventful future ahead, but this was not to start until after its assignment to the 303rd Bomb Group in October.

Also flying on operations for the first time on 29th May, were seven YB-40s of the 92nd's 327th Bomb Squadron. The first had been assigned to the Group on 8th May, with 12 being on hand by the 18th. There should have been 13, but 42-5732 had got lost on the way over from the USA, ran out of fuel and force landed on the Isle of Lewis. The aircraft was dismantled and taken the 40 miles to Stornoway. Exactly how it left the Island is not known, some reports say it was re-built on the airfield and flown out, others say it was taken out by sea. It never served in the Eighth Air Force and was subsequently returned to the USA in February 1944, and went to Dayton, Ohio for re-conditioning. Again it is not known if the journey to the USA was made by sea or air. If this aircraft was in fact re-assembled and flown back to the USA then it is the only known (B-17) serving in England that was dismantled at the site of a forced landing, moved over land and then re-built and flown again.

So ended a month when the intensity of operations is evident by the losses. The First Wing had lost 47, and the Fourth Wing 15, making a total of 61 B-17s compared with 25 in April the previous worst month. The real battle of Germany had now begun and the losses would grow, month by month, until the Spring of 1944.

The second fatal mid air collision had occurred on 7th May, when the 351st Group was returning to Polebrook from a practice bombing mission. A 508th Bomb Squadron plane, 42-29491, and a 509th Bomb Squadron plane, 42-29865, touched over the airfield and both plummeted to the ground and burst into flames, all 19 crew were killed.

B-17F 42-29819 left the 305th Group for the Air Force Service Command on the 18th May. The reason for its loss to the Group, or its subsequent fate, is not known, but there is no further record of it serving and it would seem that it was salvaged at this time.

A new Provisional Bombardment Combat Wing was established during the month. This was the 103rd with headquarters at Molesworth and it came into being by the issue of General Order No 60 dated 18th May. This new Wing had been created to absorb the new Groups which joined the First Wing during May and June, its formation brought about the first changes in Group to Wing assignments since the Provisional Wings had come into being in December 1942. The 303rd Group was transferred from the 102nd Provisional Wing into the new 103rd Provisional Wing and was joined in this new Wing by the 379th Group. The 351st Group was assigned to the 101st Provisional Wing and the 92nd Group was assigned to the 102nd Provisional Wing. The order establishing the 103rd Provisional Bombardment Combat Wing also gave orders for the movement of the Headquarters of the 102nd Provisional Bombardment Combat Wing from Chelveston to Thurleigh, this becoming effective on 18th May.

A new type joining the Wing in May was the Airspeed Oxford, the first British built aircraft to be assigned to the Wing. Four were taken on hand by the 91st Group on the 16th, for use by the Blind Approach Training Flight. New residents at Alconbury were Piper Cubs 43-713 and 43-714 which joined the 92nd on the 19th but 43-714 was re-assigned to the 95th Group the next day. Also joining the 92nd, was DB-7B, AL496 which was transferred from the 305th Group on the 31st.

May also saw a further dispersal of the remaining B-17Es in the 92nd Bomb Group. The 303rd, 305th, 306th, 351st and 379th Bomb Groups all receiving one during the month. Some of these had been modified for use as Target Tugs, they were to be used for non operational flying.

Passing through the United Kingdom during the month were two B-17Es, 41-2535 and 41-9016. These were true veterans having served originally with the Tenth Air Force in India where they had flown against the Japanese over Burma. Later they had transferred to Palestine and had flown missions against the Germans and Italians in the Eastern Mediterranean several weeks before the Eighth Air Force had flown its first missions from England. Their third theatre of operations had been North West Africa after they had joined the Twelfth Air Force. For retirement they had been alloted to the Air Transport Command for transition training of ferry pilots in the USA and were on the first leg of the ferry flight over the North Atlantic. It would seem that 41-9016 did not get to its promised destination as later in the year it was back in North Africa and was lost on a highly secret night mission out of Tunisia in December 1943.

Hangar accommodation on First Wing bases was limited and was always full with major maintenance and repairs. Much of the routine servicing was done on squadron dispersals, in this case an engine change. The weather was not always as kind as it was when this photograph was taken. *US Air Force*

			OPERATIONAL DIARY: MAY 1943				
FIELD ORDER No	**8AF MISS No**	**DAY**	**TARGET**	**No OF AIRCRAFT**			
				DESP	**BOMB**	**LOST**	
						MIA	**OTHER**
	53	1st	St. Nazaire, U-Boat Base	78	29	7	1
	54	4th	Antwerp, Industrial Transport	79	65	0	0
			Diversion	20	0	0	0
139	55	13th	Meaulte, Industrial Aviation	97	88	0	0
			St Omer/Longuenesse, Airfield	14	0	0	0
141	56	14th	Kiel, Ship Yard	115	109	3	0
			Courtrai, Airfield	18	13	2	0
142	57	15th	Heligoland, Düne and Wangerooge Islands	113	76	5	1
			Emden, Industrial Areas	19	18	1	0
	58	17th	Lorient, Port and U-Boat Base	100	80	4	0
	59	19th	Kiel, U-Boat Yard	123	103	6	0
			Diversion	24	0	0	0
	60	21st	Wilhelmshaven, U-Boat Yard	98	77	7	0
			Emden	6	0	0	0
	61	29th	St. Nazaire, U-Boat Base	169	147	8	0
				1073	805	46	2

The 94th, 95th and 96th Bomb Groups, assigned to the Fourth Bombardment Wing, Flew their first three missions on Field Orders issued by the First Bombardment Wing. The three operations are tabulated below. From the operation of 17th May, Fourth Bombardment Wing issued Field Orders for these Groups

COMBAT ORDER No	**8AF MISS No**	**DAY**	**TARGET**	**No OF AIRCRAFT**			
				DESP	**BOMB**	**LOST**	
						MIA	**OTHER**
139	55	13th	St Omer/Longuenesse Airfield	58	31	1	0
141	56	14th	Antwerp-Industrial Transport	45	38	1	0
			Courtrai Airfield	21	21	0	0
142	57	15th	Emden, Industrial Area	61	41	0	0
				185	90	2	0

The first Fourth Bombardment Wing B-17 to be listed Missing in Action was 42-29752 of 96th Bomb Group. During the take off at Grafton Underwood for the Wing's first mission on 13th May, the left waist gun accidentally discharged causing serious damage to the plane's tail section and controls and injured two gunners. As the photograph shows, most of the right horizontal stabiliser was shot away and this made the plane difficult to control. Some of the crew baled out in the vicinity of Grafton Underwood and the others abandoned the plane near the Wash, the pilot losing his life. The plane crashed in the sea. Although the plane had not entered enemy territory or been fired on by hostile forces it had failed to return to friendly territory after taking off on an operational flight and was therefore officially reported as Missing in Action. *Geoff Ward*

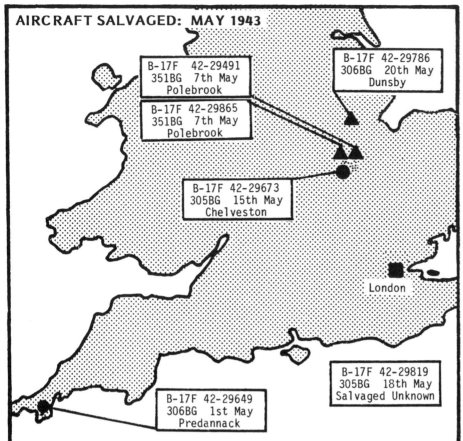

AIRCRAFT SALVAGED: MAY 1943

B-17F 42-29491
351BG 7th May
Polebrook

B-17F 42-29865
351BG 7th May
Polebrook

B-17F 42-29786
306BG 20th May
Dunsby

B-17F 42-29673
305BG 15th May
Chelveston

London

B-17F 42-29819
305BG 18th May
Salvaged Unknown

B-17F 42-29649
306BG 1st May
Predannack

AIRCRAFT MISSING IN ACTION MAY 1943			
1st	B-17F	41-24547	91BG
	B-17F	41-24610	303BG
	B-17F	42-5422	306BG
	B-17F	42-5435	305BG
	B-17F	42-5780	303BG
	B-17F	42-5784	306BG
	B-17F	42-29620	306BG
13th	B-17F	42-5406	91BG
	B-17F	42-29642	91BG
	B-17F	42-29647	305BG
14th	B-17F	41-24481	91BG
	B-17F	42-5243	303BG
	B-17F	42-29859	351BG
	B-17F	42-29862	351BG
	B-17F	42-30003	92BG
15th	B-17F	42-3173	351BG
	B-17F	42-5055	306BG
	B-17F	42-29481	303BG
	B-17F	42-29677	306BG
	B-17F	42-29744	306BG
	B-17F	42-29820	92BG
17th	B-17F	42-5063	305BG
	B-17F	42-5219	305BG
	B-17F	42-29663	305BG
	B-17F	42-29745	305BG
19th	B-17F	41-24483	91BG
	B-17F	41-24573	305BG
	B-17F	41-24590	305BG
	B-17F	41-24624	305BG
	B-17F	42-5155	305BG
	B-17F	42-29701	351BG
21st	B-17F	41-24515	91BG
	B-17F	42-3053	91BG
	B-17F	42-3214	306BG
	B-17F	42-5857	91BG
	B-17F	42-29657	91BG
	B-17F	42-29666	306BG
	B-17F	42-29806	306BG
29th	B-17F	41-24602	303BG
	B-17F	42-3113	379BG
	B-17F	42-29531	305BG
	B-17F	42-29742	305BG
	B-17F	42-29773	379BG
	B-17F	42-29792	305BG
	B-17F	42-29838	351BG
	B-17F	42-29878	379BG

FOURTH BOMBARDMENT WING AIRCRAFT MISSING IN ACTION WHILE OPERATING FROM FIRST WING BASES			
13th	B-17F	42-29752	96BG
14th	B-17F	42-3115	95BG
17th	B-17F	42-29627	94BG
	B-17F	42-29767	96BG
21st	B-17F	42-3110	95BG
	B-17F	42-3127	94BG
	B-17F	42-29682	94BG
	B-17F	42-29727	94BG
	B-17F	42-29734	96BG

Note: 42-3127, Missing in Action on 21st May was a 306th Bomb Group aircraft but is thought to have been operating with a 94th Bomb Group crew. It is listed as a 94th Bomb Group statistic and is not included on any 306th Bomb Group or First Bombardment Wing listings.

Below: the 306th Bomb Group's 42-29786 in a field at Dunsby after Lt Judas had 'bellied' it in while low flying on 20th May. Judas and crew went Missing in Action the next day. *US Air Force*

JUNE 1943

For the first time, the First Bombardment Wing despatched over 200 planes on a single mission this month. There were no operations until the 11th, but training continued and planes were still lost. On the first day of the month, the 91st's 42-3210 was taxiing at Bassingbourn, when a flare cartridge exploded in the nose, the resulting fire wrecking the aircraft. The 381st lost their first aircraft since the Group's arrival in the United Kingdom when on the 11th, 42-30020 made a belly landing at Ridgewell.

The first mission of the month, on the 11th, had Bremen as the briefed target, but this was obscured by cloud and haze, so Wilhelmshaven was attacked. Seven aircraft from the First Wing were Missing in Action. Six were from the 379th Group and another B-17F from this Group, 42-5809 was put down badly damaged at RAF Coltishall and never flew again.

The next day, the only fatal flying accident of the month occurred, when the 384th's 42-30036, crashed at Grafton Underwood following a mid air collision while on a training flight. All five crew were killed.

On the 13th, Bremen was again at the end of the target tape and this time 122 of the 151 planes despatched were able to attack. The First Wing suffered but lightly from the defences, with four planes Missing in Action. The Fourth Wing suffered their first heavy losses in action, when 22 of their planes failed to return. This was the first occasion when Fourth Wing

losses exceeded those of the First Wing, and was the heaviest loss of B-17s yet in a single day.

There followed, on the 15th an abortive mission to targets in France when the planes were recalled before reaching the French coast.

The most important operation during June was that to Hüls on the 22nd. A record force of 298 B-17s of the Eighth were despatched, 214 coming from the First Wing, the first time the Wing had despatched over 200 B-17s on one mission.

Making their first entry into the combat arena this day were the 381st and 384th Bomb Groups. Together they made up a Combat Wing to attack Antwerp. This day was the second of the three occasions during 1942/43 when all participating First Wing Groups lost aircraft in action. The two new Groups did not escape, both losing two planes and the 381st had two more crash land in England on return, 42-3226 at Manston and 42-29984 at or near Framlingham. Both were salvaged. The single 92nd Group aircraft lost was a YB-40, the only one of the type to be lost in action.

The next day, 180 planes were despatched to Villacoublay and Bernay St Martin airfields but all were recalled. It was while the aircraft of the 381st Group at Ridgewell were being bombed up for this operation, that

Brookwood Cemetery, Surrey, where many of the Eighth's personnel Killed in Action or in accidents during the first year were buried. Included were those killed in the explosion at Ridgewell on 23rd June. Later Brookwood was replaced by the cemetery at Cambridge. *US Air Force – National Air and Space Museum*

'CAREFUL VIRGIN' in flight over England, 14th June. A broken crankshaft over Idaho in September 1942 delayed her departure for England. Joining the 91st Bomb Group in early 1943. She was the oldest operational plane in the Group at 31st March 1944. *US Air Force – National Air and Space Museum*

42-30024 blew up on dispersal, killing 23 men and damaging another B-17F, 42-29992, that had to be salvaged.

After a day's rest, 197 aircraft were despatched to bomb Hamburg on the 25th, but bad weather broke up the formations and made formation flying very difficult. The 167 planes attacking sought out convoys and targets of opportunity. Fifteen aircraft failed to return.

A return was made to aviation and transport targets in France on the 26th. Once again the weather made things difficult and of the 165 aircraft despatched only 56 carried out effective sorties. Five B-17s, all from the 384th Group, were Missing in Action.

On the 28th, St Nazaire port area and Beaumont-le-Roger airfield were the targets for 147 First Wing B-17s. At St Nazaire, the 351st Group suffered its first heavy loss on a single mission, when four of the five aircraft Missing in Action came from this Group.

The last operation of the month, on 29th June, saw 148 planes airborne in two forces for attacks on airfields and other aviation targets in Northern France but 10/10 cloud was encountered and all returned without bombing.

Increasing resistance from the Luftwaffe was shown in the mounting loss rate which reached a new high of 51 for the month. The 379th Group was the worst hit, twice losing six aircraft. The new 384th, had also suffered grievously, losing ten, on its first four completed missions. For the second month running, the 92nd had come out with the lowest losses, the YB-40 lost on the 22nd, being its only loss of the month.

On joining the First Bombardment Wing, the 381st Bomb Group was assigned to the 101st Provisional Bombardment Combat Wing and the 384th Group was assigned to the 103rd Provisional Bombardment Combat Wing. Each of the Provisional Bombardment Wings now had three Groups assigned and the organisation of the First Bombardment Wing as now established, would remain unchanged until September.

There was considerable movement among the training types assigned to the Wing during the month. Two of the 91st Group's Oxfords were re-assigned, DF299 going to the 303rd, and DF399 to the 92nd Group where it was joined by four more during the month. The 92nd also received the first Cessna C-78 Bobcat to come into the Wing when 42-58434 arrived on the 5th. Aircraft moving out of the 92nd, were Oxford W6588 to the 306th on the 15th and DB-7B, AL496 to the 384th on the 14th.

Perhaps the most interesting of all the types was Tiger Moth T6369 which joined the 303rd on the 12th but its stay was short lived as it was at Polebrook for repair by the 17th. Even shorter in its stay was Lysander V9778 which was assigned to the 92nd Bomb Group on the 26th June and dropped from assignment on the 27th, it is not known if this aircraft ever joined the Group. Further movement of the B-17Es in the 92nd occurred. Two which had been on detached service with the Air Force Service Command acting as Navigational escorts for fighter aircraft ferrying to North Africa returned during the month and the 381st and 384th Bomb Groups each received one for non operational duties.

JUNE 1943

AIRCRAFT and CREW STATUS at 2000 Hours on 30th June 1943						
	OPERATIONAL AIRCRAFT			COMBAT CREWS	NON OPERATIONAL AIRCRAFT ASSIGNED	
UNIT	TYPE	ASS	ON HAND	OP		
91BG	B-17F	46	43	21	18	1 B-17E, 1 B-17F, 1 DB-7B, 2 Oxford
351BG	B-17F	41	38	19	13	1 B-17E
381BG	B-17F	44	41	17	11	1 B-17E
101PBW	B-17F	131	122	57	42	
92BG	B-17F	24	24	11	6	7 B-17E, 1 B-17F, 1 DB-7B, 1 C-78, 3 L-4B, 4 Oxford
305BG	B-17F	48	48	27	20	1 B-17E, 1 B-17F
306BG	B-17F	43	43	34	24	1 B-17E, 1 B-17F
102PBW	B-17F	115	115	72	50	
303BG	B-17F	45	37	29	18	1 B-17E, 1 B-17F, 1 DB-7B, 1 Oxford
379BG	B-17F	44	41	21	13	1 B-17E
384BG	B-17F	37	36	12	10	1 B-17E, 1 DB-7B
103PBW	B-17F	126	114	62	41	
1 BW	B-17F	372	351	191	133	
92BG	YB-40	10	8	0	8	

The old and the new. 'RIGOR MORTIS' 41-24591, an original with eight month's service, and 42-30155, with less than a month's service, ready to take off at Chelveston for the mission of 29th June. *US Air Force – National Air and Space Museum*

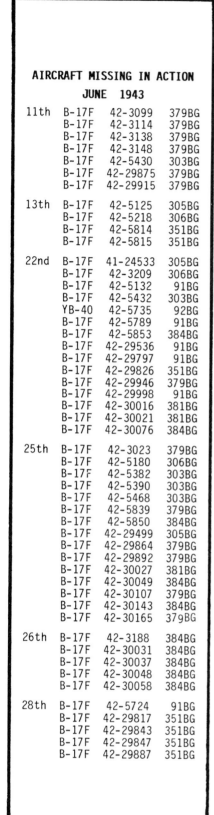

AIRCRAFT MISSING IN ACTION
JUNE 1943

11th	B-17F	42-3099	379BG
	B-17F	42-3114	379BG
	B-17F	42-3138	379BG
	B-17F	42-3148	379BG
	B-17F	42-5430	303BG
	B-17F	42-29875	379BG
	B-17F	42-29915	379BG
13th	B-17F	42-5125	305BG
	B-17F	42-5218	306BG
	B-17F	42-5814	351BG
	B-17F	42-5815	351BG
22nd	B-17F	41-24533	305BG
	B-17F	42-3209	306BG
	B-17F	42-5132	91BG
	B-17F	42-5432	303BG
	YB-40	42-5735	92BG
	B-17F	42-5789	91BG
	B-17F	42-5853	384BG
	B-17F	42-29536	91BG
	B-17F	42-29797	91BG
	B-17F	42-29826	351BG
	B-17F	42-29946	379BG
	B-17F	42-29998	91BG
	B-17F	42-30016	381BG
	B-17F	42-30021	381BG
	B-17F	42-30076	384BG
25th	B-17F	42-3023	379BG
	B-17F	42-5180	306BG
	B-17F	42-5382	303BG
	B-17F	42-5390	303BG
	B-17F	42-5468	303BG
	B-17F	42-5839	379BG
	B-17F	42-5850	384BG
	B-17F	42-29499	305BG
	B-17F	42-29864	379BG
	B-17F	42-29892	379BG
	B-17F	42-30027	381BG
	B-17F	42-30049	384BG
	B-17F	42-30107	379BG
	B-17F	42-30143	384BG
	B-17F	42-30165	379BG
26th	B-17F	42-3188	384BG
	B-17F	42-30031	384BG
	B-17F	42-30037	384BG
	B-17F	42-30048	384BG
	B-17F	42-30058	384BG
28th	B-17F	42-5724	91BG
	B-17F	42-29817	351BG
	B-17F	42-29843	351BG
	B-17F	42-29847	351BG
	B-17F	42-29887	351BG

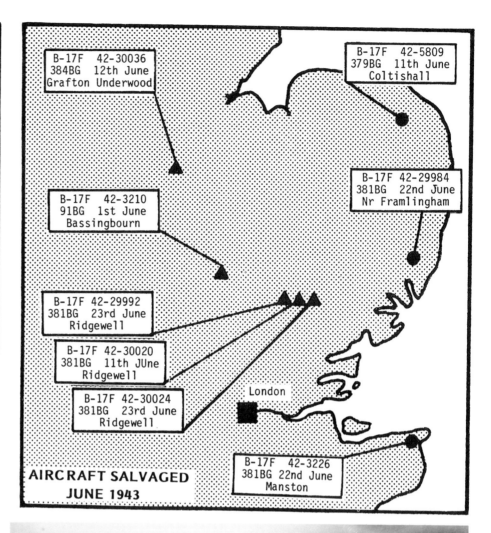

B-17F 42-30036
384BG 12th June
Grafton Underwood

B-17F 42-5809
379BG 11th June
Coltishall

B-17F 42-3210
91BG 1st June
Bassingbourn

B-17F 42-29984
381BG 22nd June
Nr Framlingham

B-17F 42-29992
381BG 23rd June
Ridgewell

B-17F 42-30020
381BG 11th JUne
Ridgewell

B-17F 42-30024
381BG 23rd June
Ridgewell

London

B-17F 42-3226
381BG 22nd June
Manston

AIRCRAFT SALVAGED
JUNE 1943

First 381st Group plane to be salvaged in England was 42-30020 which belly landed at Ridgewell on 9th June. *Ron McKay*

JUNE 1943

FIELD ORDER No	8AF MISS No	DAY	TARGET	No OF AIRCRAFT			
				DESP	BOMB	LOST	
						MIA	OTHER
	62	11th	Wilhelmshaven, U-Boat Yard	166	139	7	1
	63	13th	Bremen, U-Boat Yard	151	102	4	0
			Kiel, Harbour Area, Target of opportunity		20	0	0
	64	15th	Targets in France. Recalled before reaching French Coast	-	-	-	-
	65	22nd	Hüls, Industrial Rubber	172	134	11	0
			Antwerp, Industrial Transport	42	39	4	2
	66	23rd	Villacoublay	140	0	0	0
			Bernay/St Martin, Airfield	40	0	0	0
	67	25th	Convoys and Targets of opportunity in North West Germany	197	149	15	0
	68	26th	Villacoublay, Industrial Aviation	165	56	5	0
			Poissy, Airfield		5	0	0
			Tricoville, Airfield		39	0	0
	69	28th	St. Nazaire, Port Area	120	104	5	0
			Beaumont-Le-Roger, Airfield	50	43	0	0
	70	29th	Villacoublay Airfield	108	0	0	0
			Tricqueville, Airfield	40	0	0	0
				1391	830	51	3

Table title: OPERATIONAL DIARY: JUNE 1943

'MEMPHIS BELLE' at Bovingdon 9th June 1943, before departure for the USA. *US Air Force – National Air and Space Museum*

July 1st 1943, marked the first anniversary of the touch down at Prestwick of the first B-17E (41-9085) operated by the Eighth Air Force. The combat career of the B-17Es had been short lived. There were still 14 assigned to the First Wing. Seven were with the 92nd Bomb Group and the others were spread out through the other Groups, serving as trainers, target tugs, sometimes as air ambulances, they were still making a valuable contribution to the work of the Wing.

Operationally, July was the most active and successful month to date for the Eighth Bomber Command and culminated in the great sustained aerial offensive when beginning on the 24th and ending on the 30th, 12 major war industry targets, including two in Norway were attacked.

Early in the month, a meeting was held at Fourth Wing at which it was agreed to transfer all aircraft without Tokyo Tanks now in Fourth Wing Groups to the First Wing. Approximately 30 aircraft were involved, mostly in the 94th, 95th and 96th Bomb Groups. As replacements with the outer wing tanks became available, Fourth Wing Groups would be built up to full strength, and all replacements without the tanks would go to First Wing. The transfer had already commenced in June and most First Wing Groups had some of the aircraft transferred from Fourth Wing. By the end of the month, many of these would be 'Missing in Action'. Heaps of tangled wreckage on German soil, victims of the great air battles during the closing days of July.

Late in June, Eighth Bomber Command Headquarters had requested Groups to submit the names of all assigned aircraft. The reason for this request is not clear but many aircraft changed names as a result. In the 92nd Group only the 407th Bomb Squadron complied, with a list of YB-40 names, the Group enclosure stating that names had been removed and that new names were being allocated to the other aircraft. The 379th also reported that re-naming was under way on its aircraft.

The month's operations opened on the 4th, when 192 First Wing planes were despatched to aviation targets in France. The 101st and 103rd Provisional Wings going to Le Mans and the 102nd Provisional Wing going to Nantes. Seven aircraft failed to return and 42-5916 from 92nd Group was landed back at Portreath with severe battle damage and subsequently salvaged there. On the 10th, 185 B-17s were sent to attack airfields at Caen and Abbeville. One B-17F 'STRIC NINE' of the 91st Bomb Group was lost.

For the third successive mission this month, aviation targets in France were the objectives for the 180 planes despatched on the 14th. Four were Missing in Action. Two more, both from 381st Group were lost in England. 42-3223 'RED HOT RIDING HOOD', exploded in mid-air during assembly and crashed near Rattlesden killing six of the crew and on return from the mission, 42-3211 'TS' made a belly landing at Manston and was salvaged.

On the 17th, 207 B-17s were sent to attack industrial targets in North West Germany. This was the second occasion when the First Wing had despatched over 200 planes. Most of the force was recalled due to weather conditions and only 33 from the 101st Provisional Wing were able to bomb. The only loss was 42-29872 'SNOW BALL' an original from the 351st Group, which ditched off the Dutch coast with all the crew except the navigator being picked up by Air Sea Rescue.

It was a week before the Combat Wings were seen forming over Eastern England again. When they did on the 24th, it was to herald the start of the most intensive week's operations to date in the daylight aerial offensive. The target this day at Heroya, in Norway, was the most distant so far attempted and called for a round trip of eight and a half hours. One hundred and eighty B-17s were despatched and 166 successfully bombed the target. One 381st Group B-17F was lost, 42-3217 'GEORGIA REBEL', which was able to make a belly landing in Sweden, the first of many B-17s to land or crash in this neutral country after damage in action made the long flight home to England an uncertain or impossible proposition.

The next day, Hamburg was the target for the 182 planes the First Wing despatched. Weather disrupted assembly and the 92nd, 305th and 306th Groups abandoned the mission leaving 100 aircraft from the other two Combat Wings to bomb the target. Fifteen planes did not return, the highest loss of the month. The 384th lost seven, the highest loss the Group would suffer on a single mission up to March 1944. Six of the seven had been transferred from Fourth Wing Groups as a result of the 'Tokyo Tank' exchange, none of these having been with the Group more than nineteen days. Five were early Douglas built aircraft. Three of the aircraft lost from other Groups had also been formerly with the Fourth Wing.

Hamburg and Hannover were the targets on the 26th. The 101st and 103rd Provisional Wings despatched 121 planes to the former where only 54 were able to bomb losing two from the 91st Group. The 102nd Provisional Wing went to Hannover where 52 out of 60 despatched were able to bomb for the loss of six. The 92nd Group lost three aircraft, the Group's heaviest loss to date. Two of the three were transfers from the Fourth Wing, one, 42-29981, having come from the 96th Group only three days before. Another loss was the 306th's 41-24417, one of the Group's originals, which came down in the sea off Cromer when returning. The crew were quickly rescued.

The 384th Bomb Group suffered the heaviest losses of any First Wing Group during July with twelve B-17s Missing in Action. Seven of these were lost on the 25th including: top, 42-3024 'ROYAL FLUSH'; centre, 42-3075 'LONGHORN' and lower, 42-3122 'APRIL'S FOOL'. *Mike Gibson*

After a day's break the Fieseler Works at Kassel were the target on 28th July. Many of the 182 planes despatched abandoned the mission due to weather. Only 58 bombed the primary or targets of opportunity, seven were Missing in Action. The 306th Group lost two missing and three more in crash landings on return. One, 41-24502, crash landing at Sudbourne, was one of only four of the Group's originals that had survived after ten months of combat operations. Another, 42-29974, crash landed at Framlingham where it hit and damaged a parked B-17F of the 390th Bomb Group, and 42-3076 crash landed at Hawkinge. A fourth loss due to crash landings on return was the 379th's 42-5822 which landed at Foulsham with four injured crew members.

Kiel was the primary objective for the 168 planes despatched on the 29th. Cloud caused many of the 139 which did bomb to choose a target of opportunity. Six were missing, four from the 306th Group. 42-3221 'WHALETAIL' from 381st Group crash landed near Snetterton on return and 42-29690 of the 305th was damaged and landed at Oulton where it was salvaged. This aircraft had been assigned from the 94th Bomb Group just fifteen days before it was salvaged.

The last mission of the month, on the 30th, was a smaller effort than those of the previous six days. The 102nd Provisional Wing did not participate and the other two Wings despatched 119 planes, the smallest number despatched by the First Wing since 21st May. Ninety-four bombed the briefed target at Kassel, losing six. One of the 91st's losses, 41-24399 'MAN-OF-WAR', was the oldest of the B-17Fs assigned to the Group as an original back in the States and one of the oldest B-17Fs serving in the Eighth. The 381st Group lost 42-3100 which had come from the 95th ten days before and 42-29738 an ex-100th Bomb Group aircraft which the 303rd had acquired 17 days previously was ditched 22 miles off Felixstowe with all the crew being rescued by the ASR.

A 379th Group aircraft, 42-3212, crashed and burned while trying to land at Framlingham on return, killing all the crew and another 379th aircraft, 42-5813, crash landed near Alconbury. Two from 351st Group were crash landed, 42-3046 at Woodbridge and 42-29726 at Leiston. From 384th Group, 42-5848 was badly damaged and limped back to Boxted where it was crash landed and salvaged. A sixth aircraft to crash land on return and end up as salvage was 'HELLS BELLE', 42-30157, of 91st Bomb Group which overshot the runway when landing at Bassingbourn.

July had in many respects been a record month. The Fortresses had greatly extended their range of operations, the Fourth Wing with Tokyo Tanks going as far north as Trondheim and east to Oschersleben only 90 miles from Berlin. The cost too had been great. For the first time Eighth Bomber Command had lost over 100 B-17s in a month. Seventy-two had come from the First Wing with 56 Missing in Action and 16 salvaged in England due to damage received while on operational flights. The 384th Group had the heaviest losses with 12 Missing in Action and one salvaged in the UK and the 303rd with four Missing in Action and the 351st with two Missing in Action and two salvaged had come through with the lowest losses.

The YB-40s had continued operations. Twenty having been despatched during the month, five of them abortive. Some re-assignment of these had taken place. On the 16th, two were sent to the 91st and two to the 303rd Groups, and a third was received by the 91st on the 22nd. With this re-assignment, each of the Provisional Wing, had its own YB-40s. This change did nothing to improve the performance of these aircraft operationally and they were soon to be withdrawn from active service altogether.

Early in July, the 326th Bomb Squadron moved from Bovingdon and rejoined the 92nd Bomb Group at Alconbury. The 92nd had been scheduled to move from Alconbury to Podington about 17th July, leaving the 325th Bomb Squadron behind, to become the nucleus of a Pathfinder unit directly under Eighth Bomber Command. On 28th July the movement was postponed due to the bad condition of the runway at Podington.

Movement of the B-17Es continued during the month, 41-9107 going to the 91st Group and 41-9043 going to the 381st in exchange for 41-9019 which returned to the 92nd Bomb Group. Leaving the First Wing was 41-9042 which left the 92nd on the 26th for assignment to the 27th Air Transport Wing. The only other movement of training types was a Piper Cub 43-648 which left the 92nd and was assigned to the 381st Group on the 10th July.

FIELD ORDER No	8AF MISS No	DAY	TARGET	No OF AIRCRAFT			
				DESP	BOMB	LOST	
						MIA	OTHER
	71	4th	Le Mans, Industrial Aviation	121	105	4	0
			Nantes, Industrial Aviation	71	61	3	1
	72	10th	Caen/Carpiquet, Airfield	121	34	1	0
			Abbeville/Drucat, Airfield	64	36	0	0
	73	14th	Villacoublay, Industrial Aviation	116	101	3	0
			Amiens/Glissy, Airfield	64	53	1	2
	74	17th	Industrial Targets in North West Germany	207	33	1	0
	75	24th	Heroya, Industrial	180	166	1	0
	76	25th	Hamburg, U-Boat Yards and Targets of opportunity	182	100	15	0
	77	26th	Hanover	60	52	6	1
			Hamburg	121	54	2	0
	78	28th	Kassel, Industrial Aviation and Targets of opportunity	182	58	7	4
	79	29th	Kiel, U-Boat Yard and Targets of opportunity	168	139	6	2
	80	30th	Kassel, Industrial Aviation	119	94	6	6
				1776	1086	56	16

OPERATIONAL DIARY: JULY 1943

AIRCRAFT and CREW STATUS at 2000 Hours on 31st July 1943						
UNIT	OPERATIONAL AIRCRAFT				COMBAT CREWS	NON OPERATIONAL AIRCRAFT ASSIGNED
	TYPE	ASS	ON HAND	OP		
91BG	B-17F	40	33	10	10	1 B-17E, 1 B-17F, 1 DB-7B, 1 L-4B, 2 Oxford
351BG	B-17F	45	43	17	0	1 B-17E
381BG	B-17F	45	44	9	0	1 L-4B
101PBW	B-17F	130	120	36	10	
92BG	B-17F	36	34	12	0	5 B-17E, 1 DB-7B, 1 C-78, 2 L-4B, 4 Oxford
305BG	B-17F	42	42	20	16	1 B-17E, 1 B-17F
306BG	B-17F	34	33	26	18	1 B-17E, 1-B-17F, 1 Oxford
102PBW	B-17F	112	109	58	34	
303BG	B-17F	42	42	21	22	1 B-17E, 1 DB-7B, 1 Oxford
379BG	B-17F	40	38	17	0	1 B-17E
384BG	B-17F	37	37	15	0	1 B-17E, 1 DB-7B
103PBW	B-17F	119	117	53	22	
1 BW	B-17F	361	346	147	66	
91BG	YB-40	3	3	1		
92BG	YB-40	6	6	2		YB-40 crews are included in B-17 crews
303BG	YB-40	2	2	2		
	YB-40	11	11	5		

The right landing gear of 306th's 42-3087 gave way at Bovingdon, 31st July, causing the aircraft to ground loop. Damage was not serious and following repairs the aircraft returned to the 306th on 31st August. Note that only one landing gear gave way and this saved the aircraft from more serious damage and possible salvage. This point did not escape the top brass and at a later date instructions were issued to pilots having landing gear problems, suggesting that they land with only one gear down instead of the usual all up or all down configuration. This saved many B-17s from the salvage gangs. *US Air Force*

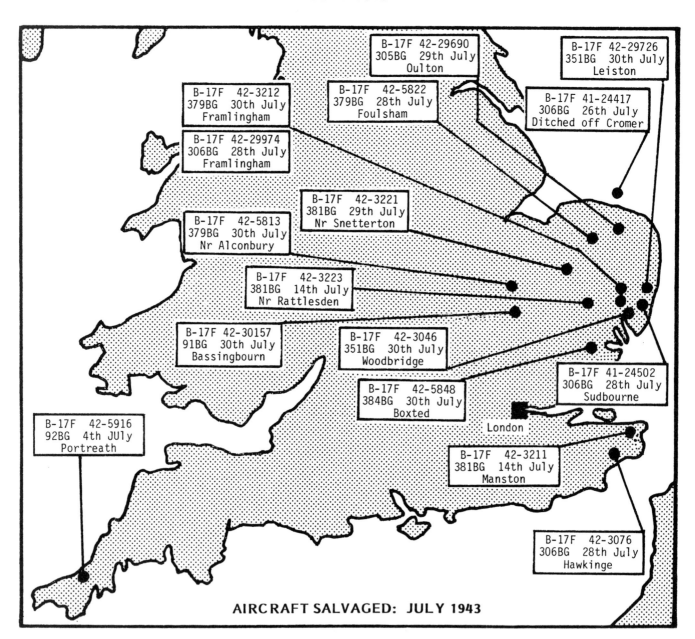

B-17F 42-29690
305BG   29th July
Oulton

B-17F 42-29726
351BG   30th July
Leiston

B-17F   42-3212
379BG   30th July
Framlingham

B-17F   42-5822
379BG   28th July
Foulsham

B-17F 41-24417
306BG   26th July
Ditched off Cromer

B-17F 42-29974
306BG   28th July
Framlingham

B-17F   42-3221
381BG   29th July
Nr Snetterton

B-17F   42-5813
379BG   30th July
Nr Alconbury

B-17F   42-3223
381BG   14th July
Nr Rattlesden

B-17F 42-30157
91BG   30th July
Bassingbourn

B-17F   42-3046
351BG   30th July
Woodbridge

B-17F   42-5848
384BG   30th July
Boxted

B-17F 41-24502
306BG   28th July
Sudbourne

B-17F 42-5916
92BG   4th July
Portreath

London

B-17F   42-3211
381BG   14th July
Manston

B-17F   42-3076
306BG   28th July
Hawkinge

AIRCRAFT SALVAGED: JULY 1943

AIRCRAFT MISSING IN ACTION: JULY 1943

4th	B-17F	42-3235	384BG	25th	B-17F	42-3024	384BG	28th	B-17F	42-3116	92BG
	B-17F	42-5053	305BG		B-17F	42-3069	384BG		B-17F	42-29777	306BG
	B-17F	42-5792	303BG		B-17F	42-3075	384BG		B-17F	42-29779	306BG
	B-17F	42-29641	305BG		B-17F	42-3088	384BG		B-17F	42-29796	379BG
	B-17F	42-29928	381BG		B-17F	42-3122	384BG		B-17F	42-29798	92BG
	B-17F	42-29960	384BG		B-17F	42-3175	379BG		B-17F	42-29970	305BG
	B-17F	42-29967	92BG		B-17F	42-3272	351BG		B-17F	42-30032	384BG
					B-17F	42-5883	384BG				
10th	B-17F	42-29475	91BG		B-17F	42-5917	379BG	29th	B-17F	42-3084	306BG
					B-17F	42-29606	303BG		B-17F	42-5426	306BG
14th	B-17F	42-3049	305BG		B-17F	42-29670	384BG		B-17F	42-5766	306BG
	B-17F	42-3330	384BG		B-17F	42-29813	91BG		B-17F	42-5810	379BG
	B-17F	42-29791	303BG		B-17F	42-29976	381BG		B-17F	42-5826	306BG
	B-17F	42-30011	381BG		B-17F	42-30013	381BG		B-17F	42-29700	384BG
					B-17F	42-30153	381BG				
17th	B-17F	42-29872	351BG					30th	B-17F	41-24399	91BG
				26th	B-17F	42-3031	91BG		B-17F	42-3100	381BG
24th	B-17F	42-3217	381BG		B-17F	42-3119	91BG		B-17F	42-5829	379BG
					B-17F	42-29612	92BG		B-17F	42-29738	303BG
					B-17F	42-29709	92BG		B-17F	42-29746	379BG
					B-17F	42-29900	306BG		B-17F	42-29916	91BG
					B-17F	42-29981	92BG				
					B-17F	42-30156	306BG				
					B-17F	42-30282	305BG				

JULY 1943

339TH BOMBARDMENT SQUADRON (H), AAF
Office of the Operations Officer

A.P.O. 634,
July 14,1943 (Date)

STATUS OF AIRCRAFT AS OF 0800 HOURS

AIRCRAFT SER No	STATUS	ESTIMATED TIME IN	REMARKS
3324	IN		
3123	IN		Pending transfer to 1st Wing
9914	IN		
0172	IN		
9945	IN		
3322	IN		
0153	IN		Pending transfer to 1st Wing
5879	IN		
3275	IN		
3180	IN		
0369	OUT	1000	Acceptance inspection
9828	OUT	Indef	Lacking armour plating

(Signed) ALFRED R. GILL Capt. Air Corps,
OPERATIONS OFFICER.

INSTRUCTIONS: This form will -----------

339th Bombardment Squadron's (96th Bomb Group) aircraft status report of 0800 hours on 14th July shows that 42-3123 and 42-30153 have already been earmarked for transfer to the First Bombardment Wing. This would have been due to their not having the Tokyo tanks fitted yet they are well into the serial range that should have had them fitted. Both went to the 381st Bomb Group on 16th July; 3123 a 96th Group original lasted until 8th October but 30153 that had been assigned to the 96th from Little Staughton on 26th May only lasted in the 381st for nine days before being Lost in Action.

These 91st Group B-17s have just returned from a mission and are taxiing back to their dispersals at Bassingbourn. The leading aircraft is past the most eastern of the four 'C' type hangars and is approaching the point where runways 25 and 31 meet the perimeter track adjacent to the trunk A14 road. Some of the aircraft will have to cross this road to gain access to their dispersals in Wimpole Park. The rear plane is just passing the Control Tower. The Oxford in front of the hangar is probably DF331 or DF335. *US Air Force – National Air and Space Museum*

An early 96th Bomb Group formation, nearest aircraft is 42-29981 **'HELL-LENA'**, which was transferred to the 92nd Bomb Group on 23rd July. Three days later on return from Hannover this plane ditched in the North Sea (photo below), all the crew were rescued. *Geoff Ward* and *Imperial War Museum*

AUGUST 1943

This month, the First Wing completed its first year of operations from British bases. Following the great offensive of blitz week, at the end of July, there was a lull in operations during the first 11 days of August. Only 147 B-17s were operational at the start of the month but the limiting factor was availability of full operational crews. There were 66 available, about half the number that had been available at the beginning of July.

Although there were no Combat Missions flown during the first 11 days of the month, training and test flying continued as Groups strived to regain their strength in aircraft and crews ready for the battle to resume later in the month. The most active day during this period, was the 9th, when each of the nine Groups averaged 48 hours flying. The first loss of the month came during this period when on the 4th, 42-3124 of 303rd Bomb Group crashed near Bala in North Wales, killing all on board. It is not known what mission the aircraft was on to bring it into this area on this day.

By the 11th, aircraft and crew availability had risen to 313 and 207 respectively, and next day, 183 planes were despatched on the first of the month's missions. Targets were Bochum, Gelsenkirchen and Recklinghausen. During the mission, the Groups became scattered and many of the 133 planes bombing did so on targets of opportunity. Twenty-three planes were Missing in Action, the highest loss the Wing had suffered in one day up to this time. The 351st was the only Group to have all its planes return to England, and one of these, 42-29874, crash landed at Leiston and was salvaged. A 379th Group aircraft, 42-3154, was badly damaged on the mission and crash landed at Bury St Edmunds on return. Another 379th aircraft salvaged this day, was 42-29933.

There was no mission on the 13th or 14th, but during local flying on the 13th, 42-3106 of 351st Group, was wrecked in a take off accident at Polebrook.

On the 15th, 180 aircraft were despatched to bomb airfields at Flushing, Poix and Amiens. There was a crash at Alconbury when the landing gear on 42-30447 was retracted too soon during the take off. This was the only loss during the day's operation, all 147 planes bombing returning safely to their bases.

The next day the airfield at Le Bourget came under attack from 171 Fortresses, four failing to return. Flying with the Wing this day was a solitary YB-40, 42-5744 'DOLLIE MADISON', on the only operation undertaken by this type this month and on what turned out to be the final operational mission for the YB-40.

It was on the 17th, the anniversary of the First Mission, that the Eighth Air Force set out on its most ambitious plan to date and one which history has recorded as one of the greatest air battles of all time. Of all the targets attacked by the Eighth, the most well known and most publicised must be Schweinfurt which was the First Wing's assigned target this day. While the Fourth Wing, again making use of the extended range afforded by the Tokyo Tanks, was to bomb Regensburg and then fly on to North Africa completing the first shuttle mission.

As on so many other occasions, carefully made plans were thwarted by the English weather, even on a mid August day. The Fourth Wing was able to take off and assemble as planned but the First Wing's take off was delayed some four hours by fog at their inland bases and thus the plan to split the Luftwaffe between two major formations at the same time was lost.

Most First Wing records were broken this day. A record 230 B-17s were despatched and a record 188 bombed the target. Never before had the wing come under such long and concentrated attack by the Luftwaffe and never before had so many planes failed to return. Thirty-six were missing from the Wing. There would only be two more occasions before the end of March 1944 when losses would be greater than on this day. The 91st Group lost ten Missing in Action and an eleventh crash landed at Manston on return. The 381st lost 11, these were the heaviest losses these two Groups would endure up to March 1944. The 11 lost by the 91st were all comparative veterans. Three were originals and none had served less than four months with the Group, they had a combined service of 74 months, or nearly seven months' each, an average even more remarkable when with the day's losses the Group had now lost 58 B-17s in action, the highest of any Group in the Eighth Air Force. The aircraft crash landing at Manston, 42-5712, was the oldest Vega built B-17 to serve in the Eighth Air Force. It had joined the Group in February 1943.

Another Group suffering heavily, was the 384th, which lost five Missing in Action and a sixth, 42-29728, made a wheels up landing at Grafton Underwood on return and was salvaged. One of the two 92nd Group losses, 42-3455, had been delivered new to the Group from Warton only five days before. One record not broken this day was the operational flying hours. This had been set at 1,192 on the 24th July mission to Norway and the hours on 17th August were 1,149.

Only one day of rest and the Wing's aircraft were back in the air on the 19th. A smaller force this day to attack the airfields at Gilze-Rijen and Flushing. One hundred and twenty-five were despatched, 93 bombed and four were Missing in Action.

Villacoublay air depot was the target for 110 101st and 102nd Provisional Wing aircraft on the 24th, and 86 were able to make an effective strike. Thirty-six planes from the 103rd Provisional Wing flew a diversion. There were no losses this day.

Two more days without operations followed. On the latter of these, the 26th, the 305th lost 42-29508 'SOUTHERN COMFORT JR' when, during maintenance, an engine caught fire and the aircraft exploded and was destroyed. This aircraft had joined the 364th Bomb Squadron on 6th April to replace the original 'SOUTHERN COMFORT' which had crashed on 31st March.

The first attack made by the First Wing and Eighth Bomber Command on new construction sites at Watten, identified as V-Weapon sites, was made on the 27th. Of the 159 planes despatched, 124 bombed and four

'KNOCK OUT DROPPER' is well away after using about half of Molesworth's runway 27. 'J' type hangar on left with technical site beyond. *Imperial War Museum*

were Missing in Action. One, 42-30617 from 92nd Bomb Group, had been delivered from Warton only six days before. Another 92nd aircraft, 42-29698, had its electrical and hydraulic systems shot out by flak and crash landed at Alconbury on return, where it was salvaged.

One more mission on the last day of the month, brought this eventful month to a close. One hundred and seventy planes were despatched to bomb the airfield at Amiens/Glisy, where 105 bombed for the loss of three. Two from the 91st Group had collided just off the English coast and fell into the sea on the way to the target. The falling debris had damaged 42-29973, which crashed at Polegate. One of the aircraft which collided was a Group original. Its loss left only five of the originals in the Group.

The last loss of the month came just 30 minutes before midnight on the 31st, when 42-5376 **'EAGER EAGLE'**, of 422nd Bomb Squadron was on a night training flight with a crew of 11 including an RAF officer. The aircraft collided in mid air with an RAF Beaufighter and crashed at Foulsham. Nine crew were killed, the two survivors being the waist gunners who parachuted to safety.

The month had seen another leap upwards in the Wing's losses to a record figure of 74. For the second month in succession the Eighth had lost more than 100 B-17s in action.

Approval for the formation of Combat Bombardment Wings within the Eighth Air Force, and the issue of Tables of Organisation for these, came through in August and signalled the end of the Provisional Bombardment Combat Wings. Personnel were assigned to the new Combat Wings during August, but were still attached to the Provisional Bomb Wings until the full changes in Wing status came into being in September.

A new Group, the 482nd Pathfinder, was formed at Alconbury on the 20th and shared this station with the 92nd Group. Crews were transferred from the 325th Bomb Squadron of the 92nd Group and the first B-17Fs, also from the 92nd were assigned on the 25th. The 482nd's function was to supply a pathfinder force of radar equipped aircraft for the three Bombardment Wings. It was assigned to the First Bombardment Wing but came under the operational control of Eighth Bomber Command. The Group's activities up to the end of August were confined to training.

On the 16th, 303rd Group's 42-29944 was despatched on a secret mission, returning on the 23rd. The nature of this mission is not known, but one can speculate that it was connected with the 17th August shuttle mission to North Africa. If this was in fact true then it is surprising, considering that this mission was an all Fourth Wing operation.

An interesting and hitherto unreported mix up in the delivery of B-17s had occurred during July and had a sequel in August. This concerned five aircraft which were destined for the Twelfth Air Force in North Africa and were flown across the North Atlantic ferry route to England, from where they should have been ferried to Marrakesh. The ingredients for a mistake were mixed before they departed the USA as orders called for the crews ferrying the planes across the Atlantic to be assigned to the Eighth Air Force when they arrived in England and no provision was made for crews to ferry the aircraft on to North Africa.

OPERATIONAL DIARY: AUGUST 1943							
FIELD ORDER No	8AF MISS	DAY	TARGET	No OF AIRCRAFT			
				DESP	BOMB	LOST	
						MIA	OTHER
	81	12th	Bochum, Gelsenkirchen Recklinghausen and Targets of opportunity	183	0 133	0 23	0 3
	82	15th	Vlissingen (Flushing) Airfield Poix and Amiens Airfields	180	147	0	1
	83	16th	Le Bourget Airfield	180	171	4	0
	84	17th	Schweinfurt, Ball Bearings	230	188	36	2
	85	19th	Gilze-Rijen and Flushing Airfields	125	93	4	0
	86	24th	Villacoublay, Industrial Aviation Diversion	110 36	86 0	0 0	0 0
	87	27th	Watten, V-Weapon Site	159	124	4	1
	88	31st	Amiens/Glissy, Airfield	170	105	3	1
				1373	1047	74	8

42-3222 **'DEUCES WILD'**, an original of the 384th Bomb Group. One of the five aircraft the Group lost at Schweinfurt on 17th August. *Mike Gibson*

AUGUST 1943

On arrival at Nutts Corner these aircraft were flown on to Prestwick, instead of south to North Africa, and were assigned via the normal channels to the Eighth Air Force. One, 42-3398, was modified to an H2S aircraft and the other four were assigned to the Fourth Bombardment Wing. Early in August the error was discovered but it was too late to re-direct the aircraft to their correct destination.

Messages flowed thick and fast between the Air Transport Command and Washington in an effort to sort out the mix up, culminating in one from Air Transport Command to Washington, dated 5th August, stating, 'We were taking five Fortresses destined for the Eighth Air Force and would deliver them to the Twelfth Air Force by the first available ferry crews unless we had instructions to the contrary from Washington'. Unfortunately, the answer to this or the subsequent action taken is not known. It is worth pointing out here that the delivery of aircraft to operational units was a complex operation, the wheels of which were set in motion even before the metal for a particular aircraft was cut. It started with the Munitions Assignment Committee in Washington, a joint British-American organisation which decided how production was to be allocated between the Allied Air Forces. This information then passed down through Material Com-

mand Statistical Section to the Ferrying Division of Air Transport Command who decided priorities of destinations and allocated crews to the factories to ferry the aircraft to modification centres and finally on to combat theatres overseas.

The major moves of non operational types during the month centred around the 92nd and 482nd Groups at Alconbury. The 92nd transferred B-17E, 41-9129 to Snetterton Heath on the 11th and 41-9013 and 9019 to the 482nd on the 27th August. Returning to the 92nd on the 11th was B-17E 41-9107 which had gone to the 91st Group in July. These moves left the 92nd with three B-17Es assigned at the end of August, the lowest total the Group had had of this type since they had been received in exchange for the B-17Fs a year before.

On 1st August Oxford LB522 was transferred from the 92nd to the 305th Group. A new type joining the Wing during the month was Miles Master DL899 which was assigned to the 92nd on the 5th. A mass transfer of training types took place at Alconbury on the 27th when C-78 42-58434, L4Bs 43-657 and 713, Oxfords DF399, LB513 and X7176 together with the newly assigned Miles Master were all transferred from the 92nd to the 482nd Group.

UNIT	TYPE	ASS	ON HAND	OP	COMBAT CREWS	NON OPERATIONAL AIRCRAFT ASSIGNED
91BG	B-17F	28	26	16	14	1 B-17E, 1 DB-7B, 1 Oxford
351BG	B-17F	38	37	16	25	1 B-17E
381BG	B-17F	29	26	15	22	1 B-17E, 1 L-4B
101PBW	B-17F	95	89	47	61	
92BG	B-17F	48	43	13	23	3 B-17E, 1 DB-7B
305BG	B-17F	34	32	18	15	1 B-17E, 1 B-17F
305(S)	B-17F	13	13	11	*	* Special Aircraft for Night Ops crews in standard B-17F totals.
306BG	B-17F	49	45	35	26	1 B-17E, 1 B-17F, 1 Oxford
102PBW	B-17F	144	133	77	64	
303BG	B-17F	35	32	19	16	1 B-17E, 1 DB-7B, 1 Oxford
379BG	B-17F	30	27	19	15	1 B-17E
384BG	B-17F	32	28	20	15	1 B-17E, 1 DB-7B
103PBW	B-17F	97	87	58	46	
1BW	B-17F	336	309	182	171	
482(S)	B-17F	9	6	6	4	2 B-17E, 1 C-78, 2 L-4B, 1 Master 4 Oxford
91BG	YB-40	3	3	3		
92BG	YB-40	5	5	3		
303BG	YB-40	1	1	1		YB-40 Crews are included in B-17F crews.
379BG	YB-40	1	1	0		
384BG	YB-40	1	1	0		
	YB-40	11	11	7		

Title: AIRCRAFT and CREW STATUS at 2000 Hours on 31st August 1943

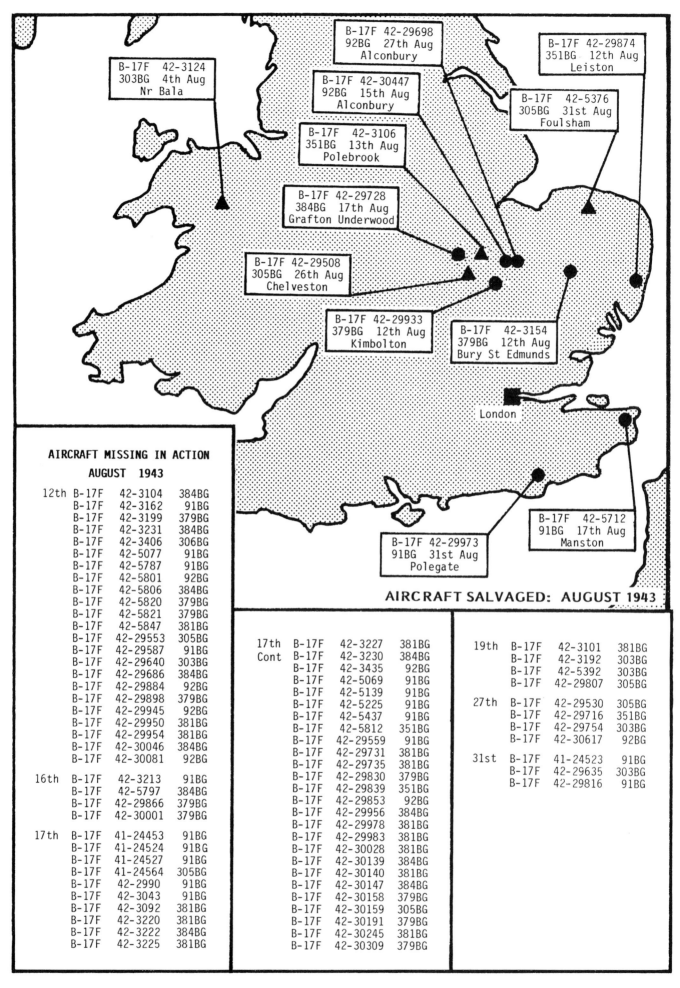

B-17F 42-29698
92BG 27th Aug
Alconbury

B-17F 42-29874
351BG 12th Aug
Leiston

B-17F 42-3124
303BG 4th Aug
Nr Bala

B-17F 42-30447
92BG 15th Aug
Alconbury

B-17F 42-5376
305BG 31st Aug
Foulsham

B-17F 42-3106
351BG 13th Aug
Polebrook

B-17F 42-29728
384BG 17th Aug
Grafton Underwood

B-17F 42-29508
305BG 26th Aug
Chelveston

B-17F 42-29933
379BG 12th Aug
Kimbolton

B-17F 42-3154
379BG 12th Aug
Bury St Edmunds

London

B-17F 42-29973
91BG 31st Aug
Polegate

B-17F 42-5712
91BG 17th Aug
Manston

AIRCRAFT MISSING IN ACTION
AUGUST 1943

12th	B-17F	42-3104	384BG
	B-17F	42-3162	91BG
	B-17F	42-3199	379BG
	B-17F	42-3231	384BG
	B-17F	42-3406	306BG
	B-17F	42-5077	91BG
	B-17F	42-5787	91BG
	B-17F	42-5801	92BG
	B-17F	42-5806	384BG
	B-17F	42-5820	379BG
	B-17F	42-5821	379BG
	B-17F	42-5847	381BG
	B-17F	42-29553	305BG
	B-17F	42-29587	91BG
	B-17F	42-29640	303BG
	B-17F	42-29686	384BG
	B-17F	42-29884	92BG
	B-17F	42-29898	379BG
	B-17F	42-29945	92BG
	B-17F	42-29950	381BG
	B-17F	42-29954	381BG
	B-17F	42-30046	384BG
	B-17F	42-30081	92BG
16th	B-17F	42-3213	91BG
	B-17F	42-5797	384BG
	B-17F	42-29866	379BG
	B-17F	42-30001	379BG
17th	B-17F	41-24453	91BG
	B-17F	41-24524	91BG
	B-17F	41-24527	91BG
	B-17F	41-24564	305BG
	B-17F	42-2990	91BG
	B-17F	42-3043	91BG
	B-17F	42-3092	381BG
	B-17F	42-3220	381BG
	B-17F	42-3222	384BG
	B-17F	42-3225	381BG

AIRCRAFT SALVAGED: AUGUST 1943

17th	B-17F	42-3227	381BG	19th	B-17F	42-3101	381BG
Cont	B-17F	42-3230	384BG		B-17F	42-3192	303BG
	B-17F	42-3435	92BG		B-17F	42-5392	303BG
	B-17F	42-5069	91BG		B-17F	42-29807	305BG
	B-17F	42-5139	91BG				
	B-17F	42-5225	91BG	27th	B-17F	42-29530	305BG
	B-17F	42-5437	91BG		B-17F	42-29716	351BG
	B-17F	42-5812	351BG		B-17F	42-29754	303BG
	B-17F	42-29559	91BG		B-17F	42-30617	92BG
	B-17F	42-29731	381BG				
	B-17F	42-29735	381BG	31st	B-17F	41-24523	91BG
	B-17F	42-29830	379BG		B-17F	42-29635	303BG
	B-17F	42-29839	351BG		B-17F	42-29816	91BG
	B-17F	42-29853	92BG				
	B-17F	42-29956	384BG				
	B-17F	42-29978	381BG				
	B-17F	42-29983	381BG				
	B-17F	42-30028	381BG				
	B-17F	42-30139	384BG				
	B-17F	42-30140	381BG				
	B-17F	42-30147	384BG				
	B-17F	42-30158	379BG				
	B-17F	42-30159	305BG				
	B-17F	42-30191	379BG				
	B-17F	42-30245	381BG				
	B-17F	42-30309	379BG				

Above: taking off for Amiens on 31st August is **'POLLY ANN'** 42-30647 of 305th Bomb Group. This aircraft crashed on the airfield at Chelveston on return from an operational mission on 23rd September 1943 killing all ten crew.

Top right: shortly after this photograph was taken, **'LADY LIBERTY'** of 305th Bomb Group was hit by flak and went down.

Lower right: one of 422nd Bomb Squadron's night flying B-17Fs, **'EAGER EAGLE'** 42-5376, collided with an RAF Beaufighter over Norfolk on 31st August and crashed at Foulsham. *Mike Gibson*

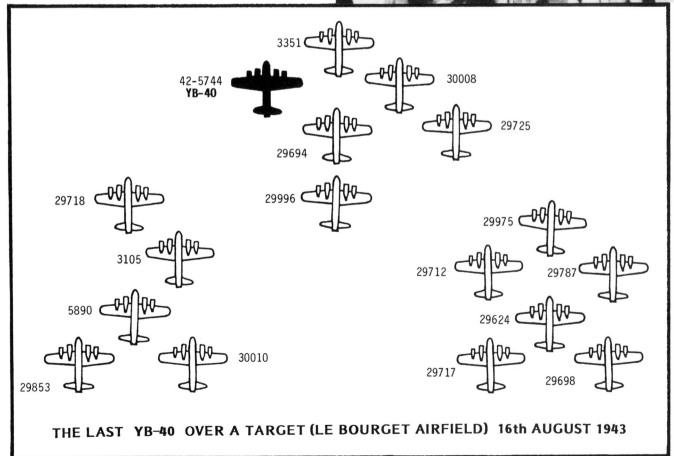

THE LAST YB–40 OVER A TARGET (LE BOURGET AIRFIELD) 16th AUGUST 1943

The month commenced with 345 B-17s assigned to the 11 Groups of the Wing. Of these, 188 were operational, and there were 175 crews available for combat. The average number of planes available had not changed much throughout the summer, 191 had been available for operations on 1st July. There had however been a marked increase in the number of combat crews reported available since July when there were 133 full crews ready for operations. There were still 11 YB-40s, which, although no longer taking part in operations, were still on hand as operational aircraft. During August the 379th and 384th Groups had each acquired one of these aircraft.

The month would see changes in the organisation of the Bombardment Wings, the Combat Bomb Wings and the introduction of new operational techniques.

Although the statistics show 17 missions despatched this month, more than in any month to date, the actual number of aircraft bombing was the lowest since June. This apparent distortion of figures being due to two despatched missions which were abandoned without bombs being dropped and to six being night missions involving no more than five planes at a time.

The night missions were the first undertaken by B-17s of Eighth Bomber Command and were carried out in conjunction with the RAF. Specially modified B-17Fs assigned to the 422nd Bomb Squadron of the 305th Bomb Group were used for these night attacks. The first was on the night of 8th September when five aircraft led by 41-24614 'WE THE PEOPLE' piloted by Maj Price were despatched at 2030 hours to join 254 of RAF Bomber Command in an attack on Boulogne and all five returned safely at 2320 hours.

Five more night missions were flown during the month and on the last of these, on 27/28th September, 42-29555 'CENTAUR', failed to return and became the first Eighth Air Force B-17 lost on a night mission.

The first day operation of the month on the 2nd met with adverse weather conditions causing two Wings to abandon and the third to be recalled. Next day, 168 planes were despatched to the Aircraft Repair Depot at Romilly-sur-Seine. Most of the 140 attacking aircraft were able to bomb the primary but some were hampered by cloud over the target area and so bombed the airfields at St Andre de L'Eure and Evreax/Fauville. Four B-17s were Missing in Action.

The largest force despatched during September was sent to Stuttgart on the 6th. Finding the primaries covered by cloud, targets of opportunity were attacked. It turned out to be the most costly day of the month with 27 aircraft Missing in Action. Three landed in Switzerland, the first B-17s from the First Wing to do so. Twelve of the missing aircraft ditched in the English Channel when they ran out of fuel on the return flight, all 118 crew members were saved by the Air Sea Rescue.

Fuel shortage was also the primary cause for the loss of five other aircraft which crash landed in southern England. One of the longest serving B-17Fs still with the 91st Group, 42-2970, crash landed at Winchelsea, it was the oldest Douglas built aircraft still serving in the First Wing. Crash landed at Wych Cross was 42-3198 from 92nd Group. The 351st had 42-29841 crash land at New Romney, it was over a month before the Group was notified that this aircraft was to be salvaged and it was carried on the Group's assigned list until 11th October. Also crash landed near New Romney was 306th Bomb Group's 42-30065 which was soon salvaged. Also salvaged was 303rd Group's 42-29944 which crash landed near West Malling. Two others, 42-5845 from 381st Group and 42-29477 from 306th Group, made forced landings near the coast in Kent but were repaired and returned to their parent groups on 22nd September.

For the 92nd Group, which up to now had not suffered as heavy losses as some of the other Groups during the summer of 1943, September 6th was a bad day. The longest serving Group in the Eighth Air Force, it was the anniversary of the Group's first mission when it had taken the B-17Es to Meaulte and lost its first aircraft in action. On the Stuttgart mission the Group lost seven Missing in Action, the heaviest in the Wing and the Group's highest loss up to March 1944. The Group's eighth loss of the day was the crash landed plane at Wych Cross.

On the 7th, 105 aircraft bombed Brussels-Evere Aircraft Repair Depot without loss, and two days later 140 bombed airfields at Lille and Vitry-en-Artois again without loss. On return, 42-3140 from 351st Group landed at West Wrattling between rows of Horsa Gliders.

The 482nd Group suffered a heavy blow on the 14th when B-17E 41-9051 crashed into a fog shrouded hillside near Keswick. All ten on board were killed in this the Group's first loss of an aircraft since its activation. Included in those killed were Capt William C Anderson, Commander of the 813rd Bomb Squadron, Maj Thomas C Henderson of 482nd Bomb Group and Maj Henry B Williams from First Bombardment Division.

On the 15th, the airfield at Romilly-sur-Seine was the target for the 93 planes which the 101st and 102nd Provisional Wings despatched and where 87 bombed without losses in action but two were crash landed and

Two Newhaven based Air Sea Rescue launches, 177 and 2548. Both played a major role in rescuing the crews of twelve First Wing B-17s which ditched off the South coast on return from the mission of 6th September. *Imperial War Museum*

salvaged on return, the 305th's 42-5910 at Hawkinge and the 351st's 42-29825 at Polebrook. The 103rd Provisional Wing did not participate in the day's mission.

Also absent from hostile skies on the 15th, was the 92nd Bomb Group which was busy making the delayed move from Alconbury to Podington. The 482nd Bomb Group took over control at Alconbury once the 92nd had moved.

The 92nd had a depleted complement of aircraft to move to Podington. The eight losses of the 6th September had not been replaced and on the 13th and 14th, four planes had been transferred to the 379th and 384th Groups leaving the Group with 31 assigned B-17s. On the 15th, two were away with the Air Force Service Command, so only 29 were on hand to transfer to Podington. Strangely the Ferry Command delivered six replacement aircraft for the Group, to Alconbury, on the day the Group moved. It is possible the weather prevented these being delivered direct to Podington as many aircraft returning from the day's mission landed away. The 482nd held these aircraft on hand until next day when they were delivered to Podington and assigned to the 92nd Bomb Group.

The 16th was the day when long planned changes to the organisation of the First Bombardment Wing became effective. These changes were not visible in the sense that units moved stations or changed their status or assignments relative to one another. The changes made were mostly on paper only and probably went unnoticed by the majority of personnel in the units concerned. The most important of these changes was that the three Provisional Wings were replaced by properly constituted units which had authorised Tables of Organisation and could have personnel and subordinate units assigned to them. The most confusing aspect of these changes concerned the organisation at Brampton Grange where a recently constituted organisation, the 'First Bombardment Division', was activated on the 13th September. It took over the functions formerly carried out by the First Bombardment Wing and the change was effected

by relieving the personnel and subordinate units from assignment to the First Bombardment Wing and then re-assigning them to the 'First Bombardment Division'.

The First Bombardment Wing did not go out of existence. It was redesignated as the First Combat Bombardment Wing (Heavy) and this designation was transferred to Bassingbourn where it assumed the functions previously carried out by the 101st Provisional Bombardment (Heavy) Combat Wing. This move was effected by assigning the personnel and subordinate units previously attached to the 101st Provisional Wing to the First Combat Bombardment Wing (H).

At Thurleigh the 102nd Provisional Bombardment Combat Wing's functions were assumed by the 40th Combat Bombardment Wing (Heavy), and at Molesworth the 103rd Provisional Bombardment Combat Wing's functions were assumed by the 41st Combat Bombardment Wing (Heavy). At both locations the changes being implemented by relieving units and men from attachment to the Provisional Units and assigning them to the new Combat Bombardment Wings. The 40th and 41st Wings were new units with no previous history or lineage within the Air Force. They had been constituted as Bombardment Wings in the USA in early 1943 and moved to England to join the Eighth Air Force.

The Headquarters Squadron of the 40th Bomb Wing had arrived at Brampton on 8th June and the Headquarters Squadron for the 41st Bomb Wing had arrived on 28th July. In August, when approval for the establishment of Combat Wings had been given, they were re-designated as Combat Bombardment Wings (Heavy) and some personnel who had been assigned prior to the 16th September were then attached to the Provisional Wings.

On the 16th, 147 B-17s set out for Nantes port area and Nantes/ Chateau-Bougon airfield. One hundred and thirty-one bombed, losing seven Missing in Action, four coming from the 379th Group, 42-30018 of 305th landed at St Just airport, Land's End, on return. The crew were

The location and details of this photograph taken on 17th September are unknown. On the ground is 324th Bomb Squadron's 42-3072 which had been assigned to the 91st Bomb Group from the 96th Group the previous day. It has numbers one, two and three engines running and number four is un-cowled. In flight is 401st Bomb Squadron's 42-3060 **'HELLS BELLE'** which had been assigned from the 385th Bomb Group four days before. Parked in the background are at least ten RAF Lancasters or Halifaxes. *US Air Force – National Air and Space Museum*

uninjured and according to reports the aircraft was not damaged. It would be interesting to know how this was accomplished as the airport was not active and was reputed to have been rendered unusable by obstacles to prevent enemy aircraft landing. Some local reports say the aircraft was dismantled and removed but it seems more likely it was flown out as it returned to the Group on the 28th September. The 92nd did not take part in the day's operations, still settling into their new base at Podington. The Group had 26 planes available for operations but it was the evening of the 16th before the Group reported crews available for operations.

A week of inaction followed and it was the 23rd before the next mission was despatched. A new record was established this day as it was the first occasion when two missions were flown in one day. The first, which was also Eighth Air Force Mission number 'One Hundred', saw 177 planes of the First and 40th Combat Wings despatched to the Nantes port area but only 46 were able to claim effective sorties. The 40th Combat Wing only got seven planes, all from the 305th Group, over the target. This should have been the 92nd's first mission from Podington, but bad weather prevented the Group assembling and their aircraft returned to base. During this attempted assembly, 42-3183 had exploded in mid air over Lincolnshire, killing three of its crew. Another plane, 42-30647 from 305th Group crashed on its base on return, killing the entire crew. There were no losses in action on this first mission of the day.

The day's second mission also had Nantes as the target. The four Groups which had put planes over the target on the earlier mission of the day did not participate in this operation. These were the three groups in the First Combat Wing and the 305th from the 40th Combat Wing. Out of 91 planes despatched, 61 attacked the primary and 19 from the 379th Group turned on to a secondary at Rennes/St Jacques airfield. The 92nd had 15 planes over the target, making it the Group's first successful mission from Podington. Two planes were Missing in Action and 42-3449 from 306th Group crashed near RAF Station Wing when attempting to land on return from the mission.

On the 26th, only 55 aircraft, all from the First Combat Wing, were despatched but shortly after crossing the French coast the weather closed in and the mission was abandoned. All aircraft returned to their bases. There were no operational losses this day but a 303rd Group aircraft, 42-5434, on a non-operational flight was abandoned in the air near Winchester.

One more mission was flown this month, when on the 27th, 167 planes were despatched to Emden. This was the first mission for the First Bombardment Division when all its assigned Groups participated. It was also the first mission for the 482nd Bomb Group (P) and the first to be led by H2S equipped B-17s. The 482nd's 813rd Bomb Squadron had despatched four Pathfinder equipped planes to the bases of the lead Groups of the First and Third Bomb Divisions. Three were despatched on the day's mission, two leading the 91st, which was the lead group for the First Division this day. The other plane went to Thorpe Abbotts to lead the Third Bomb Division. One hundred and twenty-nine planes bombed the port area of Emden and targets of opportunity. Three, all from the 91st,

OPERATIONAL DIARY: SEPTEMBER 1943

FIELD ORDER No	8AF MISS No	DAY	TARGET	No OF AIRCRAFT			
				DESP	BOMB	LOST	
						MIA	OTHER
	89	2nd	Airfields in North West France	167	0	0	0
	90	3rd	Romilly-sur-Seine, Airfield St. Andre De L'Eure, Airfield Evreux/Fauville, Airfield	168	140	4	0
	91	6th	Targets of opportunity in France and Germany	181	151	27	5
	92	7th	Brussels/Evere Airfield	114	105	0	0
	93	8th	Boulogne Area. Night with R.A.F.	5	5	0	0
	94	9th	Lille/Nord Airfield Lille/Vendeville Airfield Vitry-En-Artois, Airfield	37 52 56	37 52 51	0 0 0	0 0 0
	95	15th	Romilly-sur-Seine Airfield	93	87	0	2
	96	15/16th	Montlucon Industrial Area. Night with R.A.F.	5	5	0	0
	97	16th	Nantes, Port Area and Chateau-Bougon Airfield	147	131	7	0
	98	16/17th	Modane Marshalling Yards. Night with R.A.F.	5	5	0	0
	99	22/23rd	Hannover. Night with R.A.F.	5	5	0	0
	100	23rd	Nantes, Port Area	117	46	0	3
	101	23rd	Nantes, Port Area and Rennes/St Jacques Airfield	91	80	2	0
	102	23/24th	Mannheim. Night with R.A.F.	5	4	0	0
	103	26th	Abandoned	55	0	0	0
	104	27th	Emden Port Area and Targets of opportunity	167	129	3	0
	105	27/28th	Hannover. Night with R.A.F.	5	4	1	0
				1479	1037	44	10

Capt Hathaway and his crew with '**EAGER EAGLE**' 42-29684 of 351st Bomb Group. This aircraft was one of twelve which ran short of fuel and ditched on return from the mission of 6th September. Capt Hathaway and crew were all rescued. *Alan Dann*

'**HELLCAT**' 42-5910 of 305th Bomb Group ended up like this after running out of fuel and force landing at Hawkinge on return from the mission of 15th September. *Mike Gibson*

were missing, one, 42-30624 having been delivered to the Group only four days earlier.

The first B17Gs were delivered to the Wing early in September. The first, 42-3513, was assigned to the 92nd Group on 2nd September and two more, 42-3494 and 42-3496, were received by this Group on 4th September. On the 15th, the 305th received its first 'G' and from then on a steady flow followed so that by the end of the month there were 37 assigned, the 305th and 306th Groups having the most, with seven each.

The first B-17Gs to reach the Eighth were all Douglas built. The first were delivered from the factory on 5th July and were in fact designated as B-17F-70-DL. This has over the years led to a lot of confusion, but there is no doubt that they were B-17Gs. The Material Division were late in advising the contractor that those B-17s equipped with A-16 turrets should be designated as B-17Gs. This fact was acknowledged and Air Service Command resident representatives and modification centre personnel were advised to correct the model designation on those aircraft which were delivered before the contractor had been so informed.

The three Groups in the 41st Combat Wing did not receive any of these early B-17Gs. It was policy to concentrate the older B-17Fs without Tokyo Tanks into this Wing and many transfers of aircraft took place as a result

of this policy. The 303rd Group received ten from the 306th Group and the 379th had 11 from the 92nd during the month.

On the 25th September, the number of B-17s assigned to the First Division reached 400 for the first time. There were 367 B-17Fs and 33 B-17Gs. Two days later, the number of B-17Fs assigned reached 375, the highest number the Division would have. From now on their numbers would decline as more B-17G replacements came in.

A B-24D, 42-40987, was assigned to the 482nd Group on the 28th. The first of this type to be assigned to the First Bombardment Division. The First Bomb Wing had been all B-17 equipped since the 93rd Group had left Alconbury in December 1942.

Movements among training types was again centred on the Alconbury based 92nd and 482nd Groups. Another B-17E, 41-9051, was transferred from the 92nd to the 482nd on the 1st of the month and 41-9107 left the 92nd for Warton on the 21st, these changes left the 92nd with a single B-17E, a status it would maintain from now on. The 482nd was now the major user of the B-17E in the First Bombardment Wing having three assigned until the loss of 41-9051 reduced it to two. The only other change was at Grafton Underwood, where DB-7B AL496 left the 384th Group on the 23rd. Its new owner is not known.

AIRCRAFT and CREW STATUS at 2000 Hours on 30th September 1943					
UNIT	OPERATIONAL AIRCRAFT			COMBAT CREWS	NON OPERATIONAL AIRCRAFT ASSIGNED
	TYPE	ASS	ON HAND	OP		
91BG	B-17F/G	44	42	34	18	1 B-17E, 1 DB-7B, 2 Oxford
351BG	B-17F/G	50	45	30	27	1 B-17E
381BG	B-17F/G	47	42	32	24	1 B-17E, 1 L-4B
1 CW	B-17F/G	141	129	96	69	
92BG	B-17F/G	45	41	31	23	1 B-17E, 1 DB-7B
305BG	B-17F/G	35	32	22	22	1 B-17E, 1 B-17F
305BG	B-17F/G	11	11	11	2	Special Aircraft
306BG	B-17F/G	43	43	43	24	1 B-17E, 1 Oxford
40 CW	B-17F/G	134	127	107	71	
303BG	B-17F	44	45	31	23	1 B-17E, 1 DB-7B, 1 Oxford
379BG	B-17F	39	34	30	14	1 B-17E
384BG	B-17F	40	38	26	23	1 B-17E
41 CW	B-17F	123	117	107	60	
1 BD	B-17F/G	398	373	310	200	
482BG	B-17(S)	7	6	5	0	2 B-17E, 2 B-17F, 3 B-17F(SO), 1 B-24, 1 C-78, 2 L-4B, 1 Master, 4 Oxford.
91BG	YB-40	3	3	1		
92BG	YB-40	5	4	2		
303BG	YB-40	1	1	1		YB-40 crews are included in B-17 crews
379BG	YB-40	1	1	0		
384BG	YB-40	1	1	1		
	YB-40	11	10	5		

Many First Wing aircraft changed Groups during September. One was 42-29803 shown here displaying its twin nose guns and Triangle 'G' of the 305th Bomb Group as it flies over the patchwork English countryside. On 11th September it was transferred to the 381st Bomb Group and was the only aircraft this Group lost on the epic 14th October mission to Schweinfurt. *Mike Gibson*

SEPTEMBER 1943

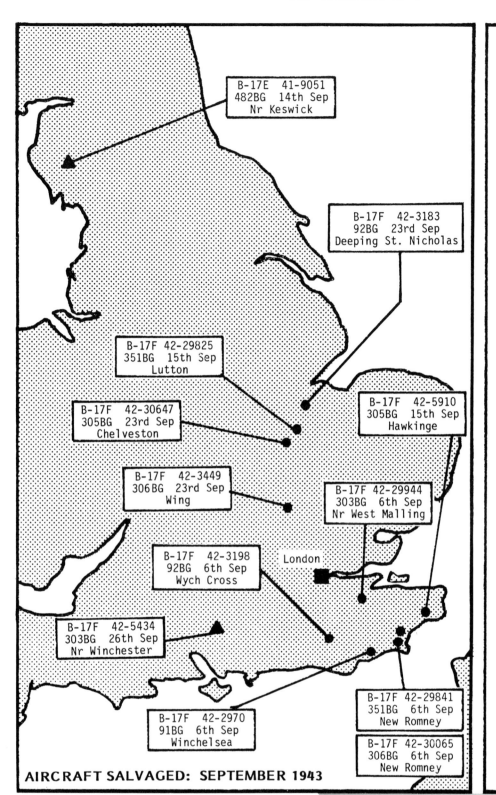

B-17E 41-9051
482BG 14th Sep
Nr Keswick

B-17F 42-3183
92BG 23rd Sep
Deeping St. Nicholas

B-17F 42-29825
351BG 15th Sep
Lutton

B-17F 42-30647
305BG 23rd Sep
Chelveston

B-17F 42-5910
305BG 15th Sep
Hawkinge

B-17F 42-3449
306BG 23rd Sep
Wing

B-17F 42-29944
303BG 6th Sep
Nr West Malling

B-17F 42-3198
92BG 6th Sep
Wych Cross

London

B-17F 42-5434
303BG 26th Sep
Nr Winchester

B-17F 42-2970
91BG 6th Sep
Winchelsea

B-17F 42-29841
351BG 6th Sep
New Romney

B-17F 42-30065
306BG 6th Sep
New Romney

AIRCRAFT SALVAGED: SEPTEMBER 1943

AIRCRAFT MISSING IN ACTION

SEPTEMBER 1943

3rd	B-17F	42-3300	379BG
	B-17F	42-29725	92BG
	B-17F	42-29789	381BG
	B-17F	42-29914	384BG
6th	B-17F	41-24497	91BG
	B-17F	41-24507	384BG
	B-17F	41-24591	305BG
	B-17F	41-24592	305BG
	B-17F	42-3002	303BG
	B-17F	42-3041	384BG
	B-17F	42-3145	379BG
	B-17F	42-3150	351BG
	B-17F	42-3428	92BG
	B-17F	42-3434	305BG
	B-17F	42-3455	384BG
	B-17F	42-5057	305BG
	B-17F	42-5720	384BG
	B-17F	42-5763	91BG
	B-17F	42-5841	306BG
	B-17F	42-5843	384BG
	B-17F	42-5890	92BG
	B-17F	42-29540	91BG
	B-17F	42-29684	351BG
	B-17F	42-29896	379BG
	B-17F	42-29965	92BG
	B-17F	42-30000	92BG
	B-17F	42-30004	305BG
	B-17F	42-30007	92BG
	B-17F	42-30010	92BG
	B-17F	42-30163	306BG
	B-17F	42-30668	92BG
16th	B-17F	42-3079	91BG
	B-17F	42-5849	384BG
	B-17F	42-29699	384BG
	B-17F	42-29876	379BG
	B-17F	42-29893	379BG
	B-17F	42-29901	379BG
	B-17F	42-29934	379BG
23rd	B-17F	42-3459	384BG
	B-17F	42-29937	379BG
27th	B-17F	42-3111	91BG
	B-17F	42-29750	91BG
	B-17F	42-30624	91BG
27/28th	B-17F	42-29555	305BG

The last two Douglas built B-17Fs to be assigned as new replacements to the 306th Bomb Group were 42-3363 and 42-3449, both joined the Group on 14th August 1943. In flight here is 449 which crashed when attempting to land at RAF Station Wing on return from the second of the 23rd September missions. *306th BG Memorial Association*

One of the most historic months in the calendar of Eighth Air Force operations. This was a decisive month, when some of the greatest air battles of the Second World War took place. A month, which nearly saw the end of the great American daylight offensive.

The month started quietly enough, with 159 planes attacking industrial areas of Emden on the 2nd. Only one aircraft was lost, this from 303rd Bomb Group. On the 4th, 155 B-17s were despatched to Frankfurt where 130 bombed successfully, but eight failed to return. One, 42-37741, from 305th Bomb Group being the Division's first loss of a B-17G.

There were no daylight operations on the 5th, 6th or 7th. The first aircraft salvaged in England during the month, was the 91st Bomb Group's 42-29793, which was struck off the Group's assigned list on the 5th. The reason for its salvage is unknown but was probably due to battle damage received on one of the late September or the two early October missions.

The 322nd Bomb Squadron of 305th Bomb Group continued night operations with the RAF. The first being to Munich on the night of 2nd/3rd, and a second to Frankfurt on the 4th/5th, when 42-3091, an old Douglas B-17F which had been an original of the 95th Bomb Group, did not return. The 422nd Bomb Squadron operated a mixture of Tokyo and non-Tokyo tank aircraft. On the longer operations, those without the extra wing tanks, carried a reduced bomb load and had extra fuel tanks in the bomb bay. 42-3091 was an aircraft fitted with the wing tanks although it had come from the 95th Bomb Group as one of the aircraft transferred during the summer as being without the tanks. On the mission of 4th/5th October each aircraft carried four 500 lb bombs and four cases of leaflets. This, the eighth night operation, was the last when bombs were carried. In future only leaflets were dropped on these night missions.

The Division set out in force for Bremen on the 8th, signalling the start of the most bloody and costly period in the history of the B-17F, 174 aircraft were despatched and 158 bombed the industrial and dock areas of the city. Thirteen did not come back, seven of them from the 381st Bomb Group. One more B-17G, again from 305th Group, was among those lost.

The mission to Anklam and Gydnia on the 9th, was the longest to date, it was also the largest of the month in terms of numbers despatched (175) and bombing (164). It also produced some of the fiercest air battles yet seen and resulted in twenty B-17s failing to return. Only the 305th escaped without losses, the 91st and 351st lost five each, and the 92nd, 306th and 379th Bomb Groups lost their first B-17Gs missing in action, the one from 379th had only been with the Group six days. Three more B-17s were written off in crash landings on return from the mission. 42-5889 of 306th Group at Matlask, 42-29890 of 379th crashed near

Kimbolton with controls out of order and 42-37759 of 306th Group crash landed back at Thurleigh, colliding with, and damaging, B-17F 42-30730. The wrecked 42-37759, became the first B-17G salvaged in the First Division. 42-30730 was repaired but did not return to service until 4th November. The 1,367 operational flying hours recorded on the 9th October mission set a new daily high for the Division.

One aircraft which should have been despatched on the 9th October mission was 41-24529, an old original of the 305th now flying with the 384th Bomb Group. It took off but aborted and returned to base. Later in the day, it went on a flight to slow time two engines but returned to Grafton Underwood when fuel was observed to be coming from number three engine. On landing it overshot the runway and was wrecked, but all four crew on board were uninjured.

Sunday the 10th, saw, for the third day running, the assembly over the East Midlands of large formations of B-17s. The target this day was Münster, where 117 from the 141 aircraft despatched bombed the city. The First Division escaped lightly this day, the only loss in action being a B-17G from the 91st, the Group's first loss of a B-17G.

Three aircraft were lost in crashes on return from the mission, 'WAHOO II', 42-5086 from the 384th Group, crashed at Eye after the crew had baled out near Ipswich, 42-29557, also from 384th Bomb Group, crash landed at RAF Desford and 42-29851, from the 351st Bomb Group, crashed in the sea off Covehithe after the crew baled out. A B-17G, 42-3506 'SIR BABOON McGOON' from the 91st Group, made a forced landing in a field at Braisworth Hall, Tannington. Only slightly damaged, it was subsequently flown out, from an improvised runway, and went to Honington for repair, it returned to the 91st Bomb Group on the 19th February 1944.

Four days' rest followed before the next mission on the following Thursday, the 14th. A day which has come to be known as Black Thursday, and for the First Bombardment Division this is an apt description. Schweinfurt was the target this day. The Division despatched 149 aircraft and 101 bombed the target. Forty-five failed to return. The highest loss the Division would sustain. Another six aircraft crashed in England when returning to their bases. The 305th Group lost 13 B-17s. The Group's highest loss and the highest single loss ever suffered by a First Wing/Division Group. The 306th lost ten, the second time this Group's losses had gone into double figures. Six B-17Gs were among those Missing in Action, including 42-31059 from 384th Group which had been delivered to the Group on 7th October, the first Boeing built B-17G assigned to the First Bomb Division and the first to go Missing in Action. Crashing in England on return were 42-3171 and 42-3351 of 92nd Bomb Group which

English children being shown round a YB-40 at Kimbolton on 2nd October. 42-5736 had served in the 303rd Bomb Group before being assigned to the 379th on 28th August. It would go to Burtonwood on 12th October for return to the USA. *Roger Freeman*

OCTOBER 1943

The day after Schweinfurt and all looks peaceful on the 401st Bomb Squadron's dispersal at Bassingbourn. In foreground is **'LIGHTNING STRIKES'** 42-3073 and at right is 42-5729. Another unidentified B-17F stands behind 729. Bomb bay tanks on ground by aircraft prove these to be non-Tokyo tank planes. These had probably been installed for the long mission to Anklam on 9th October when 073 had received damage in combat; 729 had been damaged on the mission to Münster on 10th October. It is not thought that either plane had flown the Schweinfurt mission. B-17G under nose of 073 is probably 42-37742 or 42-39802, the only two the Squadron had assigned at this time. *US Air Force – National Air and Space Museum*

crashed at Shiplake and Winkfield respectively. 42-3037, 42-5852 and 42-29784 all from 384th Bomb Group, which came down at Wakerley Woods, Chetwode and Baydon and the 303rd's 42-5482 which crashed at Riseley.

It was the 15th before the full extent of the cost in aircraft missing in action, salvaged, or out of commission for repairs could be fully assessed. On the 7th, the eve of the Bremen mission, there were 415 B-17s assigned to the Division, with 304 operational. On the 15th, this was down to 323 assigned and only 135 operational. In seven days, the Division had lost 92 B-17s from its assigned strength. Combat crew position was even more critical, there were 204 full crews available for operations on the 7th. By the 15th, this was down to 102, a loss of 50 per cent.

That the Eighth Air Force had received a heavy and painful loss was evident in that only one more heavy bomber mission was flown during the remaining two weeks of October, although weather conditions helped to keep operations at a low key. The mission to Düren on the 20th was not a successful one for the First Division. It should have been the first using an OBOE aircraft from the 482nd Bomb Group, but the failure of this equipment and bad weather conditions caused a return without bombing by most formations. Only 17 aircraft from 379th Bomb Group bombed Woensdrecht airfield as a target of opportunity. Two 303rd Group planes were Missing in Action.

The 303rd was also fated to suffer the last loss of the month, when on the 23rd, 42-29930 crashed at Keyston soon after take off from Molesworth on a local flight. All eight crew were killed.

Total losses during the month had been 91 Missing in Action and 15 salvaged due to crashes or battle damage making a total of 106, the highest monthly loss to date. Ninety-four were B-17Fs. There had been many empty hardstands on the Division's airfields when Friday, 15th October dawned. Gone were many of the veteran B-17Fs. One, 42-5714 of 91st Bomb Group, was the oldest surviving Vega built aircraft which had started its Eighth Air Force career with the 306th Bomb Group on 1st December 1942.

Some of the missing planes would eventually return to their former homes, the 303rd's 42-5360 which had landed at Biggin Hill, returned to the Group on 19th November. The 92nd had 42-3184 at Bassingbourn

and it would return on the 19th November. The badly damaged 42-29759 of 379th Bomb Group, also down at Biggin Hill, found a new home after repair, being assigned to the 91st on the 21st December. Other aircraft out for extended repairs were the 303rd's 42-3029 which was out till 30th October, and the 92nd's 42-30636 and 42-30648 which were respectively out until the 6th November and 30th October.

That the losses could be quickly replaced, was soon demonstrated. It was the 18th before they started arriving, giving the waiting ground crews time to reflect on the mounting cost of the air war and many must have been pondering on the fate of the machines they had tended so lovingly and for so long and the precious aircrews who had taken off in them only days before. On the 18th, 31 new planes arrived at First Division bases. Surprisingly the 303rd Bomb Group received 19 of these. Surprising, since this Group had only lost four aircraft Missing in Action during the previous two weeks, the lowest losses in the Division. The next day, 34 new aircraft were assigned, the 306th Bomb Group got nine of these. These new aircraft were mostly 'G's. The first Boeing and Vega built models had been assigned to the Division on the 7th October, when the 384th got the first Boeing built, and the 91st received two Vega built B-17Gs. The aircraft coming in on the 18th and 19th were from all three factories. By the 21st, the Division's assigned strength was 405 B-17s and at the end of the month stood at 417 (299 B-17F and 118 B-17G). During the month, 116 B-17Gs had been assigned to the Division, 38 from Boeing, 48 from Douglas and 30 from Vega. Twelve had gone Missing in Action, 11 Douglas and one Boeing built. Many of those assigned to the 303rd Bomb Group had left to go to Base Air Depot for modification and were not assigned at the end of the month.

October saw the departure of the YB-40s; the last two to leave being 42-5736 of 379th Group and 42-5739 of 384th Group which left for Burtonwood on the 12th. Most were returned to the USA during the next few months. During their stay in the First Wing, approximately 69 had been despatched on operational missions, many of which had been abortive; one had been lost Missing in Action. The 92nd Bomb Group which had taken these into action, had earned for itself, the distinction of being the only Air Force Heavy Bomb Group to take the three major production versions of the B-17 plus the YB-40 on combat operations.

FIELD ORDER No	8AF MISS No	DAY	TARGET	No OF AIRCRAFT			
				DESP	BOMB	LOST	
						MIA	OTHER
	106	2nd	Emden, Indusrtrial Areas	163	159	1	0
			Pathfinders	2	2	0	0
	107	2/3rd	Munich. Night with R.A.F.	2	2	0	0
	108	4th	Frankfurt/Wiesbaden, Industrial Area	104	93	5	0
			Frankfurt City	51	37	3	0
	109	4/5th	Frankfurt on Main. Night with R.A.F.	3	2	1	0
	110	7/8th	Night Leaflet Operation, France	4	4	0	0
	111	8th	Bremen, Industrial Areas and Shipyards	174	158	13	0
	112	8/9th	Night Leaflet Operation-France	2	2	0	0
	113	9th	Anklam, Industrial Area	115	106	18	3
			Gydnia, Port Area	60	58	2	0
	114	10th	Munster, Railroads and Water Ways	141	117	1	3
	115	14th	Schweinfurt	149	101	45	6
	116	20th	Duren, Idustrial Areas	103	17	2	0
	117	20/21st	Night Leaflet Operation-France	5	5	0	0
	118	24/25th	Night Leaflet Operation-France	4	4	0	0
				1082	867	91	12

OPERATIONAL DIARY: OCTOBER 1943

For the third month running activity among the non-operational types was centred around Alconbury. A first Bomb Division Flight Section was established in late September and being the nearest base to Brampton, Alconbury was chosen to house the aircraft used by this Section. It is not clear how the ownership of the aircraft used by this flight was officially covered. In the early period they appear as being assigned, variously, to the 329th Service Squadron or the 482nd Bomb Group, and it was not until early 1944 that they were charged to the First Bomb Division Flight Section. A new type to appear at Alconbury was the Fairchild UC-61A Argus one of which was assigned from Bovingdon on the 11th. Also back in the Division, this time with the 482nd, was Tiger Moth T6369, which had

been assigned to the 303rd Group so briefly in June 1943. Piper Cubs were in evidence, 43-648 moving from the 381st to the 91st on the 26th, 43-702 being assigned from Bovingdon to the 303rd on the 18th and 43-693 being assigned to the 306th on the 19th. Also on the move were DB-7Bs, AL409 which moved from the 92nd to the 305th Group on the 13th and AL452 which came into the 482nd Group from the 93rd Group on the 5th. Also coming into Alconbury for the use of the new Flight Section was Oxford DF331 which transferred from Bassingbourn on the 21st October. The 482nd now had four Oxfords charged to its care at Alconbury and they were the most numerous of the non operational types to serve in the First Wing/Division.

'FIGHTING PAPPY' 42-5407 came to the Eighth via Africa in February 1943 and served in 306th, 91st and finally 379th Bomb Groups. It did not return from Anklam on 9th October. *306th BG Memorial Association*

AIRCRAFT and CREW STATUS at 2000 Hours on 31st October 1943					
UNIT	**OPERATIONAL AIRCRAFT**			**COMBAT CREWS**	**NON OPERATIONAL AIRCRAFT ASSIGNED**
	TYPE	**ASS**	**ON HAND**	**OP**		
91BG	B-17F/G	38	37	29	17	1 B-17E, 1 DB-7B, 1 L-4B, 1 Oxford
351BG	B-17F/G	45	44	38	22	1 B-17E
381BG	B-17F/G	39	35	31	18	1 B-17E
1 CW	B-17F/G	122	116	98	57	
92BG	B-17F/G	35	29	26	20	1 B-17E
305BG	B-17F/G	33	32	26	18	1 B-17E, 1 B-17F
305BG	B-17F/G	11	11	11	3	Special aircraft
306BG	B-17F/G	40	36	36	20	1 B-17E, 1 L-4B
40 CW	B-17F/G	119	108	99		
303BG	B-17F/G	35	35	31	22	1 B-17E, 1 DB-7B, 1 L-4B, 1 Oxford
303BG	B-17F/G	26	0	0	0	GB Aircraft
379BG	B-17F/G	38	37	34	24	1 B-17E
379BG	B-17F/G	9	0	0	0	GB aircraft
384BG	B-17F/G	30	29	26	25	1 B-17E
384BG	B-17F/G	8	8	8	0	GB aircraft
41 CW	B-17F/G	146	109	99	71	
1 BD	B-17F/G	387	333	296	189	
482BG	B-17(S)	30	27	23	10	1 B-17E, 2 B-17F, 3 B-17F(S), 6 B-24D, 1 DB-7B,
482BG	B-24H	2	0	0	0	1 C-78, 2 L-4B, 1 UC-61A, 1 Master, 5 Oxford, 1 Tiger Moth

One of the first replacements received by the 381st Bomb Group, 42-29854 **'OLE FLAK SACK'**. It suffered landing gear failure July/August 43. Repaired and was one of seven aircraft the 381st lost on 8th October. *Ron Mckay*

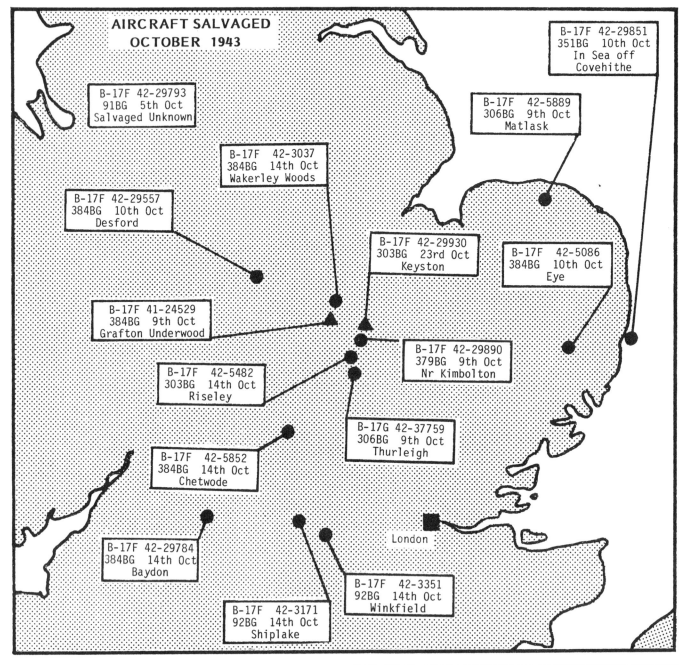

AIRCRAFT SALVAGED OCTOBER 1943

B-17F 42-29851
351BG 10th Oct
In Sea off
Covehithe

B-17F 42-29793
91BG 5th Oct
Salvaged Unknown

B-17F 42-5889
306BG 9th Oct
Matlask

B-17F 42-3037
384BG 14th Oct
Wakerley Woods

B-17F 42-29557
384BG 10th Oct
Desford

B-17F 42-29930
303BG 23rd Oct
Keyston

B-17F 42-5086
384BG 10th Oct
Eye

B-17F 41-24529
384BG 9th Oct
Grafton Underwood

B-17F 42-29890
379BG 9th Oct
Nr Kimbolton

B-17F 42-5482
303BG 14th Oct
Riseley

B-17G 42-37759
306BG 9th Oct
Thurleigh

B-17F 42-5852
384BG 14th Oct
Chetwode

London

B-17F 42-29784
384BG 14th Oct
Baydon

B-17F 42-3351
92BG 14th Oct
Winkfield

B-17F 42-3171
92BG 14th Oct
Shiplake

'ARGONAUT III' 42-29851 of 351st Bomb Group which crashed in the sea off Suffolk on return from Münster, 10th October after the crew had baled out. *Alan Dann*

On the Münster mission of 10th October, the First Bombardment Division lost one plane Missing in Action. Three more were lost in England on return. One was 42-29557 'YANKEE-GAL' of 384th Group which crash landed at Desford. *Mike Gibson*

		AIRCRAFT MISSING IN ACTION:	OCTOBER 1943				

2nd	B-17F	42-5260	303BG	9th	B-17F	42-3152	351BG
					B-17F	42-3180	381BG
4th	B-17F	42-3274	91BG		B-17G	42-3554	92BG
	B-17F	42-5807	351BG		B-17F	42-5178	91BG
	B-17F	42-29713	379BG		B-17F	42-5221	303BG
	B-17F	42-29846	303BG		B-17F	42-5407	379BG
	B-17F	42-30043	384BG		B-17F	42-29603	351BG
	B-17F	42-30646	92BG		B-17F	42-29711	91BG
	B-17G	42-37741	305BG		B-17F	42-29712	384BG
					B-17F	42-29740	91BG
4/5th	B-17F	42-3091	305BG		B-17F	42-29778	91BG
					B-17F	42-29814	384BG
8th	B-17F	42-3123	381BG		B-17F	42-29868	351BG
	B-17F	42-3258	379BG		B-17F	42-29958	381BG
	B-17F	42-5855	306BG		B-17F	42-30012	381BG
	B-17F	42-29520	91BG		B-17F	42-30772	91BG
	B-17F	42-29765	381BG		B-17F	42-30790	351BG
	B-17F	42-29854	381BG		B-17F	42-30867	351BG
	B-17F	42-29941	381BG		B-17G	42-37718	306BG
	B-17F	42-29959	306BG		B-17G	42-37728	379BG
	B-17F	42-29985	306BG				
	B-17F	42-30009	381BG	10th	B-17G	42-37737	91BG
	B-17F	42-30722	381BG				
	B-17F	42-30864	381BG				
	B-17G	42-37751	305BG				

14th	B-17F	42-3056	379BG
	B-17F	42-3176	379BG
	B-17F	42-3195	305BG
	B-17F	42-3216	384BG
	B-17F	42-3269	379BG
	B-17F	42-3436	305BG
	B-17G	42-3549	305BG
	B-17G	42-3550	305BG
	B-17F	42-5714	91BG
	B-17F	42-6096	351BG
	B-17F	42-29477	303BG
	B-17F	42-29511	379BG
	B-17F	42-29653	379BG
	B-17F	42-29776	379BG
	B-17F	42-29800	384BG
	B-17F	42-29803	381BG
	B-17F	42-29867	384BG
	B-17F	42-29870	384BG
	B-17F	42-29952	305BG
	B-17F	42-29971	306BG
	B-17F	42-29988	305BG
	B-17F	42-30175	306BG
	B-17F	42-30196	384BG
	B-17F	42-30199	306BG
	B-17F	42-30231	92BG
	B-17F	42-30242	305BG
	B-17F	42-30387	92BG
	B-17F	42-30654	92BG
	B-17F	42-30707	306BG
	B-17F	42-30708	92BG
	B-17F	42-30710	306BG
	B-17F	42-30726	92BG
	B-17F	42-30727	306BG
	B-17F	42-30779	306BG
	B-17F	42-30804	305BG
	B-17F	42-30807	305BG
	B-17F	42-30811	306BG
	B-17F	42-30813	306BG
	B-17F	42-30814	305BG
	B-17F	42-30824	92BG
	B-17F	42-30831	305BG
	B-17G	42-31059	384BG
	B-17G	42-37720	306BG
	B-17G	42-37740	305BG
	B-17G	42-37750	305BG
20th	B-17F	41-24629	303BG
	B-17F	42-29571	303BG

Serving in 305th, 381st and finally 384th Bomb Groups, 42-29784 'SMILING THRU' was one of three 384th aircraft which crashed in England on return from the 14th October Schweinfurt mission. *Mike Gibson*

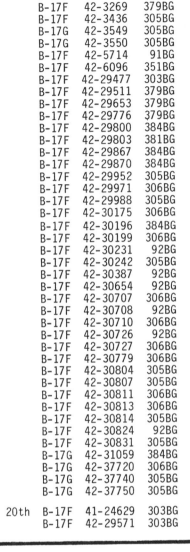

An early Douglas built B-17F, 42-3037 'WINDY CITY AVENGER' was assigned in the USA as an original to the 95th Bomb Group. Transferred to the 305th Bomb Group on 1st August and to the 384th Bomb Group on 20th September. Crashed at Wakerley Woods after the crew had baled out on return from Schweinfurt, 14th October. *Mike Gibson*

The tail of 306th Bomb Group's 42-5855 shot down near Golderstadt, Germany, 8th October. Eight chutes were reported to come from the plane but only five of the crew survived. This plane had been an original of the 95th Bomb Group and served in the 384th Group before being assigned to the 306th. *Imperial War Museum*

Matlask airfield, Norfolk. Although only a fighter station with no runways, its geographical location made it an attractive landing place for aircraft that could just make it back across the North Sea. The 306th Bomb Group's 42-5889 crash landed here on return from Gydnia on 9th October and 401st Group's 42-31090 crash landed on return from the 11th January 1944 mission. *Crown Copyright*

NOVEMBER 1943

Operations started on the 3rd, when the 40th Combat Wing led the Division to Wilhelmshaven. The 228 aircraft despatched was the largest number since the August mission to Schweinfurt. The target was covered by 10/10 cloud and bombing was done on Pathfinder aircraft of the 482nd Bomb Group. For the first time the 812nd Bomb Squadron had despatched H2X equipped B-17s, the 222 aircraft returning on effective sortie was a new record. Six planes failed to return. Two from 306th Bomb Group had collided in mid air on the way out over the North Sea, both crews being lost.

The marshalling yards at Gelsenkirchen were the target for 191 aircraft despatched on the 5th. Located in the Ruhr, an area with a reputation of being one of the most heavily defended in Germany, a rough trip was always expected to any targets in this the 'Happy Valley' as it was dubbed by RAF bomber crews. Hidden under complete cloud cover the 177 aircraft attacking did so on 482nd Bomb Group Pathfinder aircraft. Three aircraft were Missing in Action and 42-3532 from 351st Group crash landed at Ipswich airport on return and was salvaged.

This was the only occasion when a B-17 led B-24s. Capt Lister A Brumley and crew from 482nd Bomb Group acting as pathfinders for the Second Division had a rough mission. Over the target they were attacked and lost a propeller, causing the aircraft to lose speed. They then had to leave the formation, as the B-24s were over-running the B-17.

Only a small force from the First Combat Wing took part in the operation of the 7th November. Wesel was the target, and it was very much a wasted effort. From the moment of crossing the enemy coast, the bombers were over a solid cover of cloud that reached up to 20,000 feet and persisted till the target was reached. Bombing was done by use of Pathfinder equipment, and photo reconnaissance showed no sign of damage in the target area. Flak at the target was meagre and inaccurate, with no fighter opposition at all and all planes returned safely.

A severe blow struck the 482nd's 813rd Bomb Squadron on the 10th when 42-5793 crashed at Brome shortly after taking off from Thorpe Abbotts. Eleven crew and two mechanics who were in the plane and two people and a horse on the ground were killed. It is not known why the plane was at Thorpe Abbotts as no mission was flown this day. It is possible it had been the plane despatched to Framlingham to lead the Thirteenth Combat Wing on the mission of 7th November and had since been weather bound on the Third Division Base.

Bad weather persisted all through this period with fog hanging in the Division area too long in the morning to permit take off, or closing in too early in the evening to allow a landing. On the 11th, 180 aircraft were despatched, but adverse weather caused the mission to be abandoned,

with only one 482nd Pathfinder aircraft flying with the Third Bombardment Division being credited with an effective sortie.

Another mission attempted on the 13th was a disaster. During assembly heavy turbulence and icing were encountered. As a result two aircraft from 306th Group were lost; 42-3142 crashed and exploded at Great Haseley killing all the crew, and 42-31038 crashed and exploded at Princes Risborough, nine crew had baled out but the pilot was killed. 41-24575, 'SUNRISE SERENADER' an original of the 305th and now flying with the 384th Group crashed at Wargrave, only one of the crew survived and 42-30821 of 92nd Group crashed at Ferry Compton killing all ten crew. Thirty crew members had lost their lives this day, the mission was abandoned and the planes recalled before assembly was complete. Two 306th Group aircraft which formed on and flew with Third Division Groups were able to claim credit for complete missions.

The next day, the 14th, there was no mission and only 76 hours of non-operational flying were put in, 63 of these by the 381st Bomb Group. By the 15th, the weather had improved, but still not sufficient to allow combat operations, most groups flew a few hours on training and during one of these flights 42-30666 and 42-29953, both from 305th Bomb Group collided in mid air and crashed at Newton Bromshold. All crew on both planes were killed.

On the 16th, the weather cleared sufficiently to allow a full scale mission to be despatched. The target this day was Knaben in Norway. A long mission carried out without fighter escort. One hundred and eighty-nine aircraft were despatched and 130 made a successful attack. One aircraft from 92nd Group was lost. Visibility over the target was perfect with little flak to distract the bombardiers. On this mission, the 303rd's 'KNOCK OUT DROPPER' completed its 50th mission, the first heavy bomber in the Eighth Air Force to do so. Flying hours on this mission were 1,527, a new record in operational hours flown in one day.

The weather closed in following the Knaben mission and it was ten days before another major mission was launched. When it came on 26th, with Bremen as the target, there had been plenty of time to catch up on battle damage repairs, to do maintenance and to make good shortages. Also flying their first mission this day, was the Division's newest Group, the 401st; proudly displaying the Triangle 'S' on the fins of their B-17s.

It is not surprising that the numbers despatched (297) and the number bombing (266) broke all previous records. The mission met with severe fighter opposition with concentrated attacks on the lead groups. Dense persistent contrails formed as they came in to the target and the enemy used these as cover to close the range and attack the formations with rockets. A smoke screen and cloud covered the target area so bombing

Second to enemy action, the greatest hazard to flying crews was poor visibility. Conditions such as this at Ridgewell persisted through much of November keeping the Fortresses on their hardstandings or away at airfields where conditions were better. This also provided the impetus to invest heavily in research to overcome the disruption and losses that these conditions caused. *US Air Force – National Air and Space Museum*

Above: one of the 305th Bomb Group's planes involved in the Newton Bromshold mid air collision on 15th November. '**WOLFESS**' 42-29953 was an original of the 381st Bomb Group and had transferred to the 305th on 22nd August. *Mike Gibson*

was done by Pathfinder equipment. Nineteen B-17s failed to return, the heaviest loss of the month.

Four more planes were salvaged as a result of damage received on this mission or in crash landings on return. 303rd's, 42-5177 '**FAST WORKER II**', had been badly damaged and was down at or near Attlebridge. At Leiston was 42-30005 from 384th Group which had overshot on landing, and at Marham was 42-39839 of 351st Group after a crash landing. A 401st Group plane, 42-37838, had collided with a B-17 from 388th Group and was at Detling, it was the first 401st aircraft to be salvaged in the UK although it was retained on the Group's assigned list until 9th December, by which time another plane had been lost in a crash and removed from the Group's inventory.

The 303rd Bomb Group's 42-3064, was badly damaged and landed at Docking. It was repaired but did not return to the 303rd until 28th February 1944. Another aircraft thought to have been the victim of the vicious air battles of the 26th was 42-29705 of 379th Bomb Group. It is believed to have crash landed at Foulsham on return and was transferred to No 2 Strategic Air Depot on the 28th. It never returned to the 379th Group and it is almost certain that it was salvaged at this time.

Another strike at Bremen was made on the 29th, the weather had been bad for the three days since the last mission but on this day there was some lifting of the heavy fog cover over England and the mission was ordered off. The fog may have lifted off the ground, but once aloft the planes flew into a very heavy cover of cloud scattered at various altitudes up through the assembly area. Three Combat Wings took off and great difficulty was experienced during assembly. The first and 40th Combat Wings had been able to complete the assembly but as they approached the English coast the leader of the 40th, which was leading the First Division, found himself on a collision course with an unidentified Combat Wing and a quick change of course was necessary. This entailed a 360° turn, in the course of which the two Combat Wings were somewhat dispersed. They reformed and set out on the mission flying between the layers of clouds piled up to 35,000 feet, which seemed to be closing in on all sides and rather than fly over 100 planes, some of them still jostling for position in the formation, into this dense overcast, the leader decided to abandon the mission.

The 41st Combat Wing did complete the mission. They flew it not knowing that the other two Wings had aborted, because they followed a Combat Wing of the Third Division into the target mistaking it for the First Wing of the First Division.

Left: '**SALVAGE QUEEN**' 42-30005, an original of 384th Bomb Group, overshot the runway at Leiston on return from the mission of 26th November and was wrecked. *Mike Gibson*

NOVEMBER 1943

Enemy opposition on this mission was fairly heavy with 80 to 100 enemy aircraft being encountered, again using the tactics employed on the 26th November of approaching the formation under cover of the dense and persistent contrails. Flak varied from moderate to intense, accurate to inaccurate. Four bombers were lost. One more, 42-3520 from 306th Group, crash landed at Little Staughton on return and was salvaged. Badly damaged and down at Bungay was 42-5859, from 303rd Group. This plane had flown with the 379th on that Group's first mission on 29th May and had crash landed at Little Staughton on return. It had been out of the Wing/Division until 2nd October when it had been assigned to the 303rd Bomb Group. It was now back in the care of the Air Force Service Command and would not return to operations with the 303rd until February 1944.

One more mission was attempted before the end of the month. On the 30th, 224 aircraft were despatched to Solingen but the weather once again proved too much and the mission was abandoned. Only one aircraft

FIELD ORDER No	8AF MISS No	DAY	TARGET	No OF AIRCRAFT			
						LOST	
				DESP	BOMB	MIA	OTHER
	119	3rd	Wilhelmshaven, Port Area	217	211	6	0
			Pathfinders	11	11	0	0
	120	3/4th	Night Leaflet Operation-Belgium and Holland	2	2	0	0
	121	5th	Gelsenkirchen, Marshalling Yards	180	168	3	1
			Pathfinders	11	9	0	0
	122	5/6th	Night Leaflet Operation-France	5	5	0	0
	123	6/7th	Night Leaflet Operation-France	2	2	0	0
	124	7th	Wesel, Industrial Areas	59	53	0	0
			Pathfinders	3	2	0	0
	125	7/8th	Night Leaflet Operation-France	2	2	0	0
	126	10/11th	Night Leaflet Operation-France	2	2	0	0
	127	11th	Wesel. Mission Abandoned	175	0	0	0
			Pathfinders	5	1	0	0
	128	11/12th	Special Night Operation. OBOE Test, Emmerich	1	1	0	0
	129	12/13th	Special Night Operation. OBOE Test, Emmerich	1	1	0	0
	130	13th	Bremen, Port Area	5	2	0	4
	131	16th	Knaben, Industrial	189	130	1	0
	132	18th	Second Bombardment Division only	-	-	-	-
	133	18/19th	Night Leaflet Operation-France	5	5	0	0
	134	19th	Pathfinders. 482nd Bomb Group with 3rd Bomb Div	6	3	0	0
	135	19/20th	Night Leaflet Operation-France, Holland and Belgium	6	6	0	0
	136	24/25th	Night Leaflet Operation-France and Belgium	7	7	0	0
	137	25/26th	Night Leaflet Operation-France	7	7	0	0
	138	26th	Bremen, Port Area	297	266	19	4
	139	28/29th	Night Leaflet Operation-Belgium and Holland	7	7	0	0
	140	29th	Bremen Port Area	178	50	4	1
	141	29/30th	Night Leaflet Operation-France	8	8	0	0
	142	29/30th	Special Night Operation, Emmerich	1	1	0	0
	143	30th	Solingen, Industrial Area	221	1	0	1
			Pathfinders	3	1	0	0
	144	30/ 1st Dec	Night Leaflet Operation-France and Germany	6	6	0	0
				1622	970	33	11

AIRCRAFT and CREW STATUS at 2000 Hours on 30th November 1943					
UNIT	**OPERATIONAL AIRCRAFT**			**COMBAT CREWS**	**NON OPERATIONAL AIRCRAFT ASSIGNED**
	TYPE	**ASS**	**ON HAND**	**OP**	
91BG	B-17F/G	41	41	26	30	1 B-17E, 1 DB-7B, 1 L-4B, 1 Oxford
381BG	B-17F/G	42	42	41	25	1 B-17E
1 CW	B-17F/G	83	83	67	55	
92BG	B-17F/G	35	35	19	21	1 B-17E
305BG	B-17F/G	30	28	18	23	1 B-17E, 1 B-17F, 1 DB-7B
305BG	B-17F/G	10	10	8	7	Special aircraft
306BG	B-17F/G	31	31	25	29	1 B-17E, 2 B-17F
40 CW	B-17F/G	106	104	70	80	
303BG	B-17F/G	15	15	8	28	1 B-17E, 1 DB-7B, 1 L-4B, 1 Oxford
303BG	B-17F/G	39	39	28		GB aircraft
379BG	B-17F/G	13	11	8	33	1 B-17E
379BG	B-17F/G	38	37	20		GB aircraft
384BG	B-17F/G	13	13	10	30	1 B-17E
384BG	B-17F/G	42	38	25		GB aircraft
41 CW	B-17F/G	160	153	99	91	
351BG	B-17F/G	59	59	42	51	1 B-17E
401BG	B-17F/G	33	32	17	30	1 B-17E
92 CW	B-17F/G	92	91	59	81	
482BG	B-17F/G	30	30	22	15	1 B-17E, 2 B-17F, 3 B-17F(S), 5 B-24D, 2 B-24DAS, 1 DB-7B, 1 C-78, 2 L-4B, 1 UC-61A, 1 Master, 1 Tiger Moth, 5 Oxford
1 BD	B-17F/G	471	461	317	322	
482BG	B-24H	1	0	0	0	

from 303rd and one PFF from 482nd Group flying with the Third Division completed the mission.

Once again, aircraft and crews were lost on a mission which was fruitless. 42-30408 of 92nd Bomb Group exploded in mid air and crashed near Helmdon, all nine crew being killed. Another aircraft in difficulty during assembly was B-17F 42-5905 from the 388th Bomb Group of the Third Division which made an emergency landing at Polebrook.

The 422nd Bomb Squadron continued its leaflet dropping night missions during the month. It was active on 12 nights despatching up to seven aircraft each night. Also commencing night operations this month was the 482nd Bomb Group. On three nights starting on the 11/12th this Group sent a single B-17 to conduct tests of OBOE equipment and to give crews training in the use of the equipment.

Thirty-three B-17s had been lost Missing in Action during the month, the lowest losses since April. A further fifteen had been destroyed or salvaged in England.

The first aircraft of the 401st Bomb Group were reported in at Deenethorpe on 4th November. The Group's entry into combat on the

26th also resulted in the first changes to the Combat Wing Organisation in the First Division. The three existing Combat Wings in the Division, each had three Groups assigned. To cater for the introduction of the 401st and other Groups scheduled to join the Division in early 1944, a new Combat Wing, the '92nd', was activated in England on 1st November with headquarters at Polebrook. It was the 24th before this new Wing had any Groups assigned; on this day the 401st was officially assigned and the 351st Group was transferred from the First Combat Wing into the new 92nd Combat Wing.

There was not much activity among the training aircraft during the month. The B-17E, 41-9107 which had left the 92nd for Warton on 21st September, was back in the Division, being assigned to the 401st Bomb Group on the 6th. On the 10th, B-17E 41-9013 left the 482nd Group to join Third Bomb Division's 94th Group. This left the 482nd with a single B-17E and all the First Division's Groups now had one B-17E. The only other movement was Piper Cub 43-693 which left the 306th Group to go to the Air Force Service Command for repair on the 6th.

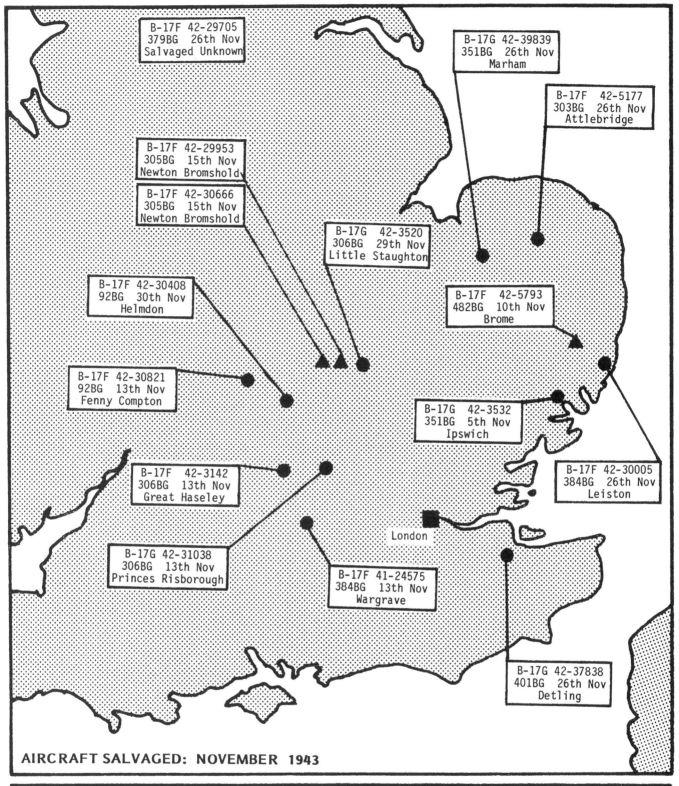

B-17F 42-29705
379BG 26th Nov
Salvaged Unknown

B-17G 42-39839
351BG 26th Nov
Marham

B-17F 42-5177
303BG 26th Nov
Attlebridge

B-17F 42-29953
305BG 15th Nov
Newton Bromshold

B-17F 42-30666
305BG 15th Nov
Newton Bromshold

B-17G 42-3520
306BG 29th Nov
Little Staughton

B-17F 42-30408
92BG 30th Nov
Helmdon

B-17F 42-5793
482BG 10th Nov
Brome

B-17F 42-30821
92BG 13th Nov
Fenny Compton

B-17G 42-3532
351BG 5th Nov
Ipswich

B-17F 42-3142
306BG 13th Nov
Great Haseley

B-17F 42-30005
384BG 26th Nov
Leiston

B-17G 42-31038
306BG 13th Nov
Princes Risborough

B-17F 41-24575
384BG 13th Nov
Wargrave

London

B-17G 42-37838
401BG 26th Nov
Detling

AIRCRAFT SALVAGED: NOVEMBER 1943

AIRCRAFT MISSING IN ACTION: NOVEMBER 1943											
3rd	B-17G	42-3533	306BG	26th	B-17F	42-3165	92BG	26th	B-17F	42-30645	305BG
	B-17F	42-29852	351BG		B-17F	42-3387	305BG	Cont	B-17F	42-30832	306BG
	B-17G	42-30776	306BG		B-17G	42-3531	305BG		B-17G	42-31042	384BG
	B-17G	42-30805	91BG		B-17G	42-3560	351BG		B-17G	42-31046	305BG
	B-17G	42-37742	91BG		B-17F	42-5051	384BG		B-17G	42-37762	384BG
	B-17G	42-39802	91BG		B-17F	42-5795	91BG		B-17G	42-37787	379BG
					B-17F	42-29694	379BG		B-17G	42-37817	351BG
5th	B-17F	41-24565	303BG		B-17F	42-29955	303BG				
	B-17F	42-30852	381BG		B-17F	42-29987	384BG	29th	B-17F	42-5483	303BG
	B-17G	42-39831	92BG		B-17F	42-30015	305BG		B-17F	42-29498	303BG
					B-17F	42-30603	306BG		B-17F	42-29787	379BG
16th	B-17F	42-29996	92BG		B-17F	42-30608	92BG		B-17F	42-29779	379BG

Above: 42-37787, a Glide Bomb equipped B-17G of the 379th Bomb Group down near Borgen, Germany, after the mission of 26th November. During its 37 day assignment to the First Division it had spent ten days at BAD undergoing modification and had been assigned to the 303rd and 384th Bomb Groups, in addition to its final assignment to the 379th. *Imperial War Museum*

Left: one of the first B-17Gs of the 401st Bomb Group to arrive was 42-31091 '**MAGGIE**', which was reported in from Prestwick on 4th November. *Mike Gibson*

he first aircraft belonging to the 401st Bomb Group, were recorded on 4th November. On the 9th, 29 more aircraft were added to the st including 42-31037 **'PISTOL PACKING MAMA'**. All were ported as transferred to Bassingbourn but were retained on the 01st's assigned and on hand status. *Mike Gibson*

Line up of 381st Bomb Group B-17s at Thurleigh (between 24th September and 5th November 1943). MS-V in upper photograph crashed near Shaftesbury on 29th December 1943. *306BG Historical Association*

truck ran into the tail of 42-37828 at Grafton Under-ood on 29th November causing the damage shown this photograph. The actual fate of the aircraft is oscure as it was not removed from the 384th's ssigned list until 3rd January 1944. *US Air Force*

DECEMBER 1943

For the first time the Division despatched over 2,000 aircraft in a month. An early start was made with four Combat Wings despatching 221 aircraft to Solingen on the first day of the month. Leverkusen had been the briefed primary but failure on the Lead Pathfinder caused the lead to be given over to the Pathfinder aircraft of another Combat Wing briefed to bomb Solingen. Enemy opposition was strong but fighter protection was excellent. Nineteen bombers failed to return. Many reported that they were low on fuel when they landed, and it is probable that this caused the loss of some of those that did not return. During assembly, 42-30714 of 306th Bomb Group crashed near Lasham. All the crew baled out except the ball turret gunner who was killed. On return, 42-39808 from 381st Group crashed at Allhallows.

was quieter still, without a single plane venturing into the air, but on the 19th training activities resumed with all Groups getting in some flying. At Molesworth, 42-39769 had its landing gear collapse when landing after a local formation flight, there were no injuries to the crew but the plane went off for salvage.

Since the 92nd Combat Wing had started operating in late November, confusion had been caused due to the existence in the Division of the 92nd Bomb Group. To overcome this confusion, a new Combat Wing, the '94th', was activated within the First Division on 12th December and on the 19th, it took over the Headquarters and staff from the 92nd Combat Wing at Polebrook. The 92nd Combat Wing transferred to the Third Bombardment Division.

Left: 42-30841 takes off at Thurleigh. This aircraft was in a mid air collision over the South coast on 27th December. It was flown back to Thurleigh where it was salvaged.
Lower photograph shows damage to number two propeller following the collision. *US Air Force*

On the 5th, 216 aircraft were despatched to airfields and air depots in France, but the weather intervened and the aircraft returned without bombing. During take off for this mission, 401st Bomb Group's **'ZENOBIA'** 42-39825 crashed in the village of Deenethorpe. The crew were able to escape and warn the inhabitants before the bomb load went off.

Bad weather persisted again for several days and it was the 11th before another mission could be flown. Emden was the target for the 219 aircraft which bombed, out of 238 despatched. Enemy opposition was not particularly severe. One aircraft was lost, this came from 306th Bomb Group. On this mission, the 351st Group despatched 40 aircraft, the first time a First Division Group had sent so many off on one mission.

The 303rd Group dropped 42-37757 from assignment on the 11th and the aircraft was recorded as salvaged on the 13th. This aircraft had flown the 1st December mission and had returned to Molesworth. It was reported to Little Staughton for repair on 9th December. The reason for its salvage is unknown but it may have crash landed at Little Staughton.

On the 15th, it was back to Bremen for the First and 41st Combat Wings, while the 40th and 92nd Wings went to Kiel. The Eighth Air Force despatched 710 bombers this day, the biggest force to date. The First Division despatched 313, the first time over 300 had been put in the air for a single mission. Opposition was very light, with moderate flak at the target. One plane, again from 306th Group, was Missing in Action. The 384th's 42-29529 **'NORA'** crashed on approach at Grafton Underwood and was salvaged.

On the 16th, Bremen was again the target. A large force of 251 bombers were despatched and 183 bombed the target. For the first time P-51s were included in the escort for the First Division. Enemy opposition to the mission was generally light and only one B-17, this time from 92nd Group, was missing. The 384th, for the second mission running, lost an aircraft on return to England. This time it was 42-29733 which overshot at Coltishall and hit some trees, fortunately without serious injuries to the crew.

The only flying on the 17th, was 16 hours turned in by the 422nd Bomb Squadron on a night leaflet mission in the early hours of the day. The 18th

Bremen port area was again the target for the 237 planes despatched on the 20th. First Division was in the lead and it was a difficult mission. The assembly of Groups, Wings and Division were carried out with a great deal of trouble due to clouds piled up to 25,000 feet all over southern England. The final Division assembly was completed at 24,000 feet, considerably higher than that called for in the field order. As a consequence the aircrews were on oxygen for much longer than they would have been, had the assembly been done as planned. Opposition was generally concentrated on the First Bomb Division and, although not considered heavy, resulted in 13 planes failing to return.

On the return from this mission the strain of flying at altitude for so long, began to tell on the pilots and as the formations approached the enemy coast they loosened. The 41st Combat Wing was dispersed in clouds and never did re-assemble on the return to their bases. The First Combat Wing, also had trouble as they approached the enemy coast on the way back from the target but managed to re-form before reaching their home bases. One 91st Group plane, 42-37767, made a wheels up landing on Cambridge airport on the return and was salvaged.

The target on the 22nd was Osnabruck, 153 aircraft from the 237 despatched bombed the target. Another difficult mission with a large amount of cloud in the assembly area. For the First and 40th Combat Wings the route was flown as planned, both Wings attacking the primary by the use of Pathfinder techniques. For the 41st and 94th Combat Wings however, the mission was far from smooth. The 41st Combat Wing flying in front of the 94th into the target, did not bomb because its Pathfinder ships aborted and the leader failed to see the First Combat Wing dropping its bombs. On the way home, two Groups of the 41st Combat Wing bombed another target. The third Group did not see the bombs dropping and brought their bombs back to base. The 94th Combat Wing was unable to find a target of opportunity and also brought the bombs back. Enemy opposition to the mission was not particularly severe. Five bombers were Missing in Action and two crashed in England on return. The 379th's 42-29891 crashed at Ubbeston and 42-37835 'CHANNEL EXPRESS' from the 401st was abandoned in the air and crashed at Washingley.

Two days after the Osnabruck mission, the Eighth turned to a new type of target. Code named 'CROSSBOW' and 'NOBALL', these were construction sites in the Pas de Calais area and were identified by numbers instead of the more familiar geographical names. These sites were being prepared to launch V-1s and V-2s at southern England, although most of the crews taking part were unaware of their true purpose. The First Division was assigned eight targets numbered 15-A, 20, 37, 51, 68, 79, 83 and 93. It was a large mission with 277 planes being despatched in four Combat Wings and 248 completed the mission. There were no losses.

There followed a five day period during which no daylight operations were flown, but training and test flying continued every day. The 27th was a day of considerable activity, especially for the 306th Group, which flew 108 hours, the highest in the Division. During the day, the 423rd Bomb Squadron mounted a formation training flight and while over the south coast, 42-30221 and 42-30841 collided in mid air. The crew abandoned 841 and it was headed out over the Channel, some reports indicating that it was shot down by Spitfires. The other aircraft was flown back to Thurleigh where it was salvaged. Both crews escaped injury.

On the 28th, the 379th made an early start to the day's training, B-17G, 42-31119 had left Kimbolton with a crew of five to carry out a navigation training exercise when at 0646 hours, the pilot, 2nd Lt George A Schuenemann, reported number one propeller feathered and requested an emergency landing. Overshooting runway 33 and turning to the left, the aircraft struck the mound forming the shooting in butts, caught fire and was destroyed. All the crew were killed.

The 29th was also a busy day, with all groups contributing to the Division's total of 670 non operational flying hours. The 381st Group's 42-30765 'CHUGALUG', was out on a slow time flight in conditions of poor visibility, and while turning near Shaftesbury, the right wing struck some trees and set up a vibration requiring a forced landing. This was successfully made at Redmond Farm, Maiden Bradley, near Warminster. There were no injuries to the crew but the plane was written off.

Operational flying started again on the 30th, with the despatch of a large force to Ludwigshafen. The First Combat Wing led the Eighth this day. Three hundred and one planes were despatched and 287 bombed the target. For the first time 'Chaff' was taken along on this mission, a task given to the 40th Combat Wing. Five B-17s were Missing in Action, including one from 401st Group, the Group's first loss in action. Three aircraft were salvaged in England as the result of crash landings. The first occurred at the start of the day when 42-39863 of 91st Group had an engine fire almost as soon as it left the runway at Bassingbourn and shortly after, made a wheels up landing on Steeple Morden airfield. On return, 42-31178, also from 91st Group made a crash landing near Windsor, both 91st crews escaped injury. The third loss was the 351st's 42-39780 'LITTLE TWINK!', which crash landed near Hawkinge, killing five of the crew.

On the last day of the month, and the year 1943, four Combat Wings were despatched to bomb Bordeaux and the blockade runner *Orsono* at Gironde. Assembly of the Combat Wings was delayed due to darkness and heavy traffic in the assembly areas, there were many reports of near collisions. Two hundred and thirty-two planes were despatched and 139 bombed. Leading the forces attacking Bordeaux, was the 94th Combat Wing with Col Hatcher, 351st Bomb Group Commander, flying the lead in 42-37731, one of the Group's oldest B-17Gs. They found the target obscured by cloud and when turning off to find a secondary target, the lead aircraft was hit. They then bombed Cognac and lost Col Hatcher's plane at this time. The First and 40th Combat Wings followed to the target and bombed without incident.

The 41st Combat Wing had been briefed to attack the *Orsono*. The route was flown as planned, but the target was found to be overcast, so a

Off the runway and bogged down at Deenethorpe on 16th December is 42-31033 'PEE TEY KUN'. It was to be one of four aircraft the Group would lose on the 11th January 1944 mission. *Alan Dann*

An ex 94th Bomb Group B-17F used by the 422nd Bomb Squadron for night leaflet operations; 42-3207 'MONKEYS UNCLE' suffered landing gear failure on 27th December. This is another case where failure of only one gear saved the aircraft from more serious damage. It was soon repaired and carried on, eventually being declared war weary. *Mike Gibson*

run was made north to Lannion, a target of opportunity, but the cloud cover persisted so the bombs were brought back to base.

On return to England, the crews found conditions very difficult, many aircraft were short of fuel and had problems finding places to land. The gathering darkness added to the difficulties. Rarely, if ever, could so many returning First Division B-17s have been put down at such a diversity of airfields. They were spread from Dorset to Lincolnshire. Many were down on Third Bomb Division bases in Suffolk and two from 401st Group were at Tibenham, a Second Air Division B-24 base in Norfolk. Worse still were those that had not found a safe haven and had been abandoned in the air, or crash landed and would never fly again. Sixteen had been Missing in Action and a further nine were destroyed on reaching England. The 91st's 41-24484 'BAD EGG', a Group original with 43 missions to its credit, was diverted from Bassingbourn to Great Dunmow but on reaching this airfield conditions were bad and it was sent on to Andrews Field, where a landing was accomplished. Unfortunately the plane collided with a jeep whose driver had been detailed to put out runway marker flares; the jeep driver was killed and the B-17 was wrecked.

The 351st Group lost seven aircraft Missing in Action this day, the Group's highest loss on any mission up to March 1944. Two more of the Group's aircraft crashed on return to England, 42-3093 'NOBODY'S DARLING' was down at Burnham-on-Sea and 42-37774 had crashed at Whitwell after all the crew had baled out safely. The 305th Group's 42-31528 crashed near Oxford and 42-31327 from 306th Group crashed between Cromer and Walkern. A 384th Group aircraft, 42-31073, crash landed at Whittlesley after eight crew had baled out. The 379th's 42-39762 landed at Rattlesden where it was salvaged. Two planes from the 401st Group were also lost: 42-31068 which crashed near Ware and 42-31198 'FANCY NANCY' was abandoned in the air and crashed and was destroyed near Kimbolton.

The difficulties experienced by those charged with keeping records of planes missing in action, crashed or landing away from base, when so much went wrong as on 31st December, is evident in the 384th Group records this day. The Group's 42-37725, a new aircraft which had been with the Group twelve days, returned to England where the crew baled out and the plane went out over the Channel and crashed in the sea. The

AIRCRAFT and CREW STATUS at 2000 Hours on 31st December 1943

UNIT	OPERATIONAL AIRCRAFT				COMBAT CREWS	NON OPERATIONAL AIRCRAFT ASSIGNED
	TYPE	ASS	ON HAND	OP		
91BG	B-17F/G	49	51*	28	23	1 B-17E, 1 DB-7B, 1 L-4B, 1 Oxford
381BG	B-17F/G	44	44	18	38	1 B-17E
1 CW	B-17F/G	93	95	46	61	* 91BG has two aircraft on DS from Little Stn.
92BG	B-17F/G	47	24	11	22	1 B-17E
305BG	B-17F/G	44	44	37	37	1 B-17E, 1 B-17F, 1 DB-7B
305BG	B-17F/G	12	10	5	5	Special aircraft
306BG	B-17F/G	45	45	28	34	1 B-17E, 1 B-17F
40 CW	B-17F/G	148	123	81	98	
303BG	B-17F/G	11	9	4	48	1 B-17E, 1 B-17F, 1 DB-7B, 1 L-4B, 1 Oxford
303BG	B-17F/G	37	37	27		GB aircraft
379BG	B-17F/G	5	4	2	47	1 B-17E
379BG	B-17F/G	48	41	35		GB aircraft
384BG	B-17F/G	7	7	2	39	1 B-17E
384BG	B-17F/G	44	38	14		GB aircraft
41 CW	B-17F/G	152	136	84	134	
351BG	B-17F/G	58	54	3	12	1 B-17E, 1 Oxford
401BG	B-17F/G	35	12	3	34	1 B-17E
94 CW	B-17F/G	93	66	6	46	
1 BD	B-17F/G	486	420	217	339	
482BG	B-17H2X	12	12	8	9	1 B-17E, 2 B-17F, 2 B-17F(S), 3 B-17G, 1 DB-7B,
482BG	B-17H2S	6	5	2		1 C-78, 2 L-4B, 2 UC-61A, 1 Master, 3 Oxford,
482BG	B-17OBOE	10	10	7		1 Tiger Moth.
482BG	B-17ASPEN	1	1	0		
482BG	B-24D	15	15	6	9	
482BG	B-24H	7	7	0		

DECEMBER 1943

OPERATIONAL DIARY: DECEMBER 1943

FIELD ORDER No	8AF MISS No	DAY	TARGET	No OF AIRCRAFT DESP	BOMB	LOST MIA	OTHER
	145	1st	Solingen, Industrial Area	221	212	19	2
			Pathfinders	6	6	0	0
	146	2/3rd	Special Night Operation-Germany	1	1	0	0
	147	3/4th	Night leaflet Operation-France	4	4	0	0
	148	4/5th	Night Leaflet Operation-France	4	4	0	0
	149	5th	La Rochelle-Laleu Air Depot, St. Jean D'Angely Air Depot, Paris-Ivry/Bois De Colombes Airfields	216	0	0	1
	150	10/11th	Special Night Operation-Knapsack	1	0	0	0
			Night Leaflet Operation-France/Belgium	6	6	0	0
	151	11th	Emden, Industrial Area	238	219	1	0
	152	11/12th	Night Leaflet Operation-France	4	4	0	0
	153	12/13th	Night Leaflet Operation-France	4	4	0	0
	154	13th	Bremen Port Area	182	171	0	1
			Kiel Port Area	119	106	1	0
			Pathfinders	12	12	0	0
	155	13/14th	Night Leaflet Operation-France	5	5	0	0
	156	16th	Bremen Port Area	240	173	1	1
			Pathfinders	11	10	0	0
	157	16/17th	Night Leaflet Operations-Germany-France-Belgium	4	4	0	0
	158	19/20th	Night Leaflet Operation-France	5	5	0	0
	159	20th	Bremen, Port Area	225	197	13	1
			Pathfinders	12	12	0	0
	160	20/21st	Night Leaflet Operation-France and Belgium	5	5	0	0
	161	22nd	Osnabruck, Communications Centre	225	147	5	2
			Pathfinders	8	6	0	0
	162	22/23rd	Night Leaflet Operation-France	6	6	0	0
	163	23/24th	Special Night Operation. OBOE Test Knapsack	1	1	0	0
	164	24th	Pas De Calais, V-Weapon Site	277	248	0	0
	165	27/28th	Night Operation-France	7	7	0	0
	166	27/28th	Special Night Operation. Quadrath	1	1	0	0
	167	29/30th	Special Night Operation. Quadrath	1	1	0	0
	168	29/30th	Night Leaflet Operation-Germany, France and Holland	6	6	0	0
	169	30th	Ludwigshaven, Port Area/Oil Refinery	289	276	5	3
			Pathfinders	12	11	0	0
	170	30/31st	Night Leaflet Operation-France and Belgium	5	5	0	0
	171	31st	Bordeaux-Merignac Airfield	175	139	16	7
			Blockade Runner at Gironde	57	0	0	2
				2595	2014	61	20

plane was listing as 'Missing in Action' in the Group's returns for 31st December and was dropped from the assigned list. It would appear that after a day or so, the crew turned up at the Group and it was then thought that the plane was down in England, so on 3rd January 1944, it was returned to the Group records as 'assigned but not on hand', being charged to the care of the Second Strategic Air Depot for repair. On the 5th January when it seems the true fate of the aircraft became known, it was restored from the Air Depot's charge to the Group's charge and was then immediately dropped as Missing in Action.

Oxfords made the news among the training types this month. LB522 went from the 305th to the 482nd Group on the 25th, DF399 went from 482nd to 351st Group on the 10th, and LB513 was transferred out from the 482nd to Honington on the 17th. A second UC-61A Argus was assigned to the 482nd on the 13th, this one coming from the disbanded 479th Anti Submarine Group. The only other movement was Piper Cub 43-657 which was transferred from the 482nd Group to No 2 Strategic Air Depot on the last day of the month.

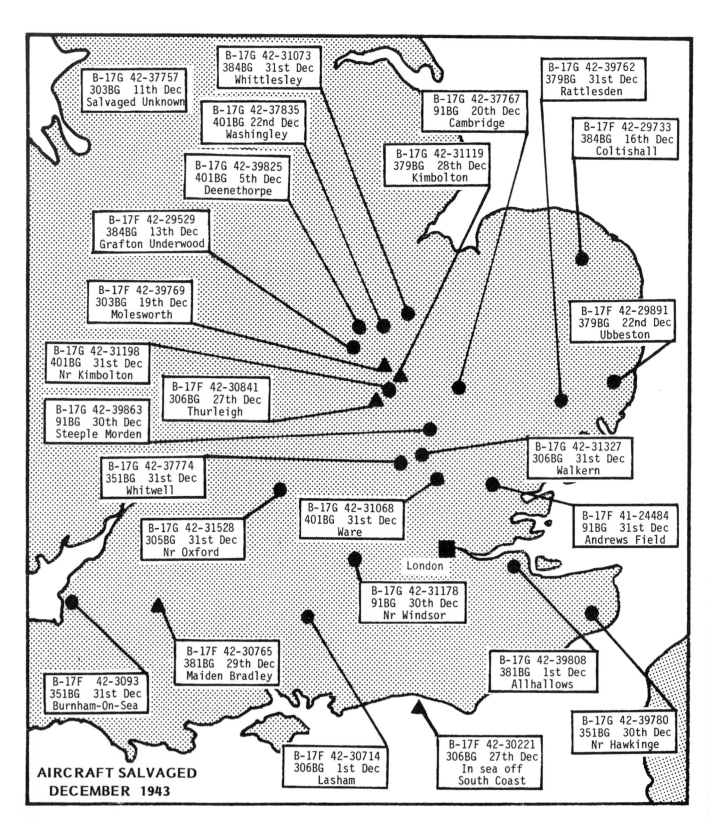

B-17G 42-31073
384BG   31st Dec
Whittlesley

B-17G 42-37757
303BG   11th Dec
Salvaged Unknown

B-17G 42-39762
379BG   31st Dec
Rattlesden

B-17G 42-37835
401BG   22nd Dec
Washingley

B-17G 42-37767
91BG   20th Dec
Cambridge

B-17F 42-29733
384BG   16th Dec
Coltishall

B-17G 42-39825
401BG   5th Dec
Deenethorpe

B-17G 42-31119
379BG   28th Dec
Kimbolton

B-17F 42-29529
384BG   13th Dec
Grafton Underwood

B-17F 42-39769
303BG   19th Dec
Molesworth

B-17F 42-29891
379BG   22nd Dec
Ubbeston

B-17G 42-31198
401BG   31st Dec
Nr Kimbolton

B-17F 42-30841
306BG   27th Dec
Thurleigh

B-17G 42-39863
91BG   30th Dec
Steeple Morden

B-17G 42-31327
306BG   31st Dec
Walkern

B-17G 42-37774
351BG   31st Dec
Whitwell

B-17G 42-31068
401BG   31st Dec
Ware

B-17F 41-24484
91BG   31st Dec
Andrews Field

B-17G 42-31528
305BG   31st Dec
Nr Oxford

London

B-17G 42-31178
91BG   30th Dec
Nr Windsor

B-17G 42-39808
381BG   1st Dec
Allhallows

B-17F 42-30765
381BG   29th Dec
Maiden Bradley

B-17F 42-3093
351BG   31st Dec
Burnham-On-Sea

B-17G 42-39780
351BG   30th Dec
Nr Hawkinge

B-17F 42-30714
306BG   1st Dec
Lasham

B-17F 42-30221
306BG   27th Dec
In sea off
South Coast

AIRCRAFT SALVAGED
DECEMBER 1943

AIRCRAFT MISSING IN ACTION: DECEMBER 1943										
1st	B-17F	41-24511	91BG	22nd	B-17F	42-3184	92BG	31st	B-17F	42-3186	92BG
	B-17F	41-24557	384BG		B-17F	42-3363	306BG		B-17G	42-3495	351BG
	B-17F	42-3060	91BG		B-17F	42-29724	379BG		B-17F	42-29630	351BG
	B-17F	42-3140	351BG		B-17G	42-37738	91BG		B-17F	42-29877	351BG
	B-17G	42-3540	381BG		B-17G	42-39778	351BG		B-17F	42-29895	91BG
	B-17G	42-3559	379BG	30th	B-17F	42-29963	379BG		B-17F	42-29921	91BG
	B-17F	42-6086	91BG		B-17G	42-31162	351BG		B-17F	42-29948	351BG
	B-17F	42-29506	381BG		B-17G	42-31274	384BG		B-17F	42-30733	92BG
	B-17F	42-29768	384BG		B-17G	42-39795	303BG		B-17F	42-30735	92BG
	B-17F	42-29794	91BG		B-17G	42-39826	401BG		B-17G	42-31064	401BG
	B-17F	42-30033	384BG						B-17G	42-31179	351BG
	B-17F	42-30803	92BG						B-17G	42-37725	384BG
	B-17G	42-31097	381BG						B-17G	42-37731	351BG
	B-17G	42-31111	381BG						B-17G	42-37770	401BG
	B-17G	42-31243	303BG						B-17G	42-39823	351BG
	B-17G	42-37847	351BG						B-17G	42-39910	381BG
	B-17G	42-39781	303BG								
	B-17G	42-39796	384BG								
	B-17G	42-39836	91BG								
11th	B-17G	42-31078	306BG								
13th	B-17G	42-39768	306BG								
16th	B-17F	42-30677	92BG								
20th	B-17F	42-3412	305BG								
	B-17G	42-3563	381BG								
	B-17F	42-5845	381BG								
	B-17F	42-5846	381BG								
	B-17F	42-29664	303BG								
	B-17F	42-29935	384BG								
	B-17F	42-30648	92BG								
	B-17F	42-30706	306BG								
	B-17G	42-31075	381BG								
	B-17G	42-31233	303BG								
	B-17G	42-37851	379BG								
	B-17G	42-37930	305BG								
	B-17G	42-39764	303BG								

42-29656 had flown on many rough missions since being assigned to the 303rd Bomb Group in March 1943. Flown to Langford Lodge on 30th June to have damage received on the mission of 25th June repaired, it did not return until September when it was assigned to the 91st Bomb Group and named **'SKUNKFACE'**. The crew are seen inspecting damage to the rudder after a Bremen mission, such damage did not prevent the sturdy and stable B-17 from returning to its home station. *US Air Force – National Air and Space Museum*

They started their journey 5,000 miles away in Seattle, Long Beach or Burbank as shining sheets, sections or extrusions of 24ST aluminium alloy. Carefully handled to preserve the surface finish, these materials were quickly transformed into the graceful contours of B-17s. This is the end of the journey, where many salvaged First Wing/Division B-17s ceased to be recognisable parts of once proud aircraft. There was no care in handling here. This is the Metal and Products Recovery Depot at Cowley controlled by Morris Motors Limited on behalf of the Minister of Aircraft Production. Here the remains were smelted down so they could be once more rolled and forged into useful sections to be re-used in the war production programme.

At left: the unloading and salvaging of sections of many types of aircraft can be seen. Above and below, the inner left mainplane section from an anonymous B-17 awaits the cutters and furnaces. With no apparent sign of damage and looking as though it has been dismantled at the production joints rather than a quick salvage job, one can only wonder how it came to be here and what was its history. *Morris Motors*

JANUARY 1944

The new year of 1944 started with many of the Division's planes and crews away from their home stations as a result of the diversions following the mission of 31st December.

Flying on the First day of the month was confined to those aircraft returning to home stations or requiring test flights after maintenance. It was on one of these flights that 42-30784 of 92nd Bomb Group became the first loss of the year. It had been damaged on the last mission of 1943 and was on a ferry flight to Little Staughton where repairs were to be carried out. After landing, and on turning off Little Staughton's Runway 25, the landing gear collapsed. The crew escaped uninjured.

On the first day of the new year, Lt Col Eugene A Romig was relieved from duty with the 41st Combat Wing and assigned as Commanding Officer of the 351st Bomb Group to replace Col Hatcher who was Missing in Action on 31st December.

It was the 4th before the first full scale mission of 1944 was flown. Two night operations had preceded this, one on 2nd/3rd when the 422nd Bomb Squadron had sent five aircraft to drop leaflets over Germany and a single aircraft operation flown by the 482nd Group on the night of 3/4th to test OBOE equipment.

On the 4th, Kiel was the target. The mission was scheduled for a pre-dawn take off and assembly was difficult. Many planes were shooting an excess of flares to identify themselves and with the numbers involved the whole assembly was very confusing. Enemy fighter opposition was very slight and support from the fighter escort was excellent; 263 planes had been despatched: 205 bombed using Pathfinder techniques. Six B-17s failed to return. One, 42-31526 from 303rd Group, had been assigned only three days before. Another, 42-31089 of 401st Group, ditched and the crew were rescued, becoming the Group's first successful ditching.

During the take off for this mission the 381st Group lost one of its longest serving crews, some of them on their 25th and last mission. The plane, 42-31278, a new B-17G that had been in the Group 14 days, piloted by Lt Cecil Clore, had a failure of some kind just after take off, turning to the left in an attempt to regain the airfield it slowly lost height and it is thought that Lt Clore attempted to crash land in a field just beyond Bloom's Farm at Sible Hedingham but in the darkness the plane hit a small wood, broke up and caught fire, killing all the crew. It was not a good day for the 381st, as on return from the mission, another of their B-17s, 42-29923, crashed at Cawston due to running out of fuel. Two crew were killed.

Next day, a double mission was flown. The 40th and 41st Combat Wings going back to Kiel and the First and 94th Combat Wings going to bomb an airfield at Tours in France. The weathermen had forecast that the Division's airfields would be closed in by 1500 hours, so another pre-dawn take off and assembly was called for, to make sure the return and landing could be accomplished in reasonable weather conditions.

As on the previous day the assembly was accomplished with great difficulty. Besides the confusion caused by the aircraft crossing each other in the dark, the wind was considerably stronger than had been forecast and the formation when assembled was five minutes early at the English coast. To delay the formation, the Combat Wing leader executed a 360° turn and in doing so he lost the composite Wing, which became boxed between two formations of B-24s, and had to fly to the target in that position. The 40th Combat Wing led to Kiel, followed by the 41st; the composite 40th and 41st as mentioned, flew to the target away from the main formation. One hundred and thirty-one planes had been despatched and 119 bombed, losing five. One of them, 42-5827 from the 379th Group, landed in Sweden.

The mission to Tours was accomplished without too much difficulty. Seventy-nine aircraft were despatched and 78 bombed the target, one from 381st Bomb Group never returned. This mission was the hundredth for the 91st, the first Eighth Air Force Group to reach the century.

The hazards of pre-dawn take off and assembly were made tragically evident this day. During the take off at Kimbolton, 42-29747 crashed at Catworth, killing seven of the crew, and at Thurleigh, 42-30767 crashed and exploded in a field a few hundred yards from the Headquarters building at Sharnbrook ammunition depot. Only the co-pilot and tail gunner survived. At Podington, 42-30580 had the right mainwheel tyre blow out during the take off run, causing the aircraft to ground loop: it came to rest with the tail section near the edge of the runway. Following was 42-31377 which attempted to stop but its right wing struck the vertical stabiliser of 580 causing extensive damage to this aircraft which was salvaged. Due to this crash blocking the runway, 42-30716 which had a number two engine failure immediately after take off was diverted to make an emergency landing at Thurleigh. Later, during assembly, the 303rd Group's 42-31441 and 379th's 42-37887, collided in mid air and crashed at Catworth and Covington respectively, killing all the crew on 441, and seven on 887.

The general feeling among crews about these early morning take offs was summed up by the report put in by the operations officer of the 92nd Group. He wrote 'Take off and assembly during darkness has proved very difficult and puts an undue strain on inexperienced pilots and navigators. On every mission where assembly was attempted before daylight, considerable confusion and distaste has been prevalent among pilots. Results of these attempts, leave on every occasion, at least three or four planes unable to make the assembly, thus jeopardising the Group defensive formation. It is felt that the thirty or forty minutes, saved in night assembly does not warrant the loss in security of the formation, confidence of the pilots and the assurance of a successful mission'.

The wreckage of crashed aircraft was removed from crash sites by working parties from the Reclamation Department of the Supply Division, Air Force Service Command at Little Staughton. Repairable or serviceable items were taken to Little Staughton for inspection and repairs. Scrap was taken to the metal and produce depot run by Morris Motors at Cowley, Oxford, where it was melted down and returned to the factories to be re-used in the war production programme.

In a spectacular runway collision at Podington, during the take off for the mission of 5th January, the right wing of 42-31377 removed the vertical stabiliser from 42-30580. Left above, the 'fin-less' 42-30580 was salvaged. Right above: part of 580's stabiliser embedded in the right wing of 42-31377 which had only been in the 92nd Group nine days and was repaired. *US Air Force*

JANUARY 1944

The 306th Group's Sharnbrook crash had occurred at 0730 hours on 5th January. At approximately 1030 hours on 6th January, a working party of nine, with T/Sgt Jesse L Rushing in charge, arrived from Little Staughton and worked until the 10th January clearing the wreckage. There is very little information available on this aspect of Eighth Air Force operations, so it is not known if this was typical or if special factors were involved in this crash which made for such speedy removal. One aspect however, which must have been unique was that when vehicle No USA 4431142-S arrived at Cowley with scrap airframe sections from the B-17, a live incendiary bomb was found in the formers of the fin section, and No 50 Maintenance Unit RAF were called in to render the bomb harmless.

The IG Farbenindustrie Chemical Works at Ludwigshaven was the target for the 210 aircraft despatched on the 7th. Cloud over the British Isles caused some difficulty during assembly. One hundred and eighty-four aircraft bombed the target using Pathfinders with unobserved results. Three planes were Missing in Action. One, 41-24525 from the 384th Group, had been one of the originals brought to England in October 1942 by the 305th Group and had been transferred to the 384th in September 1943, when the non Tokyo tank aircraft were transferred to the 41st Wing. The 351st's 42-29821, crashed at Moulton when returning from the mission, only one crew member surviving.

There followed three days when no day operations were flown, but the 422nd Bomb Squadron despatched five aircraft to drop leaflets over France and Belgium on all the nights except the 9th/10th January.

On the 9th, Little Staughton was once more the centre for a crash landing drama. This time it was B-17G 42-37924 of 384th Group, piloted by 2nd Lt Norman DeFrees, which was in trouble. Returning in the late afternoon to Grafton Underwood from a training mission the right main landing gear refused to lower by electrical or manual means, so they were directed to Little Staughton, where a crash landing was made without injury to the crew, the aircraft was salvaged.

The most important mission of the month was flown on 11th January. The target was the fighter assembly factory of AO Flugzeugwerke A/G at Oschersleben, Germany. Take off and assembly were made without difficulty and the Division, with the 41st Combat Wing leading, left the coast in correct order and on time. The 41st Combat Wing ran into some troublesome clouds over the Channel, circled them, and so lost five minutes getting to the target. The 94th Wing followed the 41st, but the First Combat Wing, seeing that the two Wings in front were going off course, did not follow and flew the course as briefed. The First Wing was followed by the composite and 40th Combat Wings.

At 1100 hours the formation was attacked by a large number of German

There were many diversions when the planes returned from the 11th January mission. The 381st Bomb Group landed at Hardwick where their planes are lined up on 12th January. At left is 42-29832 and at rear of line on right is 305th Bomb Group's 42-37726. *US Air Force – National Air and Space Museum*

OPERATIONAL DIARY: JANUARY 1944

FIELD ORDER No	8AF MISS No	DAY	TARGET	No OF AIRCRAFT			
				DESP	BOMB	LOST	
						MIA	OTHER
	172	2/3rd	Night Leaflet Operation-France and Germany	5	5	0	0
	173	3/4th	Special Night Operation-Germany	1	0	0	0
	174	4th	Keil, Port Area Pathfinders	263	205	6	2
	175	4/5th	Night Leaflet Operation-France	4	4	0	0
	176	5th	Kiel Tours Airfield Pathfinders	131 79	119 78	5 1	5 0
	177	6/7th	Night Leaflet Operation-France	5	5	0	0
	178	7th	Ludwigshaven, Industrial	210	184	3	1
	179	7/8th	Night Leaflet Operation-France	5	5	0	0
	180	8/9th	Night Leaflet Operation-France and Belgium	5	5	0	0
	181	10/11th	Night leaflet Operation-France	5	5	0	0
	182	11th	Oschersleben Pathfinders Halberstadt	177	139	36 1 5	6
	183	14th	Pas De Calais	176	169	2	0
	184	14/15th	Night Leaflet Operation-France	4	4	0	0
	185	14/15th	Night Test-OBOE Mk II	2	1	0	0
	186	20/21st	Night Leaflet Operations-France	5	4	0	0
	187	21st	Pas De Calais, V-Weapon Sites	306	156	0	0
	188	21/22nd	Night Leaflet Operation-France	5	5	0	0
	189	23/24th	Night Leaflet Operation-France	5	5	0	0
	190	23/24th	Night Test-OBOE Mk II	2	1	0	0
	191	24th	Zukunet P/S (Eschweiler)	291	2	0	1
	192	25/26th	Night Leaflet Operation-France	5	5	0	0
	193	25/26th	Night Test OBOE Mk II	1	1	0	0
	194	27/28th	Night Leaflet Operation-France	5	5	0	0
	195	28th	Pathfinders with Second Bombardment Division				0
	196	28/29th	Night Leaflet Operation-France	5	5	0	0
	197	28/29th	Night Test-OBOE Mk II	1	1	0	0
	198	29th	Frankfurt and Targets of opportunity Pathfinders	366	345	11	0 1
	199	29/30th	Night Leaflet Operation-France	5	5	0	0
	200	30th	Brunswick City Pathfinders	349	333	15	4
	201	30/31st	Night Leaflet Operation-France	5	5	0	0
	202	30/31st	Night Test OBOE Mk II	1	1	0	0
	203	31st	Pathfinders with Second Bombardment Division	1	1	0	0
				2424	1813	85	22

fighters. The attacks were heavy, carried out with exceptional daring and with great persistence. The main attacks were concentrated on the lead Group, the 303rd, and this Group suffered heavily. The attacks were continued into the target, on the bombing run and on the way back. Upon reaching the coast of England the pilots were warned that the weather was closing in over their bases and many planes were diverted to other airfields, mostly in Suffolk and Norfolk. These diversions gave rise to many problems and the next meeting of Group and Combat Wing Commanders were told that no diversions would be called for unless it was absolutely necessary.

On this mission, 177 planes had been despatched and 139 had bombed the target. Forty-two were Missing in Action. After the Black

Thursday mission of October 1943 to Schweinfurt, this was the Division's highest loss. The 303rd Bomb Group had not had a heavy loss on a mission since losing five on that epic St Nazaire mission of 23rd January 1943, almost a year before. This lucky run, was brought to an abrupt end on 11th January when ten of the Group's B-17s went down. Three, 41-24562 'SKY WOLF', 41-24587 'BAD CHECK' and 41-24619 'S FOR SUGAR', were originals that had each seen fifteen months' service with the Group. Another, 42-5360, had over 12 months' service. Another loss, 42-3448, had been the last Douglas built B-17F to be assigned to the Division. Flying the lead with the 303rd was 42-3486 of the 482nd Group, this also went down, becoming the first 482nd Group aircraft to go Missing in Action. It was the Group's 25th mission.

UNIT	OPERATIONAL AIRCRAFT				COMBAT CREWS	NON OPERATIONAL AIRCRAFT ASSIGNED
	TYPE	ASS	ON HAND	OP		
91BG	B-17F/G	56	54	29	49	1 B-17E, 1 DB-7B, 1 L-4B, 1 Oxford
381BG	B-17F/G	54	54	42	45	1 B-17E
1 CW	B-17F/G	110	108	71	94	
92BG	B-17F/G	52	51	42	38	1 B-17E
305BG	B-17F/G	52	51	32	47	1 B-17E, 1 B-17F, 1 Oxford
306BG	B-17F/G	61	60	50	41	1 B-17E, 1 B-17F, 1 DB-7B, 1 Oxford
40 CW	B-17F/G	165	162	124	126	
303BG	B-17F/G	25	24	20	40	1 B-17E, 1 B-17F, 1 DB-7B, 1 L-4B, 1 Oxford
303BG	B-17F/G	35	28	20		GB aircraft
379BG	B-17F/G	10	10	8	36	1 B-17E
379BG	B-17F/G	42	40	31		GB aircraft
384BG	B-17F/G	25	25	18	44	1 B-17E
384BG	B-17F/G	32	27	14		GB aircraft
41 CW	B-17F/G	169	154	111	120	
351BG	B-17F/G	60	56	35	35	1 B-17E, 1 Oxford
401BG	B-17F/G	53	47	24	35	1 B-17E
457BG	B-17F/G	47	3	0	0	
94 CW	B-17F/G	160	106	59	70	
1 BD	B-17F/G	604	530	365	410	
305BG	B-17F/G	12	11	9	8	422nd Bomb Squadron
482BG	B-17H2X	11	11	6	7	1 B-17E, 2 B-17F, 1 B-17F(S), 3 B-17G, 1 DB-7B,
482BG	B-17H2S	6	6	6		1 C-78, 1 L-4B, 2 UC-61A, 1 Master, 3 Oxford,
482BG	B-170BOE	10	10	9		1 Tiger Moth.
482BG	B-17ASPEN	3	3	1	0	
482BG	B-24D	23	20	10	7	
482BG	B-24H	11	11	4	4	

Title row: **AIRCRAFT and CREW STATUS at 2000 Hours on 31st January 1944**

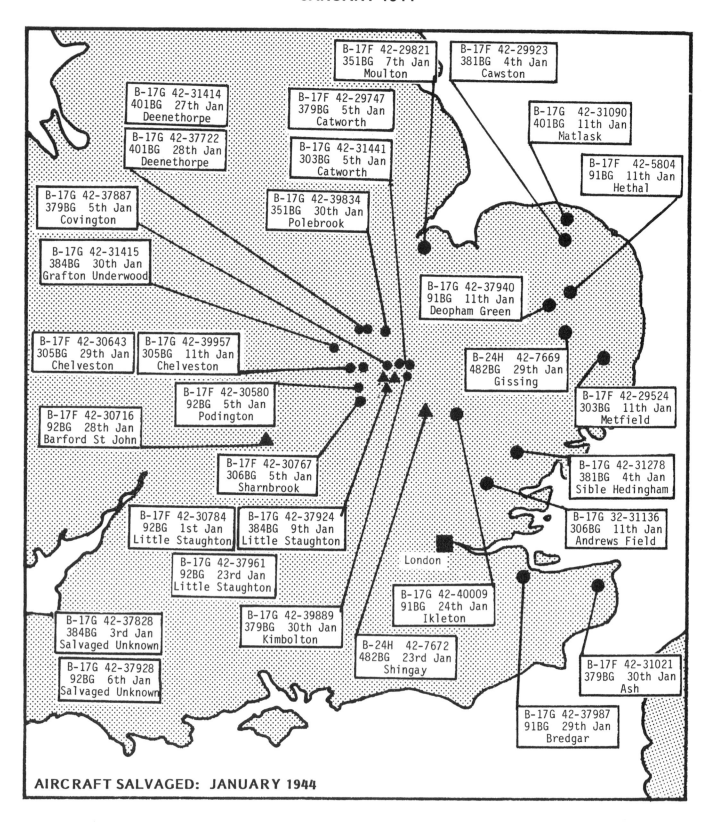

B-17F 42-29821
351BG 7th Jan
Moulton

B-17F 42-29923
381BG 4th Jan
Cawston

B-17G 42-31414
401BG 27th Jan
Deenethorpe

B-17F 42-29747
379BG 5th Jan
Catworth

B-17G 42-31090
401BG 11th Jan
Matlask

B-17G 42-37722
401BG 28th Jan
Deenethorpe

B-17G 42-31441
303BG 5th Jan
Catworth

B-17F 42-5804
91BG 11th Jan
Hethal

B-17G 42-37887
379BG 5th Jan
Covington

B-17G 42-39834
351BG 30th Jan
Polebrook

B-17G 42-31415
384BG 30th Jan
Grafton Underwood

B-17G 42-37940
91BG 11th Jan
Deopham Green

B-17F 42-30643
305BG 29th Jan
Chelveston

B-17G 42-39957
305BG 11th Jan
Chelveston

B-24H 42-7669
482BG 29th Jan
Gissing

B-17F 42-29524
303BG 11th Jan
Metfield

B-17F 42-30580
92BG 5th Jan
Podington

B-17F 42-30716
92BG 28th Jan
Barford St John

B-17F 42-30767
306BG 5th Jan
Sharnbrook

B-17G 42-31278
381BG 4th Jan
Sible Hedingham

B-17G 32-31136
306BG 11th Jan
Andrews Field

B-17F 42-30784
92BG 1st Jan
Little Staughton

B-17G 42-37924
384BG 9th Jan
Little Staughton

London

B-17G 42-37961
92BG 23rd Jan
Little Staughton

B-17G 42-40009
91BG 24th Jan
Ikleton

B-17G 42-37828
384BG 3rd Jan
Salvaged Unknown

B-17G 42-39889
379BG 30th Jan
Kimbolton

B-24H 42-7672
482BG 23rd Jan
Shingay

B-17F 42-31021
379BG 30th Jan
Ash

B-17G 42-37928
92BG 6th Jan
Salvaged Unknown

B-17G 42-37987
91BG 29th Jan
Bredgar

AIRCRAFT SALVAGED: JANUARY 1944

The return to England was not without its drama. 42-29524 of 303rd Group had been hit and set on fire and nine crew baled out over Holland. Lt Jack Watson brought the plane back to a safe landing at Metfield, where it was salvaged.

The 91st Bomb Group which had five planes Missing in Action, also lost two on return to England; 42-5804 landed at Hethal and 42-37940 landed at Deopham Green, both going for salvage. The 306th Group had also lost five Missing in Action and a sixth, 42-31136, was salvaged after crash landing at Andrews Field. The 305th Group, which had suffered so heavily on the October 1943 Schweinfurt mission, came out of the 11th January battle with no losses in action, but even then did not go unscathed, as 42-39957 collided with another aircraft, returned to England and was salvaged.

The 401st Group lost four planes Missing in Action, the heaviest loss the Group had suffered up to this time. Two were Group originals, one of them, 42-31033, had been the second B-17G to come out of the Seattle factory. The other two, were new planes which had been assigned on 2nd January. The Group's aircraft were diverted on return. Seven put down at Matlask, one of them, 42-31090 '**NASTY HABIT**', overshot the airfield blocking the road from Matlask to Wickmere and was salvaged. One of the damaged aircraft landing at Deopham Green following the mission was 91st Group's 42-31187. It took the Air Force Service Command until early March to complete repairs.

The next mission, on 14th January, was a short one to the Pas de Calais area of France. One hundred and seventy-six planes were despatched, 169 bombed and two were Missing in Action. Bad weather

		AIRCRAFT MISSING IN ACTION: JANUARY 1944					
4th	B-17F	42-3494	92BG	30th	B-17F	42-30008	92BG
	B-17F	42-5838	384BG	Cont	B-17F	42-30029	381BG
	B-17F	42-30606	306BG		B-17G	42-31047	381BG
	B-17F	42-31016	92BG		B-17G	42-31461	305BG
	B-17G	42-31089	401BG		B-17G	42-31535	379BG
	B-17G	42-31526	303BG		B-17G	42-31643	379BG
					B-17G	42-31692	379BG
5th	B-17F	42-5827	379BG		B-17G	42-37727	384BG
	B-17F	42-30155	305BG		B-17G	42-37856	401BG
	B-17F	42-30676	381BG		B-17G	42-97441	92BG
	B-17F	42-30724	305BG				
	B-17F	42-30794	306BG				
	B-17G	42-31093	379BG				
7th	B-17F	41-24525	384BG				
	B-17F	42-3078	381BG				
	B-17F	42-30386	305BG				
11th	B-17F	41-24562	303BG				
	B-17F	41-24587	303BG				
	B-17F	41-24619	303BG				
	B-17F	42-3057	91BG				
	B-17F	42-3118	381BG				
	B-17F	42-3131	303BG				
	B-17F	42-3448	303BG				
	B-17G	42-3486	482BG				
	B-17G	42-3514	381BG				
	B-17G	42-3523	351BG				
	B-17F	42-5360	303BG				
	B-17F	42-5878	381BG				
	B-17F	42-29487	91BG				
	B-17F	42-29861	351BG				
	B-17F	42-29894	303BG				
	B-17F	42-29993	306BG				
	B-17F	42-29999	381BG				
	B-17F	42-30780	351BG				
	B-17F	42-30782	306BG				
	B-17F	42-30865	303BG				
	B-17G	42-31033	401BG				
	B-17G	42-31076	91BG				
	B-17G	42-31175	92BG				
	B-17G	42-31230	91BG				
	B-17G	42-31236	306BG				
	B-17G	42-31372	91BG				
	B-17G	42-31417	381BG				
	B-17G	42-31451	306BG				
	B-17G	42-31481	351BG				
	B-17G	42-31538	306BG				
	B-17G	42-37719	381BG				
	B-17G	42-37730	381BG				
	B-17G	42-37768	379BG				
	B-17G	42-37809	401BG				
	B-17G	42-37896	303BG				
	B-17G	42-37962	381BG				
	B-17G	42-39758	92BG				
	B-17G	42-39761	351BG				
	B-17G	42-39794	303BG				
	B-17G	42-39893	401BG				
	B-17G	42-39905	351BG				
	B-17G	42-39969	401BG				
14th	B-17F	42-3029	303BG				
	B-17G	42-31246	384BG				
29th	B-17F	42-29886	379BG				
	B-17G	42-30711	92BG				
	B-17G	42-31040	379BG				
	B-17G	42-31050	379BG				
	B-17G	42-31193	401BG				
	B-17G	42-31486	401BG				
	B-17G	42-37884	381BG				
	B-17G	42-38012	401BG				
	B-17G	42-38045	381BG				
	B-17G	42-39786	303BG				
	B-17G	42-40057	401BG				
30th	B-17F	42-3325	379BG				
	B-17G	42-3509	351BG				
	B-17F	42-5404	384BG				
	B-17F	42-5444	384BG				
	B-17F	42-29761	381BG				

Top: 42-30767 of 306th Bomb Group takes off at Thurleigh. Bottom: its wreckage lies in a field at Sharnbrook after it crashed and exploded just after take off on 5th January. *306th BG Historical Association*

restricted flying during the next few days. On the 17th only five hours of non operational flying were recorded. It was the 21st before another mission was despatched, again directed at construction sites in the Pas de Calais area of Northern France. The 40th Combat Wing was unable to bomb their assigned target due to bad weather. Only 156 aircraft out of the 306 despatched were given credit sorties. All planes returned safely to their bases.

The 23rd January was a non operational day but was one of the most active of the month for training and other flying. During a ferry flight to Little Staughton 42-37961 from 92nd Bomb Group could not get the right landing gear to lower, so a crash landing had to be made which wrecked the aircraft but the crew escaped injury. Just before midnight, a 482nd Group B-24H, 42-7672, on a night training flight from Alconbury, crashed at Shingay, killing the six crew, including the 814th Bomb Squadron's Operations Officer.

On the 24th another major mission was planned, 291 planes were despatched with Zukunet as the target. Weather was bad and most of the Groups had difficulty in formating. All Groups were recalled and only two Division aircraft which had joined a Third Division formation were given credit sorties. There were no losses in action but a brand new B-17G, 42-40009, which had been assigned to the 91st Group three days earlier and was making it's first mission piloted by 1st Lt Marco Demara, had a fire develop in the top turret during assembly. The fire was soon out of control and Demara ordered the crew to bale out. Those in the rear of the aircraft and the top turret gunner did so. Demara decided to try and force land the burning bomber, and the co-pilot, bombardier and navigator elected to stay with him. The attempted force landing in a field at Ikleton Grange failed and all those in the plane were killed in the crash. While attempting to assemble, 42-3461 of 92nd Group, piloted by Lt Larson, had a failure of both left engines and at 0835 hours made an emergency landing at Barford St John, where the landing gear collapsed. This caused considerable concern, as the aircraft carried a full bomb load. Fortunately there was no fire and no casualties and the aircraft did not suffer serious damage.

There were no missions on 25th, 26th or 27th, but a considerable amount of training was carried out on all three days and on the 27th, 42-31414 of 401st Group was reduced to salvage when the landing gear was raised instead of the flaps after landing at Deenethorpe following a non-operational flight.

The 28th January was the busiest day of the month for non-operational flying with approximately 1,040 flying hours being accumulated. It also saw the loss of two more B-17s. For some unexplained reason, the 407th Bomb Squadron of the 92nd Group sent 42-30716, piloted by Lt Pickens and carrying 18 other personnel, to Barford St John, to deal with the aircraft which had crash landed on the 24th. Such incidents were normally dealt with by the Strategic Air Depot at Little Staughton. When landing, this aircraft's landing gear collapsed and the aircraft crashed on the runway. Only one occupant received minor injury, but the plane was a write off. Ironically, the aircraft which had been the cause of the trouble, 42-3461, was repaired and returned to the Group on 22nd February and survived to become an aphrodite bomber later in 1944. The second loss of the day occurred at Deenethorpe when 42-37722 caught fire on landing and was burned out.

On 29th January, the Division despatched a record 366 bombers to Frankfurt. Located in this city were the chemical works of IG Farben-industrie, and the Varenigte Deutsche Metallwerke (A/G). Assembly was accomplished with little difficulty and the formation moved out across the coast with the 40th Combat Wing leading. Fighter support was generally good, and in some places excellent. There were about 100 enemy fighter attacks and flak over the target was moderate and generally inaccurate. Ten/Tenth cloud covered Frankfurt and bombing was done on Pathfinder. A total of 351 aircraft bombed the target and 11 failed to return.

During the assembly, a 482nd Group B-24H, 42-7669, which was to lead units of the Second Bomb Division, collided in mid air with 42-100005, a B-24 of 392nd Bomb Group, and crashed at Poplar Farm, Gissing. Three crew members survived. At Chelveston the 305th's 42-30643 was preparing to leave the dispersal to taxi to the take off line, when the landing gear collapsed, there were no injuries but the plane went for salvage. On return from the mission, a 91st Group plane, 42-37987, crash landed at Bredgar and was salvaged. This was a brand new aircraft which had joined the 91st eight days before, making it the second time this month that the Group had lost a new B-17G in England.

The last mission of the month, to Brunswick on the 30th, was another major effort, with 349 aircraft being despatched. The First Combat Wing was leading this day. Over enemy territory the cloud formations caused

On the mission to Oschersleben on 11th January, the First Division lost 42 planes. Ten were from the 303rd Bomb Group and there was nearly an eleventh when 'MEAT HOUND' 42-29524 was hit and set on fire. Nine crew baled out over Holland but Lt Jack Watson (of Yankee Stadium buzzing fame) brought the plane back to Metfield where it is seen being dealt with by the fire crews. It was one of six aircraft salvaged after the mission. *US Air Force*

The 351st Group lost six planes on 11th January. The longest serving of these was 42-29861 a Group original shown here with Lt Strouse and crew. Crew on 11th January was that of Lt Cannon. *Alan Dann*

JANUARY 1943

42-30643 on its belly after the landing gear retracted as it prepared to taxi out of the dispersal at Chelveston for the mission of 29th January. Aircraft was salvaged.
Mike Gibson

trouble to both bombers and escorting fighters. Fortunately, the enemy pilots were also troubled but there were about 100 attacks on the formations. Three hundred and thirty-three planes were able to bomb using Pathfinder techniques. Just after the target, clouds scattered the formations. Fifteen bombers were lost; one, 42-5404 from 384th Group, was a 12 month veteran which had joined the 306th Group in January 1943. The 379th Group, lost four aircraft; three of these, 42-31535, 42-31643 and 42-31692, had been assigned to the Group only six days before.

Three returning planes made crash landings and a fourth which had been damaged by 20mm cannon fire had to be salvaged. The 351st Group's 42-39834 crash landed at Polebrook. The 384th's 42-31415, crash landed at Grafton Underwood and the 379th's 42-31021 crash landed at Ash. Also from the 379th was 42-39889, the plane salvaged as the result of 20mm cannon fire damage.

By the end of the month, there were 604 operational B-17s assigned to the First Division. B-17Gs were now in the majority. Forty-seven of the aircraft were assigned to the 457th Bomb Group; the newest Group to join the Division. The first of the Group's aircraft had been recorded in at Glatton on the 20th January. Most had gone to Burtonwood for modification and it would be late February before the Group was operational. The 457th joined the 351st and 401st Groups in the 94th Combat Wing.

During January, the First Bombardment Division had lost 85 B-17s in action (38 B-17Fs and 47 B-17Gs). A further 29 B-17s and two B-24s had been lost to accidents and other causes making a total of 116 for the month. By comparison the Third Bombardment Division had lost 55 Missing in Action.

Among those salvaged in England were two B-17s for which no reason for their loss can be found. The first was B-17G 42-37828 of the 384th Bomb Group. This had a truck run into the tail section at Grafton Underwood on 29th November 1943. It was placed with a Mobile Repair Unit from 1st to 4th December 1943 and then returned as assigned and on hand to its parent Group. On 3rd January 1944 it was dropped from assignment and placed with the 2nd Strategic Air Depot for salvage. It is

not known if the final salvage was due to the damage received in the incident with the truck or if the Mobile Repair Unit restored it to flying status and it had a subsequent mishap causing its salvage. The second aircraft was B-17G 42-37928 of the 92nd Bomb Group which was dropped from the Group's assignment on 6th January and transferred to the Air Force Service Command at Little Staughton.

Late in January, the first natural metal finish (silver) B-17Gs arrived in England. Vega built aircraft were the first to arrive but it was February before they had been modified and were ready for assignment to the operational groups. Also during January, the Eighth Air Force transferred 12 B-17Fs to the RAF at Sculthorpe. These were in exchange for 12 Mosquitos which were to be used for Pathfinder duties. Five of the transferred B-17Fs came from the First Bomb Division. They were 42-30809 from 305th Group; 42-3169 and 42-30812 from 306th Group; and 42-30014 from 381st Group. Some of these did not leave the Division until early February.

One aircraft scheduled for transfer to the RAF was 41-24577 **'HELLS ANGELS'** of the 303rd Group. This aircraft was dropped from assignment to the Group on 8th January but was restored on the same day. It is not known if this was connected with the proposed transfer to the RAF. It would be obvious that the news that their most famous B-17 was to be transferred out to the RAF would not have been well received at Molesworth and one suspects that there was some behind the scenes wrangling and in the end she departed on the 20th January for the USA where she went on a flag waving tour.

An unusual visitor to Kimbolton during the month was B-17F 41-24380 from the 5th Photo Group, Twelfth Air Force. It arrived on the 21st and left after repairs on the 28th, the nature of the repairs or the circumstances requiring the visit are not known.

Movement among the training aircraft was limited to DB-7B AL409 which transferred from the 305th to the 306th Group on the 28th, and the B-17E 41-2578 which joined the 482nd Group from the 1st Combat Crew Replacement Centre on the 9th, leaving for Burtonwood on the 25th.

FEBRUARY 1944

Lengthening hours of daylight, an increasingly powerful build up of strength, deeper penetrations into the German heartland and increasing losses marked this month.

The first day was quiet with only 50 hours of non operational flying being put in by a few Groups. On the second, activity increased, with all but the 381st and 401st Groups contributing to the Division's 400 hours of non operational flying. It was while landing after a local formation practice flight that the 379th's 42-38036 became the month's first casualty, when its landing gear collapsed at Kimbolton.

The first mission of the month took place on the 3rd with an attack on Wilhelmshaven. This city, with Kiel, had been the most important base for shipping and U-Boat construction in north-west Germany, since the beginning of the war and for this reason had been attacked frequently by both the RAF and USAAF heavy bombers.

For this mission, six Combat Wings were despatched with the 41st in the lead. A fairly routine mission with very little trouble at any stage. The weather over the target was completely closed in and the bombing was done by Pathfinder. Three hundred and forty-eight aircraft were despatched with 306 bombing the target. Opposition to the attack was very weak, considering the importance of the target. Two aircraft failed to return.

Late in the afternoon of the 3rd, 1st Lt Harold R Hytinen left Ridgewell in B-17F 42-30732, on a personnel ferrying mission to Little Staughton. On landing at Little Staughton, in high and gusty wind conditions, the aircraft touched down a few yards short of runway 31 shearing off the left main landing gear. Lt Hytinen opened up and made a go around, advising the tower that a crash landing would have to be made. He was advised to proceed to Alconbury where, after circling for some time while the field was prepared, the landing was made in darkness without injury to the occupants but the plane was severely damaged.

The next day, Frankfurt was the target and 287 planes were despatched with 183 bombing the primaries and 73 attacking targets of opportunity. The 40th Combat Wing flew the lead this day. Fighter opposition was completely absent and flak, though intense over the target, was inaccurate. Nine aircraft failed to return. Two of the missing aircraft were from the 482nd Bomb Group, the Group's highest loss while it served in the First Bombardment Division.

Three aircraft were salvaged in England as a result of the day's operations, 42-31494 from 92nd Group, crashed at Matching on return, six of

the crew being killed. At Ridgewell a B-17F, 42-30834, was belly landed after 1st Lt John J Kuhl had brought it back with two disabled engines. For this feat, Lt Kuhl was awarded the Distinguished Flying Cross. Also at Ridgewell, an aircraft collapsed on to runway 28 when the co-pilot hit the landing gear switch instead of the flap switch. It is almost certain that this was B-17G 42-39797 which went to No 2 Strategic Air Depot for salvage on 12th February.

Another loss on the 4th and one which has left a mystery was 306th Group's 42-31715, a new B-17G, which had joined the Group five days earlier. This aircraft had landed at Drem on the previous day and on preparing to leave, one engine refused to start. The pilot elected to take off on three engines using a short grass runway but it crashed and burned, killing all six on board. The crew consisted of four USAAF officers one of whom was 2nd Lt Roscovitch who had been the first enlisted man in the Eighth Air Force to complete a tour of 25 missions and had since become the 423rd Squadron's Gunnery Officer. The other two on board were a Royal Air Force Airman from RAF Dirleton, a radar station nearby, and a Royal Naval radar mechanic from 784 Squadron. No reason can be found to explain what the plane was doing at Drem with only a crew of four USAAF officers or for the reason why the RAF and Royal Navy passengers were on board.

For the third day in succession, a major mission was mounted on the 5th with attacks on four airfields in France. The weather over the target areas was excellent, and the bombing was visual and good. A total of 221 aircraft attacked the assigned targets. Flak was meagre and inaccurate and though ten to 15 enemy fighters were seen there were only four engagements and all planes returned safely.

Another mission was launched against airfields in France on the 6th. Three hundred and three aircraft were despatched, but over France a heavy undercast was encountered which prevented bombing of the primary targets. Sixty aircraft of the First and 94th Combat Wings identified the airfield at Caen/Carpiquet and bombed this target. One aircraft from 303rd Group was lost on the mission and 42-40025 from 381st Group was damaged and landed at Dunkeswell on return where it was salvaged.

There was no combat activity on the 7th, but on the 8th, a mission to Frankfurt was launched by the 40th and 41st Combat Wings. The total damage effected on this mission was scarcely worth the gasoline, oil, planes and men expended. Assembly was accomplished with no difficulty, but trouble started when the formations made landfall at the

As another B-17 flares out for touchdown, some of the aircraft which have already landed wait to cross the runway threshold before taxiing back to their dispersals and the waiting ground crews. It was normal for B-17s to stop inboard engines after landing. The brakes were hydraulically operated from an electrically driven pump and sufficient electrical power was available from the generators on the outboard engines. *Stan Bishop*

French coast. The leader of the high Group of the 40th Combat Wing had been unable to take off and the lead was given over to his deputy. At the French coast, the leader aborted, and although it was announced over the VHF that he was aborting, and he also gave the wheels down signal, the second deputy lead followed him as he turned away from the formation. At this point, the rest of the Combat Wing executed a 90 degree turn to the left, but the high Group (92nd) continued on a straight course, became separated from the formation, and was subjected to rather severe attacks, during which the second deputy leader was shot down. The Group finally reformed on the low Squadron Leader, who, having lost contact with the Wing, called for and received fighter protection, and led the remaining aircraft of the Group back to base.

For this mission 120 aircraft were despatched, 90 bombed and nine failed to return, one was an H2S aircraft from the 482nd Group. On return, 42-37793 of 384th Group landed at Brighton, repairs kept it out of the Group until 11th March.

A tenth loss on the 8th was 42-31045 of 384th Group. On a ferry flight from base to Little Staughton to have GEE fitted, the left main landing gear defied all attempts to extend it, electrically or manually and after returning to Grafton Underwood and then trying Alconbury the pilot was directed to make a crash landing at Little Staughton. This was successfully accomplished without injury to the crew but the plane was wrecked.

It was the 11th before another mission was despatched, this time to Frankfurt marshalling yards. Assembly and flight to the target was normal, but at Frankfurt the Pathfinder equipment in the First and 40th Combat Wings would not function properly and the two Wings flew to Ludwigshaven and bombed visually there. The 41st and 94th Combat Wings bombed Frankfurt which was hidden under 8–10/10 cloud by the use of Pathfinder equipment. Altogether, 212 aircraft out of the 223 despatched

made an effective attack. Five were Missing in Action and three were crash landed in England on return. Two of them were from the 303rd Group. 42-31314 at Shoreham where three crew were injured, and 42-39810 at West Malling where one crew man was killed and seven injured. A 351st Group B-17G, 42-31694, landed at Southend, overshot, crashed into a defence post on Warners Bridge and caught fire. The eleven crew were all taken to hospital.

Some days elapsed before the next operational mission. During this interval, another aircraft was wrecked, when on the 15th, 42-37799, from 92nd Group overshot the runway at Podington and nosed over during a training flight.

It was on the 20th, that the biggest effort of the month was mounted, when for the first time, over 400 planes were despatched. Leipzig was the target, a long flight over enemy controlled territory. The airfield at Leipzig/Mockau, housing Me-109 and Junkers assembly plants was the major target.

The assembly was accomplished with little difficulty and the flight out was very nearly as planned, with the exception that the flight plan called for the Combat Wings to fly in a column of twos, guiding to the right, but only the 40th 'A' and 'B' boxes flew out in this manner. The flight to the target was essentially as planned, but when the First Combat Wing 'B' box left the formation to bomb the designated target, the lead bombardier mistook Oschersleben for Aschersleben and bombed the wrong city. The 41st 'B' box bombed a target of opportunity, while the others bombed the primary targets.

From the 417 planes despatched, 340 dropped bombs on the targets. The opposition varied at the different targets. At Oschersleben, the flak was meagre to moderate and fairly accurate. At Bernburg the flak was moderate and accurate. At Leipzig the flak was moderate to intense, and

Some planes just could not keep out of trouble. One was 42-5859. It was assigned as an early replacement to the 379th Bomb Group and crash landed at Little Staughton on return from that Group's first mission. It was then out for repairs until it joined the 303rd Bomb Group on 2nd October 1943. Two months later it was back with the Air Force Service Command for repair after being badly damaged and landing at Bungay. It returned to the 303rd on 1st February 1944 and flew its final mission on the 20th February, crash landing and ending up across a road at Bozeat on return. *G. Darnell*

FIELD ORDER No	8AF MISS No	DAY	TARGET	No OF AIRCRAFT			
				DESP	BOMB	LOST	
						MIA	OTHER
	206	3rd	Wilhelmshaven Pathfinders	348	306	2	0
	207	3/4th	Night Leaflet Operation-France	7	7	0	0
	208	4th	Frankfurt Main, Marshalling Yards and Targets of opportunity	287	183	9	2
	209	4/5th	Night Leaflet Operation-Belgium	7	7	0	0
	210	5th	Chateauroux/Martinerie, Avord, Chateaudun and Orleans/Bricy Airfields	224	221	0	0
	211	5/6th	Night Leaflet Operation-Belgium	5	5	0	0
	212	6th	Caen/Carpiquet Airfield	303	60	1	1
	213	7/8th	Night Leaflet Operation-Belgium	6	6	0	0
	214	8th	Frankfurt Marshalling Yards and Targets of opportunity	120	90	9	0
	215	8/9th	Night Leaflet Operation-France	6	6	0	0
	217	10/11th	Night Leaflet Operation-France and Belgium	5	5	0	0
	218	11th	Frankfurt, Marshalling Yards Ludwigshaven Saarbrucken Targets of Opportunity Pathfinders	223	157 32 19 4	5	3
	219	11/12th	Night Leaflet Operation-Belgium	5	5	0	0
	225	15/16th	Night Leaflet Operation-France	6	6	0	0
	226	20th	Leipzig/Mockau Airfield Heiterblick Abtnaundorf Bernburg Oschersleben Targets of opportunity	417	239 37 44 20	7	3
	227	20/21st	Night Leaflet Operation-France	5	4	0	0
	228	21st	Achmer, Hopsten, Rheine, Diepholz, Quackenbruck Bramsche Airfields. Coevorden and Lingen Marshalling Yards.	336	285	8	2
	229	21/22nd	Night Leaflet Operation-France	5	5	0	0
	230	22nd	Aschersleben, Bernberg and Halberstadt, Industrial Aviation. Bunde, Wernegerode, Magdeburg, Marburg, Targets of opportunity	289	181	38	5
	232	23/24th	Night Leaflet Operation-France	5	5	0	0
	233	24th	Schweinfurt, Industrial Aviation	266	238	11	0
	234	24/25th	Night Leaflet Operation-France	5	5	0	0
	235	25th	Augsburg and Stuttgart, Industrial Aviation	268	246	13	1
	236	25/26th	Night Leaflet Operation-France	5	5	0	0

Table title: OPERATIONAL DIARY: FEBRUARY 1944

		OPERATIONAL DIARY: FEBRUARY 1944 (continued)				
238	28th	Pas De Calais, V-Weapon Site	134	68	2	0
		Road Junction, East of Yerville		10		
		Rail Siding, South West of Abbeville		7		
239	28/29th	Night Leaflet Operation-France	5	5	0	0
242	29th 1st Mar	Night Leaflet Operation-France	5	5	0	0
			3297	2597	105	17

First Bombardment Division did not participate in Eighth Air Force Mission Numbers 205, 216, 220, 221, 222, 223, 224, 231, 237, 240, and 241.

accurate. There were well over 100 enemy fighters seen on the flight and 67 engagements were reported. Support by friendly fighters on this mission was excellent. Seven bombers were lost.

The fighter opposition met on this mission was much less severe than could have been expected on so long a mission to a target so vital to the Luftwaffe. It did however set the stage for drama to take place when the bombers returned to their bases in England where three more B-17s were lost. Two of them carried Medal of Honour Winners and the third ended the career of 303rd's 42-5859 when it belly landed and ended up across a road at Bozeat. It had returned to the Group on 1st February after being repaired following a landing at Bungay on 29th November 1943.

Crash landing at Redhill with two engines on fire, was the 305th's 42-38109. The co-pilot had been killed over enemy territory and two other members of the crew were wounded. The pilot, 1st Lt William R Lawley was awarded the Medal of Honour for his actions in this aircraft this day. Two Medal of Honour winners, 2nd Lt Walter E Truemper and Staff Sergeant Archibald Mathies were on board 42-31763 from the 351st Group when it crashed near Glatton, the story of their heroic flight in the badly damaged aircraft is well told in Roger Freeman's 'Mighty Eight' series. General Williams in his critique of the Leipzig mission, described it as the most successful operation carried out so far by the Eighth Air Force.

The assault was continued on the 21st, with another attack on Germany. The primary targets chosen were Lippstadt, Gütersloh and Werl but a cover of clouds obscured these chosen targets and the Division bombed other targets that could be seen. The First Combat Wing bombed the airfield at Achmer, the 40th Combat Wing bombed the airfield at Hopsten, the 94th 'A' box bombed an airfield at Rheine, while the 'B' box bombed the railroad and some warehouses at Coevorden, Holland. The 41st 'A' box bombed Diepholz and Quackenbruck airfields while the 'B' box bombed the marshalling yards at Lincen and the airfield at Bromsche. A total of 285 planes from the 336 despatched, dropped bombs on these targets. Eight were lost in action.

Flying their first mission on the 21st, was the 457th Bomb Group which lost one B-17G in action and another, 42-31588, was severely damaged on the mission and salvaged after Lt Edward B. Dozier had flown it back to Glatton. One plane from the 351st Group which was Missing in Action, had ditched 30 miles from Lowestoft. Seven of the crew were rescued. Another 351st Group plane, 42-29858, had crashed after engine failure on take off. It came down at Barnwell and exploded.

For the third successive day, the bombers were out on the 22nd to attack targets deep in Germany. The targets chosen were Halberstadt, to be attacked by the 41st 'B' box, Oschersleben, to be attacked by both First and 94th Wings, Bernberg, to be attacked by the composite Combat Wing from the 94th and First; and finally Aalberg in West Denmark, to be attacked by the 40th Combat Wing. The assembly for this mission, was accomplished with considerable trouble, caused by haze and cloud formations but it was eventually carried out and the formations left the coast in correct order. During this assembly 42-38041 'HELLS ANGELS II' of 303rd Group and 42-31516 of 384th Group collided in mid air and crashed at Irthlingborough, eighteen crewmen losing their lives.

From the moment the planes crossed into Germany, the fighter escort was swamped with enemy attacks, and the bombers flew for the most part, unescorted. Halberstadt, Oschersleben and Bernberg were attacked as planned, but Oschersleben was covered with clouds so the cities of Marburg, Bunde and Magdeburg were attacked instead. The opposition met this day was very fierce indeed. Well over 200 enemy aircraft attacked the formations. The flak over any individual target was not very severe, nor very accurate, but going in to the targets, the formations passed near other heavily defended cities and were subjected to very dense and accurate fire from the guns defending these large industrial centres. Most of the flak damage suffered on the mission, came from the guns defending these areas. Two hundred and eighty-nine aircraft were despatched on this day, of which 181 bombed and 38 were Missing in Action, the month's highest daily loss. Three more were lost on return to England. All the crew were killed on 42-31322 from 305th Group which crashed and burned in Endcliffe Park, Sheffield. From the 351st Group, 42-31882 was abandoned and crashed in the sea off Cromer and 42-38023 was crash landed at Framlingham. One of the five 91st Group planes Missing in Action, 42-37939, was ditched and nine crew were rescued.

There was no mission on the 23rd, but most groups put in a few hours of non-operational flying; testing repaired planes following the heavy battle damage received on the three previous days hectic combat. The 379th Group logged only 15 hours this day. Even on a day of such low activity in the air as this, planes could still be written off, indeed they did not always have to leave the ground to do so. There were dangers inherent in the maintenance of so many closely parked planes, loaded with fuel, oil, hydraulic fluid and most dangerous of all, oxygen. So it was that during maintenance at Kimbolton this day, 42-29889, one of five originals still with the Group, caught fire and was destroyed.

After the respite of the 23rd. A large force was despatched to the ball bearing factories at Schweinfurt on the 24th. A target remembered with fear by the Division's crews. Here in two previous attacks in August and October 1943, the Division had lost 81 B-17s, more than at any other target and this must have been on the minds of many crews when the target maps were revealed at briefing on the early morning of that day. The assembly was accomplished with little difficulty, but the formation left the coast 13 minutes early, due to a sudden and unforeseen shift of wind. This caused the formation to be without fighter support for a short part of the way, but the rest of the flight had excelled cover. The 40th Combat Wing led the formation but had trouble sighting the target and made two bombing runs. For this mission, 266 planes were despatched, 238 attacked and 11 were Missing in Action.

Another major strike at the German aircraft industry followed on the 25th, with an attack on Augsburg and Stuttgart. The main effort was directed at the Messerschmitt factory in Augsburg. There was a haze at take off, but the assembly was accomplished with great efficiency and the formation left the English coast in good order and on time. Over Augsburg, the weather was clear enough to permit visual bombing with excellent results. The target at Stuttgart was the Vereinice Kugallager-Fabrik GmbH aircraft ball bearing factory. For the day's mission, 268 aircraft were despatched, 246 bombed, and 13 were Missing in Action. Three of the missing were from the 306th Group, one 42-31979 was a natural metal finish aircraft, the first to be lost in the First Bomb Division. A 457th Group plane; 42-97458, was damaged on the mission and landed at Detling, where it was salvaged. It was an extremely successful attack on an industry that was becoming more and more vital to the Germans as the war progressed.

The last operation of the month came on the 28th. The targets were defence installations in the Pas de Calais area, generally presumed to be some type of rocket defence guns. Assembly was normal, the flight to the target was essentially as planned, but over the target area a cover of clouds hid some of the places chosen for the day's bombing. Out of the 143 planes despatched, 85 were able to bomb and two failed to return.

And so the daylight operations of February came to a close. During the month for the first time, the First Bombardment Division had despatched over 3,000 aircraft. Losses too were an all time record with 105 B-17s Missing in Action. A further 24 had been written off as salvage.

AIRCRAFT SALVAGED: FEBRUARY 1944

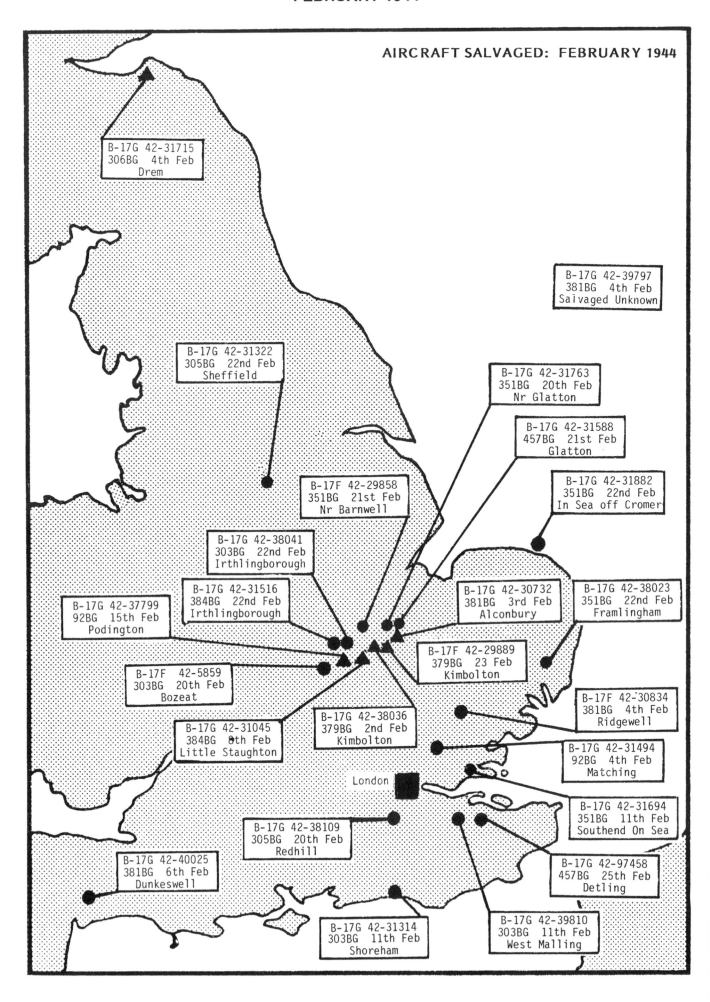

B-17G 42-31715
306BG 4th Feb
Drem

B-17G 42-39797
381BG 4th Feb
Salvaged Unknown

B-17G 42-31322
305BG 22nd Feb
Sheffield

B-17G 42-31763
351BG 20th Feb
Nr Glatton

B-17G 42-31588
457BG 21st Feb
Glatton

B-17F 42-29858
351BG 21st Feb
Nr Barnwell

B-17G 42-31882
351BG 22nd Feb
In Sea off Cromer

B-17G 42-38041
303BG 22nd Feb
Irthlingborough

B-17G 42-31516
384BG 22nd Feb
Irthlingborough

B-17G 42-30732
381BG 3rd Feb
Alconbury

B-17G 42-38023
351BG 22nd Feb
Framlingham

B-17G 42-37799
92BG 15th Feb
Podington

B-17F 42-5859
303BG 20th Feb
Bozeat

B-17F 42-29889
379BG 23 Feb
Kimbolton

B-17F 42-30834
381BG 4th Feb
Ridgewell

B-17G 42-31045
384BG 8th Feb
Little Staughton

B-17G 42-38036
379BG 2nd Feb
Kimbolton

B-17G 42-31494
92BG 4th Feb
Matching

London

B-17G 42-31694
351BG 11th Feb
Southend On Sea

B-17G 42-38109
305BG 20th Feb
Redhill

B-17G 42-40025
381BG 6th Feb
Dunkeswell

B-17G 42-97458
457BG 25th Feb
Detling

B-17G 42-31314
303BG 11th Feb
Shoreham

B-17G 42-39810
303BG 11th Feb
West Malling

FEBRUARY 1944

Three Vega built B-17Gs, 42-39767, 39779 and 39782, were assigned to the 379th Bomb Group on 21st October 1943. Only 42-39782 shown here taxiing out at Kimbolton, survived into 1944. It went down on 8th February. *Roger Freeman*

AIRCRAFT MISSING IN ACTION: FEBRUARY 1944

Date	Type	Serial	Group
3rd	B-17G	42-31056	306BG
	B-17G	42-37927	303BG
4th	B-17G	42-3500	482BG
	B-17F	42-5909	482BG
	B-17F	42-30423	92BG
	B-17F	42-31007	306BG
	B-17G	42-31036	401BG
	B-17G	42-31109	92BG
	B-17G	42-31440	306BG
	B-17G	42-39771	91BG
	B-17G	42-39803	91BG
6th	B-17G	42-97498	303BG
8th	B-17F	42-3357	482BG
	B-17F	42-29633	379BG
	B-17G	42-31387	92BG
	B-17G	42-31499	306BG
	B-17G	42-37984	92BG
	B-17G	42-39782	379BG
	B-17G	42-39784	384BG
	B-17G	42-40020	305BG
	B-17G	42-40032	92BG
11th	B-17F	42-29863	351BG
	B-17G	42-31099	381BG
	B-17G	42-31388	306BG
	B-17G	42-39962	384BG
	B-17G	42-40005	384BG
20th	B-17G	42-3562	381BG
	B-17F	42-29656	91BG
	B-17G	42-31430	305BG
	B-17G	42-31518	401BG
	B-17G	42-39770	92BG
	B-17G	42-97463	306BG
	B-17G	42-97500	305BG
21st	B-17F	42-3040	91BG
	B-17F	42-3073	91BG
	B-17F	42-30712	91BG
	B-17F	42-30866	351BG
	B-17F	42-31411	92BG
21st Cont	B-17G	42-31511	91BG
	B-17G	42-31596	457BG
	B-17G	42-31860	92BG
22nd	B-17F	41-24490	91BG
	B-17F	42-3087	387BG
	B-17F	42-5052	303BG
	B-17F	42-5788	303BG
	B-17F	42-5828	379BG
	B-17F	42-29829	379BG
	B-17F	42-29931	303BG
	B-17F	42-31028	379BG
	B-17G	42-31377	92BG
	B-17G	42-31399	303BG
	B-17G	42-31406	306BG
	B-17G	42-31409	305BG
	B-17G	42-31428	306BG
	B-17G	42-31443	381BG
	B-17G	42-31500	306BG
	B-17G	42-31510	379BG
	B-17G	42-31533	381BG
	B-17G	42-31612	351BG
	B-17G	42-31670	306BG
	B-17G	42-31695	306BG
	B-17G	42-31696	381BG
	B-17G	42-31930	401BG
	B-17G	42-37746	91BG
	B-17G	42-37939	91BG
	B-17G	42-38002	401BG
	B-17G	42-39809	384BG
	B-17G	42-39815	91BG
	B-17G	42-39857	351BG
	B-17G	42-39895	381BG
	B-17G	42-39898	91BG
	B-17G	42-39935	306BG
	B-17G	42-39945	306BG
	B-17G	42-39946	381BG
	B-17G	42-97450	384BG
	B-17G	42-97474	381BG
	B-17G	42-97488	384BG
	B-17G	42-97494	92BG
	B-17G	42-97520	379BG
24th	B-17F	42-3136	351BG
	B-17F	42-3517	351BG
	B-17G	42-31139	306BG
	B-17G	42-31180	92BG
	B-17G	42-31239	303BG
	B-17G	42-31308	305BG
	B-17G	42-31562	303BG
	B-17G	42-32034	92BG
	B-17G	42-38060	457BG
	B-17G	42-38074	306BG
	B-17G	42-40047	92BG
25th	B-17F	42-29717	384BG
	B-17F	42-30623	92BG
	B-17F	42-30678	305BG
	B-17F	42-30728	306BG
	B-17G	42-31245	306BG
	B-17G	42-31328	305BG
	B-17G	42-31517	457BG
	B-17G	42-31820	305BG
	B-17G	42-31979	306BG
	B-17G	42-37732	379BG
	B-17G	42-37755	92BG
	B-17G	42-37786	381BG
	B-17G	42-97457	457BG
28th	B-17F	42-5306	303BG
	B-17G	42-31058	384BG

FEBRUARY 1944

The third Bombardment Division had lost 86 B-17s Missing in Action.

During the month the 422nd Bomb Squadron had continued its night leaflet operations. A total of 82 aircraft had been despatched on 15 separate nights. France was the main receiver of these leaflets but some operations had taken place over Belgium. No planes had been lost on night operations.

On the 14th February, the 482nd Bomb group was transferred to the Eight Air Force Composite Command and ceased to be assigned to the First Bombardment Division. It continued to provide Pathfinder aircraft for some weeks before it changed to a training role.

The last night test of an OBOE equipped aircraft had taken place on 30/31st January and following this it had been decided to abandon further tests of this equipment in heavy bombers. Early in February the 482nd Group was instructed by Eighth Bomber Command, to despatch the B-17s and B-24s fitted with OBOE to the Ninth Air Force Depot at Stansted where the equipment would be removed for installation in B-26 Marauders. The B-17s were then re-assigned to other Groups in the First Division. The subsequent assignment of the five B-24s sent to Stansted is not known.

The 457th Group had flown it's first mission on 21st February. With this Group operational, the First Bombardment Division had reached near maturity, only one more Group was scheduled to join those already assigned. This would be the 398th Bomb Group which was to be based at Nuthampstead and would be assigned to the First Combat Wing. This Group was not scheduled to arrive until April and is therefore not part of this history. Plans for the reception of the 398th were however made during this period and one important aspect arose following experience gained with the 457th Group which would have an important bearing on

the assignment of the aircraft that the 398th would take into action with the First Division.

The 457th Group had taken a full month to get its B-17s through the Burtonwood depot and ready for operations. To obviate this same delay with the 398th, when it arrived, it was planned to have a full complement of modified aircraft ready at Nuthampstead. The 398th crews would fly their assigned planes into Nuthampstead and would only remove personal equipment. The fully modified aircraft would be flown into Nuthampstead by ferry crews who would then fly out the aircraft that the Group's crews had flown from the USA. Just how this worked out in practice is not known and since it was not to occur until April is not relevant to this book. It is however interesting to speculate on how many of the original aircraft would return to the 398th as replacements, perhaps to the same crews who had ferried them in from the USA.

The first natural metal finish (silver) B-17Gs were assigned to the groups in the Division during February. Boeing had started leaving the olive drab paint off at serial No 42-31932 and Douglas at 42-106984. The point at which Vega started is not so clear cut as several of their early silver aircraft were assigned to the 482nd Bomb Group as H2X Pathfinders and were painted olive drab after arrival in England. It is believed that the first was 42-97535 and this plane was in fact the first silver plane to join the Division when it was assigned to the 384th Group on 10th February. The next day, the 92nd received 42-97546 and by the end of the month all but the 305th and 401st Groups had received at least one or two silver planes.

There appears to be some contradiction in the way the first of these aircraft were distributed around the Groups and in the way they were introduced into combat. As early as January, when the first silver planes

Left: 'MISS B HAVEN' minus its number three propeller and off the runway at Deenethorpe after returning from the mission of 26th February. *Mike Gibson*

Below: the first Douglas built, silver B-17G to join the First Bombardment Division was 42-106998 which was assigned to the 379th Bomb Group on 28th February and was transferred to the 457th Bomb Group on 2nd March and named 'PAPER DOLL'. It had acquired a Cheyenne tail gunner's position when this photograph was taken. *Bernard Baines*

FEBRUARY 1944

had arrived in the UK, it had been noted that Groups would be reluctant to fly a few silver planes in formation with painted aircraft over Germany and it had been stated policy that they would be held back until there were sufficient to equip one squadron. The first assignments do not in fact seem to have been made with this intent in mind, as the distribution was fairly evenly spread over the Groups, and most only had one or two aircraft to start with. Perhaps it was the intention that these early silver aircraft would not be flown on operations until more were assigned although there is no known record to show this to be the case. In any event the first silver plane to be lost in the Division was the 306th Group's 42-31979 on 25th February and at this time the 306th only had one other silver plane assigned.

Early in March it did become declared policy to assign all silver aircraft to the 457th Bomb Group and as a result of this policy many of the silver planes which joined the other Groups in February were re-assigned to the 457th Group.

One of the airfields which had figured prominently in the First Bombardment Wing/Division activities during 1943 and the first two months of 1944 ceased its association with the Division on the 29th February. This was Little Staughton which had been one of the original airfields assigned to the First Bombardment Wing in September 1942 but had not been used operationally and had been transferred to the Eighth Air Force Service

Command in December 1942. It had then become the Second Strategic Air Depot. Its prime function being to service the B-17s of the First Bombardment Wing. Many of the B-17s had been to Little Staughton for repairs or modifications and some had been assigned to the Groups direct from this depot. With effect from 1st March the Second Strategic Air Depot was transferred to Abbotts Ripton using Alconbury as its airfield. Little Staughton was handed over to No 8 Pathfinder Group RAF and very soon the noise of Wright Cyclones was replaced by the deeper crackle from the Merlins of Mosquitos and Lancasters.

There was considerable activity among the training types assigned during the month, their ownership was complicated due to the transfer of the 482nd Bomb Group out of the First Bombardment Division.

Two new types appeared at Alconbury, the first, a Republic P-47D Thunderbolt, 42-7882, and the second, a Stinson L-5 Sentinal, 42-98593. This latter aircraft's stay in the First Division was short lived as it transferred out with the 482nd Group on the 14th. Also joining the 482nd was a third Fairchild UC-61A Argus. The second Cessna C-78 Bobcat to enter the Division came in on the 28th when 42-58511 was assigned to the 306th Group.

Following the transfer of the 482nd Bomb Group to the Composite Command on the 14th February the aircraft assigned to the First Bombardment Division Flight Section remained at Alconbury.

UNIT	OPERATIONAL AIRCRAFT				COMBAT CREWS	NON OPERATIONAL AIRCRAFT ASSIGNED
	TYPE	ASS	ON HAND	OP		
91BG	B-17F/G	61	59	42	39	1 B-17E, 1 DB-7B, 1 L-4B, 1 Oxford
381BG	B-17F/G	58	58	44	34	1 B-17E
1 CW	B-17F/G	119	117	86	73	
92BG	B-17F/G	52	52	37	31	1 B-17E
305BG	B-17F/G	56	55	36	41	1 B-17E, 1 B-17F
306BG	B-17F/G	55	53	29	32	1 B-17E, 1 B-17F, 1 DB-7B, 1 C-78, 1 Oxford
40 CW	B-17F/G	163	160	102	104	
303BG	B-17F/G	33	30	21	33	1 B-17E, 1 B-17FSH, 1 B-17GSH, 1 DB-7B, 1 L-4B,
303BG	B-17F/G	24	18	10		GB aircraft 1 Oxford
379BG	B-17F/G	21	21	18	30	1 B-17E
379BG	B-17F/G	35	33	26		GB aircraft
384BG	B-17F/G	24	23	21	37	1 B-17E
384BG	B-17F/G	29	23	17		GB aircraft
41 CW	B-17F/G	166	148	113	100	
351BG	B-17F/G	64	62	25	40	1 B-17E, 1 Oxford
401BG	B-17F/G	57	55	36	44	1 B-17E
457BG	B-17F/G	62	62	21	38	
94 CW	B-17F/G	183	179	92	122	
1 BD	B-17F/G	631	604	393	399	
305BG	B-17F/G	12	11	9	5	422nd Bomb Squadron
First Bomb Division Flight Section, Alconbury.						1 B-17F, 1 DB-7B, 1 C-78, 1 P-47D, 1 Master, 2 Oxford, 1 Tiger Moth.

AIRCRAFT and CREW STATUS at 2000 Hours on 29th February 1944

MARCH 1944

Operations opened on 2nd March with an attack on the Alfred Teves aircraft component factory in Frankfurt. The 41st Combat Wing was leading. Assembly was normal, except that the 94th Combat Wing arrived at the coast too early for Division assembly and had to execute a 360 degree turn to bring it into its correct position in the formation. The route to the target was flown as planned by all units. Some units in the 41st 'B' box did not bomb with the 'A' box. The Pathfinder aircraft and the lead Group released their bombs early, but the other elements in the formation, held their bombs and dropped on targets of opportunity. Opposition to the mission came in the form of moderate to intense and mostly inaccurate flak and a few enemy fighters. From the 327 bombers despatched, 293 bombed and eight were Missing in Action.

On the 3rd March the second mission of the month was executed with Erkner as the primary target and the centre of Berlin as the secondary, in case the primary was obscured by cloud. This was the first attempt by the Eighth Air Force at Berlin. The 94th Combat Wing was leading, followed by the First Combat Wing, then a composite Wing, followed by the 40th Combat Wing and lastly the 41st Combat Wing.

Assembly was normal and the planes left the English coast on time and in good formation. Because of cloud formations it was necessary to fly slightly north of course and at a higher altitude. As the formations proceeded towards the target, the cloud formations became more dense until clouds reaching up to 28,000 feet were encountered, at which point it was decided to abandon the mission. At about this time, a flight of planes from the Third Division flew through the 40th Combat Wing formation, causing the planes to scatter so widely, that they were unable to reform and they therefore returned to their bases in squadrons. The lead and second Combat Wings, approaching the enemy coast on the return, dropped their bombs on Wilhelmshaven through overcast, while the rest of the Division returned to base without bombing. Two hundred and sixty planes were despatched. Sixty-one bombed and three were lost.

In their determination to bomb Berlin, the target chosen for the 4th, was again Erkner, a suburb of that city. The 41st Combat Wing was to lead, with the 40th, the First, the 94th, and a 40th/41st composite following in that order. The weather made assembly difficult and the final Division assembly was never accomplished. Units of the 40th Combat Wing were unable to keep visual contact with the rest of the Division and abandoned the mission at the enemy coast. As the mission progressed, cloud formations became worse and again it was decided to abandon the mission. A 180 degree turn was executed to pick targets of opportunity at Bonn, Dusseldorf and Cologne. After bombing the Combat Wings picked up

their briefed routes and returned without incident. Two hundred and sixty-four planes had been despatched this day, 186 bombed and four were Missing in Action.

The first loss of the month due to an accident occurred on the 4th. It had nothing to do with the day's mission. A 91st Group plane, 42-31187, which had landed at Deopham Green on return from the 11th January mission, had finally been repaired by the Air Force Service Command and another 91st B-17 took a crew from Bassingbourn up to Deopham to collect it. On the return flight to Bassingbourn, both B-17s were flying in formation and were under a layer of cloud which got progressively lower as the flight progressed. As they crossed the RAF airfield at Newmarket, 42-31187 struck the ground and came to an abrupt halt about a mile beyond. The Service Command had put in six weeks work for nothing.

Two days later, on 6th March, the target once more was the ball bearing industrial works at Erkner. The secondary was as on the previous attempt, the industrial centre of Berlin. Leading was the First Combat Wing, then the 94th, the 41st, the 40th and finally a 40th/41st composite. The assembly was as planned with the exception of the 40th composite unit which flew as a two-Group Wing, without the 41st Wing joining it. On reaching the initial point, it was seen that visual bombing would not be possible at Erkner so the suburbs of Berlin were bombed visually.

Along the route, the fighter support was excellent. Over the target, however, the friendly fighters were greatly outnumbered by the enemy interceptors, and the bombers were subjected to a very severe series of attacks. Fighters, up to 200 in number attacked, coming in mass formations to overwhelm the defensive fire of the bombers. Two hundred and sixty-two planes had been despatched on this day and 248 were able to bomb the target. Eighteen planes were lost.

The Eighth Air Force lost 69 heavy bombers on this its first major raid on Berlin. This was to be the heaviest single day's loss the Eighth would suffer. It was also the fourth occasion when losses of heavy bombers had reached 60 or more. On the three previous occasions it had been the First Wing/Division which had suffered the heaviest losses but on the 6th March it was the turn of the Third Bomb Division to take the majority share of the losses, even so, the Third Division's losses were lower than those suffered by the First Wing on 17th August 1943, and the First Division on 14th October 1943 and 11th January 1944.

As on previous occasions, when losses in action had been heavy, the number of planes not regaining the English coast did not tell the full story. The day's losses had started, even before the planes had wheeled into their Group formations. At Bassingbourn, after 42-37761 had taken off,

The tail section of 381st Group's 42-37983 on the beach at Foreness Point. It had developed engine trouble on the 6th March Berlin mission and was landed in the sea just offshore and was later beached. *Stan Bishop*

MARCH 1944

Eighteen new planes were assigned to the 91st Bomb Group during March, nine were transfers from the 457th Bomb Group. Two that would become famous were (upper photo) 42-31636 "OUTHOUSE MOUSE', an olive drab original of the 457th that joined the 91st on 12th March, and (lower photo) 42-97061 'GENERAL IKE', a silver plane that served in the 457th for just three days before being assigned to the 91st on 16th March. Both would survive the war and return to the USA. *Barry Railton and Stan Bishop*

the crew noticed a flow of gasoline coming from the right wing. The pilot decided to land immediately, with the intention of checking and taking off again to join the formation if this were possible. As B-17s were still taking off from Bassingbourn he was directed to land at Steeple Morden but forgot to lower the landing gear and therefore made a belly landing which wrecked the aircraft. Three of the planes which returned had been so badly damaged that they were salvaged. They were: 42-31025 of 306th Group; 42-37999 of 305th Group and 42-37764 of 379th Group. A 381st Group plane, 42-37983, which developed engine trouble on the mission, landed in the sea, close to Foreness Point on return.

Early in March, it had been decided that the 457th Bomb Group would receive all-silver aircraft and that as soon as possible all camouflaged aircraft would be moved out of this Group and used as replacements in other Groups. As a result of this policy, all-silver replacements during the first week of March went to the 457th and some of the silver aircraft previously assigned to other Groups were re-assigned to this Group. By the 7th March there were sufficient at Glatton to fill a Group formation. The markings on these 'silver aircraft' as directed by A-3 at Air Force will be, 'A white group letter on a black triangle', and the aircraft and squadron letters were to be black.

During this week, Division Headquarters, notified A-3 that four RAF crews would soon arrive to observe and perhaps participate in daylight bombing operations. One would go to each station where a Combat Wing is located.

On the 4th March, 12 B-24s of Second Division, were diverted to Thurleigh. Ten arrived and two landed elsewhere en route; although First Division B-17s were frequently landing on Second Division bases in Norfolk and Suffolk when returning from operations the reverse was a much less frequent occurrence.

Another aircraft was lost to salvage on the 7th March. This was 303rd Group's 42-31052 and is another elusive case where a considerable amount of research has failed to find the reason for its demise. Assigned to the Group's 360th Bomb Squadron, but apparently it had not flown a mission with this squadron since November 1943. Some reports link this plane with the Third Bomb Division's 447th Bomb Group so it could have been salvaged at this Group's base at Rattlesden.

The second week of March opened on the 8th with another major thrust at Berlin. Once again the ball bearing works at Erkner, situated 16 miles south east of the centre of the city, was the primary target. The secondary was the centre of the city. The 94th Combat Wing was leading, with the 40th, then the 41st and last a composite First/40th.

Assembly was made without incident and the formations departed the English coast on time and in good order. Thirty miles from the target it was decided to bomb visually. A minimum of enemy opposition from a few fighters and from moderate, innaccurate flak was met. Two hundred and fifty-five planes had been despatched on this mission, 222 bombed and four were lost.

On the next day, the offensive continued with another mission to the Berlin area. This time it was the Heinkel plant at Oranienburg which was the primary with the city of Berlin as the secondary. Orders from Division headquarters called for the 40th Combat Wing to lead, with the 41st, the First and lastly the 94th to follow. Assembly and departure from the English coast was as planned. Shortly before the Initial Point, the signal for Pathfinder bombing was given and the secondary was bombed in Combat Wing formation.

The 41st Combat Wing's high Group ran into difficulty on the bombing run, when the low squadron of the lead Group flew directly under them. They did not drop their bombs until several minutes later, when they were informed that there were no aircraft below. Shortly after bombs away, the tail gunner of the lead ship of the high Group, reported a B-17 with the tail assembly knocked off, diving straight into the clouds. Apparently it had been hit by the high Group's bombs.

Flak at the target was reported as intense and inaccurate. About six enemy fighters were seen on the entire mission but no encounters were reported. Support by friendly fighters was excellent, of the 224 aircraft despatched on this mission, 208 bombed and three were Missing in Action. A fourth B-17 lost this day was 42-3536. One of the ex-482nd Group OBOE equipped B-17s that had been sent to Stansted to have the equipment removed and which had then been re-assigned to the 92nd Group, it crashed and burned just after take off at Podingdon, killing the entire crew.

The tenth of the month was a day of rest for the combat crews but on the ground there was hectic activity repairing the bombers which had been damaged during the previous eight days' operations.

On the eleventh, a small mission to the marshalling yards at Münster was undertaken. Only the 94th Combat Wing participated, despatching 62 planes, all bombed and returned without losses.

Next day, the 12th, there was no mission. A small amount of non-operational flying was carried out by some of the Groups, when returning to Molesworth from a local transition flight, the 303rd's 42-31756 had a collapse of the landing gear and was salvaged.

On the 13th, 'Crossbow' targets in France were the primaries for 85 aircraft despatched by the 41st and 94th Combat Wings. Assembly was normal but when the formation reached the French coast an undercast of 10/10 clouds were encountered. Only the low squadron of the 351st Group did any bombing. This unit, after circling Abbeville twice, was able to see a small airfield near Poix and dropped their bombs on it. The return was as briefed, the 351st Group was diverted to Molesworth because of a strong wind and runway unserviceability at their base. Opposition was only slight, friendly fighter support was as briefed. Only seven aircraft had bombed and two were Missing in Action.

During this period, a severe shortage of electrically heated flying suits was experienced in the Division. The Air Service Command was sending up to three cables a day to the States, stressing the urgency of this

OPERATIONAL DIARY: MARCH 1944

FIELD ORDER No	8AF MISS No	DAY	TARGET	No OF AIRCRAFT			
				DESP	BOMB	LOST	
						MIA	OTHER
	244	2nd	Frankfurt, Ludwigshaven, Limburg and Fischbach	327	293	8	0
	245	2/3rd	Night Leaflet Operation-France	5	5	0	0
	246	3rd	Wilhelmshaven	260	61	3	0
	247	4th	Bonn, Dusseldorf, Cologne, Frankfurt	264	186	4	0
	249	5/6th	Night Leaflet Operation-France	5	5	0	0
	250	6th	Berlin	262	248	18	5
	251	6/7th	Night Leaflet Operation	5	5	0	0
	252	8th	Berlin and Targets of opportunity	235	222	4	0
	253	9th	Berlin	224	208	3	1
	254	10/11th	Night Leaflet Operation-Belgium	5	5	0	0
	255	11th	Munster, Marshalling Yards	62	62	0	0
	257	13th	Poix	85	7	2	0
	258	13/14th	Night Leaflet Operation-France	7	7	0	0
	261	15/16th	Night Leaflet Operation-France	7	7	0	0
	262	16th	Augsburg and Gessertshausen	280	213	5	0
	264	18th	Oberpfaffenhofen, Lechfield, Landsberg, Memmingen and Targets of opportunity	290	284	8	0
	265	18/19th	Night Leaflet operation-France	6	6	0	0
	266	19th	Wizernes and Watten, V-Weapon Sites	129	117	1	0
	267	19/20th	Night Leaflet Operation-Holland	6	6	0	0
	269	20th	Frankfurt, Mannheim and targets of opportunity	231	101	3	1
	272	21/22nd	Night leaflet Operation-Holland	6	6	0	0
	273	22nd	Berlin	287	277	4	1
	274	22/23rd	Night Leaflet Operation-Holland	6	6	0	0
	275	23rd	Munster and Targets of opportunity	300	296	6	0
	276	23/24th	Night Leaflet Operation-France	5	5	0	0
	277	24th	Schweinfurt Frankfurt	230	60 162	3	3
	278	24/25th	Night Leaflet Operation-France and Belgium	5	5	0	0
	279	25/26th	Night Leaflet Operation-Belgium	6	6	0	0
	280	26th	Pas De Calais, V-Weapon Sites	243	234	4	3
	281	26/27th	Night Leaflet Operation-France	6	6	0	0
313	282	27th	St. Jean D/Angely, La Rochelle/LA Leu and Chartres Airfields. Usine Liotard and Tours/Parcay Meslay Industrial Aviation	290	285	1	0
314	283	28th	Dijon/Longvic and Reims/Champagne Airfields	182	117	0	3
	284	29th	Brunswick, Unterluss, Stedorf and Targets of opportunity	236	233	9	1

			OPERATIONAL DIARY: MARCH 1944 (continued)				
	286	30/31st	Night Leaflet Operation-France	6	6	0	0
				4272	3756	86	18

equipment. On the 12th, a very welcome 421 complete assemblies of new type F2 electrically heated flying clothing arrived at the Abbots Ripton depot and the following day, another 108 new type F2 and two type F2A assemblies arrived and were distributed to the Groups. Also arriving at this time, were electrically heated casualty bags, 30 of these were distributed to each Group.

A change of policy, concerning the assignment of natural metal finish aircraft was made during the second week of March. It was decided that the 457th Bomb Group would only have 30 of these aircraft, with 30 painted. The remaining 'silver' planes were to be distributed indiscriminately around the Division and in future, assignments of aircraft would be made, regardless of camouflage.

The most interesting aircraft coming into the Division at this time, and indeed throughout the Division's stay in England, was a B-29 Superfortress. This aircraft arrived at St Mawgan on the 7th and then flew on to Bovingdon. It visited Glatton on 12th March and left for Horsham St Faith on the 13th. According to reports, it also visited Bassingbourn before its visit to Glatton, but no proof of this has been found. At the daily staff meeting on the 14th March, Lt Col Paul Brown, Engineer, brought to the attention of those present the immense weight (the B-29's loaded weight was double that of a B-17), and the wear and tear on the runways caused by the B-29. He said that to use them in this theatre would require a very great amount of work on airfield facilities.

The First Division lost eight B-17s on 18th March. Four, including two from the 384th Bomb Group, were down in Switzerland. Upper photo shows 42-31871 which had been assigned to the 384th for less than a month, and lower photo, 42-37793 **'WINSOME WINN II'** which had returned to the 384th on 11th March following a forced landing at Brighton when returning from a mission on 8th February. *Mike Gibson*

Also coming into use during this period, were the new 'VHF' relay planes. Two B-17s had been specially modified, their function being to fly out to the coast, or further, on days a mission was being flown. They were to receive and transmit VHF messages, the prime purpose, being to keep the escorting fighters informed of the positions of the bomber formations, the messages received giving relative positions of the formations were realyed to Fighter Command or to First Bomb Division. In this way, it was possible to plan each Fighter-Bomber rendezvous easily and accurately. All Groups were notified of the existence and use of these planes.

The two 'VHF' planes had been sent to Burtonwood for modification in January. One, 42-3061, had started its Eighth Air Force career in the 95th Bomb Group and had been transferred to the 379th Group. It was assigned to the 91st Group at Bassingbourn and served as the First Bomb Division relay plane. The other, 42-3134, had served in the 92nd Group and was assigned to Eighth Fighter Command and was stationed at Ridgewell where it was maintained by the 381st Group.

Operations for the third week of March opened on the 16th, when the primary targets were Lechfeld, Landeburg and Oberpfaffenhofen, with Augsburg as the secondary. The Combat Wing order was: 41st to lead, then a 40/41st composite, the 94th, the First and last the 40th. The assembly of the First, 41st and 94th Combat Wings was as planned, the 40/41st composite had some trouble in getting the Groups together and flew in a split up formation. One squadron of the low Group of the 40th Combat Wing, failed to rendezvous and aborted.

On this mission, the secondary target was bombed by Pathfinder as a 10/10 undercast made sighting on the primary impossible. The return to base was as planned. From the 280 aircraft which were despatched, 259 bombed, losing five Missing in Action, one of the missing planes came from the 457th Group. It ditched fifteen miles from the enemy coast. All ten crew were saved by the Air Sea Rescue. This was the 457th Group's first successful ditching.

There was no operational activity on the 17th, but on the 18th, another major attack on Germany was launched. The primaries were Oberpfaffenhofen, Lechfeld and Landsberg, the secondary was Munich. Combat Wing order was: First to lead, then 41st, the 40th, then a 40/41st composite and finally the 94th. Assembly was accomplished with no difficulty and the flight to the target was essentially as briefed. On the bombing run, one of the lead squadron's bombardiers, dropped his bombs too early by mistake, and 14 aircraft of the 91st Group released with him but the rest of the First Combat Wing bombed Oberpfaffenhofen. The lead and low Groups of the 41st Combat Wing also bombed Oberpfaffenhofen. The high Group did not bomb with the rest of the Wing because the low Group was spread out below the formation. This Group later attacked an airfield north west of the city of Manningen. The composite wing and the 40th Combat Wing bombed Lechfeld. The 94th's lead and low Groups bombed Landsberg and the high Group bombed Memmingen airfield. All bombing was visual.

For this mission, 290 planes were despatched, 284 bombed and eight were Missing in Action. Four of the missing planes were down in Switzerland.

Only the 41st and 94th Combat Wings were called to provide planes for the mission on the 19th March. Targets were V-weapon sites at Wizernes and Watten. Assembly was normal and the Groups departed in good order. There was some flak from initial points to the targets, no enemy fighters were seen. From the 129 aircraft which took off, 12 returned early and 117 bombed the targets. One plane from the 384th Group was missing.

The primary target for the 20th, was the Alfred Teves factory at Frankfurt and the centre of Frankfurt was the secondary. Leading this day was the 94th Combat Wing, next came the 40th, then the First and last the 41st Combat Wing. Group assemblies were made without difficulty, but the final wing assemblies were late and the formation was three minutes late leaving the English coast.

High cirrus clouds and persistent contrails made formation flying almost impossible, the 94th Combat Wing, therefore abandoned the mission and the 40th soon followed. The First Combat Wing also met frontal conditions and after an unsuccessful attempt to climb over them, they dropped their bombs on a flak area somewhere near Mannheim. In the 41st Combat Wing, the low Group was separated from the rest of the formation by the weather, could not make contact again and so returned to base. The lead and high Groups maintained their formation and were able to bomb the city of Frankfurt.

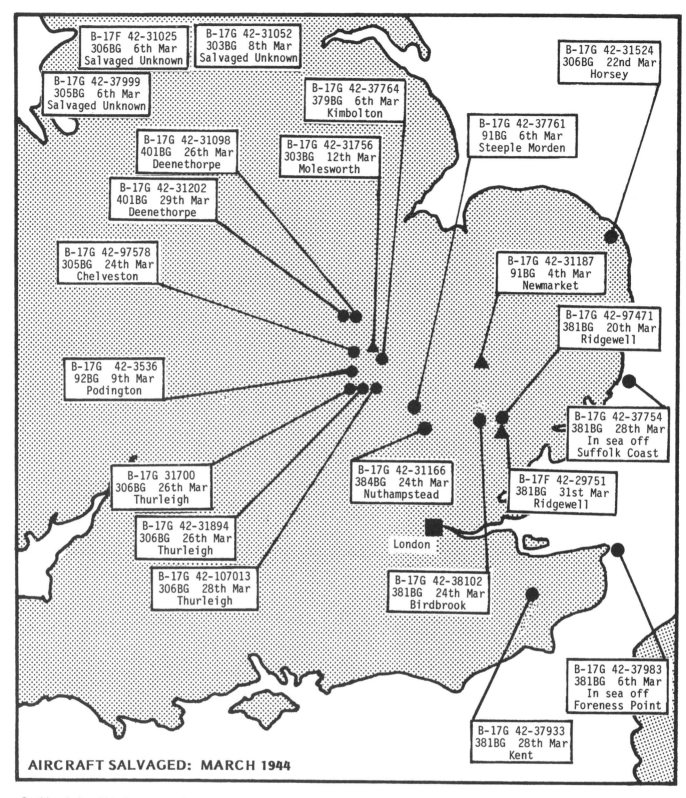

B-17F 42-31025
306BG 6th Mar
Salvaged Unknown

B-17G 42-31052
303BG 8th Mar
Salvaged Unknown

B-17G 42-31524
306BG 22nd Mar
Horsey

B-17G 42-37999
305BG 6th Mar
Salvaged Unknown

B-17G 42-37764
379BG 6th Mar
Kimbolton

B-17G 42-37761
91BG 6th Mar
Steeple Morden

B-17G 42-31098
401BG 26th Mar
Deenethorpe

B-17G 42-31756
303BG 12th Mar
Molesworth

B-17G 42-31202
401BG 29th Mar
Deenethorpe

B-17G 42-31187
91BG 4th Mar
Newmarket

B-17G 42-97578
305BG 24th Mar
Chelveston

B-17G 42-97471
381BG 20th Mar
Ridgewell

B-17G 42-3536
92BG 9th Mar
Podington

B-17G 42-37754
381BG 28th Mar
In sea off
Suffolk Coast

B-17G 31700
306BG 26th Mar
Thurleigh

B-17G 42-31166
384BG 24th Mar
Nuthampstead

B-17F 42-29751
381BG 31st Mar
Ridgewell

B-17G 42-31894
306BG 26th Mar
Thurleigh

B-17G 42-107013
306BG 28th Mar
Thurleigh

London

B-17G 42-38102
381BG 24th Mar
Birdbrook

B-17G 42-37983
381BG 6th Mar
In sea off
Foreness Point

B-17G 42-37933
381BG 28th Mar
Kent

AIRCRAFT SALVAGED: MARCH 1944

On this mission, 231 planes were despatched but only 101 returned credit sorties. Three were Missing in Action. A fourth loss was 42-97471 from 381st Group which landed normally on return to Ridgewell, but during the landing roll the landing gear collapsed, lowering the aircraft on to the runway. There were no injuries to the crew, but the aircraft was wrecked.

During this week, there was a large influx of replacement crews. Forty-one were assigned, a few were without navigators. Replacements in planes were very few, but several of the 'silver' aircraft in the 457th Group were available for re-assignment as a result of the policy change that this Group would not receive all the uncamouflaged aircraft.

An important operational change was the decision to give each Division its own Pathfinder aircraft. In the First Division, the 422nd Bomb Squadron of the 305th Bomb Group would receive 12 of these aircraft from the 482nd Bomb Group, the first arriving on the 20th March. Some of these

aircraft had arrived in the United Kingdom in natural metal finish and had been camouflaged since their arrival. The three remaining squadrons in the 305th were required to fly only one box on operations. The first mission flown by the Pathfinder Squadron would have a 482nd Group plane flying the lead position and the 422nd Bomb Squadron flying the deputy lead.

On the 15th, Lt Col Morrow, Division Ordnance Officer, accompanied Maj Frank Corbett, Divisional Chemical Officer, to Alconbury, to witness the dropping of new type pyrotechnic skymarkers. These were intended to replace the existing skymarkers then in use. There had been many cases reported where the chemicals had eaten through the plexiglass nose of planes when they flew through the smoke of the skymarkers. The tests were not completed. The bombs were loaded into the plane, and the ordnance men were checking the loading, when one of the bombs in the bomb bay went off. Smoke and fire started pouring from the plane. All

Date	Type	Serial	Group		Date	Type	Serial	Group		Date	Type	Serial	Group
2nd	B-17F	42-30636	92BG		8th	B-17G	42-31471	303BG		22nd	B-17G	42-37957	305BG
	B-17G	42-31467	401BG			B-17G	42-31488	401BG			B-17G	42-39849	351BG
	B-17G	42-31776	351BG			B-17G	42-38029	381BG			B-17G	42-97125	91BG
	B-17G	42-31799	379BG			B-17G	42-39892	91BG			B-17G	42-97523	305BG
	B-17G	42-39891	381BG										
	B-17G	42-39944	305BG		9th	B-17G	42-31564	92BG		23rd	B-17G	42-31231	92BG
	B-17G	42-39960	92BG			B-17G	42-31772	92BG			B-17G	42-31455	92BG
	B-17G	42-97509	303BG			B-17G	42-37781	384BG			B-17G	42-31532	92BG
											B-17G	42-31602	305BG
3rd	B-17G	42-37965	91BG		13th	B-17G	42-31374	401BG			B-17G	42-31888	92BG
	B-17G	42-37986	381BG			B-17G	42-39980	379BG			B-17G	42-38104	92BG
	B-17G	42-40014	92BG										
					16th	B-17F	42-31022	92BG		24th	B-17G	42-31490	381BG
4th	B-17F	42-30151	381BG			B-17G	42-31585	91BG			B-17G	42-31544	305BG
	B-17G	42-31606	384BG			B-17G	42-37801	384BG			B-17G	42-40008	381BG
	B-17G	42-32007	384BG			B-17G	42-37848	384BG					
	B-17G	42-39991	384BG			B-17G	42-97063	457BG		26th	B-17G	42-31929	303BG
											B-17G	42-37833	401BG
6th	B-17F	42-3215	381BG		18th	B-17G	42-31871	384BG			B-17G	42-97485	379BG
	B-17G	42-31079	91BG			B-17G	42-31966	351BG			B-17G	42-97663	306BG
	B-17G	42-31448	381BG			B-17G	42-37793	384BG					
	B-17G	42-31503	92BG			B-17G	42-37825	351BG		27th	B-17G	42-31363	306BG
	B-17G	42-31553	381BG			B-17G	42-37832	351BG					
	B-17G	42-31555	379BG			B-17G	42-38032	351BG		29th	B-17G	42-3506	91BG
	B-17G	42-31578	91BG			B-17G	42-39967	91BG			B-17G	42-31531	457BG
	B-17G	42-31595	457BG			B-17G	42-97515	92BG			B-17G	42-37953	306BG
	B-17G	42-31627	457BG								B-17G	42-38106	305BG
	B-17G	42-31680	92BG		19th	B-17G	42-31926	384BG			B-17G	42-38108	305BG
	B-17G	42-31869	91BG								B-17G	42-39950	306BG
	B-17G	42-31911	91BG		20th	B-17G	42-31381	381BG			B-17G	42-39965	306BG
	B-17G	42-38118	91BG			B-17G	42-31672	91BG			B-17G	42-97246	91BG
	B-17G	42-38136	401BG			B-17G	42-38033	401BG			B-17G	42-97466	305BG
	B-17G	42-40006	306BG										
	B-17G	42-40052	92BG										
	B-17G	42-97483	91BG										
	B-17G	42-97527	92BG										

AIRCRAFT MISSING IN ACTION: MARCH 1944

the men working on the plane got away safely and the fire was brought under control by the fire department, but all the bombs were destroyed.

Operations for the last ten days of March, opened on the 22nd, when Oranienburg, just outside Berlin, was the primary and Berlin itself the secondary. This was the first mission when the 422nd Squadron of the 305th Group supplied Pathfinder aircraft for the Division. Leading was the 40th Combat Wing, then 40/41st composite, third was the 94th followed by the First and finally the 41st Combat Wing.

Flight to the target was as briefed and as Oranienburg was covered in cloud, the secondary was bombed using Pathfinder technique. No enemy fighters were seen all day. Flak was intense and accurate. Friendly fighter support was excellent.

For this mission, 287 planes were despatched, 277 bombed the secondary target, four were Missing in Action. One of the planes Missing in Action was 42-97523 a H2X Pathfinder from the 422nd Bomb Squadron, which had come from the 482nd Group only two days before. A 306th Group aircraft, 42-31524, crash landed at Horsey Gap on return from the mission. Five crew had baled out over enemy territory, the other five landed safely with the aircraft.

The largest mission of March, in terms of aircraft bombing, was the one on the 23rd when 296 of 300 that were despatched bombed Münster and targets of opportunity. The 41st Combat Wing was leading, followed by a 40th/41st/94th composite, third was the 40th followed by the 94th and last the First Combat Wing. Group assemblies were made difficult by several thousand feet of icing clouds, and the rendezvous was slightly delayed. Combat Wing assembly was carried out with minimum difficulty, and the Division formation left the coast on time. The flight was as planned, except that the First and 94th Combat Wings changed places in the formation.

Upon reaching the Initial Point, it was discovered that the three primary targets were covered with clouds and course was set for the secondary. This change created some confusion in the formations and several of the units were spread out considerably. On approach to the secondary, the undercast varied and the units therefore turned to bomb targets of opportunity. The 41st bombed Beckum, Neubeckum and Ahlen. The Composite with the 40th and 41st Wings, bombed Hamm, the 94th bombed Orensteinfurt and the First bombed Ahlen. Fighters put in an appearance when the 92nd Group was over the target area and downed five of the Group's bombers. One other plane from 305th Group was also Missing in Action.

Next day, the 24th, another mission to Germany was mounted. The primary was Schweinfurt and the secondary Frankfurt.

Take off this day was marred by two bad crashes. At Chelveston, one of the Pathfinder aircraft, 42-97578 of 422nd Bomb Squadron, taking off at 0045 hours to position at Deenethorpe, from where it should have been the lead aircraft for the mission, crashed and burned at the end of its take off run. The aircraft involved had only been with the 305th Group four days. It was one of the worst flying accidents to hit the Division. All 11 crew on the plane plus eight men in a barracks and two children in a bungalow were killed. At Ridgewell, 42-38102, which had been transferred from the 457th Group 12 days before, crashed, exploded and burned at Bailey Hill Farm, Birdbrook, just two and a half miles after leaving the runway, all ten crew losing their lives. Also at Ridgewell, the perimeter track caved in blocking six aircraft from taking off. A third aircraft was lost early in the day when 42-31166, a spare from the 384th Group that had not joined the Group formation, had engine trouble and attempted to land at Nuthampstead. Two P-38s were on the runway and this caused the pilot to pull up and the plane crashed just beyond the runway.

Apart from the 381st, Group assembly was normal and the formations left the coast on time. High clouds, forced the Combat Wings to climb before reaching the target area and due to this the secondary was attacked by all units except the 94th Combat Wing which was successful in climbing over the clouds and bombed Schweinfurt through 10/10 cloud. No enemy fighters were encountered but there was flak at both targets.

For this mission, 230 aircraft had been despatched, 60 had bombed the primary target and 162 had bombed the secondary. Three were Missing in Action. Bad luck had followed the 381st Group on this mission, for two of the Missing in Action planes were from this Group and had collided in mid-air while trying to climb above the clouds in the target area. It was a bad day for the whole Division as five out of the six aircraft lost were not due to enemy action.

After a day's break, the Division was back in the air on the 26th with an attack on V-weapon sites in the Pas de Calais area. Of 243 aircraft despatched, 234 bombed the targets, which were: construction works at Watten, Mimoyecques, Wizernes and Le Grismont, all in France.

On this mission the Groups assembled without difficulty and no attempt was made to assemble as Combat Wings, bombing was done by squadrons and most squadrons flew the route back singly without reforming into Group formations. The 92nd and 305th Groups did not fly this mission.

Four planes were Missing in Action and two crash landed on return. Although no enemy fighters had been sighted on this mission, the flak over some of the targets was severe. The 306th Group which had 29 planes over the target, had 26 hit by flak, 17 of them were seriously damaged and two 42-31700 and 42-31894 crash landed back at Thurleigh as a result and were salvaged. A third aircraft salvaged as a result of the day's operations was 42-31098 from 401st Group. A spare which was not required to join the formation, it returned to Deenethorpe where it landed well down the runway and burst a tyre, causing it to swing off the runway.

Better weather next day meant more flying and 290 planes were despatched to bomb airfields in France. The units for the day's operations were divided into two task forces, the 'Third Air Task Force', comprising the First Combat Wing, flying lead with the 40th Combat Wing flying abreast and guiding left; and the 'Fourth Air Task Force', made up of the 94th Combat Wing leading a composite Wing flying abreast and guiding left, and the 41st Combat Wing third. The primary targets for the Third Air Task Force, were the airfields of St Jean D'Angely and La Rochelle and

for the Fourth Air Task Force, the airfields at Tours and Chartres. As a last resort, they were to bomb any airfield, positively identified as not being near a built up area. Two hundred and eighty-five aircraft bombed the targets. One plane from 306th Group was the only loss this day.

Airfields in France, were again the targets for the First Division on 28th March, the primary targets for the day being Dijon/Longvig and Reims/Champagne airfields. The 40th and 41st Combat Wings were scheduled to attack the former and the First Combat Wing the latter. The 94th Combat Wing did not fly on this day's operations.

The assembly was normal but the 41st was slightly late leaving the English coast. A 306th aircraft, 42-107013, left the Group's formation at 10,000 feet as the pilot was unwell and returned to Thurleigh. On landing, the landing gear collapsed and the aircraft became a salvage job. There were no injuries, this was the first Douglas built 'silver' B-17G to be lost in the Division. It had been assigned to the 306th on 24th March.

Flak at Reims was moderate and accurate, there was none at Dijon and no enemy fighters were seen. One hundred and eighty-two planes were despatched, with 117 bombing at Dijon and 59 bombing at Reims. No

AIRCRAFT and CREW STATUS at 2000 Hours on 31st March 1944

| UNIT | OPERATIONAL AIRCRAFT | | | | COMBAT CREWS | NON OPERATIONAL AIRCRAFT ASSIGNED |
	TYPE	ASS	ON HAND	OP		
91BG	B-17F/G	58	57	47	34	1 B-17E, 1 B-17F, 1 DB-7B, 1 L-4B, 1 Oxford
381BG	B-17F/G	55	51	41	31	1 B-17E
1 CW	B-17F/G	113	108	88	65	
92BG	B-17F/G	57	53	37	31	1 B-17E
305BG	B-17F/G	47	46	37	31	1 B-17E, 1 B-17F
306BG	B-17F/G	55	50	38	25	1 B-17E, 1 B-17F, 1 DB-7B, 1 C-78, 1 UC-61A 1 Oxford
40 CW	B-17F/G	159	149	112	87	
303BG	B-17F/G	32	29	26	32	1 B-17E, 1 B-17FSH, 1 B-17GSH, 1 DB-7B, 1 L-4B,
303BG	B-17F/G	28	28	25		GB aircraft 1 Oxford
379BG	B-17F/G	20	20	20	26	1 B-17E Gp records showed 63 Act Ass. 42-3167
379BG	B-17F/G	44	39	33		GB aircraft had not been picked up.
384BG	B-17F/G	20	20	15	33	1 B-17E
384BG	B-17F/G	39	39	39		GB aircraft
41 CW	B-17F/G	183	175	158	91	
351BG	B-17F/G	61	59	49	36	1 B-17E, 1 Oxford
401BG	B-17F/G	60	59	53	41	1 B-17E
457BG	B-17G	66	60	46	40	1 B-17E
94 CW	B-17F/G	187	178	148	117	
305BG	B-17F/G	9	9	8	5	422nd Bomb Squadron
305BG	B-17GSH	10	10	9	7	Pathfinder aircraft
1 BD	B-17F/G	661	629	523	372	All Groups short of crews.
First Bomb Division Flight Section at Kimbolton						1 B-17F, 1 DB-7B, 1 C-78, 1 P-47D, 1 Master, 2 Oxford, 1 Tiger Moth

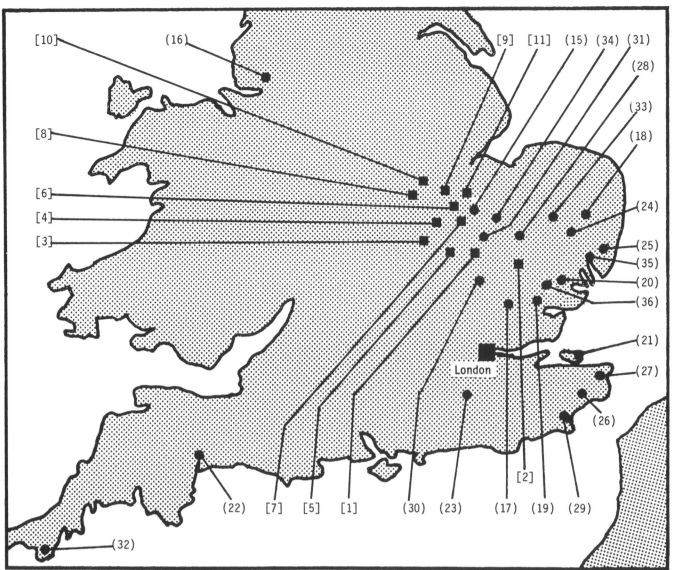

AIRCRAFT ASSIGNED AND ON HAND AT HOME STATIONS: 630 (101 B-17F and 529 B-17G)			
[1] Bassingbourn:	91BG 57(10 B-17F: 47 B-17G)	[6] Molesworth:	303BG 58(12 B-17F: 46 B-17G)
[2] Ridgewell:	381BG 51(8 B-17F: 43 B-17G)	[7] Kimbolton:	379BG 59(18 B-17F: 41 B-17G)
[3] Podington:	92BG 53(9 B-17F: 44 B-17G)	[8] Grafton Underwood:	384BG 59(13 B-17F: 46 B-17G)
[4] Chelveston:	305BG 65(11 B-17F: 54 B-17G)	[9] Polebrook:	351BG 59(13 B-17F: 46 B-17G)
[5] Thurliegh:	306BG 50(6 B-17F: 44 B-17G)	[10] Deenethorpe:	401BG 59(1 B-17F: 58 B-17G)
[11] Glatton:	457BG 60 B-17G		

AIRCRAFT ASSIGNED BUT NOT ON HAND AT HOME STATIONS: 31 (4 B-17F and 27 B-17G)		
(15) 2nd SAD Abbots Ripton:1 B-17F of 91BG: 1 B-17G of 303BG: 1 B-17G of 305BG 1 B-17G of 379BG and 4 B-17G of 457BG		
(16) 1 BAD Burtonwood: 2 B-17G of 457BG		
(17) Andrews Fld: 1 B-17F of 381BG	(24) Horham : 1 B-17G of 92BG	(30) Nuthampstead:1 B-17G of 401BG
(18) Beccles: 1 B-17G of 306BG	(25) Leiston: 1 B-17G of 306BG	(31) Oakington: 1 B-17G of 379BG
(19) Boreham: 1 B-17G of 92BG	1 B-17G of 381BG	(32) Predannack: 1 B-17G of 381BG
(20) Boxted: 1 B-17G of 351BG	(26) Lympne: 1 B-17G of 379BG	(33) Tibenham: 1 B-17G of 306BG
(21) Eastchurch: 1 B-17G of 303BG	(27) Manston: 1 B-17G of 306BG	(34) Witchford: 1 B-17F of 92BG
(22) Exeter: 1 B-17G of 381BG	(28) Mildenhall: 1 B-17G of 379BG	(35) Woodbridge: 1 B-17G of 306BG
(23) Gatwick: 1 B-17G of 379BG	(29) New Romney: 1 B-17F of 351BG	(36) Wormingford: 1 B-17G of 92BG

Serial numbers of the aircraft at each location can be found by
referring to the Group's status listings in Part Two

**LOCATION OF THE 661 (105 B-17F and 556 B-17G) OPERATIONAL AIRCRAFT ASSIGNED TO THE
FIRST BOMBARDMENT DIVISION AT 2000 HOURS ON 31st MARCH 1944**

aircraft were Missing in Action, but the Flak at Reims had caught the 381st Group. One plane was hit and its No 3 engine set on fire before the target was reached. Leaving the formation, 42-37933 made for Kent where the order to bale out was given and all the crew made a safe drop, the abandoned aircraft crashed near the coast. A direct hit in the waist position had killed both waist gunners and the rear gunner in 42-37754. This aircraft was brought back to Ridgewell but due to the damage could not be landed. Five men baled out over the airfield, watched by many of the Group's personnel who had never witnessed such a drama before. The two pilots then flew the plane to the coast, where they baled out, leaving the plane to crash in the North Sea off the Suffolk coast.

The last mission of the month was flown on the 29th. The primary target was the AG Assembly Plant at Waggum, Germany, and the secondary was the centre of Brunswick. Lead was flown by the 41st Combat Wing, with the First flying abreast and guiding right on the 41st, the 40th was third with the 94th Combat Wing flying abreast and guiding right.

All units assembled as planned, except the 41st, which assembled under the overcast and did not complete assembly until out over the sea. Two hundred and thirty-six planes were despatched and 233 bombed, some bombing on targets of opportunity. Nine were Missing in Action. Just after the target, the 40th Combat Wing was subjected to attacks by 50 to 75 aircraft, the 305th and 306th Groups each lost three planes to these attacks. A 401st Group plane, 42-31202, was damaged on the mission and was salvaged on return, this plane had been delivered to the Group as its first new replacement on 12th December 1943.

During March, the 422nd Bomb Squadron had maintained its night leaflet operations. Eighty-six aircraft had been despatched on 15 nights. France, Holland and Belgium had been visited on these operations. No planes had been lost on night operations. It was a night leaflet mission, that on 30/31st March, concluded the month's operations and also the period covered by this narrative history.

Flying on the last day of the month, was confined to training. At Ridgewell, 42-29751 was taken into the air for a short flight with a skeleton crew of five. In the co-pilot's seat sat Capt Paul H Stull Jr, a ground officer. As they were descending to land, something went wrong and the plane crashed just off the end of the runway, caught fire and was completely consumed. All five men were killed instantly. This aircraft was the '219th'

B-17 to be classed as salvage in the First Bombardment Wing/Division since the first B17E had overrun the runway at Grafton Underwood on 1st August 1942.

During March, the First Division had lost 86 B-17s in action and 22 had been lost to salvage and other causes in England. The Third Bombardment Division had lost 125 B-17s in action, the first month when its losses had exceeded those of the First Division.

Early in March the Eighth Air Force agreed to withdraw from operational service over 100 B-17Fs that had not got Tokyo Tanks fitted so they could be returned to the USA for training duties. It was inevitable that the main effect of this would fall on the First Division and on 12th March the following telex was sent from the Division to Eighth Air Force Headquarters.

RE OUR TEX E549 DATED 11 MAR THE FIRST 10 B-17 ACFT ARE READY FOR IMEDIATE TRANSFER TO A BASE DEPOT IN PREPARATION FOR RETURN TO U.S.A. 41-24359, 41-24504, 41-25505, 41-24560, 41-24578, 42-5428, 42-5729, 42-5747, 42-29636 and 42-30227.

This message signalled the end to the combat careers of the surviving veterans that had been brought to England with the pioneer Groups in 1942. Nine of the above aircraft left for Burtonwood on 15th March. More followed before the end of the month and most of the aircraft without Tokyo tanks that remained in the Division at the end of March, were transferred out during the first two weeks of April.

On 2nd March, a Fairchild UC-61A Argus, 43-14419 was assigned to the 306th Bomb Group from Alconbury, this was moved out to Abbots Ripton on the 9th and in its place on the same day came 43-14468. On the 3rd, B-17E, 41-2578 was assigned as a hack to the 457th Group, this, the oldest B-17 to serve in the Eighth Air Force, had already served in the 92nd, 97th and 482nd Bomb Groups.

On 27th March, the aircraft assigned to the First Bomb Division Flight Section which were still at Alconbury, were transferred to Kimbolton. Making the move, was: B-17F 41-24460, DB-7B AL452, C-78 Bobcat 42-58434, P-47D Thunderbolt 42-7882, UC61A's Argus 43-14469 and 43-14499, Master DL899, Oxfords DF331, LB522 and DL899 and finally Tiger Moth T6369.

A B-17G waits in its dispersal as big brother, a B-29 Superfortress 41-36963, comes in to land at Glatton on 12th March. This was the first visit of a B-29 to the United Kingdom. *Bernard Baines*

As 1944 progressed, ever larger formations of B-17s were seen in East Anglian skies. Most of the Eighth's daylight missions started with take off in the early morning, often before the sun had cleared the Eastern horizon. The heavily loaded planes would climb laboriously to the Group assembly area. When assembled the Groups would proceed to the Wing assembly point before moving out on the briefed course to the Division assembly line and the English coast. A Combat Wing formation could consist of over a hundred planes and on a clear day the observer on the ground could see several Combat Wings and therefore many hundreds of planes. Their passing could be made even more spectacular if they were leaving contrails in the blue skies.

Even on an overcast day their passage would not go un-noticed. The throb of over a million horsepower would cause the earth beneath to tremble. The vibrations set up by hundreds of propellers clawing the thin upper atmosphere would rattle doors and windows far below.

The return to base at the end of the mission was quite different. After so long breathing oxygen at high altitude the crews were pleased to come down to lower levels and the flight back over the East Anglian countryside would be made at a much lower altitude.

Above photograph shows a scene familiar to residents near Eighth Air Force bases as a Group formation returns, in this case the 379th coming home to Kimbolton. *US Air Force-National Air and Space Museum*

Right: 42-107026 **'HAM TRAMACK MAMA'** was the highest serial numbered aircraft to reach the 457th Bomb Group up to 31st March 1944. It came from Framlingham. *Bernard Bains*

Above: A B-17F takes off at Bassingbourn

Below: While the Fortresses waited for the next call to do battle with the Luftwaffe, the gathering in of the vital English grain harvest proceeded almost under the wings of the parked planes. Scenes such as this at Molesworth, were common at Eighth Air Force bases throughout East Anglia in August 1943. *US Air Force – National Air and Space Museum*

FORTRESSES OF THE BIG TRIANGLE FIRST

PART TWO

THE UNITS

15th BOMBARDMENT SQUADRON (L)

91st BOMBARDMENT GROUP (H)

92nd BOMBARDMENT GROUP (H)

93rd BOMBARDMENT GROUP (H)

97th BOMBARDMENT GROUP (H)

301st BOMBARDMENT GROUP (H)

303rd BOMBARDMENT GROUP (H)

305th BOMBARDMENT GROUP (H)

306th BOMBARDMENT GROUP (H)

351st BOMBARDMENT GROUP (H)

379th BOMBARDMENT GROUP (H)

381st BOMBARDMENT GROUP (H)

384th BOMBARDMENT GROUP (H)

401st BOMBARDMENT GROUP (H)

457th BOMBARDMENT GROUP (H)

482nd BOMBARDMENT GROUP (H)

THE UNITS

All the units assigned to the First Bombardment Wing/Division, with the exception of the 15th Bombardment Squadron (L) and the 482nd Bombardment Group (P) received an initial allocation of aircraft in the US and flew these to England.

It is at the point where these aircraft were assigned, at which this story starts, although the units were not assigned to the First Bombardment Wing/Division and the aircraft did not appear in the Wing's/Division's records until after the units had arrived at their assigned stations in England.

The 97th Bomb Group was unique in that it retained the aircraft it had used for training in the USA took them to Depots for Modification and then flew them to England. The other Groups, following training, proceeded to a staging airfield where they received new aircraft. These aircraft were almost without exception brand new, they had been delivered from the factories to an Air Depot or Modification Centre where changes to, or the installation of new equipment to suit their designated theatre of operations was carried out. From the Depots and Modification Centres they were delivered by Ferry Command crews to the new Groups at the staging airfields.

Processing and preparation for the movement overseas was also carried out at the staging airfields. The organisation responsible for this preparation for movement of the Groups up to December 1942, was the Army Air Force Foreign Service Concentration Command. This little known, and short lived organisation, was formed on 1st July 1942 with headquarters at Maritime Building, Washington, later moving to Cincinnati, Ohio. Its function was to receive the units from training, ensure the correct numbers of aircraft, personnel and equipment was assigned, write up the movement orders, and despatch the aircraft and crews to the Air Transport Command for the overseas flight.

UNITS DESTINED FOR THE EIGHTH AIR FORCE THAT WERE PROCESSED BY THE CONCENTRATION COMMAND WERE:

92nd Bomb Group (H) at Dow, Bangor, Maine
30th June to 25th August 1942

301st Bomb Group (H) at Westover, Mass
6th July to 5th August 1942

93rd Bomb Group (H) at Grenier, New Hampshire
2nd August to 8th September 1942

306th Bomb Group (H) at Westover, Mass
2nd August to 10th September 1942

91st Bomb Group (H) at Dow, Bangor, Maine
2nd September to 14th October 1942

44th Bomb Group (H) (less one Squadron) at Grenier, New Hampshire
4th September to 4th October 1942

303rd Bomb Group (H) at Kellog, Michigan and Dow, Maine
8th September to 14th October 1942

305th Bomb Group (H) at Syracuse, New York
11th September to 19th October 1942

Five Replacement B-17 Crews at Lockbourne, Ohio
October – November 1942

In addition many of the units destined for the Twelfth Air Force were also processed. The processing and despatch of the 97th Bomb Group was carried out by Eighth Fighter Command and the 92nd and 301st Bomb Groups were in the staging area when the Concentration Command was formed and they were processed in conjunction with the First Air Force.

The Concentration Command was disbanded on the 5th December 1942 and from then on all processing of units for overseas movement was done within the Air Force in which the units were trained.

Overseas destinations for aircraft were given 'Coded Shipping Designators' and units were allocated movement numbers. From 1943, project numbers were allocated to Group movements and often these numbers were stencilled on the aircraft, it normally being on the left side of the nose under the data panel. Replacement aircraft were flown over in batches which were allocated project numbers with an 'R' suffix, the 'R' indicating 'replacement'.

Very little is known about the origins and uses of these shipping codes and project numbers. The movement of the 97th Bomb Group to England was carried out under the Code BOLERO. Later Groups arriving in England in 1942 were shipped using the Code WILDFLOWER. From 1943 all these codes were of four letters and those used for Eighth Air Force B-17 deliveries were SOXO and UGLY.

The movement orders for the air echelons of the 44th, 91st, 303rd and 305th Bomb Groups was 6252 with each Headquarters and Bomb Squadron being issued a Dash letter(s) following the basic Number. Thus, the 44th Bomb Group Headquarters was movement order No 6252-A and the 422nd Bomb Squadron of the 305th Bomb Group, was movement order No 6252-CC.

The project numbers used for the movement of the air echelons of the following Groups were: 94th, 92033; 95th, 92034; 96th 92035; 351st, 92055; 379th, 92056; 381st, 92095; 384th, 92090; 401st, 92235 and the 457th, 92333.

Once processing was completed, the aircraft were despatched to the Air Transport Command who controlled the ferrying of all aircraft over the North Atlantic route.

The most commonly used airfield for B-17s departing the USA for the North Atlantic crossing was Presque Isle in Maine, but Dow Field at Bangor, Maine, and Grenier in New Hampshire, were also used. Depending on the briefed route, the first stop after leaving the US would be Gander in Newfoundland or Goose Bay in Labrador. Arrival airfield in the UK was initially Prestwick in Scotland but later Nutts Corner in Northern Ireland and Valley in Wales were also used.

Only a small number of Eighth Air Force B-17s came via the South Atlantic ferry route. All during the winter of 1942/1943 when the North Atlantic route was closed. Departure airfield for these aircraft was Morrison Field at West Palm Beach, Florida, and the terminal in the UK was St Eval in Cornwall.

The flight line at Presque Isle August 1943. B-17F in centre (between Mitchell and B-24) is 42-3465, it was assigned the 4th Combat Wings 95th Bomb Group on arrival in England. Only two more Douglas built B-17Fs followed before the B-17Gs replaced them. *US Air Force*

15th BOMBARDMENT SQUADRON (LIGHT)

Constituted as the 15th BOMBARDMENT SQUADRON (LIGHT) on 22nd December 1939
Activated on 1st February 1940
Redesignated as the 1st Pursuit Squadron (Night Fighter) on 1st April 1942
Redesignated as the 15th Bombardment Squadron (Light) on 7th May 1942
Assigned to Eighth Bomber Command on 14th May 1942
Assigned to First Provisional Bombardment Wing on 15th August 1942

STATIONS

Grafton Underwood: 14th May 1942
Molesworth: 9th June 1942
Podington: 13th September 1942

Originally part of the 27th Bomb Group (L) in the US. In October 1941 the 27th had been ordered to the Philippine Islands but a late change of orders kept the 15th Bomb Squadron in the US while the rest of the Group moved overseas. After the Japanese attack on Pearl Harbor, the Squadron flew anti-submarine patrols from Mitchell Field, New York.

On 30th April 1942, the Squadron sailed from New York and after an uneventful crossing of the North Atlantic arrived in Britain on 13th May. Next day the Squadron moved to Grafton Underwood. Total strength was 41 officers and 458 enlisted men under the command of Maj John Griffith.

Training which was carried out under RAF guidance, continued at Grafton Underwood until about 7th June, when due to Grafton having been designated as one of the first airfields to be used by heavy bombers, the 15th Squadron was moved to Molesworth.

On 4th July, the Squadron carried out the first mission in which US Air Forces in Britain officially took part. The briefing for this operation was carried out by the British at Swanton Morley and six crews using Bostons loaned from 226 Squadron RAF took part. Two of the US crewed planes failed to return.

One more mission, on 12th July, again using six Bostons borrowed from 226 Squadron, was flown and then the 15th was stood down to await the assignment of its own aircraft.

The Squadron was assigned to the First Provisional Bombardment Wing on 15th August and then to the Twelfth Air Force on 14th September. During this period it flew three more operational missions, the first on 5th September, the second on 6th September and the final one on 2nd October. No aircraft were lost on these three operations. After the 2nd October mission the Squadron concentrated on preparations for the move to North Africa, a move which was made from Predannack with 13 DB-7Bs on 15th November 1942. A full list of the 13 DB-7Bs despatched to North Africa can be found in Part One, November 1942.

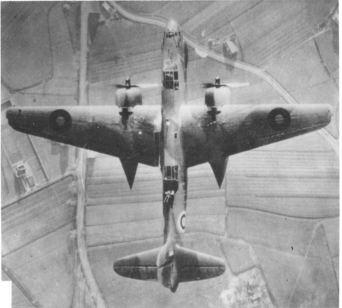

Boston III AL750 MG-Z of 226 Sqdn RAF over Ostend on 7th May 1942. This was the aircraft flown by Capt Kegelman on the 15th Bombardment Squadron (Light)'s mission of 4th July 1942. *Imperial War Museum*

'KAYO' 42-29688 with the Project No 92018R under the aft side nose window. This was a replacement which was assigned to the 305th Bomb Group on 17th March 1943. *Mike Gibson*

91st BOMBARDMENT GROUP (H)

Constituted as the 91st BOMBARDMENT GROUP (H) on 28th January 1942
Activated on 15th April 1942
Squadrons Assigned: 322nd, 323rd, 324th and 401st
Assigned to Eighth Air Force: 21st August 1942
Assigned to First Bombardment Wing: October 1942

COMBAT WING ASSIGNMENTS

First Provisional: 13th December 1942
101st Provisional Bombardment: 3rd January 1943
First Combat Bombardment: 16th September 1943

STATIONS

Kimbolton: Air Echelon from 1st October 1942
Ground Echelon in 14th September 1942
Bassingbourn: From 14th October 1942

Trained in the US on B-17Es with the Second Air Force at Walla Walla, Washington, with detachments at Redmond and Pendleton, Oregon. While at Walla Walla the Group had been assigned the second Douglas built B-17F, 42-2965, for test purposes, but about 8th August, only three days after it had arrived from Dayton, Ohio, it was wrecked in a landing accident.

The air echelon left Walla Walla for Boise, Idaho, on 24th August where the B-17Es were handed over to the Commanding Officer and six new B-17Fs were received. On 29th August they departed by air and troop train, those going by air, consisting of Col Wray and approximately 60 officers and men, flew to Denver, Colorado. Departing Denver in three flights of two aircraft each and proceeding separately, two going to Jackson, Mississippi, two to Rantoul, Illinois, and two to Selfridge, Michigan. The six aircraft had all arrived at the new base, Bangor, Maine, by 1st September. That part of the air echelon which travelled by train from Boise arrived at Bangor on the afternoon of 3rd September.

Starting 4th September more B-17Fs were assigned, and high altitude flights to check fuel consumption were started. It was the 24th before the thirty-fifth and last aircraft was assigned. The new aircraft were all of Boeing manufacture and had come from the Air Depots and Modification Centers at Middletown, Cheyenne, Tulsa and one from Denver.

On the 25th September, the 324th Bomb Squadron, flew to Gander and then on to Prestwick where it arrived without incident or loss on the 30th September. The 322nd Bomb Squadron was next, leaving for Gander on the 30th and then flew on to Prestwick, which was reached approx 1000 hrs on 1st October. All planes flew in information, except that of Lt Genheimer which left the formation about half way across and arrived at Prestwick 45 minutes ahead of the rest of the Squadron. This set up a record for the West to East crossing for the type of aircraft but Genheimer was severely reprimanded for leaving the formation.

The 401st Bomb Squadron left for Gander on 1st October and then departed for Prestwick at 2315 hrs on 2nd October. The weather deteriorated and great difficulty was experienced in finding Prestwick. One aircraft piloted by Lt Gorson landed at Stornoway and 41-24451, piloted by Capt Dale Laselle, crashed into a hill in Northern Ireland while letting down through the overcast. The Squadron flew to Kimbolton about 6th October. Last to leave Bangor was the 323rd Bomb Squadron. Starting on the 10th October with the last aircraft leaving on the 14th.

Aircraft from the 324th Bomb Squadron were the first to reach Kimbolton, the first landing about 1500 hrs on 1st October.

The ground echelon boarded the *Queen Mary* at New York and sailed on 3rd September. During the voyage the ground echelon of the 322nd Bomb Squadron were detailed duty as members of the anti-aircraft gun crew and the Squadron received a Commendation from the Commander of the vessel for the way these duties were carried out. On arrival in Scotland, they boarded trains on 13th September and travelled by the east coast route to Kimbolton where they arrived in the early morning of 14th September.

ORIGINAL B-17Fs ASSIGNED IN THE U.S.A.

41-24399	323BS		41-24459	401BS	41-24499	322BS	41-24527	401BS
41-24431	401BS	(1)	41-24479	322BS	41-24503	323BS	41-24544	323BS
41-24432	401BS	(1)	41-24480	324BS	41-24504	324BS	41-24545	322BS
41-24439	322BS		41-24481	322BS	41-24505	324BS	41-24547	323BS
41-24447	401BS	(1)	41-24482	322BS	41-24506	324BS	41-24549	323BS
41-24449	401BS		41-24483	322BS	41-24512	322BS	41-24570	323BS
41-24451	401BS	(1)(3)	41-24484	401BS	41-24515	324BS	41-24571	323BS	(2)
41-24452	401BS	(1)	41-24485	324BS	41-24523	323BS	41-24589	323BS
41-24453	322BS	(1)	41-24490	324BS	41-24524	323BS		

(1) These six aircraft assigned at Boise 29th August 1942. Remainder Assigned at
Dow Field, Bangor, 4th to 24th September 1942

(2) 41-24571: It is believed that this aircraft did not fly to U.K. with the Group;
It later served in the Twelfth Air Force

(3) 41-24451: Crashed in Northern Ireland at end of flight from Gander

---

SHORT SERVING AIRCRAFT: ASSIGNED FOR LESS THAN EIGHT DAYS

Serial No	Date In	Date Out	Reason Out	Days Ass		Serial No	Date In	Date Out	Reason Out	Days Ass
42-3321	15 June 43	16 June 43	To 95BG	1		42-30283	10 June 43	16 June 43	To 95BG	6
42-29536	15 Mar 43	22 Mar 43	MIA	7		42-30624	23 Sep 43	27 Sep 43	MIA	4
42-29699	1 June 43	5 June 43	To 94BG	4		42-40009	21 Jan 44	24 Jan 44	Crashed	3
42-30120	15 June 43	16 June 43	To 95BG	1		42-97125	16 Mar 44	22 Mar 44	MIA	6
42-30194	15 June 43	16 June 43	To 95BG	1		42-97246	25 Mar 44	29 Mar 44	MIA	4

91st BOMBARDMENT GROUP (H)

'SAD SACK' 41-24504 in an almost cloudless sky 10th July 1943. With its 'twin' 41-24505 'QUITCHURBITCHIN' was the longest serving of the Group's original aircraft. Both were among the first ten Eighth Air Force B-17Fs to be returned to the USA for training duties. They left Bassingbourn on 15th March 1944. *US Air Force–National Air and Space Museum*

42-29837 'LADY LUCK' carried on a proud tradition. Assigned to the 91st on 7th June 1943 and allocated to the 324th Bomb Squadron. It replaced 'MEMPHIS BELLE' as DF-A. On 31st March 1944 it was the second longest serving Group Act. *US Air Force–National Air and Space Museum*

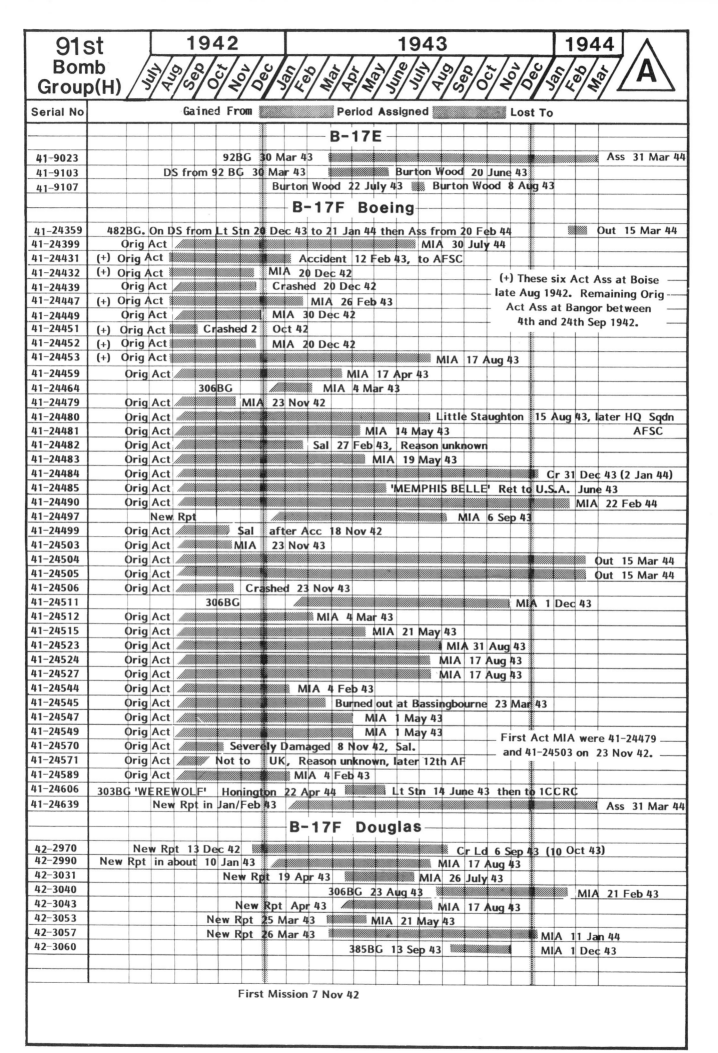

91st Bomb Group(H)

1942	1943	1944
July Aug Sep Oct Nov Dec	Jan Feb Mar Apr May June July Aug Sep Oct Nov Dec	Jan Feb Mar

△ A

Serial No	Gained From	Period Assigned	Lost To

B-17E

Serial No	Details
41-9023	92BG 30 Mar 43 ▓▓▓ Ass 31 Mar 44
41-9103	DS from 92 BG 30 Mar 43 ▓▓ Burton Wood 20 June 43
41-9107	Burton Wood 22 July 43 ▓ Burton Wood 8 Aug 43

B-17F Boeing

41-24359	482BG. On DS from Lt Stn 20 Dec 43 to 21 Jan 44 then Ass from 20 Feb 44 ▓ Out 15 Mar 44
41-24399	Orig Act ▓▓▓ MIA 30 July 44
41-24431	(+) Orig Act ▓▓ Accident 12 Feb 43, to AFSC
41-24432	(+) Orig Act ▓▓ MIA 20 Dec 42
41-24439	Orig Act ▓▓ Crashed 20 Dec 42
41-24447	(+) Orig Act ▓▓ MIA 26 Feb 43
41-24449	Orig Act ▓ MIA 30 Dec 42
41-24451	(+) Orig Act ▓ Crashed 2 Oct 42
41-24452	(+) Orig Act ▓ MIA 20 Dec 42
41-24453	(+) Orig Act ▓▓▓ MIA 17 Aug 43
41-24459	Orig Act ▓▓ MIA 17 Apr 43
41-24464	306BG ▓ MIA 4 Mar 43
41-24479	Orig Act ▓ MIA 23 Nov 42
41-24480	Orig Act ▓▓▓ Little Staughton 15 Aug 43, later HQ Sqdn
41-24481	Orig Act ▓▓ MIA 14 May 43 AFSC
41-24482	Orig Act ▓▓ Sal 27 Feb 43, Reason unknown
41-24483	Orig Act ▓▓ MIA 19 May 43
41-24484	Orig Act ▓▓▓ Cr 31 Dec 43 (2 Jan 44)
41-24485	Orig Act ▓▓ 'MEMPHIS BELLE' Ret to U.S.A. June 43
41-24490	Orig Act ▓▓▓ MIA 22 Feb 44
41-24497	New Rpt ▓▓ MIA 6 Sep 43
41-24499	Orig Act ▓ Sal after Acc 18 Nov 42
41-24503	Orig Act ▓ MIA 23 Nov 43
41-24504	Orig Act ▓▓▓ Out 15 Mar 44
41-24505	Orig Act ▓▓▓ Out 15 Mar 44
41-24506	Orig Act ▓ Crashed 23 Nov 43
41-24511	306BG ▓▓ MIA 1 Dec 43
41-24512	Orig Act ▓ MIA 4 Mar 43
41-24515	Orig Act ▓▓ MIA 21 May 43
41-24523	Orig Act ▓▓ MIA 31 Aug 43
41-24524	Orig Act ▓▓ MIA 17 Aug 43
41-24527	Orig Act ▓▓ MIA 17 Aug 43
41-24544	Orig Act ▓ MIA 4 Feb 43
41-24545	Orig Act ▓ Burned out at Bassingbourne 23 Mar 43
41-24547	Orig Act ▓ MIA 1 May 43
41-24549	Orig Act ▓ MIA 1 May 43
41-24570	Orig Act ▓ Severely Damaged 8 Nov 42, Sal.
41-24571	Orig Act ▓ Not to UK, Reason unknown, later 12th AF
41-24589	Orig Act ▓ MIA 4 Feb 43
41-24606	303BG 'WEREWOLF' Honington 22 Apr 44 ▓ Lt Stn 14 June 43 then to 1CCRC
41-24639	New Rpt in Jan/Feb 43 ▓▓▓ Ass 31 Mar 44

B-17F Douglas

Serial No	Details
42-2970	New Rpt 13 Dec 42 ▓▓ Cr Ld 6 Sep 43 (10 Oct 43)
42-2990	New Rpt in about 10 Jan 43 ▓▓ MIA 17 Aug 43
42-3031	New Rpt 19 Apr 43 ▓▓ MIA 26 July 43
42-3040	306BG 23 Aug 43 ▓▓ MIA 21 Feb 43
42-3043	New Rpt Apr 43 ▓▓ MIA 17 Aug 43
42-3053	New Rpt 25 Mar 43 ▓ MIA 21 May 43
42-3057	New Rpt 26 Mar 43 ▓▓ MIA 11 Jan 44
42-3060	385BG 13 Sep 43 ▓▓ MIA 1 Dec 43

(+) These six Act Ass at Boise late Aug 1942. Remaining Orig Act Ass at Bangor between 4th and 24th Sep 1942.

First Act MIA were 41-24479 and 41-24503 on 23 Nov 42.

First Mission 7 Nov 42

Serial No	Gained From ▨▨▨ Period Assigned ▨▨▨ Lost To

B-17F Douglas

Serial No	Timeline / Notes
42-3072	96BG 16 Sep 43 ▨ 379BG 27 Sep 43
42-3073	94BG 22 Apr 43 ▨▨▨ MIA 21 Feb 44
42-3079	95BG 16 June 43 ▨▨▨ MIA 16 Sep 43
42-3111	95BG 16 June 43 ▨▨▨ MIA 27 Sep 43
42-3119	New Rpt 4 June 43 ▨▨ MIA 26 July 43
42-3162	94BG ▨▨ MIA 12 Aug 43
42-3172	306BG – AFSC – 25 Sep 43 ▨▨▨ Ass 31 Mar 44
42-3207	94BG Act Attached for Rep Apr–May 1943
42-3210	New Rpt 18 May 43 ▨ Sal after Fire 1 June 43 (3 June 43)
42-3213	95 BG 16 June 43 ▨▨▨ MIA 16 Aug 43 (Ditched)
42-3272	New Rpt 7 June 43 ▨▨ 100BG 6 July 43
42-3274	306BG – AFSC – 14 Aug 43 ▨▨▨ MIA 4 Oct 43
42-3321	New Rpt 15 June 43 ▨ 95BG 16 June 43

B-17G Douglas

Serial No	Timeline / Notes
42-3506	New Rpt 22 Sep 43 ▨ AFSC ▨ MIA 29 Mar 44. Out for Rep 11 Oct 43 to 19 Feb 44

B-17F Boeing

Serial No	Timeline / Notes
42-5069	New Rpt ▨▨▨ MIA 17 Aug 43
42-5070	N R 14 Dec 42 ▨▨▨ MIA 17 Apr 43
42-5077	N R ▨▨▨ MIA 17 Aug 43
42-5084	N R 14 Dec 42 ▨ MIA 3 Jan 43
42-5132	303BG ▨▨▨ MIA 22 June 43 (In by 18 Jan 43)
42-5139	New Rpt ▨▨▨ MIA 17 Aug 43
42-5172	New Rpt 26 Mar 43 ▨▨ MIA 17 April 43
42-5178	303BG ▨▨▨ MIA 8 Oct 43 (In by 18 Jan 43)
42-5225	New Rpt 8 Feb 43 ▨▨▨ MIA 17 Aug 43
42-5337	New Rpt ▨▨▨ MIA 17 Apr 43
42-5362	New Rpt ▨▨ MIA 26 Feb 43
42-5370	New Rpt 26 Feb 43 ▨ MIA 4 Mar 43
42-5379	New Rpt 15 Mar 43 ▨▨▨ 379BG 1 Oct 43
42-5391	New Rpt 25 Mar 43 ▨▨ MIA 17 Apr 43
42-5406	New Rpt 19 Apr 43 ▨▨ MIA 13 May 43
42-5407	306BG 11 Sep 43 ▨ 379BG 27 Sep 43
42-5428	306BG 24 Dec 43 ▨▨▨ Out 15 Mar 44
42-5437	New Rpt 8 Mar 43 ▨▨▨ MIA 17 Aug 43

B-17F Vega

Serial No	Timeline / Notes
42-5712	▨▨▨ Crash Landed 17 Aug 43 (18 Aug 43)
42-5714	306BG 11 Sep 43 ▨▨ MIA 14 Oct 43
42-5724	New Rpt 23 Mar 43 ▨▨▨ MIA 28 June 43
42-5729	306BG 8 Sep 43 ▨▨▨ Out 15 Mar 43

YB-40

Serial No	Timeline / Notes
42-5733	92BG 17 July 43 ▨▨▨ Burtonwood 4 Oct 43
42-5734	92BG 17 July 43 ▨▨▨ Burtonwood 7 Oct 43
42-5741	92BG 22 July 43 ▨▨▨ Burtonwood 7 Oct 43

B-17F Vega

Serial No	Timeline / Notes
42-5745	482BG – Little Staughton 18 Feb 44 ▨▨ Ass 31 Mar 44
42-5763	New Rpt 9 Mar 43 ▨▨▨ MIA 6 Sep 43
42-5787	New Rpt 9 Mar 43 ▨▨▨ MIA 12 Aug 43
42-5789	New Rpt 25 Mar 43 ▨▨▨ MIA 22 June 43
42-5795	92BG No 2 AAD 5 Sep 43 ▨▨▨ MIA 26 Nov 43 (Ditched)
42-5804	306BG 11 Sep 43 ▨▨▨ Sal after Miss 11 Jan 44 (13 Jan 44)

91st Bomb Group(H)	1943 Jan Feb Mar Apr May June July Aug Sep Oct Nov Dec	1944 Jan Feb Mar	△A

Serial No	Gained From ▨ Period Assigned ▨ Lost To

Serial No	
42-5857	New Rpt 19 Apr 43 ▨ MIA 21 May 43
42-5893	New Rpt 4 June 43 ▨ 95BG 16 June 43
42-6086	New Rpt 21 Oct 43 ▨ MIA 1 Dec 43

B-17F Boeing

Serial No	
42-29475	New Rpt 7 Mar 43 ▨ MIA 10 July 43
42-29487	New Rpt 9 Mar 43 ▨ MIA 11 Jan 44
42-29520	303BG Burtonwood 7 Sep 43 ▨ MIA 8 Oct 43
42-29536	New Rpt 19 Apr 43 ▨ MIA 22 June 43
42-29537	New Rpt 7 Mar 43 ▨ MIA 28 Mar 43
42-29540	303BG AFSC 24 Aug 43 ▨ MIA 6 Sep 43
42-29559	N R 25 Feb 43 ▨ MIA 17 Aug 43
42-29574	N R 27 Feb 43 ▨ MIA 17 Apr 43
42-29587	New Rpt 19 Apr 43 ▨ MIA 12 Aug 43
42-29591	95BG 16 June 43 ▨ Ass 31 Mar 44
42-29642	New Rpt 15 Mar 43 ▨ MIA 13 May 43
42-29656	303BG AFSC 8 Sep 43 ▨ MIA 20 Feb 44
42-29657	▨
42-29659	New Rpt 15 Mar 43 ▨ MIA 22 Mar 43 With a 92BG crew.
42-29679	95BG 16 June 43 ▨ Ass 31 Mar 44
42-29711	94BG 29 Aug 43 ▨ MIA 8 Oct 43
42-29739	306BG 11 Sep 43 ▨ Ass 31 Mar 43
42-29740	95BG AFSC 21 Sep 43 ▨ MIA 9 Oct 43
42-29741	306BG 11 Sep 43 ▨ Ass 31 Mar 43
42-29750	96BG 24 Aug 43 ▨ MIA 27 Sep 43
42-29759	379BG 2SAD 21 Dec 43 ▨ Ass 31 Mar 43
42-29778	96BG 24 Aug 43 ▨ MIA 9 Oct 43
42-29793	306BG 11 Sep 43 ▨ Sal Reason unknown (5 Oct 43)
42-29794	306BG 11 Sep 43 ▨ MIA 1 Dec 43
42-29797	New Rpt 18 May 43 ▨ MIA 26 June 43
42-29813	95BG 16 June 43 ▨ MIA 25 July 43
42-29815	306BG 14 Sep 43 ▨ Ass 31 Mar 44
42-29816	New Rpt 19 Apr 43 ▨ MIA 31 Aug 43
42-29837	New Rpt 7 June 43 ▨ Ass 31 Mar 43
42-29895	New Rpt 23 May 43 ▨ MIA 31 Dec 43
42-29916	New Rpt 7 June 43 ▨ MIA 30 July 43
42-29921	New Rpt 23 May 43 ▨ MIA 31 Dec 43
42-29947	100BG 6 July 43 ▨ Ass 31 Mar 44
42-29973	New Rpt 11 June 43 ▨ Crashed 31 Aug 43
42-29998	New Rpt 7 June 43 ▨ MIA 22 June 43
42-30120	New Rpt 15 June 43 ▨ 95BG 16 June 43
42-30157	New Rpt 10 June 43 ▨ Crash Landed 30 July 43 (7 Aug 43)
42-30194	New Rpt 15 June 43 ▨ 95BG 16 June 43
42-30235	New Rpt 6 June 43 ▨ 95BG 16 June 43
42-30283	New Rpt 10 June 43 ▨ 95BG 16 June 43
42-30624	New Rpt 23 Sep 43 ▨ MIA 27 Sep 43
42-30712	New Rpt 27 Sep 43 ▨ MIA 21 Feb 44
42-30772	New Rpt 23 Sep 43 ▨ MIA 9 Oct 43
42-30773	New Rpt 26 Sep 43 ▨ Sculthorpe 19 Jan 44
42-30805	New Rpt 24 Sep 43 ▨ MIA 3 Nov 43

91st Bomb Group(H)	1943						1944			Ⓐ
	July	Aug	Sep	Oct	Nov	Dec	Jan	Feb	Mar	
Serial No	Gained From ▓▓▓ Period Assigned ▓▓▓ Lost To									

B-17G Boeing

Serial No										
42-31070	New Rpt 14 Dec 43									Ass 31 Mar 44
42-31076	New Rpt 16 Oct 43						MIA 11 Jan 44			
42-31079	401BG 20 Nov 43								MIA 6 Mar 44	
42-31178	New Rpt 20 Dec 43						Cr Landed 30 Dec 43 (3 Jan 44)			
42-31187	401BG 20 Nov 43								Cr 4 Mar 44 (5 Mar 44)	
42-31230	New Rpt 22 Dec 43						MIA 11 Jan 44			
42-31333	New Rpt 20 Dec 43									Ass 31 Mar 44
42-31353	New Rpt 20 Dec 43									Ass 31 Mar 44
42-31367	New Rpt 25 Jan 44									Ass 31 Mar 44
42-31372	New Rpt 20 Dec 43						MIA 11 Jan 44			
42-31513	New Rpt 24 Feb 44									Ass 31 Mar 44
42-31515	New Rpt 21 Jan 44									Ass 31 Mar 44
42-31542	457BG 12 Mar 44									Ass 31 Mar 44
42-31572	457BG 23 Jan 44							MIA 21 Feb 44		
42-31578	New Rpt 29 Dec 43								MIA 6 Mar 44	
42-31579	New Rpt 1 Feb 44									Ass 31 Mar 44
42-31580	New Rpt 29 Jan 44									Ass 31 Mar 44
42-31585	New Rpt 1 Feb 44								MIA 16 Mar 44	
42-31610	New Rpt 1 Feb 44									Ass 31 Mar 44
42-31634	New Rpt 23 Jan 44									Ass 31 Mar 44
42-31636	457BG 12 Mar 44									Ass 31 Mar 44
42-31672	New Rpt 23 Jan 44								MIA 20 Mar 44	
42-31673	New Rpt 27 Jan 44									Ass 31 Mar 44
42-31678	New Rpt 27 Jan 44									Ass 31 Mar 44
42-31812	New Rpt 20 Feb 44									Ass 31 Mar 44
42-31869	New Rpt 25 Feb 44								MIA 6 MAR 44	
42-31883	New Rpt 22 Mar 44									Ass 31 Mar 44
42-31909	New Rpt 24 Feb 44									Ass 31 Mar 44
42-31911	New Rpt 24 Feb 44								MIA 6 Mar 44	
42-31982	New Rpt 24 Feb 44									Ass 31 Mar 44
42-32072	New Rpt 31 Mar 44									Ass 31 Mar 44
42-32076	NMF New Rpt 23 Mar 44									Ass 31 Mar 44
42-32095	457BG 16 Mar 44									Ass 31 Mar 44
42-32116	457BG 16 Mar 44									Ass 31 Mar 44

B-17G Douglas

Serial No										
42-37736	New Rpt 24 Sep 43									Ass 31 Mar 44
42-37737	New Rpt 26 Sep 43		MIA 10 Oct 43							
42-37738	New Rpt 24 Sep 43					MIA 22 Dec 43				
42-37742	New Rpt 22 Sep 43			MIA 3 Nov 43						
42-37746	401BG 20 Nov 43							MIA 22 Feb 44		
42-37761	New Rpt 4 Oct 43								Cr Landed 6 Mar 44 (8 Mar 44)	
42-37767	New Rpt 5 Nov 43					Cr Landed 20 Dec 43 (21 Dec 43)				
42-37779	401BG 20 Nov 43									Ass 31 Mar 44
42-37911	New Rpt 10 Jan 44									Ass 31 Mar 44
42-37938	Bovingdon 30 Mar 44									Ass 31 Mar 44
42-37939	New Rpt 20 Dec 43							MIA 22 Feb 44 (Ditched)		
42-37940	New Rpt 13 Dec 43						Sal after Op Miss 11 Jan 44 (15 Jan 44)			
42-37958	New Rpt 20 Dec 43									Ass 31 Mar 44
42-37965	New Rpt 20 Dec 43								MIA 3 Mar 44	
42-37987	New Rpt 21 Dec 43						Cr Landed 29 Jan 44 (30 Jan 44)			
42-38006	New Rpt 8 Jan 44									Ass 31 Mar 44
42-38027	New Rpt 10 Jan 44									Ass 31 Mar 44
42-38083	New Rpt 1 Feb 44									Ass 31 Mar 44
42-38118	New Rpt 25 Feb 44								MIA 6 Mar 44	
42-38128	New Rpt 25 Feb 44									Ass 31 Mar 44
42-38144	New Rpt 28 Feb 44									Ass 31 Mar 44

91st Bomb Group(H) — A

	1943			1944		
Serial No	Oct	Nov	Dec	Jan	Feb	Mar

Gained From ▨ Period Assigned ▨ Lost To

B-17G Vega

Serial No	Notes
42-39771	401BG 20 Nov 43 — MIA 4 Feb 44
42-39774	N R 18 Oct 43 — Ass 31 Mar 44
42-39802	New Rpt (— MIA 3 Nov 43
42-39803	7 Oct 43 (— MIA 4 Feb 44
42-39815	N R 16 Oct 43 — MIA 22 Feb 44
42-39836	401BG 20 Nov 43 — MIA 1 Dec 43
42-39863	New Rpt 22 Dec 43 — Crash Landed 30 Dec 43 (31 Dec 43)
42-39892	New Rpt 13 Dec 43 — MIA 8 Mar 44
42-39898	New Rpt 13 Dec 43 — MIA 22 Feb 44
42-39929	New Rpt 20 Dec 43 — Ass 31 Mar 44
42-39967	New Rpt 25 jan 44 — MIA 18 Mar 44
42-39975	New Rpt 10 Jan 44 — Ass 31 Mar 44
42-39996	New Rpt 14 Jan 44 — Ass 31 Mar 44
42-40000	New Rpt 4 Jan 44 — Ass 31 Mar 44
42-40009	New Rpt 21 Jan 44 — Crashed 24 Jan 44

B-17G Boeing

Serial No	Notes
42-97061	457BG 16 Mar 44 — Ass 31 Mar 44
42-97125	457BG 16 Mar 44 — MIA 22 Mar 44
42-97151	New Rpt 22 Mar 44 — Ass 31 Mar 44
42-97246	New Rpt 25 Mar 44 — MIA 29 Mar 44

B-17G Vega

Serial No	Notes
42-97455	457BG 12 Mar 44 — Ass 31 Mar 44
42-97467	457BG 12 Mar 44 — Ass 31 Mar 44
42-97483	New Rpt 24 Feb 44 — MIA 6 Mar 44
42-97504	New Rpt 23 Jan 44 — Ass 31 Mar 44
42-97519	New Rpt 12 Feb 44 — Ass 31 Mar 44
42-97563	NMF 457BG 16 Mar 44 — Ass 31 Mar 44

B-17G Douglas

Serial No	Notes
42-107030	New Rpt 26 Mar 44 — Ass 31 Mar 44
42-107033	NMF New Rpt 24 Mar 44 — Ass 31 Mar 44
42-107075	New Rpt 22 Mar 44 — Ass 31 Mar 44

	1943											1944		
Serial No	Jan	Feb	Mar	Apr	May	June	July	Aug	Sep	Oct	Nov	Dec	Jan	Feb	Mar

Gained From ▨ Period Assigned ▨ Lost To

DB-7B Douglas

Serial No	Notes
AL397	17 Apr 43 — Ass 31 Mar 44
AL441	Not Known — AFSC 4 Mar 43 Wrecked in taxying Acc

Piper L-4B Cub

Serial No	Notes
43-648	381BG 26 Oct 43 — Ass 31 Mar 44

Airspeed Oxford

Serial No	Notes
DF-299	16 May 43 — 303BG 12 June 43
DF331	16 May 43 — First Bomb Division 21 Oct 43
DF335	16 May 43 — Ass 31 May 44
DF399	16 May 43 — First Bomb Wing 8 June 43

91st BOMBARDMENT GROUP (H)

None of the original aircraft were with the Group on 31st March 1944. Three had survived into 1944; 41-24490 'JACK THE RIPPER'; 41-24504 'THE SAD SACK'; and 41-24505 'QUITCHURBITCHIN'. All three had served side by side in the 324th Bomb Squadron. The 'Ripper' had flown on the Group's first Mission and was the last of the originals to go Missing in Action when it failed to return on 22nd February 1944. The other two had flown on the Group's first two missions. They were among the first ten First Division B-17Fs earmarked for return to the USA and departed for Burtonwood on 15th March.

The oldest operational aircraft assigned on 31st March was 41-24639 'THE CAREFULL VIRGIN'. She had joined the Group in January/February 1943. Her operational days with the 91st were now numbered, but her fate was not to be a westbound flight to the relative safe training fields of the USA with the other veterans. Her final epitaph would be 'Missing in Action' but the manner of her going would be dramatically different to that which had taken so many of the B-17s that had graced the hardstands beside her at Bassingbourn.

The next in line for long service was 42-29837 'LADY LUCK', which had joined the Group on 7th June 1943, followed closely by 42-29591 'SHAMROCK SPECIAL' and 42-29679 both having joined from the 95th Bomb Group on 16th June 1943. All three now had less than a week to serve in the 91st, before they would be transferred out to BAD for return to the USA or for other duties within the Eighth Air Force.

LONG SERVING AIRCRAFT ASSIGNED FOR ONE YEAR OR MORE				
Serial No	Date In	Date Out	Reason Out	Months Ass
41-24484	Orig Act	31 Dec 43	Crashed	15
41-24490	Orig Act	22 Feb 44	MIA	17
41-24504	Orig Act	15 Mar 44	Ret to USA	18
41-24505	Orig Act	15 Mar 44	Ret to USA	18
41-24639	Jan/Feb 43	Still Ass		13/14

STATUS OF AIRCRAFT ASSIGNED AT 2000 HOURS on 31st MARCH 1944

Operational: 58 B-17 (11 B-17F: 47 B-17G)

Non Operational: 5 (1 B-17E: 1 B-17F: 1 DB-7B: 1 L-4B: 1 Oxford)

Operational Aircraft Assigned and on hand at Bassingbourn

B-17F

42-3172	42-29591 *	42-29741 *	42-29837 *
	42-29679 *	42-29759 *	42-29947
42-5745 *	42-29739 *	42-29815 *	

B-17G

42-31070	42-31636	42-37736	42-39774	42-97455
42-31333	42-31673	42-37779	42-39929	42-97467
42-31353	42-31678	42-37911	42-39975	42-97504
42-31367	42-31812	42-37938	42-39996	42-97519
42-31513	42-31883	42-37958	42-40000	42-97563 NMF
42-31515	42-31909	42-38006		
42-31542	42-31982 NMF	42-38027	42-97061 NMF	42-107030 NMF
42-31579	42-32072 NMF	42-38083	42-97151 NMF	42-107033 NMF
42-31580	42-32076 NMF	42-38128		42-107075 NMF
42-31610	42-32095 NMF	42-38144		
42-31634	42-32116 NMF			

Assigned but not on hand: B-17F 41-24639 * at 2 SAD

Non Operational Aircraft on hand at Bassingbourn: B-17E 41-9023: B-17F 42-3061 (V.H.F. Relay Aircraft)

DB-7B AL397: L-4B 43-648: Oxford DF335

* These nine Aircraft without Tokyo tanks

AIRCRAFT AND OPERATIONAL STATISTICS

Total Aircraft Assigned

B-17E:	30 Mar 43 to 31 Mar 44	3	DB-7B:	42/43 to 31 Mar 44	2
B-17F:	24 Aug 42 to 31 Mar 44	137	L-4B:	26 Oct 43 to 31 Mar 44	1
B-17G:	22 Sep 43 to 31 Mar 44	84	Oxford:	16 May 43 to 31 Mar 44	5
YB-40:	17 July 43 to 7 Oct 43	3			

Operational Statistics

First Miss flown on: 7 Nov 42

First Act MIA: B-17Fs 41-24479 and 41-24503 on 22 Nov 42

First B-17G Ass: 42-3506 and 42-37742 on 22 Sep 43

First B-17G MIA: 42-37737 on 10 Oct 43

First NMF Ass: 42-31982 on 24 Feb 44

First NMF MIA: 42-97125 on 22 Mar 44

Total Act MIA: 119 (90 B-17F and 29 B-17G)

Highest Days Losses: Ten on 17 Aug 43

Other Losses (Salvaged) 23 B-17s 1 DB-7B

B-17F: 15 (9 Op, 4 Non Op and 2 Unknown)

B-17G: 8 (7 Op, 1 Non Op)

DB-7B: 1 (Non Op)

92nd BOMBARDMENT GROUP (H)

Constituted as the 92nd BOMBARDMENT GROUP (H) on 28th January 1942
Activated on 1st March 1942
Squadrons Assigned: 325th, 326th, 327th and 407th
Assigned to Eighth Air Force: Prior to 8th July 1942
Assigned to First Provisional Bombardment Wing: By order of 15th August 1942
Came under the control of Eighth Bomber Command
Moved into First Bombardment Wing (less 326th Bomb Squadron): 6th January 1943

COMBAT WING ASSIGNMENTS

102nd Provisional Bombardment: May 1943
40th Combat Bombardment: 16th September 1943

STATIONS

Bovingdon: Air Echelon in 16th to 27th August 1942
Ground Echelon in 18th August 1942
Alconbury: 6th January 1943 (less 326th Bomb Squadron)
326th Bomb Squadron in July 1943
Podington: 15th September 1943

Trained in the US using B-17Es. Air echelon moved to Wendover, Massachusetts, 20th June 1942, and then to Bangor, Maine, where from late June, new B-17Fs were assigned. All the new aircraft were of Boeing manufacture. Most came from the Air Depot at Middletown, with the remainder coming from the Air Depot at San Antonio and the Modification Center at Cheyenne in Wyoming. It was early August before the last of the 36 B-17Fs were on hand.

During the stay at Bangor, two of the new aircraft were involved in landing accidents. One, 41-24365, being damaged to the extent it had to leave the Group and go to the Rome Air Depot in New York, for repair. It was March 1943 before it finally joined the Eighth Air Force in England.

The ground echelon moved from Sarasota, Florida, to Fort Dix, New Jersey, and boarded the USS *West Point* which sailed from Staten Island, New York, on 6th August as part of the convoy which also brought the First Bombardment Wing to England. The *West Point* docked at Liverpool on 18th August, and on the 19th and 20th, all units travelled to Bovingdon, Herts.

The Group's air echelon was the first Eighth Air Force unit to make the direct flight across the North Atlantic from Gander in Newfoundland to Prestwick in Scotland. The first Squadron to leave Bangor, was the 326th, which left for Gander on 12th August and reached Prestwick on 16th August. The 325th left Bangor on 16th August with the 327th following two

days later. Both squadrons flew Gander to Prestwick on 19th/20th August. Lt Haas of the 327th landed in Northern Ireland due to weather, but re-joined the Squadron at Prestwick for the flight to Bovingdon.

Finally the 407th departed Bangor 25th August, arriving at Prestwick on 27th August and then flew on to Bovingdon. For the conduct and execution of the transatlantic ferry flight which had been accomplished without serious problems or losses, the Group received a Special Commendation.

The Group had been assigned to the First Provisional Bombardment Wing by the order of 15th August, but by the time of the Group's arrival at Bovingdon, the Provisional Wing had become the First Bombardment Wing and had started combat operations. It had been decided that the 92nd would be a training unit to give newly arrived crews indoctrination into combat and procedures in the European Theatre, and the Group came under the direct control of Eighth Bomber Command. Although the Group would fly on some of the Eighth Air Force missions of September and October 1942 and additionally carry out a few diversions for the main force, it would be May 1943 before it became a fully equipped Combat Group assigned to the First Bombardment Wing. An additional frustration dictated by operational logic was that the Group's new B-17Fs were exchanged for the B-17Es of the 97th Bomb Group.

The 92nd received new B-17Fs in April 1943. Eight were assigned on the 25th including 42-30008 shown here being used as a Guinea pig for experiments in camouflaging dispersed aircraft on 26th May 1943. It was the longest surviving of the Group's second generation B-17Fs. *US Air Force–National Air and Space Museum*

92nd BOMBARDMENT GROUP (H)

ORIGINAL B-17Fs ASSIGNED AT BANGOR JUNE TO AUGUST 1942

41-24342	41-24376	41-24388	41-24414	41-24437
41-24343	41-24377	41-24392	41-24415	41-24441
41-24344	41-24378	41-24400	41-24416	41-24442
41-24345	41-24379	41-24406	41-24417	41-24443
41-24365 (1)	41-24380 (2)	41-24411	41-24419	41-24444
41-24370	41-24382	41-24412	41-24421	41-24445
41-24373	41-24385	41-24413	41-24435	41-24473

(1) 41-24365: In landing Acc at Bangor 20 July 42. Not to UK with 92BG

(2) 41-24380: In landing Acc at Bangor 26th July 42. Not known if to UK with 92BG

The longest serving B-17 Group in the Eighth Air Force. The original B-17Fs had of course been taken over by the 97th Bomb Group and most had joined the Twelfth Air Force in North Africa in November 1942 and many were still serving.

It was April 1943 before the 92nd Group started to receive B-17Fs for combat operations. None of the aircraft assigned during April/May 1943 survived until March 1944. The longest lived had been 42-30008 which went Missing in Action on 30th January 1944 after nine months of combat operations.

The longest serving operational aircraft still assigned at 31st March 1944 was 42-29975 which had come from the 96th Bomb Group on 23rd July 1943. Still serving in the Group in a training role was B-17E 41-9154 which had been one of the aircraft involved in the exchange of aircraft with the 97th Bomb Group in August 1942 and now had been assigned to the same Group longer than any other B-17 in the Eighth Air Force.

AIRCRAFT AND OPERATIONAL STATISTICS

Total Aircraft Assigned

B-17E:	Aug 42 to 31 Mar 44	37	C-78:	5 June 43 to 27 Aug 43	1
B-17F:	June 42 to 31 Mar 44	132	L-4B:	8 Apr 43 to 27 Aug 43	4
B-17G:	2 Sep 43 to 31 Mar 44	89	Oxford:	5 June 43 to 27 Aug 43	5
YB-40:	8 May 43 to 5 Oct 43	12	Master:	5 Aug 43 to 27 Aug 43	1
DB-7B:	Early 43 to 13 Oct 43	2			

Operational Statistics

First Miss flown on:	6 Sep 42	Total Act MIA:	83 (2 B-17E: 47 B-17F: 33 B-17G: 1 YB-40)
First Act MIA:	B-17E 41-9026 on 6 Sep 42	Highest Days Losses:	Seven on 6 Sep 43
First B-17G Ass:	42-3513 on 2 Sep 43	Other Losses (Salvaged)	20
First B-17G MIA:	42-3554 on 9 Oct 43	B-17E:	3 (1 Op, 2 Non Op)
First NMF Ass:	42-97546 on 11 Feb 44	B-17F:	12 (10 Op, 2 Non Op)
First NMF MIA:	42-32034 on 24 Feb 44	B-17G:	5 (2 Op, 2 Non Op, 1 Unknown)

42-38156 comes in past the checkered runway controller's trailer at Podington. This aircraft reached England about a month later than other aircraft which came off the Douglas production lines at the same time. It was assigned to the 92nd on 23rd March 1944 and was probably the last olive drab B-17G the Group received. *Stan Bishop*

Serial No	Gained From	Period Assigned	Lost To

B-17E

Serial No	Notes
41-2578	97BG — 11 CCRC — 482BG 9 Jan 44
41-2626	97BG — Sal after Op Miss 9 Oct 42
41-2628	97BG — 11 CCRC To B Wd then 305BG 29 May 43
41-2629	305BG 14 Dec 42 — Unknown later 100BG
41-9013	97BG — 11 CCRC — 482BG 27 Aug 43
41-9017	305BG 6 Dec 42 — Unknown, later 94BG
41-9018	97BG — MIA 9 Oct 42
41-9019	305BG then unknown to 92BG 13 May 43 — 482BG 27 Aug 43
41-9020	97BG — 303BG 1 May 43
41-9021	97BG 28 Au 42 — Dam 9 Oct 42 To AFSC for Rep then to 2CCRC and later to 390BG
41-9022	97BG — 384BG 4 June 43
41-9023	97BG 28 Au 42 — 91BG 30 Mar 43 (BAT Flight)
41-9025	97BG — To 11 CCRC
41-9026	97BG — MIA 6 Sep 42
41-9030	305BG 2 Dec 42 — Unknown then 310 Ferrying Squadron Nov 43
41-9042	97BG — 27 Air Transport Wing 26 July 43
41-9043	97BG — 381BG July 43
41-9044	97BG — Crashed 11 Feb 43
41-9045	97BG — Crashed in Eire 15 Jan 43
41-9051	97BG — 482BG 1 Sep 43 Loaned to AFSC Mar/June 1943
41-9082	97BG — To MTO 23 Jan 43
41-9085	97BG — Unknown after 16 Dec 42
41-9089	97BG 28 Au 43 — 11 CCRC
41-9100	97BG 28 Au 43 — 11 CCRC To B Wd then 379BG
41-9103	97BG 28 Au 43 — 91BG 30 Mar 43 (BAT Flight)
41-9107	97BG — Warton 21 Sep 43.
41-9112	97BG — 8th Bomber Command. Ret to U.S.A. 14 Feb 43. First 8th AF B-17 to do so.
41-9114	97BG — TO MTO 14 Feb 43
41-9119	97BG — 11 CCRC
41-9121	97BG — 11 CCRC B Wd then 351BG 27 May 43
41-9125	97BG — Unknown
41-9129	305BG — Snetterton Heath 11 Aug 43
41-9132	97BG — Unknown
41-9148	97BG — 306BG 1 May 43
41-9154	97BG — Ass 31 Mar 44
41-9174	97BG — 11 CCRC Crashed June 43
41-9175	97BG — Unknown then 27 Air Transport Wing Nov 43

B-17F Boeing

Serial No	Notes
41-24342	Or Ac — 97BG 24 Aug 42
41-24343	Or Ac — 97BG
41-24344	Or Ac — 97BG
41-24345	Or Ac — 97BG
41-24359	305BG 20 Apr 43 — 482BG 25 Aug 43
41-24365	Or Ac — Acc at Bangor 20 July 42. To Rome AD for Rep. To 8th AF March 43
41-24370	Or Ac — 97BG
41-24373	Or Ac — 97BG
41-24376	Or Ac — 97BG
41-24377	Or Ac — 97BG
41-24378	Or Ac — 97BG
41-24379	Or Ac — 97BG
41-24380	Or Ac — Acc at Bangor 26 July 42. Remained in U.S.A. Later to 12AF
41-24382	Or Ac — 97BG
41-24385	Or Ac — 97BG
41-24388	Or Ac — 97BG
41-24392	Or Ac — 97BG 24 Aug 42
41-24400	Or Ac — 97BG 24 Aug 42

Original Aircraft (Or Ac) Ass at Bangor, Maine, Late June to early Aug 1942

92nd Bomb Group(H)		1942 July Aug Sep Oct Nov Dec	1943 Jan Feb Mar Apr May June July Aug Sep Oct Nov Dec	1944 Jan Feb Mar	△ B

Serial No		Gained From	Period Assigned	Lost To
41–24406	Or Ac	97BG 24 Aug 42		
41–24411	Or Ac	97BG		
41–24412		97BG	Probably from 301BG in U.S.A.	
41–24413	Or Ac	97BG 24 Aug 42		
41–24414	Or Ac	97BG		
41–24415	Or Ac	97BG 24 Aug 42		
41–24416	Or Ac	97BG		
41–24417	Or Ac	97BG 24 Aug 42 Later 306BG		
41–24419	Or Ac	97BG		
41–24421	Or Ac	97BG		
41–24435	Or Ac	97BG		
41–24437	Or Ac	97BG		
41–24441	Or Ac	97BG		
41–24442	Or Ac	97BG		
41–24443	Or Ac	97BG		
41–24444	Or Ac	97BG		
41–24445	Or Ac	97BG		
41–24473	Or Ac	97BG 24 Aug 42		

B-17F Douglas

42–3105		96BG May 43	DS to 11 CCRC 30 Aug 43 then unknown
42–3116		96BG May 43	MIA 28 July 43
42–3134		New Rpt 23 May 43	Bwd 29 Jan 44
42–3165		New Rpt 23 Apr 43	MIA 26 Nov 43
42–3171		95BG AFSC 11 Aug 43	Crashed 14 Oct 43 (15 Oct 43)
42–3183		96BG 19 July 43	Crashed 23 Sep 43
42–3184		New Rpt 24 Apr 43	MIA 22 Dec 43
42–3186		New Rpt 23 May 43	MIA 31 Dec 43
42–3198		306BG – AFSC 25 July 43	Crash Landed 6 Sep 43
42–3202		New Rpt 24 Apr 43 95BG 15 May 43	
42–3213		New Rpt 24 Apr 43 95BG May 43	
42–3277		New Rpt 15 June 43 95BG 16 June 43	
42–3351		New Rpt 24 July 43	Crashed 14 Oct 43 (15 Oct 43)
42–3385	SO Act	New Rpt 11 Aug 43 482BG 25 Aug 43 (°)	Ass 31 Mar 44
42–3428		New Rpt 14 Aug 43 MIA 6 Sep 43	(°) From Stansted 21 Feb 44
42–3435		New Rpt 12 Aug 43 MIA 17 Aug 43	
42–3461		New Rpt 23 Aug 43	(*) Ass 31 Mar 44

B-17G Douglas

(*) At Barford St John

42–3493		New Rpt 28 Sep 43	Ass 31 Mar 44
42–3494		New Rpt 4 Sep 43	MIA 4 Jan 44
42–3496		New Rpt 4 Sep 43	Ass 31 Mar 44
42–3513		New Rpt 2 Sep 43	Ass 31 Mar 44
42–3536		482BG – Stansted 20 Feb 44	Crashed 9 Mar 44
42–3554		New Rpt 16 Sep 43 MIA 9 Oct 43	

YB-40

42–5733		U.S.A. (+)	91BG 16 July 43
42–5734		U.S.A. (+)	91BG 16 July 43
42–5735		U.S.A. (+)	MIA 22 June 43. Only YB-40 MIA
42–5736		U.S.A. 14 May 43	303BG 3 Aug 43
42–5737		U.S.A. 11 May 43	303BG 16 July 43
42–5738		U.S.A. (+)	Bwd 5 Oct 43
42–5739		U.S.A. (+)	303BG 16 July 43
42–5740		U.S.A. (+)	Bwd 5 Oct 43
42–5741		U.S.A. (+)	91BG 22 July 43
42–5742		U.S.A. 11 May 43	Bwd 5 Oct 43
42–5743		U.S.A. 11 May 43	Bwd 5 Oct 43
42–5744		U.S.A. 18 May 43	Bwd 5 Oct 43

(+) Six Act Ass on 8 May 43 and One Ass on 15 May 43

42-5744 Flew last YB-40 Mission on 16 Aug 43

92nd Bomb Group(H)		1943									1944			
	Apr	May	Jun	Jly	Aug	Sep	Oct	Nov	Dec	Jan	Feb	Mar		

Serial No	Gained From ▒▒▒▒ Period Assigned ▒▒▒▒ Lost To

B-17F Vega

42-5745	* 20 Apr 43 ▒▒▒▒▒▒▒▒▒▒ 482BG 25 Aug 43
42-5793	* 20 Apr 43 ▒▒▒▒▒▒▒▒▒▒ 482BG 25 Aug 43
42-5801	94BG 28 July 43 ▒▒ MIA 12 Aug 43
42-5819	New Rpt 12 Aug 43 ▒▒ 482BG 25 Aug 43
42-5890	New Rpt 7 Aug 43 ▒▒▒ MIA 6 Sep 43
42-5916	New Rpt 6 June 43 ▒▒▒ Sal after Dam on Op Miss 4 July 43 (7 July 43)
42-5919	New Rpt 28 June 43 ▒▒▒ Bovingdon 22 July 43

B-17F Boeing

42-29511	* May 43 ▒▒▒▒▒▒▒▒ 379BG 4 Sep 43
42-29612	* 25 Apr 43 ▒▒▒▒▒▒▒▒▒ MIA 26 July 43 (Ditched)
42-29624	303BG 27 July 43 ▒▒▒▒ 379BG 13 Sep 43
42-29653	96BG 19 July 43 ▒▒▒▒ 379BG 4 Sep 43
42-29694	AFSC 7 July 43 ▒▒▒▒ 379BG 4 Sep 43
42-29698	94BG 3 Aug 43 ▒▒ Dam on Op Miss 27 Aug 43 and Sal (29 Aug 43)
42-29709	95BG 17 June 43 ▒▒▒ MIA 26 July 43
42-29712	95BG 17 June 43 ▒▒▒▒▒ 384BG 14 Sep 43
42-29713	94BG 26 July 43 ▒▒▒ 379BG 5 Sep 43
42-29717	94BG – AFSC 1 Aug 43 ▒▒▒▒ 384BG 13 Sep 43
42-29718	94BG 26 July 43 ▒▒▒ 379BG 5 Sep 43
42-29724	94BG 3 Aug 43 ▒▒▒ 379BG 4 Sep 43
42-29725	94BG 30 July 43 ▒▒▒ MIA 3 Sep 43
42-29776	305BG 22 July 43 ▒▒▒ 379BG 4 Sep 43
42-29780	95BG-AFSC 12 June 43 ▒ 95BG 26 June 43
42-29787	95BG 6 Aug 43 ▒▒▒ 379BG 4 Sep 43
42-29798	* 25 Apr 43 ▒▒▒▒▒▒▒ MIA 28 July 43
42-29802	305BG 22 July 43 ▒▒▒▒ 379BG 13 Sep 43
42-29820	* 24 Apr 43 ▒▒ MIA 15 May 43
42-29853	95BG 17 June 43 ▒▒▒▒▒ MIA 17 Aug 43
42-29884	* 23 May 43 ▒▒▒▒▒▒ MIA 12 Aug 43
42-29897	* 26 May 43 ▒▒▒▒▒ 379BG 4 Sep 43
42-29945	96BG 23 July 43 ▒▒▒ MIA 12 Aug 43
42-29962	94BG 26 July 43 ▒▒▒▒▒▒▒ AFSC Bovingdon 16 Oct 43
42-29965	94BG 26 July 43 ▒▒▒▒▒ MIA 6 Sep 43
42-29967	95BG 17 June 43 ▒▒▒ MIA 4 July 43
42-29975	96BG 23 July 43 ▒▒▒▒▒▒▒▒▒▒▒▒▒ Ass 31 Mar 44
42-29981	96BG – AFSC 23 July 43 ▒ MIA 26 July 43 (Ditched)
42-29994	* 25 Apr 43 ▒▒▒▒▒▒▒▒ 482BG 25 Aug 43
42-29996	* 24 Apr 43 ▒▒▒▒▒▒▒▒▒▒▒ MIA 16 Nov 43
42-30000	* 24 Apr 43 ▒▒▒▒▒▒▒▒ MIA 6 Sep 43
42-30003	* 25 Apr 43 ▒▒ MIA 14 May 43 First B-17F MIA
42-30006	* 25 Apr 43 ▒▒▒▒▒▒▒ 482BG 25 Aug 43
42-30007	* 25 Apr 43 ▒▒▒▒▒▒▒▒ MIA 6 Sep 43
42-30008	* 25 Apr 43 ▒▒▒▒▒▒▒▒▒▒ MIA 30 Jan 44
42-30010	* 25 Apr 43 ▒▒▒▒▒▒▒▒ MIA 6 Sep 43
42-30081	* 23 May 43 ▒▒▒▒▒▒ MIA 12 Aug 43
42-30154	New Rpt 13 June 43 ▒ 95BG 16 June 43
42-30211	New Rpt 13 June 43 ▒ 95 BG 16 June 43
42-30231	New Rpt 6 June 43 ▒▒▒▒▒ MIA 14 Oct 43 (Not Ass 1–10 Sep 43)
42-30261	New Rpt 27 Sep 43 ▒▒▒▒▒▒▒▒▒ Ass 31 Mar 44
42-30328	New Rpt 7 Aug 43 ▒▒ 482BG 25 Aug 43
42-30387	New Rpt 21 Aug 43 ▒▒▒▒▒ MIA 14 Oct 43
42-30408	New Rpt 14 Aug 43 ▒▒▒▒▒▒ Crashed 30 Nov 43

* New B-17Fs ass when the Group resumed Combat Operations in May 1943

First Mission with B-17Fs 14th May 1943

92nd Bomb Group(H)	1943						1944			B
	July	Aug	Sep	Oct	Nov	Dec	Jan	Feb	Mar	

Serial No	Gained From — Period Assigned — Lost To
42-30423	New Rpt 7 Aug 43 — MIA 4 Feb 44
42-30447	New Rpt 7 Aug 43 — Crashed 15 Aug 43 (17 Aug 43)
42-30580	New Rpt 14 Aug 43 — In Take Off Acc 4 Jan 44 (6 Jan 44)
42-30608	New Rpt 31 Aug 43 — MIA 26 Nov 43
42-30617	New Rpt 21 Aug 43 — MIA 27 Aug 43 (Ditched)
42-30623	New Rpt 16 Sep 43 — MIA 25 Feb 44
42-30636	New Rpt 31 Aug 43 — MIA 2 Mar 44
42-30638	New Rpt 30 Aug 43 — Ass 31 Mar 44
42-30644	New Rpt 7 Sep 43 — Ass 31 Mar 44
42-30646	New Rpt 2 Sep 43 — MIA 4 Oct 43
42-30648	New Rpt 30 Aug 43 — MIA 20 Dec 43
42-30649	New Rpt 31 Aug 43 — Ass 31 Mar 44
42-30654	New Rpt 16 Sep 43 — MIA 14 Oct 43
42-30668	New Rpt 15 Aug 43 — MIA 6 Sep 43
42-30677	New Rpt 30 Aug 43 — MIA 16 Dec 43
42-30708	New Rpt 31 Aug 43 — MIA 14 Oct 43
42-30711	New Rpt 31 Aug 43 — MIA 29 Jan 44
42-30716	New Rpt 2 Sep 43 — Crash Landed 28 Jan 44 (30 Jan 44)
42-30726	New Rpt 18 Sep 43 — MIA 14 Oct 43
42-30733	New Rpt 16 Sep 43 — MIA 31 Dec 43
42-30735	New Rpt 26 Sep 43 — MIA 31 Dec 43
42-30784	New Rpt 27 Sep 43 — Landing Gear collapsed 1 Jan 44 (6 Jan 44)
42-30803	New Rpt 27 Sep 43 — MIA 1 Dec 43
42-30821	New Rpt 16 Sep 43 — Crashed 13 Nov 43 (14 Nov 43)
42-30824	New Rpt 26 Sep 43 — MIA 14 Oct 43
42-30849	New Rpt 27 Sep 43 — Ass 31 Mar 44
42-31016	New Rpt 17 Oct 43 — MIA 4 Jan 44
42-31022	New Rpt 23 Nov 43 — MIA 16 Mar 44

B-17G Boeing

Serial No	Gained From — Period Assigned — Lost To
42-31109	New Rpt 17 Oct 43 — MIA 4 Feb 44
42-31175	New Rpt 2 Dec 43 — MIA 11 Jan 44
42-31180	New Rpt 23 Nov 43 — MIA 24 Feb 44
42-31231	New Rpt 23 Nov 43 — MIA 23 Mar 44
42-31248	New Rpt 30 Nov 43 — Ass 31 Mar 44
42-31250	New Rpt 2 Dec 43 — Ass 31 Mar 44
42-31277	New Rpt 21 Jan 44 — Ass 31 Mar 44
42-31326	New Rpt 30 Nov 43 — Ass 31 Mar 44
42-31362	New Rpt 30 Dec 43 — Ass 31 Mar 44
42-31377	New Rpt 27 Dec 43 — MIA 22 Feb 44
42-31387	New Rpt 4 Jan 44 — MIA 8 Feb 44
42-31408	New Rpt 27 Dec 43 — Ass 31 Mar 44
42-31411	New Rpt 2 Dec 43 — MIA 21 Feb 44
42-31455	New Rpt 23 Jan 44 — MIA 23 Mar 44
42-31494	New Rpt 31 Dec 43 — Crashed 4 Feb 44 (6 Feb 44)
42-31503	New Rpt 30 Dec 43 — MIA 6 Mar 44
42-31529	New Rpt 23 Jan 44 — Ass 31 Mar 44
42-31532	New Rpt 4 Jan 44 — MIA 23 Mar 44
42-31536	New Rpt 27 Jan 44 — Ass 31 Mar 44
42-31548	457BG 11 Mar 44 — Ass 31 Mar 44
42-31564	New Rpt 30 Dec 43 — MIA 9 Mar 43
42-31587	457BG 11 Mar 44 — Ass 31 Mar 44
42-31613	457BG 11 Mar 44 — Ass 31 Mar 44
42-31635	457BG 11 Mar 44 — Ass 31 Mar 44
42-31680	New Rpt Feb 44 — MIA 6 Mar 44
42-31687	New Rpt 28 Jan 44 — Ass 31 Mar 44
42-31713	New Rpt 1 Feb 44 — Ass 31 Mar 44
42-31765	New Rpt 2 Mar 44 — Ass 31 Mar 44
42-31771	New Rpt 2 Mar 44 — Ass 31 Mar 44

92nd Bomb Group(H)	1943						1944				B
	July	Aug	Sep	Oct	Nov	Dec	Jan	Feb	Mar		
Serial No	Gained From			Period Assigned					Lost To		
42-31772							New Rpt 1 Feb 44		MIA 9 Mar 44		
42-31783							New Rpt 5 Feb 44		Ass 31 Mar 44		
42-31828							New Rpt 2 Mar 44		Ass 31 Mar 44		
42-31860							New Rpt 5 Feb 44	MIA 21 Feb 44			
42-31888							New Rpt 19 Feb 44		MIA 23 Mar 44		
42-31898							New Rpt 2 Mar 44		Ass 31 Mar 44		
42-31907							New Rpt 19 Feb 44		Ass 31 Mar 44		
42-31914							New Rpt 11 Feb 44		Ass 31 Mar 44		
42-31921							New Rpt 5 Feb 44		Ass 31 Mar 44		
42-31978							New Rpt 2 Mar 44		Ass 31 Mar 44		
42-31984	NMF						New Rpt 2 Mar 44		Ass 31 Mar 44		
42-31995							New Rpt 23 Mar 44		Ass 31 Mar 44		
42-32034							Stansted 20 Feb 44	MIA 24 Feb 44			

B-17G Douglas

42-37735						482BG – Stansted 20 Feb 44			Ass 31 Mar 44		
42-37753						482BG – Stansted 21 Feb 44			Ass 31 Mar 44		
42-37755		New Rpt 16 Sep 43						MIA 25 Feb 44			
42-37799			New Rpt 21 Oct 43					Wrecked 15 Feb 44 (17 Feb 44)			
42-37877						New Rpt 20 Jan 44			Ass 31 Mar 44		
42-37928				New Rpt 1 Dec 43			To Sal reason unknown (6 Jan 44)				
42-37934				New Rpt 30 Nov 43					Ass 31 Mar 44		
42-37961					New Rpt 30 Dec 43		Cr Landed 23 Jan 44 (25 Jan 44)				
42-37976						New Rpt 8 Jan 44			Ass 31 Mar 44		
42-37984						New Rpt 6 Jan 44		MIA 8 Feb 44			
42-38025						New Rpt 4 Jan 44			Ass 31 Mar 44		
42-38101							New Rpt 20 Feb 44		Ass 31 Mar 44		
42-38104							457BG 11 Mar 44	MIA 23 Mar 44			
42-38110							457BG 11 Mar 44		Ass 31 Mar 44		
42-38156							New Rpt 23 Mar 44		Ass 31 Mar 44		

B-17G Vega

42-39758						New Rpt 2 Dec 43		MIA 11 Jan 44			
42-39770						New Rpt 25 Dec 43		MIA 20 Feb 44			
42-39831			New Rpt 21 Oct 43	MIA 5 Nov 43							
42-39851					New Rpt 2 Dec 43				Ass 31 Mar 44		
42-39958						New Rpt 27 Dec 43			Ass 31 Mar 44		
42-39960							New Rpt 23 Jan 44		MIA 2 Mar 44		
42-40014						New Rpt 6 Jan 44			MIA 2 Mar 44		
42-40032							New Rpt 27 Jan 44	MIA 8 Feb 44			
42-40047						New Rpt 31 Dec 43		MIA 24 Feb 44			
42-40052						New Rpt 30 Dec 43			MIA 6 Mar 44		

B-17G Boeing

42-97141							New Rpt 22 Mar 44		Ass 31 Mar 44		
42-97203							New Rpt 22 Mar 44		Ass 31 Mar 44		
42-97217	NMF						New Rpt 23 Mar 44		Ass 31 Mar 44		
42-97218							New Rpt 24 Mar 44		Ass 31 Mar 44		
42-97227							New Rpt 27 mar 44		Ass 31 Mar 44		
42-97243							New Rpt 23 Mar 44		Ass 31 Mar 44		

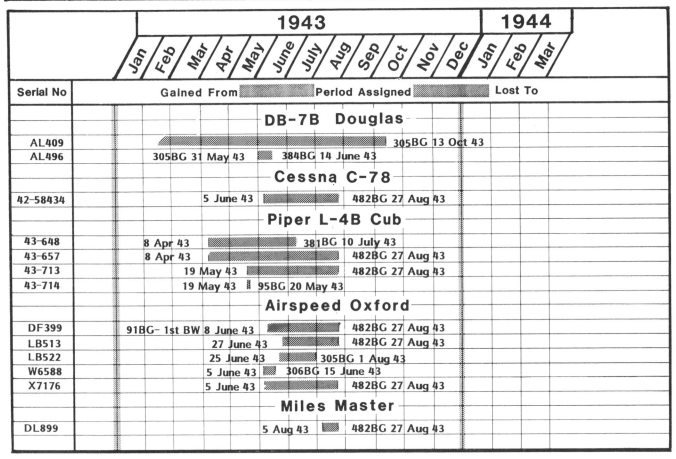

92nd Bomb Group(H)	1943			1944				B
	Oct	Nov	Dec	Jan	Feb	Mar		
Serial No	Gained From ▒▒▒ Period Assigned ▒▒▒ Lost To							
	B-17G Vega							
42-97441			New Rpt 10 Jan 44		▒ MIA 30 Jan 44			
42-97479			New Rpt 27 Jan 44			Ass 31 Mar 44		
42-97489			New Rpt 23 Jan 44			Ass 31 Mar 44		
42-97494			New Rpt 20 Jan 44		MIA 22 Feb 44			
42-97515			New Rpt 28 Jan 44			MIA 18 Mar 44		
42-97527			New Rpt 5 Feb 44		MIA 6 Mar 44			
42-97546	NMF		New Rpt 11 Feb 44 ▒ 457BG 24 Feb 44					
	B-17G Douglas							
42-107012	NMF			New Rpt 22 Mar 44 ▒ Ass 31 Mar 44				
42-107044				New Rpt 25 Mar 44 ▒ Ass 31 Mar 44				

	1943												1944		
Serial No	Jan	Feb	Mar	Apr	May	June	July	Aug	Sep	Oct	Nov	Dec	Jan	Feb	Mar
	Gained From ▒▒ Period Assigned ▒▒ Lost To														
	DB-7B Douglas														
AL409									305BG 13 Oct 43						
AL496	305BG 31 May 43 ▒ 384BG 14 June 43														
	Cessna C-78														
42-58434					5 June 43		482BG 27 Aug 43								
	Piper L-4B Cub														
43-648		8 Apr 43				381BG 10 July 43									
43-657		8 Apr 43						482BG 27 Aug 43							
43-713				19 May 43				482BG 27 Aug 43							
43-714				19 May 43	95BG 20 May 43										
	Airspeed Oxford														
DF399	91BG- 1st BW 8 June 43						482BG 27 Aug 43								
LB513					27 June 43		482BG 27 Aug 43								
LB522					25 June 43		305BG 1 Aug 43								
W6588					5 June 43	306BG 15 June 43									
X7176					5 June 43		482BG 27 Aug 43								
	Miles Master														
DL899							5 Aug 43	482BG 27 Aug 43							

SHORT SERVING AIRCRAFT: ASSIGNED FOR LESS THAN EIGHT DAYS. (From April 1943)									
Serial No	Date In	Date Out	Reason Out	Days Ass	Serial No	Date In	Date Out	Reason Out	Days Ass
42-3277	15 June 43	16 June 43	To 96BG	1	42-30154	13 June 43	16 June 43	To 95BG	3
42-3435	12 Aug 43	17 Aug 43	MIA	5	42-30211	13 June 43	16 June 43	To 95BG	3
42-29981	23 July 43	26 July 43	MIA	3	42-30617	21 Aug 43	27 Aug 43	MIA	6
42-30114	8 Sep 43	13 Sep 43	To 95BG	5	42-32034	20 Feb 44	24 Feb 44	MIA	4

92nd BOMBARDMENT GROUP (H)

STATUS OF AIRCRAFT ASSIGNED AT 2000HOURS ON 31st MARCH 1944

Operational: 57 B-17 (10 B-17F: 47 B-17G)

Non Operational: 1 B-17E

Operational Aircraft Assigned and on hand at Podington

B-17F

42-3385	42-3493	42-29975	42-30261	42-30649
42-3461	42-3496		42-30638	42-30849

B-17G

42-3513	42-31613	42-31914	42-38025	42-97217 NMF
	42-31635	42-31921	42-38101	42-97218 NMF
42-31248	42-31687	42-31978 NMF	42-38110	42-97227 NMF
42-31250	42-31713	42-31984 NMF	42-38156	42-97243 NMF
42-31326	42-31765	42-31995 NMF		
42-31362	42-31771		42-39851	42-97479
42-31408	42-31783	42-37753	42-39958	42-97489
42-31536	42-31828	42-37877		
42-31548	42-31898	42-37934	42-97141 NMF	42-107012 NMF
42-31587	42-31907	42-37976	42-97203 NMF	42-107044 NMF

Assigned but not on hand

B-17F 42-30644: At Witchford. B-17G 42-31277: At Wormingford.

B-17G 42-31529: At Boreham. B-17G 42-37735: At Horham

Non Operational Aircraft on hand at Podington: B-17E 41-9154

'BUNDLES FOR BERLIN', **'SOCIETY GAL'** and **'TIGER ROSE'**. Original B-17Fs of the 92nd Bomb Group at Bangor, 9th August 1942. Serial numbers are not known.

93rd's **'KATY BUG'** 41-23745 was the last B-24D to be lost while assigned to the First Bombardment Wing when it crashed near Alconbury on return from the mission of 18th November 1942. *Mike Bailey*

93rd BOMBARDMENT GROUP (H)

Constituted as the 93rd BOMBARDMENT GROUP (H) on 28th January 1942
Activated on 1st March 1942
Squadrons Assigned: 328th, 329th, 330th and 409th
Assigned to Eighth Air Force: About 1st August 1942
Assigned to First Bombardment Wing: September 1942

STATION

Alconbury: Air Echelon in 5th to 12th September 1942
Ground Echelon in 6th September 1942

Trained in the USA on B-24Ds based at Fort Myers, Florida. Engaged in anti-submarine patrols over the Gulf of Mexico and the Caribbean Sea, May–June 1942.

The air echelon departed Fort Myers for Grenier Field, on 2nd August with four planes per Squadron. The ground echelon left Fort Myers on 13th August and entrained for Fort Dix, New Jersey.

At Grenier, each Squadron was assigned nine new B-24Ds, these coming from the depot at St Paul, Minnesota. Four weeks were spent in transition training, equipping the aircraft and processing of personnel.

On 1st September they flew from Grenier to Gander on the initial leg of the flight to England. One B-24D, 41-23713, was lost over the Atlantic and no trace of aircraft or crew were ever found.

The only Group to use B-24s on operations while assigned to the First Bombardment Wing. The Group was transferred to the Second Bombardment Wing in December 1942.

AIRCRAFT AND OPERATIONAL STATISTICS		
Aircraft Assigned		
B-24D:	Aug 42 to Dec 42	35
Operational Statistics		
First Mission flown on:		9 Oct 42
Last Mission flown on:		23 Nov 42
Act MIA:	1 B-24D 41-23678 on 9 Oct 42	
Other Losses: 3 B-24D (2 Op and 1 Non Op)		

93rd Bomb Group(H)	1942					
	July	Aug	Sep	Oct	Nov	Dec
Serial No	Gained From ▓▓▓ Period Assigned ▓▓▓ Lost To					

B-24H Consolidated

Serial No	Sqdn					
41-23658	329BS	Orig Act				2nd Bomb Wing 6 Dec 42
41-23665	330BS	Orig Act				2nd Bomb Wing 6 Dec 42
41-23666	330BS	Orig Act				2nd Bomb Wing 6 Dec 42
41-23667	328BS	Orig Act				2nd Bomb Wing 6 Dec 42
41-23672	328BS	Orig Act				2nd Bomb Wing 6 Dec 42
41-23674	329BS	Orig Act				2nd Bomb Wing 6 Dec 42
41-23675	330BS	Orig Act				2nd Bomb Wing 6 Dec 42
41-23678	330BS	Orig Act			MIA 9 Oct 42 Only B-24 MIA While Ass to 1BW/BD	
41-23679		Orig Act	Left at Grenier, Details unknown			
41-23682	329BS	Orig Act				2nd Bomb Wing 6 Dec 42
41-23683	329BS	Orig Act				2nd Bomb Wing 6 Dec 42
41-23686	329BS	Orig Act				2nd Bomb Wing 6 Dec 42
41-23689	329BS	Orig Act				2nd Bomb Wing 6 Dec 42
41-23692	330BS	Orig Act				2nd Bomb Wing 6 Dec 42
41-23707	HQ Sqdn	Orig Act				2nd Bomb Wing 6 Dec 42
41-23710	329BS	Orig Act			Cr Exeter 7 Nov 42	
41-23711	328BS	Orig Act				2nd Bomb Wing 6 Dec 42
41-23712	330BS	Orig Act		Cr 27 Oct 42		
41-23713	328BS	Orig Act	Lost in Atlantic 10 Sep 42			
41-23717	329BS	Orig Act				2nd Bomb Wing 6 Dec 42
41-23721	330BS	Orig Act				2nd Bomb Wing 6 Dec 42
41-23722	328BS	Orig Act				2nd Bomb Wing 6 Dec 42
41-23723	329BS	Orig Act			Cr Exeter 8 Nov 42	
41-23724	409BS	Orig Act				2nd Bomb Wing 6 Dec 42
41-23728	330BS	Orig Act				2nd Bomb Wing 6 Dec 42
41-23729	328BS	Orig Act				2nd Bomb Wing 6 Dec 42
41-23732	409BS	Orig Act				2nd Bomb Wing 6 Dec 42
41-23734	409BS	Orig Act				2nd Bomb Wing 6 Dec 42
41-23737	328BS	Orig Act				2nd Bomb Wing 6 Dec 42
41-23738	409BS	Orig Act				2nd Bomb Wing 6 Dec 42
41-23740	409BS	Orig Act				2nd Bomb Wing 6 Dec 42
41-23742	409BS	Orig Act				2nd Bomb Wing 6 Dec 42
41-23744	409BS	Orig Act				2nd Bomb Wing 6 Dec 42
41-23745	328BS	Orig Act			Cr on Ret from Op Miss 18 Nov 42	
41-23748	409BS	Orig Act				2nd Bomb Wing 6 Dec 42
41-23754	409BS	Orig Act				2nd Bomb Wing 6 Dec 42

— Bomb Sqdn Ass given at time Act were Ass to Group —

97th BOMBARDMENT GROUP (H)

Constituted as the 97th BOMBARDMENT GROUP (H) on 28th January 1942
Activated on 3rd February 1942
Squadrons Assigned: 340th, 341st, 342nd and 414th
Assigned to Eighth Air Force: 20th May 1942
Assigned to First Provisional Bombardment Wing: 15th August 1942

STATIONS

Polebrook: Ground Echelons of the 340th and 341st Bomb Squadrons and Group Headquarters in 13th June 1942
Air Echelons in 2nd to 28th July 1942. Ground and Air Echelons of 342nd and 414th Bomb Squadrons in from Grafton Underwood 8th September 1942
Grafton Underwood: (Satellite Station). Ground Echelons of 342nd and 414th Bomb Squadrons in 13th June 1942
Air Echelons in 2nd to 28th July 1942. Both Squadrons moved to Polebrook 8th September 1942

First Heavy Bombardment Group to be assigned to the Eighth Air Force and the only Group to fly B-17Es across the Atlantic to England.

The 97th received B-17Es for training when based at McDill, Florida in March 1942. On 29th March, 14 of these aircraft were taken with the Group to its new base at Sarasota, also in Florida, where the strength was brought up to 35 B-17Es.

Between 13th and 16th May, the air echelon left Sarasota, the 340th and 341st Bomb Squadrons going to the Air Depot at San Antonio, Texas, and the 342nd and 414th Bomb Squadrons going to the Air Depot at Middletown, Pennsylvania. At these depots the aircraft were modified ready for the forthcoming flight overseas. The modifications being mostly to armament and radio equipment.

At the end of May the 340th and 341st Bomb Squadrons flew to Bangor, Maine, and the 342nd and 414th Squadrons flew to Grenier, New Hampshire. At this time, the battle of Midway was looming in the mid-Pacific and to strengthen the air defences on the US Pacific coast the 97th was directed to fly across the USA. The 340th and 341st Squadrons going to Hammer Field, California, and the 342nd and 414th Squadrons going to McChord in Washington where they came under the control of the Second Air Force.

Once the Midway crisis had passed, the Group returned to the East coast, the 340th and 341st Squadrons once more to Bangor and the 342nd and 414th Squadrons to Grenier.

The Group's ground echelon left Sarasota by train on 15th May for the Plant Park Fair Grounds staging area and then on 19th May left for Fort Dix, New Jersey. They sailed from Brooklyn aboard the *Queen Elizabeth* on 6th June and arrived at Liverpool on 12th June. On the 13th they were taken to their stations in England. Group Headquarters, the 340th and 341st Squadrons going to Polebrook and the 342nd and 414th Squadrons to the satellite at Grafton Underwood.

The planning for the deployment of the 97th Bombardment Group, to the Eighth Air Force in England had started as early as April 1942. The actual movement was conducted under the code name BOLERO which also included other air and ground units. Among these were P-38s of the First Fighter Group which lacked the navigation and communications equipment needed for such a long overwater flight and it was planned that these would fly in flights of four accompanied by a B-17E which would provide navigational and communications facilities.

The planning for and preparation of the units for despatch overseas was allocated to Eighth Fighter Command with Headquarters at Grenier Field in New Hampshire. This organisation prepared the movement orders and assembled the units at their points of departure where they were handed over to Air Transport Command, North Atlantic Division for the final briefing for the overseas movement.

After much discussion, the route chosen was Goose Bay in Labrador, Blui West One or Blui West Eight in Greenland then to Reykjavik in Iceland and on to Prestwick in Scotland. The final departure point in the USA being Presque Isle in north-east Maine.

One aspect which troubled the planners and received much attention was the problem of forecasting the weather over the ferry route and frantic efforts were made throughout the spring and summer of 1942 to improve forecasting facilities at the staging airfields. To assist the weather forecasters on the ground a plan was worked out to have a number of specially equipped B-17Es positioned at the staging airfields and these were to fly a pre-planned set of legs along the route and radio back weather conditions.

By early May, it had been determined that 53 B-17s would be required to furnish the escort for the P-38s and to provide the weather ships. The 97th Bomb Group had 35 aircraft assigned so a further 18 were requested by Eighth Fighter Command. On orders from Headquarters AAF to Second Air Force at Fort George Wright on 7th May, five B-17Es from the 301st Bomb Group at Gieger Field, Washington, were transferred to the Fairfield Air Depot, Ohio, and on further orders dated 20th May, 13 B-17Es were sent from the 303rd Bomb Group at Gowen Field, Idaho, to the Air Depot at Mobile, Alabama.

The orders called for the aircraft to be moved from their present stations to the Air Depots for the installation of special radio equipment. Once modified they were to proceed to Bolling Field, Washington, where they would come under the control of the Eighth Air Force for the purpose of weather observation flights over the BOLERO route.

The original orders were for a temporary move from their stations not to exceed 30 days after which, crews and aircraft were to return to their assigned units in the USA. These orders were soon changed to make the move of aircraft and crews a permanent one. Sometime between the issue of these orders and the arrival of the aircraft at the staging area, four of the aircraft were diverted to Alaska leaving 14 to make up the weather

Lt Lee's 41-2588 after it had ground looped at the end of runway 28 at Presque Isle on 28th June 1942. The accident which was put down to brake failure, occurred at the end of the landing roll following a ferry flight from Houlton accompanied by four P-38s which had peeled off and landed in front of the B-17E. It was estimated that it would take 9,200 man hours to repair the damage and the aircraft was salvaged, the second of the 97th Group's B-17Es to be wrecked before leaving the US *US Air Force*

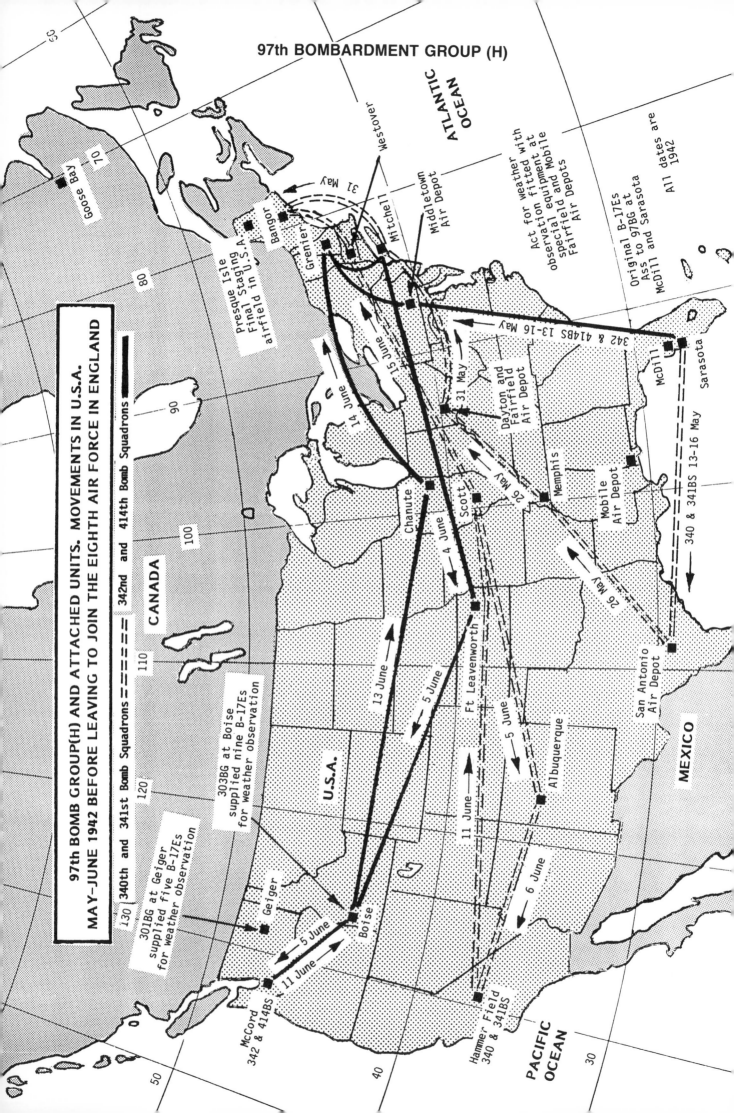

97th BOMBARDMENT GROUP (H)

97th BOMB GROUP(H) AND ATTACHED UNITS. MOVEMENTS IN U.S.A.
MAY-JUNE 1942 BEFORE LEAVING TO JOIN THE EIGHTH AIR FORCE IN ENGLAND

340th and 341st Bomb Squadrons ====
342nd and 414th Bomb Squadrons ▬▬▬

301BG at Geiger supplied five B-17Es for weather observation

303BG at Boise supplied nine B-17Es for weather observation

Act for weather with observation equipment at special equipment Mobile Fairfield Air Depots

Original B-17Es Ass to 97BG at McDill and Sarasota

All dates are All 1942

ATLANTIC OCEAN

CANADA

U.S.A.

MEXICO

PACIFIC OCEAN

Goose Bay

Presque Isle
Final Staging U.S.A.
airfield in U.S.A.

Bangor

Grenier

Westover

Mitchel

Middletown
Air Depot

31 May

15 June

14 June

Dayton and
Fairfield
Air Depot

31 May

26 May

Memphis

Mobile
Air Depot

342 & 414BS 13-16 May

340 & 341BS 13-16 May

Sarasota

McDill

San Antonio
Air Depot

Chanute

Scott

4 June

5 June

26 May

13 June

Ft Leavenworth

11 June

5 June

Albuquerque

6 June

Geiger

Boise

5 June

11 June

McCord
342 & 414BS

Hammer Field
340 & 341BS

97th Bomb Group(H)	1942									
	Mar	Apr	May	June	July	Aug	Sep	Oct	Nov	

Serial No — Gained From ▨ Period Assigned ▨ Lost To

B-17E

35 Ass in U.S.A. plus 14 from 301st and 303rd BGs for weather flights over ferry route.

Serial No	Notes
41-2578	Orig Act — 92BG
41-2588	Orig Act — Cr Presque Isle 28 June 42
41-2626	Orig Act — 92BG
41-2628	Orig Act — 92BG
41-2629	Orig Act — 305BG 5 Nov 42
41-9013	Orig Act — 92BG
41-9017	Orig Act — 305BG 6 Nov 42
41-9018	Orig Act — 92BG
41-9019	Orig Act — 305BG 6 Nov 42
41-9020	Orig Act — 92BG
41-9021	Orig Act — 92BG 24 Aug 42
41-9022	Orig Act — 92BG
41-9023	Orig Act — 92BG 24 Aug 42
41-9024	Orig Act — Wrecked 1 Aug 42. First 8th AF B-17 Sal in U.K.
41-9025	Orig Act — 92BG
41-9026	Orig Act — 92BG
41-9030	Orig Act — 305BG 6 Nov 42
41-9032	Orig Act — Cr Greenland 26 June 42
41-9042	Orig Act — 92BG
41-9043	Orig Act — 92BG
41-9044	Orig Act — 92BG
41-9045	Orig Act — 92BG 24 Aug 42
41-9051	Orig Act — 92BG
41-9073	303BG — Wrecked at Houlton 27 June 42
41-9074	303BG to 97BG 28 July 42 — Sal after Op Miss 7 Sep 42. First Op Sal.
41-9082	301BG — 92BG
41-9085	303BG — 92BG
41-9089	Orig Act — 92BG 24 Aug 42
41-9090	Orig Act — Landed in Water near Greenland 26 June 42
41-9098	303BG — Cr Wales 11 Aug 42
41-9100	Orig Act — 92BG 24 Aug 42
41-9101	Orig Act — Cr Landed Greenland 15 July 42
41-9103	Orig Act — 92BG 24 Aug 42
41-9105	Orig Act — Cr Landed Greenland 15 July 42
41-9107	Orig Act — 92BG
41-9108	Orig Act — Cr Landed Greenland 26 June 42
41-9112	301BG Not known if Ass to 97BG while in U.K. — 8th Bomber Command, Later U.S.A.
41-9114	Orig Act — 92BG
41-9115	Orig Act — Cr 14 Aug 42
41-9119	301BG — 92BG
41-9121	303BG — 92BG
41-9125	303BG — 92BG
41-9127	301BG — O/Shot Runway at Houlton 26 June 42. Not to U.K.
41-9129	303BG — 305BG 6 Nov 42
41-9132	303BG — 92BG
41-9148	303BG — 92BG
41-9154	301BG — 92BG
41-9174	Orig Act — 92BG
41-9175	Orig Act — 92BG

Ass to 8th AF 20 May 42

To U.K. June–July 42

Ass to 1st Prov Bombardment Wing 15 Aug 42
First 8th AF Heavy Bomber Mission 17 Aug 42-—Act taking part ■

97th Bomb Group(H)	1942						
	July	Aug	Sep	Oct	Nov	Dec	
Serial No	Gained From ▨▨▨ Period Assigned ▨▨▨ Lost To						

B-17F Boeing

Serial No	Gained From / Lost To
41-24342	92BG 24 Aug 42 — MTO 20 Nov 42
41-24343	92BG — MTO 22 Nov 42
41-24344	92BG — MIA 21 Oct 42
41-24345	92BG — MTO 20 Nov 42
41-24370	92BG — MTO 20 Nov 42
41-24373	92BG — MTO 17 Nov 42
41-24376	92BG — MTO 15 Nov 42
41-24377	92BG — MTO 5 Nov 42
41-24378	92BG — MTO 20 Nov 42
41-24379	92BG — MTO 17 Nov 42
41-24380	92BG — MTO 10 Nov 42
41-24382	92BG — MTO 17 Nov 42
41-24385	92BG — MTO 10 Nov 42
41-24388	92BG — MTO 6 Nov 42
41-24392	92BG 24 Aug 42 — MTO 20 Nov 42
41-24400	92BG 24 Aug 42 — Sal after Op Miss 21 Oct 42
41-24406	92BG 24 Aug 42 — MTO 20 Nov 42
41-24411	92BG — Sal after Op Miss 21 Oct 42
41-24412	92BG — MTO 10 Nov 42
41-24413	92BG 24 Nov 42 — MTO 20 Nov 42
41-24414	92BG — MTO 20 Nov 42
41-24415	92BG 24 Nov 42 — MTO 20 Nov 42
41-24416	92BG — Unknown, Later 4th Combat Wing
41-24417	92BG — Bwd 24 Oct 42, Later 306BG
41-24419	92BG — MTO 17 Nov 42
41-24421	92BG — MTO 17 Nov 42
41-24435	92BG — MTO 11 Nov 42
41-24437	92BG — MTO 17 Nov 42
41-24441	92BG — MIA 21 Oct 42
41-24442	92BG — MTO 20 Nov 42
41-24443	92BG 24 Aug 42 — MIA 21 Oct 42
41-24444	92BG — MTO 5 Nov 42
41-24445	92BG — MIA 6 Sep 42. First 8th AF B-17 MIA
41-24473	92BG 24 Aug 42 — MTO 20 Nov 42
41-24477	306BG — MTO 10 Nov 42
41-24532	305BG 4 Nov 42 — MTO 20 Nov 42
41-24572	305BG 4 Nov 42 — MTO 20 Nov 42
41-24576	305BG 4 Nov 42 — MTO 17 Nov 42
42-2969	305BG 4 Nov 42 — MTO 17 Nov 42
42-5087	Probably New Replacement from U.S.A. — MTO 11 Nov 42
42-5090	Probably New Replacement from U.S.A. — MTO 20 Nov 42
42-5713	305BG 4 Nov 42 — MTO 20 Nov 42
42-5715	Probably New Replacement from U.S.A. — MTO 20 Nov 42

— Ass to 12th AF 14 Sep 42 —

— Final Mission with 8th AF 21 Oct 42 —

— From U.K. to 12AF in North Africa Nov 42 —

154

97th BOMBARDMENT GROUP (H)

AIRCRAFT AND OPERATIONAL STATISTICS

Total Aircraft Assigned

B-17E: U.S.A. June 42, 35 Ass plus 14 Attached
U.K. Late July 42. (Not all Ass)   41
On Ass to First Prov BW on 15 Aug 42,   35

B-17F: Late Aug 42 to Nov 42   43

Operational Statistics

First   17 Aug 42
Total Act MIA: Four B-17F
Last Mission flown on: 21 Oct 42

First Act MIA: B-17F   41-24445 on 6 Sep 42
Highest Days losses: 3 on 21 Oct 42

Other Losses

3 B-17Es: Cr in U.S.A. Prior to leaving for U.K.
3 B-17Es: Cr in U.K. Prior to 15th Aug 42 (these 3 are included in First BW Statistics in this book)

5 B-17Es: Lost on ferry flight to U.K.
1 B-17E: Sal as result of Battle Dam (Op Loss)
2 B-17F: Sal as result of Battle Dam (Op Loss)

detachment and therefore making a total of 49 B-17Es scheduled to make the crossing to England. It was planned that on arrival in England the 14 aircraft would be based at Thurleigh and Chelveston and be used for training and as spares.

Being the first movement of a full Bomb Group over an unproven route, coupled with the need to co-ordinate the P-38 escort mission, the movement of the 97th was complicated and extended and did not take place without incident. Accidents in the USA resulted in two aircraft being written off and a third damaged to the extent it was left behind for repairs, so only 46 B-17Es started out from the USA. Two others were damaged in landing incidents and had to be repaired before setting out on the Atlantic crossing.

The first aircraft to depart the USA were the weather ships followed by those from the 342nd and 414th Squadrons which were not escorting P-38s. Ten of these arrived at Goose Bay on the afternoon of 26th June and later that day, departed for Blui West One, but on arrival over Greenland, the weather had closed in and six returned to Goose Bay. One made it to Blui West Eight and the other three made forced landings and were lost, but fortunately there were no serious injuries to their crews who were all rescued.

The first aircraft to arrive at Prestwick was the weather ship 41-9085 piloted by Lt Johnson which came in on 1st July and so became the first Eighth Air Force B-17 to touch down on British soil. This aircraft had been allotted the Prestwick–Iceland sector and during the next three weeks made several flights back and forth to observe weather

conditions for the following planes. A second aircraft arrived at Preswick on 4th July. This was probably the weather ship 41-9098 flown by Maj Thomas which had been allotted the Iceland–Prestwick sector and which also made several flights between Iceland and Prestwick.

The first of the main group reached Prestwick on 6th July when 41-9017, 41-9019, 41-9023, 41-9024, 41-9026, 41-9042, 41-9103 and 41-9115 arrived. Two more of the B-17Es were lost on the Greenland Icecap on 15th July, so only 41 B-17Es arrived in England. Most had completed the crossing by 27th July and it is believed the last to arrive was 41-9022 which was delayed at Presque Isle for repairs following a landing accident on 27th June.

Group was assigned to Twelfth Air Force on 14th September 1942 but continued to operate under the First Bombardment Wing until after the mission of 21st October. Moved to North Africa in November 1942 taking 35 B-17Fs.

B-17Es parked at Meeks Field, Iceland, during the ferry flight to England 21st July 1942. Nearest aircraft is 41-9051. On left is 41-9021 and in centre (above 9051) is 41-9125. *US Air Force–National Air and Space Museum*

ALLOCATION of WEATHER AIRCRAFT, BASES and ROUTES for BOLERO MOVEMENT– PRESQUE ISLE; 23rd June 1942				
BASE	SHIP No	PILOT	Act No	ROUTE
Goose Bay	1	Lt Traylor	41-9119	Goose Bay to BW1
	6	Lt Teague	41-9082	Goose Bay to BW8
BW1	2	Lt Stoddard	41-9112	BW1 to Iceland
	7	Lt Conners	41-9148	BW1 to Goose Bay
BW8	3	Lt Coulter	41-9154	BW8 to Goose Bay
	8	Lt Pett	41-9132	BW8 to Iceland
Iceland	4	Lt Blair	41-9125	Iceland to BW8
	9	Capt Hughes	41-9074	Iceland to BW1
	10	Maj Thomas	41-9098	Iceland to Prestwick
Prestwick	5	Lt Johnson	41-9085	Prestwick to Iceland

97th BOMBARDMENT GROUP (H)

SERIAL NUMBERS, SQUADRON ASSIGNMENTS and PILOTS OF THE
49 B-17Es
SCHEDULED FOR THE BOLERO MOVEMENT AS AT 16th JUNE 1942

340th Bomb Squadron 97th Bomb Group		341st Bomb Squadron 97th Bomb Group		342nd Bomb Squadron 97th Bomb Group	
41-2578	Lt Beasley	41-2628	Lt Taylor	41-9017	Lt Kelly
41-2588	Lt Lee (1)	41-9013	Lt McCorkle	41-9026	Lt Sammons
41-2626	Lt Wikle	41-9018	Lt Kimmel	41-9032	Lt Stinson (2)
41-2629	Lt Aenschbacher	41-9022	Lt Paine	41-9042	Lt Burges
41-9020	Lt Karas	41-9025	Lt Cronkhite	41-9043	Lt Dallas
41-9051	Lt Summers	41-9044	Lt Duncan	41-9090	Lt Nichols (4)
41-9107	Lt Hoffman	41-9101	Lt Hanna (5)	41-9108	Lt Holmes (7)
41-9174	Lt Rockett	41-9105	Lt Staples (6)	41-9115	Lt Schwarzenbeck
41-9175	Lt Lipsky	41-9114	Lt Ijams		

414th Bomb Squadron 97th Bomb Group		359th Bomb Squadron 303rd Bomb Group		419th Bomb Squadron 301st Bomb Group	
41-9019	Lt Baker	41-9073	Lt Riley (3)	41-9082	Lt Teague
41-9021	Lt Smartt	41-9074	Capt Hughes	41-9112	Lt Stoddard
41-9023	Lt Dowswell	41-9085	Lt Johnson	41-9119	Lt Traylor (CO)
41-9024	Lt Thacker	41-9098	Maj Thomas (CO)	41-9127	Lt Wilson (8)
41-9030	Lt Sauders	41-9121	Lt Bennett	41-9154	Lt Coulter
41-9045	Lt Schley	41-9125	Lt Blair		
41-9089	Lt Starks	41-9129	Lt Schmoldt		
41-9100	Lt Borders	41-9132	Lt Pett		
41-9103	Lt Lawrence	41-9148	Lt Connors		

(1) 41-2588 Cr in U.S.A. Prior to Departure   (5) 41-9101 Cr in Greenland on route to U.K.
(2) 41-9032 Cr in Greenland on route to U.K.   (6) 41-9105 Cr in Greenland on route to U.K.
(3) 41-9073 Cr in U.S.A. Prior to departure   (7) 41-9108 Cr in Greenland on route to U.K.
(4) 41-9090 Cr in Greenland on route to U.K.   (8) 41-9127 Dam in U.S.A. Did not fly to U.K.

A 97th Bomb Group B-17E under guard at Meeks Field, Iceland, 21st July 1942. *US Air Force–National Air and Space Museum*

301st BOMBARDMENT GROUP (H)

Constituted as the 301st BOMBARDMENT GROUP (H) on 28th January 1942
Activated on 3rd February 1942
Squadrons Assigned: 32nd, 352nd, 353rd and 419th
Assigned to Eighth Air Force: Prior to 8th July 1942
Assigned to First Provisional Bombardment Wing: 15th August 1942

STATIONS

Bovingdon: That part of the Air Echelon that arrived prior to 9th August 1942
Chelveston: Air Echelon from 9th August 1942 (including the element from Bovingdon)
Ground Echelons in from 19th August 1942
Air and Ground Echelons of the 352nd Bomb Squadron from 7th September 1942
Podington: 352nd Bomb Squadron, Ground Echelon in 20th August 1942, Air Echelon in 21st August 1942, both Air and Ground Echelons moved to Chelveston on 7th September 1942

Trained in the US with B-17Es. In May 1942, five B-17Es were detached and fitted with special equipment for weather observation flights along the BOLERO route (see 97th Bomb Group).

Moved to Brainard, Hartford, Connecticut, on 10th June and then to Westover, Massachusetts at end of June. Here the B-17Es were handed over to the 306th Bomb Group and starting on 9th July, new B-17Fs from the Air Depots at San Antonio and Middletown were assigned, the last arriving on 16th July. All these aircraft were from the Boeing factory at Seattle.

The first aircraft of the 419th Bomb Squadron left Westover on 21st July on the first stage of the flight to the UK. They were followed by the 352nd, the 353rd and the 32nd Bomb Squadrons, in that order. The route was Presque Isle, Goose Bay, Blui West One, Iceland, Prestwick, from where the first aircraft flew to Bovingdon, where they stayed until the 9th of August and then flew to the Group's permanent base at Chelveston.

It was during the ferry flight from Bovingdon to Chelveston that 2nd Lt James M Hair's aircraft 41-24347 got into difficulties and crash landed at RAF Church Lawford and earned the distinction of becoming the first US operated B-17F to be salvaged in England.

On the 15th August when the Group was assigned to the First Provisional Bombardment Wing there were 19 B-17Fs at Chelveston. The wrecked plane at Church Lawford was still regarded as a Group aircraft so the records showed 20 B-17Fs assigned on this date.

All aircraft were in by 26th August except for Lt Sylvestor's 41-24348 which had been damaged in a parking accident with a P-38 at ³lui West

One. Some of his crew returned to the USA for another aircraft but returned to Blui West One three weeks later without one. Meanwhile the aircraft had been repaired sufficiently to fly and it was flown to Chelveston arriving on 9th September. Two days later it was flown to Burtonwood for permanent repair and returned to Chelveston on 1st October.

The ground echelon had been separated from the air echelon since 17th June when it had moved by train from Alamogordo, New Mexico, to Richmond, Virginia, where it stayed for about three weeks and then went to Fort Dix for final overseas processing. Leaving Fort Dix on 4th August they boarded the USS *Uruquay* at Staten Island and sailed on the 6th August arriving at Swansea, Wales, on 18th August.

Travelling by train they were taken to Higham Ferrers arriving on the 19th August and were then trucked to Chelveston to be re-united with the air echelon. The ground echelon of the 352nd Bomb Squadron went straight to Podingdon arriving on the 20th August. The air echelon of the Squadron joined them next day. The Squadron moved to Chelveston on the 7th September, the operation of a single Squadron on a satellite airfield had not been a great success.

The Group was assigned to the Twelfth Air Force on 14th September 1942 but continued to operate under the First Bombardment Wing until after the mission of 8th November 1942. Moved to North Africa later in November taking 35 B-17Fs. The serial numbers, dates and airfields of departure of the B-17Fs taken to North Africa is tabulated in Part One, November 1942.

AIRCRAFT AND OPERATIONAL STATISTICS		
Total Aircraft Assigned		
B-17E: May-July 1942, Five Attached to 97BG to provide weather flights over the BOLERO Ferry route. See 97BG for details		
B-17F: July - Nov 1942		41
Operational Statistics		
First Mission flown on: 5 Sep 42	Other Losses (Salvaged): One B-17F Cr Ld in England prior to Gp being Ass to the First BW.	
Act MIA: 1 B-17F 41-24362	This Act is included in First BW statistics in this book.	
Last Mission flown on: 8 Nov 42	2 B-17F: After Ass to First BW. (1 Op and 1 Non Op)	

P-38s of the First Fighter Group which were escorted over the North Atlantic by the 97th Bomb Group's B-17Es, parked at Meeks Field, Iceland, on 6th July 1942. On left of photograph the tail of B-17E 41-2578 is visible. *US Air Force–National Air and Space Museum*

301st Bomb Group(H)	1942										
	Mar	Apr	May	June	July	Aug	Sep	Oct	Nov		
Serial No	Gained From	Period Assigned					Lost To				

B-17E

Serial No									
41-9082	To Fairfield Air Depot, Ohio, May 1942 for Installation of Special Equipment				97BG				
41-9112					97BG				
41-9119					97BG				
41-9127					Dam In U.S.A. Not to U.K.				
41-9154					97BG				

B-17F Boeing

Serial No									
41-24346	419BS			Orig Act					MTO 24 Nov 42.
41-24347	352BS			Orig Act	Cr Ld 9 Aug 42. Sal. First B-17F Sal in U.K.				
41-24348	353BS			Orig Act					MTO 24 Nov 42.
41-24350	352BS			Orig Act					MTO 24 Nov 42.
41-24351	353BS			Orig Act					MTO 24 Nov 42.
41-24352	352BS			Orig Act					MTO 24 Nov 42.
41-24359				Orig Act			Unknown, Later 305BG.		
41-24360	419BS			Orig Act					MTO 24 Nov 42.
41-24361				Orig Act					MTO 24 Nov 42.
41-24362	419BS			Orig Act			MIA 9 Oct 42. (Ditched)		
41-24363				Orig Act					MTO 24 Nov 42.
41-24364	353BS			Orig Act					MTO 24 Nov 42.
41-24366	353BS			Orig Act					MTO 24 Nov 42.
41-24367	419BS			Orig Act					MTO 25 Nov 42.
41-24368	352BS			Orig Act					MTO 24 Nov 42.
41-24369				Orig Act					MTO 24 Nov 42.
41-24371	353BS	All Original Aircraft Assigned at Westover Mass. Between 9th and 16th July 1942		Orig Act					MTO 24 Nov 42.
41-24372	352BS			Orig Act					MTO 24 Nov 42.
41-24374	353BS			Orig Act					MTO 24 Nov 42.
41-24386	353BS			Orig Act					MTO 24 Nov 42.
41-24390	419BS			Orig Act					MTO 23 Nov 42.
41-24393	419BS			Orig Act					MTO 28 Nov 42.
41-24394	419BS			Orig Act					MTO 24 Nov 42.
41-24395	419BS			Orig Act					MTO 24 Nov 42.
41-24396	419BS			Orig Act					MTO 24 Nov 42.
41-24397	352BS			Orig Act			Sal After Op Miss. 2 Oct 42.		
41-24398	419BS			Orig Act			Cr Ld 3 Oct 42. Sal.		
41-24404	352BS			Orig Act					MTO 24 Nov 42.
41-24405	353BS			Orig Act					MTO 24 Nov 42.
41-24407	352BS			Orig Act					MTO 24 Nov 42.
41-24408				Orig Act					MTO 24 Nov 42.
41-24409	352BS			Orig Act					MTO 24 Nov 42.
41-24412				Orig Act		Probably to 92BG in U.S.A.			
41-24418				Orig Act					MTO 24 Nov 42.
41-24422	352BS			Orig Act					MTO 24 Nov 42.
41-24423	353BS			Orig Act					MTO 24 Nov 42.
41-24618					New Rpt				MTO 24 Nov 42.

B-17F Boeing

Serial No									
42-5061					New Rpt				MTO 24 Nov 42.
42-5082					Prestwick 7 Nov 42				MTO 24 Nov 42.
42-5085					Prestwick 7 Nov 42				MTO 24 Nov 42.
42-5131					New Rpt				MTO 24 Nov 42.

Flew North Atlantic Route to England 21 July to 26 Aug 1942

First Mission 5 Sep 1942

Last Mission 8 Nov 1942

Ass to First Provisional Bombardment Wing 15 Aug 1942

303rd BOMBARDMENT GROUP (H)

Constituted as the 303rd BOMBARDMENT GROUP (H) on 28th January 1942
Activated on 3rd February 1942
Squadrons Assigned: 358th, 359th, 360th and 427th
Assigned to Eighth Air Force: 21st August 1942
Assigned to First Bombardment Wing: October 1942

COMBAT WING ASSIGNMENTS

Second Provisional: 13th December 1942
102nd Provisional Bombardment: 3rd January 1943
103rd Provisional Bombardment: 18th May 1943
41st Combat Bombardment: 16th September 1943

STATIONS

Molesworth: Air Echelon in 21st to 26th October 1942
Ground Echelon in 12th September 1942

Trained in US using B-17Es, 13 B-17Es were detached in May 1942 to make up a Squadron of weather aircraft for the BOLERO movement. (See 97th Bomb Group for details.)

Moved from Biggs Field, Texas, to Kellogg Field at Battle Creek, Michigan, where new B-17Fs were assigned. First three, 41-24581, 41-24582 and 41-24577 were assigned on 11th September 1942 and the last, 41-24559, on 2nd October. Included in the new planes were 42-2966 and 2967, the first Douglas built B-17s assigned to the Eighth Air Force. Most of the aircraft had come from the Douglas Modification Centers at Tulsa, but others came from Cheyenne and Denver Modification Centers.

The air echelon flew to Bangor Maine, with some aircraft staging through Westover. From Bangor they flew the direct North Atlantic route via Gander to Prestwick. Most planes made the Gander–Prestwick flight on 20–21st October with the last aircraft, 42-2966, leaving Bangor on the 28th October. From Prestwick they flew to Molesworth, the first aircraft to arrive being 41-24608 of the 359th Bomb Squadron which touched down

at 1551 hours on 21st October. Several planes made an attempt to fly Prestwick–Molesworth on the 22nd October but had to return to Prestwick due to bad weather. A similar attempt on the 23rd, resulted in some planes diverting to Silloth, and on the 24th, 41-24582 diverted to Croydon. Last plane landed at Molesworth on 5th November.

The ground echelon left Biggs by train on 24th August, arriving at Fort Dix, New Jersey, on 28th August where final preparations for the overseas movement were made.

The 359th Bomb Squadron were the first to entrain for Port of Embarkation as they had been selected to operate the mess hall aboard ship. They left Fort Dix on 2nd September and boarded the *Queen Mary*. The remainder of the Group followed on 4th September and the 'Queen' left New York early on the 5th and docked at Glasgow on the 11th.

From Glasgow they were taken by train to Thrapston where they arrived early on 12th September and then boarded British trucks for the last few miles to Molesworth.

'**BAD CHECK**' at dispersal beside a cornfield August 1943. She survived for over a year and was one of three of the Group's original aircraft among the ten B-17s the 303rd lost on 11th January 1944. *US Air Force–National Air and Space Museum*

| 303rd Bomb Group(H) | 1942 July Aug Sep Oct Nov Dec | 1943 Jan Feb Mar Apr May June July Aug Sep Oct Nov Dec | 1944 Jan Feb Mar | C |

Serial No — Gained From █ Period Assigned █ Lost To

B-17E

Nine detached to 97BG in May 1942 to make up a Weather Squadron
for the BOLERO movement. See 97BG for details.

Serial No	Gained From	Notes	Lost To
41-9020		92BG 1 May 43	Ass 31 Mar 44
41-24416		95BG 17 June 43 At Framlingham At Woodbridge	out 30 Mar 44
41-24517	Orig 24 Sep 42	MIA 3 Jan 43	
41-24526	Orig 19 Sep 42	MIA 3 Jan 43	
41-24539	Orig 16 Sep 42	Bovingdon 27 July 43 (1CCRC)	
41-24541	Orig 16 Sep 42	MIA 16 Feb 43	
41-24558	Orig 16 Sep 42	MIA 18 Mar 43. With 92BG crew	
41-24559	Orig 2 Oct 42	Crashed 31 Mar 43	
41-24561	Orig 17 Sep 42		Ass 31 Mar 44
41-24562	Orig 16 Sep 42	MIA 11 Jan 44	
41-24563	Orig 17 Sep 42	Sal after belly landing 11 Nov 42	
41-24565	Orig 18 Sep 42	MIA 5 Nov 43	
41-24566	Orig 18 Sep 42	MIA 20 Dec 43	
41-24567	Orig 18 Sep 42	MIA 23 Jan 43	
41-24568	Orig 18 Sep 42	MIA 23 Nov 42 First Group Act MIA	
41-24569	Orig 18 Sep 42	MIA 4 Feb 43	
41-24577	Orig 13 Sep 42	To U.S.A. 20 Jan 44	
41-24579	Orig Act	Sal after belly landing 21 Jan 43 (Hells Angels)	
41-24580	Orig Act	MIA 23 Jan 43	
41-24581	Orig Act	Sal after belly landing 20 Dec 42	
41-24582	Orig 13 Sep 42	MIA 12 Dec 42	
41-24584	Orig 17 Sep 42	MIA 23 Jan 43	
41-24585	Orig 1 Oct 42	MIA 12 Dec 42	
41-24587	Orig 1 Oct 42	MIA 11 Jan 44	
41-24602	Orig 21 Sep 42	MIA 29 May 43	
41-24603	Orig 21 Sep 42	MIA 23 Jan 43	
41-24605	Orig 22 Sep 42		Ass 31 Mar 44
41-24606	Orig 18 Sep 42	Landed in field (Dawlish) 23 Jan 43. To 91BG	
41-24607	Orig 24 Sep 42	MIA 23 Jan 43	
41-24608	Orig 23 Sep 42	MIA 3 Jan 43	
41-24609	Orig 23 Sep 42	MIA 4 Apr 43	
41-24610	Orig 24 Sep 42	MIA 1 May 43	
41-24612	Orig 26 Sep 42	To AFSC 20 May 43 then to 1CCRC	
41-24619	Orig Act	MIA 11 Jan 44	
41-24620	Orig 28 Sep 42	MIA 3 Jan 43	
41-24629		306BG 25 Sep 43 MIA 20 Oct 43	
41-24635	Dec 42		Ass 31 Mar 44

B-17F Douglas

Serial No	Gained From	Notes	Lost To
42-2966	Orig 16 Sep 42	Bovingdon 4 July 43	First Douglas
42-2967	Orig 18 Sep 42	MIA 16 Feb 43	built to 8AF
42-2973	New Rpt 14 Dec 42		Out 26 Mar 44
42-3002		New Rpt 8 Apr 43 MIA 6 Sep 43	
42-3029		New Rpt 9 Apr 43 MIA 14 Jan 44	
42-3040		New Rpt 9 Apr 43 306BG 17 Apr 43 then to 91BG	
42-3041		New Rpt 9 Apr 43 306BG 17 Apr 43 then to 384BG	
42-3064		100BG 13 July 43 At Docking	Ass 31 Mar 44
42-3105		On loan from 92BG 3 Sep 43 19 Oct 43	
42-3124		New Rpt 2 June 43 Crashed 4 Aug 43 (6 Aug 43)	
42-3131		New Rpt 4 June 43 MIA 11 Jan 44	
42-3158		New Rpt 2 June 43	Ass 31 Mar 44
42-3192		New Rpt 16 May 43 MIA 19 Aug 43	
42-3448		18 Oct 43 MIA 11 Jan 44	

303rd Bomb Group(H)

1942			1943												1944			△C
Oct	Nov	Dec	Jan	Feb	Mar	Apr	May	June	July	Aug	Sep	Oct	Nov	Dec	Jan	Feb	Mar	

Serial No — Gained From ▓▓▓ Period Assigned ▓▓▓ Lost To

B-17F Boeing

Serial No	Entry
42-5052	306BG 25 Sep 43 ▓▓▓ MIA 22 Feb 44
42-5054	306BG 25 Sep 43 ▓▓▓ Out 30 Mar 44
42-5081	New Rpt 15 Feb 43 ▓▓▓ Ass 31 Mar 44
42-5132	New Rpt 21 Dec 42 ▓ 91BG. Out by 18 Jan 43
42-5177	▓▓▓ Sal after Op Miss 26 Nov 43 (28 Nov)
42-5178	New Rpt 21 Dec 43 ▓ 91BG. Out by 18 Jan 43
42-5221	New Rpt 8 Apr 43 ▓▓▓ MIA 9 Oct 43
42-5243	▓▓ MIA 14 May 43
42-5257	New Rpt 19 Feb 43 ▓▓▓ Out 29 Mar 44
42-5260	▓▓▓ MIA 2 Oct 43
42-5262	▓▓ MIA 6 Mar 43
42-5264	New Rpt 1 Feb 43 ▓▓▓ Ass 31 Mar 44
42-5306	306BG 25 Sep 43 ▓▓▓ MIA 28 Feb 44
42-5341	▓▓▓ Ass 31 Mar 44
42-5360	New Rpt 8 Jan 43 ▓▓▓ MIA 11 Jan 44
42-5382	New Rpt 25 Feb 43 ▓▓ MIA 25 June 43. Ass to 379BG 31 May to 3 June.
42-5390	New Rpt 26 Mar 43 ▓▓ MIA 25 June 43
42-5392	New Rpt 26 Mar 43 ▓▓ MIA 19 Aug 43
42-5393	New Rpt 25 Feb 43 ▓▓▓ Ass 31 Mar 44
42-5430	New Rpt 25 Feb 43 ▓▓ MIA 11 June 43
42-5432	New Rpt 25 Feb 43 ▓▓ MIA 22 June 43
42-5434	New Rpt 6 Mar 43 ▓▓ Crashed 26 Sep 43
42-5444	2 June 43 ▓ L Lodge 5 July 43 then to 384BG
42-5468	New Rpt 8 Apr 43 ▓▓ MIA 25 June 43, Crashed in Sea.
42-5482	New Rpt 6 Mar 43 ▓▓ Crashed 14 Oct 43
42-5483	New Rpt 7 Mar 43 ▓▓ MIA 29 Nov 43

B-17F Vega

Serial No	Entry
42-5723	New Rpt 13 Feb 43 ▓ Crash Landed 18 Mar 43

YB-40

Serial No	Entry
42-5736	92BG 3 Aug 43 ▓ 379BG 28 Aug 43
42-5737	92BG 16 July 43 ▓▓ AFSC 10 Oct 43
42-5739	92BG 16 July 43 ▓▓ 384BG 28 Aug 43

B-17F Vega

Serial No	Entry
42-5780	New Rpt 8 Apr 43 ▓ MIA 1 May 43
42-5788	New Rpt 8 Apr 43 ▓▓▓ MIA 22 Feb 44
42-5792	New Rpt 8 Apr 43 ▓▓ MIA 4 July 43
42-5854	100BG 13 July 43 ▓▓▓ Ass 31 Mar 44
42-5859	379BG to AFSC then to 303BG 2 Oct 43 ▓▓ Crash Landed 20 Feb 44 Rep at Bungay 29 Nov 43 to 1 Feb 44

B-17F Boeing

Serial No	Entry
42-29477	306BG 25 Sep 43 ▓ MIA 14 Oct 43
42-29481	New Rpt 6 Apr 43 ▓ MIA 15 May 43
42-29498	306BG 25 Sep 43 ▓▓ MIA 29 Nov 43
42-29520	New Rpt 6 Mar 43 ▓ AFSC 20 May 43 then to 91BG
42-29524	306BG to AFSC then to 303 BG 30 July 43 ▓▓ Sal after Miss 11 Jan 44 (12 Jan 44)
42-29540	New Rpt 25 Feb 43 ▓▓ AFSC 1 June 43 then to 91BG
42-29570	New Rpt 21 Mar 43 ▓▓ BAD 22 May 43, Then to 381BG
42-29571	New Rpt 6 Apr 43 ▓▓▓ MIA 20 Oct 43
42-29573	New Rpt 6 Mar 43 ▓ Crashed after mid air Collision 31 Mar 43
42-29606	New Rpt 6 Apr 43 ▓▓ MIA 25 June 43
42-29620	New Rpt 15 Apr 43 ▓ 306BG 17 Apr 43
42-29624	New Rpt 6 Apr 43 ▓▓ 92BG 27 Feb 43

| 303rd Bomb Group(H) | 1943 — Jan Feb Mar Apr May June July Aug Sep Oct Nov Dec | 1944 — Jan Feb Mar | △ C |

Serial No	Gained From ▨ Period Assigned ▨ Lost To
42-29629	306BG 25 Sep 43 ▨▨▨▨ BAD 28 Mar 44
42-29635	New Rpt 26 Mar 43 ▨▨▨ MIA 31 Aug 43
42-29640	New Rpt 26 Mar 43 ▨▨▨ MIA 12 Aug 43
42-29656	New Rpt 21 Mar 43 ▨▨ AFSC 30 June 43 then 91BG
42-29664	New Rpt 21 Mar 43 ▨▨▨ MIA 20 Dec 43, Ditched
42-29738	100BG 13 July 43 ▨ MIA 30 July 43
42-29741	New Rpt 15 Apr 43 ▮ 306BG 17 Apr 43
42-29754	95BG 17 June 43 ▨▨ MIA 27 Aug 43
42-29791	95BG 17 June 43 ▨▨ MIA 14 July 43, Ditched
42-29795	306BG 25 Sep 43 ▨▨▨ Ass 31 Mar 44
42-29823	306BG 26 Sep 43 ▨▨▨ Ass 31 Mar 44
42-29846	New Rpt 16 May 43 ▨▨▨ MIA 4 Oct 43
42-29894	306BG 25 Sep 43 ▨▨▨ MIA 11 Jan 44
42-29930	306BG 25 Sep 43 ▨ Crashed 23 Oct 43 (24 Oct 43)
42-29931	100BG 13 July 43 ▨▨▨ MIA 22 Feb 44
42-29944	New Rpt 9 June 43 ▨▨▨ Crashed 6 Sep 43 (7 Sep 43)
42-29955	New Rpt 16 May 43 ▨▨▨ MIA 26 Nov 43
42-29994	482BG 15 Jan 44 ▨▨ Ass 31 Mar 44
42-30161	New Rpt 16 June 43 ▮ 95BG 18 June 43
42-30273	New Rpt 16 June 43 ▮ 95BG 17 June 43
42-30300	New Rpt 16 June 43 ▮ 95BG 17 June 43
42-30865	New Rpt 18 Oct 43 ▨▨▨ MIA 11 Jan 44

B-17G Boeing

Serial No	Gained From ▨ Period Assigned ▨ Lost To
42-31042	New Rpt 19 Oct 43 ▨ BAD 23 Oct 43, then to 384BG
42-31052	(°) Reason Unknown — New Rpt 11 Oct 43 ▨▨▨ To Sal 8 Mar 44 (°)
42-31055	New Rpt 18 Oct 43 ▨▨▨ Ass 31 Mar 44
42-31060	New Rpt 18 Oct 43 ▨▨▨ Ass 31 Mar 44
42-31177	New Rpt 18 Nov 43 ▨▨▨ Ass 31 Mar 44
42-31183	New Rpt 18 Nov 43 ▨▨▨ Ass 31 Mar 44
42-31200	New Rpt 1 Jan 44 ▨▨ Ass 31 Mar 44
42-31213	New Rpt 18 Nov 43 ▨▨▨ Ass 31 Mar 44
42-31224	New Rpt 13 Jan 44 ▨▨ Ass 31 Mar 44
42-31233	New Rpt 18 Nov 43 ▨ MIA 20 Dec 43
42-31239	New Rpt 18 Nov 43 ▨▨ MIA 24 Feb 44
42-31241	New Rpt 18 Nov 43 ▨▨▨ Ass 31 Mar 44
42-31243	New Rpt 18 Nov 43 ▨ MIA 1 Dec 43 (Ditched)
42-31314	(+) (13 Feb 44) — New Rpt 18 Nov 43 ▨▨ Crash Landed 11 Feb 44 (+)
42-31340	New Rpt 27 Dec 43 ▨▨ Ass 31 Mar 44
42-31386	New Rpt 18 Jan 44 ▨▨ Ass 31 Mar 44
42-31399	New Rpt 27 Dec 43 ▨▨ MIA 22 Feb 44
42-31405	New Rpt 14 Jan 44 ▨▨ Ass 31 Mar 44
42-31423	New Rpt 18 Jan 44 ▨▨ Ass 31 Mar 44
42-31432	New Rpt 18 Jan 44 ▨▨ Ass 31 Mar 44
42-31441	New Rpt 1 Jan 44 ▨ Crashed 5 Jan 44
42-31471	New Rpt 1 Jan 44 ▨▨ MIA 8 Mar 44
42-31483	New Rpt 1 Jan 44 ▨▨ Ass 31 Mar 44
42-31526	New Rpt 1 Jan 44 ▨ MIA 4 Jan 44
42-31562	New Rpt 13 Jan 44 ▨▨ MIA 24 Feb 44
42-31574	New Rpt 13 Jan 44 ▨▨ Ass 31 Mar 44
42-31583	New Rpt 13 Jan 44 ▨▨ Ass 31 Mar 44
42-31616	New Rpt 14 Jan 44 ▨▨ Ass 31 Mar 44
42-31669	New Rpt 15 Feb 44 ▨ Ass 31 Mar 44
42-31739	New Rpt 15 Feb 44 ▨ Ass 31 Mar 44
42-31754	New Rpt 28 Feb 44 ▨ Ass 31 Mar 44
42-31756	(*) (13 Mar 44) — New Rpt 1 Mar 44 ▨ Wrecked 12 Mar 44 (*)
42-31830	New Rpt 20 Feb 44 ▨ Ass 31 Mar 44
42-31929	New Rpt 1 Mar 44 ▨ MIA 26 Mar 44

Serial No	1943 Oct	Nov	Dec	1944 Jan	Feb	Mar		
	Gained From			Period Assigned			Lost To	
42-31997					New Rpt 22 Feb 44		Ass 31 Mar 44	
42-32027	NMF				New Rpt 1 Mar 44		Ass 31 Mar 44	
42-32037					New Rpt 28 feb 44		Ass 31 Mar 44	

B-17G Douglas

Serial No								
42-37727	N R 18 Oct 43	BAD 23 Oct 43 Then to		384BG				
42-37757	N R 18 Oct 43		To	Salvage (11 Dec 43) Reason unknown.				
42-37762	N R 22 Oct 43	BAD 30 Oct 43. Then to		384BG				
42-37776	N R 18 Oct 43	BAD 23 Oct 43. Then to		384BG				
42-37781	N R 19 Oct 43	BAD 23 Oct 43. Then to		384BG				
42-37785	N R 18 Oct 43	BAD 23 Oct 43. Then to		384BG				
42-37787	N R 19 Oct 43	BAD 23 Oct 43. Then to		384BG				
42-37789	N R 18 oct 43	BAD 23 Oct 43. Then to		384BG				
42-37791	N R 19 Oct 43	BAD 23 Oct 43. Then to		384BG				
42-37841	New Rpt 18 Nov 43						Ass 31 Mar 44	
42-37875	New Rpt 18 Nov 43						Ass 31 Mar 44	
42-37893	New Rpt 18 Nov 43						Ass 31 Mar 44	
42-37896			New Rpt 27 Dec 43	MIA 11 Jan 44				
42-37927	New Rpt 18 Nov 43				MIA 3 Feb 44			
42-38020			New Rpt 20 Jan 44				Ass 31 Mar 44	
42-38041			New Rpt 18 Jan 44		Crashed 22 Feb 44 (24 Feb 44)			
42-38050			New Rpt 18 Jan 44				Ass 31 Mar 44	
42-38051			New Rpt 13 Jan 44				Ass 31 Mar 44	
42-38154				New Rpt 18 Feb 44			Ass 31 Mar 44	
42-38168				New Rpt 22 Feb 44			Ass 31 Mar 44	
42-38204				New Rpt 29 Feb 44			Ass 31 Mar 44	

B-17G Vega

42-39764	N R 18 Oct 43			MIA 20 Dec 43				
42-39769	N R 18 Oct 43			Landing Acc, 19 Dec 43 (22 Dec 43)				
42-39781	N R 18 Oct 43		MIA 1 Dec 43. First Group B-17G MIA.					
42-39783	N R 19 Oct 43	BAD 23 Oct 43. Then to		384BG				
42-39785	N R 18 Oct 43						Ass 31 Mar 44	
42-39786	N R 18 Oct 43				MIA 29 Jan 44			
42-39787	N R 18 Oct 43						Ass 31 Mar 44	
42-39794	N R 18 Oct 43			MIA 11 Jan 44				
42-39795	N R 18 Oct 43			MIA 30 Dec 43				
42-39796	N R 21 Oct 43	BAD 23 Oct 43. Then to		384BG				
42-39800	N R 18 Oct 43	BAD 23 Oct 43. Then to		384BG				
42-39807	New Rpt 19 Nov 43						Ass 31 Mar 44	
42-39810	N R 18 Oct 43				Crash Landed 11 Feb 44 (14 Feb 44)			
42-39875			New Rpt 14 Jan 44				Ass 31 Mar 44	
42-39885			New Rpt 31 Dec 43				Ass 31 Mar 44	

B-17G Boeing

Serial No								
42-97058						New Rpt 27 Mar 44	Ass 31 Mar 44	
42-97187	NMF					New Rpt 26 Mar 44	Ass 31 Mar 44	
42-97254						New Rpt 26 Mar 44	Ass 31 Mar 44	
42-97260						New Rpt 26 Mar 44	Ass 31 Mar 44	

303rd Bomb Group(H)	1943			1944			△ C
	Oct	Nov	Dec	Jan	Feb	Mar	
Serial No	Gained From ▓▓▓ Period Assigned ▓▓▓ Lost To						

B-17G Vega

Serial No							
42-97498		New Rpt 14 Jan 44		MIA 6 Feb 44			
42-97509				New Rpt 28 Feb 44 ▓ MIA 2 Mar 44			
42-97546				457BG 12 Mar 44 ░░░ Ass 31 Mar 44			
42-97552				457BG 12 Mar 44 ░░░ Ass 31 Mar 44			
42-97590				457BG 13 Mar 44 ░░░ Ass 31 Mar 44			
42-97617				New Rpt 23 Feb 44 ░░░ Ass 31 Mar 44			
42-97622	NMF			New Rpt 23 Feb 44 ░░░ Ass 31 Mar 44			

B-17G Douglas

42-107002				New Rpt 24 Mar 44 ░░ Ass 31 Mar 44			
42-107048				New Rpt 23 Mar 44 ░░ Ass 31 Mar 44			

B-24D Consolidated

42-40748	On Loan from 93BG	(On hand 6 Feb 44 to 13 Mar 44 ▓▓▓ Ass 31 Mar 44					
		(Then Ass from 14 Mar 44					

	1943												1944		
	Jan	Feb	Mar	Apr	May	June	July	Aug	Sep	Oct	Nov	Dec	Jan	Feb	Mar
Serial No	Gained From ▓▓▓ Period Assigned ▓▓▓ Lost To														

DB-7B Douglas

| AL491 | Not Known | ▓▓▓▓▓▓▓▓▓▓▓▓▓▓▓▓▓ Ass 31 Mar 44 | | | | | | | | | | | | | |

Piper L-4B Cub

| 43-702 | | | | | BOVINGDON 18 Oct 43 ▓▓▓▓▓ Ass 31 Mar 44 | | | | | | | | | | |

Airspeed Oxford

| DF299 | | | 91BG 12 June 43 ▓▓▓▓▓▓▓▓▓ Ass 31 Mar 44 | | | | | | | | | | | | |

De Haviland Tiger Moth

| T6369 | | | 12 June 43 ▓ To R.A.F. Polebrook for Repair 17 June 43 | | | | | | | | | | | | |

ORIGINAL B-17Fs ASSIGNED AT KELLOGG BETWEEN 11th SEP and 2nd OCT 1942							
41-24517	427BS	41-24565	359BS	41-24582	358BS	41-24608	359BS
41-24526	358BS	41-24566	359BS	41-24584	427BS	41-24609	359BS
41-24539	358BS	41-24567	360BS	41-24585	360BS	41-24610	427BS
41-24541	358BS	41-24568	359BS	41-24587	427BS	41-24612	427BS
41-24558	358BS	41-24569	427BS	41-24602	360BS	41-24619	427BS
41-24559	360BS	41-24577	358BS	41-24603	359BS	41-24620	360BS
41-24561	359BS	41-24579	360BS	41-24605	359BS		
41-24562	358BS	41-24580	358BS	41-24606	358BS	42-2966	427BS
41-24563	360BS	41-24581	359BS	41-24607	427BS	42-2967	360BS

303rd BOMBARDMENT GROUP (H)

At the beginning of 1944 the 303rd Bomb Group had more of its original aircraft still assigned than did the other three Groups which had started operations in late 1942.

There were six remaining when the New Year commenced but three went down on the 11th January, leaving 'THE DUCHESS', 'HELLS ANGELS', and 'KNOCKOUT DROPPER' to continue. 'HELLS ANGELS' left the Group to return to the USA on 20th January. 'THE DUCHESS', the oldest operational B-17 in the Eighth Air Force, survived until April when she was retired along with most of the other non-Tokyo tank aircraft. Only the 'DROPPER' would survive after 5th April.

Some of the replacement aircraft had also set records for longevity. Eight had served for 12 months or more and five of these were still serving at the end of March. Helping the Group achieve its record for long serving aircraft was its lower Missing in Action rate than the other three pioneer Groups. Another important factor was that being in the 41st Combat Wing, the Group had escaped having its old non-Tokyo tank aircraft transferred out in September/October 1943.

The 303rd Bomb Group lost a quarter of its assigned aircraft during the first eleven days of 1944. To make up these losses many new planes were assigned during the following seven days including 42-31432 'OLD GLORY' which arrived on 18th January. *Ben Smith*

LONG SERVING AIRCRAFT: ASSIGNED FOR ONE YEAR OR MORE				
Serial No	Date In	Date Out	Reason Out	Months Ass
41-24561	Sep 42	Still Ass		18
41-24562	Sep 42	11 Jan 44	MIA	15
41-24565	Sep 42	5 Nov 43	MIA	13
41-24566	Sep 42	20 Dec 43	MIA	15
41-24577	Sep 42	20 Jan 44	Ret to USA	15
41-24587	Sep 42	11 Jan 44	MIA	15
41-24605	Sep 42	Still Ass		18
41-24619	Sep 42	11 Jan 44	MIA	15
41-24635	Dec 42	Still Ass		15
42-2973	14 Dec 42	26 Mar 44	To BAD	13
42-5081	14 Feb 43	Still Ass		13
42-5257	19 Feb 43	29 Mar 44	To BAD	13
42-5264	1 Feb 43	Still Ass		14
42-5341	Feb 43	Still Ass		13
42-5360	8 Jan 43	11 Jan 44	MIA	12
42-5393	25 Feb 43	Still Ass		13

SHORT SERVING AIRCRAFT: ASSIGNED FOR LESS THAN EIGHT DAYS				
Serial No	Date In	Date Out	Reason Out	Days Ass
42-29620	15 Apr 43	17 Apr 43	To 306BG	2
42-29741	15 Apr 43	17 Apr 43	To 306BG	2
42-30161	16 June 43	18 June 43	To 95BG	2
42-30273	16 June 43	17 June 43	To 95BG	1
42-30300	16 June 43	17 June 43	To 95BG	1
42-31042	19 Oct 43	23 Oct 43	To BAD	4
42-31441	1 Jan 44	5 Jan 44	Crashed	4
42-31526	1 Jan 44	4 Jan 44	MIA	3
42-37727	18 Oct 43	23 Oct 43	To BAD	5
42-37776	18 Oct 43	23 Oct 43	To BAD	5
42-37781	19 Oct 43	23 Oct 43	To BAD	4
42-37785	18 Oct 43	23 Oct 43	To BAD	5
42-37787	19 Oct 43	23 Oct 43	To BAD	4
42-37789	18 Oct 43	23 Oct 43	To BAD	5
42-37791	19 Oct 43	23 Oct 43	To BAD	4
42-39783	19 Oct 43	23 Oct 43	To BAD	4
42-39796	21 Oct 43	23 Oct 43	To BAD	5
42-39800	18 Oct 43	23 Oct 43	To BAD	5
42-97509	28 Feb 44	2 Mar 44	MIA	2

AIRCRAFT AND OPERATIONAL STATISTICS		
Total Aircraft Assigned		
B-17E: June-July 1942. Nine attached to 97BG to provide weather flights over the BOLERO ferry route. See 97BG for details. 1 May 43 to 31 Mar 44 — 1	YB-40: 16 July 43 to 10 Oct 43 — 3	
	DB-7B: 1942/1943 to 31 Mar 44 — 1	
	L-4B: 18 Oct 43 to 31 Mar 44 — 1	
	Oxford: 12 June 43 to 31 Mar 44 — 1	
B-17F: Sep 42 to 31 Mar 44 — 117	Tiger Moth: 12 June 43 to 17 June 43 — 1	
B-17G: 11 Oct 43 to 31 Mar 44 — 86	B-24D: 14 Mar 44 to 31 Mar 44 — 1	

Operational Statistics

First Miss flown on: 17 Nov 42
First Act MIA: 41-24568 on 23 Nov 43
First B-17G Ass: 42-31052 on 11 Oct 43
First B-17G MIA: 42-39781 on 1 Dec 43
First NMF Ass: 42-97617 on 23 Feb 43
First NMF MIA: None up to 31 Mar 44

Total Act MIA: 81 (64 B-17F and 17 B-17G)
Highest Days Losses: Ten on 11 Jan 44
Other Losses (Salvaged)
  B-17F: 15 (11 Op, 4 Non Op)
  B-17G: 7 (3 Op, 2 Non Op, 2 Unknown)

303rd BOMBARDMENT GROUP (H)

STATUS OF AIRCRAFT ASSIGNED AT 2000 HOURS on 31st MARCH 1944

Operational: 60 B-17 (12 B-17F: 48 B-17G)

Non Operational: 1 B-17E: 1 B-17F: 1 B-17G: 1 B-24D: 1 DB-7B: 1 L-4B: 1 Oxford

Operational Aircraft Assigned and on hand at Molesworth

B-17F

41-24561 * Orig Act	42-3064 *	42-5081 *	42-5393 *	42-29795 *
41-24605 * Orig Act	42-3158	42-5264 *	42-5854 *	42-29823 *
41-24635 *		42-5341 *		

B-17G

42-31060	42-31423	42-32027 NMF	42-38168	42-97260 NMF
42-31177	42-31432	42-32037 NMF	42-38204	
42-31183	42-31483			42-97546 NMF
42-31200	42-31574	42-37841	42-39785	42-97552 NMF
42-31213	42-31583	42-37875	42-39807	42-97590 NMF
42-31224	42-31616	42-37893	42-39875	42-97617 NMF
42-31241	42-31669	42-38020	42-39885	42-97622 NMF
42-31340	42-31739	42-38050		
42-31386	42-31754	42-38051	42-97058 NMF	42-107002 NMF
42-31405	42-31830	42-38154	42-97187 NMF	42-107048 NMF
			42-97254 NMF	

Assigned but not on hand

B-17G: 42-31055, At Abbots Ripton for Rep.　　　　B-17G: 42-31997 NMF, At Eastchurch for Rep.

Non Operational Aircraft on hand at Molesworth

B-17E 41-9020:　B-17F 42-29994:　B-17G 42-39787:　DB-7B AL491:　L-4B 43-702:

B-24D 42-40748:　Assigned and on hand, on temporary loan from Hethel.

Assigned but not on hand: Oxford DF299, At Cheddington on temporary loan.

* These 12 B-17Fs without Tokyo tanks

THE ORIGINAL PIONEERS

The four pioneer Groups (91st, 303rd, 305th and 306th) had 140 B-17Fs assigned when they left the U.S.A. for England in 1942. By January 1944, after more than a year on operations, only seventeen of these original aircraft remained on operational status. During the first three months of 1944, fourteen more were taken off assigned status for various reasons leaving only three still assigned at 31st March. The chart below shows how these seventeen aircraft finally finished their operational careers. Of the three still assigned at 31st March 1944: 'THE DUTCHESS' was first to go, leaving on 7th April. Next was 'KNOCK OUT DROPPER' which left on 20th April and finally 'WE THE PEOPLE' left for BAD on 4th May.

Serial No		1944			
		Jan	Feb	Mar	
41-24484	91BG 'BAD EGG'	Crashed 31 Dec 43 but remained Ass until 2 Jan 44			
41-24490	91BG 'JACK THE RIPPER'		MIA 22 Feb 44		
41-24504	91BG 'THE SAD SACK'			To BAD 15 Mar 44	
41-24505	91BG 'QUITCHURBITCHIN'			To BAD 15 Mar 44	
41-24525	305BG 'WHATS COOKING DOC' To 384BG	MIA 7 Jan 44			
41-24560	306BG 'LITTLE AUDREY' To 384BG			To BAD 15 Mar 44	
41-24561	303BG 'THE DUTCHESS'			Ass 31 Mar 44	
41-24562	303BG 'SKY WOLF'	MIA 11 Jan 44			
41-24577	303BG 'HELLS ANGELS'	RET to U.S.A. 20 Jan 44			
41-24578	305BG 'OLD RELIABLE' To 384BG			To BAD 15 Mar 44	
41-24586	305BG 'WHAM BAM'			To BAD 20 Mar 44	
41-24587	303BG 'BAD CHECK'	MIA 11 Jan 44			
41-24605	303BG 'KNOCK OUT DROPPER'			Ass 31 Mar 44	
41-24614	305BG 'WE THE PEOPLE'			Ass 31 Mar 44	
41-24615	305BG 'TARGET FOR TONITE'			To BAD 22 Mar 44	
41-24616	305BG 'SAMS LITTLE HELPER'			To BAD 21 Mar 44	
41-24619	303BG 'S FOR SUGAR'	MIA 11 Jan 44			

305th BOMBARDMENT GROUP (H)

Constituted as the 305th BOMBARDMENT GROUP (H) on 25th January 1942
Activated on 1st March 1942
Squadrons Assigned: 364th, 365th, 366th and 422nd
Assigned to Eighth Air Force: 21st August 1942
Assigned to First Bombardment Wing: October 1942

COMBAT WING ASSIGNMENTS

Second Provisional: 13th December 1942
102nd Provisional Bombardment: 3rd January 1943
40th Combat Bombardment: 16th September 1943

STATIONS

Grafton Underwood: Air Echelon in from 27th October 1942
Ground Echelon in 12th September 1942
Chelveston: From 26th November 1942

After training on B-17Es, the air echelon moved by train from Tucson to Syracuse, New York. Some crews went to Cheyenne where they were to pick up new aircraft but these were not available so they travelled on to Syracuse by train.

The first new B-17F was delivered to the Group at Syracuse on 14th September 1942 and the last arrived on 14th October. The aircraft came from the Depots and Modification Centers at Ogden, Tucson, Tulsa, Lowry, Denver and Cheyenne.

Although mostly of Boeing manufacture the new inventory included a single Douglas built aircraft (42-2969) and 42-5713 from Vega, the first from this manufacturer to be assigned to a Group in the Eighth Air Force. The Group thus became the first to have aircraft from all three manufacturers assigned.

The ground echelon moved to Fort Dix on 23rd August 1942 and boarded the liner *Queen Mary* at New York. They arrived at Greenock, Scotland on 11th September and were taken by train to Grafton Underwood.

The air echelon departed Syracuse for Presque Isle on 19th October and then flew on to Gander and Prestwick. First aircraft to reach the Group's new base at Grafton Underwood were from 366th Bomb Squadron, the first one landing at 1151 hours on 27th October with most of the Group following on that day but some were delayed by weather along the route and did not arrive until early November.

Two 366th Bomb Squadron aircraft were lost on the flight from the USA. 41-24530 crashed while making a night take off at Gander and 42-5059 came down in the sea off Nova Scotia. Both crews were able to return to Presque Isle and pick up new aircraft to ferry to England.

On arrival in England, several aircraft were transferred to the 97th Bomb Group and the 305th received five B-17Es in return. Included in the transfer were the Douglas and Vega built planes and so the Group became an all Boeing equipped unit, a status it would maintain for nearly three months.

'**WHAM BAM**' 41-24586 was one of the four originals still assigned to the 305th in 1944. It was among several B-17Fs that left the Group in late March 1944 for return to the USA *Mike Gibson*

ORIGINAL B-17Fs ASSIGNED AT SYRACUSE BETWEEN 14th SEP and 14th Oct 1942							
41-24467	422BS	41-24573	365BS	41-24593	364BS	41-24624	366BS
41-24525	422BS	41-24575	365BS	41-24601	365BS	42-2969	366BS (Dgls)
41-24529	422BS	41-24576	365BS	41-24604	366BS	42-5056	364BS
41-24532	422BS	41-24578	365BS	41-24611	422BS	42-5057	364BS
41-24533	365BS	41-24586	365BS	41-24614	422BS	42-5058	364BS
41-24530	366BS (2)	41-24588	364BS	41-24615	422BS	42-5059	366BS (1)
41-24553	422BS	41-24590	364BS	41-24616	422BS	42-5078	366BS
41-24564	365BS	41-24591	366BS	41-24617	364BS	42-5713	366BS(Vega)
41-24572	364BS	41-24592	366BS	41-24623	365BS		
(1) Force landed off Nova Scotia 26 Oct 42:		(2) Crashed on TO at Gander 25 Oct 42					

305th Bomb Group(H)

1942	1943	1944	G
July Aug Sep Oct Nov Dec	Jan Feb Mar Apr May June July Aug Sep Oct Nov Dec	Jan Feb Mar	

Serial No	Gained From — Period Assigned — Lost To

B-17E

Serial No	
41-2628	Burtonwood 29 May 43 — Ass 31 Mar 44
41-2629	97BG 6 Nov 42 — 92BG 14 Dec 42
41-9017	97BG 6 Nov 42 — 92BG 6 Dec 42
41-9019	97BG 6 Nov 42 — Lost to and date unknown, later 92BG
41-9030	97BG 6 Nov 42 — 92BG 2 Dec 42
41-9129	97BG 6 Nov 42 — 92BG

B-17F Boeing

Serial No	
41-24359	305BG 25 Nov 42 — 92BG 17 Apr 43
41-24365	New Rpt 6 Apr 43 — Warton 7 Nov 43 then 2 CCRC
41-24467	Orig Act — 306BG
41-24525	Orig Act — 384BG 22 Sep 43
41-24529	Orig Act — 384BG 22 Sep 43
41-24530	Orig Act — Crashed 25 Oct 42 at Gander
41-24532	Orig Act — 92BG 4 Nov 42
41-24533	Orig Act — MIA 22 June 43
41-24553	Orig Act — MIA 6 Dec 42 First Group Act MIA
41-24564	Orig Act — MIA 17 Aug 43
41-24572	Orig Act — 97BG 4 Nov 42
41-24573	Orig Act — MIA 19 May 43
41-24575	Orig Act — 384BG 19 Sep 43
41-24576	Orig Act — 97BG 4 Nov 42
41-24578	Orig Act — 384BG 7 Oct 43
41-24586	Orig Act — Bwd 20 Mar 44
41-24588	Orig Act — MIA 8 Mar 43
41-24590	Orig Act — MIA 19 May 43
41-24591	Orig Act — MIA 6 Sep 43
41-24592	Orig Act — MIA 6 Sep 43
41-24593	Orig Act — MIA 4 Feb 43
41-24601	Orig Act — MIA 13 Jan 43
41-24604	Orig Act — MIA 26 Jan 43
41-24611	Orig Act — MIA 16 Feb 43
41-24614	Orig Act — Ass 31 Mar 44
41-24615	Orig Act — Bwd 22 Mar 44
41-24616	Orig Act — Bwd 21 Mar 44
41-24617	Orig Act — Crashed 31 Mar 43 (1 Apr 43)
41-24623	Orig Act — MIA 26 Feb 43
41-24624	Orig Act — MIA 19 May 43
41-24637	New Rpt 12 Dec 42 — MIA 27 Jan 43

Original Aircraft Ass at Syracuse 14 Sep to 14 Oct 42

B-17F Douglas

Serial No	
42-2969	Orig Act — 97BG 4 Nov 42
42-3037	95BG 1 Aug 43 — 384BG 20 Sep 43
42-3048	New Rpt 21 Mar 43 — 381BG 22 Aug 43
42-3049	New Rpt 25 Mar 43 — MIA 14 July 43
42-3051	New Rpt 31 May 43 — 384BG 19 Sep 43
42-3087	95BG 25 Mar 43 — 306BG 11 Apr 43
42-3091	95BG 17 June 43 — MIA 4 Oct 43
42-3181	95BG 1 Aug 43 — Ass 31 Mar 44
42-3195	MIA 14 Oct 43
42-3207	94BG 14 July 43 — Ass 31 Mar 44
42-3387	New Rpt 30 Aug 43 — MIA 26 Nov 43
42-3412	New Rpt 30 Aug 43 — MIA 21 Dec 43
42-3434	New Rpt 12 Aug 43 — MIA 6 Sep 43 Switzerland
42-3436	New Rpt 18 Sep 43 — MIA 14 Oct 43

305th Bomb Group(H)	1942 July Aug Sep Oct Nov Dec	1943 Jan Feb Mar Apr May June July Aug Sep Oct Nov Dec	1944 Jan Feb Mar	G

Serial No	Gained From	Period Assigned	Lost To

B-17G Douglas

Serial No	Event
42-3531	New Rpt 17 Sep 43 — MIA 26 Nov 43
42-3549	New Rpt 1 Oct 43 — MIA 14 Oct 43
42-3550	New Rpt 1 Oct 43 — MIA 14 Oct 43

B-17F Boeing

Serial No	Event
42-5052	New Rpt 8 Nov 42 — AFSC then 306BG
42-5053	MIA 4 July 43
42-5056	Orig Act — MIA 26 Feb 43
42-5057	Orig Act — MIA 6 Sep 43
42-5058	ORig Act — MIA 16 Feb 43
42-5059	Orig Act — Force landed in sea off Novia Scotia 26 Oct 42
42-5060	MIA 4 Feb 43
42-5063	MIA 17 May 43
42-5078	Orig Ac — MIA 30 Dec 42
42-5125	New Rpt 17 Dec 42 — MIA 13 June 43
42-5146	New Rpt 12 Dec 42 — MIA 4 Apr 43
42-5155	New Rpt 21 Mar 43 — MIA 19 May 43
42-5156	BAD 20 Mar 44
42-5219	New Rpt 18 Feb 43 — MIA 17 May 43
42-5220	New Rpt 25 Mar 43 — MIA 16 Apr 43
42-5232	New Rpt 12 Dec 42 — MIA 4 Apr 43
42-5253	MIA 4 Apr 43
42-5376	New Rpt 25 Feb 43 — Crashed 31 Aug 43
42-5435	New Rpt 25 Feb 43 — MIA 1 May 43

B-17F Vega

Serial No	Event
42-5713	Orig Act — 97BG 4 Nov 42. First Vega Built B-17 Ass to 8AF
42-5725	New Rpt 8 Feb 43 — 381BG 22 Aug 43
42-5745	Out 17 Apr 43 Then to 92BG 20 Apr 43
42-5747	New Rpt 25 Mar 43 — 381BG 22 Aug 43
42-5793	New Rpt 17 Mar 43 — Out 18 Apr 43 then to 92BG 23 Apr 43
42-5910	New Rpt 10 June 43 — Crash Landed 15 Sep 43 (16 Sep 43)
42-6174	New Rpt 7 Nov 43 — Ass 31 Mar 44

B-17F Boeing

Serial No	Event
42-29499	New Rpt 7 Mar 43 — MIA 25 June 43
42-29506	New Rpt 2 Mar 43 — 381BG 22 Aug 43
42-29508	New Rpt 6 Apr 43 — Sal after fire 26 Aug 43
42-29529	New Rpt — 384BG 6 Nov 43
42-29530	New Rpt 8 Apr 43 — MIA 27 Aug 43
42-29531	New Rpt 8 Apr 43 — MIA 29 May 43
42-29553	New Rpt 4 Mar 43 — MIA 12 Aug 43
42-29555	New Rpt 6 Apr 43 — MIA 27 Sep 43, On night Mission
42-29557	New Rpt 25 Feb 43 — 384BG 20 Sep 43
42-29632	26 June 43 — 384BG 8 Oct 43
42-29633	New Rpt — 381BG 11 Sep 43
42-29634	New Rpt 21 Mar 43 — Bovingdon 30 June 43 (1 CCRC)
42-29636	New Rpt 24 Mar 43 — 384BG 30 Sep 43
42-29641	New Rpt 21 Mar 43 — MIA 4 July 43
42-29647	New Rpt 8 Apr 43 — MIA 13 May 43
42-29663	New Rpt 2 Mar 43 — MIA 17 May 43
42-29673	New Rpt 6 Apr 43 — Sal after Dam on Op Miss 15 May 43 (16 May 43)
42-29688	New Rpt 17 Mar 43 — 384 BG 6 Nov 43
42-29690	94BG 14 July 43 — Sal after Op Miss 29 July 43

305th Bomb Group(H)	1943 Apr May Jun Jly Aug Sep Oct Nov Dec	1944 Jan Feb Mar	△G

Serial No	Gained From	Period Assigned	Lost To
42-29733	94BG 14 July 43	384BG 6 Nov 43	
42-29742	* MIA 29 May 43	* New Rpt 8 Apr 43	
42-29745	* MIA 17 May 43	* New Rpt 16 Apr 43	
42-29776	BAD 19 July 43 92BG 22 July 43		
42-29784	* 18 May 43 381BG 11 Sep 43	* New Rpt	
42-29792	* MIA 29 may 43	* New Rpt 8 Apr 43	
42-29800	95BG 17 June 43 384BG 7 Oct 43		
42-29802	BAD 19 July 43 92BG 22 July 43		
42-29803	95BG 17 June 43 381BG 11 Sep 43		
42-29807	95BG 17 June 43 MIA 19 Aug 43		
42-29819	* DS to Burtonwood 3 May 43. To AFSC 18 May 43	No further record.	* New Rpt 16 Apr 43
42-29832	* 18 May 43 381BG 22 Aug 43	* New Rpt	
42-29867	Lt Stm 12 July 43 381BG 22 Aug 43		
42-29870	New Rpt 23 June 43 384BG 29 Sep 43		
42-29923	* 18 May 43 381BG 11 Sep 43	* New Rpt	
42-29943	New Rpt 15 June 43 95BG 16 June 43		
42-29952	AFSC 31 May 43 + MIA 14 Oct 43	(Originally 96BG)	+ Out to AFSC for Rep 29 July to 16 Aug 43.
42-29953	381BG 22 Aug 43 Crashed 15 Nov 43		
42-29970	94BG 14 July 43 MIA 28 July 43		
42-29987	* 18 May 43 384BG 19 Sep 43		
42-29988	381BG 22 Aug 43 MIA 14 oct 43		
42-30004	381BG 22 Aug 43 MIA 6 Sep 43		
42-30015	381BG 22 Aug 43 MIA 26 Nov 43		
42-30018	381BG 22 Aug 43		BAD 20 Mar 44
42-30034	381BG 22 Aug 43 ○		Ass 31 Mar 44
42-30155	New Rpt 31 May 43 MIA 5 Jan 44		
42-30159	* 24 May 43 MIA 17 Aug 43	* New Rpt	○ With 100 Group R.A.F. 28 Dec 43 to 13 Jan 44.
42-30242	New Rpt 10 June 43 MIA 14 Oct 43		
42-30282	New Rpt 10 June 43 MIA 26 July 43		
42-30305	New Rpt 24 June 43 100BG 30 June 43		
42-30375	New Rpt 3 Sep 43		Ass 31 Mar 44
42-30386	New Rpt 6 Sep 43 MIA 7 Jan 44		
42-30422	New Rpt 12 Aug 43		Ass 31 Mar 44
42-30643	New Rpt 2 Sep 43	Acc 29 Jan 44 (31 Jan 44)	
42-30645	New Rpt 22 Aug 43 MIA 26 Nov 43		
42-30647	New Rpt 17 Aug 43 Crashed 23 Sep 43		
42-30650	New Rpt 12 Aug 43		BAD 20 Mar 44
42-30652	New Rpt 15 Sep 43		BAD 20 Mar 44
42-30656	New Rpt 1 Oct 43		Ass 31 Mar 44
42-30666	New Rpt 18 Sep 43 Crashed 15 Nov 43		
42-30678	New Rpt 6 Sep 43	MIA 25 Feb 44	
42-30704	New Rpt 18 Sep 43		Ass 31 Mar 44
42-30724	New Rpt 31 Aug 43 MIA 5 Jan 44		
42-30775	New Rpt 18 Sep 43		Ass 31 Mar 44
42-30791	New Rpt 1 Oct 43		Ass 31 Mar 44
42-30804	New Rpt 18 Sep 43 MIA 14 Oct 43		
42-30807	New Rpt 18 Sep 43 MIA 14 Oct 43		
42-30809	New Rpt 6 Sep 43	R.A.F. 22 Feb 44	
42-30814	New Rpt 21 Sep 43 MIA 14 Oct 43		
42-30831	New Rpt 15 Sep 43 MIA 14 Oct 43		
42-30838	New Rpt 1 Oct 43		Ass 31 Mar 44
42-31019	New Rpt 18 Oct 43		BAD 20 Mar 44

Serial No	Gained From — Period Assigned — Lost To

B-17G Boeing

Serial No	Notes
42-31032	New Rpt 25 Nov 43 — Ass 31 Mar 44
42-31046	New Rpt 18 Oct 43 — MIA 26 Nov 43
42-31255	New Rpt 3 Dec 43 — Ass 31 Mar 44
42-31308	New Rpt 23 Nov 43 — MIA 24 Feb 44
42-31322	New Rpt 30 Jan 44 — Crashed 22 Feb 44 (25 Feb 44)
42-31328	New Rpt 22 Dec 43 — MIA 25 Feb 44
42-31342	New Rpt 3 Dec 43 — Ass 31 Mar 44
42-31365	New Rpt 3 Jan 44 — Ass 31 Mar 44
42-31402	New Rpt 22 Dec 43 — Ass 31 Mar 44
42-31409	New Rpt 22 Jan 44 — MIA 22 Feb 44
42-31427	New Rpt 21 Dec 43 — Ass 31 Mar 44
42-31430	New Rpt 6 Jan 44 — MIA 20 Feb 44
42-31461	New Rpt 28 Dec 43 — MIA 30 Jan 44
42-31475	New Rpt 28 Dec 43 — Ass 31 Mar 44
42-31480	New Rpt 22 Dec 43 — Ass 31 Mar 44
42-31501	New Rpt 24 Dec 43 — Ass 31 Mar 44
42-31528	New Rpt 28 Dec 43 — Crashed 31 dec 43 (3 Jan 44)
42-31544	New Rpt 21 Jan 44 — MIA 24 Mar 44
42-31602	New Rpt 22 Feb 44 — MIA 23 Mar 44
42-31611	New Rpt 29 Jan 44 — Ass 31 Mar 44
42-31794	New Rpt 22 Feb 44 — Ass 31 Mar 44
42-31801	H2X Acft — 482BG 20 Mar 44 — Ass 31 Mar 44
42-31816	New Rpt 15 Feb 44 — Ass 31 Mar 44
42-31820	New Rpt 22 Feb 44 — MIA 25 Feb 44

B-17G Douglas

Serial No	Notes
42-37717	New Rpt 20 Dec 43 — Ass 31 Mar 44
42-37726	New Rpt 1 Oct 43 — Ass 31 Mar 44
42-37740	New Rpt 15 Sep 43 — MIA 14 Oct 43
42-37741	New Rpt 18 Sep 43 — MIA 4 Oct 43. First Group and First Division B-17G MIA.
42-37750	New Rpt 18 Sep 43 — MIA 14 Oct 43
42-37751	New Rpt 16 Sep 43 — MIA 8 Oct 43
42-37771	New Rpt 18 Oct 43 — Ass 31 Mar 44
42-37778	New Rpt 30 Nov 43 — Ass 31 Mar 44
42-37793	New Rpt 23 Nov 43 — 384 BG 2 Dec 43
42-37870	New Rpt 23 Nov 43 — Ass 31 Mar 44
42-37881	New Rpt 23 Nov 43 — Ass 31 Mar 44
42-37930	New Rpt 3 Dec 43 — MIA 20 Dec 43
42-37931	New Rpt 5 Jan 44 — Ass 31 Mar 44
42-37944	New Rpt 12 Dec 43 — Ass 31 Mar 44
42-37945	New Rpt 21 Dec 43 — Ass 31 Mar 44
42-37957	New Rpt 12 Dec 43 — MIA 22 Mar 44
42-37978	New Rpt 5 Jan 44 — Ass 31 Mar 44
42-37979	New Rpt 5 jan 44 — Ass 31 Mar 44
42-37999	482BG 10 Dec 43 — Sal (6 Mar 44) reason Unknown
42-38037	New Rpt 22 Jan 44 — Ass 31 Mar 44
42-38098	New Rpt 22 Feb 44 — Ass 31 Mar 44
42-38106	New Rpt 16 Feb 44 — MIA 29 Mar 44
42-38108	New Rpt 16 Feb 44 — MIA 29 Mar 44
42-38109	Stansted 10 Feb 44 — Cr Landed 20 Feb 44 (23 Feb 44)
42-38149	New Rpt 22 Feb 44 — Ass 31 Mar 44
42-38167	New Rpt 22 Feb 44 — Ass 31 Mar 44
42-38176	New Rpt 16 Feb 44 — Ass 31 Mar 44
42-38206	New Rpt 1 Mar 44 — Ass 31 Mar 44

305th Bomb Group(H)		1943			1944			G
		Oct	Nov	Dec	Jan	Feb	Mar	
Serial No		Gained From ▨▨ Period Assigned ▨▨ Lost To						

B-17G Vega

Serial No		Gained / Period	Lost To
42-39766	(H2X)	482BG 25 mar 44	Ass 31 Mar 44
42-39790	N R 18 Oct 43		Ass 31 Mar 44
42-39811	N R 19 Oct 43		Ass 31 Mar 44
42-39818	N R 19 Oct 43		Ass 31 Mar 44
42-39829	N R 18 Oct 43		Ass 31 Mar 44
42-39832	N R 18 Oct 43		Ass 31 Mar 44
42-39843	N R 16 Oct 43		Ass 31 Mar 44
42-39878		New Rpt 3 Jan 44	Ass 31 Mar 44
42-39944		New Rpt 3 Dec 43	MIA 2 Mar 44
42-39947		New Rpt 39947	Ass 31 Mar 44
42-39948		New Rpt 3 Dec 43	Ass 31 Mar 44
42-39949		New Rpt 30 Nov 43	Ass 31 Mar 44
42-39957		New Rpt 12 Dec 43 Dam on Op Miss 11 Jan 44. Sal (16 Jan 44)	
42-39966		New Rpt 5 Jan 44	Ass 31 Mar 44
42-39992		New Rpt 21 Jan 44	Ass 31 Mar 44
42-40018	(H2X)	482BG 20 Mar 44	Ass 31 Mar 44
42-40020		New Rpt 22 Jan 44 MIA 8 Feb 44	

B-17G Boeing

Serial No		Gained / Period	Lost To
42-97077		New Rpt 31 Mar 44	Ass 31 Mar 44
42-97097	NMF	New Rpt 31 Mar 44	Ass 31 Mar 44
42-97321		New Rpt 31 Mar 44	Ass 31 Mar 44

B-17G Vega

Serial No		Gained / Period	Lost To
42-97466		New Rpt 8 Feb 44	MIA 29 Mar 44
42-97475		Stansted 11 Feb 44	Ass 31 Mar 44
42-97500		New Rpt 22 Jan 44 MIA 20 Feb 44	
42-97514	(H2X)	482BG 20 Mar 44	Ass 31 Mar 44
42-97523	(H2X)	482BG 20 Mar 44	MIA 22 Mar 44
42-97532	(H2X)	482BG 26 Mar 44	Ass 31 Mar 44
42-97533	(H2X)	482BG 20 Mar 44	Ass 31 Mar 44
42-97543	(H2X)	Some or all	482BG 20 Mar 44	Ass 31 Mar 44
42-97557	(H2X)	Camouflaged	482BG 20 Mar 44	Ass 31 Mar 44
42-97574	(H2X) NMF	after	482BG 20 Mar 44	Ass 31 Mar 44
42-97578	(H2X)	arrival	482BG 20 Mar 44	Crashed 24 Mar 44
42-97592	(H2X)	in U.K.	482BG 20 Mar 44	Ass 31 Mar 44

	1943											1944		
	Jan	Feb	Mar	Apr	May	June	July	Aug	Sep	Oct	Nov	Dec	Jan	Feb	Mar
Serial No	Gained From ▨▨ Period Assigned ▨▨ Lost To													

DB-7B Douglas

Serial No		Gained / Period	Lost To
AL409		92BG 13 Oct 43	306BG 28 Jan 44
AL496	Unknown	92BG 31 May 43	

Airspeed Oxford

Serial No		Gained / Period	Lost To
LB522		92BG 1 Aug 43	482BG 25 Dec 43

305th BOMBARDMENT GROUP (H)

AIRCRAFT AND OPERATIONAL STATISTICS

Total Aircraft Assigned

B-17E:	November 1942	5	DB-7B: 1942/1943 to 28 Jan 44	2
	29 May 43 to 31 Mar 44	1	Oxford: 1 Aug 43 to 25 Dec 43	1
B-17F:	14 Sep 42 to 31 Mar 44	140		
B-17G:	15 Sep 43 to 31 Mar 44	87		

Operational Statistics

First Mission flown on: 17 Nov 42
First Act MIA: 41-24553 on 6 Dec 42
First B-17G Ass: 42-37740 on 15 Sep 43
First B-17G MIA: 42-37741 on 4 Oct 43
First NMF Ass: Five, 42-97543, 97557, 97574, 97578 and 97592 Ass on 20 Mar 44 were NMF ex factory but may have been painted OD in U.K. Three more 42-97077, 97097, and 97321 Ass on 31 Mar 44, were probably first used in action.

Total Act MIA: 90 (66 B-17F: 24 B-17G)
Highest Days Losses: 13 On 14 Oct 43
Other Losses: 17 B-17s
    B-17F: 11 (6 Op, 4 Non Op, 1 Unknown)
    B-17G: 6 All Op losses

Four of the Group's original aircraft survived into 1944. 41-24586 'WHAM BAM': 41-24614 'WE THE PEOPLE': 41-24615 'TARGET FOR TONITE' and 41-24616 'SAMS LITTLE HELPER'. These four had escaped being transferred out in September/October 1943 when the other aircraft without Tokyo tanks had gone. 'WHAM BAM' had been on training status since November 1943 and the other three were in the 422nd Bomb Squadron. Only 'WE THE PEOPLE' would remain at 31st March, the other three having been transferred out for re-deployment to the USA on the 20th March. The longest serving replacement aircraft still assigned on 31st March was 42-3207 'MONKEY'S UNCLE' which had come from the 94th Bomb Group on 14th July 1943.

SHORT SERVING AIRCRAFT: ASSIGNED FOR LESS THAN EIGHT DAYS

Serial No	Date In	Date Out	Reason Out	Days Ass
42-29776	19 July 43	22 July 43	To 92BG	3
42-29802	19 July 43	22 July 43	To 92BG	3
42-29943	15 June 43	16 June 43	To 95BG	1
42-30305	24 June 43	30 June 43	To 100BG	6
42-31528	28 Dec 43	31 Dec 43	Crashed	3(6)
42-31820	22 Feb 44	25 Feb 44	MIA	3
42-97523	20 Mar 44	22 Mar 44	MIA	2
42-97578	20 Mar 44	24 Mar 44	Crashed	4

LONG SERVING AIRCRAFT: ASSIGNED FOR ONE YEAR OR MORE

Serial No	Date In	Date Out	Reason Out	Months Ass
41-24578	Orig Act	7 Oct 43	To 384BG	12
41-24586	Orig Act	20 Mar 44	To BAD	16
41-24614	Orig Act	Still Ass		18
41-24615	Orig Act	22 Mar 44	To BAD	17
41-24616	Orig Act	21 Mar 44	To BAD	17

STATUS OF AIRCRAFT ASSIGNED AT 2000 HOURS on 31st MARCH 1944

Operational: 66 B-17 (11 B-17F: 55 B-17G)
Non Operational: 2 (1 B-17E: 1 B-17F)
Operational Aircraft Assigned and on hand at Chelveston

B-17F

41-24614 *(Orig Act)	42-3181	42-6174	42-30422	42-30775
	42-3207		42-30656	42-30791
		42-30375	42-30704	42-30838

B-17G

42-31032	42-31801 H2X	42-37945	42-39811	42-97077 NMF
42-31255	42-31816	42-37978	42-39818	42-97097 NMF
42-31342		42-37979	42-39829	42-97321 NMF
42-31365	42-37717	42-38037	42-39832	
42-31402	42-37726	42-38098	42-39843	42-97475
42-31427	42-37771	42-38149	42-39878	42-97514 H2X
42-31475	42-37778	42-38167	42-39947	42-97532 H2X
42-31480	42-37870	42-38176	42-39948	42-97533 H2X
42-31501	42-37881	42-38206	42-39966	42-97543 NMF H2X (2)
42-31611 (1)	42-37931		42-39992	42-97557 NMF H2X (2)
42-31794	42-37944	42-39766 H2X	42-40018 H2X	42-97574 NMF H2X (2)
		42-39790		42-97592 NMF H2X (2)

Assigned but not on hand: B-17G 42-39949: At 2 SAD

Non Operational Aircraft on hand at Chelveston: B-17E 41-2628: B-17F 42-30034

(1) Gp had reported 42-31611 as MIA on 29 Mar 44 in error for 42-97466. This was corrected on 2 Apr 44

(2) These Four Aircraft probably painted OD after arrival in UK

* 41-24614 without Tokyo tanks

306th BOMBARDMENT GROUP (H)

Constituted as the 306th BOMBARDMENT GROUP (H) on 28th January 1942
Activated on 1st March 1942
Squadrons Assigned: 367th, 368th, 369th and 423rd
Assigned to Eighth Air Force: About 1st August 1942
Assigned to First Bombardment Wing: September 1942

COMBAT WING ASSIGNMENTS

First Provisional: 13th December 1942
101st Provisional Bombardment: 3rd January 1943
102nd Provisional Bombardment: 18th May 1943
40th Combat Bombardment: 16th September 1943

STATION

Thurleigh: Air Echelon in 7th to 12th September 1942
Ground Echelon in 6th September 1942

Trained on B-17Es at Wendover, Utah. In early July 1942 many crews were sent to Westover, Massachusetts, to ferry B-17Es, handed over by the 301st Bomb Group back to Wendover and by 21st July about 40 B-17Es were on hand.

The air echelon left Wendover on 1st August for Westover, stopping at Chanute Field, Illinois, on the way, and arriving at Westover on 2nd and 3rd August.

The ground echelon left Wendover on 1st August for Richmond, Virginia, arriving on the 5th and left for Fort Dix on the 13th. On 30th the ground echelon boarded the *Queen Elizabeth* in New York and next day sailed for England, arriving at Gourock, Scotland on 5th September. On the 6th and 7th, they trained down to Thurleigh.

The first B-17F for the air echelon arrived at Westover on 15th August,

and by 28th August, 35 were assigned. The new planes came from the Air Depots at San Antonio, Middletown and Ogden and were all from the Boeing factory.

The air echelon left Westover on 1st September and flew by way of Presque Isle and Gander, to Prestwick and then on to Thurleigh. The first aircraft arrived at Thurleigh on the 8th September and the movement was completed by the 13th.

One of the new B-17Fs, 41-24462, was damaged before leaving the USA and had to be replaced, another, 41-24463, exploded in mid air 150 miles out from Gander and was lost with all its crew, and 41-24516 ditched in the Irish Sea at the end of the flight from Gander, but all the crew were saved.

'BANSHEE' 41-24488, an original of the 306th Bomb Group, was one of ten planes the Group lost on 17th April 1943. *306th Historical Association*

ORIGINAL B-17Fs ASSIGNED AT WESTOVER BETWEEN 15th and 28th AUGUST 1942

41-24460	423BS	41-24471	369BS	41-24489	367BS	41-24502	368BS
41-24461	369BS	41-24472	369BS	41-24491	423BS	41-24507	368BS
41-24462	369BS (1)	41-24474	367BS	41-24492	367BS	41-24508	423BS
41-24463	423BS (3)	41-24475	423BS	41-24493	368BS	41-24509	423BS
41-24464	367BS	41-24476	423BS	41-24494	367BS	41-24510	423BS
41-24465	368BS	41-24478	369BS	41-24495	367BS	41-24511	423BS
41-24466	368BS	41-24486	367BS	41-24496	423BS	41-24514	368BS
41-24468	369BS	41-24487	368BS	41-24498	369BS	41-24516	368BS (4)
41-24469	367BS	41-24488	369BS	41-24501	368BS	41-24470	369BS (2)

(1) 41-24462: Tail wheel collapsed about 5th Sep, Act did not go overseas with Group

(2) 41-24470: It is believed this Act replaced 41-24462

(3) 41-24463: Lost over Atlantic 5 Sep 42

(4) 41-24516: Ditched in Irish sea on arrival from Gander, 12 Sep 42

306th Bomb Group(H)	1942	1943	1944	H

Months across top: July Aug Sep Oct Nov Dec | Jan Feb Mar Apr May June July Aug Sep Oct Nov Dec | Jan Feb Mar

Serial No	Gained From	Period Assigned	Lost To

B-17E

Serial No	Notes
41-9148	92BG 1 May 43 — Ass 31 Mar 44

B-17F Boeing

Serial No		Notes
41-24417		97BG Bwd 26 Feb 43 — Ditched 26 July 43 (Not listed as MIA)
41-24460	Orig Act	482BG 22 Sep 43
41-24461	Orig Act	Sal 27 Feb 43, reason unknown
41-24462	Orig Act	Acc in U.S.A. Not to England
41-24463	Orig Act	Crashed in Atlantic 5 Sep 42
41-24464	Orig Act	91BG
41-24465	Orig Act	MIA 5 Apr 43
41-24466	Orig Act	SBA Trainer 11 Apr 43. To AFSC 16 Apr 43, later to 11CCRC
41-24467		305BG AFSC — MIA 17 Apr 43
41-24468	Orig Act	AFSC 26 Mar 43 Then to 1CCRC
41-24469	Orig Act	Lost on Non Op flight 6 Jan 43
41-24470	Orig Act	MIA 3 Jan 43
41-24471	Orig Act	MIA 13 Jan 43
41-24472	Orig Act	MIA 8 Nov 42
41-24474	Orig Act	MIA 18 Nov 42
41-24475	Orig Act	Sal 5 Dec 42, reason unknown
41-24476	Orig Act	Wheels up landing 1 Mar 43, Sal
41-24477	Orig Act	97BG Sep 42
41-24478	Orig Act	MIA 23 Nov 42
41-24486	Orig Act	MIA 9 Nov 42
41-24487	Orig Act	Ass 31 Mar 44
41-24488	Orig Act	MIA 17 Apr 43
41-24489	Orig Act	MIA 20 Dec 42
41-24491	Orig Act	MIA Nov 42
41-24492	Orig Act	Crashed 2 Oct 42
41-24493	Orig Act	SBA Trainer 11 Apr 43 to AFSC 16 Apr 43 then unknown
41-24494	Orig Act	Sal after crash landing 9 Nov 42
41-24495	Orig Act	MIA 20 Dec 42
41-24496	Orig Act	Badly Dam on Op Miss 17 Nov 42. Sal on return
41-24498	Orig Act	MIA 13 Jan 43
41-24501	Orig Act	MIA 3 Jan 43
41-24502	Orig Act	Crashed 28 July 43
41-24507	Orig Act	(+) (+) 384BG 22 Aug 43 (+) SBA Trainer 11 Apr 43, To L.Ldg 16Apr 43. Ret to Group 1 July 43 (+)
41-24508	Orig Act	Sal after hitting trees in flight 27 Oct 42
41-24509	Orig Act	MIA 9 Nov 42
41-24510	Orig Act	MIA 9 Oct 42. First Group Act MIA
41-24511	Orig Act	91BG by Feb 43
41-24514	Orig Act	MIA 8 Mar 43
41-24516	Orig Act	Lost in Irish Sea 12 Sep 42
41-24542		Exact dates unknown — Could be wrong serial on records
41-24557	New Rpt 28 Nov 42	384BG 22 Aug 43
41-24560	New Rpt 28 Nov 42	384BG 5 Sep 43
41-24629	New Rpt 28 Feb 43	303BG 25 Sep 43

B-17F Douglas

Serial No		Notes
42-2975	New Rpt 29 Nov 42	MIA 30 Dec 42, First Douglas built MIA.
42-2978		381BG 19 Nov 43
42-3034	New Rpt 12 Mar 43	MIA 17 Apr 43
42-3040	303BG 17 Apr 43	Lt Stn 18June 43 then 91BG (not Ass 21-29 May)
42-3041	303BG 17 Apr 43	384BG 22 Aug 43
42-3074	(At Burtonwood 30 Nov 43 to 2 Feb 44)	384BG 22 Aug 43 — Cheddington 29 Feb 44
42-3076	New Rpt 20 Apr 43	Sal Hawkhinge 28 July 43

306th Bomb Group(H)

1942	1943	1944	H
Oct Nov Dec	Jan Feb Mar Apr May June July Aug Sep Oct Nov Dec	Jan Feb Mar	

Serial No	Gained From — Period Assigned — Lost To
42-3084	New Rpt 10 Apr 43 — MIA 29 July 43
42-3087	305BG 11 Apr 43 — 384BG 4 Sep 43
42-3127	New Rpt 5 May 43 — MIA 21 May 43. With 94BG Crew. Not listed as MIA in 1st BW.
42-3142	New Rpt 18 May 43 — Crashed 13 Nov 43
42-3167	New Rpt 19 Apr 43 — AFSC 16 June 43 Then 379BG
42-3169	(Not Ass 30 June to 13 July) 18 June 43 — R.A.F. 3 Feb 44
42-3172	New Rpt 5 May 43 — AFSC for Rep 25 June 43 Then 91BG
42-3198	New Rpt 5 May 43 — AFSC 15 May 43. Then 92BG
42-3209	New Rpt 23 May 43 — MIA 22 June 43
42-3214	New Rpt 5 May 43 — MIA 21 May 43
42-3274	New Rpt 4 June 43 — AFSC for Rep 29 June 43. Then 91BG
42-3301	New Rpt 21 Sep 43 — Cheddington 29 Feb 44
42-3363	New Rpt 14 Aug 43 — MIA 22 Dec 43
42-3382	482BG – Stansted 22 Feb 44 — Ass 31 Mar 44
42-3406	New Rpt 4 Aug 43 — MIA 12 Aug 43
42-3449	New Rpt 14 Aug 43 — Crashed 24 Sep 43

B-17G Douglas

Serial No	
42-3515	New Rpt 21 Sep 43 — L Ldg 25 Mar 44
42-3520	New Rpt 16 Sep 43 — Crashed 29 Nov 43 (30 Nov 43)
42-3521	482BG – Stansted 22 Feb 44 — Ass 31 Mar 44
42-3527	482BG – Stansted 22 Feb 44 — Ass 31 Mar 44
42-3533	New Rpt 21 Sep 43 — MIA 3 Nov 43

B-17F Boeing

Serial No	
42-5052	New Rpt 19 Apr 43 — 303BG 25 Sep 43
42-5054	5 Aug 43 — 303BG 25 Sep 43
42-5055	New Rpt 7 May 43 — MIA 15 May 43
42-5071	N R 30 Nov 42 — MIA 20 Dec 42
42-5072	N R 28 Nov 42 — MIA 5 Apr 43
42-5086	N R 29 Nov 42 — 384BG 5 Sep 43
42-5129	N R 2 Dec 42 — MIA 4 Mar 43
42-5130	NR 29 Nov 42 — MIA 6 Mar 43
42-5171	N R 8 Dec 42 — MIA 17 Apr 43
42-5175	NR 28 Nov 42 — MIA 16 Feb 43
42-5180	NR 28 Nov 42 — MIA 25 June 43
42-5218	New Rpt 25 Feb 43 — MIA 13 June 43
42-5251	Date in Unknown — MIA 17 Apr 43
42-5306	Date in Unknown — 303BG 25 Sep 43
42-5378	Date in Unknown — MIA 6 Mar 43
42-5394	New Rpt 2 Mar 43 — MIA 17 Apr 43
42-5404	Date in Unknown — 384BG 22 Aug 43
42-5407	New Rpt 25 Feb 43 — 91BG 11 Sep 43
42-5422	New Rpt 25 Feb 43 — MIA 1 May 43
42-5426	New Rpt 25 Mar 43 — MIA 29 July 43
42-5428	New Rpt 24 Mar 43 — (+) 91BG 24 Dec 43 (+) Out for
42-5431	New Rpt 25 Feb 43 — MIA 5 Apr 43 — Rep 6 Sep to 9 Nov.

B-17F Vega

Serial No	
42-5714	NR 1 Dec 42 — 91BG 11 Sep 43
42-5717	NR 1 Dec 42 — MIA 16 Feb 43
42-5720	Date in Unknown — 384BG 22 Aug 43
42-5729	New Rpt 18 Feb 43 — 91BG 8 Sep 43
42-5766	New Rpt 2 June 43 — MIA 29 July 43
42-5784	New Rpt 12 Mar 43 — MIA 1 May 43
42-5804	96BG – Hitcham – 6 Aug 43 — 91BG 11 Sep 43
42-5826	New Rpt 7 May 43 — MIA 29 July 43
42-5841	New Rpt 22 Apr 43 — MIA 6 Sep 43

Serial No	Gained From / Period Assigned / Lost To
42-5855	384BG 22 Aug 43 — MIA 8 Oct 43
42-5889	384BG 22 Aug 43 — Crash Landed 9 Oct 43

B-17F Boeing

Serial No	Gained From / Period Assigned / Lost To
42-29477	N R 27 Feb 43 — 303BG 25 Sep 43
42-29498	N R 2 Mar 43 — 303BG 25 Sep 43
42-29524	N r 2 Mar 43 — AFSC for Repair 21 May then 303BG
42-29554	New Rpt 25 Mar 43 — 384BG 22 Aug 43
42-29620	303BG 17 Apr 43 — MIA 1 May 43
42-29625	New Rpt 16 Mar 43 — MIA 17 Apr 43
42-29629	New Rpt 12 Mar 43 — 303BG 25 Sep 43
42-29631	New Rpt 25 Mar 43 — MIA 17 Apr 43
42-29643	New Rpt 13 Mar 43 — MIA 17 Apr 43
42-29649	New Rpt 24 Mar 43 — Sal due to Battle Dam after Op Miss 1 May 43. (2 May 43)
42-29658	New Rpt 16 Mar 43 — MIA 17 Apr 43
42-29660	New Rpt 22 Mar 43 — MIA 5 Apr 43
42-29666	New Rpt 25 Mar 43 — MIA 21 May 43 (Ditched)
42-29677	New Rpt 20 Apr 43 — MIA 15 May 43
42-29739	95BG – AFSC 4 Aug 43 — 91BG 11 Sep 43
42-29741	303BG 17 Apr 43 — 91BG 11 Sep 43
42-29744	New Rpt 20 Apr 43 — MIA 15 May 43
42-29777	New Rpt 19 May 43 — MIA 28 July 43
42-29779	New Rpt 4 June 43 — MIA 28 July 43
42-29786	New Rpt 20 Apr 43 — Crashed 20 May 43 (21 May 43)
42-29793	New Rpt 20 Apr 43 — 91BG 11 Sep 43
42-29794	New Rpt 19 Apr 43 — 91BG 11 Sep 43
42-29795	New Rpt 20 Apr 43 — Date out unknown then to 303BG 25 Sep 43
42-29806	New Rpt 19 May 43 — MIA 21 May 43
42-29809	New Rpt 20 Apr 43 — 384BG 4 Sep 43
42-29815	New Rpt 20 Apr 43 — 91BG 14 Sep 43
42-29823	New Rpt 19 Apr 43 — 303BG 26 Sep 43
42-29824	Date in Unknown — AFSC for Rep 30 July 43 then 379BG
42-29894	New Rpt 18 May 43 — 303BG 25 Sep 43
42-29900	New Rpt 23 May 43 — MIA 26 July 43
42-29930	New Rpt 17 June 43 — 303BG 25 Sep 43
42-29937	New Rpt 23 May 43 — AFSC for Rep 27 June 43 then 379BG
42-29959	New Rpt 23 May 43 — MIA 8 Oct 43
42-29971	New Rpt 23 May 43 — MIA 14 Oct 43
42-29974	New Rpt 4 June 43 — Crash Landed 28 July 43
42-29985	384BG 21 Aug 43 — MIA 8 Oct 43
42-29993	New Rpt 19 Apr 43 — MIA 11 Jan 44
42-30065	384BG 22 Aug 43 — Sal after Crash Landing 6 Sep 43 (11 Sep 43)
42-30145	384BG 22 Aug 43 — (+) (+) Ass 31 Mar 44
42-30156	New Rpt 22 June 43 — MIA 26 July 43
42-30163	New Rpt 23 May 43 — MIA 6 Sep 43
42-30175	New Rpt 18 June 43 — MIA 14 Oct 43
42-30199	New Rpt 31 Aug 43 — MIA 14 Oct 43
42-30221	New Rpt 18 June 43 — Crashed in Sea 27 Dec 43
42-30431	New Rpt 19 Oct 43 — Ass 31 Mar 44
42-30451	New Rpt 3 Sep 43 — R.A.F. 3 Feb 44
42-30586	New Rpt 7 Aug 43 — Ass 31 Mar 44
42-30603	New Rpt 7 Aug 43 — MIA 26 Nov 43
42-30606	New Rpt 4 Aug 43 — MIA 4 Aug 44
42-30706	New Rpt 31 Aug 43 — MIA 20 Aug 43
42-30707	New Rpt 31 Aug 43 — MIA 14 Oct 43

(+) To R.A.F. Farnborough 7 Jan to 13 Mar 44 (+)

306th Bomb Group(H)	1943						1944			
	July	Aug	Sep	Oct	Nov	Dec	Jan	Feb	Mar	

Serial No	Gained From ▓▓▓ Period Assigned ▓▓▓ Lost To
42-30710	New Rpt 6 Sep 43 ▓▓▓ MIA 14 Oct 43
42-30714	New Rpt 31 Aug 43 ▓▓▓ Crashed 1 Dec 43
42-30727	New Rpt 2 Sep 43 ▓▓▓ MIA 14 Oct 43
42-30728	New Rpt 2 Sep 43 ▓▓▓ MIA 25 Feb 44
42-30730	New Rpt 20 Sep 43 ▓▓▓ ± + ▓▓▓ Ass 31 Mar 44
42-30767	New Rpt 21 Sep 43 ▓▓▓ Crashed 5 Jan 44
42-30776	New Rpt 20 Sep 43 ▓▓▓ Crashed 3 Nov 43 + At Horsham St Faith for Rep
42-30779	New Rpt 18 Sep 43 ▓▓▓ MIA 14 Oct 43 12 Jan to 7 Feb 44 +
42-30782	New Rpt 2 Sep 43 ▓▓▓ MIA 11 Jan 44
42-30794	New Rpt 2 Sep 43 ▓▓▓ MIA 5 Jan 44
42-30811	New Rpt 2 Sep 43 ▓▓▓ MIA 14 Oct 43
42-30812	New Rpt 4 Sep 43 ▓▓▓ R.A.F. 29 Jan 44
42-30813	new Rpt 2 Sep 43 ▓▓▓ MIA 14 Oct 43
42-30832	New Rpt 18 Sep 43 ▓▓▓ MIA 26 Nov 43
42-30841	New Rpt 19 Sep 43 ▓▓▓ Sal after Mid air Coll. 27 Dec 43
42-30939	New Rpt 21 Oct 43 ▓▓▓ Ass 31 Mar 44
42-31007	New Rpt 21 Oct 43 ▓▓▓ MIA 4 Feb 44
42-31025	New Rpt 19 Oct 43 ▓▓▓ Dam on Op Miss 6 Mar 44 (8 Mar 44)

B-17G Boeing

Serial No	Period Assigned / Lost To
42-31038	New Rpt 19 Oct 43 ▓▓▓ Crashed 13 Nov 43
42-31056	New Rpt 19 Oct 43 ▓▓▓ MIA 3 Feb 44
42-31065	New Rpt 19 Oct 43 ▓▓▓ Ass 31 Mar 44
42-31078	New Rpt 19 Oct 43 ▓▓▓ MIA 11 Dec 43
42-31136	New Rpt 19 Oct 43 ▓▓▓ Dam On Op Miss 11 Jan 44 (12 Jan 44)
42-31139	New Rpt 19 Oct 43 ▓▓▓ MIA 24 Feb 44
42-31143	New Rpt 19 Oct 43 ▓▓▓ Ass 31 Mar 44
42-31158	+ At Foulsham for Rep New Rpt 12 Dec 43 ▓▓▓ + + ▓▓▓ Ass 31 Mar 44
42-31172	12 Jan to 31 Jan 44 + 457BG 12 Mar 44 ▓▓▓ Ass 31 Mar 44
42-31196	New Rpt 14 Dec 43 ▓▓▓ Ass 31 Mar 44
42-31236	New Rpt 21 Dec 43 ▓▓▓ MIA 11 Jan 44
42-31245	New Rpt 14 Dec 43 ▓▓▓ MIA 25 Feb 44
42-31327	New Rpt 12 Dec 43 ▓▓▓ Crashed 31 Dec 43 (1 Jan 44)
42-31363	New Rpt 19 Dec 43 ▓▓▓ MIA 27 Mar 44
42-31385	New Rpt 4 Jan 44 ▓▓▓ Ass 31 Mar 44
42-31388	New Rpt 21 Dec 43 ▓▓▓ MIA 11 Feb 44
42-31406	New Rpt 21 jan 44 ▓▓▓ MIA 22 Feb 44
42-31418	New Rpt 27 Dec 43 ▓▓▓ Ass 31 Mar 44
42-31428	New Rpt 21 Jan 44 ▓▓▓ MIA 22 Feb 44
42-31440	New Rpt 4 Jan 44 ▓▓▓ MIA 4 Feb 44
42-31444	New Rpt 8 Jan 44 ▓▓▓ Ass 31 Mar 44
42-31445	New Rpt 21 Jan 44 ▓▓▓ Ass 31 Mar 44
42-31451	New Rpt 30 Dec 43 ▓▓▓ MIA 11 Jan 44
42-31454	New Rpt 27 Dec 43 ▓▓▓ Ass 31 Mar 44
42-31469	(*) At Foulsham 12-31 Jan 44 New Rpt 27 Dec 43 ▓▓▓ (*) ▓▓▓ Ass 31 Mar 44
42-31499	New Rpt 21 jan 44 ▓▓▓ MIA 8 Feb 44
42-31500	New Rpt 4 Jan 44 ▓▓▓ MIA 22 Feb 44
42-31524	New Rpt 21 Jan 44 ▓▓▓ Cr Landed 22 Mar 44
42-31538	New Rpt 4 Jan 44 ▓▓▓ MIA 11 Jan 44 (23 Mar 44)
42-31539	New Rpt 4 Jan 44 ▓▓▓ Ass 31 Mar 44
42-31556	New Rpt 4 Jan 44 ▓▓▓ Ass 31 Mar 44
42-31558	New Rpt 21 Jan 44 ▓▓▓ Ass 31 Mar 44
42-31670	New Rpt 14 Jan 44 ▓▓▓ MIA 22 Feb 44
42-31690	New Rpt Date in nknown but in before 6 mar 43 ▓▓▓ Ass 31 Mar 44
42-31695	New Rpt 29 Jan 44 ▓▓▓ MIA 22 Feb 44
42-31700	New Rpt 29 Jan 44 ▓▓▓ Cr Ld 26 Mar 44 (27 Mar 44)
42-31715	New Rpt 29 Jan 44 ▓▓▓ Crashed 4 Feb 44 (5 Feb 44)
42-31726	New Rpt date in nknown but in before 6 Mar 44 ▓▓▓ Ass 31 Mar 44
42-31737	New Rpt 28 Feb 44 ▓▓▓ Ass 31 Mar 44
42-31758	New Rpt 3 Mar 44 ▓▓▓ Ass 31 Mar 44

306th Bomb Group(H)	1943						1944			H
	July	Aug	Sep	Oct	Nov	Dec	Jan	Feb	Mar	
Serial No	Gained From				Period Assigned				Lost To	
42-31768	New Rpt, Date in unknown. In before 6 Feb 44.									Ass 31 Mar 44
42-31894								New Rpt 28 Feb 44		Cr Ld 26 Mar 44 (27 Mar 44)
42-31897								New Rpt 25 Feb 44		Ass 31 Mar 44
42-31901								New Rpt 25 Feb 44		Ass 31 Mar 44
42-31969							New Rpt 22 Feb 44			Ass 31 Mar 44
42-31979	First NMF MIA in 1st BD			NMF			New Rpt 22 Feb 44	MIA 25 Feb 44		
42-32099							457BG 12 Mar 44			Ass 31 Mar 44
42-32113							457BG 12 Mar 44			Ass 31 Mar 44

B-17G Douglas

Serial No	July	Aug	Sep	Oct	Nov	Dec	Jan	Feb	Mar	Lost To
42-37718		New Rpt 19 Sep 43		MIA 9 Oct 43			(First Group B-17G MIA)			
42-37720		New Rpt 18 Sep 43		MIA 14 Oct 43			(First B-17G Ass to Group)			
42-37724		New Rpt 20 Sep 43								Ass 31 Mar 44
42-37759		New Rpt 19 Sep 43		Crash Landed 9 Oct 43						
42-37765					New Rpt 14 Dec 43					Ass 31 Mar 44
42-37836					New Rpt 30 Dec 43					Ass 31 Mar 44
42-37840							457BG 12 Mar 44			Ass 31 Mar 44
42-37942					New Rpt 19 Dec 43					Ass 31 Mar 44
42-37943					New Rpt 12 Dec 43					Ass 31 Mar 44
42-37953					New Rpt 27 Dec 43					MIA 29 Mar 44
42-38008					New Rpt 21 Jan 44			At 2 SAD 4 Mar 44		
42-38019					New Rpt 21 Jan 44					Ass 31 Mar 44
42-38042					New Rpt 9 Jan 44					Ass 31 Mar 44
42-38074					New Rpt 23 Jan 44			MIA 24 Feb 44		
42-38093								New Rpt 28 Feb 44		Ass 31 Mar 44
42-38129								New Rpt 25 Feb 44		Ass 31 Mar 44
42-38155								New Rpt 25 Feb 44		Ass 31 Mar 44
42-38163								New Rpt 29 Feb 44		Ass 31 Mar 44

B-17G Vega

Serial No	July	Aug	Sep	Oct	Nov	Dec	Jan	Feb	Mar	Lost To
42-39768				New Rpt 21 Oct 43			MIA 13 Dec 43			
42-39776				New Rpt 6 Nov 43						Ass 31 Mar 44
42-39827				New Rpt 24 Nov 43						Ass 31 Mar 44
42-39850				New Rpt 22 Oct 43						Ass 31 Mar 44
42-39935						New Rpt 6 Jan 44		MIA 22 Feb 44		
42-39945						New Rpt 12 Dec 43		MIA 22 Feb 44		
42-39950						New Rpt 28 Dec 43				MIA 29 Mar 44
42-39963						New Rpt 30 Dec 43				Ass 31 Mar 44
42-39965						New Rpt 19 Dec 43				MIA 29 Mar 44
42-40006						New Rpt 8 Jan 44		MIA 6 Mar 44		
42-40053						New Rpt 27 Dec 43				Ass 31 Mar 44

B-17G Boeing

Serial No	July	Aug	Sep	Oct	Nov	Dec	Jan	Feb	Mar	Lost To
42-97133									New Rpt 26 Mar 44	Ass 31 Mar 44
42-97146	NMF								New Rpt 24 Mar 44	Ass 31 Mar 44
42-97185									New Rpt 31 Mar 44	Ass 31 Mar 44
42-97327									New Rpt 31 Mar 44	Ass 31 Mar 44

B-17G Vega

Serial No	July	Aug	Sep	Oct	Nov	Dec	Jan	Feb	Mar	Lost To
42-97463							New Rpt 27 Jan 44	MIA 20 Feb 44		
42-97505				New Rpt, date in unknown						Ass 31 Mar 44
42-97588	NMF						457BG 12 Mar 44			Ass 31 Mar 44
42-97663	NMF						457BG 12 Mar 44			MIA 26 Mar 44

B-17G Douglas

Serial No	July	Aug	Sep	Oct	Nov	Dec	Jan	Feb	Mar	Lost To
42-107013	NMF								New Rpt 24 Mar 44	Cr Ld 28 Mar 44 (29 Mar 44)

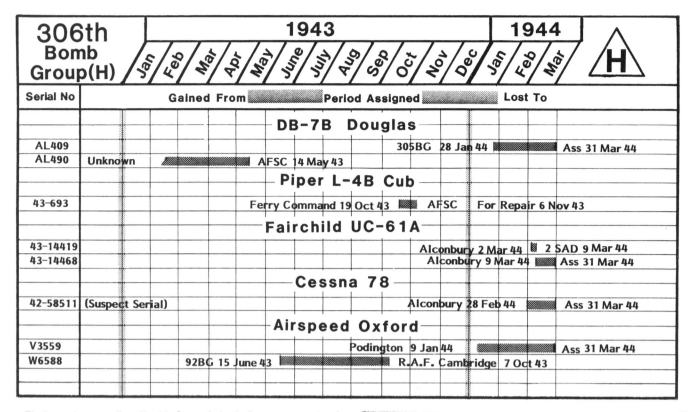

306th Bomb Group(H)	1943 Jan / Feb / Mar / Apr / May / June / July / Aug / Sep / Oct / Nov / Dec	1944 Jan / Feb / Mar	H

Serial No	Gained From ▓▓▓ Period Assigned ▓▓▓ Lost To

DB-7B Douglas

| AL409 | | 305BG 28 Jan 44 ▓▓▓ Ass 31 Mar 44 |
| AL490 | Unknown ▓▓▓ AFSC 14 May 43 | |

Piper L-4B Cub

| 43-693 | Ferry Command 19 Oct 43 ▓ AFSC For Repair 6 Nov 43 |

Fairchild UC-61A

| 43-14419 | Alconbury 2 Mar 44 ▓ 2 SAD 9 Mar 44 |
| 43-14468 | Alconbury 9 Mar 44 ▓▓ Ass 31 Mar 44 |

Cessna 78

| 42-58511 | (Suspect Serial) | Alconbury 28 Feb 44 ▓▓ Ass 31 Mar 44 |

Airspeed Oxford

| V3559 | Podington 9 Jan 44 ▓▓▓ Ass 31 Mar 44 |
| W6588 | 92BG 15 June 43 ▓▓▓ R.A.F. Cambridge 7 Oct 43 |

The heavy losses suffered by this Group during its first seven months of combat are reflected by the fact that at the end of April 1943 only four of the original B-17Fs remained. They were 41-24460, 41-24487 'EAGER BEAVER', 41-24502 and 41-24507.

The first of these to go was 41-24502 which crashed when returning from an operational mission on 28th July 1943. A month later, on 22nd August, 41-24507, which had spent the latter half of April and all of May and June 1943 on maintenance at Langford Lodge, was transferred to the 384th Bomb Group. Next to go had been 41-24460 which went to the 482nd Bomb Group on 22nd September.

The sole survivor of the four, 41-24487, had been badly damaged on the Group's first mission and very nearly written off after landing at Manston on return. It had then spent over two months at Honington undergoing repairs. This aircraft survived operations until October 1943 when it was transferred to training duties and was still serving in this role on 31st March 1944. It had been assigned to the same Group longer than any other B-17F in the Eighth Air Force.

The early replacement B-17Fs had not fared any better than the originals had. The oldest of these still serving operationally on 31st March was 42-30586 which had joined the Group on 7th August 1943.

LONG SERVING AIRCRAFT: ASSIGNED FOR ONE YEAR OR MORE				
Serial No	Date In	Date Out	Reason Out	Months Ass
41-24460	Orig Act	22 Sep 43	To 482BG	13
41-24487	Orig Act	Still Ass		19½

SHORT SERVING AIRCRAFT: ASSIGNED FOR LESS THAN EIGHT DAYS				
Serial No	Date In	Date Out	Reason Out	Days Ass
42-29806	19 May 43	21 May 43	MIA	2
42-31538	4 Jan 44	11 Jan 44	MIA	7
42-31715	29 Jan 44	4 Feb 44	Crashed	6(7)
42-31979	22 Feb 44	25 Feb 44	MIA	3
42-107013	24 Mar 44	29 Mar 44	Cr Ld	5(6)

AIRCRAFT AND OPERATIONAL STATISTICS					
Total Aircraft Assigned					
B-17E:	1 May 43 to 31 Mar 44	1	UC-61A:	2 Mar 44 to 31 Mar 44	2
B-17F:	Aug 42 to 31 Mar 44	166	C-78:	28 Feb 44 to 31 Mar 44	1
B-17G:	18 Sep 43 to 31 Mar 44	91	L-4B:	19 Oct 43 to 31 Mar 44	1
DB-7B:	42/43 to 31 Mar 44	2	Oxford:	15 June 43 to 31 Mar 44	2

Operational Statistics

First Mission flown on:	9 Oct 42	Total Act MIA:	111 (81 B-17F and 30 B-17G)
First Act MIA:	B-17F 41-24510 on 9 Oct 42	Highest Days Losses:	Ten on 17 Apr 43 and Ten on 14 Oct 43
First B-17G Ass:	42-37720 on 18 Sep 43		
First B-17G MIA:	42-37718 on 9 Oct 43	Other Losses (Salvaged)	33 B-17
First NMF Ass:	42-31969 and 31979 on 22 Feb 44	B-17F:	23 (12 Op, 9 Non Op, 2 Unknown)
First NMF MIA:	42-31979 on 25 Feb 44 (First in First BD)	B-17G:	10 (9 Op, 1 Non Op)

306th BOMBARDMENT GROUP (H)

STATUS OF AIRCRAFT ASSIGNED AT 2000 HOURS on 31st MARCH 1944

Operational: 55 B-17 (6 B-17F: 49 B-17G)

Non Operational: 6 (1 B-17E: 1 B-17F: 1 DB-7B: 1 UC-61A: 1 C-78: 1 Oxford)

Operational Aircraft Assigned and on hand at Thurleigh

B-17F

42-3382	42-30145	42-30586	42-30939
	42-30431	42-30730	

B-17G

42-3521	42-31445	42-31768	42-38019	42-39963
42-3527	42-31454	42-31897	42-38042	42-40053
	42-31469	42-31901	42-38093	
42-31143	42-31539	42-32099 NMF	42-38129	42-97133
42-31158	42-31556	42-32113 NMF	42-38155	42-97146
42-31172	42-31558		42-38163	42-97185 NMF
42-31196	42-31690	42-37724		42-97327 NMF
42-31385	42-31726	42-37765	42-39776	
42-31418	42-31737	42-37840	42-39827	42-97505
42-31444	42-31758	42-37943	42-39850	

Assigned but not on hand:

B-17Gs: 42-31065 at Manston: 42-31969 at Woodbridge: 42-37836 at Leiston:
42-37942 at Beccles and 42-97588 (NMF) at Tibenham

Non Operational Aircraft on hand at Thurleigh:

B-17E 41-9148: B-17F 41-24487 *: DB-7B AL409: UC-61A 43-14468: C-78 42-58511 and Oxford V3559

Note: B-17G 42-38008 was at 2 SAD from 5 Mar 44 to 5 Apr 44 and was not Ass on 31 Mar 44.

* B-17F 41-24487 was without Tokyo tanks

42-31894 was one of the last Boeing built olive drab B-17Gs to join the 306th Bomb Group. It crash landed at Thurleigh on return from the mission of 26th March 1944, just 27 days after it had been assigned. *306th Historical Association*

351st BOMBARDMENT GROUP (H)

Constituted as the 351st BOMBARDMENT GROUP (H) on 25th September 1942
Activated on 1st October 1942
Squadrons Assigned: 508th, 509th, 510th and 511th
Assigned to Eighth Air Force: April 1943
Assigned to First Bombardment Wing: April 1943

COMBAT WING ASSIGNMENTS

101st Provisional Bombardment: May 1943
92nd Combat Bombardment: 16th September 1943
94th Combat Bombardment: 11th December 1943

STATIONS

Polebrook: Air Echelon in 15th April 1943
Ground Echelon in 12th May 1943

Trained in USA using B-17Fs. Third phase training at Pueblo, Colorado, where during March 1943, new B-17Fs were assigned. These came from the Modification Centers at Denver, Long Beach and Cheyenne.

Air echelon moved to Kearney, Nebraska, on 2nd April where checks and processing for the overseas movement took place.

Flew to Selfridge Field, Michigan, on 6th April and to Presque Isle on 7th April where final processing and repairs to the aircraft were carried out. Left Presque Isle for Gander on 15th April and departed for Prestwick the next day. Prestwick was reached on 17th April and the planes were refuelled and flown on to Polebrook. First aircraft to reach Polebrook was 42-29491 which carried the advance party, Lt Col Bowles, Maj Milton and Maj Scott who arrived on 15th April. By the 2nd May, 40 aircraft had arrived.

The ground echelon left Pueblo on 17th April for Camp Williams, Wisconsin, and then went on to Camp Shanks, New York, where they arrived on 26th April. Final processing took place here. On 4th May they boarded the *Queen Elizabeth* in New Jersey docks and reached Greenock, Scotland, on 11th May. They then travelled on to join the air echelon at Polebrook which was reached on the evening of 12th May.

The 351st Bomb Group had ten of its original aircraft complete one year's service with the Group. One was 42-5824 **'SCREW BALL'** which left the Group on 31st March 1944 to be returned to the USA *Alan Dann*

ORIGINAL B-17Fs ASSIGNED AT PUEBLO, MARCH 1943				
42-3120	42-5756	42-29491	42-29847	42-29862
42-3136	42-5812	42-29684	42-29848	42-29863
42-3140	42-5814	42-29701	42-29849	42-29865
42-3141	42-5815	42-29817	42-29850	42-29868
42-3150	42-5823	42-29821	42-29852	42-29872
42-3152	42-5824	42-29838	42-29858	42-29874
42-3173		42-29839	42-29859	42-29877
		42-29841	42-29860	42-29882
		42-29843	42-29861	42-29887

SHORT SERVING AIRCRAFT: ASSIGNED FOR LESS THAN EIGHT DAYS									
Serial No	Date In	Date Out	Reason Out	Days Ass	Serial No	Date In	Date Out	Reason Out	Days Ass
42-30244	9 June 43	12 June 43	To 4CW	3	42-31882	17 Feb 44	22 Feb 44	Crashed	5
42-30255	10 June 43	16 June 43	To 95BG	6	42-97063	29 Feb 44	1 Mar 44	To 457BG	1
42-31776	25 Feb 44	2 Mar 43	MIA	6	42-97552	25 Feb 44	1 Mar 44	To 457BG	5

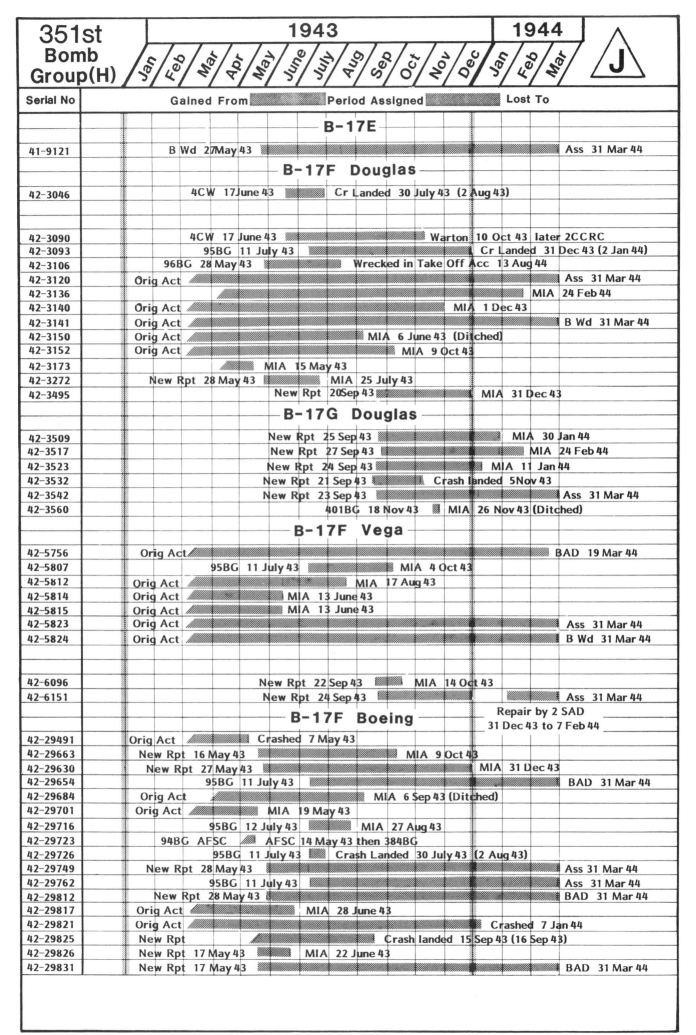

351st Bomb Group(H)	1943												1944			J
	Jan	Feb	Mar	Apr	May	June	July	Aug	Sep	Oct	Nov	Dec	Jan	Feb	Mar	
Serial No	Gained From　　　　Period Assigned　　　　Lost To															

B-17E

41-9121	B Wd 27 May 43 ▓▓▓▓▓▓▓▓▓▓▓▓▓▓▓▓▓▓ Ass 31 Mar 44

B-17F Douglas

42-3046	4CW 17 June 43 ▓▓▓ Cr Landed 30 July 43 (2 Aug 43)

42-3090	4CW 17 June 43 ▓▓▓▓▓▓▓▓ Warton 10 Oct 43 later 2CCRC
42-3093	95BG 11 July 43 ▓▓▓▓▓▓▓▓▓ Cr Landed 31 Dec 43 (2 Jan 44)
42-3106	96BG 28 May 43 ▓▓▓▓▓▓ Wrecked in Take Off Acc 13 Aug 44
42-3120	Orig Act ▓▓▓▓▓▓▓▓▓▓▓▓▓▓▓▓▓▓▓▓▓▓▓▓ Ass 31 Mar 44
42-3136	▓▓▓▓▓▓▓▓▓▓▓▓▓▓▓▓▓▓▓▓▓▓▓ MIA 24 Feb 44
42-3140	Orig Act ▓▓▓▓▓▓▓▓▓▓▓▓▓▓▓▓▓ MIA 1 Dec 43
42-3141	Orig Act ▓▓▓▓▓▓▓▓▓▓▓▓▓▓▓▓▓▓▓▓▓▓▓▓ B Wd 31 Mar 44
42-3150	Orig Act ▓▓▓▓▓▓▓▓▓ MIA 6 June 43 (Ditched)
42-3152	Orig Act ▓▓▓▓▓▓▓▓▓▓▓▓ MIA 9 Oct 43
42-3173	▓▓▓ MIA 15 May 43
42-3272	New Rpt 28 May 43 ▓▓▓▓▓▓▓ MIA 25 July 43
42-3495	New Rpt 20 Sep 43 ▓▓▓▓ MIA 31 Dec 43

B-17G Douglas

42-3509	New Rpt 25 Sep 43 ▓▓▓▓▓ MIA 30 Jan 44
42-3517	New Rpt 27 Sep 43 ▓▓▓▓▓▓ MIA 24 Feb 44
42-3523	New Rpt 24 Sep 43 ▓▓▓▓ MIA 11 Jan 44
42-3532	New Rpt 21 Sep 43 ▓▓▓ Crash landed 5 Nov 43
42-3542	New Rpt 23 Sep 43 ▓▓▓▓▓▓▓▓ Ass 31 Mar 44
42-3560	401BG 18 Nov 43 ▓ MIA 26 Nov 43 (Ditched)

B-17F Vega

42-5756	Orig Act ▓▓▓▓▓▓▓▓▓▓▓▓▓▓▓▓▓▓▓▓▓▓ BAD 19 Mar 44
42-5807	95BG 11 July 43 ▓▓▓▓▓▓ MIA 4 Oct 43
42-5812	Orig Act ▓▓▓▓▓▓▓▓▓ MIA 17 Aug 43
42-5814	Orig Act ▓▓▓▓▓ MIA 13 June 43
42-5815	Orig Act ▓▓▓▓▓ MIA 13 June 43
42-5823	Orig Act ▓▓▓▓▓▓▓▓▓▓▓▓▓▓▓▓▓▓▓▓▓▓ Ass 31 Mar 44
42-5824	Orig Act ▓▓▓▓▓▓▓▓▓▓▓▓▓▓▓▓▓▓▓▓▓▓ B Wd 31 Mar 44

42-6096	New Rpt 22 Sep 43 ▓▓ MIA 14 Oct 43
42-6151	New Rpt 24 Sep 43 ▓▓▓▓ ▓▓▓ Ass 31 Mar 44

B-17F Boeing

Repair by 2 SAD
31 Dec 43 to 7 Feb 44

42-29491	Orig Act ▓▓▓▓ Crashed 7 May 43
42-29663	New Rpt 16 May 43 ▓▓▓▓▓▓▓ MIA 9 Oct 43
42-29630	New Rpt 27 May 43 ▓▓▓▓▓▓▓▓▓▓ MIA 31 Dec 43
42-29654	95BG 11 July 43 ▓▓▓▓▓▓▓▓▓▓▓▓▓ BAD 31 Mar 44
42-29684	Orig Act ▓▓▓▓▓▓▓ MIA 6 Sep 43 (Ditched)
42-29701	Orig Act ▓▓▓▓ MIA 19 May 43
42-29716	95BG 12 July 43 ▓▓▓ MIA 27 Aug 43
42-29723	94BG AFSC ▓ AFSC 14 May 43 then 384BG
42-29726	95BG 11 July 43 ▓ Crash Landed 30 July 43 (2 Aug 43)
42-29749	New Rpt 28 May 43 ▓▓▓▓▓▓▓▓▓▓▓▓▓▓▓▓▓▓ Ass 31 Mar 44
42-29762	95BG 11 July 43 ▓▓▓▓▓▓▓▓▓▓▓▓▓▓▓ Ass 31 Mar 44
42-29812	New Rpt 28 May 43 ▓▓▓▓▓▓▓▓▓▓▓▓▓▓▓▓▓ BAD 31 Mar 44
42-29817	Orig Act ▓▓▓▓▓▓ MIA 28 June 43
42-29821	Orig Act ▓▓▓▓▓▓▓▓▓▓▓▓ Crashed 7 Jan 44
42-29825	New Rpt ▓▓▓▓ Crash landed 15 Sep 43 (16 Sep 43)
42-29826	New Rpt 17 May 43 ▓▓▓ MIA 22 June 43
42-29831	New Rpt 17 May 43 ▓▓▓▓▓▓▓▓▓▓▓▓▓▓▓▓ BAD 31 Mar 44

351st Bomb Group(H)	1943											1944			J
	Jan	Feb	Mar	Apr	May	June	July	Aug	Sep	Oct	Nov	Dec	Jan	Feb	Mar

Serial No	Gained From · · · Period Assigned · · · Lost To
42–29835	New Rpt 17 June 43 · · · Ass 31 Mar 44
42–29838	Orig Act · · · MIA 29 May 43
42–29839	Orig Act · · · MIA 17 Aug 43
42–29841	Orig Act · · · Crash Landed 6 Sep 43 (11 Oct 43)
42–29843	Orig Act · · · MIA 28 June 43
42–29847	Orig Act · · · MiA 28 June 43
42–29848	Orig Act · · · BAD 19 Mar 44
42–29849	Orig Act · · · Ass 31 Mar 44
42–29850	Orig Act · · · Ass 31 Mar 44
42–29851	New Rpt 16 May 43 · · · Crashed in Sea 10 Oct 43
42–29852	Orig Act · · · MIA 3 Nov 43
42–29858	Orig Act · · · Crash landed 21 Feb 44 (22 Feb 44)
42–29859	Orig Act · · · MIA 14 May 43
42–29860	Orig Act · · · Ass 31 Mar 44
42–29861	Orig Act · · · MIA 11 Jan 44
42–29862	Orig Act · · · MIA 14 May 43
42–29863	Orig Act · · · MIA 11 Feb 44
42–29865	Orig Act · · · Crashed 7 May 43
42–29868	Orig Act · · · MIA 9 Oct 43
42–29872	Orig Act · · · MIA 17 July 43 (Ditched)
42–29874	Orig Act · · · Crash Landed 12 Aug 43 (16 Aug 43)
42–29877	Orig Act · · · MIA 31 Dec 43
42–29882	Orig Act · · · Ass 31 Mar 44
42–29887	Orig Act · · · MIA 28 June 43
42–29925	New Rpt · · · Ass 31 Mar 44
42–29948	New Rpt 28 May 43 · · · MIA 31 Dec 43
42–30135	New Rpt 28 May 43 · · · 95BG 16 June 43
42–30244	New Rpt 9 June 43 · · · 4 Combat Wing 17 June 43
42–30255	New Rpt 10 June 43 · · · 95BG 16 June 43
42–30499	New Rpt 27 Sep 43 · · · Ass 31 Mar 44
42–30780	New Rpt 21 Sep 43 · · · MIA 11 Jan 44
42–30785	New Rpt 23 Sep 43 · · · MIA 4 Oct 43
42–30790	New Rpt 22 Sep 43 · · · MIA 9 Oct 43
42–30857	New Rpt 22 Sep 43 · · · Ass 31 Mar 44
42–30866	401BG 21 Nov 43 · · · MIA 21 Feb 44
42–30867	New Rpt 27 Sep 43 · · · MIA 9 Oct 43
42–30994	401BG 21 Nov 43 · · · Ass 31 Mar 44

B-17G Boeing

42–31162	New Rpt 7 Nov 43 · · · MIA 30 Dec 43
42–31179	New Rpt 23 Dec 43 · · · MIA 31 Dec 43
42–31192	401BG 3 Dec 43 · · · Ass 31 Mar 44
42–31238	New Rpt 23 Dec 43 · · · Ass 31 Mar 44
42–31384	New Rpt 20 Jan 44 · · · Ass 31 Mar 44
42–31481	New Rpt 2 Jan 44 · · · MIA 11 Jan 44
42–31509	New Rpt 14 Jan 44 · · · Ass 31 Mar 44
42–31560	New Rpt 25 Feb 44 · · · Ass 31 Mar 44
42–31612	New Rpt 30 Jan 44 · · · MIA 22 Feb 44
42–31694	New Rpt 30 Jan 44 · · · Cr 11 Feb 44 (13 Feb 44)
42–31702	New Rpt 30 Jan 44 · · · Ass 31 Mar 44
42–31711	New Rpt 30 Jan 44 · · · Ass 31 Mar 44
42–31714	New Rpt 29 Jan 44 · · · Ass 31 Mar 44
42–31721	New Rpt 29 Jan 44 · · · Ass 31 Mar 44
42–31725	New Rpt 30 Jan 44 · · · Ass 31 Mar 44
42–31748	New Rpt 19 Feb 44 · · · Ass 31 Mar 44
42–31757	New Rpt 25 Feb 44 · · · Ass 31 Mar 44
42–31763	New Rpt 30 Jan 44 · · · Cr 20 Feb 44 (21 Feb 44)

351st Bomb Group(H)	1943						1944				△J
	July	Aug	Sep	Oct	Nov	Dec	Jan	Feb	Mar		
Serial No	Gained From ▓▓▓ Period Assigned ▓▓▓ Lost To										
42-31776							New Rpt 25 Feb 44		MIA 2 Mar 44		
42-31875							New Rpt 25 Feb 44		Ass 31 Mar 44		
42-31879							New Rpt 25 Feb 44		Ass 31 Mar 44		
42-31882						New Rpt 17 Feb 44	Cr in Sea 22 Feb 44				
42-31899							New Rpt 29 Feb 44		Ass 31 Mar 44		
42-31955							New Rpt 29 Feb 44		Ass 31 Mar 44		
42-31966	NMF						New Rpt 29 Feb 44	MIA 18 Mar 44			
42-31975							New Rpt 22 Feb 44		Ass 31 Mar 44		
42-31988							New Rpt 30 Mar 44		Ass 31 Mar 44		

B-17G Douglas

Serial No	July	Aug	Sep	Oct	Nov	Dec	Jan	Feb	Mar		
42-37714				401BG 18 Nov 43					Ass 31 Mar 44		
42-37731	New Rpt 22 Sep 43					MIA 31 Dec 43					
42-37774				401BG 21 Nov 43		Crashed 31 Dec 43 (1 Jan 44)					
42-37780				401 BG 18 Nov 43					Ass 31 Mar 44		
42-37817			New Rpt 24 Oct 43		MIA 26 Nov 43						
42-37825			379BG 21 Oct 43					MIA 18 Mar 44			
42-37827			New Rpt 27 Oct 43						Ass 31 Mar 44		
42-37832			New Rpt 24 Oct 43					MIA 18 Mar 44			
42-37845			New Rpt 25 Nov 43						Ass 31 Mar 44		
42-37847			New Rpt 24 Oct 43		MIA Dec 43						
42-38005				New Rpt 4 Jan 44					Ass 31 Mar 44		
42-38023				New Rpt 1 Jan 44				Crash Landed 22 Feb 44 (24 Feb 44)			
42-38028				New Rpt 1 Jan 44					Ass 31 Mar 44		
42-38032				New Rpt 14 Jan 44				MIA 18 Mar 44			
42-38038				New Rpt 14 Jan 44					Ass 31 Mar 44		
42-38146							New Rpt 29 Feb 44		Ass 31 Mar 44		
42-38153							New Rpt 25 Feb 44		Ass 31 Mar 44		

B-17G Vega

Serial No	July	Aug	Sep	Oct	Nov	Dec	Jan	Feb	Mar		
42-39760				401BG 25 Nov 43					Ass 31 Mar 44		
42-39761				401BG 18 Nov 43		MIA 11 Jan 44					
42-39778				401BG 18 Nov 43		MIA 22 Dec 43 (Ditched)					
42-39780				401BG 18 Nov 43		Crash Landed 30 Dec 43 (2 Jan 44)					
42-39823				401BG 18 Nov 43		MIA 31 Dec 43					
42-39834				401BG 18 Nov 43				Crash Landed 30 Jan 44 (5 Feb 44)			
42-39835				401BG 18 Nov 43					Ass 31 Mar 44		
42-39839				401BG 18 Nov 43	Crash Landed 26 Nov 43 (28 Nov 43)						
42-39848				401BG 18 Nov 43					MIA 22 Mar 44		
42-39849				401BG 18 Nov 43					Ass 31 Mar 44		
42-39853				401BG 18 Nov 43				MIA 22 Feb 44			
42-39857				New Rpt 2 Jan 44		MIA 11 Jan 44					
42-39905				New Rpt 20 Jan 44					Ass 31 Mar 44		
42-39914				New Rpt 30 Jan 44					Ass 31 Mar 44		
42-39987											

B-17G Boeing

Serial No	July	Aug	Sep	Oct	Nov	Dec	Jan	Feb	Mar		
42-97063							New Rpt 29 Feb 44	457BG 1 Mar 44			
42-97066									New Rpt 26 Mar 44 Ass 31 Mar 44		
42-97144									New Rpt 26 Mar 44 Ass 31 Mar 44		
42-97149									New Rpt 26 Mar 44 Ass 31 Mar 44		
42-97157	NMF								New Rpt 24 Mar 44 Ass 31 Mar 44		
42-97169									New Rpt 24 Mar 44 Ass 31 Mar 44		
42-97191									New Rpt 25 Mar 44 Ass 31 Mar 44		
42-97193									New Rpt 24 Mar 44 Ass 31 Mar 44		
42-97196									New Rpt 24 Mar 44 Ass 31 Mar 44		
42-97258									New Rpt 24 Mar 44 Ass 31 Mar 44		

351st Bomb Group(H)	1943			1944				J
	Oct	Nov	Dec	Jan	Feb	Mar		
Serial No	Gained From ▓▓▓▓ Period Assigned ▓▓▓▓							
			B-17G Vega					
42-97472					New Rpt 25 Feb 44 ▓▓▓▓	Ass 31 Mar 44		
42-97492				New Rpt 14 Jan 44 ▓▓▓▓		Ass 31 Mar 44		
42-97552	NMF			New Rpt 25 Feb 44 ░░ 457BG 1 Mar 44				
			B-17G Douglas					
42-107005	NMF				New Rpt 24 Mar 44 ░░ Ass 31 Mar 44			
42-107046					New Rpt 26 Mar 44 ░░ Ass 31 Mar 44			
			Airspeed Oxford					
DF-399		482BG 10 Dec 43 ▓▓▓▓				Ass 31 Mar 44		
			B-17F Vega					
42-5905	Landed Polebrook 30 Nov 43 ▓▓▓ Ret to 388BG 10 Jan 44 (On Hand only, Ass to 388BG)							

STATUS OF AIRCRAFT ASSIGNED AT 2000 HOURS on 31st MARCH 1944

Operational: 61 B-17 (14 B-17F: 47 B-17G)

Non Operational: 2 (1 B-17E: 1 Oxford)

Operational Aircraft Assigned and on hand at Polebrook

B-17F

42-5823*(Orig Act)	42-29749 *	42-29849*(Orig Act)	42-29882*(Orig Act)	42-30499
42-6151	42-29762*	42-29850*(Orig Act)	42-29925*	42-30857
	42-29835*	42-29860*(Orig Act)		42-30994

B-17G

42-3542	42-31725	42-37714	42-39760	42-97169 NMF
	42-31748	42-37780	42-39835	42-97191 NMF
42-31192	42-31757	42-37827	42-39848	42-97193 NMF
42-31238	42-31875	42-37845	42-39853	42-97196 NMF
42-31384	42-31879	42-38005	42-39914	42-97258 NMF
42-31509	42-31899	42-38028	42-39987	
42-31560	42-31955 NMF	42-38038		42-97472
42-31711	42-31975 NMF	42-38146	42-97066 NMF	42-97492
42-31714	42-31988 NMF	42-38153	42-97144 NMF	
42-31721			42-97149 NMF	42-107005 NMF
			42-97157 NMF	42-107046 NMF

Assigned but not on hand

B-17F 42-3120 (Orig Act), At New Romney for Rep: B-17G 42-31702: At Boxted for Rep

Non Operational Act on hand at Polebrook: B-17E 41-9121: Oxford DF399

* These nine Act without Tokyo tanks

351st BOMBARDMENT GROUP (H)

Fourteen of the Group's original aircraft survived into 1944; they were 42-3120, 3141, 5756, 5823, 5824, 29821, 29848, 29849, 29850, 29858, 29860, 29861, 29863 and 29882. Lost in January 1944 were 29821 and 29861 and in February 29858 crashed and 29863 went MIA. During March 3141, 5756, 5824 and 29848 were transferred out for ret to the USA. They had all completed 12 months' service with the Group. Remaining at 31st March were 42-3120, 5823, 29849, 29850, 29860 and 29882 all having completed over 12 months' service with the Group since being assigned at Pueblo, Colorado in March 1943. The Group had therefore had ten aircraft which had completed a full year's service, this was a record for the First Division up to 31st March 1944. The longest serving replacement aircraft still serving on 31st March was 42-29749 which had been assigned on 28th May 1943.

LONG SERVING AIRCRAFT: ASSIGNED FOR ONE YEAR OR MORE				
Serial No	Date In	Date Out	Reason Out	Months Ass
42-3120	Orig Act	Still Ass		12
42-3141	Orig Act	31 Mar 44	To BAD	12
42-5756	Orig Act	19 Mar 44	To BAD	12
42-5823	Orig Act	Still Ass		12
42-5824	Orig Act	31 Mar 44	To BAD	12
42-29848	Orig Act	19 Mar 44	To BAD	12
42-29849	Orig Act	Still Ass		12
42-29850	Orig Act	Still Ass		12
42-29860	Orig Act	Still Ass		12
42-29882	Orig Act	Still Ass		12

'MY PRINCESS' 42-30499. One of the last B-17s to join the 351st. It was still assigned on 31st March 1944. *Alan Dann*

'BEDLAM BALL' 42-38153, assigned to the 351st on 25th February 1944 and still serving on 31st March 1944. *Alan Dann*

AIRCRAFT AND OPERATIONAL STATISTICS				
Total Aircraft Assigned				
B-17E:	27 May 43 to 31 Mar 44	1	B-17G: 22 Sep 43 to 31 Mar 44	80
B-17F:	Mar 43 to 31 Mar 44	75	Oxford: 10 Dec 43 to 31 Mar 44	1

Operational Statistics

First Mission flown on: 13 May 43
First Act MIA: 42-29859 and 29862 on 14 May 43
First B-17G Ass: 42-37731 on 22 Sep 43
First B-17G MIA: 42-37817 on 26 Nov 43
First NMF Ass: 42-31975 on 22 Feb 44
First NMF MIA: 42-31966 on 18 Mar 44

Total Act MIA: 59 (36 B-17F and 23 B-17G)
Highest Days Losses: Seven on 31 Dec 43
Other Losses: (Salvaged) 21 B-17
  B-17F: 12 (9 Op, 3 Non Op)
  B-17G: 9 Op

379th BOMBARDMENT GROUP (H)

Constituted as the 379th BOMBARDMENT GROUP (H) on 28th October 1942
Activated on 3rd November 1942
Squadrons Assigned: 524th, 525th, 526th and 527th
Assigned to Eighth Air Force: April 1943
Assigned to First Bombardment Wing: April 1943

COMBAT WING ASSIGNMENTS

103rd Provisional Bombardment: May 1943
41st Combat Bombardment: 16th September 1943

STATIONS

Bovingdon: Air Echelon in 26th April 1943
Kimbolton: Air Echelon in May 1943
Ground Echelon in 19th May 1943

Trained in the USA on B-17Fs. Moved to Sioux City, Iowa, for third phase training on 2nd February 1943. On 2nd March, the 524th Bomb Squadron moved to Watertown, South Dakota, the 525th Bomb Squadron went to Mitchell, also in South Dakota and the 526th moved to Scribner, Nebraska. Group Headquarters and the 527th Bomb Squadron stayed at Sioux City.

From 14th to 20th March, new B-17Fs were assigned, these coming from the Modification Centers at Denver, Cheyenne and Long Beach. On 3rd April, Headquarters moved to Mitchell and the 527th Bomb Squadron moved to Watertown.

The air echelon moved to Kearney, Nebraska, on 9th April where final processing and checks for overseas movement took place. One of the new planes, 42-29879, was wrecked here, and did not proceed overseas

with the Group. The air echelon flew to Selfridge, Michigan, and then on to Bangor, Maine.

Leaving Bangor on 15th April for Gander from where they took off for Prestwick which most aircraft reached on 23rd April. One plane, 42-3132, was lost over the Atlantic with all its crew, another, 42-3143, crashed at Bunderan in Ireland and 42-29942 crashed at Prestwick when landing at the end of the transatlantic flight. On 26th April they flew to Bovingdon where they stayed almost a month before moving to their permanent station at Kimbolton.

The ground echelon went to Camp Williams, Wisconsin, and then boarded trains for the journey to Camp Shanks, New York. On 9th May, they boarded a train to take them to the docks where they embarked on the *Aquitania*. They arrived at Greenock, Scotland, on the 18th May.

42-29876 returning from Le Bourget on 16th August 1943. Exactly one month later it would be one of four B-17Fs that did not return to Kimbolton from Nantes. *US Air Force–National Air and Space Museum*

```
          ORIGINAL B-17Fs ASSIGNED AT SIOUX CITY BETWEEN APPROX 16th and 20th MARCH 1943
    42-3099         42-5809         42-29772        42-29875        42-29891
    42-3113         42-5813         42-29773        42-29876        42-29892
    42-3114         42-5816         42-29829        42-29878        42-29893
    42-3132 (2)     42-5821         42-29830·       42-29879 (1)    42-29896
    42-3138         42-5822         42-29864        42-29886        42-29898
    42-3143 (3)     42-5827         42-29866        42-29889        42-29901
    42-3145         42-5828         42-29869        42-29890        42-29942 (4)
    42-3148         42-5829
    42-3154         42-5830

            (1) 42-29879: Wrecked at Kearney about 9 Apr, not to UK
               (2) 42-3132: Lost in Atlantic Ocean, 23 Apr 43
           (3) 42-3143: Crashed in Northern Ireland on arrival from Gander
        (4) 42-29942: Crashed landing at Prestwick at end of Transatlantic ferry flight
    NOTE: Only 39 aircraft are listed, there is possibly one more that could not be located
```

379th Bomb Group(H)	1943												1944			K
	Jan	Feb	Mar	Apr	May	June	July	Aug	Sep	Oct	Nov	Dec	Jan	Feb	Mar	

Serial No	Gained From	Period Assigned	Lost To

B-17E

41-2629	Ass from Burtonwood on 27 May 43 but Ass cancelled on	28 May 43
41-9100	1 CCRC 28 May 43	Ass 31 Mar 44

B-17F Boeing

41-24583	Lt Stn 8 June 43	Bovingdon 3 July 43 (1 CCRC)

B-17F Douglas

42-3023	New Rpt 8 June 43	MIA 25 June 43
42-3048	381BG 26 Sep 43	Ass 31 Mar 44
42-3056	New Rpt 20 June 43	
42-3061	95BG 28 June 43	Bwd 21 Jan 44 as VHF Act
42-3072	91BG 27 Sep 43	Ass 31 Mar 44

42-3099	Orig Act	MIA 11 June 43	
42-3113	Orig Act	MIA 29 May 43	
42-3114	Orig Act	MIA 11 June 43	
42-3132	Orig Act	Lost in Atlantic 23 Apr 43 (+)	(+) Not Ass to Group while in First Bomb Wing (42-3132 and 42-3143)
42-3138	Orig Act	MIA 11 June 43	
42-3143	Orig Act	Crash Landed in Ireland 9 May 43 (+)	
42-3145	Orig Act	MIA 6 May 43	
42-3148	Orig Act	MIA 11 June 43	
42-3154	Orig Act	Crash Landed 12 Aug 43 (13 Aug 43)	
42-3167	306BG - AFSC 18 Aug 43	(*) Ass 31 Mar 44	
42-3175	95BG	MIA 25 July 43	(*) Out from 4 to 29 Mar 44
42-3176	95BG 27 June 43	MIA 14 Oct 43	
42-3199	New Rpt 20 May 43	MIA 12 Aug 43	
42-3212	Date in Unknown	Crashed 30 July 43	
42-3258	New Rpt 11 June 43	MIA 8 Oct 43	
42-3269	New Rpt 6 June 43	MIA 14 Oct 43	
42-3300	New Rpt 11 June 43	MIA 3 Sep 43	
42-3325	New Rpt 11 June 43	MIA 30 Jan 44	

B-17G Douglas

42-3524	New Rpt 3 Oct 43	Ass 31 Mar 44
42-3559	New Rpt 22 Nov 43	MIA 1 Dec 43

B-17F Boeing

42-5379	96BG 27 Sep 43	Ass 31 Mar 44
42-5382	303 BG - AFSC 31 May 43	3 June 43, Probably never on hand. Ret to 303BG
42-5407	91BG 27 Sep 43	MIA 9 Oct 43

YB-40

42-5736	303BG 28 Aug 43	Burtonwood 12 Oct 43

B-17F Vega

42-5809	Orig Act	Crash Landed 11 June 43 (12 June 43)
42-5810	Date in Unknown	MIA 29 July 43
42-5813	Orig Act	Crash landed 30 July 43
42-5816	Orig Act	Ass 31 Mar 44
42-5820	New Rpt 8 June 43	MIA 12 Aug 43
42-5821	Orig Act	MIA 12 Aug 43
42-5822	Orig Act	Crash Landed 28 July 43 (30 July 43)
42-5827	Orig Act	MIA 5 Jan 44 (Sweden)
42-5828	Orig Act	MIA 22 Feb 44
42-5829	Orig Act	MIA 30 July 43
42-5830	Orig Act	Ass 31 Mar 44

379th Bomb Group(H)

	1943	1944	K
	Jan Feb Mar Apr May June July Aug Sep Oct Nov Dec	Jan Feb Mar	

Serial No — Gained From — Period Assigned — Lost To

Serial No	Entry
42-5836	MIA 25 June 43
42-5859	New Rpt 20 May 43, AFSC 29 May 43, Later to 303BG
42-5917	New Rpt 21 June 43, MIA 25 July 43

B-17F Boeing

Serial No	Entry
42-29511	92BG 4 Sep 43, MIA 14 Oct 43
42-29624	92BG 13 Sep 43, Ass 31 Mar 44
42-29633	92BG 26 Sep 43, MIA 8 Feb 44
42-29653	92BG 4 Sep 43, MIA 14 Oct 43
42-29694	92BG 4 Sep 43, MIA 26 Nov 43
42-29705	Knettishall 27 Sep 43, Out 28 Nov 43, fate unknown
42-29713	92BG 5 Sep 43, MIA 4 Oct 43
42-29718	92BG 4 Sep 43, Ass 31 Mar 44
42-29724	92BG 4 Sep 43, MIA 22 Dec 43
42-29746	96BG 12 July 43, MIA 30 July 43
42-29747	96BG 12 July 43, Crashed 5 Jan 44
42-29759	96BG 12 July 43, 2 SAD 15 Oct 43, later to 91BG
42-29772	Orig Act, Ass 31 Mar 44
42-29773	Orig Act, MIA 29 May 43
42-29776	92BG 4 Sep 43, MIA 14 Oct 43
42-29787	92BG 4 Sep 43, MIA 29 Nov 43
42-29796	New Rpt 20 June 43, MIA 28 July 43
42-29802	92BG 13 Sep 43, Ass 31 Mar 44
42-29824	306BG – BAD 3 Oct 43, Ass 31 Mar 44
42-29829	Orig Act, MIA 22 Feb 44
42-29830	Orig Act, MIA 17 Aug 43
42-29864	Orig Act, MIA 25 June 43
42-29866	Orig Act, MIA 16 Aug 43
42-29869	Orig Act, Ass 31 Mar 44
42-29875	Orig Act, MIA 11 June 43
42-29876	Orig Act, MIA 16 Sep 43
42-29878	Orig Act, MIA 29 May 43
42-29879	Orig Act, Wrecked in U.S.A. about 9 April 43. Not to U.K.
42-29886	Orig Act, MIA 29 Jan 44
42-29889	Orig Act, Dest, fire, 23 Feb 44
42-29890	Orig Act, Crashed 9 Oct 43 (10 Oct 43)
42-29891	Orig Act, Crashed 22 Dec 43
42-29892	Orig Act, MIA 25 June 43
42-29893	Orig Act, MIA 16 Sep 43
42-29896	Orig Act, MIA 6 Sep 43
42-29897	92BG 4 Sep 43, Ass 31 Mar 44
42-29898	Orig Act, MIA 12 Aug 43
42-29901	Orig Act, MIA 16 Sep 43
42-29905	New Rpt 21 May 43, Ass 31 Mar 44
42-29915	New Rpt, MIA 11 June 43
42-29933	96BG 12 July 43, Dam on Op Miss 12 Aug 43, Sal on Ret. (15 Aug 43)
42-29934	New Rpt 6 June 43, MIA 16 Sep 43
42-29937	306BG – AFSC 18 Aug 43, MIA 23 Sep 43
42-29942	Orig Act, Landing Gear Coll at end of flight from U.S.A. 1 May 43. Sal.
42-29946	New Rpt 9 June 43, MIA 22 June 43
42-29963	New Rpt 11 June 43, MIA 30 Dec 43
42-29997	New Rpt 6 July 43, Ass 31 Mar 44
42-30001	New Rpt 23 June 43, MIA 16 Aug 43
42-30107	New Rpt 20 June 43, MIA 25 June 43
42-30158	New Rpt 23 June 43, MIA 17 Aug 43
42-30165	New Rpt 21 June 43, MIA 25 June 43
42-30191	New Rpt 6 June 43, MIA 17 Aug 43

Serial No	Gained From	Period Assigned	Lost To
42-30192	New Rpt 20 June 43	95BG 27 June 43	
42-30237	New Rpt June 43		Ass 31 Mar 44
42-30271	New Rpt 6 June 43	95BG 30 June 43	
42-30298	New Rpt 13 Aug 43		Ass 31 Mar 44
42-30309	New Rpt 21 June 43	MIA 17 Aug 43	
42-30720	New Rpt 19 Oct 43		Ass 31 Mar 44
42-31021	New Rpt 22 Nov 43		Cr Landed 30 Jan 44 (3 Feb 44)
42-31028	New Rpt 19 Nov 43		MIA 22 Feb 44

B-17G Boeing

42-31040	New Rpt 22 Oct 43		MIA 29 Jan 44
42-31043	New Rpt 19 Oct 43		Ass 31 Mar 44
42-31050	New Rpt 22 Oct 43		MIA 29 Jan 44
42-31083	New Rpt 19 Oct 43		Ass 31 Mar 44
42-31085	New Rpt 19 Oct 43		Ass 31 Mar 44
42-31093	New Rpt 19 Oct 43		MIA 5 Jan 44
42-31119	New Rpt 22 Nov 43		Crashed and burned 28 Dec 43
42-31189	New Rpt 22 Nov 43		Ass 31 Mar 44
42-31228	New Rpt 22 Nov 43		Ass 31 Mar 44
42-31394	New Rpt 20 Jan 44		Ass 31 Mar 44
42-31510	New Rpt 9 Jan 44		MIA 22 Feb 44
42-31535	New Rpt 24 Jan 44		MIA 30 Jan 44
42-31555	New Rpt 31 Jan 44		MIA 6 Mar 44
42-31592	457BG 18 Mar 44		Ass 31 Mar 44
42-31597	New Rpt 31 Jan 44		Ass 31 Mar 44
42-31643	New Rpt 24 Jan 44		MIA 30 Jan 44
42-31648	New Rpt 17 Feb 44		Ass 31 Mar 44
42-31663	New Rpt 2 Feb 44		Ass 31 Mar 44
42-31692	New Rpt 24 Jan 44		MIA 30 Jan 44
42-31720	New Rpt 27 Jan 44		Ass 31 Mar 44
42-31779	New Rpt 6 Feb 44		Ass 31 Mar 44
42-31799	New Rpt 7 Feb 44		MIA 2 Mar 44
42-31915	New Rpt 6 Feb 44		Ass 31 Mar 44
42-31927	New Rpt 8 Feb 44		Ass 31 Mar 44
42-31972	New Rpt 22 Feb 44		Ass 31 Mar 44
42-32000	NMF	New Rpt 21 Mar 44	Ass 31 Mar 44
42-32024	New Rpt 20 Feb 44		Ass 31 Mar 44
42-32091	New Rpt 30 Mar 44		Ass 31 Mar 44

B-17G Douglas

42-37728	New Rpt 3 Oct 43	MIA 9 Oct 43	
42-37732	New Rpt 19 Oct 43		MIA 25 Feb 44
42-37764	New Rpt 21 Oct 43		Sal after Op Miss 6 Mar 44
42-37768	New Rpt 19 Oct 43		MIA 11 Jan 44 (8 Mar 44)
42-37784	New Rpt 19 Oct 43		Ass 31 Mar 44
42-37787	384BG 11 Nov 43	MIA 26 Nov 43	
42-37791	384BG 7 Nov 43		Ass 31 Mar 44
42-37805	New Rpt 2 Dec 43		Ass 31 Mar 44
42-37825	New Rpt 19 Oct 43	351BG 21 Oct 43	
42-37851	New Rpt 13 Dec 43	MIA 20 Dec 43	
42-37887	New Rpt 22 Nov 43		Crashed 5 Jan 44
42-37888	New Rpt 6 Dec 43		Ass 31 Mar 44
42-38036	New Rpt 21 Jan 44		Cr Ld 2 Feb 44 (4 Feb 44)
42-38057	457BG 18 Mar 44		Ass 31 Mar 44
42-38058	457BG 18 Mar 44		Ass 31 Mar 44
42-38082	New Rpt 29 Jan 44		Ass 31 Mar 44
42-38111	New Rpt 12 Feb 44		Ass 31 Mar 44
42-38141	New Rpt 28 Feb 44		Ass 31 Mar 44

379th Bomb Group(H)	1943			1944			K
	Oct	Nov	Dec	Jan	Feb	Mar	

Serial No	Gained From	Period Assigned	LOST TO
42-38161		New Rpt 19 Feb 44	Ass 31 Mar 44
42-38183		New Rpt 19 Feb 44	Ass 31 Mar 44
42-38185		New Rpt 22 Feb 44	Ass 31 Mar 44
42-38192		New Rpt 1 Mar 44	Ass 31 Mar 44

B-17G Vega

Serial No	Gained From	Period Assigned	LOST TO
42-39762	N R 21 Oct 43	Sal after Op Miss 31 Dec 43 (8 Jan 44)	
42-39779	N R 21 Oct 43	MIA 29 Nov 43	
42-39782	N R 21 Oct 43	MIA 8 Feb 44	
42-39783	384BG 11 Nov 43		Ass 31 Mar 44
42-39789	N R 19 Oct 43		Ass 31 Mar 44
42-39800	384BG 7 Nov 43		Ass 31 Mar 44
42-39828	New Rpt 19 Nov 43		Ass 31 Mar 44
42-39889	New Rpt 22 Nov 43	Dam on Op Miss 30 Jan 44 and Sal. (1 Feb 44)	
42-39980		New Rpt 14 Jan 44	MIA 13 Mar 44
42-40003		New Rpt 20 Jan 44	Ass 31 Mar 44

B-17G Boeing

Serial No	Gained From	Period Assigned	LOST TO
42-97087		New Rpt 1 Mar 44	457BG 2 Mar 44
42-97128	NMF	New Rpt 23 Mar 44	Ass 31 Mar 44
42-97170		New Rpt 30 Mar 44	Ass 31 Mar 44
42-97229		New Rpt 23 Mar 44	Ass 31 Mar 44

B-17G Vega

Serial No	Gained From	Period Assigned	LOST TO
42-97462		New Rpt 9 Jan 44	Ass 31 Mar 44
42-97469		457BG 18 Mar 44	Ass 31 Mar 44
42-97485		New Rpt 29 Jan 44	MIA 26 Mar 44
42-97502		New Rpt 18 Feb 44	Ass 31 Mar 44
42-97520		New Rpt 8 Feb 44	MIA 22 Feb 44

B-17G Douglas

Serial No	Gained From	Period Assigned	LOST TO
42-106985		New Rpt 1 Mar 44	457BG 2 Mar 44
42-106998		New Rpt 28 Feb 44	457BG 2 Mar 44
42-107004	NMF	New Rpt 23 Mar 44	Ass 31 Mar 44
42-107014		New Rpt 30 Mar 44	Ass 31 Mar 44
42-107082		New Rpt 23 Mar 44	Ass 31 Mar 44

FIRST BOMBARDMENT DIVISION SPECIAL FLIGHT SECTION

Serial No	Gained From	Period Assigned	LOST TO
41-24460	B-17F	Alconbury 27 Mar 44	Ass 31 Mar 44
AL452	DB-7B	Alconbury 27 Mar 44	Ass 31 Mar 44
42-58434	UC-78	Alconbury 27 Mar 44	Ass 31 Mar 44
42-7882	P-47D	Alconbury 27 Mar 44	Ass 31 Mar 44
DL899	Master II	Alconbury 27 Mar 44	Ass 31 Mar 44
DF331	Oxford II	Alconbury 27 Mar 44	Ass 31 Mar 44
LB522	Oxford I	Alconbury 27 Mar 44	Ass 31 Mar 44
T6369	Tiger Moth	Alconbury 27 Mar 44	Ass 31 Mar 44
7147	Spitfire	Ass from Alconbury 27 Mar 44 but not on hand until Apr 44	

B-17F Boeing

Serial No	Gained From	Period Assigned	LOST TO
41-24380	B-17F. From 5th Photo Group 12AF	21 Jan 44	28 Jan 44. On hand only, Not Ass

379th BOMBARDMENT GROUP (H)

Nine of the Group's original aircraft survived the first nine months of service and were still with the Group in January 1944. They were 42-5816, 5827 '**LAKANUKI**', 5828, 5830, 29772, 29829, 29869, 29886 and 29889. First to go was 42-5827 which landed in Sweden following the mission of 5th January, next was 29886 which did not return on 29th January and then the vicious battle of 22nd February took out 5828 and 29829. On the 23rd February 29889 was destroyed by fire at Kimbolton during an engine run.

The four remaining aircraft, 42-5816, 5830, 29772 and 29869, survived until the end of March and thus completed one year's service with the Group.

The longest serving replacement aircraft still assigned on the 31st March was 42-29905 which had joined the Group as one of the first replacements on 21 May 1943 and had therefore survived the Group's full operational period.

Also resident at Kimbolton was the First Bombardment Division Flight Section which had moved in from Alconbury on the 27th March. Among the interesting types on hand with this unit, was a P-47D, a Miles Master and a Tiger Moth, the only examples of these types serving in the Division. Also on hand was B-17F 41-24460, the oldest B-17F still serving in the Eighth Air Force.

SHORT SERVING AIRCRAFT: ASSIGNED FOR LESS THAN EIGHT DAYS				
Serial No	Date In	Date Out	Reason Out	Days Ass
42-5382	31 May 43	3 June 43	Transferred	3
42-30107	20 June 43	25 June 43	MIA	5
42-30165	21 June 43	25 June 43	MIA	4
42-30192	20 June 43	27 June 43	To 95BG	7
42-31535	24 Jan 44	30 Jan 44	MIA	6
42-31643	24 Jan 44	30 Jan 44	MIA	6
42-31692	24 Jan 44	30 Jan 44	MIA	6
42-37728	3 Oct 43	9 Oct 43	MIA	6
42-37825	19 Oct 43	21 Oct 43	To 351BG	2
42-37851	13 Dec 43	20 Dec 43	MIA	7
42-97087	1 Mar 44	2 Mar 44	To 457BG	1
42-106985	1 Mar 44	2 Mar 44	To 457BG	1
42-106998	28 Feb 44	2 Mar 44	To 457BG	3

LONG SERVING AIRCRAFT: ASSIGNED FOR ONE YEAR OR MORE										
Serial No	Date In	Date Out	Reason Out	Months Ass		Serial No	Date In	Date Out	Reason Out	Months Ass
42-5816	Orig Act	Still Ass		12		42-29772	Orig Act	Still Ass		12
42-5830	Orig Act	Still Ass		12		42-29869	Orig Act	Still Ass		12

STATUS OF AIRCRAFT ASSIGNED AT 2000 HOURS on 31st MARCH 1944

Operational: 64 B-17 (18 B-17F: 46 B-17G)

Non Operational: 1 B-17E

Operational Aircraft Assigned and on hand at Kimbolton

B-17F

42-3048*	42-5379*	42-29624*	42-29869* (Orig Act)	42-30237
42-3072*	42-5816* (Orig Act)	42-29718*	42-29897*	42-30298
42-3167 (1)	42-5830* (Orig Act)	42-29772* (Orig Act)	42-29905*	42-30720
		42-29802*	42-29997	
		42-29824*		

B-17G

42-3524	42-31648	42-37784	42-39783	42-97462
	42-31663	42-37791	42-39789	42-97469
42-31043	42-31720	42-37805	42-39800	42-97502
42-31083	42-31779	42-38057	42-39828	
42-31085	42-31915	42-38058	42-40003	42-107004 NMF
42-31189	42-31972 NMF	42-38141		42-107014 NMF
42-31228	42-32000 NMF	42-38161	42-97128 NMF	42-107082 NMF
42-31394	42-32024 NMF	42-38183	42-97170 NMF	
42-31597	42-32091 NMF	42-38185	42-97229 NMF	
		42-38192		

Assigned but not on hand

B-17Gs: 42-31592 at Mildenhall: 42-31927 at Lympne: 42-37888 at 2 SAD:
42-38082 at Gatwick: and 42-38111 at Oakington

Non Operational Aircraft on hand at Kimbolton: B-17E 41-9100

(1) B-17F 42-3167 had left the Group on 4th March and was re-assigned on 29 Mar. Due to an error, it was not picked up on the Group's records until 5 April 44 so the records actually showed only 63 operational aircraft assigned.

First Bombardment Division Flight Section aircraft at Kimbolton

B-17F 41-24460: DB-7B AL452: UC-78 42-58434: P-47D 42-7882: Master DL899:
Oxford LB522: Oxford DF331: Tiger Moth T6369:
Spitfire 7147 was Assigned but was not on hand until April 1944

* These 13 B-17Fs were without Tokyo tanks

379th BOMBARDMENT GROUP (H)

AIRCRAFT AND OPERATIONAL STATISTICS				
Total Aircraft Assigned				
B-17E:	28 May 43 to 31 Mar 44	1	B-17G: 3 Oct 43 to 31 Mar 44	76
B-17F:	Mar 43 to 31 Mar 44	100	YB-40: 28 Aug 43 to 12 Oct 43	1
Operational Statistics				

First Mission flown on: 19 May 43
First Act MIA: B-17Fs 42-3113, 29773 and 29878
                  on 29 May 43
First B-17G Ass: 42-37728 on 3 Oct 43
First B-17G MIA: 42-37728 on 9 Oct 43
First NMF Ass: 42-32024 on 20 Feb 44
First NMF MIA: None up to 31 Mar 44

Total Act MIA: 80 (61 B-17F and 19 B-17G)
Highest Days Losses: 6 on 11 June 43, 6 on
            25 June 43 and 6 on 14 Oct 43
Other Losses: (Salvaged) 18 B-17s
  B-17F: 12 (11 OP and 1 Unknown)
  B-17G: 6 (3 Op and 3 Non Op)

B-17Fs in their natural element: There are over two hundred crewmen aloft in the aircraft in this photograph. *US Air Force–National Air and Space Museum*

381st BOMBARDMENT GROUP (H)

Constituted as the 381st BOMBARDMENT GROUP (H) on 28th October 1942
Activated on 3rd November 1942
Squadrons Assigned: 532nd, 533rd, 534th and 535th
Assigned to Eighth Air Force: May 1943
Assigned to First Bombardment Wing: June 1943

COMBAT WING ASSIGNMENTS

101st Provisional Bombardment: June 1943
First Combat Bombardment: 16th September 1943

STATIONS

Bovingdon: Air Echelon only, May 1943
Ridgwell: Ground Echelon in 1st June 1943
Air Echelon in from 5th June 1943

After initial training at Pyote, Texas, the Group moved to Pueblo, Colorado, in early April 1943 where 41 new B-17Fs were received. Most of these coming from the Modification Center at Cheyenne with a few coming from Denver and Long Beach.

The first plane, piloted by Col Joe Nazzaro with Col Hall as co-pilot, left Pueblo for Salina, Kansas, on 4th May and over the next two days the remaining planes of the air echelon followed. At Salina, final modifications for the flight overseas were carried out. One plane, 42-3092, flown by Lt Lord, lost a wheel on take off at Pueblo and was directed to make a landing at Oklahoma City where there was a repair depot.

On 15th May, the first aircraft departed Salina for the trip overseas. Most of the planes flew first to Selfridge Field, Michigan, and then on to Bangor, from where they finally departed the USA and headed for Gander on the first leg of the Atlantic crossing. They then flew to Prestwick and finally to Bovingdon.

The ground echelon left Pueblo in four trains on 9th and 10th May for Camp Kilmer, New Jersey, which was reached on 12th May. From there, they were taken on board the *Queen Elizabeth* in New York harbour from where they made an uneventful crossing to Scotland which was reached on 1st June. They were transported by train to Ridgewell, which would be their home for the next two years.

The first aircraft of the air echelon moved from Bovingdon to Ridgewell on 15th June and by the 16th there were 45 B-17Fs assigned the Group, with 44 of them on hand at Ridgewell.

A waist gunner's view of a B-17F when in close formation. A comforting sight when in hostile skies. 42-3220 was an original 381st Bomb Group aircraft.
Douglas

ORIGINAL B-17Fs ASSIGNED AT PUEBLO APRIL 1943							
42-3092	532BS	42-5845	534BS	42-29978	534BS	42-30016	532BS
42-3211	535BS	42-5846	533BS	42-29988	535BS	42-30020	532BS
42-3215	533BS	42-5847	535BS	42-29992	533BS	42-30021	533BS
42-3217	535BS					42-30024	533BS
42-3219	534BS	42-29789	532BS	42-30009	532BS	42-30025	534BS (1)
42-3220	535BS	42-29888	532BS	42-30011	535BS	42-30026	534BS
42-3221	534BS	42-29950	535BS	42-30012	534BS	42-30027	533BS
42-3223	533BS	42-29953	535BS	42-30013	532BS	42-30028	532BS
42-3225	535BS	42-29954	534BS	42-30014	533BS	42-30029	535BS
42-3226	535BS	42-29958	534BS	42-30015	533BS	42-30034	Gp Comm
42-3227		42-29976	532BS				
(1) 42-30025 : Did not proceed to England with the Group							

381st Bomb Group(H)	1943								1944			L
	Apr	May	Jun	Jly	Aug	Sep	Oct	Nov	Dec	Jan	Feb	Mar

Serial No	Gained From ▓▓▓ Period Assigned ▓▓▓ Lost To

B-17E

41-9019	92BG 11 June 43 ▓▓ 92BG 10 July 43
41-9043	Date in unknown ▓▓▓▓▓▓▓▓▓▓▓ Ass 31 Mar 44
41-24500	15 June 43 ▓▓ Bovingdon 18 July 43

B-17F Douglas

42-2978	306BG 19 Nov 43 ▓▓▓▓ Ass 31 Mar 44
42-3033	Date in unknown ▓▓▓▓▓▓▓▓ 2 SAD 9 Jan 44, then 2 CCRC
42-3048	305BG 22 Aug 43 ▓▓ 379BG 26 Sep 43
42-3078	New Rpt 15 June 43 ▓▓▓▓▓▓▓▓ MIA 7 Jan 44
42-3092	Or Ac ▓▓▓▓▓▓ MIA 17 Aug 43
42-3100	95BG 20 July 43 ▓▓ MIA 30 July 43
42-3101	New Rpt 21 July 43 ▓▓ MIA 19 Aug 43
42-3118	96BG 6 July 43 ▓▓▓▓▓▓▓▓ MIA 11 Jan 44
42-3123	96BG 16 July 43 ▓▓▓▓ MIA 8 Oct 43
42-3177	96BG 15 July 43 ▓▓▓▓▓▓▓ R.A.F. 25 Jan 44
42-3180	96BG 16 July 43 ▓▓▓▓ MIA 9 Oct 43
42-3211	Or Ac ▓▓▓ Crash Landed 14 July 43
42-3215	Or Ac ▓▓▓▓▓▓▓▓▓▓▓ MIA 6 Mar 44
42-3217	Or Ac ▓▓▓▓ MIA 24 July 43. Landed in Sweden. First 8th AF B-17 to do so.
42-3219	Or Ac ▓▓ Not To UK with Group. Later with 94BG.
42-3220	Or Ac ▓▓▓▓▓▓ MIA 17 Aug 43
42-3221	Or Ac ▓▓▓▓ Crash Landed 29 July 43
42-3223	Or Ac ▓▓▓ Crashed 14 july 43
42-3225	Or Ac ▓▓▓▓▓▓ MIA 17 Aug 43
42-3226	Or Ac ▓▓ Crash Landed 22 June 43
42-3227	Or Ac ▓▓▓▓▓▓ MIA 17 Aug 43
42-3268	Date in Unknown ▓▓ 96BG 6 July 43
42-3411	New Rpt 21 Sep 43 ▓▓▓▓▓▓ Ass 31 Mar 44

B-17G Douglas

42-3514	New Rpt 24 Sep 43 ▓▓▓▓ MIA 11 Jan 44
42-3522	New Rpt 27 Sep 43 ▓▓▓▓▓ Ass 31 Mar 44
42-3525	Ex 482BG Stansted 22 Feb 44 ▓▓ Ass 31 Mar 44
42-3540	New Rpt 16 Sep 43 ▓▓▓ MIA 1 Dec 43
42-3562	401BG 2 Nov 43 ▓▓▓▓ MIA 20 Feb 44
42-3563	New Rpt 24 Sep 43 ▓▓(*) (*) ▓ MIA 20 Dec 43 (*) Out for Rep/Main 9 Oct – 12 Dec 43 (*)

B-17F Vega

42-5725	305BG 22 Aug 43 ▓▓▓▓▓ Ass 31 Mar 44
42-5747	305BG 22 Aug 43 ▓▓▓ 384BG 5 Oct 43
42-5845	Or Ac ▓▓▓▓▓▓▓ MIA 20 Dec 43
42-5846	Or Ac ▓▓▓▓▓▓▓ MIA 20 Dec 43
42-5847	Or Ac ▓▓▓▓ MIA 12 Aug 43
42-5878	New Rpt 18 Sep 43 ▓▓▓▓ MIA 11 Jan 44

B-17F Boeing

42-29506	306BG 22 Aug 43 ▓▓▓▓ MIA 1 Dec 43
42-29570	303BG – AFSC 7 Sep 43 ▓▓▓▓▓ Ass 31 Mar 44
42-29633	305BG 11 Sep 43 ▓ 379BG 26 Sep 43
42-29731	96BG 16 July 43 ▓▓ MIA 17 Aug 43
42-29735	96BG 16 July 43 ▓▓ MIA 17 Aug 43 (Ditched)
42-29751	96BG – AFSC 7 Sep 43 ▓▓▓▓▓▓ Crashed 31 Mar 44
42-29755	96BG 14 July 43 ▓▓▓▓▓▓▓ Ass 31 Mar 44
42-29761	96BG 14 July 43 ▓▓▓▓▓▓ MIA 30 Jan 44
42-29765	96BG 14 July 43 ▓▓▓▓ MIA 8 Oct 43

381st Bomb Group(H)

	1943		1944	L
	Apr May Jun Jly Aug Sep Oct Nov Dec		Jan Feb Mar	

Serial No	Gained From — Period Assigned — Lost To
42-29784	305BG 11 Sep 43 ... 384BG 4 Oct 43
42-29789	Or Ac ... MIA 3 Sep 43
42-29803	305BG 11 Sep 43 ... MIA 14 Oct 43
42-29832	305BG 22 Aug 43 ... Ass 31 Mar 44
42-29854	New Rpt 16 June 43 ... MIA 8 Oct 43
42-29867	305BG 22 Aug 43 ... 384BG 4 Oct 43
42-29888	Or Ac ... Ass 31 Mar 44
42-29923	305BG 11 Sep 43 ... Crashed 4 Jan 44 (5 Jan 44)
42-29928	New Rpt 23 June 43 ... MIA 4 July 43
42-29941	96BG 15 July 43 ... MIA 8 Oct 43
42-29950	Or Ac ... MIA 12 Aug 43
42-29953	Or Ac ... MIA 22 Aug 43
42-29954	Or Ac ... MIA 12 Aug 43
42-29958	Or Ac ... MIA 9 Oct 43
42-29976	Or Ac ... MIA 25 July 43
42-29978	Or Ac ... MIA 17 Aug 43
42-29983	96BG 14 july 43 ... MIA 17 Aug 43
42-29984	New Rpt 16 June 43 ... Crash Landed 22 June 43
42-29988	Or Ac ... 305BG 22 Aug 43
42-29992	Or Ac ... Dam by Explosion of 42-30024 23 June 43 (1 July 43)
42-29999	96BG 16 July 43 ... MIA 11 Jan 44
42-30004	New Rpt 15 June 43 ... 305BG 22 Aug 43
42-30009	Or Ac ... MIA 8 Oct 43
42-30011	Or Ac ... MIA 14 July 43
42-30012	Or Ac ... MIA 9 Oct 43
42-30013	Or Ac ... MIA 25 July 43
42-30014	Or Ac ... R.A.F. 29 Jan 44
42-30015	Or Ac ... 305BG 22 Aug 43
42-30016	Or Ac ... MIA 22 June 43
42-30018	Or Ac ... 305BG 22 Aug 43
42-30020	Or Ac ... Cr Landed 9 June 43 (16 June 43). First Group Act Sal in U.K.
42-30021	Or Ac ... MIA 22 June 43
42-30024	Or Ac ... Exploded on Ground 23 June 43 and Destroyed.
42-30025	Or Ac ... Not to U.K. with Group.
42-30026	Or Ac ... 384BG 30 May 43
42-30027	Or Ac ... MIA 25 June 43
42-30028	Or Ac ... MIA 17 Aug 43
42-30029	Or Ac ... MIA 30 Jan 44
42-30034	Or Ac ... 305BG 22 Aug 43
42-30140	New Rpt 23 June 43 ... MIA 17 Aug 43
42-30151	New Rpt 15 june 43 ... MIA 4 Mar 44
42-30153	96BG 16 July 43 ... MIA 25 July 43
42-30245	New Rpt 15 June 43 ... MIA 17 Aug 43
42-30613	Ex 482BG – Stansted 28 Feb 44 ... Ass 31 Mar 44
42-30676	New Rpt 19 Sep 43 ... MIA 5 Jan 44
42-30721	New Rpt 19 Sep 43 ... Ass 31 Mar 44
42-30722	482BG 20 Sep 43 ... MIA 8 Oct 43
42-30732	New Rpt 26 Sep 43 ... Crash Landed 3 Feb 44 (5 Feb 44)
42-30765	New Rpt 20 Sep 43 ... Force Landed 29 Dec 43 (30 Dec 43)
42-30834	New Rpt 23 Sep 43 ... Crash Landed 4 Feb 44 (7 Feb 44)
42-30852	New Rpt 24 Sep 43 ... MIA 5 Nov 43
42-30864	New Rpt 19 Sep 43 ... MIA 8 Oct 43

381st Bomb Group(H)	1943						1944			(L)
	July	Aug	Sep	Oct	Nov	Dec	Jan	Feb	Mar	

Serial No	Gained From ▨▨▨ Period Assigned ▨▨▨ Lost To

B-17G Boeing

Serial No	Notes
42-31047	New Rpt 20 Oct 43 — MIA 30 Jan 44
42-31067	New Rpt 20 Oct 43 — Ass 31 Mar 44
42-31075	New Rpt 20 Oct 43 — MIA 20 Dec 43
42-31097	401BG 21 Nov 43 — MIA 1 Dec 43
42-31099	401 BG 21 Nov 43 — MIA 11 Feb 44
42-31111	New Rpt 19 Oct 43 — MIA 1 Dec 43
42-31197	New Rpt 13 Jan 44 — Ass 31 Mar 44
42-31278	New Rpt 20 Dec 43 — Crashed 4 Jan 44
42-31291	New Rpt 11 Dec 43 — Ass 31 Mar 44
42-31357	New Rpt 13 Dec 43 — Ass 31 Mar 44
42-31381	New Rpt 22 Jan 44 — MIA 20 Mar 44
42-31417	New Rpt 13 Dec 43 — MIA 11 Jan 44
42-31443	New Rpt 6 Jan 44 — MIA 22 Feb 44
42-31448	New Rpt 23 Jan 44 — MIA 6 Mar 44
42-31490	New Rpt 10 Jan 44 — MIA 24 Mar 44
42-31497	New Rpt 22 Jan 44 — Ass 31 Mar 44
42-31533	New Rpt 5 Jan 44 — MIA 22 Feb 44
42-31550	New Rpt 13 Jan 44 — Ass 31 Mar 44
42-31553	New Rpt 19 Feb 44 — MIA 6 Mar 44
42-31569	New Rpt 19 Feb 44 — Ass 31 Mar 44
42-31570	New Rpt 2 Feb 44 — Ass 31 Mar 44
42-31575	New Rpt 20 Feb 44 — Ass 31 Mar 44
42-31614	New Rpt 22 Jan 44 — Ass 31 Mar 44
42-31696	New Rpt 20 Feb 44 — MIA 22 Feb 44
42-31698	New Rpt 23 Feb 44 — Ass 31 Mar 44
42-31761	New Rpt 31 Jan 44 — Ass 31 Mar 44
42-31878	New Rpt 20 Feb 44 — Ass 31 Mar 44
42-32025	NMF — New Rpt 25 Feb 44 — Ass 31 Mar 44
42-32102	New Rpt 25 Mar 44 — Ass 31 Mar 44

B-17G Douglas

Serial No	Notes
42-37719	New Rpt 1 Oct 43 — MIA 11 Jan 44
42-37721	New Rpt 1 Oct 43 — Ass 31 Mar 44
42-37730	New Rpt 20 Sep 43 — MIA 11 Jan 44
42-37733	Ex 482BG — Stansted 22 Feb 44 — Ass 31 Mar 44
42-37754	New Rpt 20 Sep 43 — Crashed 28 Mar 44
42-37760	New Rpt 20 Sep 43 — Ass 31 Mar 44
42-37786	401BG 21 Nov 43 — MIA 25 Feb 44
42-37884	New Rpt 20 Dec 43 — MIA 29 Jan 44
42-37933	New Rpt 20 Dec 43 — Crashed 28 Mar 44
42-37962	New Rpt 20 Dec 43 — MIA 11 Jan 44
42-37969	(+) Out for Repair 12 Jan 44 to 15 Mar 44 (+) — New Rpt 23 Dec 43 — (+) (+) Ass 31 Mar 44
42-37983	New Rpt 22 Jan 44 — MIA 6 Mar 44
42-37986	New Rpt 15 Jan 44 — MIA 3 Mar 44
42-38004	New Rpt 6 Jan 44 — Ass 31 Mar 44
42-38009	New Rpt 8 Jan 44 — Ass 31 Mar 44
42-38010	New Rpt 13 Jan 44 — Ass 31 Mar 44
42-38029	Ex 482BG — Stansted 1 Mar 44 — MIA 8 Mar 44
42-38045	New Rpt 22 Jan 44 — MIA 29 Jan 44
42-38061	New RPt 2 Feb 44 — Ass 31 Mar 44
42-38079	Stansted 20 Feb 44 — Ass 31 Mar 44
42-38102	457BG 12 Mar 44 — Crashed 24 Mar 44
42-38103	457BG 12 Mar 44 — Ass 31 Mar 44
42-38117	New Rpt 26 Feb 44 — Ass 31 Mar 44
42-38159	New Rpt 28 Feb 44 — Ass 31 Mar 44
42-38194	New Rpt 25 Mar 44 — Ass 31 Mar 44

381st Bomb Group(H)	1943			1944			⚠ L
	Oct	Nov	Dec	Jan	Feb	Mar	

B-17G Vega

Serial No	Gained From	Period		Lost To
42-39797		New Rpt 22 Jan 44	Crashed on Take off 4 Feb 44 (12 Feb 44)	
42-39798		New Rpt 24 Jan 44		Ass 31 Mar 44
42-39808	N R 19 Oct 43	Crashed 1 Dec 43 (2 Dec 43)		
42-39890	New Rpt 20 Dec 43			Ass 31 Mar 44
42-39891	New Rpt 13 Jan 44		MIA 2 Mar 44	
42-39895	New Rpt 22 Dec 43		MIA 22 Feb 44	
42-39906	Ne Rpt 20 Dec 43			Ass 31 Mar 44
42-39910	New Rpt 20 Dec 43	MIA 31 Dec 43		
42-39946	New Rpt 22 Jan 44		MIA 22 Feb 44	
42-39997	New Rpt 13 Jan 44			Ass 31 Mar 44
42-40007	New Rpt 22 Jan 44			Ass 31 Mar 44
42-40008	New Rpt 8 Jan 44		MIA 24 Mar 44	
42-40011	New Rpt 22 Jan 44			Ass 31 Mar 44
42-40017	New Rpt 5 Jan 44			Ass 31 Mar 44
42-40025	New Rpt 6 Jan 44		Dam On Op Miss 6 Feb 44 (8 Feb 44)	

B-17G Boeing

42-97059		457BG 17 Mar 44	Ass 31 Mar 44
42-97076	NMF	457BG 17 Mar 44	Ass 31 Mar 44
42-97214		New Rpt 25 Mar 44	Ass 31 Mar 44

B-17G Vega

42-97442	New Rpt 21 Feb 44		Ass 31 Mar 44
42-97454	New Rpt 13 Jan 44		Ass 31 Mar 44
42-97471	457BG 12 Mar 44	Wrecked 20 Mar 44 (21 Mar 44)	
42-97474	New Rpt 15 Jan 44	MIA 22 Feb 44	
42-97503	New Rpt 13 Jan 44		Ass 31 Mar 44
42-97511	New Rpt 22 Feb 44		Ass 31 Mar 44

B-17G Douglas

42-107018	NMF	New Rpt 25 Mar 44	Ass 31 Mar 44
42-107023		New Rpt 25 Mar 44	Ass 31 Mar 44

Piper L-4B Cub

43-648	* ▨▨▨ 91BG 26 Oct 43	* Gained from 92BG on 10 July 43.

42-3134	B-17F	Special VHF Aircraft Ass to 8th Fighter Command	6 Mar 44	On hand at 31 Mar 44

43-666	L-4B Cub	25 Nov 43 ▨ 3 Dec 43	Assigned to 56th Fighter Group. Made emergency landing.

381st BOMBARDMENT GROUP (H)

Four of the Group's original aircraft survived into 1944, 42-3215 **'LINDA MARY'**, 42-29888 **'THE JOKER'**, 42-30014 and 42-30029 **'CHAPS FLYING CIRCUS'**. The first to go was 30014 which was transferred to the RAF on 29th January and the next day the **'FLYING CIRCUS'** went MIA. **'LINDA MARY'** became the last of the originals to go MIA when she failed to return from Berlin on 6th March. This left **'THE JOKER'** as the only original still with the Group on 31st March, and this aircraft then had only five more days to serve before retirement and return to the USA.

The longest serving replacement aircraft was 42-29755 which had come from the 96th Bomb Group on 14th June 1943.

Also assigned on 31st March were 42-2978 and 42-5725; respectively the oldest operational Douglas and Vega built B-17s then serving in the Eighth Air Force.

SHORT SERVING AIRCRAFT: ASSIGNED FOR LESS THAN EIGHT DAYS				
Serial No.	Date In	Date Out	Reason Out	Days Ass
42-29984	16 June 43	22 June 43	Cr Ld	6
42-31696	20 Feb 44	22 Feb 44	MIA	2
42-38029	1 Mar 44	8 Mar 44	MIA	7
42-38045	22 Jan 44	29 Jan 44	MIA	7

LONG SERVING AIRCRAFT: ASSIGNED FOR TEN MONTHS OR MORE										
Serial No	Date In	Date Out	Reason Out	Months Ass		Serial No	Date In	Date Out	Reason Out	Months Ass
42-3215	Orig Act	6 Mar 44	MIA	11		42-29888	Orig Act	Still Ass		11

AIRCRAFT AND OPERATIONAL STATISTICS

Total Aircraft Assigned

B-17E:	11 June 43 to 31 Mar 44	2	B-17G:	16 Sep 43 to 31 Mar 44	86
B-17F:	Apr 43 to 31 Mar 44	91	L-4B:	10 July 43 to 26 Oct 43	1

Operational Statistics

First Mission flown on: 22 June 43

First Act MIA: 42-30016 and 30021 on 22 June 43

First B-17G Ass: 42-3540 on 16 Sep 43

First B-17G MIA: 42-31097 and 31111 on 1 Dec 43

First NMF Ass: 42-32025 on 25 Feb 44

First NMF MIA: None up to 31 Mar 44

Total Act Mia: 82 (51 B-17F and 31 B-17G)

Highest Days Losses: 11 on 17 Aug 43

Other Losses: (Salvaged) 22 B-17s

  B-17F: 12 (7 Op, 5 Non Op)

  B-17G: 10 (8 Op, 1 Non Op, 1 Unknown)

STATUS OF AIRCRAFT ASSIGNED AT 2000 HOURS on 31st MARCH 1944

Operational: 55 B-17 (9 B-17F: 46 B-17G)

Non Operational: 1 B-17E

Operational Aircraft Assigned and on hand at Ridgewell

B-17F

42-2978*	42-29750*	42-29832*	42-30613
42-3411	42-29755*	42-29888* (Orig Act)	42-30721

B-17G

42-3522	42-31575	42-37760	42-39798	42-97214 NMF
42-3525	42-31614	42-37969	42-39890	
	42-31698	42-38004	42-39906	42-97442
42-31197	42-31761	42-38010	42-39997	42-97454
42-31291	42-31878	42-38061	42-40007	42-97503
42-31357	42-32025 NMF	42-38103	42-40011	42-97511
42-31497	42-32102 NMF	42-38117	42-40017	
42-31550		42-38159		42-107018 NMF
42-31569	42-37721	42-38194	42-97059 NMF	42-107023 NMF
42-31570	42-37733		42-97076 NMF	

Assigned but not on hand

B-17F 42-5725* At Andrews Field for Rep: B-17Gs: 42-31067 at Predannack for Rep:

42-38009 at Exeter for Rep: 42-38079 at Leiston for Rep.

Non Operational Aircraft on hand at Ridgewell: B-17E 41-9043

On hand but not Assigned: B-17F 42-3134. Special VHF Act Ass to Eighth Fighter Command

* These six Act without Tokyo tanks

384th BOMBARDMENT GROUP (H)

Constituted as the 384th BOMBARDMENT GROUP (H) on 25th November 1942
Activated on 1st December 1942
Squadrons Assigned: 544th, 545th, 546th and 547th
Assigned to Eighth Air Force: May 1943
Assigned to First Bombardment Wing: May 1943

COMBAT WING ASSIGNMENTS

103rd Provisional Bombardment: June 1943
41st Combat Bombardment: 16th September 1943

STATION

Grafton Underwood: Air Echelon in 26th May 1943
Ground Echelon in 3rd June 1943

Trained in USA on B-17Fs. Moved from Wendover, Utah, to Sioux City, Iowa, on 1st April 1943. Here new B-17Fs were assigned. These came from the Modification Centers at Cheyenne, Long Beach and Denver.

On 2nd May an advance party moved to Atlantic City, New Jersey, and on 3rd May the air echelon left for Kearney, Nebraska, for final phase training.

On 9th May the ground echelon boarded trains for Camp Kilmer where final preparations for the journey overseas were made. It was Wednesday 26th May before they left Camp Kilmer and made the trip through New Jersey countryside and across the Hudson river by ferry to board the *Queen Elizabeth*.

The 'Queen' sailed shortly after noon on 27th May and arrived in the Firth of Clyde on Wednesday 2nd June. Early next morning the ground echelon disembarked and boarded trains for the journey south to Kettering where trucks were waiting to take them to their new home at Grafton Underwood.

The air echelon flew from Kearney to Bangor and then on to Prestwick during the last week of May. Some aircraft routed via Goose Bay and others via Gander. From Prestwick they flew to Grafton Underwood. One plane, 42-30074, was wrecked before leaving the USA, another, 42-5851, crashed when landing at Gander and a third, 42-30041, crashed in the sea off Greenland.

The first nine aircraft, 42-5848, 5849, 5850, 5852, 5853, 30033, 30040, 30046 and 30065, reported in at Grafton Underwood on 26th May. Twenty-five were in by the end of May and there were 40 assigned and on hand by 23rd June.

A B-17E, 41-9022, was assigned for training duties on 5th June. This came from the 92nd Bomb Group and had until shortly before been on detached service to the Air Force Service Command who had used it as a navigational escort for ferrying fighters to North Africa.

The first replacement B-17F was assigned on 9th June and the first loss of a plane in England occurred on 12th June when 42-30036 crashed after a mid air collision which killed all five crew.

Another addition was DB-7B AL496 which was assigned from the 92BG for training and target towing duties on 14th June.

Damage to the nose of 42-31871 after it had flown through the smoke emission from Skymarkers on 2nd March 1944. The combat life of this aircraft lasted 26 days and was terminated by a crash landing in Switzerland following the mission of 18th March 1944. *US Air Force*

ORIGINAL B-17Fs ASSIGNED AT SIOUX CITY APRIL 1943				
42-3216	42-5838	42-29956	42-30036	42-30049
42-3218	42-5843	42-29960	42-30037	42-30065
42-3222	42-5848		42-30039	42-30073
42-3230	42-5849	42-30005	42-30040	42-30074 (1)
42-3231	42-5850	42-30026	42-30041 (3)	42-30076
42-3235	42-5851 (2)	42-30030	42-30043	42-30131
	42-5852	42-30031	42-30045	42-30139
	42-5853	42-30032	42-30046	42-30142
		42-30033	42-30048	42-30143

(1) Wrecked in the U.S.A. about 1st May 43
(2) Crashed at Bangor, 19th May 1943
(3) Crashed in the sea, 9th June 1943

Serial No	Gained From — Period Assigned — Lost To
	B-17E
41-9022	92BG 4 June 43 — Ass 31 Mar 44
	B-17F Boeing
41-24507	306BG 22 Aug 43 — MIA 6 Sep 43
41-24525	305BG 22 Sep 43 — MIA 7 Jan 44
41-24529	305BG 22 Sep 43 — Crash landed 9 Oct 43 (11 Oct 43)
41-24557	306BG 22 Aug 43 — MIA 1 Dec 43
41-24560	306BG 5 Sep 43 — Burtonwood 15 Mar 44
41-24575	305BG 19 Sep 43 — Crashed 13 Nov 43
41-24578	305BG 8 Oct 43 — Burtonwood 15 Mar 44
	B-17F Douglas
42-3024	New Rpt 28 June 43 — MIA 25 July 43
42-3037	305BG 20 Sep 43 — Crashed 14 oct 43 (15 Oct 43)
42-3041	306BG 22 Aug 43 — MIA 6 Sep 43
42-3051	305BG 19 Sep 43 — Ass 31 Mar 44
42-3069	94BG 12 July 43 — MIA 25 July 43
42-3074	94BG 12 July 43 — 306BG 22 Aug 43
42-3075	94BG 12 July 43 — MIA 25 July 43
42-3087	306BG 4 Sep 43 — MIA 22 Feb 44
42-3088	94BG 12 July 43 — MIA 25 July 43
42-3104	94BG 12 July 43 — MIA 12 Aug 43
42-3122	96BG 6 July 43 — MIA 25 July 43
42-3188	New Rpt 9 June 43 — MIA 26 June 43
42-3216	Or Ac — MIA 14 Oct 43
42-3218	Or Ac — Burtonwood 4 Jan 44 Then to R.A.F.
42-3222	Or Ac — MIA 17 Aug 43
42-3230	Or Ac — MIA 17 Aug 43
42-3231	Or Ac — MIA 12 Aug 43
42-3235	Or Ac — MIA 4 July 43
42-3259	94BG 16 july 43 — Cheddington 1 Mar 43
42-3317	New Rpt 10 June 43 — 95BG 28 June 43
42-3330	New Rpt 27 June 43 — MIA 14 July 43
42-3429	New Rpt 11 Aug 43 — Ass 31 Mar 44
42-3440	In before 6 June 43 — Ass 31 Mar 44
42-3441	New Rpt 9 Aug 43 — Ass 31 Mar 44
42-3455	New Rpt 11 Aug 43 — MIA 6 Sep 43
42-3459	New Rpt 9 Aug 43 — MIA 23 Sep 43
	B-17F Boeing
42-5051	New Rpt 26 July 43 — MIA 26 Nov 43
42-5086	306BG 5 Sep 43 — Crashed 10 Oct 43 (11 Oct 43)
42-5404	306BG 22 Aug 43 — MIA 30 Jan 44
42-5444	303BG – L Lodge 11 Aug 43 — MIA 30 Jan 44
	B-17F Vega
42-5720	306B 22 Aug 43 — MIA 6 Sep 43
	YB-40
42-5739	303BG 28 Aug 43 — Burtonwood 12 Oct 43
	B-17F Vega
42-5747	381BG 5 Oct 43 — (+) (+) Bwd 15 Mar 44
42-5797	Date in unknown — MIA 16 Aug 43 (+) At 2 SAD 1 Dec 43 to 4 Mar 44 (+)
42-5806	New Rpt 3 July 43 — MIA 12 Aug 43
42-5838	Or Ac — MIA 4 Jan 44

384th Bomb Group(H) △P

1943: Apr May Jun Jly Aug Sep Oct Nov Dec **1944:** Jan Feb Mar

Serial No		Gained From — Period Assigned — Lost To
42-5843	Or Ac	MIA 6 Sep 43
42-5848	Or Ac	Dam on Op Miss 30 July 43 (6 Aug 43)
42-5849	Or Ac	MIA 16 Sep 43
42-5850	Or Ac	MIA 25 June 43
42-5851	Or Ac	Crashed 19 May 43 at Bangor, Maine, U.S.A.
42-5852	Or Ac	Crashed 14 Oct 43 (15 Oct 43)
42-5853	Or Ac	MIA 22 June 43
42-5855		95BG 28 June 43 — 306BG 22 Aug 43
42-5883		96BG 6 July 43 — MIA 25 July 43
42-5889		New Rpt 23 June 43 — 306BG 22 Aug 43

B-17F Boeing

Serial No	Event / Notes
42-29529	305BG 6 Nov 43 — Crash Landed 13 Dec 43 (16 Dec 43)
42-29554	306BG 22 Aug 43 — Farnborough 19 feb 44
42-29557	305B 20 Sep 43 — Crash Landed 10 Oct 43 (11 Oct 43)
42-29632	305BG 8 Oct 43 — Ass 31 Mar 44
42-29636	305BG 30 Sep 43 — BAD 15 Mar 44
42-29651	New Rpt 27 June 43 — (*) — Ass 31 Mar 44
42-29670	94BG 16 July 43 — 25 July 43 — (*) At Metfield 23 Feb to 9 Mar 44
42-29686	94BG 12 July 43 — MIA 12 Aug 43
42-29688	305BG 6 Nov 43 — Ass 31 Mar 44
42-29699	94BG 16 July 43 — MIA 6 Sep 43
42-29700	94BG 12 July 43 — MIA 29 July 43
42-29703	95BG 10 July 43 — Ass 31 Mar 44
42-29712	92BG 14 Sep 43 — MIA 9 Oct 43
42-29717	92BG 13 Sep 43 — MIA 25 Feb 44
42-29723	94BG – BAD 16 Oct 43 — Ass 31 Mar 44
42-29728	94BG 12 July 43 — Crash Landed 17 Aug 43 (19 Aug 43)
42-29733	305BG 6 Nov 43 — Over Shot 16 Dec 43 (19 Dec 43)
42-29768	95BG 28 une 43 — MIA 1 Dec 43
42-29784	381BG 4 Oct 43 — Crashed 14 Oct 43 (15 Oct 43)
42-29800	305BG 8 Oct 43 — MIA 14 Oct 43
42-29809	306BG 4 Sep 43 — Ass 31 Mar 44
42-29814	New Rpt 26 July 43 — MIA 9 Oct 43
42-29828	96BG 14 July 43 — Ass 31 Mar 44
42-29867	381BG 4 Oct 43 — MIA 14 Oct 43
42-29870	305BG 29 Sep 43 — MIA 14 Oct 43
42-29914	96BG 14 Aug 43 — MIA 3 Sep 43
42-29927	96BG 6 July 43 — Ass 31 Mar 44
42-29935	96BG 14 Aug 43 — MIA 20 Dec 43
42-29956	Or Ac — MIA 17 Aug 43
42-29960	Or Ac — MIA 4 July 43
42-29985	New Rpt 28 June 43 — 306BG 22 Aug 43
42-29987	305BG 19 Sep 43 — MIA 26 Nov 43
42-30005	Or Ac — Over Shot 26 Nov 43 (9 Dec 43)
42-30026	Or Ac — Ass 31 Mar 44
42-30030	Or Ac — AFSC 31 July 43 then to 388 BG
42-30031	Or Ac — MIA 26 June 43
42-30032	Or Ac — MIA 28 July 43
42-30033	Or Ac
42-30036	Or Ac — Crashed 12 June 43
42-30037	Or Ac — MIA 26 June 43
42-30039	Or Ac — To Little Staughton 14 Aug 43, then unknown
42-30040	Or Ac — 96BG 6 July 43
42-30041	Or Ac — Crashed in Sea off Greenland 9 June 43

384th Bomb Group(H)

	1943	1944	△ P
	Apr May Jun Jly Aug Sep Oct Nov Dec	Jan Feb Mar	

Serial No	Gained From ▨▨▨ Period Assigned ▨▨▨ Lost To
42-30034	Or Ac — MIA 4 Oct 43 (Ditched)
42-30045	Or Ac — 95BG 28 June 43
42-30046	Or Ac — MIA 12 Aug 43
42-30048	Or Ac — MIA 26 June 43
42-30049	Or Ac — MIA 25 June 43
42-30058	New Rpt 26 June 43 MIA 26 June 43
42-30065	Or Ac — 306BG 22 Aug 43
42-30073	Or Ac — 96BG 6 July 43
42-30074	Or Ac Wrecked in U.S.A. about 1 May 43
42-30076	Or Ac — MIA 22 June 43
42-30131	Or Ac — AFSC 17 July 43. Then to Bovingdon
42-30139	Or Ac — MIA 17 Aug 43
42-30142	Or Ac — Lt Stn 14 Aug 43. Then to 388BG
42-30143	Or Ac — MIA 25 June 43
42-30145	94BG 12 July 43 — 306BG 22 Aug 43
42-30147	New Rpt 28 June 43 MIA 17 Aug 43
42-30180	New Rpt 10 June 43 96BG 6 July 43
42-30196	New Rpt 23 June 43 MIA 14 Oct 43

B-17G Boeing

Serial No	
42-31042	New Rpt 2 Nov 43 MIA 26 Nov 43
42-31045	305BG 29 Nov 43 Crash landed 8 Feb 44 (17 Feb 44)
42-31048	New Rpt 1 Mar 44 Ass 31 Mar 44
42-31058	New Rpt 18 Oct 43 MIA 28 Feb 44
42-31059	New Rpt 7 Oct 43 MIA 14 Oct 43. (First Group B-17G MIA)
42-31073	New Rpt 18 Oct 43 Crashed 31 Dec 43 (5 Jan 43)
42-31166	482BG – Stansted 5 Feb 44 Crashed 24 Mar 44
42-31211	New Rpt 23 Nov 43 Ass 31 Mar 44
42-31222	New Rpt 23 Nov 43 Ass 31 Mar 44
42-31235	New Rpt 6 Jan 44 Ass 31 Mar 44
42-31246	New Rpt 27 Nov 43 MIA 14 Jan 44
42-31274	New Rpt 22 Nov 43 MIA 30 Dec 43 (Ditched)
42-31346	New Rpt 20 Jan 44 Ass 31 Mar 44
42-31364	New Rpt 10 Jan 44 Ass 31 Mar 44
42-31375	New Rpt 21 Jan 44 Ass 31 Mar 44
42-31415	New Rpt 8 Jan 44 Crash Landed 30 Jan 44 (2 Feb 44)
42-31433	New Rpt 8 Jan 44 Ass 31 Mar 44
42-31435	New Rpt 2 Mar 44 Ass 31 Mar 44
42-31484	New Rpt 20 Jan 44 Ass 31 Mar 44
42-31495	New Rpt 21 Jan 44 Ass 31 Mar 44
42-31516	New Rpt 8 Feb 44 Crashed 22 Feb 44 (23 Feb 44)
42-31606	New Rpt 6 Jan 44 MIA 4 Mar 44
42-31740	New Rpt 1 Mar 44 Ass 31 Mar 44
42-31871	New Rpt 22 Feb 44 MIA 18 Mar 44
42-31926	New Rpt 19 Feb 44 MIA 19 Mar 44
42-32007	First Group NMF MIA New Rpt 1 Mar 44 MIA 4 Mar 44
42-32106	NMF New Rpt 24 Mar 44 Ass 31 Mar 44

B-17G Douglas

Serial No	
42-37725	New Rpt 19 Dec 43 MIA 31 Dec 43 (Crashed in Sea)
42-37727	New Rpt 2 Nov 43 MIA 30 Jan 44
42-37758	New Rpt 3 Oct 43 Ass 31 Mar 44
42-37762	New Rpt 2 Nov 43 MIA 26 Nov 43
42-37776	New Rpt 2 Nov 43 Ass 31 Mar 44
42-37781	New Rpt 2 Nov 43 MIA 9 Mar 44
42-37785	New Rpt 2 Nov 43 Ass 31 Mar 44
42-37787	New Rpt 2 Nov 43 379BG 11 Nov 43
42-37788	New Rpt 7 Nov 43 Ass 31 Mar 44

384th Bomb Group(H)		1943			1944				
		Oct	Nov	Dec	Jan	Feb	Mar		P
Serial No		Gained From			Period Assigned			Lost To	
42-37789	New Rpt 2 Nov 43							Ass 31 Mar 44	
42-37791	New Rpt 2 Nov 43		379BG 7 Nov 43						
42-37792	New Rpt 2 Nov 43							Ass 31 Mar 44	
42-37793	New Rpt 2 Nov 43						MIA 18 Mar 44		
42-37801		New Rpt 25 Nov 43						MIA 16 Mar 44	
42-37816	N R 18 Oct 43							Ass 31 Mar 44	
42-37825	N R 21 Oct 43						MIA 18 Mar 44		
42-37828	N R 18 Oct 43				Out to Sal 3 Jan 44	Reason unknown.			
42-37848	N R 18 Oct 43						MIA 16 Mar 44		
42-37885		New Rpt 22 Nov 43						Ass 31 Mar 44	
42-37924			New Rpt 2 Dec 43		Crash Landed 9 Jan 44 (16 Jan 44)				
42-37974				New Rpt 21 Jan 44				Ass 31 Mar 44	
42-37982				New Rpt 21 Jan 44				Ass 31 Mar 44	
42-38013				New Rpt 21 Jan 44				Ass 31 Mar 44	
42-38014				New Rpt 6 Jan 44				Ass 31 Mar 44	
42-38112					New Rpt 20 Feb 44			Ass 31 Mar 44	
42-38158						New Rpt 1 Mar 44		Ass 31 Mar 44	
42-38208						New Rpt 1 Mar 44		Ass 31 Mar 44	

B-17G Vega

Serial No		Oct	Nov	Dec	Jan	Feb	Mar	Lost To	
42-39783	New Rpt 2 Nov 43		379BG 11 Nov 43						
42-39784	New Rpt 2 Nov 43					MIA 8 Feb 44			
42-39796	303BG 2 Nov 43			MIA 8 Dec 43					
42-39797	New Rpt 2 Nov 43			Out 24 Dec 43, later to 381BG					
42-39800	New Rpt 2 Nov 43		379BG 7 Nov 43						
42-39809				New Rpt 6 Jan 44		MIA 22 Feb 44			
42-39888		New Rpt 23 Nov 43						Ass 31 Mar 44	
42-39962				New Rpt 21 Jan 44	MIA 11 Feb 44				
42-39991				New Rpt 8 Jan 44		MIA 4 Mar 44			
42-40005				New Rpt 6 Jan 44	MIA 11 Feb 44				

B-17G Boeing

Serial No		Oct	Nov	Dec	Jan	Feb	Mar	Lost To	
42-97072							New Rpt 24 Mar 44	Ass 31 Mar 44	
42-97081						457BG 12 Mar 44		Ass 31 Mar 44	
42-97124						457BG 12 Mar 44		Ass 31 Mar 44	
42-97136						457BG 12 Mar 44		Ass 31 Mar 44	
42-97139						457BG 12 Mar 44		Ass 31 Mar 44	
42-97142						457BG 12 Mar 44		Ass 31 Mar 44	
42-97150	NMF					New Rpt 12 Mar 44		Ass 31 Mar 44	
42-97201							New Rpt 31 Mar 44	Ass 31 Mar 44	
42-97204							New Rpt 30 Mar 44	Ass 31 Mar 44	
42-97228							New Rpt 31 Mar 44	Ass 31 Mar 44	
42-97231							New Rpt 24 mar 44	Ass 31 Mar 44	
42-97237						New Rpt 24 Mar 44		Ass 31 Mar 44	
42-97251						New Rpt 24 Mar 44		Ass 31 Mar 44	

B-17G Vega

Serial No		Oct	Nov	Dec	Jan	Feb	Mar	Lost To	
42-97449					New Rpt 20 Jan 44			Ass 31 Mar 44	
42-97450						New Rpt 20 Feb 44 MIA 22 Feb 44			
42-97477					New Rpt 20 Jan 44			Ass 31 Mar 44	
42-97488						New Rpt 19 Feb 44 MIA 22 Feb 44			
42-97510						New Rpt 18 Feb 44		Ass 31 Mar 44	
42-97521						New Rpt 10 Feb 44		Ass 31 Mar 44	
42-97535						New Rpt 10 Feb 44 457BG 20 Feb 44			

		1943							
		May	June	July	Aug	Sep	Oct		

DB-7B Douglas

		May	June	July	Aug	Sep	Oct		
AL496		92BG 14 June 43				OUT 23 Sep 43			

384th BOMBARDMENT GROUP (H)

AIRCRAFT AND OPERATIONAL STATISTICS

Total Aircraft Assigned

B-17E:	4 June 43 to 31 Mar 44	1	YB-40: 28 Aug 43 to 12 Oct 43 — 1
B-17F:	Apr 43 to 31 Mar 44	113	DB-7B: 14 June 43 to 23 Sep 43 — 1
	B-17G: 3 Oct 43 to 31 Mar 44	84	

Operational Statistics

First Mission flown on: 22 June 43
First Act MIA: B-17Fs 42-5833 and 30076 on 22 June 43
First B-17G Ass: 42-37758 on 3 Oct 43
First B-17G MIA: 42-31059 on 14 Oct 43
First NMF Ass: 42-32007 on 1 Mar 44
First NMF MIA 42-32007 on 4 Mar 44

Total Act MIA: 86 (62 B-17F and 24 B-17G)
Highest Days losses: 7 on 25 July 43
Other Losses (Salvaged): 20 B-17s
    B-17F: 13 (11 Op, 2 Non Op)
    B-17G: 7 (4 Op, 2 Non Op, 1 Unknown)

SHORT SERVING AIRCRAFT: ASSIGNED FOR LESS THAN EIGHT DAYS

Serial No	Date In	Date out	Reason Out	Days Ass
42-29800	8 Oct 43	14 Oct 43	MIA	6
42-31059	7 Oct 43	14 Oct 43	MIA	7
42-31516	18 Feb 44	22 Feb 44	Crashed	4(5)
42-32007	1 Mar 44	4 Mar 44	MIA	3
42-37791	2 Nov 43	7 Nov 43	To 379BG	5
42-39800	2 Nov 43	7 Nov 43	To 379BG	5
42-97450	20 Feb 44	22 Feb 44	MIA	2
42-97488	19 Feb 44	22 Feb 44	MIA	3

LONG SERVING AIRCRAFT: ASSIGNED FOR TEN MONTHS OR MORE

Serial No	Date In	Date Out	Reason Out	Months Ass
42-30026	Orig Act	Still Ass		11

Damage sustained to **'THE SAINT'** following a tail wheel collapse on 20th February 1944. The aircraft was soon repaired and back in service and was still assigned to the 384th Bomb Group on 31st March 1944. *US Air Force*

Only three of the Group's original aircraft survived into 1944. They were 42-3218 **'DORIS MAE'**, 42-5838 **'MAD MONEY II'**, and 42-30026 **'BATTLE WAGON'**. **'DORIS MAE'** and **'MAD MONEY'** did not see much of the New Year at Grafton Underwood, both leaving on the 4th January. The former departing to Burtonwood and more operations with the RAF and the latter earning the double distinction of being the last of the Group's originals to go MIA and the first Group plane lost in 1944. **'BATTLE WAGON'** served on and became the only original still serving on 31st March.

The longest serving replacement aircraft was 42-29651 **'STELLA'**, which had joined the Group on 27th June 1943. She had been rescued from a forced landing in a field at Lytchet Minster in March 1943. Her days with the Group were now numbered as on 4th April she would be flown out to Warton for return to the USA.

STATUS OF AIRCRAFT ASSIGNED AT 2000 HOURS on 31st MARCH 1944

Operational: 59 B-17 (13 B-17F: 46 B-17G)
Non Operational: 1 B-17E

Operational Aircraft Assigned and on hand at Grafton Underwood

B-17F

42-3051*	42-3441	42-29651*	42-29723*	42-29927*
42-3429		42-29688*	42-29809*	
42-3440	42-29632	42-29703	42-29828	42-30026 Orig Act

B-17G

42-31048	42-31495	42-37816	42-39888	42-97204 NMF
42-31211	42-31740	42-37885		42-97228 NMF
42-31222	42-32106 NMF	42-37974	42-97072 NMF	42-97231 NMF
42-31235		42-37982	42-97081 NMF	42-97237 NMF
42-31346	42-37758	42-38013	42-97124 NMF	42-97251 NMF
42-31364	42-37776	42-38014	42-97136 NMF	
42-31375	42-37785	42-38112	42-97139 NMF	42-97449
42-31433	42-37788	42-38158	42-97142 NMF	42-97477
42-31435	42-37789	42-38208	42-97150 NMF	42-97510
42-31484	42-37792		42-97201 NMF	42-97521

Non Operational Aircraft on hand at Grafton Underwood: B-17E 41-9022

* These nine Aircraft without Tokyo tanks

401st BOMBARDMENT GROUP (H)

Constituted as the 401st BOMBARDMENT GROUP (H) on 20th March 1943
Activated on 1st April 1943
Squadrons Assigned: 612th, 613th, 614th and 615th
Assigned to Eighth Air Force: October 1943
Assigned to First Bombardment Division: November 1943

COMBAT WING ASSIGNMENTS

92nd Combat Bombardment: 24th November 1943
94th Combat Bombardment: 12th December 1943

STATION

Deenethorpe: Air Echelon in from 4th November 1943
Ground Echelon in 3rd November 1943

Trained in the USA using B-17Fs. The Group moved to Great Falls, Montana, on 1st July 1943. Early in August, three of the Squadrons were dispersed to satellite fields. The 613th went to Cutbank, the 614th to Glasgow, and the 615th to Lewistown, all in Montana. The 612th Bomb Squadron and Group Headquarters remained at Great Falls.

In late September and early October new B-17s were assigned. The Group received 60 B-17Gs and two B-17Fs. The Groups that had departed the States for England in the Spring of 1943 had had only 40 aircraft assigned.

On 18th October the air echelon left for Scott Field, Illinois, where processing for overseas movement took place. From Scott, some aircraft flew to Baer Field, Fort Wayne, Indiana, and others went to Syracuse, New York. Final departure point from the US was Presque Isle or Bangor. Some planes flew direct to Prestwick, others flew via Goose Bay and Greenland.

The ground echelon left Great Falls and the satellite fields on 19th October and travelled by train to Camp Shanks, which was reached on the 22nd. On the 27th October they were taken to New York City to board the *Queen Mary* which sailed on the evening of that day and docked at Greenock on the evening of 2nd November. Disembarking on the morn-ing of 3rd November they were entrained for Geddington station, near Kettering, where a truck convoy was waiting to transport them to Deenethorpe their new home in the European Theatre of Operations.

On arrival in England, the air echelon had flown to Polebrook and Bassingbourn. On 16th November, with the arrival from Prestwick of 42-31089, 42-31187 and 42-39835 the Group was able to report an assigned strength of 60 aircraft. More than any other Group then in the First Bombardment Division. Sixty-two planes had composed the Group's air echelon on departure from the USA but two planes, 42-31192 and 42-39760, were assigned to the 351st Bomb Group on the day of their arrival and were never recorded as being assigned to the 401st Bomb Group in England. Two days after the arrival of the last planes from Prestwick, 14 were transferred to the 351st Bomb Group, and more transfers out followed, which with other losses saw the Group's strength decline to 31 planes by the 9th December.

At the end of the year, the Group had only 35 B-17s assigned, the lowest of any First Division Group. Following the mission of 31st December, many aircraft had landed at other bases and there were only 12 aircraft on hand at Deenethorpe of which only three were available for operations.

'DRY RUN' on dispersal at Deenethorpe. It was one of 18 originals still assigned to the 401st Bomb Group on 31st March 1944. *Stan Bishop*

Serial No	Gained From	Period Assigned	Lost To

B-17E

Serial No	Gained From	Lost To
41-9107	Framlingham 6 Nov 43	Ass 31 Mar 44

B-17G Douglas

Serial No	Gained From	Lost To
42-3507	Or Ac	Ass 31 Mar 44
42-3560	Or Ac	351BG 18 Nov 43
42-3562	Or Ac	381BG 21 Nov 43

B-17F Boeing

Serial No	Gained From	Lost To
42-30227	96BG 13 Dec 43	BAD 17 Mar 44
42-30855	New Rpt 22 Dec 43	Ass 31 Mar 44
42-30866	Or Ac	351BG 21 Nov 43
42-30994	Or Ac	351BG 21 Nov 43

B-17G Boeing

Serial No	Gained From	Lost To
42-31033	Or Ac	MIA 11 Jan 44
42-31034	Or Ac	Ass 31 Mar 44
42-31036	Or Ac	MIA 4 Feb 44
42-31037	Or Ac	Ass 31 Mar 44
42-31064	Or Ac	MIA 31 Dec 43
42-31068	Or Ac	Crashed 31 Dec 43
42-31069	Or Ac	Ass 31 Mar 44
42-31072	Or Ac	Ass 31 Mar 44
42-31077	Or Ac	Ass 31 Mar 44
42-31079	Or Ac	91BG 20 Nov 43
42-31081	Or Ac	Ass 31 Mar 44
42-31087	Or Ac	Ass 31 Mar 44
42-31089	Or Ac	Ditched 4 Jan 44
42-31090	Or Ac	Dam on Op Miss 11 Jan 44, Sal, (21 Jan 44)
42-31091	Or Ac	Ass 31 Mar 44
42-31097	Or Ac	381BG 21 Nov 43
42-31098	Or Ac	Crash Landed 26 Mar 44
42-31099	Or Ac	381BG 21 Nov 43
42-31116	Or Ac	Ass 31 Mar 44
42-31187	Or Ac	91BG 20 Nov 43
42-31192	Or Ac	351BG 3 Dec 43, Direct from U.S.A. Not Ass to 401BG in First B Div.
42-31193	Or Ac	MIA 29 Jan 44
42-31198	New Rpt 24 Dec 43	Crashed 31 Dec 43
42-31202	New Rpt 12 Nov 43	Sal after Op Miss 29 Mar 44
42-31226	New Rpt 22 Dec 43	Ass 31 Mar 44
42-31315	New Rpt 23 Dec 43	Ass 31 Mar 44
42-31369	New Rpt 14 Jan 44	Ass 31 Mar 44
42-31374	New Rpt 14 Jan 44	MIA 13 Mar 44
42-31414	New Rpt 14 Jan 44	Dam in Landing Acc 27 Jan 44 (30 Jan 44)
42-31467	New Rpt 6 Jan 44	MIA 2 Mar 44
42-31485	New Rpt 6 Jan 44	Ass 31 Mar 44
42-31486	New Rpt 14 Jan 44	MIA 29 Jan 44
42-31488	New Rpt 2 Jan 44	MIA 8 Mar 44
42-31496	New Rpt 1 Feb 44	Ass 31 Mar 44
42-31508	New Rpt 21 Jan 44	Ass 31 Mar 44
42-31511	New Rpt 1 Jan 44	Ass 31 Mar 44
42-31518	New Rpt 14 Jan 44	MIA 20 Feb 44
42-31521	New Rpt 1 Feb 44	Ass 31 Mar 44
42-31557	New Rpt 21 Jan 44	Ass 31 Mar 44
42-31591	457BG 11 Mar 44	Ass 31 Mar 44
42-31593	New Rpt 1 Feb 43	Ass 31 Mar 44
42-31619	New Rpt 31 Jan 44	Ass 31 Mar 44
42-31662	New Rpt 31 Jan 44	Ass 31 Mar 44

401st Bomb Group(H)	1943			1944			△S
Serial No	Oct	Nov	Dec	Jan	Feb	Mar	

Gained From ▨▨▨ Period Assigned ▨▨▨ Lost To

Serial No		Gained From / Period Assigned					Lost To
42-31730				New Rpt 31 Jan 44			Ass 31 Mar 44
42-31863				New Rpt 6 Feb 44			Ass 31 Mar 44
42-31891				New Rpt 18 Feb 44			Ass 31 Mar 44
42-31930				New Rpt 7 Feb 44	MIA 22 Feb 44		
42-31983					New Rpt 7 Mar 44		Ass 31 Mar 44
42-32005	NMF				New Rpt 7 Mar 44		Ass 31 Mar 44
42-32012					New Rpt 5 Mar 44		Ass 31 Mar 44
42-32086					New Rpt 3 Mar 44	457BG 5 Mar 44	

B-17G Douglas

42-37714	Orig Act	351BG 18 Nov 43					
42-37722			New Rpt 21 Jan 44	Salvaged after Fire, 28 Jan 44 (30 Jan 44)			
42-37746	Orig Act	91BG 20 Nov 43					
42-37770	Orig Act		MIA 31 Dec 43				
42-37774	Orig Act	351BG 21 Nov 43					
42-37779	Orig Act	91BG 20 Nov 43					
42-37780	Orig Act	381BG 18 Nov 43					
42-37786	Orig Act	381BG 21 Nov 43					
42-37809	Orig Act			MIA 11 Jan 44			
42-37833	Orig Act					MIA 26 Mar 44	
42-37835	Orig Act		Crashed 22 Dec 43				
42-37838	Orig Act	Mid Air Collision 26 Nov 43 (9 Dec 43)					
42-37843	Orig Act						Ass 31 Mar 44
42-37856		New Rpt 23 Dec 43		MIA 30 Jan 44			
42-38002			New Rpt 21 Jan 44		MIA 22 Feb 44		
42-38012			New Rpt 21 Jan 44	MIA 29 Jan 44			
42-38026				New Rpt 2 Feb 44			Ass 31 Mar 44
42-38033			New Rpt 6 Jan 44			MIA 20 Mar 44	
42-38136					New Rpt 23 Feb 44	MIA 6 Mar 44	
42-38162						New Rpt 22 Mar 44	Ass 31 Mar 44

B-17G Vega

42-39760	Orig Act	351BG 25 Nov 43, Direct from U.S.A. Not Ass to 401BG in First B Div.					
42-39761	Orig Act	351BG 18 Nov 43					
42-39765	Orig Act						Ass 31 Mar 44
42-39771	Orig Act	91BG 20 Nov 43					
42-39778	Orig Act	351BG 18 Nov 43					
42-39780	Orig Act	351BG 18 Nov 43					
42-39820	Orig Act						Ass 31 Mar 44
42-39823	Orig Act	351BG 18 Nov 43					
42-39825	Orig Act		Crashed 5 Dec 43				
42-39826	Orig Act		MIA 30 Dec 43				
42-39833	Orig Act	Subsequent History not known					
42-39834	Orig Act	351BG 18 Nov 43					
42-39835	Orig Act	351BG 18 Nov 43					
42-39836	Orig Act	91BG 19 Nov 43					
42-39837	Orig Act						Ass 31 Mar 44
42-39839	Orig Act	351BG 18 Nov 43					
42-39840	Orig Act						Ass 31 Mar 44
42-39846	Orig Act						Ass 31 Mar 44
42-39847	Orig Act						Ass 31 Mar 44
42-39848	Orig Act	351BG 18 Nov 43					
42-39849	Orig Act	351BG 18 Nov 43					
42-39853	Orig Act	351BG 18 Nov 43					
42-39857	Orig Act	351BG 18 Nov 43					
42-39873	Orig Act						Ass 31 Mar 44
42-39881		New Rpt 13 Dec 43					Ass 31 Mar 44
42-39893			New Rpt 2 Jan 44	MIA 11 Jan 44			

401st Bomb Group(H)	1943			1944			⚠S
	Oct	Nov	Dec	Jan	Feb	Mar	

Serial No	Gained From ▓▓▓ Period Assigned ▓▓▓ Lost To						
42-39904			New Rpt 19 Dec 43 ▓▓				Ass 31 Mar 44
42-39932			New Rpt 2 Jan 44 ▓▓				Ass 31 Mar 44
42-39943			New Rpt 2 Jan 44 ▓▓				Ass 31 Mar 44
42-39969			New Rpt 2 Jan 44 ▓ MIA 11 Jan 44				
42-39979			New Rpt 5 Jan 44 ▓▓				Ass 31 Mar 44
42-39993			New Rpt 1 Jan 44 ▓▓				Ass 31 Mar 44
42-40001			New Rpt 5 Jan 44 ▓▓				Ass 31 Mar 44
42-40002			New Rpt 29 Dec 43 ▓▓				Ass 31 Mar 44
42-40050			New Rpt 1 Jan 44 ▓▓				Ass 31 Mar 44
42-40057			New Rpt 5 Jan 44 ▓▓ MIA 29 Jan 44				
			B-17G Boeing				
42-97073	NMF					New Rpt 23 Mar 44 ▓	Ass 31 Mar 44
			B-17G Vega				
42-97440			New Rpt 1 Jan 44 ▓▓				Ass 31 Mar 44
42-97448			New Rpt 1 Jan 44 ▓▓				Ass 31 Mar 44
42-97464					457BG 11 Mar 44 ▓▓		Ass 31 Mar 44
42-97478					457BG 11 Mar 44 ▓▓		Ass 31 Mar 44
42-97487			New Rpt 12 Jan 44 ▓▓				Ass 31 Mar 44
42-97496			New Rpt 31 Jan 44 ▓▓				Ass 31 Mar 44
			B-17G Douglas				
42-107009						New Rpt 23 Mar 44 ▓	Ass 31 Mar 44
42-107039	NMF					New Rpt 23 Mar 44 ▓	Ass 31 Mar 44
42-107043						New Rpt 23 Mar 44 ▓	Ass 31 Mar 44
42-107092						New Rpt 23 Mar 44 ▓	Ass 31 Mar 44

ORIGINAL B-17s ASSIGNED AT GREAT FALLS AND SATELLITES SEP/OCT 1943

B-17F

42-30866　　　　　　　　　　42-30994

B-17G

42-3507	42-31072	42-31192 (1)	42-37838	42-39834
42-3560	42-31077	42-31193	42-37843	42-39835
42-3562	42-31079			42-39836
	42-31081	42-37714	42-39760 (1)	42-39837
42-30866	42-31087	42-37746	42-39761	42-39839
42-30994	42-31089	42-37770	42-39765	42-39840
42-31033	42-31090	42-37774	42-39771	42-39846
42-31034	42-31091	42-37779	42-39778	42-39847
42-31036	42-31097	42-37780	42-39780	42-39848
42-31037	42-31098	42-37786	42-39820	42-39849
42-31064	42-31099	42-37809	42-39823	42-39853
42-31068	42-31116	42-37833	42-39825	42-39857
42-31069	42-31187	42-37835	42-39826	42-39873

(1) 42-31192 and 42-39760 were assigned to 351st BG on Arr in England and were not recorded as being assigned to the Group while it was in the First BD.

42-39833 May have been ass as an orig in the U.S.A. but it's subs history is not known

With just over four months in combat, there were no long serving veterans in the 401st Bomb Group. Although losses in action had not been heavy, only 18 of the 62 planes flown over from the USA remained with the Group at the end of March 1944.

Twenty-nine of the originals had been transferred to other Groups soon after the 401st had arrived in the UK. These losses were not made up by the few new replacements which trickled in during December 1943. However this trend was reversed in January 1944 when 31 new planes were assigned which brought the Group's inventory of assigned aircraft up to 53 by the end of the month.

SHORT SERVING ACT: ASS FOR LESS THAN EIGHT DAYS				
Serial No	Date In	Date Out	Reason Out	Days Ass
42-31198	24 Dec 43	31 Dec 43	Crashed	7
42-32086	3 Mar 44	5 Mar 44	To 457BG	2
42-37722	21 Jan 44	28 Jan 44	Salvaged	7(9)

42-31090 lands at Deenethorpe. Ended its combat career with a crash landing at Matlask on return from the mission of 11th January 1944. *Mike Gibson*

AIRCRAFT AND OPERATIONAL STATISTICS

Total Aircraft Assigned

B-17E: 6 Nov 43 to 31 Mar 44	1	B-17F: Sep 43 to 31 Mar 44	4
	B-17G: Sep 43 to 31 Mar 44	121	

Operational Statistics

First Mission flown on: 26 Nov 43	Total Act MIA: 23 B-17G
First Act MIA: 42-39826 on 30 Dec 43	Highest Days Losses: 4 on 11 Jan 44 and
First NMF Ass: 42-32086 on 3 Mar 44	4 on 29 Jan 44
First NMF MIA: None up to 31 Mar 44	Other losses: (Salvaged) 10 B-17s
	B-17G: (8 Op, 2 Non Op)

STATUS OF AIRCRAFT ASSIGNED AT 2000 HOURS on 31st MARCH 1944

Operational: 60 B-17 (1 B-17F: 59 B-17G)

Non Operational: 1 B-17E

Operational Aircraft assigned and on hand at Deenethorpe

B-17F 42-30855

B-17G

42-3507 (Orig Act)	42-31369	42-31891	42-39847 (Orig Act)	42-97073 NMF
	42-31485	42-31983 NMF	42-39873 (Orig Act)	
42-31034 (Orig Act)	42-31496	42-32005 NMF	42-39881	42-97440
42-31037 (Orig Act)	42-31508	42-32012 NMF	42-39904	42-97448
42-31069 (Orig Act)	42-31511		42-39932	42-97464
42-31072 (Orig Act)	42-31521	42-37843 (Orig Act)	42-39943	42-97478
42-31077 (Orig Act)	42-31557	42-38026	42-39979	42-97487
42-31081 (Orig Act)	42-31591	42-38162	42-39993	42-97496
42-31087 (Orig Act)	42-31593		42-40001	
42-31091 (Orig Act)	42-31619	42-39765 (Orig Act)	42-40002	42-107009 NMF
42-31116 (Orig Act)	42-31662	42-39820 (Orig Act)	42-40050	42-107039 NMF
42-31226	42-31730	42-39840 (Orig Act)		42-107043 NMF
42-31315	42-31863	42-39846 (Orig Act)		42-107092 NMF

Assigned but not on hand: B-17G 42-39837 (Orig Act) at Nuthampstead

Non Operational Aircraft on hand at Deenethorpe: B-17E 41-9107

401st BOMBARDMENT GROUP (H)

THE RISE AND FALL OF THE BIG 'TRIANGLE S'

With the arrival from Prestwick of B-17Gs: 42-31089, 31187 and 39835 on 16th November 1943, the 401st Bombardment Group had 60 B-17s assigned. A greater number than any of the other Groups then in the First Bombardment Division. Twenty three days later on 9th December the Group's inventory of assigned aircraft was down to 31; then the lowest number of any of the Division's Groups. Just how this rise and fall came about will be seen by the following diary of the Group's gains and losses during November and December 1943.

AIRCRAFT STATUS

Nov 1943	Operational			Non Op		Details and Explanatory Notes
	Ass	On Hd	Op	Ass	On Hd	
1st	0	0	0	0	0	
2nd	0	0	0	0	0	Air Echelon with original aircraft on route from U.S.A.
3rd	0	0	0	0	0	
4th	12	12	0	0	0	Gained from Pwk: 42-3560, 31081, 31090, 31091, 31193, 37833, 39778, 39823, 39825, 39848, 39849 and 39857. (All orig Act from the U.S.A.)
5th	12	12	0	0	0	No change in Act status
6th	12	12	0	1	1	Gained: B-17E 41-9107 from Framlingham
7th	12	12	0	1	1	No change in Act status
8th	19	19	0	1	1	Gained: 42-31034, 31036, 31068, 31087, 31099, 37838 and 39834. (All orig Act from the U.S.A.)
9th	48	48	0	1	1	Gained: 42-3507, 3562, 30866(B-17F), 42-30994(B-17F), 31033, 31037, 31064, 31072, 31077, 31097, 31098, 31116, 37746, 37770, 37774, 37780, 37786, 37809, 37835, 37843, 39761, 39826, 39836, 39839, 39846, 39847, 39853, 39873, (All orig Act from the U.S.A.) These 29 Act were transferred to Bassingbourn, but still retained on ass and on hand status.
10th	48	48	0	1	1	No Change in Act status
11th	47	47	0	1	1	Gained: 42-31069 and 37714. (Both orig Act from the U.S.A.). Lost to Lt Stn: 42-31036, 31081 and 39857. (Dropped from Ass)
12th	47	47	0	1	1	No change in Act status
13th	50	50	0	1	1	Gained from Lt Stn: 42-31036, 31081 and 39857. The three Act lost to to Lt Stn on the 11th. Normally Act away for such a short time would not have been dropped from ass but would have been carried as 'DS Ass but not on hand.'
14th	54	54	11	1	1	Gained: 42-31079, 37779, 39765, 39771, 39780, 39820 and 39837 (All orig Act from the U.S.A.) Lost to Lt Stn: 42-3560, 39825 and 39849. First day that Act reported operational.
15th	57	55	16	1	1	Gained from Lt Stn: 42-3560, 39825 and 39849. (The 3 Act lost to Lt Stn on 14th Nov) DS to Lt Stn: 42-31069 and 31091 (Carried as ass but not on Hd)
16th	60	58	16	1	1	Gained from Pwk: 42-31089, 31187 and 39835. (Orig Act from the U.S.A.)
17th	60	58	39	1	1	
18th	46	44	29	1	1	Transferred to 351st BG: 42-3560, 37714, 37780, 39761, 39778, 39780, 39823, 39834, 39835, 39839, 39848, 39849, 39853 and 39857.
19th	46	44	29	1	1	No change in Act status.
20th	40	38	29	1	1	Trans to 91BG: 42-31079, 31187, 37746, 37779, 39771 and 39836.
21st	33	26		1	1	Trans to 351BG: 42-30866(B-17F), 30994(B-17F) and 37774. Trans to 381BG: 42-3562, 31097, 31099 and 37786. DS to Polebrook: 42-31193, 37833 and 39825. DS to Bassingbourn: 42-31098 and 39765.
22nd	33	31	17	1	1	From DS at Polebrook: 42-31193, 37833 and 39825. From DS at Lt Stn: 42-31069 and 31091 (Went to Lt Stn on 15th Nov).
23rd	33	33	22	1	1	From DS at Bassingbourn: 42-31098 and 39765.
24th	33	33	22	1	1	No change in Act status. First day Group in 92nd Combat Wing.
25th	33	33	29	1	1	42-39760(Orig Act arr from U.S.A) Ass to 351BG, Never ass to 401BG in U.K.
26th	33	33	12	1	1	Group flies it's first operational mission.
27th	33	32	14	1	1	42-37838 Dam on Op miss 26th Nov, at R.A.F. Detling,(Carried as ass but not on hand).
28th	33	32	17	1	1	
29th	33	32	20	1	1	
30th	33	32	17	1	1	Group's second Op miss.

401st BOMBARDMENT GROUP (H)

						THE RISE AND FALL OF THE BIG 'TRIANGLE S' CONTINUED
1st Dec 1943	33	28	8	1	1	Group's third Op Miss. Away on DS: 42-31064 at Nuthampstead for Rep. 42-37843 at Addelburg?* for Rep. 42-39840 at Manston for Rep(Ret on 15 Feb 44). 42-39765 at Wakerley?* for Rep(Ret on 14 Jan 44) ?* These two locations not identified and probably errors on records.
2nd	33	30	8	1	1	Ret from DS 42-31064 from Addelburg?* and 37843 from Nuthampstead.
3rd	33	30	16	1	1	42-31192 Arr: (Orig from the U.S.A.) Ass to 351BG , never ass to 401BG in UK.
4th	33	30	20	1	1	
5th	32	29	12	1	1	Group's fourth Op Miss. Lost: 42-39875 Cr and exploded, dropped from Ass. Note: This was the first Act to be lost to sal, although 42-37838 Dam on Op Miss of 26th Nov was at Detling and being carried as Ass but not on hand It would not fly again and was sal on 9th Dec.
6th	32	29	21	1	1	
7th	32	29	22	1	1	
8th	32	29	21	1	1	
9th	31	29	21	1	1	Lost: 42-37838 Sal at Detling and dropped from Ass. (Was dam on Op Miss of 26th Nov)
10th	31	29	19	1	1	
11th	31	24		1	1	Group's fifth Op Miss. Away on DS: 42-31098 at Lindholme (Ret on 10 Jan 44 42-31116 at Kingscliff. DS to Lt Stn: 42-31068, 39826 and 39847.
12th	32	25		1	1	Gained: 42-31202(First new replacement operational plane ass in U.K.)
13th	34	27		1	1	Group's sixth Op Miss: Gained 42-30227 and 39881. (New replacements)
14th	34	27	20	1	1	
15th	34	27		1	1	
16th	34	27	19	1	1	Group's seventh Op Miss
17th	34	29		1	1	From DS at Lt Stn: 42-31068. From DS at Kingscliff: 42-31116.
18th	34	29		1	1	
19th	35	32	22	1	1	Group re-assigned to the 94th Combat Wing. Gained: 42-39904 (new Rpt). From DS at Lt Stn: 42-39826 ans 39847.
20th	35	30		1	1	Group's Eighth Op Miss. DS to Lt Stn: 42-31037 and 31089. DS to Lt Stn: B-17E 41-9107 for GEE installation.
21st	35	30	17	1	0	
22nd	35	30	12	1	0	Group's Ninth Op Miss. Lost: 42-37835 (Cr). Gained 42-30855 (New Rpt)
23rd	38	35	20	1	0	Gained: 42-31226, 31315 and 37856 (New Rpt's) From DS at Lt Stn: 42-31037 and 31089.
24th	39	35	17	1	1	Group's Tenth Op Miss. Gained: 42-31198 (New Rpt). DS to Lt Stn: 42-31077. From DS at Lt Stn: B-17E 41-9107.
25th	39	35	17	1	1	
26th	39	35	23	1	1	From DS at Lt Stn: 42-31077. DS to Lt Stn: 42-31033.
27th	39	35	27	1	1	
28th	39	35	28	1	1	
29th	40	35	27	1	1	Gained:42-40002 (New Rpt). From DS at Lt Stn: 42-31033. DS to Lt Stn: 42-31072 and 31116.
30th	39	34	21	1	1	Group's Eleventh Op Miss. Lost: 42-39826 MIA. (First Group Act MIA).
31st Dec 1943	35	12	3	1	1	Group's Twelfth Op Miss. Lost: 42-31064 and 37770 (MIA). Lost: 42-31068 and 31198 (Cr) (These four Act dropped from Ass). Landed away: 18 Act. 42-3507 at Hemswell: 30855 and 31087 at Tibenham: 31034 at Marham: 31037 at Bury St Edmunds: 31077 at Knettishall: 31089 at Downham Market: 31069 and 31090 at Great Ashfield: 31091 at Mildenhall: 31193 at Molesworth: 31202 at Nuthampstead: 37809 at Waterbeach: 39820 at Leiston: 39846 at Framlingham: 39881 and 39904 at Keevil: and 31226 at Framlingham. Status of these 18 Act is (Ass but not on hand).

457th BOMBARDMENT GROUP (H)

Constituted as the 457th BOMBARDMENT GROUP (H) on 19th May 1943
Activated on 1st July 1943
Squadrons Assigned: 748th, 749th, 750th and 751st
Assigned to Eighth Air Force: January 1944
Assigned to First Bombardment Division: January 1944

COMBAT WING ASSIGNMENTS

94th Combat Bombardment: February 1944

STATION

Glatton: Air Echelon in from 22nd January 1944
Ground Echelon in: 2nd February 1944

Trained in the USA on B-17Fs. Completed third phase training at Wendover, Utah, where new aircraft were assigned. Moved to Grand Island, Nebraska, early in January 1944, where final preparations for the overseas movement was completed.

The ground echelon, left Wendover by train on 1st January and proceeded to the East coast where they embarked aboard the troopship SS *Mormactide* for the crossing to the United Kingdom. After a seven day voyage, the *Mormactide* entered the Clyde and on disembarking, the men were taken by train to Holme station which was reached during the early morning of 2nd February. From Holme they were trucked the short distance to their new station at Glatton.

The air echelon left Grand Island on the 17th January, some aircraft proceeded via Presque Isle and others went via Grenier. The transatlantic flight was made via Gander or Goose Bay and arrival in the United Kingdom was made at Prestwick, Nutts Corner or Valley. Two aircraft, 42-97443 and 42-97459, crash landed on arrival at Nutts Corner. The first nine aircraft were reported as arrived from the USA on 20th January but when the first daily report of aircraft assigned was made on 22nd January only eight planes were listed. It is thought the ninth was 42-31572 which was assigned to the 91st Group on 23rd January. Most of the remaining aircraft arrived during the next week but some were delayed into February.

The planes were despatched to Burtonwood over the next three weeks for modifications, some making two visits, as related elsewhere in this book, the extended period over which the aircraft were being modified at Burtonwood resulted in alternative plans being made to get the 398th Bomb Group, due to arrive in the First Division in April, more speedily into combat.

All the originals of the 457th were olive drab finished, many of these were transferred out to other Groups during early March 1944. One that was retained and served the Group for several months was 42-97470 'OH KAY'. *US Air Force*

457th Bomb Group(H)	1943			1944			U
	Oct	Nov	Dec	Jan	Feb	Mar	

Serial No	Gained From	Period Assigned	Lost To

B-17E

Serial No			
41-2578		Burtonwood 3 Mar 44	Ass 31 Mar 44

B-17G Boeing

Serial No			
42-31154		New Rpt 20 Feb 44	Ass 31 Mar 44
42-31172		New Rpt 20 Feb 44	306BG 12 Mar 44
42-31505	Orig Act		Ass 31 Mar 44
42-31517	Orig Act		MIA 25 Feb 44
42-31520	Orig Act		Ass 31 Mar 44
42-31531	Orig Act		MIA 29 Mar 44
42-31541	Orig Act	Crashed in U.S.A. about 24 Dec 43	
42-31542	Orig Act		91BG 12 Mar 44
42-31545	Orig Act		Ass 31 Mar 44
42-31547	Orig Act	Crashed in U.S.A. about 5 Jan 44	
42-31548	Orig Act		92BG 11 Mar 44
42-31551	Orig Act		Ass 31 Mar 44
42-31552	Orig Act		Ass 31 Mar 44
42-31568	Orig Act		Ass 31 Mar 44
42-31572	Orig Act	91BG 23 Jan 44	
42-31586	Orig Act	Accident in U.S.A. about 11 Dec 43.	
42-31587	Orig Act		92BG 11 Mar 44
42-31588	Orig Act	Damaged on Op Miss 21 Feb 44 (25 Feb 44)	
42-31591	Orig Act		401BG 11 Mar 44
42-31592	Orig Act		379BG 18 Mar 44
42-31594	Orig Act		Ass 31 Mar 44
42-31595	Orig Act		MIA 6 Mar 44
42-31596	Orig Act		MIA 21 Feb 44
42-31607	Orig Act		Ass 31 Mar 44
42-31613	Orig Act		92BG 11 Mar 44
42-31615	Orig Act		Ass 31 Mar 44
42-31618	Orig Act		Ass 31 Mar 44
42-31620	Orig Act		Ass 31 Mar 44
42-31627	Orig Act		MIA 6 Mar 44
42-31629	Orig Act		Ass 31 Mar 44
42-31630	Orig Act		Ass 31 Mar 44
42-31633	Orig Act		Ass 31 Mar 44
42-31635	Orig Act		92BG 11 Mar 44
42-31639	Orig Act		91BG 12 Mar 44
42-31656			Ass 31 Mar 44
42-31706			Ass 31 Mar 44
42-31923		New Rpt 23 Mar 44	Ass 31 Mar 44
42-32051		New Rpt 27 Feb 44	Ass 31 Mar 44
42-32079		New Rpt 9 Mar 44	Ass 31 Mar 44
42-32084		New Rpt 3 Mar 44	Ass 31 Mar 44
42-32086		401BG 6 Mar 44	Ass 31 Mar 44
42-32095	NMF	New Rpt 14 Mar 44	91BG 16 Mar 44
42-32098		388BG 4 Mar 44	Ass 31 Mar 44
42-32099		390BG 4 Mar 44	306BG 12 Mar 44
42-32101		New Rpt 6 Mar 44	Ass 31 Mar 44
42-32113		385BG 3 Mar 44	306BG 12 Mar 44
42-32116		452BG 11 Mar 44	91BG 16 Mar 44

457th Bomb Group(H)	1943			1944			△U
	Oct	Nov	Dec	Jan	Feb	Mar	

Serial No	Gained From	Period Assigned	Lost To

B-17G Douglas

Serial No							
42-37840				New Rpt 20 Feb 44		306BG	12 mar 44
42-38021		Orig Act					Ass 31 Mar 44
42-38055		Orig Act					Ass 31 Mar 44
42-38056		Orig Act	No further record.				
42-38057		Orig Act				379BG	18 Mar 44
42-38058		Orig Act				379BG	18 Mar 44
42-38060		Orig Act			MIA 24 Feb 44		
42-38063		Orig Act					Ass 31 Mar 44
42-38064		Orig Act					Ass 31 Mar 44
42-38065		Orig Act	No further record.				
42-38066		Orig Act	No further record.				
42-38073		Orig Act					Ass 31 Mar 44
42-38102		Orig Act				381BG	12 Mar 44
42-38103		Orig Act				381BG	12 Mar 44
42-38104		Orig Act				92BG	11 Mar 44
42-38110		Orig Act				92BG	11 Mar 44
42-38113		Orig Act					Ass 31 Mar 44

B-17G Boeing

Serial No							
42-97059				New Rpt 20 Feb 44		381BG	15 Mar 44
42-97060				New Rpt 4 Mar 44			Ass 31 Mar 44
42-97061				New Rpt 13 Mar 44		91BG	16 Mar 44
42-97062				New Rpt 15 Mar 44			Ass 31 Mar 44
42-97063				351BG 1 Mar 44		MIA	16 Mar 44
42-97067				94BG 4 Mar 44			Ass 31 Mar 44
42-97070				New Rpt 15 Mar 44			Ass 31 Mar 44
42-97075				New Rpt 7 Mar 44			Ass 31 Mar 44
42-97076				New Rpt 8 Mar 44		381BG	15 Mar 44
42-97081				New Rpt 11 mar 44		384BG	12 Mar 44
42-97087				379BG 2 Mar 44			Ass 31 Mar 44
42-97088				New Rpt 9 Mar 44			Ass 31 Mar 44
42-97122	NMF			New Rpt 17 Mar 44			Ass 31 Mar 44
42-97123				New Rpt 8 Mar 44			Ass 31 Mar 44
42-97124				New Rpt 11 Mar 44		384BG	12 Mar 44
42-97125				New Rpt 13 Mar 44		91BG	16 Mar 44
42-97131				New Rpt 8 Mar 44			Ass 31 Mar 44
42-97136				New Rpt 11 Mar 44		384BG	12 Mar 44
42-97137				New Rpt 9 Mar 44			Ass 31 Mar 44
42-97139				New Rpt 11 Mar 44		384BG	12 Mar 44
42-97142				New Rpt 11 Mar 44		384BG	12 Mar 44
42-97162				New Rpt 8 Mar 44			Ass 31 Mar 44
42-97164				New Rpt 15 Mar 44			Ass 31 Mar 44
42-97190				New Rpt 24 Mar 44			Ass 31 Mar 44
42-97236				New Rpt 31 Mar 44			Ass 31 Mar 44

457th Bomb Group(H)	1943			1944			U
	Oct	Nov	Dec	Jan	Feb	Mar	
Serial No	Gained From		Period Assigned			Lost To	

B-17G Vega

Serial No	Gained From / Period / Lost To
42-97443	Orig Act — Crashed 24 Jan 44. (In Ireland)
42-97450	Orig Act — 384BG 20 Feb 44
42-97451	Orig Act — Ass 31 Mar 44
42-97452	Orig Act — Ass 31 Mar 44
42-97455	Orig Act — 91BG 11 Mar 44
42-97456	Orig Act — Ass 31 Mar 44
42-97457	Orig Act — MIA 25 Feb 44
42-97458	Orig Act — Dam on Op Miss 25 Feb 44 (29 Feb 44)
42-97459	Orig Act — Crashed in Northern Ireland 23 Feb 44
42-97460	Orig Act — Ass 31 Mar 44
42-97464	Orig Act — 401BG 11 Mar 44
42-97465	Orig Act — Ass 31 Mar 44
42-97466	Orig Act — 305BG 8 Feb 44
42-97467	Orig Act — 91BG 11 Mar 44
42-97468	Orig Act — Ass 31 Mar 44
42-97469	Orig Act — 379BG 18 Mar 44
42-97470	Orig Act — Ass 31 Mar 44
42-97471	Orig Act — 381BG 11 Mar 44
42-97473	Orig Act — No further record with Group. Later with 390BG.
42-97477	Orig Act — 384BG 20 Jan 44
42-97478	Orig Act — 401BG 11 Mar 44
42-97481	Orig Act — Ass 31 Mar 44
42-97488	Orig Act — 384BG 19 Feb 44
42-97535	384BG 20 Feb 44 — Ass 31 Mar 44
42-97537	New Rpt 25 Feb 44 — Ass 31 Mar 44
42-97546	92BG 24 Feb 44 — 303BG 13 Mar 44
42-97552	351BG 1 Mar 44 — 303BG 12 Mar 44
42-97558	New Rpt 15 Feb 44 — Ass 31 Mar 44
42-97563	New Rpt 13 Mar 44 — 91BG 16 Mar 44
42-97571	New Rpt 24 Feb 44 — Ass 31 Mar 44
42-97579	New Rpt 23 Feb 44 — Ass 31 Mar 44
42-97587	New Rpt — Ass 31 Mar 44
42-97588	New Rpt 7 Mar 44 — 306BG 12 Mar 44
42-97590	NMF — New Rpt 22 Feb 44 — 303BG 13 Mar 44
42-97591	New Rpt 2 Mar 44 — Ass 31 Mar 44
42-97624	Reported as Assigned but not on hand 22 Feb 44 — No further record.
42-97662	306BG 3 Mar 44 — Ass 31 Mar 44
42-97663	452BG 4 Mar 44 — 306BG 12 Mar 44

B-17G Douglas

Serial No	Gained From / Period / Lost To
42-106985	379BG 2 Mar 44 — Ass 31 Mar 44
42-106998	379BG 2 Mar 44 — Ass 31 Mar 44
42-107001	New Rpt 2 Mar 44 — Ass 31 Mar 44
42-107015	New Rpt 3 Mar 44 — Ass 31 Mar 44
42-107026	New Rpt 4 Mar 44 — Ass 31 Mar 44

Boeing YB-29-BW Superfortress

Serial No	Gained From / Period / Lost To
41-36963	VISITING AIRCRAFT. ON HAND ONLY. NOT ASSIGNED 12 Mar 44 — HORSHAM St FAITH 13 Mar 44

457th BOMBARDMENT GROUP (H)

AIRCRAFT AND OPERATIONAL STATISTICS			
Total Aircraft Assigned			
B-17E:	3 Mar 44 to 31 Mar 44	1	B-17G: Late 1943 to 31 Mar 44	123
Operational Statistics			

First Mission flown on:	21 Feb 44	Total Act MIA:	8
First Act MIA:	B-17G 42-31596 on 21 Feb 44	Highest Days Losses: 2 on 25 Feb 44 and	
First NMF Act Ass:	42-97558 on 15 Feb 44	2 on 6 Mar 44	
First NMF Act MIA:	42-97063 on 6 Mar 44	Other Losses (Salvaged) 2 B-17G Op	

At the end of March 1944, the 457th had been operational for just six weeks. The Group's most noticeable statistics was that despite being the junior of the Division, it had had more B-17Gs assigned than any of the other Groups and also had more natural metal finished planes assigned.

Both these factors were due to the decision taken early in March that the 457th would become the Eighth's first 'all silver' Group and as a result many of the original painted aircraft were transferred out. Later in March, a change of plans was made and it was decided that the Group would only have half its complement of aircraft 'silver' and as a result many of the silver planes assigned in as part of the original policy were then transferred to other Groups.

42-97537, one of several Vega NMF aircraft assigned to the 457th in late February 1944. *US Air Force*

ORIGINAL B-17Gs ASSIGNED AT WENDOVER DECEMBER 1943

42-31505	42-31588	42-31633	42-38102	42-97459 (2)
42-31517	42-31591	42-31635	42-38103	42-97460
42-31520	42-31592	42-31636	42-38104	42-97464
42-31531	42-31594		42-38110	42-97465
42-31541 (1)	42-31595	42-38021	42-38113	42-97466
42-31542	42-31596	42-38055		42-97467
42-31545	42-31607	42-38056 (3)	42-97443 (2)	42-97468
42-31547 (1)	42-31613	42-38057	42-97450	42-97469
42-31548	42-31615	42-38058	42-97451	42-97470
42-31551	42-31618	42-38060	42-97452	42-97471
42-31552	42-31620	42-38063	42-97455	42-97473
42-31568	42-31627	42-38064	42-97456	42-97477
42-31572	42-31629	42-38065 (3)	42-97457	42-97478
42-31586 (1)	42-31630	42-38066 (3)	42-97458	42-97481
42-31587		42-38073		42-97488

(1) 42-31541, 31547 and 31586 Crashed in U.S.A. before departure

(2) 42-97443 and 97459 Crash landed in Northern Ireland on Arr in U.K.

(3) 42-38056, 38065 and 38066 Allocated in the U.S.A. but no evidence of service in U.K. prior to 31st March 1944

457th BOMBARDMENT GROUP (H)

	SHORT SERVING AIRCRAFT: ASSIGNED FOR LESS THAN EIGHT DAYS									
Serial No	Date In	Date Out	Reason Out	Days Ass		Serial No	Date In	Date Out	Reason Out	Days Ass
42-32095	14 Mar 44	16 Mar 44	To 91BG	2		42-97125	13 Mar 44	16 Mar 44	To 91BG	3
42-32116	11 Mar 44	16 Mar 44	To 91BG	5		42-97136	11 Mar 44	12 Mar 44	To 384BG	1
42-97061	13 Mar 44	16 Mar 44	To 91BG	3		42-97139	11 Mar 44	12 Mar 44	To 384BG	1
42-97063	1 Mar 44	6 Mar 44	MIA	5		42-97142	11 Mar 44	12 Mar 44	To 384BG	1
42-97076	8 Mar 44	15 Mar 44	To 381BG	7		42-97563	13 Mar 44	16 Mar 44	To 91BG	3
42-97081	11 Mar 44	12 Mar 44	To 384BG	1		97588	7 Mar 44	12 Mar 44	To 306BG	5
42-97124	11 Mar 44	13 Mar 44	To 384BG	1						

Another of the nine Vega NMF aircraft assigned the 457th during late February 1944 was 42-97571, see here settling down gracefully at Glatton. *US Air Force*

```
STATUS OF AIRCRAFT ASSIGNED AT 2000 HOURS on 31st MARCH 1944
                Operational:  66 B-17G
              Non Operational:  1 B-17E
   Operational Aircraft Assigned and on hand at Glatton.  All B-17Gs
```

42-31505 *	42-31656	42-38064 *	42-97164 NMF	42-97558 NMF
42-31520 *	42-31706	42-38073 *	42-97190 NMF	42-97571 NMF
42-31545 *	42-31923	42-38113 *	42-97236 NMF	42-97579 NMF
42-31551 *	42-32051 NMF			42-97587 NMF
42-31552 *	42-32079 NMF	42-97062 NMF	42-97451 *	42-97591 NMF
42-31568 *	42-32084 NMF	42-97067 NMF	42-97452 *	42-97662 NMF
42-31594 *	42-32086 NMF	42-97070 NMF	42-97456 *	
42-31607 *	42-32098 NMF	42-97075 NMF	42-97460 *	42-106985 NMF
42-31615 *	42-32101 NMF	42-97087 NMF	42-97468 *	42-106998 NMF
42-31620 *		42-97088 NMF	42-97470 *	42-107001 NMF
42-31629 *	42-38021 *	42-97122 NMF	42-97481 *	42-107015 NMF
42-31630 *	42-38055 *	42-97123 NMF	42-97535 NMF	42-107026 NMF
42-31633 *	42-38063 *	42-97137 NMF	42-97537 NMF	

```
                Assigned but not on hand:
      B-17Gs:  42-97060, 31618, 97131 and 97162 at 2 SAD
        B-17Gs:  42-31154 and 97465 at Burtonwood
   Non Operational Aircraft on hand at Glatton:  B-17E 41-2578
           *  These 26 were Original Group Aircraft
```

482nd BOMBARDMENT GROUP (P)

Constituted as the 482nd BOMBARDMENT GROUP (P) on 10th August 1943
Activated on 20th August 1943
Squadrons Assigned: 812th, 813th, 814th (from 21st October 1943), 819th (20th August 1943 to 21st October 1943)
Assigned to Eighth Air Force: 20th August 1943
Assigned to First Bombardment Wing: 20th August 1943

STATION

Alconbury: From 20th August 1943

Activated at Alconbury, the 482nd was the only Bomb Group to be formed in England. Although assigned to the First Bombardment Wing, tactical control was exercised by the Commanding General, Eighth Bomber Command.

The Group's function was to provide a Pathfinder force of Radar equipped aircraft to precede bomber formations and to find and mark targets obscured by bad weather conditions.

The nucleus of combat crews were transferred from the 325th Bomb Squadron of the 92nd Bomb Group, where they had been training with special equipment. Ground personnel came mainly from the disbanded Squadrons of the 479th Anti-Submarine Group.

The first eight B-17Fs were assigned on 25th August, all came from the 92nd Bomb Group. They were: 41-24359, 42-3385, 42-5745, 42-5793, 42-5819, 42-29994, 42-30006 and 42-30328. At the time of their assignment, 42-5745 was on detached service at Farnborough and 42-5819 was at Defford having H2S fitted. All eight were assigned to the 813rd Bomb Squadron (Pathfinder) and excepting for 42-30006 had either OBOE Mk 1, or H2S fitted. It would be these aircraft which would fly the first Pathfinder missions starting on 27th September.

During June 1943, a Radar officer and other senior personnel from the 92nd Bomb Group were sent to the USA to study H2X equipment and to help in the installation and in the training of a squadron of aircraft. Twelve B-17s were modified at the Rome Air Depot, New York, and were later flown to Boston where the sets were fitted and test flights carried out. These aircraft flew to England via the North Atlantic, the first arriving at Alconbury on 2nd October where they were assigned to the 812th Bomb Squadron. The Squadron flew its first operation on 3rd November 1943.

The Group's third Squadron, the 819th, was renumbered as the 814th Bomb Squadron (Pathfinder) on 21st October and was equipped with B-24 aircraft, the first of this type to be assigned to the First Bombardment Division, and the first to come under the control of Brampton Grange since the departure from Alconbury of the 93rd Bomb Group in December 1942.

The first Liberator, a B-24D 41-40987, arrived from Burtonwood on 28th September and several more followed in October. These came mostly from the disbanded 479th Anti-Submarine Group at Dunkeswell. Spares for the B-24s were furnished from the Third Strategic Air Depot at Watton. In October this depot was directed to furnish Alconbury with a ten day supply of B-24 spares immediately.

42-5793 started out with the 305th Bomb Group before transferring to the 92nd Bomb Group. In May 1943 it went to Defford to have the Eighth Air Force's first H2S installed. Photograph shows the aircraft in flight on 25th August 1943, the day it was transferred from the 92nd to the 482nd Bomb Group. *US Air Force–National Air and Space Museum*

The burnt-out remains of 42-5793 after it had crashed at Brome, Suffolk, shortly after taking off from Thorpe Abbotts on 10th November 1943. *Stan Bishop*

```
┌─────────────────────────────────────────────────────────────────────────────┐
│         STATUS OF AIRCRAFT ASSIGNED AT 2000 HOURS on 14th FEBRUARY 1944        │
│         WHEN THE 482nd BOMB GROUP WAS TRANSFERRED TO COMPOSITE COMMAND          │
│                           B-17E   41-9019                                       │
│                              B-17F                                              │
│  41-24460 Training      42-5819 H2S          42-30006 Training    42-30328      │
│                         42-5970 H2S          42-30280 H2S         42-30729      │
│  42-3398 H2S                                                      42-30731      │
│                                                                                 │
│                              B-17G                                              │
│  42-3483 H2X     42-3492 H2X     42-37745 H2X      42-97514 H2X    42-97545 H2X  │
│  42-3484 H2X     42-3511 H2X                       42-97523 H2X    42-97554 H2X  │
│  42-3485 H2X                     42-39766 H2X      42-97532 H2X    42-97555 H2X  │
│  42-3487 H2X     42-31801        42-39880 H2X      42-97534 H2X    42-97556 H2X  │
│  42-3490 H2X                     42-39915          42-97542 H2X    42-97565 H2X  │
│  42-3491 H2X                                                       42-97567 H2X  │
│                                                                                 │
│                              B-24D                                              │
│  41-23674 SA     42-40538 SA     42-63773 SA       42-63784 SA     42-63792 SA   │
│                  42-40549        42-63775          42-63786 SA     42-63798 SA   │
│  42-40362 SA     42-40550 SA     42-63776 SA       42-63788 SA     42-63801 SA   │
│  42-40478        42-40618 SA     42-63781          42-63789 SA                   │
│  42-40501 SA     42-40713 SA                                       42-72863 SA   │
│  42-40530 SA     42-40987 SH                                                     │
│                                                                                 │
│                              B-24H                                              │
│  41-28639        41-28690        41-29120          41-29177 SH     42-7644 SH    │
│  41-28653        41-28700        41-29163 SH       41-29783        42-7645 SH    │
│  41-28676                                                          42-7646 SH    │
│                              OTHER TYPES                                         │
│  DB-7B: AL452     C-78: 42-58434    L-4B: 43-713     L-5: 42-98593   P-47D: 42-7882 │
│  UC-61: 43-14469 and 43-14484          Oxfords: DF331 and LB522      Master: DL899 │
│                           Tiger Moth:  T6369                                     │
└─────────────────────────────────────────────────────────────────────────────┘
```

482nd Bomb Group(H)

	1943						1944		
	July	Aug	Sep	Oct	Nov	Dec	Jan	Feb	Mar

Serial No — Gained From ▒▒▒ Period Assigned ▒▒▒ Lost To

B-17E

Serial No	Gained From / Notes
41-2578	1 C.C.R.C. 9 Jan 44 — Burtonwood 25 Jan 44, then to 457BG
41-9013	92BG 27 Aug 43 — 94BG 10 Nov 43
41-9019	92BG 27 Aug 43 — Ass 14 Feb 44
41-9051	92BG 1 Sep 43 — Crashed 14 Sep 43

B-17F Boeing

Serial No	Gained From / Notes
41-24359	92BG 25 Aug 43 — Lt Stn 20 Dec 43 then 91BG

B-17F Douglas

Serial No	Gained From / Notes
42-3357	(H2S) New Rpt 8 Sep 43 — MIA 8 Feb 44
42-3382	(SO) New Rpt 8 Sep 43 — Stansted 5 Feb 44, then to 306BG
42-3385	(SO) 92BG 25 Aug 43 — Stansted 5 Feb 44, then to 92BG
42-3398	(H2S) 21 Oct 43 — Ass 14 Feb 44

B-17G Douglas

Serial No	Gained From / Notes
42-3483	(H2X) U.S.A. 2 Oct 43 — Ass 14 Feb 44
42-3484	(H2X) U.S.A. 2 Oct 43 — Ass 14 Feb 44
42-3485	(H2X) U.S.A. 19 Oct 43 — Ass 14 Feb 44
42-3486	(H2X) U.S.A. 18 Oct 43 — MIA 11 Jan 44
42-3487	(H2X) U.S.A. 7 Oct 43 — Ass 14 Feb 44
42-3490	(H2X) U.S.A. 7 Oct 43 — Ass 14 Feb 44
42-3491	(H2X) U.S.A. 2 Oct 43 — Ass 14 Feb 44
42-3492	(H2X) U.S.A. 2 Oct 43 — Ass 14 Feb 43
42-3500	(H2X) U.S.A. 2 Oct 43 — MIA 4 Feb 44
42-3511	(H2X) U.S.A. 2 Oct 43 — Ass 14 Feb 44
42-3521	(SO) 16 Oct 43 — Stansted 5 Feb 44, then to 306BG
42-3525	(SO) Mk 2 15 Oct 43 — Stansted 11 Feb 44, then to 381BG
42-3527	(SO) 16 Oct 43 — Stansted 5 Feb 44, then to 306BG
42-3536	(SO) 21 Oct 43 — Stansted 5 Feb 44, then to 92BG

B-17F Vega

Serial No	Gained From / Notes
42-5745	(SOT) 92BG 25 Aug 43 — Lt Stn 20 Dec 43, then to 91BG
42-5793	(H2S) 92BG 25 Aug 43 — Crashed 10 Nov 43
42-5819	(H2S) 92BG 25 Aug 43 — Ass 14 Feb 44
42-5909	(H2S) 92BG 26 Aug 43 — MIA 4 Feb 44
42-5970	(H2S) 7 Oct 43 — Ass 14 Feb 44

B-17F Boeing

Serial No	Gained From / Notes
42-29994	(SOT) 92BG 25 Aug 43 — 303BG 15 Jan 44
4230006	92BG 25 Aug 43 — Ass 14 Feb 44 Training Act
42-30280	(H2X) U.S.A. 19 Oct 43 — Ass 14 Feb 44 (MIA 22 Feb 44)
42-30328	(SO) 92BG 25 Aug 43 — Stansted 5 Feb 44. To 482BG 14 Feb
42-30613	(SO) 7 Sep 43 — Stansted 5 Feb 44 Then to 381BG
42-30676	15 Sep 43 — 381BG 20 Sep 43
42-30721	10 Sep 43 — 381BG 20 Sep 43
42-30722	10 Sep 43 — 381BG 20 Sep 43
42-30729	5 Oct 43 — Ass 14 Feb 44
42-30731	9 Oct 43 — Ass 14 Feb 44
42-31166	(SO) Mk 2 25 Dec 43 — Stansted 5 Feb 44, then to 384BG
42-31801	U.S.A. 10 Feb 44 — Ass 14 Feb 44, to 305BG 20 Mar 44

Group Activated on 20 Aug 43

First Mission flown on 27th Sep 43

482nd Bomb Group(H)		1943			1944				
		Oct	Nov	Dec	Jan	Feb	Mar		
Serial No		Gained From ▓▓▓ Period Assigned ▓▓▓ Lost To							

B-17G Douglas

Serial No			
42-37733	(SO) N R 3 Nov 43 ▓▓▓▓▓▓▓▓▓▓▓▓▓▓▓	Stansted 9 Feb 44	then to 381BG
42-37735	(SO)N R 23 Nov 43 ▓▓▓▓▓▓▓▓▓▓▓	Stansted 5 Feb 44,	then to 92BG
42-37745	(H2X) ** ▓▓▓▓▓▓▓▓▓▓▓▓	Ass 14 Feb 44.	** New Rpt 2 Oct 43
42-37753	(SO) ** ▓▓▓▓▓▓▓▓▓▓	Stansted 5 Feb 44, then to 92BG. **N R 20 Oct 44	
42-37999	New Rpt 6 Dec 43 ▓ 305BG 10 Dec 43		

B-17G Vega

Serial No			
42-39766	(H2X)	30 Jan 44 ▓▓▓ Ass 14 Feb 44. To 305BG 26 Mar 44	
42-39880	(H2X)	30 Dec 4 ▓▓▓▓▓ Ass 14 Feb 44	
42-39915	U.S.A. 29 Dec 43 ▓▓▓▓▓ Ass 14 Feb 44		
42-40018	(H2X)	U.S.A. 9 Feb 44 ▓ Ass 14 Feb 44	To 305BG 20 Mar 44
42-97475	OBOE MK 2	New Rpt 29 Jan 44 ▓ Stansted 5 Feb 44, then to 305BG	
42-97514	(H2X)	New Rpt 6 Feb 44 ▓ Ass 14 Feb 44, To 305BG 20 Mar 44	
42-97523	(H2X)	U.S.A. 6 Feb 44 ▓ Ass 14 Feb 44, To 305BG 20 Mar 44	
42-97532	(H2X)	8 Feb 44 ▓ Ass 14 Feb 44, To 305BG 26 ar 44	
42-97533	(H2X)	In after 14 Feb 44	To 305BG 20 Mar 44
42-97534	(H2X)	6 Feb 44 ▓ Ass 14 Feb 44	To 96BG
42-97542	(H2X)	6 Feb 44 ▓ Ass 14 Feb 44	To 96BG
42-97543	(H2X)	In after 14 Feb 44	To 305BG 20 Mar 44
42-97545	(H2X)	6 Feb 44 ▓ Ass 14 Feb 44	To 96BG
42-97554	(H2X)	New Rpt 7 Feb 44 ▓ Ass 14 Feb 44	To 96BG
42-97555	(H2X)	U.S.A. 10 Feb 44 ▓ Ass 14 Feb 44	To 96BG
42-97556	(H2X)	New Rpt 7 Feb 44 ▓ Ass 14 Feb 44	To 96BG
42-97565	(H2X)	U.S.A. 8 Feb 44 ▓ Ass 14 Feb 44	To 96BG
42-97567	(H2X)	6 Feb 44 ▓ Ass 14 Feb 44	
42-97574	(H2X)	In after 14 Feb 44	To 305BG 20 Mar 44
42-97578	(H2X)	In after 14 Feb 44	To 305BG 20 Mar 44
42-97592	(H2X)	In after 14 Feb 44	To 305BG 20 Mar 44

NMF
Some or all
Camouflaged
after arrival
in U.K.

B-24D Consolidated

Serial No			
41-23674	(SA)	BADA 20 Dec 43 ▓▓▓▓▓▓▓▓▓ Ass 14 Feb 44	

B-24H Douglas

41-28617	Warton 24 Jan 44 ▓ 9AF Stansted 7 Feb 44		
41-28636	(SO)	U.S.A. 31 Jan 44 ▓ 9AF Stansted 7 Feb 44	
41-28639	U.S.A. 12 Feb 44 ▓ Ass 14 Feb 44		
41-28648	(SO)	Warton 29 Jan 44 ▓ 9AF Stansted 7 Feb 44	
41-28651	(SO)	Warton 26 Jan 44 ▓ 9AF Stansted 7 Feb 44	
41-28652	(SO)	Warton 26 Jan 44 ▓ 9AF Stansted 7 Feb 44	
41-28653	U.S.A. 7 Feb 44 ▓ Ass 14 Feb 44		
41-28676	U.S.A. 9 Feb 44 ▓ Ass 14 Feb 44		
41-28690	U.S.A. 9 Feb 44 ▓ Ass 14 Feb 44		
41-28700	U.S.A. 9 Feb 44 ▓ Ass 14 Feb 44		
41-29120	(SH)	BADA 20 Dec 43 ▓▓▓▓▓ Ass 14 Feb 44	
41-29163	(SH)	BADA 15 Dec 43 ▓▓▓▓▓ Ass 14 Feb 44	
41-29177	(SH)	BADA 15 Dec 43 ▓▓▓▓▓ Ass 14 Feb 44	
41-29183	U.S.A. 12 Feb 44 ▓ Ass 14 Feb 44		

To Composite Command 14th Feb 44

482nd Bomb Group(H)			1943			1944			
			Oct	Nov	Dec	Jan	Feb	Mar	
Serial No			Gained From			Period Assigned			Lost To

B-24H Ford

Serial No			Oct	Nov	Dec	Jan	Feb	Mar	Lost To
42-7499	(SO)	***				93BG 31 Dec 43			
42-7629		** *		93BG 12 Nov 43					
42-7644	(SH)			BADA 20 Dec 43			Ass 14 Feb 44		
42-7645	(SH)			BADA 4 Jan 44			Ass 14 Feb 44		
42-7646	(SH)			BADA 21 Dec 43			Ass 14 Feb 44		
42-7669	(SH)			BADA 26 Dec 43		Crashed 29 Jan 44			
42-7672	(SH)			BADA 29 Dec 43		Crashed 23 Jan 44			

B-24D Consolidated

Serial No			Oct	Nov	Dec	Jan	Feb	Mar	Lost To
42-40362	(SA)				BADA 28 jan 44		Ass 14 Feb 44		
42-40474				BADA 25 Dec 43	Crashed 27 Dec 43 (28 Dec 43)				
42-40478	(SA)				BADA 4 jan 44		Ass 14 Feb 44		
42-40501	(SA)				BADA 30 Dec 43		Ass 14 Feb 44		
42-40530	(SA)			BADA 17 Dec 43			Ass 14 Feb 44		
42-40538	(SA)				BADA 28 Jan 44		Ass 14 Feb 44		
42-40549	(SA)		BADA 17 Nov 43				ASS 14 Feb 44		
42-40550	(SA)			BADA 5 Dec 43			Ass 14 Feb 44		
42-40618	(SA)			BADA 30 Dec 43			Ass 14 Feb 44		
42-40713	(SA)			BADA 5 Dec 43			Ass 14 Feb 44		
42-40840	(AS)		31 Oct 43	BADA 24 Nov 43					
42-40859	(AS)		6 Nov 43	BADA 3 Dec 43					
42-40919	(AS)		31 Oct 43	BADA 24 Nov 43					
42-40921	(AS)		31 Oct 43	Burtonwood 18 Nov 43					
42-40925	(AS)		3 Nov 43	BADA 24 Nov 43					
42-40926	(AS)		6 Nov 43	BADA 1 Dec 43					
42-40931			8 Nov 43	Burtonwood 18 Nov 43					
42-40937	(AS)		31 Oct 43	BADA 24 Nov 43					
42-40939	(AS)		3 Nov 43	Burtonwood 18 nov 43					
42-40944	(AS)		31 Oct 43	Burtonwood 20 Nov 43					
42-40959	(AS)		3 Nov 43	BADA 24 Nov 43					
42-40987	(SH)	++					Ass 14 Feb 44		

B-24D Ford

Serial No			Oct	Nov	Dec	Jan	Feb	Mar	Lost To
42-63773	(SA)			BADA 20 Dec 43			Ass 14 Feb 44		
42-63775					BADA 28 Jan 44		Ass 14 Feb 44		
42-63776	(SA)			BADA 20 Dec 43			Ass 14 Feb 44		
42-63781			Date in Unknown				Ass 14 Feb 44		
4263784			Burtonwood 20 Nov 43				Ass 14 Feb 44		
42-63786				BADA 30 Dec 43			Ass 14 Feb 44		
42-63787									
42-63788	(SA)				BADA 29 Jan 44		Ass 14 Feb 44		
42-63789	(SA)		Bwd 17 Nov 43				Ass 14 Feb 44		
42-63792	(SA)			BADA 5 Jan 44			Ass 14 Feb 44		
42-63798	(SA)			BADA 3 Jan 44			Ass 14 Feb 44		
42-63801	(SA)			BADA 3 Jan 44			Ass 14 Feb 44		

B-24D Consolidated

Serial No			Oct	Nov	Dec	Jan	Feb	Mar	Lost To
42-72863	(SA)		8 Nov 43				Ass 14 Feb 44		

First B-24 Mission flown on 11th Jan 44

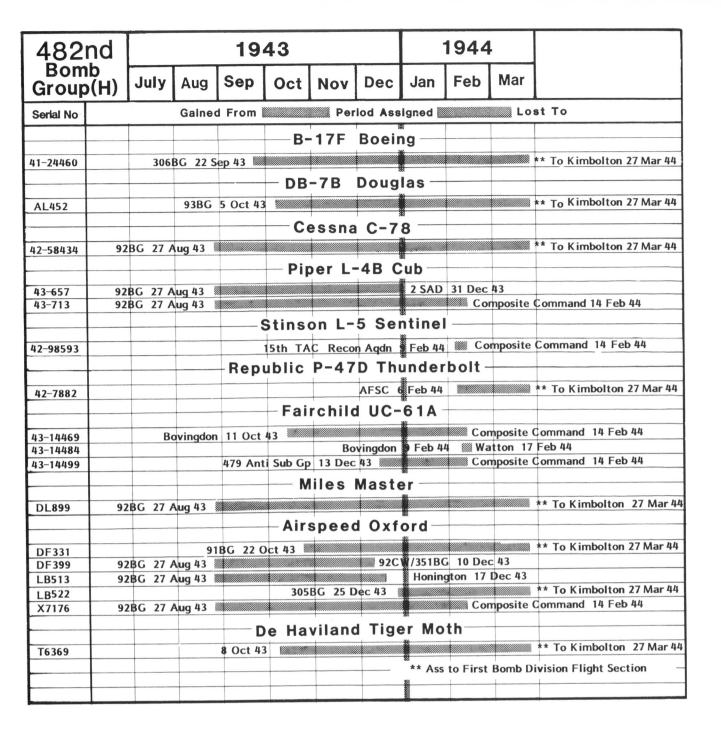

482nd Bomb Group(H)	1943						1944			
Serial No	July	Aug	Sep	Oct	Nov	Dec	Jan	Feb	Mar	

B-17F Boeing

41-24460 — 306BG 22 Sep 43 — ** To Kimbolton 27 Mar 44

DB-7B Douglas

AL452 — 93BG 5 Oct 43 — ** To Kimbolton 27 Mar 44

Cessna C-78

42-58434 — 92BG 27 Aug 43 — ** To Kimbolton 27 Mar 44

Piper L-4B Cub

43-657 — 92BG 27 Aug 43 — 2 SAD 31 Dec 43
43-713 — 92BG 27 Aug 43 — Composite Command 14 Feb 44

Stinson L-5 Sentinel

42-98593 — 15th TAC Recon Aqdn 8 Feb 44 — Composite Command 14 Feb 44

Republic P-47D Thunderbolt

42-7882 — AFSC 6 Feb 44 — ** To Kimbolton 27 Mar 44

Fairchild UC-61A

43-14469 — Bovingdon 11 Oct 43 — Composite Command 14 Feb 44
43-14484 — Bovingdon 9 Feb 44 — Watton 17 Feb 44
43-14499 — 479 Anti Sub Gp 13 Dec 43 — Composite Command 14 Feb 44

Miles Master

DL899 — 92BG 27 Aug 43 — ** To Kimbolton 27 Mar 44

Airspeed Oxford

DF331 — 91BG 22 Oct 43 — ** To Kimbolton 27 Mar 44
DF399 — 92BG 27 Aug 43 — 92CW/351BG 10 Dec 43
LB513 — 92BG 27 Aug 43 — Honington 17 Dec 43
LB522 — 305BG 25 Dec 43 — ** To Kimbolton 27 Mar 44
X7176 — 92BG 27 Aug 43 — Composite Command 14 Feb 44

De Haviland Tiger Moth

T6369 — 8 Oct 43 — ** To Kimbolton 27 Mar 44

** Ass to First Bomb Division Flight Section

B-17G 42-3527 landing at Thurleigh. It was one of the aircraft sent to the 9th Air Force at Stansted for the removal of special equipment in February 1944. It was later assigned to the 306th Bomb Group. It is still carrying the codes of the 813th Bomb Squadron and it is not known if this photograph was taken before or after its assignment to the 306th Bomb Group. *306th Historical Association*

482nd BOMBARDMENT GROUP (H)

B-24D 42-40921 '**WHITE SAVAGE**' of 479th Anti Submarine Group. Was assigned to the 482nd Bomb Group on 31st October 1943 and left for Burtonwood on 18th November 1943. *Mike Bailey.*

AIRCRAFT AND OPERATIONAL STATISTICS

Total Aircraft Assigned

B-17E:	27 Aug 43 to 14 Feb 44	4	DB-7B:	5 Oct 43 to 14 Feb 44	1
B-17F:	25 Aug 43 to 14 Feb 44	21	C-78:	27 Aug 43 to 14 Feb 44	1
B-17G:	2 Oct 43 to 14 Feb 44	37	L-4B:	27 Aug 43 to 14 Feb 44	2
B-24D:	28 Sep 43 to 14 Feb 44	36	L-5:	9 Feb 44 to 14 Feb 44	1
B-24H:	8 Oct 43 to 14 Feb 44	21	P-47D:	6 Feb 44 to 14 Feb 44	1
Master:	27 Aug 43 to 14 Feb 44	1	UC-61A:	11 Oct 43 to 14 Feb 44	3
Oxford:	27 Aug 43 to 14 Feb 44	5	Tiger Moth:	8 Oct 43 to 14 Feb 44	1

Operational Statistics

First Mission flown on: 27 Sep 43	Total Act MIA: 4 (2 B-17F and 2 B-17G)
First Act MIA: B-17G 42-3486 on 11 Jan 44	Highest Days Losses: 2 on 4 Feb 44
First B-17G Ass: 42-3483, 3484, 3491, 3492, 3500, 3511 and 37745 on 2 Oct 43	Other Losses: (Salvaged) 2 B-17s and 3 B-24s
	B-17E: 1 (Non Op) B-17F: 1 (Non Op)
First NMF Ass: 42-97542, 97545 and 97567 on 6 Feb 44.(These were probably painted OD in U.K.)	B-24D: 1 (Non Op)
	B-24H: 2 (1 Op and 1 Non Op)
First NMF MIA None while in First BD	

Some of the above aircraft were reported as Ass to the 329th Service Group and later were assigned to the First Bomb Division Flight Section

42-7644, a Ford built B-24H of 44th Bomb Group in 1944. This aircraft had been assigned to the 482nd Bomb Group on 20th December 1943 and was still assigned when the 482nd left the First Bombardment Wing in February 1944. *Mike Bailey*

FORTRESSES OF THE BIG TRIANGLE FIRST

PART THREE

THE AIRCRAFT

B-17E

B-17F

B-17G

YB-40

B-24D

B-24H

DB-7B

C-78

L-4B

L-5

P-47D

UC-61

Lysander

Master

Oxford

Spitfire

Tiger Moth

B-17E BOEING

41-2578 To 97BG May 42 340BS 'BUTCHER SHOP'. To UK July 42. On 8AFs first Miss 17 Aug 42. To 92BG then to 1CCRC. To 482BG 9 Jan 44. To 457BG 3 Mar 44. Ass 31 Mar 44. Oldest B-17 in 8AF, served to end of war.

41-2626 To 97BG 340BS. To UK July 1942. To 92BG 407BS. Dam on Op Miss 9 Oct 42, Ld at Gatwick on ret and sal.

41-2628 To 97BG 341BS. To UK July 42. To 92BG then to 1CCRC 1943. To 305BG 29 May 43. Ass 31 Mar 44.

41-2629 To 97BG 340BS. To UK July 42. To 305BG 6 Nov 42. To 92BG 14 Dec 42. Was Ass to 379BG on 27 May 43 but this was cancelled on 28 May 43. Later served in 100BG.

41-9013 To 97BG 341BS. To UK July 42. To 92BG 327BS. Made courier flight to North Africa 18 Dec 42. To 1CCRC. Ret to 92BG 13 May 43. To 482BG 27 Aug 43. To 94BG 10 Nov 43.

41-9017 To 97BG 342BS 'HEIDI HO'. To UK, Arr Pwk 6 July 42. On 8AFs first Miss 17 Aug 42. To 305BG 6 Nov 42. To 92BG 6 Dec 42. Later 94BG. Sal at Great Ashfield Sep 43.

41-9018 To 97BG 341BS. To UK July 42. To 92BG 327BS, MIA 9 Oct 42. Lt Francis H Chorak.

41-9019 To 97BG March 42 414BS 'LITTLE SKUNK FACE'. To UK, Arr Pwk 6 July 42. To 305BG 6 Nov 42 then unknown. To 92BG 13 May 43, used as TT. To 381BG 11 June 43, ret to 92BG 10 July 43 327BS. To 482BG 27 Aug 43. Still with 482BG on 14 Feb 44 when the Gp trans to Com Cmd.

41-9020 To 97BG 340BS 'PHYLLIS'. To UK July 42. To 92BG. Made several courier flights to North Africa late 42, early 43. In use as TT Apr 43. To 303BG 1 May 43. Ass 31 Mar 44.

41-9021 To 97BG March 42 414BS 'HANGAR QUEEN'. To UK July 42. On 8AFs first Miss 17 Aug 42. To 92BG 327BS 24 Aug 42. Was in 8AFs first mid air coll when it hit 41-9051 while on Op Miss 9 Oct 42. Piloted by Lt James C Dempsey. Act was badly dam but ret to Bovingdon where rep was done by outside working party from Bwd. Did not fly again until Feb 43. Later served in 2CCRC and 390BG.

41-9022 To 97BG 341BS 'ALABAMA EXTERMINATOR'. Over-shot runway when landing at Presque Isle 27 June 42, Lt Paine. Rep using parts from the sal 41-2588. To UK, date of arrival unknown, probably last of the B-17Es to arr. To 92BG, loaned on DS to AFSC Mar-Apr 43 for use as Navigation Act for fighter ferry flights to North Africa. To 384BG 4 June 43, used as TT. Ass 31 Mar 44.

41-9023 To 97BG 414BS 'YANKEE DOODLE'. To UK, Arr Pwk 6 July 43. On 8AFs first Miss 17 Aug 42. To 92BG 24 Aug 42. Made courier flight to North Africa 14 Feb 43. To 91BG 30 Mar 43. Used for Blind Approach Training. Ass 31 Mar 44.

41-9024 To 97BG Mar 42 414BS 'KING CONDOR'. To UK, Arr Pwk 6 July 42. Dam beyond rep when landing at Grafton Underwood 1650hrs 1 Aug 42. Piloted by 2nd Lt Lawrence with ten other crew on board. Ld on the East Runway with an eight mile an hour tailwind and continued past the end of the runway through a hedge and on to an Air Ministry road where the number four engine struck a lorry. None of the crew were inj but the two men in the truck were inj, one fatally. This was the first 8AF B-17 to be sal in England. It was also the first loss to the 414BS.

41-9025 To 97BG Mar 42 341BS 'LITTLE JOHN'. To UK July 42. To 92BG. Made courier flight to North Africa 23 Dec 43. Later to 11CCRC.

41-9026 To 97BG 342BS. To UK, Arr Pwk 6 July 42. On 8AFs first Miss 17 Aug 42. To 92BG. It is believed this is the 92BG B-17E MIA on 6 Sep 42. No confirmation can be found but it is the only one of the 41 B-17Es that reached England that cannot be accounted for after Sept 42. 2nd Lt Leigh E Stewart.

41-9030 To 97BG Mar 42 414BS 'BIG PUNK'. To UK, Arr Pwk 15 July 42. On 8AFs first Miss 17 Aug 42. To 305BG 6 Nov 42. To 92BG 2 Dec 42. To 310th Ferrying Squadron, 27th Air Transport Group Nov 43.

41-9042 To 97BG 342BS. To UK, Arr Pwk 6 July 42. On 8AFs first Miss 17 Aug 42. To 92BG 325BS-B then to 310th Ferrying Squadron, 27th Air Transport Group 26 July 43.

41-9043 To 97BG 342BS 'PEGGY D'. To UK, Arr Pwk 15 July 42. On 8AFs first Miss 17 Aug 42. To 92BG then to 381BG June/July 43. Ass 31 Mar 44.

41-9018 keeps company with two P-38s at Meeks Field, Iceland, 21st July 1942. Assigned to the 341st Bomb Squadron and flown to England by Lt Kinnel and crew. Transferred to the 327th Bomb Squadron of the 92nd Bomb Group. It was the second and last Eighth Air Force B-17E to go Missing in Action. *US Air Force – National Air and Space Museum*

Lt Schley's 41-9045 **'STINK Y'** undergoing an engine change at Meeks Field, Iceland, 25th July 1942. Later named **'TENESSEE BELLE'** and ended its career in an Irish field when returning from a courier flight to North Africa, 15th January 1943. *US Air Force – National Air and Space Museum*

41-9044 To 97BG 341BS. To UK July 42. To 92BG 325BS. Made a courier flight to North Africa 22 Jan 43. Left Portreath on a courier flight to Gibraltar on 11 Feb 43. Engine trouble developed after TO and the aircraft returned and was diverted to Chivenor where difficulty was experienced in landing the heavily loaded plane. On the first approach the aircraft hit something in the darkness and after landing on the second attempt the landing gear was retracted, the aircraft stopping just short of the end of the runway. The crew were uninjured but the aircraft was badly dam and sal. 1st Lt Alan E Hermance. The Act had flown a total of 485.35 hours prior to the incident. (14 Feb 43)

41-9045 To 97BG Mar 42 414BS **'TENESSEE BELLE'**. To UK July 42. To 92BG. Made courier flight to North Africa 6 Dec 43. Cr Ld at Athenry, Ireland 15 Jan 43 on flight from North Africa to Portreath. On board was Gen Devers and three other Gens, one Col, one Maj, one Capt, two Lts, two Tech Sgts and five Sgts. No one was injured, all were driven up to Northern Ireland. Act was dismantled and taken to L. Ldg. Pilot was Tom Hulin.

41-9051 To 97BG 340BS. To UK, Arr Pwk 15 July 42. To 92BG. Was in mid air collision with 41-9021 while on Op Miss 9 Oct 42. Although badly dam, landed safely at Detling. Made courier flight to North Africa 14 Feb 43. Loaned to AFSC March/June 43 and used as lead Act for ferrying fighters to North Africa. Ret to 92BG 18 June 43. To 482BG 2 Sep 43. Cr into hillside near Keswick 14 Sep 43. Capt William C Anderson CO of 813BS. All ten on act kld. Served in 326 and 327BSs while in 92BG.

41-9074 To 303BG 359BS. To UK, Arr Pwk 23 July 43. To 97BG 340BS-N 28 July 42. Flew on Miss 7 Sep 42, was dam, sal after this Miss. Remains to Bwd for spares. First B-17 sal as a result of dam sustained on an Op Miss. Capt Hughes.

41-9082 To 301BG 419BS. To UK July 42. To 97BG. To 92BG. Made courier flight to North Africa 6 Dec 42. Later trans to 12AF and used as personal Act by Maj Gen Bernard Montgomery.

41-9085 To 303BG 359BS. To UK, Arr Pwk 1 July 42. First US operated B-17 to arrive in UK. To 97BG **'JARRIN JENNY'**. To 92BG. With AFSC for rep 16 Dec 42. No record after this date.

41-9089 To 97BG Apr 42 414BS **'JOHNNY REB'**. To UK, Arr Pwk 15 July 42. On 8AFs first Miss 17 Aug 42. On Op Miss of 21 Aug 42, the Co-Pilot, 2nd Lt Donald A Walter was kld. First 8AF combat fatality. To 92BG and later served with 11CCRC.

41-9098 To 303BG 359BS. To UK, Arr Pwk 8 July 42. Cr in mountains at Llanrhawdr 11 Aug 42. Burnt out. All crew kld. 2nd Lt Robert E Beers.

41-9100 To 97BG 414BS **'BIRMINGHAM BLITZKREIG'**. Apr 42. To UK, Arr Pwk 24 July 42. On 8AFs first Miss 17 Aug 42. To 92BG 24 Aug 42. To 1CCRC. To 379BG 28 May 43. Ass 31 Mar 44.

41-9103 To 97BG Apr 42 414BS **'DIXIE DEMO'**. To UK, Arr Pwk 6 July 42. To 92BG 24 Aug 42. DS to 91BG 30 Mar 43. To Bwd 20 June 43. Later to 385BG.

41-9107 To 97BG 340BS. To UK, Arr Pwk 22 July 42. To 92BG, made at least five courier flights to North Africa Nov 42-Jan 43. On DS to AFSC. Used as lead Act for fighter ferry flights to North Africa. Ret to 92BG and fitted as TT June 43. To 91BG 22 Jul 43. Ret to 92BG 29 Aug 43. 407BS-P and then to Warton 21 Sep 43. To 401BG 6 Nov 43. 613BS. Ass 31 Mar 44. May have served in 390BG prior to Ass to 401BG.

41-9112 To 301BG 419BS. To UK, Arr Pwk 15 July 42. Not known if Ass to 97th or 92BS while in UK. Ass to 8th Bomber Command. Ret to USA via North Africa 14 Feb 43. First 8AF B-17 known to have ret to USA. Went to Wright Field while in USA. Ret to UK Oct 43. Had B-24 nose and tail turrets fitted.

41-9114 To 97BG 341BS. To UK, Arr Pwk 24 July 42. To 92BG. To 11CCRC. Made special courier flight to North Africa 14 Feb 43. Probably did not ret from this flight. Ass to 12AF.

42-9115 To 97BG 342BS. To UK, Arr Pwk 6 July 42. Cr ld on Berners Heath, Elvedon, 14 Aug 42. When on practice flight. 1st Lt Francis Schwarzenbeck. One crew man kld, eight baled out.

41-9119 To 301BG 419BS. To UK July 1942. To 97BG. To 92BG. To 11CCRC 1943. Later to 96BG.

41-9121 To 303BG 359BS. To UK July 1942. To 97BG 'THE BIG BITCH'. To 92BG. To 11CCRC 1943. Made courier flights to North Africa 17 and 26 Nov 42, 23 Dec 42, 5 and 13 Jan 43 and 18 Feb 43. To 351BG 27 May 43. Ass 31 Mar 44. (Flew Op Miss with 97BG on 6 Sep 42).

41-9125 To 303BG 359BS. To UK, Arr Pwk 24 July 42. To 97BG 342BS. On 8AFs first Miss 17 Aug 42. To 92BG. Made courier flights to North Africa, 15 and 20 Nov 42, 23 Dec 42 and 16 Feb 43. TT Act May 43. Unknown after this date.

41-9129 To 303BG 359BS. Left Presque Isle for Goose Bay 22 June 42. Had trouble finding Goose Bay due to weather and Ld in a large field at Bathurst, New Brunswick, where a large boulder demolished the tail wheel. Pilot was Lt H D Schmoldt. Act stayed at Bathurst for two weeks during which time it was rep. It was stripped and a 1400ft steel mat runway was laid out on which the TO was made. This was the first of several such occasions where a temporary runway was laid to rescue an 8AF B-17 from the site of a forced landing.

While the aircraft was being rep, orders had been issued to the crew to ret to their Ass unit at Gowen Field. When it was learned that the rep and rescue of the aircraft had been successful these orders were rescinded and the Act and crew made a successful crossing to the UK, Arr Pwk 24 July 42. To 97BG. To 305BG 6 Nov 42. To 92BG 327BS. To Snetterton Heath 11 Aug 43.

41-9132 To 303BG 359BS. To UK, Arr Pwk 24 July 42. To 97BG. To 92BG. Made courier flight to North Africa 18 Dec 42. No further information. Probably sal 1943.

41-9148 To 303BG 359BS. To UK, Arr Pwk 24 July 42. To 97BG 'BOOMERANG'. To 92BG. Made courier flights to North Africa 1 Dec 42 and 23 Dec 42. To 306BG 1 May 43. Used as TT. Ass 31 Mar 44.

41-9154 To 301BG 419BS. To UK July 42. To 97BG. To 92BG. Used as TT. Ass 31 Mar 44.

41-9174 To 97BG 340BS. To UK July 42. To 92BG. To 1CCRC. Cr on TO at Bovingdon June 43. Lt Buford, no inj to crew.

41-9175 To 97BG 340BS. To UK July 42. Ld Manston on ret from Op Miss 24 Aug 42. First US operated B-17 to land at this airfield. To 92BG. To 1CCRC. To 310th Ferrying Sqdn, 27th Air Transport Group Nov 43.

41-9129 at dispersal in bright sunshine. One of the B-17Es belonging to the 359th Bomb Squadron of the 303rd Bomb Group, forming the BOLERO weather flight, nearly finished its days in a New Brunswick field. Went on to serve in the 97th, 92nd and 305th Groups before leaving the First Wing in August 1943. *Mike Bailey*

B-17F BOEING

41-24342 Orig of 92BG. To 97BG 24 Aug 42 414BS. To 12AF. Dep Hurn 20 Nov 42.

41-24343 Orig of 92BG. To 97BG 342BS-D 'PEGGY D II'. Later to 414BS. To 12AF. Dep Hurn 22 Nov 42.

41-24344 Orig of 92BG 326BS. To 97BG 414BS. MIA 21 Oct 42. Capt Bennett.

41-24345 Orig of 92BG 326BS. To 97BG. To 12AF. Dep Hurn 20 Nov 42.

41-24346 Orig of 301BG 419BS. To 12AF. Dep Hurn 24 Nov 42.

41-24347 Orig of 301BG 347BS 'STORK'. Made a wheels up landing on Church Lawford airfield after developing engine trouble on a flight from Bovingdon to Chelveston 9 Aug 42. 2nd Lt James M Hair. No inj to crew. First 8AF B-17F sal in UK.

41-24348 Orig of 301BG 353BS. Was dam in parking Acc with a P-38 at BW-1, Greenland 3 Aug 42 while on ferry flight to UK. Rep and flown to UK. To 12AF. Dep Hurn 24 Nov 42.

41-24350 Orig of 301BG. To 12AF. Dep Hurn 24 Nov 42.

41-24351 Orig of 301BG 352BS. To 12AF. Dep Hurn 24 Nov 42.

41-24352 Orig of 301BG 352BS. To 12AF. Dep Hurn 24 Nov 42.

41-24359 Orig of 301BG. To 305BG 25 Nov 42. On DS to Wyton Mar 43 for installation of OBOE Mk 1. Also used as SBA trainer. To 92BG 20 Apr 43 325BS. To 482BG 25 Aug 43 813BS. Out to Lt Stn 20 Dec 43 then on DS to 91BG 20 Dec 43 to 21 Jan 44. Ass to 91BG 20 Feb 44. Out to BAD 15 Mar 44 for ret to USA. (Served in five First Wing/Division Groups.)

41-23460 Orig of 301BG 419BS. To 12AF. Dep Hurn 24 Nov 42.

41-24361 Orig of 301BG. To 12AF. Dep Hurn 24 Nov 42.

41-24362 Orig of 301BG 419BS. MIA 9 Oct 42. Ditched in Channel on ret from Op Miss. The only 301BG Act lost to enemy action while the Gp was operating with 8AF. Also first successful ditching of a US operated B-17 in European Theatre. All crew rescued, 1st Lt Donald M Swenson.

41-24363 Orig of 301BG. To 12AF. Dep Hurn 24 Nov 42.

41-24364 Orig of 301BG 353BS. To 12AF. Dep Hurn 24 Nov 42.

41-24365 Orig of 92BG. In landing Acc at Bangor, 20 Jul 42. To Rome Air Depot for rep. To UK Mar 43. To 305BG 6 Apr 43 365BS-E. Used as SBA trainer. To Warton 7 Nov 43. Later to 2CCRC.

41-24367 Orig of 301BG 419BS. To 12AF. Dep Hurn 25 Nov 42.

41-24344, the fifth B-17F off the Boeing Seattle line. Went to the Middletown Air Depot on 28th June 1942 and then assigned to the 92nd Bomb Group in the USA. Transferred to the 97th Bomb Group in England and went Missing in Action on that Group's final mission with the Eighth Air Force, 21st October 1942. *US Air Force. Via Mike Bailey*

41-24368 Orig of 301BG 352BS. To 12AF. Dep Hurn 24 Nov 42.

42-24369 Orig of 301BG. To 12AF. Dep Hurn 24 Nov 42.

41-24370 Orig of 92BG 'PALE FACE'. To 97BG 342BS 'BERLIN SLEEPER'. To 12AF. Dep Hurn 20 Nov 42.

41-24371 Orig of 301BG. To 12AF. Dep Hurn 14 Nov 42.

41-24372 Orig of 301BG. To 12AF. Dep Hurn 24 Nov 42.

41-24373 Orig of 92BG 326BS. To 97BG 341BS. To 12AF. Dep Predannack 17 Nov 42.

41-24374 Orig of 301BG. To 12AF. Dep Hurn 24 Nov 42.

41-24376 Orig of 92BG. To 97BG 341BS. To 12AF. Dep Predannack 15 Nov 42.

41-24377 Orig of 92BG. To 97BG 342BS-E 'BOOMERANG'. Made secret flight to Gibraltar 19 Oct 42. To 12AF. Dep Hurn 5 Nov 42. Carried Gen Mark Clark to Gibraltar.

41-24378 Orig of 92BG 326BS. To 97BG 342BS. To 12AF. Dep Hurn 20 Nov 42.

41-24379 Orig of 92BG. To 97BG 341BS. To 12AF. Dep Predannack 17 Nov 42.

41-24380 Orig of 92BG. To 97BG 340BS. To 12AF. Dep Predannack 10 Nov 42.

41-24382 Orig of 92BG. To 97BG 341BS. To 12AF. Dep Predannack 17 Nov 42.

41-24385 Orig of 92BG 326BS. To 97BG 340BS. To 12AF. Dep Hurn for Gibraltar 5 Nov 42. Carried Allied Commanders for TORCH Operation. Ret to Predannack 9 Nov 42 and then dep for North Africa 10 Nov 42.

41-24386 Orig of 301BG. To 12AF. Dep Predannack 24 Nov 42.

41-24388 Orig of 92BG. To 97BG 340BS. To 12AF. Dep Hurn for Gibraltar 6 Nov 42. Carried Generals Doolittle and Lemnitzer, was attacked by Ju-88s on the flight from England. Pilot was John C Summers.

41-24390 Orig of 301BG 419BS. To 12AF. Dep Portreath 23 Nov 42.

41-24392 Orig of 92BG. To 97BG 28 Aug 42. 414BS. To 12AF. Dep Hurn 20 Nov 42.

41-24393 Orig of 301BG 419BS. To 12AF. Dep Hurn 28 Nov 42.

41-24394 Orig of 301BG. To 12AF. Dep Hurn 24 Nov 42.

41-24395 Orig of 301BG 419BS. To 12AF. Dep Hurn 24 Nov 42.

41-24396 Orig of 301BG 419BS. To 12AF. Dep Hurn 24 Nov 42.

41-24397 Orig of 301BG. Dam by enemy action on Op Miss 2 Oct 42. Made wheels up landing at Gatwick on ret. Nose was cut off to facilitate removal of wounded top turret gunner. Sal and remains to Bwd for spares.

41-24398 Orig of 301BG 419BS up to 15 Sep 42 then Sqdn unknown. Cr Ld at Newmarket 3 Oct 42 due to LG trouble. 1st Lt Clement Bird. Sal by 1SAD. Remains to Bwd for spares.

41-24399 Orig of 91BG 325BS-V 'MAN-OF-WAR'. MIA 30 July 43. 2nd Lt Keene C McCammon.

41-24400 Orig of 92BG. To 97BG. Dam on Op Miss 21 Oct 42. Sal on ret and remains to Bwd for spares.

41-24404 Orig of 301BG. To 12AF. Dep Hurn 24 Nov 42.

41-24405 Orig of 301BG. To 12AF. Dep Hurn 24 Nov 42.

41-24406 Orig of 92BG. To 97BG 24 Aug 42 414BS. To 12AF. Dep Hurn 20 Nov 42.

41-24407 Orig of 301BG 352BS. To 12AF. Dep Hurn 24 Nov 42.

41-24408 Orig of 301BG. To 12AF. Dep Hurn 24 Nov 42.

41-24409 Orig of 301BG. To 12AF. Dep Hurn 24 Nov 42.

41-24411 Orig of 92BG. To 97BG. Dam on Op Miss 21 Oct 42. Sal, remains to Bwd for spares.

41-24412 Possibly to 301BG in July 42, but trans to 92BG prior to leaving the USA. To 97BG 340BS-D. To 12AF. Dep Predannack 10 Nov 42.

41-24413 Orig of 92BG. To 97BG 24 Aug 42 414BS. To 12AF. Dep Hurn 20 Nov 42.

41-24414 Orig of 92BG. To 97BG 342BS. To 12AF. Dep Hurn 20 Nov 42.

41-24415 Orig of 92BG. To 97BG 24 Aug 42 414BS. To 12AF. Dep Hurn 20 Nov 42.

41-24416 Orig of 92BG 326BS. To 97BG, but left before Gp dep for 12AF in Nov 42. Probably due to dam received on Op Miss of 2 Oct 42 when Act landed back at Oakington. Unknown till with 95BG June 43. To 303BG 17 June 43 359BS-V 'BLACK DIAMOND EXPRESS'. To BAD for ret to USA 30 Mar 44.

41-24417 Orig of 92BG. To 97BG 24 Aug 42. 414BS. Dam on Op Miss 21 Oct 42. To Bwd. To 306BG 26 Feb 43 369BS. Landed in sea on ret from Op Miss 26 July 43. Came down about 500 yards off Cromer Beach at 1500hrs. Lt Alphonse M Maresh. (Listed as Op Loss).

41-24418 Orig of 301BG. To 12AF. Dep Hurn 24 Nov 42.

41-24419 Orig of 92BG. To 97BG 341BS. To 12AF. Dep Predannack 17 Nov 42.

41-24421 Orig of 92BG. To 97BG 341BS. To 12AF. Dep Predannack 17 Nov 42.

41-24422 Orig of 301BG. To 12AF. Dep Hurn 24 Nov 42.

41-24423 Orig of 301BG. To 12AF. Dep Hurn 24 Nov 42.

41-24431 Orig of 91BG 401BS-G 'THE SAINT'. Dam in taxiing Acc at Bassingbourn 12 Feb 43. Wind lifted tail as Act taxied for TO on flight to Honington. 1st Lt Earl F Riley.

41-24432 Orig of 91BG 401BS-E 'DANELLEN'. MIA 20 Dec 42. 1st Lt Dan W Corson.

41-24435 Orig of 92BG. To 97BG 340BS. To 12AF. Dep Hurn for Gibraltar 5 Nov 42. Carried Allied Commanders for TORCH operations. Ret to Predannack 9 Nov 42 and then dep for North Africa 11 Nov 42.

41-24437 Orig of 92BG. To 97BG 341BS. To 12AF. Dep Predannack 17 Nov 42.

41-24439 Orig of 91BG 322BS-Q 'CHIEF SLY'. Cr at Parsonage Farm, Fletchling, on ret from Op Miss 20 Dec 42. Crew safe. Maj Bruce Barton.

41-24441 Orig of 92BG 326BS. To 97BG 342BS. MIA 21 Oct 42. 1st Lt Francis Schwarzenbeck.

41-24442 Orig of 92BG 326BS. To 97BG 342BS. To 12AF. Dep Hurn 20 Nov 42.

41-24443 Orig of 92BG. To 97BG 24 Aug 42 414BS. MIA 21 Oct 42. 1st Lt Milton M Stenstrom.

41-24444 Orig of 92BG. To 97BG 340BS-R 'THE RED GREMLIN'. Paul Tibbets flew this Act to Gibraltar 19 Oct 42. Carried Gen Mark Clark for meeting with French Generals in North Africa. Accompanied by 41-24377 was first visit by US operated B-17s to Gibraltar. Ret to Polebrook 24 Oct 42. To 12AF. Dep Hurn 5 Nov 42 for Gibraltar, carrying Gen Eisenhower, Supreme Commander of the TORCH operation.

41-24445 Orig of 92BG 326BS. To 97BG. MIA 6 Sep 42. 2nd Lt Clarence W Lipsky. Down near Flasselles. First 8AF B-17 lost in action.

41-24447 Orig of 91BG 401BS 'KICKA POO'. MIA 26 Feb 44. Capt John T Swais.

41-24449 Orig of 91BG 401BS 'SHORT SNORTER'. MIA 30 Dec 42. 1st Lt William D Bloodgood.

41-24452 Orig of 91BG 401BS-E. MIA 20 Dec 42. 1st Lt Robert S English.

41-24453 Orig of 91BG 322BS-O 'MIZPAH' and 'THE BEARDED BEAUTY'. In mid air coll with 41-24499 18 Nov 42. Ld at Yeovilton and rep. MIA 17 Aug 43. 2nd Lt Everett L Kenner.

41-24459 Orig of 91BG 401BS-B 'INVASION II'. MIA 17 Apr 43. 1st Lt John W Wilson.

41-24460 Orig of 306BG 423BS-A. Used as SBA trainer 43. to 482BG 22 Sep 43. To 379BG 27 Mar 44. Ass to 1BD Special Purpose Flight at Kimbolton. Ass 31 Mar 44. Oldest B-17F still Ass to 8AF and 1BD on 31 Mar 44.

41-24461 Orig of 306BG 369BS. Sal 27 Feb 43. Reason unknown.

41-24464 Orig of 306BG 367BS. To 91BG 'EXCALIBUR'. MIA 4 Mar 43. 1st Lt Alan Brill. Ditched. 7 crew picked up by ASR.

41-24465 Orig of 306BG 368BS. MIA 5 Apr 43. 2nd Lt Robert W Seelos.

41-24466 Orig of 306BG 368BS. To SBA trainer 11 Apr 43. To L Ldg for overhaul 16 Apr 43. Then to 11CCRC 3 July 43.

41-24467 Orig of 305BG 422BS. To 306BG, probably about 20 Jan 43. MIA 17 Apr 43. Lt Glen J Lally.

41-24468 Orig of 306BG 369BS. To AFSC 26 Mar 43 then to 1CCRC.

41-24469 Orig of 306BG 367BS. Lost 6 Jan 43. Group had ld at St Eval on ret from Op Miss 3 Jan 43. On 6 Jan this Act left St Eval to ret to Thurleigh. Unable to Ld at Thurleigh due to weather, it ret to St Eval but never Ld there. No trace of Act or crew were found. 1st Lt Robert E Brandon. This Act is listed as MIA in most records. The reason for this probably being that, as it had not returned to its home station, it was still considered to be on an operational flight.

41-24470 To 306BG 369BS 'SONS OF FURY'. MIA 3 Jan 43. 1st Lt Charles W Cranmer. Down in sea after repeated fighter attacks about 40 miles N West of Brest. All crew lost. Believed to have been Ass to 306BG in USA as a replacement for 41-24462 before Group dep for UK.

41-24471 Orig of 306BG 369BS. MIA 13 Jan 43. Capt James A Johnston. Mid air coll with 41-24498 over France.

41-24472 Orig of 306BG. MIA 6 Nov 42. Capt Richard D Adams.

41-24473 Orig of 92BG. To 97BG 24 Aug 42 414BS 'KISSY-ME-KOWBOY'. To 12AF. Dep Hurn 20 Nov 42.

41-24474 Orig of 306BG 367BS 'FLOOZY'. MIA 18 Nov 42. 1st Lt Ralph J Gaston. Ditched 2 miles off Ile D'Quessant, crew picked up by French fishing boat.

41-24475 Orig of 306BG 423BS. Sal 5 Dec 42, reason unknown, but probably due to dam rec in action on one of the late Nov 42 missions.

41-24476 Orig of 306BG 369BS-D 'ADORABLE'. In mid air coll with 42-5251 of 306BG 1 Mar 43. Made wheels up landing at Chelveston and sal. 1st Lt Ralph W Jones.

41-24477 Orig of 306BG 369BS 'JOAN OF ARC'. To 97BG Sep 42 340BS, possibly as replacement for 41-24445 (MIA on 6 Sep 42). To 12AF. Dep Hurn for Gibraltar 5 Nov 42, carrying Commanders for TORCH operation. Ret to Predannack 9 Nov 42, and then left for North Africa on 10 Nov 42.

41-24478 Orig of 306BG 369BS. MIA 23 Nov 42. 1st Lt Clay M Isbell.

41-24479 Orig of 91BG 322BS 'SAD SACK'. MIA 23 Nov 42. Maj Victor S Zienowicz.

41-24480 Orig of 91BG 324BS-C, 'B' in May 43, later 322BS 'BAD PENNY'. To Lt Stn 15 Aug 43. Ass to Hq and Hq Sqdn 8AFSC.

41-24481 Orig of 91BG 322BS 'HELLS ANGELS'. MIA 14 May 43. 1st Lt William H Broley.

41-24482 Orig of 91BG 322BS 'HEAVY WEIGHT ANNIHILATORS'. Sal 27 Feb 43 reason not known.

41-24483 Orig of 91BG 322BS-U 'SPIRIT OF ALCOHOL'. MIA 19 May 43. 1st Lt Baxley.

41-24484 Orig of 91BG 401BS-C 'BAD EGG'. Cr Ld at Andrews Field after being diverted on ret from Op Miss 31 Dec 43. Collided with Jeep, driver, Corporal Gillies kld. Act piloted by 1st Lt Hilary H Evers Jr. Act had done 43 Miss. (2 Jan 44).

41-24485 Orig of 91BG 324BS-A 'MEMPHIS BELLE'. Most well known 8AF B-17. First to complete 25 Op Miss. Ret to USA 8 June 43. Now preserved at Memphis Tenessee. Film made with Act name as title.

41-24486 Orig of 306BG 367BS 'MAN O'WAR'. MIA 9 Nov 42. 2nd Lt James M Stewart. Down in sea, 11 crew kld.

41-24487 Orig of 306BG 368BS-Q 'EAGER BEAVER'. Dam on Op Miss 9 Oct 42. Ld at Manston on ret. Out for rep till Dec 42. Served as Training Act from Oct 43. Still Ass 31 Mar 44. Only orig Act still Ass to 306BG at 31 Mar 44. Ass to same Gp longer than any other B-17 in 8AF. (Up to 31 Mar 44).

'CHENNAULT'S PAPPY' at Exeter, 18th November 1942. It had landed after suffering extensive battle damage on the mission to St Nazaire on the previous day. It never flew again and so became the fourth of the 306th Group's original B-17Fs to be salvaged in England. *US Air Force – National Air and Space Museum*

41-24488 Orig of 306BG 369BS. Later 367BS **'BANSHEE II'**. MIA 17 Aug 43. Capt William J Casey.

41-24489 Orig of 306BG 367BS. MIA 20 Dec 43. 1st Lt Lewis R McKesson.

41-24490 Orig of 91BG 324BS-C **'JACK THE RIPPER'**. MIA 22 Feb 44. 1st Lt James I Considine. Last orig of 91BG to go MIA.

41-24491 Orig of 306BG 423BS. MIA 9 Nov 42. 1st Lt Loyal M Felts.

41-24492 Orig of 306BG 367BS. Cr near Spalding 2 Oct 42. Broke up in air due to excessive speed when diving to a lower altitude after crew member had oxygen trouble. Was on training flight, 6 kld. 1st Lt William W Ely. First 306BG lost since group Ass to 1BW. Also first B-17 lost in an Acc in UK since Gps were Ass to 1st BW on 15 Aug 42.

41-24493 Orig of 306BG 368BS. To SBA Trainer 11 Apr 43. To AFSC 16 Apr 43. Then unknown. Possibly ret to USA Oct 43.

41-24494 Orig of 306BG 367BS. Cr Ld at Portreath on ret from Op Miss 9 Nov 42. Maj Harry J Holt.

41-24495 Orig of 306BG 367BS **'ROSE O'DAY'**. MIA 20 Dec 42. 1st Lt John R McKee.

41-24496 Orig of 306BG 423BS **'CHENNAULT's PAPPY'**. Badly dam on Op Miss 17 Nov 42. Landed at Exeter on ret and sal. Capt Robert C Williams.

41-24497 To UK 3 Dec 42. To 91BG 322BS-P **'MIZPAH II'**. MIA 6 Sep 43. 1st Lt William R Cox. Ditched, crew rescued. With 42-5125 was last B-17 across North Atlantic route in 42.

41-24498 Orig of 306BG 369BS. MIA 13 Jan 43. 2nd Lt Jack A Spaulding. In mid air coll with 41-24471 over France.

41-24499 Orig of 91BG 322BS **'FURY'**. Sal after mid air coll with 41-24453 of 91BG while on Op Miss 18 Nov 42. Ld at Turweston. Maj Victor S Zienowicz.

41-24500 Early history is obscure. To UK about May 43. To 381BG 15 June 43 535BS **'ANNIE FREEZE'**. To Bovingdon 18 July 43.

41-24501 Orig of 306BG 368BS. MIA 3 Jan 43. Lt James M Ferguson.

41-24502 Orig of 306BG 368BS-B later 'O' then 'E'. Cr Ld at Sudbourne on ret from Op Miss 28 July 43. 2nd Lt William A Dooley.

41-24503 Orig of 91BG 324BS. MIA 23 Nov 42. Maj Harold C Smelser.

41-24504 Orig of 91BG 324BS-D **'THE SAD SACK'**. Left for BAD 15 Mar 44.

41-24505 Orig of 91BG 324BS-E **'QUITCHURBITCHIN'**. Used as SBA trainer 43. To BAD for ret to USA 15 Mar 44.

41-24506 Orig of 91BG 324BS. Cr at Leavesden on ret from Op Miss 23 Nov 42. 1st Lt Natman H Carman.

41-24507 Orig of 306BG 368BS. To SBA trainer 11 Apr 43. To L Ldg for overhaul 16 Apr 43. Ret to 306BG 1 July 43. To 384BG 22 Aug 43 545BS **'YANKEE RAIDER'**. MIA 6 Sep 43. 2nd Lt James E Armstrong.

41-24508 Orig of 306BG 423BS. Struck trees during low level two plane formation flight 27 Oct 42. Caused extensive dam to nose and flight controls. Remained airborne and Ld at RAF Graveley. 1st Lt Raymond J Check. Slight inj to crew, Act sal.

41-24509 Orig of 306BG 423BS **'MISS SWOOSE'**. MIA 9 Nov 42. 1st Lt John R Barnett. Down in sea, 5 kld.

41-24510 Orig of 306BG 367BS. MIA 9 Oct 42. Capt John W Olson. First 306BG Act MIA.

41-24511 Orig of 306BG 423BS. To 91BG (before 16 Apr 43) 322BS-W **'WHEEL AND DEAL'**. MIA 1 Dec 43. 2nd Lt John T Wennerberg.

41-24512 Orig of 91BG 322BS **'ROSE O'DAY'**. MIA 4 Mar 43. 1st Lt Ralph A Felton Jr.

41-24514 Orig of 306BG. Flew courier Miss to North Africa 12, 20 and 23 Nov 42. MIA 8 Mar 43. 2nd Lt Otto A Buddenbaum.

41-24515 Orig of 91BG 324BS-H. MIA 21 May 43. 1st Lt Phillips S Fischer.

41-24517 Orig of 303BG 427BS-O. MIA 3 Jan 43. 1st Lt D E Gletz.

41-24523 Orig of 91BG 323BS-N **'LIL AUDREY'** later **'SNOOKS'**. MIA 31 Aug 43. 1st Lt Richard C Rodman. Col. with 42-29816 shortly after leaving Sussex coast. 10 crew lost.

41-24524 Orig of 91BG 323BS-O **'EAGLES WRATH'**. MIA 17 Aug 43. Lt Anthony G Arcaro.

41-24525 Orig of 305BG 422BS-O. To 384BG 22 Sep 43 547BS-Y **'WHATS COOKING DOC'**. MIA 7 Jan 44. 2nd Lt Walter E Garner.

41-24526 Orig of 303BG 358BS-J **'LEAPING LIZ'**. MIA 3 Jan 43. 1st Lt J B Clark.

41-24527 Orig of 91BG 401BS later 324BS-Y **'SKY WOLF'** to **'THE GREAT SPECKLED BIRD'** July 43. MIA 17 Aug 43. 1st Lt William S Munger.

41-24529 Orig of 305BG 422BS-T. To 384BG 22 Sep 43 546BS-E. Took off for Op Miss 9 Oct 43 but aborted. Later that day, went on local flight to slow time two engines. Ret to Grafton Underwood due to fuel coming from No 3 engine. Overshot on Ld and was wrecked. 2nd Lt John M Berbrich. (11 Oct 43).

Damage to the nose and flight controls, caused by hitting trees while on a practice flight, resulted in the 306th Bomb Group's 41-24508 landing at RAF Graveley, 27th October 1942. It was the second of the Group's original aircraft to be lost in a flying accident in England. *US Air Force*

41-24532 Orig of 305BG 422BS. To 97BG 4 Nov 42 414BS. To 12AF. Dep Hurn 20 Nov 42.

41-24533 Orig of 305BG 365BS-T. MIA 22 June 43. Lt John J Hall.

41-24539 Orig of 303BG 358BS-K 'JERSEY BOUNCE'. To 1CCRC Bovingdon 27 July 43.

41-24541 Orig of 303BG 358BS-B 'SPOOK'. MIA 16 Feb 43. Capt Lawrence G Dunnica.

41-24542 By Sth Fy Rt. To UK May 43. 306BG. Dates and fate not known.

41-24544 Orig of 91BG 323BS 'PENNSYLVANIA POLKA'. MIA 4 Feb 43. 1st Lt Alan L Bobrow.

41-24545 Orig of 91BG 322BS 'MATSIE'. Burned at Bassingbourn 23 Mar 43, during rep to oxygen system. Interior of fuselage burned out. First 8AF B-17 destroyed in a ground Acc, where an aircrew was not in control of the Act.

41-24547 Orig of 91BG 323BS 'VERTIGO'. MIA 1 May 43. 1st Lt Robert D Rand.

41-24549 Orig of 91BG 323BS 'STUPN TAKIT'. MIA 4 Mar 43. Lt McCarthy.

41-24553 Orig of 305BG 422BS. MIA 6 Dec 42. Lt William A Prentice. First 305BG MIA.

41-24557 Dep Gander for UK 22 Nov 42. To 306BG 28 Nov 42 423BS-T. To 384BG 22 Aug 43 545BS-O 'DAMN YANKEE'. MIA 1 Dec 43. 2nd Lt Bruce G Sundlum.

41-24558 Orig of 303BG 358BS-F 'HUNGA DUNGA'. MIA 18 Mar 43 with a 92BG crew. 1st Lt Charles N Austin.

41-24559 Orig of 303BG 360BS-C 'OOOLD SOLJER'. Flew a courier Miss to North Africa Dec 42. In mid air coll with 42-29573 of 303BG while forming for Op Miss 31 Mar 43. Cr at Mears Ashby. Dest. 1st Lt Keith O Barlett. 8 kld, 2 sur.

41-24560 To 306BG 28 Nov 42. To 384BG 5 Sep 43 544BS-A. To BAD for ret to USA 15 Mar 44.

41-24561 Orig of 303BG 359BS-T 'THE DUCHESS'. Jack Mathis won medal of honour on this Act 18 Mar 43. Ass 31 Mar 44. Oldest operational B-17 in 8AF at 31 Mar 44.

'HUNGA DUNGA' 41-24558, an original assigned to the 303rd Bomb Group. 1st Lt Joe Haas waves from the cockpit. 25th January 1943. Went Missing in Action with a 92nd Bomb Group crew, 18th March 1943. *Roger Freeman*

41-24562 Orig of 303BG 358BS-A 'SKY WOLF'. MIA 11 Jan 44. 1st Lt Aubrey D Emerson.

41-24563 Orig of 303BG 360BS 'GARBAGE'. Dam in forced Ld at Luton 11 Nov 42. Hit Anson EF939. Sal.

41-24564 Orig of 305BG 365BS-W 'PATCHES'. MIA 17 Aug 43. 2nd Lt Mutschler Goodrich.

41-24565 Orig of 303BG 359BS-P 'IDAHO POTATO PEELER'. Renamed 'THE RAMBLING WRECK'. MIA 5 Nov 43. 2nd Lt Ambrose G Grant.

41-24566 Orig of 303BG 359BS-W 'ZOMBIE'. MIA 20 Dec 42. 1st Lt O S Wilt.

41-24567 Orig of 303BG 360BS-U later 'J' 'BEATS ME'. MIA 23 Jan 43. 1st Lt J E Haas.

41-24568 Orig of 303BG 359BS-U 'LADY FAIRWEATHER'. MIA 23 Nov 42. Capt Charles G Miller. First 303BG Act MIA.

41-24569 Orig of 303BG 427BS-W later 'V'. MIA 4 Feb 43. Capt L R Cole.

41-24570 Orig of 91BG 323BS 'PANHANDLE DOGY'. Badly dam on Op Miss 8 Nov 42. Probably sal after this Miss. Lt Anderson.

41-24572 Orig of 305BG 364BS. To 97BG 4 Nov 42 414BS. To 12AF. Dep Hurn 20 Nov 42.

41-24573 Orig of 305BG 365BS later 364BS-N. MIA 19 May 43. Lt Carrol L McCauley.

41-24575 Orig of 305BG 365BS-S 'SUNRISE SERENADER'. To 384BG 19 Sep 43 544BS-J 'SUNRISE SERENADER'. Cr Wargrave 13 Nov 43. 2nd Lt Ralph J Connell. 9 kld, 1 sur.

41-24576 Orig of 305BG 365BS. To 97BG 4 Nov 43 341BS. To 12AF. Dep Predannack 17 Nov 42.

41-24577 Orig of 303BG 358BS-D 'HELLS ANGELS'. One of 8AFs most famous B-17s. Left Gp to ret to USA 20 Jan 44 and then went on publicity tour. Had done 48 Miss. Was allocated to RAF in early Jan 44, was taken off Ass to 303BG on 8 Jan 44 but was re-Ass same day. Reason for this is unknown.

41-24578 Orig of 305BG 365BS-R 'F' from Sep 43 'OLD RELIABLE'. To 384BG 8 Oct 43 547BG-U 'OLD RELIABLE'. To BAD for ret to USA 15 Mar 44.

41-24579 Orig of 303BG 360BS-F 'THUMPER'. Belly Ld at Lulsgate Bottom on ret from Op Miss 23 Jan 43. 1st Lt John A Castle.

41-24580 Orig of 303BG 358BS-C 'HELLCAT'. MIA 23 Jan 43. 1st Lt O T O'Connor.

41-24581 Orig of 303BG 359BS-O 'THE 8 BALL'. Belly Ld at Bovingdon on ret from Op Miss 20 Dec 42. 8 crew baled out. Capt William R Calhoun Jr.

41-24582 Orig of 303BG 358BS-G 'ONE O'CLOCK JUMP'. MIA 12 Dec 43. Capt W N Frost.

41-24583 Ass to UK Nov 42, but no known history until it was Ass to 379BG from Lt St on 8 Jun 43. To 1CCRC Bovington 4 July 43. Did not fly on Ops.

41-24584 Orig of 303BG 427BS-Q. MIA 23 Jan 43. 1st Lt H A Kobey Jr.

41-24585 Orig of 303BG 360BS-B 'WULF HOUND'. MIA 12 Dec 42. 1st Lt Paul F Flickinger. Landed with little damage in enemy territory and was later flown by the Luftwaffe.

41-24586 Orig of 305BG 365BS-U 'A' from Sep 43 'WHAM BAM'. To BAD for ret to USA 20 Mar 44.

41-24587 Orig of 303BG 427BS-P 'BAD CHECK'. MIA 11 Jan 44. 1st Lt George S McClellan Jr.

41-24588 Orig of 305BG 364BS. MIA 8 Mar 43. Capt Joseph W Carter.

41-24589 Orig of 91BG 323BS 'TEXAS BRONCO'. MIA 4 Feb 43. 2nd Lt Eugene B Ellis.

41-24590 Orig of 305BG 364BS-B. MIA 19 May 43. Lt Harvey J Kohler.

41-24591 Orig of 305BG 366BS-B 'RIGOR MORTIS'. MIA 6 Sep 43. F/O Raymond E Halliday.

41-24592 Orig of 305BG 366BS-C 'G' from Aug 43. MIA 6 Sep 43. Lt Floyd E Macspadden. Ld in Switzerland.

41-24593 Orig of 305BG 364BS 'EL LOBO'. MIA 4 Feb 43. 1st Lt Cornelius A Jenkins. Down in North Sea.

41-24601 Orig of 305BG 365BS. MIA 13 Jan 43. 1st Lt Conrad J Hilbinger.

41-24602 Orig of 303BG 360BS-A 'YARDBIRD'. MIA 25 May 43. 1st Lt Joseph E Trojan.

41-24603 Orig of 303BG 359BS-Y. MIA 23 Jan 43. 1st Lt Ellis J Sanderson.

41-24604 Orig of 305BG 366BS. MIA 26 Feb 43. Capt Everett E Tribbett.

41-24605 Orig of 303BG 359BS-R 'KNOCK OUT DROPPER'. First 8AF B-17 to complete 50 Miss 16 Nov 43 and 75 Miss 27 Mar 44. Ass 31 Mar 44.

41-24606 Orig of 303BG 358BS-H 'WEREWOLF'. Ld in field at Dawlish on ret from Op Miss 23 Jan 43. Lt George J Oxrider. Rep on site and flown out on improvised runway. Did not ret to 303BG. Went to Honington and then to 91BG 22 Apr 43 401BS 'WEREWOLF'. To L Ldg 11 June 43, then to Lt St 14 June 43. Then 1CCRC.

'WE THE PEOPLE' 41-24614. Assigned as an original to the 305th Bomb Group. Would lead the first Eighth Air Force night bombing mission on 8th September 1943 and was the only original aircraft still with the 305th at 31st March 1944. *Mike Gibson*

41-24607 Orig of 303BG 427BS-W. MIA 23 Jan 43. 1st Lt E H Reber.

41-24608 Orig of 303BG 359BS-S. First Gp Act in to Molesworth 1551hrs 21 Oct 42. MIA 3 Jan 43. 1st Lt Frank A Saunders.

41-24609 Orig of 303BG 359BS-Q. MIA 4 Apr 43. 1st Lt Ercil F Eyster.

41-24610 Orig of 303BG 427BS-T 'JOE BTFSPLK'. MIA 1 May 43. 1st Lt V X Walsh.

41-24611 Orig. of 305BG 422BS 'BOOMERANG'. Carried Gen Eaker to Casablanca Conference 15 Jan 43. Ret 24 Jan 43 and force Ld at Eglington. MIA 16 Feb 43. Lt Charles J Steenbarger.

41-24612 Orig of 303BG 427BS-R. Went to L Ldg Feb 43 for prototype LH and RH nose guns on ball mounting installation. To AFSC 20 May 43. Then to 1CCRC.

41-24614 Orig of 305BG 422BS-R 'A' from Sep 43 'WE THE PEOPLE'. Ass 31 Mar 44. Only orig of 305BG still with Gp at 31 Mar 44.

Awaiting attention at the Douglas Modification Center at Tulsa are 14 Boeing built B-17Fs. These had positioned at Tulsa between 26th and 30th August 1942. All were later assigned to the Eighth Air Force. Ten going as originals to the 303rd Bomb Group at Kellogg Field and four to the 305th Bomb Group at Syracuse. All safely made the North Atlantic crossing to England.
The Aircraft are:

Rear Row, left to right
41-24614 To 305BG 'WE THE PEOPLE' (tail just visible). Only orig still serving in 305th at 31 Mar 44.
41-24611 To 305BG 'BOOMERANG'. Carried Gen Eaker to Casablanca Jan 43. MIA 16 Feb 43.
41-24623 To 305BG. MIA 26 Feb 43.
41-24615 To 305BG 'TARGET FOR TONITE'. Ret to USA 1944.

Centre Row
41-24606 To 303BG 'WEREWOLF'. Ld in field at Dawlish, 23 Jan 43.
41-24605 To 303BG 'KNOCK OUT DROPPER'. Still ass to Gp 31 Mar 44.
41-24607 To 303BG. MIA 23 Jan 43.
41-24608 To 303BG. Would be first 303rd Act in to Molesworth. MIA 3 Jan 43.

Front Row
41-24612 To 303BG. Left Gp for AFSC 20 May 43.
41-24616 To 305BG. Ret to USA 1944.
41-24619 To 303BG 'S FOR SUGAR'. MIA 11 Jan 44.
41-24620 To 303BG 'SNAP CRACKLE POP'. MIA 3 Jan 43. (With 41-24608 was first of the 14 to be lost).
41-24609 To 303BG. MIA 4 Apr 43.
41-24610 To 303BG 'JOE BTFSPLK'. MIA 1 May 43.

Behind hangar at top left is the tail of 42-2971, the eighth B-17F to be built by Douglas. This aircraft was assigned to the Eighth Air Force in October 1942 but no details of it ever having served can be found.

US Air Force – National Air and Space Museum

41-24615 Orig of 305BG 422BS-P 'F' from Sep 43 **'TARGET FOR TONIGHT'**. To BAD for ret to USA 22 Mar 44.

41-24616 Orig of 305BG 422BS-U 'K' from Sep 43 **'SAMS LITTLE HELPER'**. To BAD for ret to USA 21 Mar 44.

41-24617 Orig of 305BG 364BS **'SOUTHERN COMFORT'**. Cr at Wickham Bishops on ret from Op Miss 31 Mar 43. 1st Lt Hugh G Ashcroft. (1 Apr 43).

41-24619 Orig of 303BG 427BS-S **'S FOR SUGAR'**. MIA 11 Jan 44. 2nd Lt Thomas L Simmons.

41-24620 Orig of 303BG 360BS-D **'SNAP CRACKLE POP'**. MIA 3 Jan 43. 1st Lt A T Adams.

41-24623 Orig of 305BG 365BS. MIA 26 Feb 43. 1st Lt George E Stallman.

41-24624 Orig of 305BG 366BS-J. MIA 19 May 43. Capt Charles D Clark.

41-24629 By Sth Fy Rt. Mrk to UK Feb 43. To 306BG 28 Feb 43 369BS-O. To 303BG 25 Sep 43 358BS-G. MIA 20 Oct 43. 1st Lt John W Hendry Jr.

41-24635 To 303BG Dec 42 359BS-O **'THE 8 BALL'**. Ass 31 Mar 44.

41-24637 To 305BG 12 Dec 43 366BS. MIA 27 Jan 43. Lt Vance W Beckham.

41-24639 To 91BG 323BS-W **'CAREFUL VIRGIN'**. Probably in to 91st early Feb 43. Ass but not on hand 31 Mar 44. (At 2 SAD).

B-17F DOUGLAS

42-2966 Orig of 303BG 427BS-U. Trans to 1CCRC at Bovingdon 4 July 43.

42-2967 Orig of 303BG 360BS-G **'SHAK HACK'**. MIA 16 Feb 43. Capt William H Breed.

42-2969 Orig of 305BG 366BS. To 97BG 4 Nov 42 341BS. To 12AF. Dep Predannack 17 Nov 42. Cr in sea and all on board were lost. Piloted by Maj John Knox, Squadron Commander of 341BS. Brig Gen Duncan was a passenger. First Douglas built B-17 lost in European Theatre.

42-2970 To 91BG 13 Dec 42 324BS-E later 'C' **'CONNECTICUT YANKEE'**. Cr Ld at Pitt Level, Winchelsea 6 Sep 43. 2nd Lt William G Pegram. (10 Sep 43).

42-2973 To UK Dec 42. To 303BG 14 Dec 42 360BS-K **'IZA VAILABLE'**. To BAD for ret to USA 26 Mar 44.

42-2975 To 306BG 29 Nov 42. MIA 30 Dec 42. Capt John B Brady. Flying with 305BG formation. First Douglas built B-17 MIA.

42-2978 By Sth Fy Rt. Arr St Eval 12 Jan 43. To 306BG 369BS-M. To 381BG 18 Nov 43 Ass 31 Mar 44. Oldest Douglas built B-17F still operational in 8AF at 31 Mar 44.

42-2990 By Sth Fy Rt. Arr St Eval 8 Jan 43. To 91BG 322BS-R **'DAME SATAN'**. MIA 17 Aug 43. 2nd Lt Jack A Hargis.

42-3002 By Sth Fy Rt. From Mrk to UK after 23 Mar 43. To 303BG 8 Apr 43 359BS-Z **'OLD SQUAW'**. MIA 6 Sep 43. Ditched. Crew rescued.

42-3023 To 379BG 8 Jun 43. MIA 25 Jun 43. 1st Lt Thomas V Simones.

42-3024 By Sth Fy Rt. Mrk to UK 2 May 43. To 384BG 546BS-K **'ROYAL FLUSH'**. MIA 25 July 43. 2nd Lt P J Ward.

42-3029 To 303BG 9 Apr 43 359BS-N **'WALLARO'**. MIA 14 Jan 44. Capt Merle R Hungerford Jr.

42-3031 By Sth Fy Rt. To 91BG 19 Apr 43 324BS-F **'NIGHTMARE'**. MIA 26 July 43. 1st Lt James W Randall.

One of the B-17Fs to reach England by the Southern Ferry Route during the winter of 1942/43. 42-3057 became **'PICCADILLY COMMANDO'** of the 91st Bomb Group and was one of five aircraft the Group lost on the epic Oschersleben mission on 11th January 1944. *US Air Force – National Air and Space Museum*

42-3033 By Sth Fy Rt. To 381BG Aug 43. To 2 SAD 9 Jan 44. Then to 2CCRC.

42-3034 By Sth Fy Rt. Mrk to UK 11 Mar 43. To 306BG 12 Mar 44. MIA 17 Apr 43. Capt Walter N Smiley.

42-3037 95BG to 305BG 1 Aug 43 366BS-N. To 384BG 20 Sep 43 544BS-Z 'WINDY CITY AVENGER'. Cr Wakerley Woods, Corby 14 Oct 43. 1st Lt William M Price. (18 Oct 43).

42-3040 By Sth Fy Rt. To 303BG 9 Apr 43. To 306BG 17 Apr 43 369BS-R. To AFSC for rep 21 May 43 to 29 May 43. Not Ass to 306BG between these dates. To Lt Stn 18 June 43. To 91BG 23 Aug 43 323BS-Q 'MISS QUACHITA'. MIA 22 Feb 44. 2nd Lt Spencer K Osterberg.

42-3041 By Sth Fy Rt. To 303BG 9 Apr 43. To 306BG 17 Apr 43 369BS-U. To 384BG 22 Aug 43 544BS-H. MIA 6 Sep 43. 2nd Lt James J McMahon.

42-3043 By Sth Fy Rt. To 91BG April 43 401BS-B 'HITLERS GREM-LIN'. MIA 17 Aug 43. 1st Lt Eugene M Lockhart. Ditched 45 miles from English coast, crew rescued.

42-3046 From 4th Wing to 351BG 17 June 43 510BS-X 'OLD JACK-SON'. Cr Ld at Woodbridge on ret from Op Miss 30 July 43. (2 Aug 43).

42-3048 By Sth Fy Rt. Mrk to UK 18 Mar 43. To 305BG 21 Mar 43 366BS-A. To 381BG 22 Aug 43. To 379BG 26 Sep 43 524BS. Ass 31 Mar 44.

42-3049 To 305BG 25 Mar 43 422BS-W 'WINDY CITY CHAL-LENGER'. MIA 14 July 43. 1st Lt John H Perkins Jr.

42-3051 By Sth Fy Rt. Mrk to UK 18 Mar 43. To 305BG 31 May 43 366BS-M 'HELLS ANGELS'. To 384BG 19 Sep 43 546BS-C. 'HELLS ANGELS'. Ass 31 Mar 44.

42-3053 By Sth Fy Rt. Mrk to UK 18 Mar 43. To 91BG 25 Mar 43 324BS-Z. MIA 21 May 43. 1st Lt Norbert D Koll.

42-3056 To 379BG 20 June 43 527BS. MIA 14 Oct 43. 2nd Lt Matthew A Zack. (524BS crew).

42-3057 By Sth Fy Rt. Mrk to UK 20 Mar 43. To 91BG 26 Mar 43 322BS-N 'PICCADILLY COMMANDO'. Also 'BLOND BOMBER'. MIA 11 Jan 44. 2nd Lt Wayne E Murdoch.

42-3060 385BG to 91BG 13 Sep 43 401BS-G 'HELLS BELLE'. MIA 1 Dec 43. 2nd Lt Charles A Guinn.

42-3061 95BG to 379BG 28 June 43. To Bwd 20 Jan 44 for special VHF Installation. To 91BG 1 Mar 44. Used as 1st BD VHF Relay Act. Ass 31 Mar 44.

42-3064 100BG to 303BG 17 July 43 358BS-O 'STARDUST'. Badly dam on Miss 26 Nov 43. Ld at Docking. Out of Gp for rep till 28 Feb 44. Ass 31 Mar 44.

42-3069 94BG to 384BG 12 Jul 43 544BS-F 'PASSES CANCELLED'. MIA 25 July 43. Lt Gordon J Hankinson.

42-3072 96BG to 91BG 16 Sep 43. To 379BG 27 Sep 43 525BS. Ass 31 Mar 44.

42-3073 94BG to 91BG 22 Apr 43 401BS-A 'LIGHTNING STRIKES'. MIA 21 Feb 44. 1st Lt William P Gibbons.

WITH TOKYO TANKS

42-3074 94BG to 384BG 12 July 43 545BS-B 'LOMA LEE'. To 306BG 22 Aug 43 at Bwd 30 Nov 43 to 2 Feb 44, when Act not Ass to 306BG. To Cheddington 29 Feb 44.

42-3075 94BG to 384BG 12 July 43 546BS-M 'LONGHORN'. MIA 25 July 43. Lt John M Hegewald.

42-3076 To 306BG 20 Apr 43. Cr Ld at Hawkinge on ret from Op Miss 28 July 43. 1st Lt Woodrow W Thomas.

42-3078 To 381BG 15 June 43 534BS-M 'WINSOME WINN'. MIA 7 Jan 44. 2nd Lt Arden D Wilson.

42-3077 'WINSOME WINN'. One of four replacement B-17Fs assigned to the 381st Bomb Group from Little Staughton on 15th June 1943. This aircraft survived until 7th January 1944 when it was lost on a mission to Ludwigshaven. *US Air Force – National Air and Space Museum*

42-3079 95BG to 91BG 16 June 43 323BS-X. MIA 16 Sep 43. 1st Lt Eldon J Smith.

42-3084 95BG from Mrk 20 Mar 43. To 306BG 10 Apr 43. MIA 29 July 43. F/O Carl D Brown.

42-3087 95BG from Mrk 20 Mar 43. To 305BG then to 306BG 11 Apr 43 367BS-W. Cr Ld at Bovingdon 31 July 43. Rep and ret to 306BG 31 Aug 43. To 384BG 3 Sep 43 547BS-O later 'A'. MIA 22 Feb 44. 2nd Lt William J Kew.

42-3088 94BG to 384BG 12 July 43 544BS-G 'SUGAR PUSS'. MIA 25 July 43. 1st Lt Clarence R Christman.

42-3090 Landed at Clonakilty, Ireland on 7 Apr 43. Flown out on 2 May 43. 4th Wing to 351BG 17 June 43 508BS-N 'TAINT A BIRD'. To Warton 10 Nov 43. To 2CCRC 44.

42-3091 95BG to 305BG 17 June 43 422BS-S 'H' from Sep 43. MIA 4 Oct 43. Lt Thomas S Seay.

42-3092 Orig of 381BG 532BS later 533BS 'STRATO SAM'. MIA 17 Aug 43. F/O James C Hudson.

42-3093 96BG to 351BG 11 July 43 510BS-K 'NOBODYS DARLING'. Cr Ld Burnham-on-Sea, on ret from Op Miss 31 Dec 43. Lt Robert P Chalmers. Crew safe. (2 Jan 44).

42-3099 Orig of 379BG 527BS-R. MIA 11 June 43. 1st Lt William H Pinson.

42-3100 95BG to 381BG 20 July 43 532BS. MIA 30 July 43. Maj Robert F Post.

42-3101 95BG to 381BG 21 July 43 533BS. MIA 19 Aug 43. 1st Lt Orlando H Koenig.

42-3104 94BG to 384BG 12 July 43 547BS-A. MIA 12 Aug 43. 1st Lt George B Keck.

42-3105 96BG to 92BG May 43 407BS-N. DS to 11CCRC 30 Aug 43. Later loaned to 303BG for experimental purposes. Was fitted with a mechanical control for Supercharger Waste Gates, later to 2CCRC.

42-3106 96BG to 351BG 28 May 43 508BS-M. Wrecked on TO on Non Op Flight at Polebrook 13 Aug 43. Lt Joseph S Peck.

42-3111 95BG to 91BG 16 June 43 324BS-A1 'LOCAL GIRL'. MIA 27 Sep 43. 2nd Lt William G Pegram.

42-3113 Orig of 379BG 525BS-F. MIA 29 May 43. 1st Lt Arthur P Hale.

42-3114 Orig of 379BG 525BS-T. MIA 11 June 43. 1st Lt Noel R Britten.

42-3116 96BG to 92BG May 43 407BS-U. MIA 28 July 43. 2nd Lt Harold W Porter.

42-3118 96BG to 381BG 6 July 43 534BS 'GREEN HORNET'. MIA 11 Jan 44. 2nd Lt Austin G Larson.

42-3119 To 91BG 4 June 43 322BS-M. MIA 26 July 43. 2nd Lt Jack A Hargis. Ditched in North Sea, crew rescued by ASR.

42-3120 Orig of 351BG 509BS-O 'GREMLINS DELIGHT'. Ass but not on hand 31 Mar 44. (At New Romney for rep).

42-3122 96BG to 384BG 6 July 43 545BS-N 'APRILS FOOL'. MIA 25 July 43. 2nd Lt Ralph J Hall.

42-3123 96BG to 381BG 16 July 43 535BS. MIA 8 Oct 43. 1st Lt Jack S Fry.

42-3124 To 303BG 2 June 43 427BS-N. Cr Arenig Fawr, Bala, North Wales 4 Aug 43. (6 Aug 43).

42-3127 To 306BG 5 May 43 367BS-M. MIA 21 May 43. It is believed that this aircraft was being flown by the crew of Lt Ecklund of 94BG. It was not one of the Act scheduled by the 306BG for this days Miss and is not included in the three 306BG Act officially listed as MIA this day.

42-3131 To 303BG 4 June 43 427BS-U 'FLAK WOLF'. MIA 11 Jan 44. 2nd Lt John W Carother.

42-3134 To 92BG 23 May 43 407BS-P. To Bwd 29 Jan 44, for special VHF Installation. To Ridgewell 6 Mar 44. Assigned to Eighth Fighter Command as VHF Relay Act. Maintained by 381BG. Ass 31 Mar 44.

42-3136 To 351BG 511BS-P 'EIGHT BALL'. Later 'NO BALLS AT ALL'. MIA 24 Feb 44. 2nd Lt Walter B Le Clerc.

42-3138 Orig of 379BG 527BS-M. MIA 11 June 43. 1st Lt Burrel F Newman.

42-3140 Orig of 351BG 509BS-P 'PATTY ANN II'. MIA 1 Dec 43. Capt Eugene P Harris. Ditched.

42-3141 Orig of 351BG 508BS-A 'HITLERS HEADACHE'. To BAD for ret to USA 31 Mar 44.

42-3142 To 306BG 18 May 43 368BS-I. Cr Great Haseley 13 Nov 43. Caught in turbulence and icing when forming for Op Miss. Blew up and dest on hitting ground. All crew kld. 2nd Lt Floyd O Scudder.

42-3145 Orig of 379BG 527BS-B. MIA 6 Sep 43. Lt Alden C Johnson. Ditched, crew rescued by HSL 156 off English coast.

42-3148 Orig of 379BG 526BS-A. MIA 11 June 43. 1st Lt William F Brinkman.

42-3150 Orig of 351BG 511BS-Q 'FOUL BALL'. MIA 6 Sep 43. Lt Clarence F Norris. Ditched just off Beachy Head on ret from the Miss. Crew swam ashore.

42-3152 Orig of 351BG 510BS-A 'SLEEPY LAGOON'. MIA 9 Oct 43. F/O William H Warring.

42-3154 Orig of 379BG 526BS-B. Cr Ld Bury St Edmunds on ret from Op Miss 12 Aug 43. (13 Aug 43).

42-3158 To 303BG 2 June 43 427BS-Y 'MAX'. Ass 31 Mar 44.

42-3162 94BG to 91BG 324BS-A. MIA 12 Aug 43. 1st Lt Talmidge G Wilson.

42-3165 To 92BG 23 Apr 43 325BS-G later 327BS. MIA 26 Nov 43. 2nd Lt Hugh Dougherty Jr.

42-3167 To 306BG 19 Apr 43 423BS-Z. Out to Depot 16 June 43 then to 379BG 18 Aug 43 527BS-S. Out of 379th 4 Mar 44, but re-Ass on 29 Mar 44. Ass 31 Mar 44.

42-3169 To 306BG 18 June 43. To AFSC for rep 30 June 43 to 13 July 43. Not Ass to 306BG at this time. To RAF 214 Sqdn at Sculthorpe 3 Feb 44.

42-3171 95BG to AFSC. To 92BG 11 Aug 43 326BS. Cr Shiplake on ret from Op Miss 14 Oct 43. 2nd Lt Frank W Wolf. (15 Oct 43).

42-3172 To 306BG 5 May 43 423BS-R. To AFSC for rep 27 June 43, then to 91BG 25 Sep 43 323BS-R later 'X' 'CHENNAULTS PAPPY'. Ass 31 Mar 44.

42-3173 To 351BG 511BS-R 'SPAREBALL'. MIA 15 May 43. 1st Lt Joseph A Meli Jr.

42-3175 95BG to 379BG 524BS-T. MIA 25 July 43. 1st Lt Frank A Hildebrandt.

42-3176 95BG to 379BG 27 June 43. MIA 14 Oct 43. 1st Lt Alden G Johnson.

42-3177 96BG to 381BG 15 July 43 535BS. To 214 Sqdn RAF at Sculthorpe 25 Jan 44.

42-3180 96BG to 381BG 16 July 43 'FORGET ME NOT II'. MIA 9 Oct 43. 1st Lt Herbert Carqueville.

42-3183 95BG to 305BG 1 Aug 43 366BS-L. Ass 31 Mar 44.

42-3183 96BG to 92BG 19 July 43 327BS. Cr Deeping St Nicholas while assembling for Op Miss 23 Sep 43. Three crew kld. 2nd Lt Henly M Ogburn.

42-3184 To 92BG 24 Apr 43 407BS-Q 'ALI QUIPPA'. MIA 22 Dec 43. 2nd Lt Harry J Roeber.

B-17Fs at Meeks Field, Iceland, 23rd April 1943. They are about to depart on the final leg of the North Atlantic crossing to England. Nearest is 42-3186 which was assigned to the 92nd Bomb Group on 23rd May 1943. Next aircraft has **'CALAMITY JANE'** on nose but serial No is not known. *US Air Force – National Air and Space Museum*

42-3186 To 92BG 23 May 43 407BS-Y. MIA 31 Dec 43. 2nd Lt Coleman Goldstein.

42-3188 To 384BG 9 June 43 544BS-F **'MISS CARRIAGE'**. MIA 26 June 43. Lt Thomas A Cuddeback.

42-3192 To 303BG 16 May 43 358BS-G. MIA 18 Aug 43. 1st Lt J S Nix.

42-3195 To 305BG 26 June 43 366BS-O. MIA 14 Oct 43. Lt Veal D Fisher.

42-3198 To 306BG 5 May 43 368BS-Z. To AFSC 15 May 43. Probably left 306BG at this time. To 92BG 25 July 43. 407BS-M. Cr Ld at Wych Cross on ret from Op Miss 6 Sep 43. 2nd Lt Basil M Jones.

42-3199 To 379BG 20 May 43 324BS. MIA 12 Aug 43. 1st Lt Robert P Paulin. Carried 11 crew, two from 2AF.

42-3202 To 92BG 24 Apr 43. To 95BG 15 May 43.

42-3207 94BG to 305BG 14 July 43 422BS-Q1 'G' from Sept 43. **'MONKEYS UNCLE'**. Ass 31 Mar 44.

42-3209 To 306BG 23 May 43 367BS-Q. MIA 22 June 43. 2nd Lt J W Johnson.

42-3210 To 91BG 18 May 43. Flare cartridges exploded in nose while taxiing at Bassingbourne 1 June 43. 1st Lt Jerold D Kethley. (3 June 43).

42-3211 Orig of 381BG 535BS **'TS'**. Belly Ld at Manston on ret from Op Miss 14 July 43. 2nd Lt Edwin R Manchester. Had collided with FW 190 while on the Miss.

42-3212 To 379BG. Cr at Parham on ret from Op Miss 30 July 43. Burned out, crew of ten kld. 1st Lt Melton D Wallace.

42-3213 To 92BG 23 Apr 43. To 95BG 19 May 43. Then to 91BG 16 June 43. 323BS-M. Ditched on ret from Op Miss 16 Aug 43. Crew rescued. Listed as MIA. Lt Smith.

42-3214 To 306BG 5 May 43 423BS-F. MIA 21 May 43. 1st Lt Maxwell V Judas.

42-3215 Orig of 381BG 533BS-T **'LINDA MARY'**. MIA 6 Mar 44. 2nd Lt Richard W Coyle.

42-3216 Orig of 384BG 545BS **'THE JOKER'**. MIA 14 Oct 43. 2nd Lt William E Kopf.

42-3217 Orig of 381BG 535BS-T **'GEORGIA REBEL'**. MIA 24 July 43. Belly Ld in Sweden. First B-17 in Sweden. 1st Lt Osce V Jones.

42-3218 Orig of 384BG 545BS **'DORIS MAE'**. To Bwd 4 Jan 44, then to RAF.

42-3220 Orig of 381BG 535BS **'DAMFINO'**. MIA 17 Aug 43. Lt Harry M Smith.

42-3221 Orig of 381BG 534BS-E **'WHALETAIL'**. Cr Ld near Snetterton 29 July 43 on ret from Op Miss. 1st Lt Dexter Lishon.

42-3222 Orig of 384BG 545BS-P **'DEUCES WILD'**. MIA 17 Aug 43. Lt Frank G Mattes.

42-3223 Orig of 381BG 533BS **'RED HOT RIDING HOOD'**. Exploded in mid air and cr near Rattlesden while assembling for Op Miss 14 July 43. Six kld, four parachuted to safety. 1st Lt Charles B Radin.

42-3225 Orig of 381BG 353BS **'CHUG-A-LUG LULU'**. MIA 17 Aug 43. Lt Lorin C Disbrow.

42-3226 Orig of 381BG 535BS. Cr Ld North Foreland 22 June 43. On ret from Op Miss. 2nd Lt Inman G Jobe.

42-3227 Orig of 381BG 534BS. MIA 17 Aug 43. Lt Hamden L Forkner.

42-3230 Orig of 384BG 545BS-U **'YANKEE POWERHOUSE II'**. (**'MARY KATHLEEN'** at 19 July 43). MIA 17 Aug 43. Lt Drewry T Wofford.

42-3231 Orig of 384BG 545BS-M **'THE INFERNO'**. MIA 12 Aug 43. Capt Richard T Carrington.

42-3235 Orig of 384BG 545BS-T **'LAKANUKI'**. MIA 4 July 43. 2nd Lt Lawrence W Meyer.

42-3220 on test flight near Long Beach, early April 1943. The 257 on decking aft of cockpit is the Douglas line No. Was assigned as an original to the 381st Bomb Group at Pueblo and named 'DAMFINO'. Was one of 11 planes the 381st lost at Schweinfurt 17th August 1943. *Douglas*

42-3258	To 379BG 11 June 43. MIA 8 Oct 43. 2nd Lt William L Hickey.	42-3330	To 384BG 27 June 43 544BS-N. MIA 14 July 43. 1st Lt James S Munday.
42-3259	94BG. To 384BG 16 July 43 546BS-N. To 545BS-T 'SNAFU' later 'ALABAMA WHIRLWIND'. To Cheddington 1 Mar 44.	42-3351	To 92BG 24 July 43 407BS-E 'Z' from Sep/Oct 43. Cr Winkfield on ret from Op Miss 14 Oct 43. 1st Lt Richard W Lyng. (15 Oct 43).
42-3268	381BG date Ass not known 534BS 'MESSIE BESSIE'. To 96BG 6 July 43.	42-3357	To 482BG 8 Sep 43 (H2S) 813BS-S. MIA 8 Feb 44. 1st Lt Joe M Gold.
42-3269	To 379BG 6 June 43 527BS. MIA 14 Oct 43. Capt Walter F Carnal Jr.	42-3363	To 306BG 14 Aug 43 367BS 'PUNCHY'. MIA 22 Dec 43. 1st Lt James E Winter.
42-3271	To 91BG 7 June 43. To 100BG 6 July 43.	42-3382	To 482BG 8 Sep 43 (SO) 813BS-I. To 9AF Stansted 5 Feb 44. Then to 306BG 22 Feb 44. Ass 31 Mar 44.
42-3272	To 351BG 28 May 43 510BS-M 'CAPTAIN BILL'. MIA 25 July 43. 1st Lt Edwin S Boyd.	42-3385	To 92BG 11 Aug 43. To 482BG 25 Aug 43 (SO) 813BS-C. To 9AF Stansted 5 Feb 44. Then to 92BG 21 Feb 44 407BS-K. Ass 31 Mar 44.
42-3274	To 306BG 4 June 43 367BS-L. To AFSC for rep for battle damage 29 June 43. Then to 91BG 14 Aug 43 323BS-U. MIA 4 Oct 43. 1st Lt Lloyd S Schaper.	42-3387	To 305BG 30 Aug 43 364BS-O. MIA 26 Nov 43. Lt George Sartis.
42-3277	To 92BG 15 June 43 325BS. To 95BG 16 June 43.		
42-3300	To 379BG 11 June 43 526BS. MIA 3 Sep 43. 2nd Lt Julius W Kraff. (524BS crew).	42-3398	One of five B-17Fs Ass to 12AF but delivered in error to 8AF (the other four served in 3BD). This was due to confusion in orders issued in USA. The crews who ferried the Act were destined for 8AF, but the Act were for 12AF. By the time the error was discovered the Act had been modified and Ass to tactical units. ATC suggested that five Act destined for 8AF should be diverted for 12AF, but it is not known if this was done. This Act Arr at Nutts Corner 25 July 43 and went on to Pwk 26 July 43. It was Ass to 482BG 21 Oct 43 (H2S). Still Ass on 14 Feb 44. Later served in 303BG.
42-3301	Orig of 390BG. Delayed in USA due to Acc. To 306BG 21 Sep 43 367BS 'CAVALIER'. To Cheddington 29 Feb 44.		
42-3317	To 384BG 10 June 43. To 95BG 28 June 43.		
42-3321	To 91BG 15 June 43. To 95BG 16 June 43.		
42-3325	To 379BG 12 June 43. MIA 30 Jan 44. 2nd Lt Kenneth Davis.		

'YANKEE POWERHOUSE II' or 'MARY KATHLEEN'? 42-3230 an original of the 384th Bomb Group appears to have been re-named following a request by 8th Bomber Command in June 1943 for Groups to submit details of all names carried on B-17s. She was one of five planes the 384th lost on the Schweinfurt mission 17th August 1943. *Mike Gibson*

42-3406	To 306BG 4 Aug 43 367BS-V. MIA 12 Aug 43. 1st Lt William J Cunningham.
42-3411	To 381BG 21 Sep 43. Ass 31 Mar 44.
42-3412	To 305BG 30 Aug 43 365BS-M. MIA 21 Dec 43. Lt William E Nordyke.
42-3428	To 92BG 14 Aug 43. MIA 6 Sep 43. Ditched. Crew rescued.
42-3429	To 384BG 11 Aug 43 544BS-F 'FLAK HOUSE'. Ass 31 Mar 44.
42-3434	To 305BG 12 Aug 43 364BS-E. MIA 6 Sep 43. Ld in Switzerland. Lt David J Engler.
42-3435	To 92BG 12 Aug 43 327BS. MIA 17 Aug 43. Capt Roland L Sargent.
42-3436	To 305BG 18 Sep 43 364BS-R. MIA 14 Oct 43. Lt Dennis J McDarby.
42-3440	To 384BG Aug 43 544BS-B 'BROADWAY ROSE'. Ass 31 Mar 44.
42-3441	To 384BG 9 Aug 43 547BS-E 'PATCHES II'. Ass 31 Mar 44.
42-3448	To 303BG 19 Oct 43 359BS. MIA 11 Jan 44. 2nd Lt Henry J Eich Jr. (Last Douglas built B-17F Ass to 1BD).
42-3449	To 306BG 14 Aug 369BS. Cr trying to Ld at RAF Sta Wing, on ret from Op Miss 23 Sep 43. 1st Lt Immanuel J Klette.
42-3455	To 384BG 11 Aug 43 546BS-M 'LUCKY THIRTEEN'. MIA 6 Sep 43. 1st Lt Russell R Faulkiner.
42-3459	To 384BG 9 Aug 43 546BS-F. MIA 23 Sep 43. 1st Lt Phillip E Higdon.
42-3461	To 92BG 23 Aug 43 407BS-S. Ass 31 Mar 44.

B-17G DOUGLAS

42-3483	To 482BG 2 Oct 43 812BS-A (H2X). Ass 14 Feb 44.
42-3484	To 482BG 2 Oct 43 812BS-B (H2X). Ass 14 Feb 44.
42-3485	To 482BG 19 Oct 43 812BS-C (H2X). Ass 14 Feb 44.
42-3486	To 482BG 18 Oct 43 812BS-D (H2X). MIA 11 Jan 44. 1st Lt James J McGinnis. Was flying with 303BG. First 482BG Act MIA.
42-3487	To 482BG 7 Oct 43 812BS-E (H2X). Ass 14 Feb 44.
42-3490	To 482BG 7 Oct 43 812BS-F (H2X). Ass 14 Feb 44.
42-3491	To 482BG 2 Oct 43 812BS-G (H2X). Ass 14 Feb 44.
42-3492	To 482BG 2 Oct 43 812BS-H (H2X). Ass 14 Feb 44.
42-3493	To 92BG 28 Sep 43 325BS-H. Ass 31 Mar 44.
42-3494	To 92BG 4 Sep 43 407BS-F. MIA 4 Jan 44. 2nd Lt Raymond J Mancu.
42-3495	To 351BG 20 Sep 43. MIA 31 Dec 43. 1st Lt Ralph M Saville.
42-3496	To 92BG 4 Sep 43 327BS. Ass 31 Mar 44.
42-3500	To 482BG 2 Oct 43 812BS-J (H2X). MIA 5 Feb 44. 1st Lt Warren E Bock.

Six H2X equipped B-17s lined up at Grenier Field in September 1943, prior to making the North Atlantic crossing to join the 482nd Bomb Group in England. The second aircraft along the line is 42-3484. The serials of the remaining aircraft are unknown, they are almost certainly early Douglas-built B-17Gs. *US Air Force – National Air and Space Museum*

42-3506 To 91BG 22 Sep 43 324BS-B 'SIR BABOON McGOON'. Made Emergency Ld in field at Braisworth Hall, Tannington, on ret from Op Miss 10 Oct 43. Was flown out on improvised runway. Went to Honington. Ret to 91BG 19 Feb 44. MIA 29 Mar 44. 2nd Lt Edgar C Downing. 11 Miss.

42-3507 Orig of 401BG 613BS-O 'DUFFYS TAVERN'. Ass 31 Mar 44.

42-3509 To 351BG 25 Sep 43 511BS-Z. MIA 30 Jan 44. 1st Lt Charles E Robertson.

42-3511 To 482BG 2 Oct 43 812BS-K (H2X). Ass 14 Feb 44.

42-3513 To 92BG 2 Sep 43 326BS. Ass 31 Mar 44. First B-17G Ass to 1st BD.

42-3514 To 381BG 24 Sep 43 513BS. MIA 11 Jan 44. 1st Lt Billy F Chason.

42-3515 To 306BG 21 Sep 43 423BS-O. To L Lodge 25 Mar 44. Later to 482BG.

42-3517 To 351BG 27 Sep 43 508BS-O 'HAPPY WARRIOR'. MIA 24 Feb 44. 1st Lt Richard B Caughman.

42-3520 To 306BG 16 Sep 43 368BS. Cr Ld at Lt Stn on ret from Op Miss 29 Nov 43. Lt John Gassler. (30 Nov 43).

42-3521 To 482BG 16 Oct 43 813BS (SO). To 9AF Stansted 5 Feb 44, then to 306BG 22 Feb 44. Ass 31 Mar 44.

42-3522 To 381BG 27 Sep 43. Ass 31 Mar 44.

42-3523 To 351BG 24 Sep 43 510BS-M 'APRIL GIRL'. MIA 11 Jan 44. 1st Lt George J Procak.

42-3524 To 379BG 3 Oct 43. Ass 31 Mar 44.

42-3525 To 482BG 15 Oct 43 813BS-D (SO). To 9AF Stansted 11 Feb 44. Then to 381BG 22 Feb 44. Ass 31 Mar 44.

42-3527 To 482BG 16 Oct 43 813BS-G (SO). To 9AF Stansted 5 Feb 44. Then to 306BG 22 Feb 44. Ass 31 Mar 44.

42-3531 To 305BG 17 Sep 43 365BS-N. MIA 26 Nov 43. Harold S Elliott.

42-3532 To 351BG 21 Sep 43 511BS-O 'LUCILLE BALL'. Made wheels up Ld on Ipswich Airport on ret from Op Miss 5 Nov 43. 1st Lt Donald Gaylord.

42-3533 To 306BG 21 Sep 43 368BS. MIA 3 Nov 43. Cr in sea after mid air coll with 42-30776. 1st Lt Donald L Wadley.

42-3536 To 482BG 21 Oct 43 831BS (SO). To 9AF Stansted 5 Feb 44. Then to 92BG 20 Feb 44 325BS. Cr and burned just after TO from Podington 9 Mar 44. On Op Miss, dest, crew of ten kld. 2nd Lt William L Webb.

42-3540 To 381BG 16 Sep 43 535BS 'BACTA-TH'SAC'. MIA 1 Dec 43. 2nd Lt Warren C Hess.

42-3542 To 351BG 23 Sep 43 509BS-V 'SHADY LADY II'. Ass 31 Mar 44.

42-3549 To 305BG 1 Oct 43 366BS-H. MIA 14 Oct 43. 2nd Lt Charles W Willis Jr.

42-3550 To 305BG 9 Oct 43 365BS-H. MIA 14 Oct 43. Lt Alden C Kincaid.

42-3554 To 92BG 16 Sep 43 325BS. MIA 9 Oct 43. 1st Lt William F Whelan.

42-3559 To 379BG 22 Nov 43 526BS. MIA 1 Dec 43. 2nd Lt Charles E Thomson Jr.

42-3560 Orig of 401BG. To 351BG 18 Nov 43 508BS-H. MIA 26 Nov 43. Lt Lawrance H Blaisdell. Ditched, crew rescued.

42-3562 Orig of 401BG. To 381BG 21 Nov 43. MIA 20 Feb 44. 1st Lt Kirch J Cogswell.

42-3563 To 381BG 24 Sep 43. MIA 20 Dec 43. 1st Lt Bernard F Hollencamp.

B-17F — BOEING
WITHOUT TOKYO TANKS

42-5051 Allocated to 8AF Oct 42, but no record in UK until Ass to 384BG 26 July 43 544BS-M 'BARREL HOUSE BESSIE'. MIA 26 Nov 43. Maj William F Gilmore. Ditched.

42-5052 To 305BG 8 Nov 42. To 306BG 19 Apr 43. To 303BG 25 Sep 43 358BS, and 427BS 'MIZPAH'. MIA 22 Feb 44. 2nd Lt Jack McVay.

42-5053 To 305BG 366BS-L. MIA 4 July 43. Lt William C Wetzel.

42-5054 Allocated to 8AF Nov 42, but no record in UK until Ass to 306BG 5 Aug 43. To 303BG 25 Sep 43 360BS-I 'BELLE OF SAN JOAQUIN'. Out of BAD for ret to USA 30 Mar 44.

42-5055 Allocated to 8AF Nov 42, but no record in UK until Ass to 306BG 7 May 43 367BS-H. MIA 15 May 43. Lt Gaylord O Ritland.

42-5056 Orig of 305BG 364BS 'DEVILS PLAYMATE'. MIA 26 Feb 43. 1st Lt Isaac D Benson.

42-5057 Orig of 305BG 364BS later 422BS-M. MIA 6 Sep 43. Lt Dahly. Ditched, crew rescued.

42-5058 Orig of 305BG 364BS. MIA 16 Feb 43. Lt Henry Burman.

42-5060 Dep Gander for UK 27 Oct 42. To 305BG. MIA 4 Feb 43. Capt William K Davidson. Ditched Waddenzee, 10km east of Texel. 2 kld, 7 POW.

42-5063 To 305BG 366BS-K. MIA 17 May 43. 1st Lt Joe H Roney Jr.

42-5069 To 91BG 324BS-G 'OUR GANG'. MIA 17 Aug 43. Lt William H Wheeler.

42-5070 To 91BG 14 Dec 42. MIA 17 Apr 43. Capt Oscar D O'Neil.

42-5071 To 306BG 30 Nov 42. MIA 20 Dec 42. 1st Lt Danton J Nygaard.

42-5072 Dep Gander for UK 22 Nov 42. To 306BG 28 Nov 42. MIA 5 Apr 43. 1st Lt William H Parker.

42-5077 To 91BG 323BS-T 'DELTA REBEL No 2'. MIA 12 Aug 43. 2nd Lt Robert W Thompson.

42-5078 Orig of 305BG 366BS. MIA 30 Dec 42. Ditched. 1st Lt Floyd E Love.

42-5081 By Sth Fy Rt. Arr Watchfield 10 Feb 43. To 303BG 15 Feb 43 427BS-V 'LUSCIOUS LADY'. Ass 31 Mar 44.

42-5084 To 91BG 14 Dec 42. MIA 3 Jan 43. Lt Anderson.

42-5086 To 306BG 29 Nov 42 369BS-J. Badly dam on Op Miss 24 July 43. To 384BG 5 Sep 43 546BS-B 'WAHOO II'. Cr at Eye on ret from Op Miss 10 Oct 43. 2nd Lt William M Wilson. Crew baled out near Ipswich. (11 Oct 43).

42-5125 From Gander 3 Dec 42, with 41-24497 was last US B-17 across Nth Atlantic in 42. To 305BG 365BS-T (In by 17 Dec 42). MIA 13 June 43. 1st Lt Grant B Higgs.

42-5129 To 306BG 2 Dec 42. MIA 4 Mar 43. Capt William E Friend.

42-5130 To 306BG 29 Nov 42 367BS 'SWEET PEA'. MIA 6 Mar 43. Capt John L Ryan.

42-5132 From Gander 23 Nov 42. To 303BG 21 Dec 42. To 91BG (In by 18 Jan 43) 401BS-E. MIA 22 June 43. 1st Marcell E Fountain.

42-5139 By Sth Fy Rt. Arr St Eval 15 Jan 43. To 91BG 322BS-V **'CHIEF SLY II'**. MIA 17 Aug 43. 2nd Lt Joel W Gatewood.

42-5146 To 305BG 12 Dec 42 422BS. MIA 4 Apr 43. Lt Herschel B Ellis.

42-5155 By Sth Fy Rt. Dep Mrk 18 Mar 43. To 305BG 21 Mar 43 365BS-Q. MIA 19 May 43. Lt William F Higgins.

42-5156 By Sth Fy Rt. Dep Mrk Jan 43. To 305BG 364BS-B. Out for rep 29 July 43. To Oct 43. To BAD for ret to USA 20 Mar 44.

42-5171 To 306BG 8 Dec 42. MIA 17 Apr 43. Lt Robert C Miller.

42-5172 By Sth Fy Rt. Dep Mrk 19 Mar 43. To 91BG 26 Mar 43. MIA 17 Apr 43. 1st Lt William D Beasley.

42-5175 To 306BG 28 Nov 42. MIA 11 Feb 43. 1st Lt Joseph A Downing.

42-5177 To 303BG 359BS-U **'FAST WORKER Mk II'**. Dam on Op Miss 26 Nov 43, put down at or near Attlebridge and sal. (28 Nov 43).

42-5178 To 303BG 21 Dec 42. To 91BG Jan 43 322BS-L **'THE OLD STAND BY'**. MIA 9 Oct 43. 1st Lt James D Judy.

42-5180 From Gander 22 Nov 42. To 306BG 28 Nov 42 423BS-B. MIA 25 June 43. Lt Thomas E Logan.

42-5218 By Sth Fy Rt. Dep Mrk 22 Feb 43. To 306BG 25 Feb 43 3423BS-J. MIA 13 June 43. Lt William H Marcotte.

42-5219 By Sth Fy Rt. Dep Mrk 16 Feb 43. To 305BG 18 Feb 43 364BS-K. MIA 17 May 43. Lt Harry W Indiere.

42-5220 By Sth Fy Rt. Dep Mrk 20 Mar 43. To 305BG 25 Mar 43. MIA 16 Apr 43. 1st Lt Lawrence L Leach.

42-5221 By Sth Fy Rt. March 43. To 303BG 8 Apr 43 427BS-Z. MIA 9 Oct 43. 2nd Lt Bernard J Clifford.

42-5225 By Sth Fy Rt. To 91BG 8 Feb 43 323BS-S **'STORMY WEATHER'**. (**'V-PACKETTE'** July 43). Overshot runway at Bassingbourn on ret from Op Miss 4 Mar 43. MIA 17 Aug 43. 2nd Lt Don Van Der Heyde.

42-5232 To 305BG 12 Dec 42. MIA 4 Apr 43. 1st Lt Morris M Jones.

42-5243 By Sth Fy Rt. Dep Mrk 24 Jan 43. To 303BG. MIA 14 May 43. Capt Ross C Bales.

42-5251 By Sth Fy Rt. Arr St Eval 12 Jan 43. To 306BG. In mid air coll with 41-24476 of 306BG on 1 Mar 43. To AFSC for rep 3 Mar 43 to 9 Apr 43. MIA 17 Apr 43. Lt Theodore Jankowski.

42-5253 By Sth Fy Rt. To 305BG. MIA 4 Apr 43. 1st Harold P O'Neill.

42-5257 By Sth Fy Rt. To 303BG 19 Feb 43 359BS-S **'MISS BEA HAVEN'**. Out to BAD 29 Mar 44 for ret to USA.

42-5260 By Sth Fy Rt. Dep Mrk 24 Jan 43. To 303BG 360BS-A **'YARDBIRD'**. MIA 2 Oct 43. 1st Lt Paul S Tippett.

42-5262 By Sth Fy Rt. Dep Mrk 24 Jan 43. To 303BG. MIA 6 Mar 43. 1st Lt M E Plocher.

42-5264 By Sth Fy Rt. Dep Mrk 26 Jan 43. To 303BG 358BS-J **'YANKEE DOODLE DANDY'**. Ass 31 Mar 44.

42-5306 By Sth Fy Rt. To 306BG 367BS-P. To 303BG 25 Sep 43 359BS. MIA 28 Feb 44. 1st Lt Noel E Shoup.

42-5337 By Sth Fy Rt. Arr St Eval 8 Jan 43. To 91BG. MIA 17 Apr 43. 1st Lt Nathan F Lindsey.

42-5341 By Sth Fy Rt. To 303BG 427BS-Q **'VICIOUS VIRGIN'**. Ass 31 Mar 44.

42-5360 By Sth Fy Rt. Arr Portreath 5 Jan 43. To 303BG 8 Jan 43 358BS. MIA 11 Jan 44. 2nd Lt Harry A Schwaebe.

42-5362 By Sth Fy Rt. To 91BG Jan 43 401BS. MIA 26 Feb 43. 1st Lt Beman E Smith.

42-5370 By Sth Fy Rt. Dep Mrk 22 Feb 43. To 91BG 26 Feb 43. MIA 4 Mar 43. Lt H H Henderson.

42-5376 By Sth Fy Rt. Dep Mrk 20 Feb 43. To 305BG 25 Feb 43 422BS-X **'EAGER EAGLE'**. Cr at Foulsham after mid-air coll with RAF Beaufighter V8715 31 Aug 43. 1st Lt Floyd H Truesdell. 9 kld including Sqdn Ldr E R Appleton (RAF) who was in the B-17. 2 parachuted to safety. (1 Sep 43).

42-5378 By Sth Fy Rt. To 306BG. MIA 6 Mar 43. 1st Lt Earl C Tunnell.

42-5379 By Sth Fy Rt. Dep Mrk 13 Mar 43. To 91BG 15 Mar 43 401BS-D. To Bwd 20 Sep 43. To 96BG. Then to 379BG 27 Sep 43 527BS-W. Was re-Ass to 91BG 30 Sep 43, but ret to 379BG 1 Oct 43. Ass 31 Mar 43.

42-5382 By Sth Fy Rt. Dep Mrk 20 Feb 43. To 303BG 25 Feb 43 **'WITCHES TIT'**. Out to AFSC 3 May 43. To 379BG 31 May 43 but taken off Ass 3 June 43. Act was most likely at Lt Stn at this time and possibly never on hand with 379BG. To 303BG 7 June 43. MIA 25 June 43. 1st Lt D W Mack.

42-5390 By Sth Fy Rt. To 303BG 26 Mar 43 360BS-L. MIA 25 June 43. 1st Lt Joseph F Palmer.

42-5391 By Sth Fy Rt. Dep Mrk 18 Mar 43. To 91BG 25 Mar 43 401BS. MIA 17 Apr 43. Lt Walker.

42-5392 By Sth Fy Rt. To 303BG 26 Mar 43 427BS-X **'STRICK NINE'**. MIA 19 Aug 43. 2nd Lt L H Quillin.

42-5393 By Sth Fy Rt. Dep Mark 20 Feb 43. To 303BG 25 Feb 43 360BS-G **'THUMPER AGAIN'**. Ass 31 Mar 44.

42-5394 By Sth Fy Rt. Dep Mrk 28 Feb 43. To 306BG 2 Mar 43. MIA 17 Apr 43. Lt Raymond W Fortin.

42-5404 By Sth Fy Rt. Arr Portreath 5 Jan 43. To 306BG 369BS-M. To 384BG 22 Aug 43 545BS-M **'THE GEEZIL'**. MIA 30 Jan 44. 2nd Lt Horace F Writz.

42-5406 By Sth Fy Rt. To 91BG 19 Apr 43. MIA 13 May 43. 1st Lt Homer C Biggs.

42-5407 By Sth Fy Rt. Dep Mrk 22 Feb 43. To 306BG 25 Feb 43. To 91BG 11 Sep 43 **'FIGHTING PAPPY'**. To 379BG 27 Sep 43 526BS. MIA 9 Oct 43. 2nd Lt Vernon R Smith.

The 306th Bomb Group received nine new replacement aircraft at the end of November 1942. One was 42-5086 which served until it was transferred to the 384th Bomb Group on 5th September 1943. It ended its career on a Sunday evening just over a month later, when on returning from Münster it was abandoned near Ipswich and then crashed on the bank of the river Dove at Eye. *Gordon Richards*

42-5422 By Sth Fy Rt. Dep Mrk 20 Feb 43. To 306BG 25 Feb 43. MIA 1 May 43. Lt Edwin G Pipp.

42-5426 By Sth Fy Rt. Dep Mrk 19 Mar 43. To 306BG 25 Mar 43 369BS-X. MIA 29 July 43. 1st Lt Donald R Winter.

42-5428 By Sth Fy Rt. Dep Mrk 19 Mar 43. To 306BG 24 Mar 43 368BS. Landed at High Halden on ret from Op Miss 6 Sep 43. Ret to 306BG 9 Nov 43. To 91BG 24 Dec 43. To BAD 15 Mar 44 for ret to USA.

42-5430 By Sth Fy Rt. Dep Mrk 22 Mar 43. To 303BG 25 Feb 43 359BS-V 'PAPPY'. MIA 11 June 43. 1st Lt Rolland M Haines.

42-5431 By Sth Fy Rt. Dep Mrk 20 Feb 43. To 306BG 25 Feb 43. MIA 5 Apr 43. 2nd Lt Clarence R Fischer.

42-5432 By Sth Fy Rt. Dep Mrk 20 Feb 43. To 303BG 25 Feb 43 358BS-B 'THE HUNTING CLUB' (name carried on fin). MIA 20 June 43. 1st Lt Ray W Jess.

42-5434 By Sth Fy Rt. Dep Mrk 20 Feb 43. To 303BG 6 Mar 43 360BS-J 'LADY LUCK'. Cr near Winchester 26 Sep 43. 1st Lt R Cogswell. Crew baled out.

42-5435 By Sth Fy Rt. Dep Mrk 20 Feb 43. To 305BG 25 Feb 43 366BS. MIA 1 May 43. 1st Lt Einar H Suomi.

42-5437 By Sth Fy Rt. Dep Mrk 5 Mar 43. To 91BG 8 Mar 43 401BS-H 'FRANKS NIGHTMARE'. MIA 17 Aug 43. Lt Arlynn E Weieneth.

Some 303rd Bomb Group aircraft carried names or artwork on the fin in early 1943. Two were 42-5432 'THE HUNTING CLUB' above and 42-5434 'LADY LUCK' below. Both came via the Southern Ferry route in February 1943. The LADY's luck ran out on 26th September 1943 when the crew baled out and it crashed near Winchester and the CLUB went Missing in Action on 20th June 1943. *Mike Gibson*

42-5444 By Sth Fy Rt. Mar/Apr 43. To 303BG 2 June 43 369BS-C. To L Ldg 5 July 43. To 384BG 11 Aug 43 545BS-N 'WE DOOD IT'. MIA 30 Jan 44. 1st Lt Burton R Ross.

42-5468 By Sth Fy Rt. Mar/Apr 43. To 303BG 8 Apr 43 360BS-I 'QUININE THE BITTER DOSE'. Cr in sea off Norfolk on ret from Op Miss 25 June 43. Capt George V Stallings. This Act listed as MIA.

42-5482 By Sth Fy Rt. Dep Mrk 28 Feb 43. To 303BG 6 Mar 43 359BS-W 'CAT-O-NINE TAILS'. Cr at Riseley on ret from Op Miss 14 Oct 43. Crew baled out in Aylesbury area.

42-5483 By Sth Fy Rt. Dep Mrk 28 Feb 43. To 303BG 7 Mar 43 360BS-F 'RED ASS'. MIA 29 Nov 43. 2nd Lt P A Brumbeloe.

B-17F VEGA
WITHOUT TOKYO TANKS

42-5712 By Sth Fy Rt. Dep Mrk 24 Jan 43. To 91BG 322BS-S 'MY PRAYER'. Cr Ld at Manston on ret from Op Miss 17 Aug 43. 2nd Lt James D Judy. Oldest VEGA built B-17 to serve in 8AF. (18 Aug 43).

42-5713 Orig of 305BG 366BS. To 97BG 4 Nov 42 342BS. To 12AF MTO. Dep Hurn 20 Nov 42. First VEGA built B-17F to reach England.

42-5714 To 306BG 1 Dec 42 423BS-S. To 91BG 11 Sep 43 401BS. MIA 14 Oct 43. 2nd Lt Robert M Slane.

42-5717 To 306BG 1 Dec 42 423BS-F. MIA 16 Feb 43. 1st Lt William H Warner. First 8AF VEGA built B-17F MIA.

42-5720 By Sth Fy Rt. Arr St Eval 12 Jan 43. To 306BG 367BS-Y. To 384BG 22 Aug 43 544BS-A. MIA 6 Sep 43. 2nd Lt Lester Aufmuth.

42-5723 By Sth Fy Rt. Arr Yeovilton 10 Feb 43. To 303BG 13 Feb 43 360BS. Cr Ld 3 miles SW of Molesworth 18 Mar 43, on ret from Op Miss. Lt Griffin.

42-5724 By Sth Fy Rt. Dep Mrk 19 Mar 43. To 91BG 23 Mar 43 322BS-T 'THUNDERBIRD'. MIA 28 June 43. 1st Lt Edward Brodnax Jr.

42-5725 By Sth Fy Rt. To 305BG 8 Feb 43 365BS-P 'FLAPPER'. To 381BG 22 Aug 43 532BS-C 'THIS IS IT'. Ass but not on hand 31 Mar 44 (at Andrews Field for rep). Oldest VEGA built B-17 still operational in 8AF at 31 Mar 44.

42-5729 By Sth Fy Rt. Dep Mrk 16 Feb 43. To 306BG 18 Feb 43. To 91BG 8 Sep 43 401BS-E. To BAD 15 Mar 44 for ret to USA.

YB-40
VEGA BUILT B-17F CONVERTED BY
DOUGLAS WITHOUT TOKYO TANKS

42-5733 To 92BG May 43 327BS-F 'PEORIA PROWLER'. To 91BG 16 Jul 43 322BS-T. To Bwd 4 Oct 43. Ret to USA Nov 43.

42-5734 To 92BG May 43 327BS-D 'SEYMOUR ANGEL'. To 91BG 16 July 43 325BS-R 'OLD IRONSIDES'. To Bwd 17 Oct 43. Ret to USA Feb 44.

42-5735 To 92BG May 43 327BS-B. MIA 22 June 43. 1st Lt Andrew G Bilek. Only YB-40 lost in action.

42-5736 To 92BG 14 May 43 327BS-C 'TAMPA TORNADO'. To 303BG 3 Aug 43 359BS-Q. To 379BG 28 Aug 43 524BS-P. To Bwd 12 Oct 43. To USA Nov 43.

42-5737 To 92BG 11 May 43 327BS-K 'DAKOTA DEMON'. To 303BG 16 July 43. 360BS-D. To AFSC for mod 10 Oct 43. No record that Act ret to 303BG. Fate not known but believed sal in UK.

42-5738 To 92BG May 43 327BS-G 'BOSTON TEA PARTY'. To Bwd 5 Oct 43. Ret to USA Nov 43.

Three YB-40s, at front is 42-5736 '**TAMPA TORNADO**'. Unfortunately the identity of the other two are unknown. Twelve of these aircraft were assigned to the 92nd Bomb Group in May 1943. One was Missing in Action, the others were withdrawn from the First Bombardment Division in October 1943 and most returned to the USA in late 1943 or early 1944. *US Air Force – National Air and Space Museum*

42-5739	To 92BG May 43 327BS-J '**LUFKIN RUFFIAN**'. To 303BG 16 July 43. 427BS-D. Then to 384BG 28 Aug 43 545BS-P. To Bwd 12 Oct 43. Ret to USA March 44.
42-5740	To 92BG May 43 327BS-E '**MONTICELLO**'. To Bwd 5 Oct 43. Ret to USA Nov 43.
42-5741	To 92BG May 43 327BS-H '**CHICAGO**'. To 91BG 22 Jul 43 401BS-Y. To Bwd 7 Oct 43. Ret to USA Nov 43.
42-5742	To 92BG 11 May 43. 327BS-L '**PLAIN DEALING EXPRESS**'. To Bwd 5 Oct 43. Ret to USA March 44.
42-5743	To 92BG 11 May 43 327BS-M '**WOOLAROC**'. To Bwd 5 Oct 43. Ret to USA Nov 43.
42-5744	To 92BG 18 May 43 327BS-A '**DOLLIE MADISON**'. To Bwd 5 Oct 43. Ret to USA Nov 43. Flew last YB-40 Miss on 16 Aug 43.

B-17F VEGA WITHOUT TOKYO TANKS

42-5745	By Sth Fy Rt. Arr St Eval 14 Jan 43. To 305BG. To Wyton March 43. For installation of OBOE. To 92BG 20 Apr 43 325BS-H. On DS to Farnborough Aug 43. To 482BG 25 Aug 43 813BS. On DS to Farnborough Nov 43. To 91BG 18 Feb 44. Ass 31 Mar 44. Was with 91BG. On DS from Lt Stn from 20 Dec 43, to 21 Jan 44, but not Ass to 91BG until 18 Feb 44.
42-5747	By Sth Fy Rt. Dep Mrk 20 Mar 43. To 305BG 25 Mar 43 364BS-F '**HANGAR QUEEN**'. To 381BG 22 Aug 43 then to 384BG 5 Oct 43 547BS-M '**HANGAR QUEEN**'. At 2SAD 1 Dec 43 to 4 Mar 44 to BAD 15 Mar 44 for ret to USA.
42-5756	Orig of 351BG 509BS-R '**KAY L II**'. To BAD 19 Mar 44 for ret to USA.
42-5763	By Sth Fy Rt. Dep Mrk 7 Mar 43. To 91BG 9 Mar 43 401BS-F '**BOMBOOGIE**'. MIA 6 Sep 43. 1st Lt Elwood D Arp.
42-5766	By Sth Fy Rt. Apr 43. To 306BG 2 June 43 367BS-G. MIA 29 July 43. F/O Berryman H Browns.
42-5780	By Sth Fy Rt. Late March 43. To 303BG 8 Apr 43. MIA 1 May 43. 1st Lt J R Sterling.
42-5784	By Sth Fy Rt. Dep Mrk 11 Mar 43. To 306BG 12 Mar 43 423BS. MIA 1 May 43. 1st Lt Bart Wigginton.
42-5787	By Sth Fy Rt. Early March 43. To 91BG 9 Mar 43 323BS-U '**BILLIE KAY**'. MIA 12 Aug 43. 1st Lt Jerold D Kethley.
42-5788	By Sth Fy Rt. To 303BG 8 Apr 43 360BS-H '**A.O.G. NOT IN STOCK**'. On DS to Farnborough late June 43. MIA 22 Feb 44. 2nd Lt John R Morris.
42-5789	By Sth Fy Rt. Dep Mrk 18 Mar 43. To 91BG 25 Mar 43 322BS-X. MIA 22 June 43. 2nd Lt Paul D Kahl.
42-5792	By Sth Fy Rt. To 303BG 8 Apr 43 358BS-I '**THE MUGGER**'. MIA 4 July 43. 1st Lt Robert S O'Connor.
42-5793	By Sth Fy Rt. Dep Mrk 14 Mar 43. To 305BG 17 Mar 43. Transferred out 18 Apr 43, and to 92BG 23 Apr 43 325BS-M. To Defford May 43 for 8AFs initial H2S modification. To 482BG 25 Aug 43 813BS-M. Cr at Brome 10 Nov 43. 1st Lt Arthur J Reynolds. 13 crew kld.
42-5795	95BG to 91BG 5 Sep 43 401BS-B. MIA 26 Nov 43. 1st Lt Bob Tibbetts Jr. Ditched. All crew rescued.
42-5797	To 384BG Aug 43 546BS-E. MIA 16 Aug 43. 1st Lt David Magowan Jr.
42-5801	94BG to 92BG 28 July 43 327BS. MIA 12 Aug 43. 1st Lt Paul S Casey.

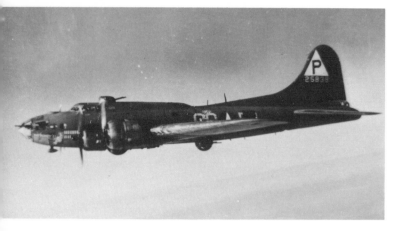

42-5838 'MAD MONKEY II'. An original of the 384th Bomb Group was the last of the Group's originals to go Missing in Action, 4th January 1944. *Mike Gibson*

42-5804 96BG to 306BG 6 Aug 43 423BS-Z. To 91BG 11 Sep 43 322BS-R. Dam on Op Miss 11 Jan 44. Ld at Hethel on ret and sal. (13 Jan 44).

42-5806 To 384BG 3 July 43 547BS-Y/545BS-Z. MIA 12 Aug 43. 2nd Lt Robert D Swank.

42-5807 95/96BG to 351BG 11 July 43 511BS-T 'MINOR BALL'. MIA 4 Oct 43. 1st Lt Daniel D Nauman.

42-5809 Orig of 379BG 526BS-D. Sal at Coltishall as result of dam received on Op Miss 11 June 43. (12 June 43).

42-5810 To 379BG. MIA 29 July 43. 2nd Lt Richard F Johnson.

42-5812 Orig of 351BG 511BS-O 'CANNON BALL'. MIA 17 Aug 43. Lt Max A Pinkerton.

42-5813 Orig of 379BG 525BS-S. Cr Ld near Alconbury 30 Jul 43. Lt W C Breiner.

42-5814 Orig of 351BG 508BS-B. MIA 13 June 43. 1st Willard T Forrest.

42-5815 Orig of 351BG 509BS-Q. MIA 13 June 43. 1st Lt Robert W Jackson.

42-5816 Orig of 379BG 527BS-Q. Ass 31 Mar 44.

42-5819 To 92BG 12 Aug 43. To 482BG 25 Aug 43 (H2S) 813BS-R. Ass 31 Mar 44.

42-5820 To 379BS 8 June 43. MIA 12 Aug 43. 2nd Lt Kurt W Freund.

42-5821 Orig of 379BG 527BS-O. MIA 12 Aug 43. F/O David W Bees.

42-5822 Orig of 379BG 525BS-G. Cr Ld at Foulsham A/F on 28 July 43 on ret from Op Miss. 4 crew inj. (30 July 43).

42-5823 Orig of 351BG 508BS-C. Ass 31 Mar 44.

42-5824 Orig of 351BG 511BS-S 'SCREW BALL'. To BAD 31 Mar 44 for ret to USA.

42-5826 To 306BG 7 May 43 369BS-W. MIA 29 July 43. 1st Lt Keith Conley.

42-5827 Orig of 379BG 526BS 'LAKANUKI'. MIA 5 Jan 44. Ld in Sweden. 1st Lt Allen E Grissom.

42-5828 Orig of 379BG 524BS-O 'SWEATER GIRL'. MIA 22 Feb 44. 1st Lt John E Morse.

42-5829 Orig of 379BG 525BS. MIA 30 July 43. 1st Lt Lawrence D Hoveland.

42-5830 Orig of 379BG. Ass 31 Mar 44.

42-5838 Orig of 384BG 547BS-P 'MAD MONKEY II'. MIA 4 Jan 44. 1st Lt William Karzaraba. (Last Gp original to go MIA).

42-5839 To 379BG 525BS-X. MIA 25 June 43. F/O Kenneth A Quack.

42-5841 To 306BG 22 Apr 43 423BS-Y. MIA 6 Sep 43. 1st Lt Martin Andrews.

42-5843 Orig of 384BG 547BS-S 'BLACK GHOST'. MIA 6 Sep 43. 1st Lt Ralph K Pulcipher.

42-5845 Orig of 381BG 534BS-A 'WHALE TAIL'. Force Ld near Ashford, Kent 6 Sep 43 on ret from Op Miss. Ret to 381BG 22 Sep 43. MIA 20 Dec 43. 2nd Lt Leo Canelake.

42-5846 Orig of 381BG 533BS later 535BS 'TINKERTOY'. MIA 20 Dec 43. 2nd Lt Dorman F Lane.

42-5847 Orig of 381BG 535BS later 532BS 'MARGIE MAE'. MIA 12 Aug 43. 2nd Lt Theodore L Moon.

42-5848 Orig of 384BG 547BS-R 'PATCHES'. Badly dam on Op Miss 30 July 43. Cr Ld at Boxted on ret. 2nd Lt William R Harry. (6 Aug 43).

42-5849 Orig of 384BG 547BS-N 'HELLS BELLS II'. MIA 16 Sep 43. 1st Lt John A Butler.

42-5850 Orig of 384BG 547BS-M. MIA 25 June 43. Maj Seldon L McMillin.

42-5852 Orig of 384BG 547BS-T 'THE NATURAL'. Cr Chetwade on ret from Op Miss 14 Oct 43. 1st Lt Edmund A Goulder. (15 Oct 43).

42-5853 Orig of 384BG 547BS-U. MIA 22 June 43. Lt Disney.

42-5854 100BG to 303BG 13 July 43 360BS-C. Ass 31 Mar 44.

WITH TOKYO TANKS

42-5855 95BG to 384BG 28 June 43 545BS-V. To 306BG 22 Aug 43 423BS-T. MIA 8 Oct 43. 1st Lt Dean C Rodman.

42-5857 To 91BG 19 Apr 43 324BS-J. MIA 21 May 43. 1st Lt John H Miller.

42-5859 To 379BG 20 May 43. Cr Ld at Lt Stn on ret from first Miss, 29 May 43. Did not ret to 379BG, to 303BG 2 Oct 43 360BS-M. Ld Bungay on ret from Op Miss 29 Nov 43. To AFSC for rep. Ret to 303BG 1 Feb 44. Cr Ld at Bozeat on ret from Op Miss 20 Feb 44. Lt J B Morris.

42-5878 To 381BG 18 Sep 43 533BS. MIA 11 Jan 44. 2nd Lt Alfred R Perot.

42-5883 From 96BG to 384BG 6 July 43 544BS-D 'NO NAME JIVE'. Changed to 'WEARY WILLEY'. MIA 25 July 43. 1st Lt Thomas J Estes.

42-5889 To 384BG 23 June 43 544BS-A. To 306BG 22 Aug 43. Cr Ld at Matlask, o/shot (Little Barningham) 9 Oct 43.

305th Bomb Group's **'HELLCAT'** 42-5910, takes off from Chelveston. Assigned on 10th June 1943 it was salvaged after crash landing at Hawkinge on return from an operational mission, 15th September 1943. *Mike Gibson*

42-5890 To 92BG 7 Aug 43. MIA 6 Sep 43. 1st Lt Richard A Christenson.

42-5893 To 91BG 3 June 43 323BS-M. To 95BG 16 June 43.

42-5909 To 482BG 26 Aug 43 813BS-N (H2S). MIA 4 Feb 44. Capt Lyman I Collis.

42-5910 To 305BG 10 June 43 365BS-Z later 'N' **'HELLCAT'**. Force Ld at Hawkinge on ret from Op Miss 15 Sep 43, due to fuel shortage. (16 Sep 43).

42-5916 To 92BG 6 June 43 325BS-N **'RUTHIE'**. Ld at Portreath on ret from Op Miss 4 July 43 with severe battle dam and was sal. 1st Lt Robert L Campbell. (7 July 43).

42-5917 To 379BG 21 June 43. MIA 25 July 43. 2nd Lt Phillip A Mohr.

42-5919 To 92BG 28 June 43 327BS-N. To Bovingdon 22 July 43.

42-5970 To 482BG 7 Oct 43 813BS-T (H2S). Force Ld Eye with fire aboard on 13 Dec 43. Crew uninjured. (Ass 14 Feb 44).

42-6086 To 91BG 21 Oct 43 401BS-P. MIA 1 Dec 43. 1st Lt Jens T Weiby Jr.

42-6096 To 351BG 22 Sep 43 511BS-W **'ONDA BALL'**. MIA 14 Oct 43. 1st Lt Oliver W Crimson.

42-6151 To 351BG 24 Sep 43 508BS-M **'ROUND TRIP'**. Cr Ld at Feltwell on ret from Op Miss 31 Dec 43. Out for rep until 7 Feb 44. At Sculthorpe 23 Feb–12 Mar 44. Ass 31 Mar 44.

42-6174 To 305BG 7 Nov 43. Ass 31 Mar 44. Last VEGA built B-17F Ass to 1BD.

B-17F BOEING
WITHOUT TOKYO TANKS

42-29475 By Sth Fy Rt. Dep Mrk 1 Mar 43. To 91BG 1 July 43 323BS-R **'STRIC-NINE'**. MIA 10 July 43. 1st Lt Leland E Forsblad.

42-29477 By Sth Fy Rt. Dep Mrk 20 Feb 43. To 306BG 369BS-H. Ld at Deanland 6 Sep 43. Ret to 306BG 21 Sep 43. To 303BG 25 Sep 43. 358BS-B. MIA 14 Oct 43. 2nd Lt Roy C Sanders.

42-29481 By Sth Fy Rt. Dep Mrk 23 Mar 43. To 303BG 6 Apr 43 427BS. MIA 15 May 43. 1st Lt Chester D Jacques.

42-29487 By Sth Fy Rt. Dep Mrk 6 Mar 43. To 91BG 9 Mar 43 324BS-K **'RITZY BLITZ'**. MIA 11 Jan 44. 2nd Lt Wayne D Heglin. 48 Miss.

42-29491 Orig of 351BG 509BS. Was Groups command Act. Arr Polebrooke 15 Apr 43. In mid air coll with 42-29865 of 351BG over Polebrooke while on practice formation flight 7 May 43. 1st Lt Roy Snipes. All crew kld. Act dest.

42-29498 By Sth Fy Rt. Dep Mrk 28 Feb 43. To 306BG 2 Mar 43 368BS-L. To 303BG 25 Sep 43 360BS-D. MIA 29 Nov 43. 1st Lt Carl J Fyler. 11 crew inc photographer on Act.

42-29499 By Sth Fy Rt. Dep Mrk 28 Feb 43. To 305BG 7 Mar 43 422BS-Q **'MA MA CHANG'**. MIA 26 June 43. Lt Lawrence R Wilcox.

42-29506 By Sth Fy Rt. Dep Mrk 28 Feb 43. To 305BG 2 Mar 43 365BS-V **'YE WHITE SWAN'**. To 381BG 22 Aug 43 532BS **'FULL BOOST'**. MIA 1 Dec 43. 2nd Lt Jason H Duncan.

42-29508 By Sth Fy Rt. To 305BG 6 Apr 43 364BS-D **'SOUTHERN COMFORT JNR'**. Engine caught fire during maintenance at Chelveston 26 Aug 43. Act exploded and destroyed.

42-29511 By Sth Fy Rt. To 92BG about 23 May 43 407BS-W. To 379BG 4 Sep 43 525BS **'THE IRON MAIDEN'**. MIA 14 Oct 43. 2nd Lt Roland H Martin Jr.

42-29520 By Sth Fy Rt. Dep Mrk 28 Feb 43. To 303BG 6 Mar 43 427BS-O. To AFSC 20 May 43. To 91BG 7 Sep 43 323BS-S. MIA 8 Oct 43. 1st Lt John J Kamp.

42-29524 By Sth Fy Rt. Dep Mrk 28 Feb 43. To 306BG 2 Mar 43 423BS-D. To AFSC for rep 21 May 43. Then to 303BG 30 July 43 359BS-Q **'MEAT HOUND'**. On Op Miss 11 Jan 44, was hit and set on fire. 9 crew baled out over Holland. 2nd Lt Jack W Watson brought Act back to Metfield where it was sal. (12 Jan 44).

42-29529 By Sth Fy Rt. To 305BG 364BS-L **'NORA'**. To 384BG 6 Nov 43. 545BS-U. **'NORA'**. Cr Ld Grafton Underwood 13 Dec 43. 2nd Lt G J Poole. (16 Dec 43).

42-29530 By Sth Fy Rt. To 305BG 8 Apr 43 365BS-Y. MIA 27 Aug 43. Lt Don W Moore.

42-29531 By Sth Fy Rt. To 306BG 8 Apr 43 422BS-Z. MIA 29 May 43. 1st Lt Marshall R Peterson.

42-29536 By Sth Fy Rt. To 91BG 19 Apr 43 401BS-A **'MARY RUTH MEMORIES OF MOBILE'**. MIA 22 June 43. 1st Lt Kenneth L Brown.

42-29537 By Sth Fy Rt. Dep Mrk 28 Feb 43. To 91BG 7 Mar 43. MIA 28 Mar 43. 1st Lt John A Coen.

42-29540 By Sth Fy Rt. Dep Mrk 22 Feb 43. To 303BG 25 Feb 43 427BS-O. To AFSC 1 June 43 then to 91BG 24 Aug 43 323BS. MIA 6 Sep 43. 1st Lt Lloyd S Schaper. Ditched – 7 crew rescued.

42-29553 By Sth Fy Rt. Dep Mrk 28 Feb 43. To 305BG 4 Mar 43 366BS-D **'ARKY'**. MIA 12 Aug 43. 2nd Lt Wright F Gerke.

42-29554 By Sth Fy Rt. Dep Mrk 19 Mar 43. To 306BG 25 Mar 43 367BS-X. To 384BG 22 Aug 43 545BS-Y. To Farnborough 19 Feb 44.

42-29555 By Sth Fy Rt. To 305BG 6 Apr 43 422BS-Y 'D' from Sep 43 **'CENTAUR'**. MIA on night Miss 27/28 Sep 43. Capt Harvey B Rodgers. First 8AF B-17 MIA on a night Miss.

42-29557 By Sth Fy Rt. Dep Mrk 22 Feb 43. To 305BG 25 Feb 43 365BS-O. To 384BG 20 Sep 43 547BS-S **'YANKEE GAL'**. Cr Lld at Desford 10 Oct 43. Hit hangar. 2nd Lt William E Kopf. (11 Oct 43).

42-29559 By Sth Fy Rt. Dep Mrk 20 Feb 43. To 91BG 25 Feb 43 323BS-Q **'STUP-N-TAKIT'**. MIA 17 Aug 43. Lt Charles A Bennett.

42-29570 By Sth Fy Rt. Dep Mrk 14 Mar 43. To 303BG 21 Mar 43 360BS-D. To AFSC 22 May 43. Then to 381BG 7 Sep 43. Ass 31 Mar 44.

42-29571 By Sth Fy Rt. To UK late Mar/early Apr 43. To 303BG 6 Apr 43 358BS-L **'CHARLEY HORSE'**. MIA 20 Oct 43. 2nd Lt William R Hartigan.

42-29573 By Sth Fy Rt. Dep Mrk 28 Feb 43. To 303BG 6 Mar 43 358BS **'TWO BEAUTS'**. In mid air coll with 41-24559 of 303BG, while forming for Op Miss 31 Mar 43. Cr at Mears Ashby. Act destroyed. 1st Lt J K Dunn. 7 kld – 3 survived.

42-29574 By Sth Fy Rt. Dep Mrk 20 Feb 43. To 91BG 27 Feb 43. MIA 17 Apr 43. Lt Nicholas P Stoffel.

42-29587 To 91BG 19 Apr 43 401BS-J **'JOLLY ROGER'**. MIA 12 Aug 43. 1st Lt Robert C Heller.

42-29591 95BG to 91BG 16 June 43 401BS-Z **'SHAMROCK SPECIAL'**. Ass 31 Mar 44.

42-29603 To 351BG 16 May 43 511BS-R **'SPITBALL'**. MIA 9 Oct 43. 1st Lt Howard G Maser.

42-29606 By Sth Fy Rt. To 303BG 6 Apr 43 360BS-M **'TOOTS'**. MIA 25 July 43. Capt John A Van Wie.

42-29612 To 92BG 25 Apr 43 325BS-J. MIA 26 July 43. Ditched off Sheringham. Capt Blair G Belognia. All crew rescued.

42-29620 By Sth Fy Rt. Dep Mrk 14 Mar 43. To 303BG 15 Apr 43. 306BG 17 Apr 43 367BS. MIA 1 May 43. 1st Lt Owen C Luby.

42-29624 To 303BG 6 Apr 43. To 92BG 27 Apr 43 326BS. To 379BG 13 Sep 43 527BS-N **'PAPPY'**. Ass 31 Mar 44.

42-29625 By Sth Fy Rt. Dep Mrk 14 Mar 43. To 306BG 16 Mar 43 369BS-B. MIA 17 Apr 43. Capt Craig J Harwood.

42-29629 By Sth Fy Rt. Dep Mrk 11 Mar 43. To 306BG 12 Mar 43 369BS-A. To 303BG 25 Sep 43. To BAD 28 Mar 44 for ret to USA.

42-29630 By Sth Fy Rt. To UK Mar 43. To 351BG 27 May 43. 509BS **'PICADILLY COMMANDO'**. MIA 31 Dec 43. 1st Lt Willis D Smith.

42-29631 By Sth Fy Rt. Dep Mrk 19 Mar 43. To 306BG 25 Mar 44 **'UNMENTIONABLE'**. MIA 17 Apr 43. 1st Lt Warren George Jr.

42-29632 To 305BG 23 June 43 422BS-N. To 384BG 8 Oct 43 545BS-K **'CASED ACE'**. Ass 31 Mar 44.

42-29633 By Sth Fy Rt. Dep Mrk 18 Mar 43. To 305BG 364BS-J. To 381BG 11 Sep 43. To 379BG 26 Sep 43 525BS. MIA 8 Feb 44. 2nd Lt Doris R Beam.

42-29634 By Sth Fy Rt. Dep Mrk 18 Mar 43. To 305BG 21 Mar 43 364BS-A. Designated for training only 2 June 43. To 1CCRC Bovingdon 30 June 43. 9 Miss.

42-29635 By Sth Fy Rt. Dep Mrk 18 Mar 43. To 303BG 26 Mar 43 358BS-M **'AUGERHEAD'**. MIA 31 Aug 43. 1st Lt William J Monahan. (Crew of 11).

42-29591 came to the Eighth Air Force as an original of the 95th Bomb Group. Transferred to the 91st Bomb Group on 16th June 1943 and named 'SHAMROCK SPECIAL'. It apparently was the loser in a collision with another B-17. Fitted with a new tail section it carried on and was one of nine B-17Fs without Tokyo Tanks still with the 91st on 31st March 1944. The identity of the other B-17 and the date of this incident are unknown. *US Air Force*

42-29636 By Sth Fy Rt. Dep Mrk 20 Mar 43. To 305BG 24 Mar 43 **'X-VIRGIN'**. To 384BG 30 Sep 43 546BS-F **'X-VIRGIN'**. To BAD 15 Mar 44 for ret to USA.

42-29640 By Sth Fy Rt. Dep Mrk 18 Mar 43. To 303BG 26 Mar 43 359BS-X **'OLD IRONSIDES'**. MIA 12 Aug 43. 1st Lt A H Pentz.

42-29641 By Sth Fy Rt. To 305BG 21 Mar 43 422BS-V **'BLACK SWAN'**. MIA 4 July 43. Lt Frank Scott.

42-29642 By Sth Fy Rt. Dep Mrk 14 Mar 43. To 91BG 15 Mar 43 323BS. MIA 13 May 43. Lt Stark.

42-29643 By Sth Fy Rt. Dep Mrk 12 Mar 43. To 306BG 13 Mar 43. MIA 17 Apr 43. 1st Lt Frank K Watson.

42-29647 By Sth Fy Rt. Dep Mrk 20 Mar 43. To 305BG 8 Apr 43 365BS. MIA 13 May 43. 1st Lt Harold C Pierce.

42-29649 By Sth Fy Rt. To 306BG 24 Mar 43. Sgt Maynard Smith won Medal of Honour on this Act 1 May 43. Act was Ld at Predannack on ret from Op Miss this day and sal. 1st Lt Lewis P Johnson. (2 May 43).

42-29651 By Sth Fy Rt. Ld in field at Lytchett Minster on Arr in UK 7 Apr 43. Rep and flown out on improvised rwy. To 384BG 27 June 43 544BS-G **'STELLA'**. At Lt St 9 July 43 to 11 Aug 43. At Metfield 23 Feb to 9 Mar 44. Ass 31 Mar 44.

42-29653 96BG to 92BG 19 July 43 327BS. To 379BG 4 Sep 43 525BS. MIA 14 Oct 43. 2nd Lt Richard W Jones.

42-29654 95BG to 351BG 11 July 43 508BS-B **'DOTTIE J'**. To BAD for ret to USA 31 Mar 44.

42-29656 By Sth Fy Rt. Dep Mrk 14 Mar 43. To 303BG 21 Mar 43 358BS-F **'TERRIBLE TEN'**. To L Ldg for rep 30 June 43. Then to 91BG 8 Sep 43 322BS-S **'SKUNKFACE'**. MIA 20 Feb 44. 2nd Lt Earnest B Kidd.

42-29657 By Sth Fy Rt. Dep Mrk 18 Mar 43. To 91BG 26 Mar 43 323BS-X. MIA 21 May 43. 1st Lt Norman Retchin.

42-29658 By Sth Fy Rt. Dep Mrk 14 Mar 43. To 306BG 16 Mar 43. MIA 17 Apr 43. 1st Lt Frank K Watson.

42-29659 By Sth Fy Rt. Mar 43. To 91BG 15 Mar 43 324BS. MIA 22 Mar 43 with a 92BG crew. Capt Hascall C McClellan.

42-29660 By Sth Fy Rt. Dep Mrk 14 Mar 43. To 306BG 27 Mar 43. MIA 5 Apr 43. Lt Kelly G Ross.

42-29663 By Sth Fy Rt. Dep Mrk 28 Feb 43. To 305BG 2 Mar 43 364BS-H. MIA 17 May 43. Lt John W Tuttle.

42-29664 By Sth Fy Rt. Dep Mrk 14 Mar 43. To 303BG 21 Mar 43 358BS-C **'JERSEY BOUNCE JR'**. MIA 20 Dec 43. T Sgt Vosler won Medal of Honour on this Act this day. Ditched off Cromer. Lt Alex.

42-29666 By Sth Fy Rt. Dep Mrk 19 Mar 43. To 306BG 25 Mar 43 423BS-Z **'DEARLY BELOVED'**. MIA 21 May 43. 1st Lt Robert H Smith. Ditched, all crew picked up by British minesweeper.

42-29670 94BG 16 July 43 544BS-K. MIA 25 July 43. 1st Lt Kelmer J Hall.

42-29673 By Sth Fy Rt. Dep Mrk 19 Mar 43. To 305BG 6 Apr 43 422BS-S **'OLD BILL'**. Badly dam on Op Miss 15 May 43. Lt William D Whitson. To AFSC for sal. (16 May 43).

42-29677 96BG to 306BG 20 Apr 43 367BS **'BATTLING B'**. MIA 15 May 43. 1st Lt Alden T Mann.

42-29679 95BG to 91BG 16 June 43 401BS-A1 **'RAMBLING WRECK'**. Ass 31 Mar 44.

42-29684 Orig of 351BG 509BS-T **'EAGER EAGLE'**. MIA 6 Sep 43. Capt Richard E Hathaway. Ditched 20 miles off English coast. Crew rescued.

42-29686 94BG to 384BG 12 July 43 547BS-B **'PIE EYED PIPER'**. MIA 12 Aug 43. 2nd Lt William H Bigelow.

'KAYO' 42-29688. Came to England via the Southern Ferry route in mid March 1943. Assigned first to the 305th Bomb Group and then from 6th November 1943 to the 384th Bomb Group. It put in over a year's service before returning to the USA. *Mike Gibson*

42-29688 By Sth Fy Rt. Dep Mrk 14 Mar 43. To 305BG 17 Mar 43 365BS-X **'KAYO'**. To 384BG 6 Nov 43 546BS-X. Later 547BS-S **'KAYO'**. Ass 31 Mar 44.

42-29690 94BG to 305BG 14 July 43 366BS-L. Ld at Oulton on ret from Op Miss 29 July 43. Sal.

42-29694 To 92BG 7 July 43. To 379BG 4 Sep 43 527BS-X. MIA 26 Nov 43. 2nd Lt Lawrence F Malarin.

42-29698 94BG to 92BG 3 Aug 43 326BS. Cr Ld at Alconbury on ret from Op Miss 27 Aug 43. Had hydraulic and electrical system shot out by flak and 20mm cannon. Sal. (29 Aug 43).

42-29699 94BG Act. Probably remained at Bassingbourn for rep after 94BG moved out. Not Ass to 91BG. Ret to 94BG 5 June 43. Then to 384BG 16 July 43 547BS-D **'OLD BATTLE AXE'**. MIA 16 Sep 43. 2nd Lt William H Price. Ditched, crew picked up by ASR.

42-29700 94BG to 384BG 12 July 43. MIA 29 July 43. 1st Lt James R Roberts.

42-29701 Orig of 351BG 510BS-B **'IN THE MOOD'**. MIA 19 May 43. 2nd Lt Robert W Mansfield.

42-29703 95BG to 384BG 10 July 43 544BS-E **'KATHY JANE'**. Ass 31 Mar 44.

42-29705 From Knettishall to 379BG 27 Sep 43 524BS-G. To 2SAD 28 Nov 43. No record after this date. It is believed that this Act was dam on the Op Miss of 26 Nov 43 and was cr Ld at Foulsham on ret. It left the 379BG at this time. It was still at Foulsham in early Jan 44. It is not known if it was sal at this time or if it was rep and Ass to other duties.

42-29709 95BG to 92BG 17 June 43 325BS. MIA 26 July 43. 1st Lt Alan E Hermance.

42-29711 94BG to 91BG 29 Aug 43 322BS-V. MIA 9 Oct 43. 1st Lt Charles B Pinning.

42-29712 95BG to 92BG 17 June 43 325BS-R later 326BS. To 384BG 14 Sep 43 546BS-O **'PHILLY-BROOKLYN'**. MIA 9 Oct 43. 2nd Lt Mark B Calnon.

42-29713 94BG to 92BG 26 July 43 407BS-K. To 379BG 525BS 5 Sep 43. MIA 4 Oct 43. 2nd Lt Joseph Ondo.

42-29716 95BG to 351BG 12 July 43 508BS-A. MIA 27 Aug 43. 1st Lt William J Suit.

42-29717 94BG to 92BG 1 Aug 43 326BS. To 384BG 13 Aug 43 544BS-H later 'M' **'MR FIVE BY FIVE'**. MIA 25 Feb 44. 1st Lt Jack K Larsen.

42-29718 94BG to 92BG 26 July 43 327BS. To 379BG 4 Sep 43 524BS. Ass 31 Mar 44.

42-29723 94BG to AFSC. To 351BG. To AFSC 14 May 43. To 384BG 16 Oct 43 546BS-B **'WOLF PACK'**. Ass 31 Mar 44.

42-29724 94BG to 92BG 3 Aug 43 327BS. To 379BG 4 Sep 43 524BS. MIA 22 Dec 43. 2nd Lt Edward T Mueller.

42-29725 94BG to 92BG 30 July 43 407BS-U. MIA 3 Sep 43. 2nd Lt Ralph Bruce.

42-29726 96BG to 351BG 17 July 43 509BS-Q. Cr Ld at Leiston on ret from Op Miss 30 July 43. 1st Lt James J Maginis. (2 Aug 43).

42-29728 94BG to 384BG 12 July 43 544BS-J **'EL RAUNCHO'**. Cr Ld at Grafton Underwood on ret from Op Miss 17 Aug 43. F O Randolph G E Jacobs. (19 Aug 43).

42-29731 96BG to 381BG 16 July 43 534BS. MIA 17 Aug 43. Lt Leo Jarvis.

42-29733 94BG to 305BG 14 July 43. To 384BG 6 Nov 43 544BS **'LOUISIANA PURCHASE'**. Overshot on Ld at Coltishall 16 Dec 43. Lt George Cosentine. (19 Dec 43).

42-29735 96BG to 381BG 16 July 43 532BS. MIA 17 Aug 43. F O George R Darrow. Ditched 20 miles east of Felixstowe. Crew rescued.

42-29738 100BG to 303BG 13 July 43. MIA 30 July 43. Lt Cogswell. Ditched 22 miles off Felixstowe. All crew picked up by ASR.

42-29739 95BG to 306BG 4 Aug 43 369BS-F. To 91BG 11 Sep 43 323BS-N **'THE VILLAGE FLIRT'**. Ass 31 Mar 44.

42-29740 95BG to AFSC then to 91BG 21 Sep 43 323BS-P. MIA 9 Oct 43. 1st Lt Morris L Gutta.

42-29741 By Sth Fy Rt. To 303BG 15 Apr 43. To 306BG 17 Apr 43 368BS-V. To 91BG 11 Sep 43 324BS-F. Ass 31 Mar 44.

42-29742 By Sth Fy Rt. To 305BG 8 Apr 43 366BS-M. MIA 29 May 43. 1st Lt James C Stevenson. Ditched off Start Point. 9 rescued.

42-29744 By Sth Fy Rt. To 306BG 20 Apr 43 367BS. MIA 15 May 43. 1st Lt Frank B Clemons.

42-29745 To 305BG 16 Apr 43 364BS-M. MIA 17 May 43. 1st Lt Varney D Cline. Ditched. 5 parachuted and were lost. 5 saved.

42-29746 96BG to 379BG 12 July 43 524BS. MIA 30 July 43. 2nd Lt George A Kayn.

42-29747 96BG to 379BG 12 July 43. Cr at Catworth after TO for Op Miss 5 Jan 44. 2nd Lt Dale C Killian. All crew kld.

42-29749 By Sth Fy Rt. To 351BG 28 May 43 509BS-Z **'BELLE OF THE BAYOUS'**. Ass 31 Mar 43.

42-29750 96BG to 91BG 24 Aug 43 323BS-L **'REBELS REVENGE'**. MIA 27 Sep 43. 1st Lt John M Perritt.

42-29751 96BG to 381BG 7 June 43. 534BS-D **'MIS ABORTION'** later **'STUFF'**. Stalled and cr on approach to Ridgewell after test flight 31 Mar 44. 1st Lt Wayne G Schoenburg. All 6 crew kld.

42-29754 95BG to 303BG 17 June 43 360BS-B. MIA 27 Aug 43. 2nd Lt George A Crockett Jr.

42-29755 96BG to 381BG 14 July 43. Ass 31 Mar 44.

42-29759 96BG to 379BG 12 July 43 **'GAY CAVALLEROS'**. Badly dam on Op Miss 14 Oct 43. Ld at Biggin Hill on ret. Out of Gp to 2SAD 15 Oct 43. To 91BG 21 Dec 43. Ass 31 Mar 44.

42-29761 96BG to 381BG 14 July 43 533BS-W. MIA 30 Jan 44. 2nd Lt Henry D Steele.

42-29762 95BG to 351BG 11 July 43 510BS-D **'COUP DE GRACE'**. Ass 31 Mar 44.

42-29765 96BG to 381BG 14 July 43 533BS. MIA 8 Oct 43. 2nd Lt James Bartje.

One of the Fourth Bombardment Wing aircraft, based at Bassingbourn, April/May 1943 was 42-29733 of the 94th Bomb Group. It joined the First Wing's 305th Bomb Group on 14th July 1943 and on 6th November 1943 was transferred to the 384th Bomb Group and named **'LOUISIANA PURCHASE'**. Photo shows salvage party preparing to remove the left outer wing panel at Coltishall where it had crash landed on return from the mission of 16th December 1943. *RAF Museum*

42-29779 in trouble after running off the taxi strip at Meeks Field, Iceland, 1st May 1943. It survived and made it safely to England where it was assigned to the 306th Bomb Group on 4th June. Carries the name **'BABS BEST'** on nose. It is not known if this name was carried on to the 306th Bomb Group. Went Missing in Action, 28th July 1943. *US Air Force – National Air and Space Museum*

42-29768 95BG to 384BG 28 June 43 547BS-X **'WINSOME WYNN II'**. MIA 1 Dec 43. 2nd Lt Darwin G Nelson.

42-29772 Orig of 379BG 524BS-R. Ass 31 Mar 44.

42-29773 Orig of 379BG 526BS-F. MIA 29 May 43. Capt John O Hall.

42-29776 To 303BG 19 July 43. To 92BG 22 July 43. 326BS. To 379BG 4 Sep 43 524BS. MIA 14 Oct 43. 2nd Lt Samuel P Gaffield Jr.

42-29777 To 306BG 19 May 43 423BS-H **'PECKS BAD BOYS'**. MIA 28 July 43. 2nd Lt Stephen W Peck.

42-29778 96BG to 91BG 24 Aug 43 323BS-M. MIA 9 Oct 43. 2nd Lt Alexander W Stewart.

42-29779 To 306BG 4 June 43 423BS-A. MIA 28 July 43. 2nd Lt Jack Harris.

42-29780 95BG to 92BG 12 June 43. To 95BG 26 June 43.

42-29784 By Sth Fy Rt. To 305BG 18 May 43 366BS-K **'SMILIN THRU'**. To 381BG 11 Sep 43. Then to 384BG 4 Oct 43 545BS-V **'SMILIN THRU'**. Cr at Blaydon 14 Oct 43 on ret from Op Miss. 2nd Lt Erwin C Johnson. (15 Oct 43).

42-29786 By Sth Fy Rt. To 306BG 20 Apr 43 368BS-N. Cr at Dunsby, 20 May 43 on ret from a practice bombing Miss on the Wash. Was in a 5 plane attack formation at low altitude when it struck the ground causing extensive dam to No 3 engine cowl and losing the ball turret. Act gained altitude and the crew prepared for a cr Ld. Completely wrecked but no inj to crew. 1st Lt Maxwell V Judas. (21 May 43). Lt Judas and crew went MIA next day in 42-3214.

42-29787 95BG to 92BG 6 Aug 43 326BS. To 379BG 4 Sep 43 525BS. MIA 29 Nov 43. 2nd Lt Charles H Lefevre.

42-29789 Orig of 381BG 532BS **'BIG TIME OPERATOR'**. MIA 3 Sep 43. 2nd Lt Benjamin J Zum.

42-29791 95BG to 303BG 17 June 43 358BS-B. MIA 14 July 43. 1st Lt Calvin A Swaffer. Ditched 30 miles off Shoreham, crew rescued.

42-29792 By Sth Fy Rt. To 305BG 8 Apr 43 366BS-G. MIA 29 May 43. 1st Lt James C Perry.

42-29793 By Sth Fy Rt. To 306BG 20 Apr 43 368BS-P. To 91BG 11 Sep 43. Sal Oct 43, reason unknown. (5 Oct 43).

42-29794 To 306BG 19 Apr 43 367BS-K. To 91BG 11 Sep 43 322BS-O. MIA 1 Dec 43. 2nd Lt Leonard F Anderson.

42-29795 To 306BG 20 Apr 43 368BS. To 303BG 25 Sep 43 427BS-O. Ass 31 Mar 44.

42-29796 By Sth Fy Rt. To 379BG 20 June 43. MIA 28 July 43. 1st Lt Charles L Taylor.

42-29797 By Sth Fy Rt. To 91BG 18 May 43 401BS-Y **'OLD IRON-SIDES'**. MIA 22 June 43. 1st Lt Buster Peek. Ditched.

42-29798 To 92BG 25 Apr 43 325BS-L. MIA 28 July 43. 1st Lt Benjamin Smotherman.

42-29800 95BG to 305BG 17 June 43 422BS-Z later 'E'. To 384BG 7 Oct 43 546BS. **'ME AND MY GAL'**. MIA 14 Oct 43. Lt William R Harry.

42-29802 To 305BG 19 July 43. To 92BG 22 July 43 326BS-C **'RUTHIE II'**. John C Morgan won Medal of Honour on this Act 26 July 43. To 379BG 13 Sep 43. Ass 31 Mar 44.

42-29803 95BG to 305BG 17 June 43. To 381BG 11 Sep 43. MIA 14 Oct 43.

42-29806 To 306BG 19 May 43 368BS-D. MIA 21 May 43. 1st Lt Floyd J Fields. Came down in sea, five of crew picked up by German seaplane.

42-29807 95BG to 305BG 17 June 43 364BS-O **'LADY LIBERTY'**. MIA 19 Aug 43. Lt Ralph R Miller.

42-29809 To 306BG 20 Apr 43 368BS-T. To 384BG 4 Sep 43 545BS-X **'QUEEN JEANIE'** to **'DAM YANKEE II'**. Ass 31 Mar 44.

42-29812 To 351BG 28 May 43 509BS-U **'LUCIFIER Jr'**. To BAD for ret to USA 31 Mar 44.

42-29813 95BG to 91BG 16 June 43 323BS-B1. MIA 25 July 43. 2nd Lt Pilert.

42-29814 By Sth Fy Rt. To 384BG 26 July 43 544BS-D **'DALLAS REBEL'**. MIA 9 Oct 43. 1st Lt John T Ingles.

42-29815 To 306BG 20 Apr 43 367BS-N. To 91BG 14 Sep 43. Ass 31 Mar 44.

42-29816 By Sth Fy Rt. To 91BG 19 Apr 43 401BS-K **'EAGER BEAVER'**. MIA 31 Aug 43. 1st Lt Buster Peek. Coll with 41-24523 off Sussex coast. 10 crew lost, 1 sur.

42-29817 Orig of 351BG 508BS-D **'ARGONAUT'**. MIA 28 June 43. 2nd Lt William C King.

42-29819 By Sth Fy Rt. To 305BG 16 Apr 43. DS to Bwd 3 May 43 then to AFSC 18 May 43. No further record. Probably sal at this time.

42-29820 To 92BG 24 Apr 43 407BS-V. MIA 15 May 43. 1st Lt Larche M Washer.

42-29821 Orig of 351BG 508BS-F **'ARGONAUT I'**. Cr Moulton 7 Jan 44. 1st Lt Harvey J Anderson. Was caught in prop wash.

42-29823 To 306BG 19 Apr 43 368BS-Y. To 303BG 26 Sep 43 427BS-X. Ass 31 Mar 44.

42-29824 To 306BG June/July 43 369BS-B. To AFSC for rep 30 July 43 then to 379BG 3 Oct 43. Cr Ld at Leiston on ret from Op Miss 29 Nov 43. With AFSC for rep until 14 Jan 44 but remained Ass to 379BG during this time. Ass 31 Mar 44.

42-29825 To 351BG 511BS-Z **'MAJOR BALL'** to **'MEAT BALL'** July 43. Cr Ld at Lutton on approach to Polebrook 15 Sep 43. Maj James T Stewart. Ran out of fuel on ret from Op Miss. (16 Sep 43).

42-29826 To 351BG 17 May 43 502BS-H. MIA 22 June 43. 2nd Lt Leo P Turgeon.

42-29828 96BG to 384BG 14 July 43 545BS-Q. Ass 31 Mar 44.

42-29829 Orig of 379BG 527BS-P. MIA 22 Feb 44. 1st Lt Robert W Haston.

42-29830 Orig of 379BG 525BS-A **'PETER WABBIT'**. MIA 17 Aug 43. 1st Lt Erwalt D Wagner.

42-29831 To 351BG 17 May 43 510BS-H **'THE INVADER'**. To BAD 31 Mar 44 for ret to USA.

42-29832 To 305BG 18 May 43 364BS-H **'SPIRIT OF A NATION'**. To 381BG 22 Aug 43. Ass 31 Mar 44.

42-29835 From 4th CW to 351BG 17 June 43 511BS-Y **'PISTOL BALL'**. Ass 31 Mar 44.

42-29837 To 91BG 7 June 43 324BS-A **'LADY LUCK'**. Ass 31 Mar 44.

42-29838 Orig of 351BG 509BS-U **'THE CONCHO CLIPPER'**. MIA 29 May 43. 1st Lt Colonel J Russel Jr.

42-29839 Orig of 351BG 510BS-C **'CHEROKEE GIRL'**. MIA 17 Aug 43. Lt Helmutt F Hansen.

42-29841 Orig of 351BG 509BS-V **'SHADY LADY'**. Cr Ld near New Romney on ret from Op Miss 6 Sep 43. Lt Robert M Spika.

42-29843 Orig of 351BG 510BS-D. MIA 28 June 43. 1st Lt John M Moss.

42-29846 To 303BG 16 May 43 359BS-P. MIA 4 Oct 43. 1st Lt Victor J Longnan.

42-29847 Orig of 351BG 511BS-T **'HIGHBALL'**. MIA 28 June 43. 1st Lt Robert W Adams.

42-29848 Orig of 351BG 510BS-F **'AMATOL'**. To BAD for ret to USA 19 Mar 44.

42-29849 Orig of 351BG 511BS-U **'LINDA BALL'**. Ass 31 Mar 44.

42-29850 Orig of 351BG 510BS-G **'GREMLIN CASTLE'**. Ass 31 Mar 44.

42-29851 To 351BG 16 May 43 508BS-J **'ARGONAUT III'**. Cr in sea off Covehithe on ret from Op Miss 10 Oct 43. 2nd Lt Theodore Argiropulos. Crew baled out. Not classed as MIA.

42-29852 Orig of 351BG 511BS-V **'FIREBALL'**. MIA 3 Nov 43. 1st Lt Elmer J Nardi.

42-29853 95BG to 92BG 17 June 43 407BS-J. MIA 17 Aug 43. Lt James D Stewart.

42-29854 To 381BG 16 June 43 532BS-B **'OLD FLAK SACK'**. MIA 8 Oct 43. 1st Lt Arthur M Sample.

42-29858 Orig of 351BG 508BS-G **'MURDER INCORPORATED'** then **'CENSORED'**. Cr Ld near Barnwell 21 Feb 44. Lt Howard R Evans. (22 Feb 44).

42-29859 Orig of 351BG 510BS-H **'THE ANNIHILATOR'**. MIA 14 May 43. Capt William P Forsythe.

42-29860 Orig of 351BG 509BS-W **'SNOOZIN SUSAN'**. Ass 31 Mar 44.

42-29861 Orig of 351BG 509BS-X **'BUCK SHOT'**. MIA 11 Jan 44. 1st Lt Harold C Cannon.

The 351st Group's 42-29825 after crash landing at Lutton when it ran out of fuel on approach to Polebrook following the mission of 15th September 1943. *US Air Force*

42-29890; delivered on 3rd March 1943, went to the Modification Center at Denver and was then assigned as an original to the 526th Bomb Squadron of the 379th Bomb Group at Scribner, Nebraska.

'STUPIFIER' as the plane was named, met its end in a field near Kimbolton when returning from the long mission to Anklam on 9th October 1943.

42-29862 Orig of 351BG 508BS-H. MIA 14 May 43. 1st Lt Clifford J McCoy.

42-29863 Orig of 351BG 509BS-Y 'AINT IT GRUESOME' later 'KENTUCKY BABE'. MIA 11 Feb 44. Capt John P Carson Jr.

42-29864 Orig of 379BG 525BS-E. MIA 25 June 43. 1st Lt Courtney T Browne.

42-29865 Orig of 351BG 508BS. In mid air coll with 42-29491 of 351BG over Polebrook while on practice formation flight 7 May 43. Maj Keith G Birlem. Act dest, all crew kld.

42-29866 Orig of 379BG 524BS-L. MIA 16 Aug 43. 2nd Lt Charles R Bigler.

42-29867 To 305BG 12 July 43. To 381BG 22 Aug 43. To 384BG 4 Oct 43 544BS-C. MIA 14 Oct 43. Lt Walter C Williams.

42-29868 Orig of 351BG 508BS-K 'FLAP RAISER' (the 'VENUS' July 43). MIA 9 Oct 43. 1st Lt Joseph H Turley.

42-29869 Orig of 379BG 525BS-J. Ass 31 Mar 44.

42-29870 To 305BG 23 June 43 365BS-T 'H' from Sep 'BIG MOOSE'. To 384BG 29 Sep 43 545BS-U 'TS'. MIA 14 Oct 43. Lt Giles Kauffman.

42-29872 Orig of 351BG 511BS-W 'SNOW BALL'. MIA 17 July 43. 1st Lt W E Peters. Ditched off Dutch coast. Crew rescued by ASR. Nav lost.

42-29874 Orig of 351BG 510BS-J 'EL CONQUISTADOR I'. Cr Ld at Leiston on ret from Op Miss 12 Aug 43. Lt Jose A Garcia. (16 Aug 43).

42-29875 Orig of 379BG 527BS-L. MIA 11 June 43. Capt George A Hamrick Jr.

42-29876 Orig of 379BG 525BS-B. MIA 16 Sep 43. 1st Lt Elton Hoyt III.

42-29877 Orig of 351BG 511BS-X 'SPEEDBALL'. MIA 31 Dec 43. Lt Albert Jones. Ditched 12 miles North of Guernsey.

42-29878 Orig of 379BG 526BS-G. MIA 29 May 43. 1st Lt Theodore M Peterson.

42-29882 Orig of 351BG 508BS-L 'SHARON ANN'. Ass 31 Mar 44.

42-29884 To 92BG 23 May 43 325BS later 326BS. MIA 12 Aug 43. 1st Lt Hans C Johnson.

42-29886 Orig of 379BG 525BS. MIA 29 Jan 44. 1st Lt Harry Mosses.

42-29887 Orig of 351BG 510BS-K 'MEHITABEL'. MIA 28 June 43. 2nd Lt Derward R Copeland.

42-29888 Orig of 381BG 532BS 'THE JOKER'. Ass 31 Mar 44.

42-29889 Orig of 379BG 526BS-H. Caught fire while being serviced at Kimbolton 23 Feb 44. (24 Feb 44).

42-29890 Orig of 379BG 526BS-J 'STUPEFIER'. Cr near Kimbolton on ret from Op Miss 9 Oct 43.

42-29891 Orig of 379BG 524BS-N 'DANGEROUS DAN'. Cr Ubbeston 22 Dec 43. 2nd Lt Kenneth Davis. Dest.

42-29892 Orig of 379BG 527BS-N. MIA 25 June 43. 1st Lt Douglas K Groom.

42-29893 Orig of 379BG 524BS-Q. MIA 16 Sep 43. 2nd Lt Floyd H Jamerson.

42-29894 To 306BG 18 May 43 367BS-O. To 303BG 25 Sep 43. MIA 11 Jan 44. 2nd Lt William A Pursell.

42-29895 To 91BG 23 May 43 324BS-H 'BLACK SWAN'. MIA 31 Dec 43. 1st Lt Stuart B Mendelsohn.

42-29896 Orig of 379BG 527BS-Y. MIA 6 Sep 43. Ditched.

42-29897 To 92BG 26 May 43 325BS-D to 379BG 524BS 4 Sep 43. Ass 31 Mar 44.

42-29898 Orig of 379BG 524BS-K. MIA 12 Aug 43. 2nd Lt Ralph H Osborne.

42-29900 To 306BG 23 May 43 432BS-U 'UNBEARABLE II'. MIA 26 July 43. F/O Norman A Armbrust.

42-29901 Orig of 379BG 526BS-K. MIA 16 Sep 43. 2nd Lt Walter C Euwer.

42-29905 To 379BG 21 May 43 526BS. Ass 31 Mar 44.

42-29914 96BG to 384BG 14 Aug 43 546BS-H. MIA 3 Sep 43. 2nd Lt Justin R Jones.

Tuesday 4th January 1944, was a bad day for the 381st Bomb Group. After losing a crew in a crash after take off for the day's mission, another aircraft, 42-29927 '**LUCKY STRIKE**' crashed at Cawston, Norfolk, on return, killing two more crew members. '**LUCKY STRIKE**' had started out as the 305th's '**PAPPY'S HELIONS III**' before transferring to the 381st on 11th September 1943. *US Air Force*

42-29915 To 379BG 524BS-U. MIA 11 June 43. 1st Lt Raymond J Zucker.

42-29916 To 91BG 7 June 43 323BS-L '**YANKEE DANDY**'. MIA 30 July 43. Lt Miles.

42-29921 To 91BG 23 May 43 324BS-Z '**OKLAHOMA OKIE**'. MIA 31 Dec 43. 2nd Lt Bayard T G Dudley.

42-29923 To 305BG 18 May 43 364BS-K '**PAPPY'S HELIONS III**'. To 381BG 11 Sep 43 525BS-K '**LUCKY STRIKE**'. Cr at Cawston on ret from Op Miss 4 Jan 44. Lt Evans. (5 Jan 44).

42-29925 To 351BG 510BS-L '**THE DUCHESS**'. Ass 31 Mar 44.

42-29927 96BG to 384BG 6 July 43 546BS-B later 547BS-R '**HOMESICK SAL**'. Ass 31 Mar 44.

42-29928 To 381BG 23 June 43 533BS. MIA 4 July 43. 1st Lt Olef M Ballinger.

42-29930 To 306BG 17 June 43 423BS-J. To 303BG 360BS 25 Sep 43. Cr at Keyston, soon after TO from Molesworth on local flight 23 Oct 44. 1st Lt Leonard E Jokerst. All 8 crew kld. (24 Oct 43).

42-29931 100BG to 303BG 13 July 43 360BS-L '**SATANS WORK-SHOP**'. MIA 22 Feb 44. 1st Lt George E Underwood.

ALL SUBSEQUENT AIRCRAFT HAVE TOKYO TANKS

42-29933 96BG to 379BG 12 July 43. Dam on Op Miss 12 Aug 43 and sal on ret. (15 Aug 43).

42-29934 To 379BG 6 June 43 526BS. MIA 16 Sep 43. 1st Lt Donald M Murray.

42-29935 96BG to 384BG 14 Aug 43 546BS-K. MIA 20 Dec 43. 2nd Lt James P Carnes. Crew on first Miss.

42-29937 To 306BG 23 May 43 368BS-K. To AFSC for rep 27 June 43. Then to 379BG 18 Aug 43 525BS. MIA 23 Sep 43. 2nd Lt Leslie T Broidenthal.

42-29941 96BG to 381BG 15 July 43 535BS-R. MIA 8 Oct 43. Capt Edwin R Manchester.

42-29943 To 305BG 15 June 43. To 95BG 16 June 43.

42-29944 To 303BG 9 June 43 427BS-E '**BUZZING BRONCO**'. Went on secret Miss 16 Aug 43 to 23 Aug 43. Probably connected with 17 Aug 43 shuttle Miss to North Africa. Cr near West Malling 6 Sep 43 on ret from Op Miss. Out of fuel. (7 Sep 43).

42-29945 96BG to 92BG 23 July 43 326BS. MIA 12 Aug 43. F/O George W Davis Jr.

42-29946 To 379BG 9 June 43. MIA 22 June 43. Capt Erzeine S Dollarhyde.

42-29947 100BG to 91BG 6 July 43. 322BS-U '**WABASH CANNON-BALL**'. Ass 31 Mar 44.

42-29948 To 351BG 28 May 43 510BS-B '**JENNIE**'. MIA 31 Dec 43. 1st Lt Homer B Wells.

42-29950 Orig of 381BG 535BS '**FORGET ME NOT**'. MIA 12 Aug 43. F/O Fred G Evans.

42-29952 96BG to 305BG 31 May 43 366BS-J. Out to AFSC for rep 29 July 43 to 19 Aug 43. MIA 14 Oct 43. Lt Douglas L Murdock.

42-29953 Orig of 381BG 535BS '**MAN O' WAR**'. To 305BG 22 Aug 43 364BS-F '**WOLFESS**'. Dest in mid air coll with 42-30666 of 305BG 15 Nov 43 when on training flight. Cr at Newton Bromshold, all crew kld. 2nd Lt Wetzel F Mays.

42-29954 Orig of 381BG 534BS '**DEVILS ANGEL**'. MIA 12 Aug 43. 1st Lt William Groblicka.

42-29955 To 303BG 16 May 43 427BS-I '**MR FIVE BY FIVE**'. MIA 26 Nov 43. Capt Addell A Cote.

42-29985, 'Cracked up' in Iceland, 17th April 1943, when on the way to England. Assigned to the Carter Provisional Group for the ferry flight, it eventually made it and was one of four replacements assigned to the 384th Bomb Group on 28th June 1943. Another of those aircraft which appears to have changed names about the time of the Eighth Bomber Command's 'purge on names', June/July 1943. It carried '**KATHLEEN**' and '**BARREL HOUSE BESSIE**'. Went to the 306th Group on 22nd August 1943 and was lost on 8th October 1943. *US Air Force – National Air and Space Museum*

42-29956 Orig of 384BG 544BS '**VERTICAL SHAFT**'. MIA 17 Aug 43. Lt Jesse D Hausenfluck.

42-29958 Orig of 381BG 534BS-J '**BATTLIN BOMB SPRAYER**'. MIA 9 Oct 43. 1st Lt James L Loftin.

42-29959 To 306BG 23 May 43 367BS-M. Fin badly dam in coll with another Gp Act on Op Miss 14 July 43. Out for rep till 21 July 43. MIA 8 Oct 43. 1st Lt Lawrence W Kooima.

42-29960 Orig of 384BG 544BS-J '**NYMOKYMI**'. MIA 4 July 43. F/O Gordon B Erickson.

42-29962 94BG to 92BG 26 July 43 326BS. To AFSC Bovingdon 16 Oct 43. Later with 390BG.

42-29963 To 379BG 11 June 43 527BS-I. MIA 30 Dec 43. 2nd Lt Glenn E Camp Jr.

42-29965 94BG to 92BG 26 July 43 407BS-L. MIA 6 Sep 43. Ditched. Crew rescued.

42-29967 95BG to 92BG 17 June 43. MIA 4 July 43. 1st Lt John J Campbell.

42-29970 94BG to 305BG 14 July 43 364BS. MIA 28 July 43. Lt George Dragasavac.

42-29971 To 306BG 23 May 43 423BS-F. MIA 14 Oct 43. 1st Lt Vernon K Cole.

42-29973 To 91BG 11 June 43 322BS-Q. Cr Polegate 31 Aug 43. Was dam by debris from 91BGs 41-24523 and 42-29816 which coll in mid air off Sussex coast while outbound on Op Miss. Attempted cr Ld. 8 crew kld. Lt Jess D Rodgers.

42-29974 To 306BG 4 June 43. Cr Ld at Framlingham on ret from Op Miss 28 July 43. Hit 390BGs 42-30302 which was also sal. 1st Lt Lawrence W Kooima. Crew safe.

42-29975 96BG to 92BG 23 July 43 326BS. Ass 31 Mar 44.

42-29976 Orig of 381BG 532BS '**SAD SACK**'. MIA 25 July 43. 1st Lt Jack H Owen.

42-29978 Orig of 381BG 534BS '**HELLS ANGELS**'. MIA 17 Aug 43. Lt Reinhardt M King.

42-29981 96BG to 92BG 23 July 43. MIA 26 July 43. 1st Lt Paul S Casey. Ditched. Crew rescued.

42-29983 96BG to 381BG 14 July 43 533BS. MIA 17 Aug 43. Lt Challen P Atkinson.

42-29984 To 381BG 16 June 43. Cr Ld at Framlingham on ret from Op Miss 22 June 43. Lt Schenk.

42-29985 To 384BG 28 June 43 545BS-Y '**KATHLEEN**' was '**BARREL HOUSE BESSIE**' July 43). To 306BG 22 Aug 43 367BS. MIA 8 Oct 43. 1st Lt Thomas E Ledgerwood.

42-29987 To 305BG 18 May 43 366BS-F. To 384BG 16 Sep 43 547BS-Q. MIA 2 Nov 43. 2nd Lt Leslie O Amundsen.

42-29988 Orig of 381BG 535BS '**LUCIFER JR**'. To 305BG 22 Aug 43 364BS-A. MIA 14 Oct 43. Robert W Holt.

42-29992 Orig of 381BG 533BS-J. Was dam when 42-30024 exploded at Ridgewell 23 June 43 and sal. (1 July 43).

42-29993 To 306BG 19 Apr 43 369BS-K. To Bwd for mods 23 Sep 43 to 27 Sep 43. MIA 11 Jan 44. 2nd Lt Donald W Tattershall.

42-29994 To 92BG 25 Apr 43 325BS-K. DS to Boscombe Down 10 July 43 to 23 July 43. Special equipment fitted. To 482BG 25 Aug 43. To 303BG 15 Jan 44. Ass 31 Mar 44.

42-29996 To 92BG 24 Apr 43 407BS-R. MIA 16 Nov 43. 2nd Lt Joseph F Thornton.

42-29997 To 379BG 6 July 43 527BS-A. Ass 31 Mar 44.

42-29998 To 91BG 7 June 43 324BS. MIA 22 June 43. 1st Lt Joseph E Slattery.

42-29999 96BG to 381BG 16 July 43 533BS. MIA 11 Jan 44. 2nd Lt Matthew J McEvoy.

42-30000 To 92BG 24 Apr 43 325BS-C later 327BS. MIA 6 Sep 43. 1st Lt Wayne C Bocard.

42-30001 To 379BG 23 June 43. MIA 16 Aug 43. 2nd Lt Raymond H Bidwell.

42-30003 To 92BG 25 Apr 43 407BS-S. MIA 14 May 43. 1st Lt Lowell Walker.

42-30004 To 381BG 15 June 43. To 305BG 22 Aug 43. MIA 6 Sep 43. Lt M Lieursi. Ditched – crew rescued by HSL 156 off South coast.

42-30005 Orig of 384BG 546BS-A '**SALVAGE QUEEN**'. Overshot rwy at Leiston 26 Nov 43 on ret from Op Miss. (9 Dec 43).

42-30006 To 92BG 25 Apr 43 325BS-A. Went to Defford 30 June to 3 July 43 and to Boscombe Down 23-26 July 43. To 482BG 25 Aug 43. Ass 14 Feb 44.

42-30007 To 92BG 25 Apr 43 325BS-E later 327BS. MIA 6 Sep 43.

42-30008 To 92BG 25 Apr 43 407BS-T. MIA 30 Jan 44. 2nd Lt Wayne H Larsen.

42-30009 Orig of 381BG 532BS-S '**FEATHER MERCHANT**'. MIA 8 Oct 43. 1st Lt Jack G Fry.

42-30010 To 92BG 25 Apr 43 407BS-X. MIA 6 Sep 43. Ditched. Crew safe. 1st Lt Coleman R Asher.

42-30011 Orig of 381BG 535BS. MIA 14 July 43. 1st Lt Robert J Holdom.

42-30012 Orig of 381BG 534BS later 533BS. MIA 9 Oct 43. Maj Landon C Hendricks.

42-30013 Orig of 381BG 532BS-E. MIA 25 July 43. 1st Lt William R Moore.

42-30014 Orig of 381BG 533BG-O. To RAF 30 Jan 44.

42-30015 Orig of 381BG 533BS. To 305BG 22 Aug 43 366BS-A. MIA 26 Nov 43. Lt Frederick Jones.

42-30016 Orig of 381BG 532BS. MIA 22 June 43. 2nd Lt Earl R Horr.

42-30018 Orig of 381BG 532BS-L '**OLD COFFIN**'. To 305BG 22 Aug 43 365BS-J. Landed at St Just Airport on ret from Op Miss 16 Sep 43. To BAD for ret to USA 20 Mar 44.

42-30020 Orig of 381BG 532BS. Belly landed at Ridgewell 9 June 43. First 381BG Act sal in UK. (16 June 43).

42-30021 Orig of 381BG 533BS. MIA 22 June 43. 2nd Lt John J Martin.

42-30024 Orig of 381BG 533BS. On Gp's first Miss carried Brig Gen Frank O'Donnell Hunter CO of 8th Fighter Command. Exploded when being loaded with bombs at Ridgewell 23 June 43. 24 US personnel and one British civilian kld, 42-30024 completely dest, 42-29992 severely dam and sal. 42-30014, 42-30015 and 42-3223 dam but rep.

42-30026 Orig of 381BG 534BS. To 384BG late May 43 546BS-J '**BATTLE WAGON**'. Ass 31 Mar 43.

42-30027 Orig of 381BG 533BS. MIA 25 June 43. 1st Lt Robert K Schrader.

42-30028 Orig of 381BG 532BS later 534BS '**GREAT IN LANI**'. MIA 17 Aug 43. 2nd Lt Neil H Wright.

42-30029 Orig of 381BG 535BS-P '**CHAPS FLYING CIRCUS**'. MIA 30 Jan 44. 1st Lt Carl O Baer.

42-30030 Orig of 384BG 546BS-F. To AFSC 31 July 43 then to 388BG.

42-30031 Orig of 384BG 544BS-D. MIA 26 June 43. Lt Howard C Burgoon.

42-30032 Orig of 384BG 546BS-D '**SKY QUEEN**'. MIA 28 July 43. 1st Lt William Dietel Jr.

42-30033 Orig of 384BG 546BS-G '**LITTLE AMERICA**'. MIA 1 Dec 43. 1st Lt Edmund A Goulder.

42-30034 Orig of 381BG 532BS-K. (Was Group Commanders Act when Ass in USA). To 305BG 22 Aug 43 365BS-D to 100 Gp RAF 28 Dec 43. Ret to 381BG 13 Jan 44. To training Act 20 Mar 44. Ass 31 Mar 44.

42-30036 Orig of 384BG. Cr after mid air coll at Grafton Underwood 12 June 43. Lt Kowalski. All 5 crew kld. On non Op flight.

42-30037 Orig of 384BG 546BS-F. MIA 26 June 43. 1st Lt Lykes S Henderson.

42-30039 Orig of 384BG 544BS-H '**LIBERTY BELLE**'. To Lt Stn 14 Aug 43, then unknown. Later to Aphrodite Project.

42-30040 Orig of 384BG 546BS-B '**PICADILLY COMMANDO**'. To 96BG 6 July 43.

42-30043 Orig of 384BG 547BS-V '**RUTHLESS**'. MIA 4 Oct 43. 1st Lt Giles F Kauffman. Ditched, crew picked up by HM Drifter *Lord Keith* and transferred to ST443.

42-30045 Orig of 384BG 545BS to 96BG 28 June 43.

42-30046 Orig of 384BG 546BS-K '**MERRIE HELL**'. MIA 12 Aug 43. 1st Lt Ernest J Sierens.

42-30048 Orig of 384BG 544BS-K '**FLAK DODGER**'. MIA 26 June 43. 2nd Lt Delton G Wheat.

42-30049 Orig of 384BG 544BS-F '**MISS DEAL**'. MIA 25 June 43. 2nd Lt John R Way.

42-30058 To 384BG 17 June 43 546BS-M. MIA 26 June 43. Lt Joseph Rosio.

42-30065 Orig of 384BG 547BS-O. To 306BG 22 Aug 43. Cr Ld near New Romney 6 Sep 43. 1st Lt William A Price. (11 Sep 43).

42-30073 Orig of 384BG. To 96BG 6 July 43.

42-30076 Orig of 384BG 545BS-V. MIA 22 June 43. 2nd Lt Robert J Oblinksi.

42-30081 To 92BG 23 May 43 407BS-O '**USS ALIQUIPPA**'. MIA 12 Aug 43. 1st Lt Eugene M Wiley.

42-30107 To 379BG 20 June 43. MIA 25 June 43. 1st Lt Weldon F Holmes.

42-30120 To 91BG 15 June 43. To 95BG 16 June 43.

42-30131 To 384BG 9 June 43 547BS-Q. To AFSC 17 July 43. Then to Bovingdon.

42-30135 To 351BG 28 May 43. To 95BG 16 June 43.

42-30139 To 384BG 14 June 43 545BS-O '**SNUFFY**'. MIA 17 Aug 43. 2nd Lt Oliver Sweningsen.

42-30140 To 381BG 23 June 43 532BS (533BS Aug 43) '**KING MALFUNCTION II**'. MIA 17 Aug 43. Lt Jack B Painter.

'**RUTHLESS**' 42-30043, an original of the 384th Bomb Group. Ditched on return from mission of 4th October 1943, crew were rescued. *Mike Gibson*

42-30142 Orig of 384BG 544BS-L. To Lt Stn 14 Aug 43. Then 388BG.

42-30143 Orig of 384BG 545BS-Q **'YANKEE POWERHOUSE'**. MIA 25 June 43. Lt George W Riches.

42-30145 94BG to 384BG 12 July 43. To 306BG 22 Aug 43. To RAF 100 Gp Farnborough 7 Jan 44. Re-Ass to 306BG 13 Mar 44. Ass 31 Mar 44.

42-30147 To 384BG 28 June 43 544BS-O **'M'HONEY'** (**'FLAK DANCER'** July 43). MIA 17 Aug 43. Lt Clayton R Wilson.

42-30151 To 381BG 15 June 43 **'SPARE PARTS'**. MIA 4 Mar 44. 2nd Lt Robert Somero.

42-30153 96BG to 381BG 532BS. MIA 35 July 43. Capt Joseph E Alexander.

42-30154 To 92BG 13 June 43. To 95BG 16 June 43.

42-30155 To 305BG 31 May 43 366BS-E. MIA 5 Jan 44. Lt Percy H Hoag.

42-30156 To 306BG 22 June 43 423BS-Z. MIA 26 July 43. 2nd Lt Wesley E Courson.

42-30157 To 91BG 10 June 43 323BS-P **'HELLS BELLE'**. Overshot rwy at Bassingbourne 30 July 43. 2nd Lt Donald S Van Der Heyde. (7 July 43).

42-30158 To 379BG 23 June 43 525BS-X **'MARY JANE II'**. 1st Lt Howard O Koeppen.

42-30159 To 305BG 24 May 43 366BS-H **'SETTIN BULL'**. Lt Rothery McKeegan.

42-30161 To 303BG 16 June 43. To 95BG 18 June 43.

42-30163 To 306BG 23 May 43 368BS-D. MIA 6 Sep 43. 2nd Lt Wesley D Peterson.

42-30165 To 379BG 21 June 43 524BS. MIA 25 June 43. 2nd Lt Paul W Hartman.

42-30175 To 306BG 18 June 43 367BS. MIA 14 Oct 43. 1st Lt Richard Butler.

42-30180 To 384BG 10 June 43. To 96BG 6 July 43.

42-30191 To 379BG 6 June 43 525BS **'THE BOLEVICH'**. MIA 17 Aug 43. 1st Lt Donald W Merchant.

42-30192 To 379BG 20 June 43. To 95BG 27 June 43.

42-30194 To 91BG 15 June 43. To 95BG 16 June 43.

42-30196 To 384BG 23 June 43 546BS-Y **'SAD SACK'**. MIA 14 Oct 43. Lt Lawrence L Keller.

42-30199 To 306BG 31 Aug 43 369BS. MIA 14 Oct 43. 1st Lt George C Bettinger.

42-30211 To 92BG 13 June 43. To 95BG 16 June 43.

42-30221 To 306BG 18 June 43 423BS. In mid air coll with 42-30841 of 306BG 27 Dec 43 when on Sqdn formation flight. Crew baled out. Act headed out to sea and shot down by Spitfires. 1st Lt J P Toombs. Crew uninjured.

42-30227 96BG to 401BG 13 Dec 43. To BAD 17 Mar 44 for ret to USA.

42-30231 To 92BG 6 June 43 325BS-Z later 326BS. MIA 14 Oct 43. 2nd Lt Ray E Clough.

42-30235 To 91BG 6 June 43 401BS-Z. To 95BG 16 June 43.

42-30237 To 379BG June 43 524BS-V. Ass 31 Mar 44.

42-30242 To 305BG 10 June 43 364BS-N **'LALLAH-V III'**. MIA 14 Oct 43. Ellsworth E Kenyon.

42-30244 To 351BG 9 June 43. To 4CW 17 June 44.

42-30245 To 381BG 15 June 43 534BS **'LUCKY LADY'**. MIA 17 Aug 43. Lt Weldon L Simpson.

42-30255 To 351BG 10 June 43. To 95BG 16 June 43.

42-30261 To 92BG 27 Sep 43 325BS-C. Ass 31 Mar 44.

42-30271 To 379BG 6 June 43. To 95BG 28 June 43. (In exchange for 42-3061).

42-30273 To 303BG 16 June 43. To 95BG 17 June 43.

42-30280 To 482BG 19 Oct 43 812BS-L (H2X). Ass 14 Feb 44. (MIA 21 Feb 44).

42-30282 To 305BG 10 June 43 366BS-N. MIA 26 July 43. 1st Lt Otto W Kuhlmann.

42-30283 To 91BG 10 June 43 324BS. To 95BG 16 June 43.

42-30298 To 379BS 13 Aug 43. Ass 31 Mar 44.

42-30300 To 303BG 16 June 43. To 95BG 17 June 43.

42-30305 To 305BG 24 June 43. To 100BG 30 June 43.

42-30309 To 379BG 21 June 43 525BS-P **'RAGING RED'**. MIA 17 Aug 43. F/O James N Sexton.

42-30328 To 92BG 7 Aug 43. To 482BG 25 Aug 43 813BS-B (SO). Ass 14 Feb 44.

42-30375 To 305BG 3 Sep 43 365BS-B. Ass 31 Mar 44.

Two 384th Group B-17Fs. Nearest is 42-30030 an original which went to Air Force Service Command 31st July 1943 and then to the 388th Bomb Group. The other is 42-30196, one of the first new replacements the Group received after arriving in England. It was one of six aircraft the Group lost at Schweinfurt on 14th October 1943. *Mike Gibson*

42-30386 To 305BG 6 Sep 43 364BS-E. MIA 7 Jan 44.

42-30387 To 92BG 21 Aug 43 326BS. MIA 14 Oct 43.

42-30408 To 92BG 14 Aug 43 327BS. Blew up in air and cr between Syresham and Helmdon 30 Nov 43. Act had TO for Op Miss which had been recalled. 9 crew kld. Capt Richard W Pugh.

42-30422 To 305BG 12 Aug 43 365BS-B '**ANY TIME ANNIE**'. To 422BS-B Sep 43. Ass 31 Mar 44.

42-30423 To 92BG 7 Aug 43 326BS. MIA 4 Feb 44. 2nd Lt Lawrence H Cook.

42-30431 To 306BG 19 Oct 43. Ass 31 Mar 44.

42-30447 To 92BG 7 Aug 43. LG retracted during TO for Op Miss Alconbury 15 Aug 43. (17 Aug 43).

42-30451 To 306BG 3 Sep 43 368BS. To RAF Sculthorpe 3 Feb 44.

42-30499 To 351BG Oct 43 509BS-Q '**MY PRINCESS**'. Ass 31 Mar 44.

42-30580 To 92BG 19 Aug 43 326BS-N. Right main wheel tyre blew out during TO at Podington 5 Jan 44. Was on Op Miss. Act ground looped and came to rest with tail section on edge of runway. Following Act, 42-31377, tried to stop but its right wing hit the tail of 580, which was extensively dam and sal. 2nd Lt William B Lock. (6 Jan 44).

42-30586 To 306BG 7 Aug 43. Ass 31 Mar 44.

42-30603 To 306BG 6 Aug 43 '**LAS VEGAS AVENGER**'. MIA 26 Nov 43. 1st Lt Virgil H Jeffries.

42-30606 To 306BG 4 Aug 43 369BS-U. MIA 4 Jan 44. 2nd Lt Charles E Tucker Jr.

42-30608 To 92BG 31 Aug 43 326BS. MIA 26 Nov 43. 2nd Lt Truman A Shannon.

42-30613 To 482BG 7 Sep 43 813BS-J (SO). To 9AF Stansted 5 Feb 44. Then to 381BG 28 Feb 44. Ass 31 Mar 44.

42-30617 To 92BG 21 Aug 43. MIA 27 Aug 43. 1st Lt Winston J Tucker. Ditched off Sheppey, crew safe. Sal and beached at Marine Parade on 31 Aug 43.

42-30623 To 92BG 16 Sep 43 326BS. MIA 25 Feb 44. 2nd Lt Charles G Nasheld.

42-30624 To 91BG 23 Sep 43 322BS. MIA 27 Sep 43. 1st Lt Cleo C Struble.

42-30636 To 92BG 31 Aug 43 327BS. MIA 2 Mar 44. 2nd Lt Bernard R Swart.

42-30638 To 92BG 30 Aug 43 327BS-N. Ass 31 Mar 44.

42-30643 To 305BG 2 Sep 43 364BS-P. LG retracted as plane prepared to taxi out of dispersal for Op Miss 29 Jan 44. 1st Lt Harry A Patterson. (31 Jan 44).

42-30644 To 92BG 7 Sep 43 327BS-V̇. Ass but not on hand 31 Mar 44 (at Witchford).

42-30645 To 305BG 22 Aug 43 365BS-K. MIA 25 Nov 43. Robert M Jackman.

42-30646 To 92BG 2 Sep 43 326BS. MIA 4 Oct 43. 2nd Lt Carson Fleming.

42-30647 To 305BG 17 Aug 43 365BS-H '**POLLY ANN**'. Cr on Chelveston Afd on ret from Op Miss 23 Sep 43. All 10 crew kld. 1st Lt Norman A Drouin.

42-30648 To 92BG 30 Aug 43 327BS. MIA 20 Dec 43. 2nd Lt Edward M Cole.

42-30649 To 92BG 31 Aug 43 327BS. Ass 31 Mar 44.

42-30650 To 305BG 12 Aug 43 365BS-D. To BAD 20 Mar 44 for ret to USA.

A mixed olive drab and silver formation flies over Kimbolton. In front of T2 Hangar is 42-30720 a B-17F equipped to drop Glide Bombs. Assigned to the 379th on 19th October 1943 it was one of the last B-17Fs to join the Group. *US Air Force – National Air and Space Museum*

Two 381st Bomb Group B-17Fs that came to grief on non-operational flights. In both cases there were no injuries to crew members. Above is 42-30732 which damaged its landing gear during an attempted landing at Little Staughton on 3rd February 1944 and was then diverted to crash land at Alconbury. Below is 'CHUGALUG' 42-30765 lying on a hillside at Redmead Farm, Maiden Bradley, after hitting trees on a slow timing flight on 29th December 1943. *US Air Force Photos*

42-30652 To 305BG 15 Sep 43 364BS-J. To BAD 20 Mar 44 for ret to USA.

42-30654 To 92BG 15 Sep 43 327BS. MIA 14 Oct 43. 1st Lt Julian T Brown.

42-30656 To 305BG 1 Oct 43 422BS-D. Ass 31 Mar 44.

42-30666 To 305BG 18 Sep 43 364BS-M. In mid air coll with 42-29953 of 305BG 15 Nov 43. Cr at Newton Bromshold. All crew kld. Was on training flight. 2nd Lt Denzel M Smith.

42-30668 To 92BG 15 Aug 43. MIA 6 Sep 43. Ditched, crew rescued.

42-30676 To 482BG 15 Sep 43. To 381BG 19 Sep 43 532BS. MIA 5 Jan 44. 2nd Lt Jack R Zeman.

42-30677 To 92BG 30 Aug 43 326BS. MIA 16 Dec 43. 1st Lt Edward C Walsh.

42-30678 To 305BG 6 Sep 43 366BS-B. MIA 25 Feb 44. Robert H Safranek.

42-30704 To 305BG 18 Sep 43 422BS-M. Ass 31 Mar 44.

42-30706 To 306BG 31 Aug 43. MIA 20 Dec 43. 2nd Lt Ray W Ryther.

42-30707 To 306BG 31 Aug 43 369BS-B 'PICCADILLY COMMANDO'. MIA 14 Oct 43. 1st Lt Gustave S Holmstrom.

42-30708 To 92BG 31 Aug 43 407BS-L. MIA 14 Oct 43. 2nd Lt William J Byrne.

42-30710 To 306BG 6 Sep 43 423BS-I. MIA 14 Oct 43. 1st Lt John D Jackson.

42-30711 To 92BG 31 Aug 43 407BS-H. MIA 29 Jan 44. 2nd Lt James F Holdren.

42-30712 To 91BG 27 Sep 43 323BS-O later 'R' 'MISS MINOOKIE'. MIA 21 Feb 44. 22 Miss. 1st Lt Neal P Ward.

42-30714 To 306BG 31 Aug 43 423BS. Cr College Farm Lasham when assembling for Op Miss 1 Dec 43. Capt George Reese. BTG kld. Rest of crew safe.

42-30716 To 92BG 2 Sep 43 407BS-G. Was sent to Barford St John with 19 personnel on board 28 Jan 44. This was in connection with the earlier cr Ld of 42-3461. On Ld the LG collapsed and the Act was sal as a result. Lt Pickens. (30 Jan 44).

42-30720 To 379BG 19 Oct 43. Ass 31 Mar 44.

42-30721 To 482BG 10 Sep 43. To 381BG 20 Sep 43 534BS 'SWEET AND LOVELY'. Ass 31 Mar 44.

42-30722 To 482BG 10 Sep 43. To 381BG 20 Sep 43 534BS 'BOBBY T'. MIA 8 Oct 43. Capt Dexter Lishon.

42-30724 To 305BG 31 Aug 43 364BS-D. MIA 5 Jan 44. 1st Lt Stephen W Barker.

42-30726 To 92BG 18 Sep 43 407BS-X. MIA 14 Oct 43. 1st Lt Stafford W Webb.

42-30727 To 306BG 2 Sep 43 367BS-Z. MIA 14 Oct 43. 1st Lt William C Bisson.

42-30728 To 306BG 2 Sep 43 367BS-S. MIA 25 Feb 44. 1st Lt Joseph M Gay Jr.

42-30729 To 482BG 5 Oct 43 813BS-V (H2S). Ass 14 Feb 44.

42-30730 To 306BG 20 Sep 43. Was hit by 42-37759 which cr Ld at Thurleigh 9 Oct 43. Was rep and ret to 306BG 4 Nov 43. Dam on Op Miss 11 Jan 44. Ld at Horsham St Faith on ret. Out for rep till 6 Feb 44. Ass 31 Mar 44.

42-30731 To 482BG 9 Oct 43. 813BS-U (H2S). Ass 14 Feb 44.

42-30732 To 381BG 26 Sep 43 534BS-B. Was Ld at Lt Stn during passenger carrying Miss on 3 Feb 44. Touched down short of runway shearing off left LG. Made a go-around and was directed to cr Ld at Alconbury. This was done in darkness with no inj to crew. 1st Lt Harold R Hytinen. (5 Feb 44).

42-30733 To 92BG 16 Sep 43 326BS. MIA 31 Dec 43. 2nd Lt James A Grumbler.

42-30735 To 92BG 26 Sep 43 327BS. MIA 31 Dec 43. 2nd Lt Michael J Stroff Jr.

42-30765 To 381BG 20 Sep 43 535BS-U 'CHUGALUG'. Hit trees near Shaftsbury while on a slow time Miss, 29 Dec 43 and then force Ld at Redmead Farm, Maiden Bradley near Warminster. 1st Lt Bill B Ridley. No inj to crew. (30 Dec 43).

42-30767 To 306BG 21 Sep 43 367BS-Y. Cr at Sharnbrook soon after TO from Thurleigh on Op Miss 5 Jan 44. Exploded and dest. Capt Ian R Elliott. 8 crew kld. CP and TG survived. Remains to metal recovery unit, Cowley.

42-30772 To 91BG 23 Sep 43 323BS. MIA 9 Oct 43. 1st Lt Thomas E Walsh.

42-30773 To 91BG 26 Sep 43 324BS-B. To Sculthorpe 19 Jan 44.

42-30775 To 305BG 18 Sep 43 422BS-P. Ass 31 Mar 44.

42-30776 To 306BG 20 Sep 43 368BS. MIA 3 Nov 43. 1st Lt George L Goris Jr. In mid air coll with 42-3533 of 306BG while outbound on Op Miss. Cr in North Sea. All crew lost.

42-30779 To 306BG 18 Sep 43. MIA 14 Oct 43. 1st Lt William H Lockyear.

42-30780 To 351BG 21 Sep 43 509BS-T 'EAGER BEAVER II'. MIA 11 Jan 44. 2nd Lt William H Myers.

42-30782 To 306BG 2 Sep 43 368BS-O. MIA 11 Jan 44. 1st Lt William D Reed.

42-30784 To 92BG 27 Sep 43 325BS-C. LG collapsed at end of Ld run at Lt Stn after ferry flight from Bovingdon 1 Jan 44. 2nd Lt Clifford P Beach. No inj. (6 Jan 44). Note, reported as on flight from Bovingdon but its possible it should have been Podington.

42-30785 To 351BG 22 Sep 43 508BS-H. MIA 4 Oct 43. 1st Lt Theodore W Reed Jr.

42-30790 To 351BG 22 Sep 43 511BS-Q 'CUE BALL'. MIA 9 Oct 43. Capt Harry B Morse Jr.

42-30792 To 305BG 1 Oct 43 422BS-J 'PISTOL PACKIN MAMA'. Ass 31 Mar 44.

42-30794 To 306BG 2 Sep 43. MIA 5 Jan 44. 2nd Lt Sidney Wolfe.

42-30803 To 92BG 27 Sep 43 325BS. MIA 1 Dec 43. 2nd Lt George C Hale.

42-30804 To 305BG 18 Sep 43 365BS-G. MIA 14 Oct 43. 2nd Lt Victor C Maxwell.

42-30805 To 91BG 24 Sep 43 401BS-H. MIA 3 Nov 43. 1st Lt Robert A Pitts.

42-30807 To 305BG 18 Sep 43 364BS-K. MIA 14 Oct 43. Lt Gerald B Eakle.

42-30809 To 305BG 6 Sep 43 366BS-G. To RAF Sculthorpe 22 Jan 44.

42-30811 To 306BG 2 Sep 43 369BS-D. MIA 14 Oct 43. 1st Lt Ralph T Peters.

42-30812 To 306BG 4 Sep 43 423BS. To RAF Sculthorpe 29 Jan 44.

42-30813 To 306BG 2 Sep 43 423BS-L 'QUEEN JEANNIE'. MIA 14 Oct 43. 2nd Lt Robert McCallum.

42-30814 To 305BG 21 Sep 43 366BS-F. MIA 14 Oct 43. Lt Robert A Skerry.

42-30821 To 92BG 16 Sep 43 407BS-U. Cr at Fenny Compton 13 Nov 43 while forming for Op Miss. 10 kld. (14 Nov 43).

42-30824 To 92BG 26 Sep 43 327BS. MIA 14 Oct 43. 2nd Lt Frank M Talbot.

42-30831 To 305BG 15 Sep 43 364BS-H. MIA 14 Oct 43. Belly Ld in Switzerland. Lt Edward W Diehardt.

42-30832 To 306BG 18 Sep 43 368BS. MIA 26 Nov 43. 2nd Lt Francis J Hoey.

42-30834 To 381BG 23 Sep 43 535BS. Badly dam on Op Miss, 4 Feb 44, Ret on two engines and cr Ld at Ridgewell. 1st Lt John J Kuhl. (7 Feb 44).

42-30838 To 305BG 1 Oct 43 422BS-N. Ass 31 Mar 44.

42-30841 To 306BG 19 Sep 43 423BS. In mid air coll with 42-30221 of 306BG when on Sqdn formation training flight 27 Dec 43. Ret to Thurleigh and was sal. 2nd Lt Nelson W Hardin. Crew uninjured.

42-30849 To 92BG 27 Sep 43 325BS-F. Ass 31 Mar 44.

42-30852 To 381BG 24 Sep 43 535BS 'BLOWIN BESSIE'. MIA 5 Nov 43. 1st Lt Donald K Hopp.

42-30855 To 401BG 22 Dec 43 613BS-N 'OL' MASA'. Ass 31 Mar 44.

42-30857 To 351BG 22 Sep 43 510BS-J 'MY DEVOTION'. Ass 31 Mar 44.

42-30864 To 381BG 19 Sep 43 535BS-T. MIA 8 Oct 43. 1st Lt William R Cormany.

42-30865 To 303BG 18 Oct 43 358BS. MIA 11 Jan 44. 1st Lt Paul N Campbell.

'MY DEVOTION' 42-30857. Assigned to the 351st Bomb Group on 22nd September 1943. Flew 34 missions and returned to the USA in late 1944. *Alan Dann*

The last operational B-17F to join the 379th Bomb Group was 42-31021 on 22nd November 1943. It is shown here after crash landing at Ash, Kent, on return from operational mission, 30th January 1944. *Roger Freeman*

42-30866 Orig Act of 401BG. To 351BG 21 Nov 43. 508BS-S 'PISTOL PACKIN MAMA'. MIA 21 Feb 44. Lt Albert M Kogelman.

42-30867 To 351BG 27 Sep 43 510BS-N. MIA 9 Oct 43. 1st Lt Lloyd A Christman.

42-30939 To 306BG 21 Oct 43. Ass 31 Mar 44.

42-30994 Orig Act of 401BG. To 351BG 21 Nov 43 508BS-T 'VOX POP II'. Ass 31 Mar 44.

42-31007 To 306BG 21 Oct 43 369BS. MIA 4 Feb 44. 1st Lt Charles E Berry.

42-31016 To 92BG 17 Oct 43 326BS. MIA 4 Jan 44. 2nd Lt Joseph C Hughes. Took off as ordered but failed to make Gp assembly, no further information.

42-31019 To 305BG 18 Oct 43 366BS-F. To BAD 20 Mar 44 for ret to USA.

42-31021 To 379BG 22 Nov 43. 524BS-K. Cr Ld at Ash on ret from Op Miss 30 Jan 44. (3 Feb 44).

42-31022 To 92BG 23 Nov 43 407BS. MIA 16 Mar 44. 2nd Lt George W Starks.

42-31025 To 306BG 19 Oct 43. Dam by enemy action on Op Miss 6 Mar 44. Sal on ret. Believed to have Ld away from Thurleigh. Possibly Alconbury or a 2BD Base. Lt A Adams. (8 Mar 44).

42-31028 To 379BG 19 Nov 43 524BS. MIA 22 Feb 44. Capt Harry R Simons.

B-17G BOEING

42-31032 To 305BG 25 Nov 43 422BS. Ass 31 Mar 44.

42-31033 Orig of 401BG 613BS-B 'PEE TEY KUN'. MIA 11 Jan 44. 1st Lt Stephen J Nasen.

42-31034 Orig of 401BG 612BS-G 'BONNIE DONNIE'. Ass 31 Mar 44.

42-31036 Orig of 401BG 614BS-X 'NOBODY'S BABY'. MIA 4 Feb 44. 2nd Lt Frank J Zitkovic.

42-31037 Orig of 401BG 613BS-F 'PISTOL PACKIN MAMA'. Ass 31 Mar 44.

42-31038 To 306BG 19 Oct 43 367BS-N. Encountered severe turbulence and icing when forming for Op Miss 13 Nov 43. Cr at Princes Risborough. Crew baled out except Pt, 1st Lt Clyde W Cosper who was kld attempting cr Ld.

42-31040 To 379BG 22 Oct 43 527BS-A 'DUFFY'S TAVERN'. MIA 29 Jan 44. Capt Douglas H Hoverkamp.

42-31042 To 303BG 19 Oct 43. To 384BG 2 Nov 43 544BS-L. MIA 26 Nov 43. 2nd Lt John B Holland.

42-31043 To 379BG 19 Oct 43. Ass 31 Mar 44.

42-31045 To 384BG 29 Nov 43 546BS-M. Cr Ld at Lt Stn 8 Feb 44. Was being ferried from Grafton Underwood for GEE installation and left main LG would not extend. No inj. 2nd Lt Henry V Markow. (17 Feb 44).

42-31046 To 305BG 18 Oct 43 365BS-E. MIA 26 Nov 43. Lt Robert E Reid.

42-31047 To 381BG 20 Oct 43 535BS-T 'WOLVERINE'. MIA 30 Jan 44. 2nd Lt Robert P Deering.

42-31048 To 384BG 1 Mar 44 545BS-L. Ass 31 Mar 44. This Act not to 8AF till Feb 44.

42-31050 To 379BG 19 Oct 43 527BS-R. MIA 29 Jan 44. 1st Lt Jack O Rayner.

On 8th February 1944, 2nd Lt Henry Markow and six other crew were taking 384th Bomb Group's 42-31045 to Little Staughton for installation of GEE. The left landing gear would not extend electrically or manually and after flying back to Grafton Underwood to inform the tower of the problem a return was made to Little Staughton, where they were directed to go to Alconbury. However the aircraft then flew back to Little Staughton where a wheels up landing was made without injury to the crew. The aircraft was salvaged but it was 17th February before it was officially dropped from the Group's inventory. *US Air Force*

'WOLVERINE' 42-31047. One of the first Boeing-built B-17Gs assigned to the 381st Bomb Group. It was lost on 30th January 1944. *Mike Bailey*

42-31052 To 303BG 11 Oct 43 360BS. History of this Act is obscure. It flew on Miss of 16 Nov 43 and 26 Nov 43. Both piloted by Lt Brinkley. There is no record of it flying any further Miss with 360BS. It was still Ass to 360BS on 1 Mar 44 with only six Miss credited, three of which had been abortive. Reported to Abbotts Ripton for sal on 8 Mar 44. The whereabouts of this Act from Nov 43 to March 44 and the reason for its sal is unknown.

42-31055 To 303BG 18 Oct 43 360BS-J 'ALOHA'. Badly dam on Op Miss 6 Mar 44. To 2SAD for rep. Ass but not on hand 31 Mar 44. (At Abbots Ripton).

42-31056 To 306BG 19 Oct 43 369BS-U. MIA 3 Feb 44. 2nd Lt Richard S Wong.

42-31058 To 384BG 18 Oct 43 546BS-T 'LIBERTY RUN'. MIA 28 Feb 44. 2nd Lt Austin D Rinne.

42-31059 To 384BG 7 Oct 43. MIA 14 Oct 43. 1st Lt Donald P Ogilvie. First Boeing built B-17G Ass to 1BD and first MIA. First 384BG B-17G MIA.

42-31060 To 303BG 18 Oct 43 427BS-N 'POGUE MA HONE'. Ass 31 Mar 44.

42-31064 Orig of 401BG 614BS-H 'HEY LOU'. MIA 31 Dec 43. Cr in sea off Isle of Wight on ret from Op Miss. 2nd Lt Donald H Lawry. All 10 crew lost.

42-31065 To 306BG 19 Oct 43. Ass but not on hand 31 Mar 44. (At Manston).

42-31067 To 381BG 19 Oct 43 'PHYLLIS'. Ass but not on hand 31 Mar 44. (At Predannack for rep).

42-31068 Orig of 401BG 612BS-D 'FOOL'S LUCK'. Cr near Ware on ret from Op Miss 31 Dec 43. Capt Jere Maupin.

42-31069 Orig of 401BG 615BS-K 'LITTLE MOE'. Ass 31 Mar 44.

42-31070 To 91BG 14 Dec 43. Ass 31 Mar 44.

42-31072 Orig of 401BG 613BS-K 'BETTY J'. Ass 31 Mar 44.

42-31073 To 384BG 18 Oct 43 547BS. Cr Ld at Whittlesey 31 Dec 43 on ret from Op Miss. 1st Lt George Stier. (5 Jan 44).

42-31075 To 381BG 19 Oct 43. MIA 20 Dec 43. 1st Lt Waldo B Crosson.

42-31076 To 91BG 16 Oct 43 323BS-L 'CHIEF SLY'S SON'. MIA 11 Jan 44. 2nd Lt J C Page. (18 Miss).

42-31077 Orig of 401BG 615BS-A 'PAKAWALUP II'. Ass 31 Mar 44.

42-31078 To 306BG 19 Oct 43 369BS-R. MIA 11 Dec 43. 1st Lt John P Noack.

42-31079 Orig of 401BG. To 91BG 20 Nov 43 401BS. MIA 6 Mar 44. 1st Lt Paris R Coleman.

42-31081 Orig of 401BG 613BS-C 'SON OF A BLITZ'. Ass 31 Mar 44.

42-31083 To 379BG 19 Oct 43. Ass 31 Mar 44.

42-31085 To 379BG 19 Oct 43. Ass 31 Mar 44.

42-31087 Orig of 401BG 612BS-K 'BOCHE BUSTER'. Ass 31 Mar 44.

42-31089 Orig of 401BG 612BS-M 'CAROLYNE'. MIA 4 Jan 44. Ditched about 20 miles from English Coast after engine caught fire on way to target. Capt C Garland. Also on board was Maj Malcolm Martin CO of 612BS. Bd and one WG lost. 8 res by RN Minesweepers *Monique*, *Camille* and *T   yphoon*.

42-31090 Orig of 401BG 613BS-L 'NASTY HABIT'. Dam on Op Miss 11 Jan 44. Ld at Matlask on ret and sal there. (21 Jan 44).

42-31091 Orig of 401BG 615BS-O 'MAGGIE'. Ass 31 Mar 44.

42-31093 To 379BG 19 Oct 43 525BS. MIA 5 Jan 44. 1st Lt Thomas E Eaton.

42-31097 Orig of 401BG. To 381BG 21 Nov 43 535BS. MIA 1 Dec 43. F/O Harland V Sunde. With 42-31111 was first loss of B-17G in 381BG.

42-31098 Orig of 401BG 614BS-B 'PENNYS THUNDERBIRD'. Cr Ld at Deenethorpe 26 Mar 44. Lt C L Wilson. Was a spare for Miss. Ret and Ld with full bomb load, blew out left tyre and slewed off runway. (29 Mar 44).

42-31099 Orig of 401BG. To 381BG 21 Nov 43. MIA 11 Feb 44. 2nd Lt Robert V Laux.

42-31109 To 92BG 17 Oct 43 327BS. MIA 4 Feb 44. 2nd Lt Robert E Walther.

42-31111 To 381BG 19 Oct 43 535BS. MIA 1 Dec 43. 2nd Lt Donald E Noxon. With 42-31097 was first loss of B-17G in 381BG.

42-31116 Orig of 401BG 614BS-D 'CAWNT MISS'. Ass 31 Mar 44.

42-31119 To 379BG 22 Nov 43 524BS. Cr and burned while attempting a three engine Ld at Kimbolton while on training flight, 28 Dec 43. 2nd Lt George A Schuenemann. All 5 crew kld.

42-31136 To 306BG 19 Oct 43 369BS. Dam on Op Miss 11 Jan 44. Cr Ld at Andrews Field on ret and sal. Lt Kenneth F Dowell. (12 Jan 44).

42-31139 To 306BG 19 Oct 43 423BS. MIA 24 Feb 44. 1st Lt Norwood L Garrett.

42-31143 To 306BG 19 Oct 43 'SATANS LADY'. Ass 31 Mar 44.

42-31154 To 457BS 20 Feb 44. Ass but not on hand 31 Mar 44. (At Burtonwood).

Fog had probably caused the take off to be delayed after planes of the 381st Bomb Group had taxied to the take off line. The rear aircraft, 42-31111, was one of two B-17Gs the Group lost on 1st December 1943, the first losses of B-17Gs in the 381st Group. Photo probably taken November 1943. *US Air Force – National Air and Space Museum*

42-31158 To 306BG 12 Dec 43. Dam on Op Miss 11 Jan 44. Ld at Foulsham on ret. Out till 31 Jan 44. Ass 31 Mar 44.

42-31162 To 351BG 7 Nov 43 511BS-V '**VICTORY BALL**'. MIA 30 Dec 43. 1st Lt Roy A Parsons.

42-31166 To 482BG 25 Dec 43 813BS-K/Z (SO). To 9AF Stansted 5 Feb 44. Then to 384BG 10 Feb 44 545BS-Z '**MISS BILLIE JR**'. Cr Nuthampstead 24 Mar 44. 2nd Lt Scott A Briley.

42-31172 To 457BG 20 Feb 44. To 306BG 12 Mar 44. Ass 31 Mar 44.

42-31175 To 92BG 2 Dec 43 326BS. MIA 11 Jan 44. 1st Lt William B Lock.

42-31177 To 303BG 18 Nov 43 359BS-L. Ass 31 Mar 44.

42-31178 To 91BG 20 Dec 43 324BS. Cr Ld Old Windsor on ret from Op Miss 31 Dec 43. 2nd Lt Wayne D Hedglin. (3 Jan 44).

42-31179 To 351BG 23 Dec 43 511BS-B. MIA 31 Dec 43. 1st Lt Warren L Putnam.

42-31180 To 92BG 23 Nov 43 407BS. MIA 24 Feb 44. 2nd Lt Robert L Clayton.

42-31183 To 303BG 18 Nov 43. Ass 31 Mar 44.

42-31187 Orig of 401BG. To 91BG 20 Nov 43 401BS. Ld at Deopham Green on ret from Op Miss 11 Jan 44. Left Deopham after repairs on 4 Mar 44. Cr near Newmarket. Struck ground when flying low. Capt Donald W Garrett. (5 Mar 44).

42-31189 To 379BG 22 Nov 43. Ass 31 Mar 44.

42-31192 Orig of 401BG 612BS. To 351BG 3 Dec 43 508BS-R. (On arrival in UK, never joined 401BG in UK). Ass 31 Mar 44.

42-31193 Orig of 401BG '**LITTLE BOOTS**'. MIA 29 Jan 44. Capt Robert W Beers.

42-31196 To 306BG 14 Dec 43. Ass 31 Mar 44.

42-31197 To 381BG 13 Jan 44. Ass 31 Mar 44.

42-31198 To 401BG 24 Dec 43 612BS-N '**FANCY NANCY**'. Abandoned over England on ret from Op Miss 31 Dec 43. Cr near Kimbolton and dest. Lt Scribner C Dailey.

42-31200 To 303BG 1 Jan 44. 427BS '**THE BAD PENNY**'. Ass 31 Mar 44.

42-31202 To 401BG 12 Nov 43 613BS-D. Dam on Op Miss 29 Mar 44 and sal on ret. Was first new replacement Act Ass to 401BG in England.

42-31211 To 384BG 23 Nov 43 546BS-H. Ass 31 Mar 44.

42-31213 To 303BG 18 Nov 43 '**PISTOL PACKIN MAMA**'. Ass 31 Mar 44.

42-31222 To 384BG 23 Nov 43 546BS-D '**LAZY DAISY**'. Ass 31 Mar 44.

42-31224 To 303BG 13 Jan 44 358BS-F '**HELEN HEAVEN**'. Ass 31 Mar 44.

42-31226 To 401BG 22 Dec 43 613BS-G. Ass 31 Mar 44.

42-31228 To 379BG 22 Nov 43. Ass 31 Mar 44.

42-31230 To 91BG 22 Dec 43 324BS. MIA 11 Jan 44. 2nd Lt Allen A Uskala.

42-31231 To 92BG 23 Nov 43 325BS. MIA 23 Mar 44. 2nd Lt Homer C Wall.

42-31233 To 303BG 18 Nov 43 427BS. MIA 20 Dec 43. 1st Lt Franklin Leve.

42-31235 To 384BG 6 Jan 44 544BS-C '**GOING DOG**'. Ass 31 Mar 44.

42-31236 To 306BG 21 Dec 43 367BS. MIA 11 Jan 44. 1st Lt George Campert.

42-31238 To 351BG 23 Dec 43 511BS-A '**DEVILS BALL**'. Ass 31 Mar 44.

42-31239 To 303BG 18 Nov 43 358BS. MIA 24 Feb 44. 1st Lt Marshall L Smith.

42-31241 To 303BG 18 Nov 43 427BS '**SPIRIT OF WANETT**'. Ass 31 Mar 44.

42-31243 To 303BG 18 Nov 43. MIA 1 Dec 43. Ditched in Pegwell Bay. Lt Eckart.

42-31245 To 306BG 14 Dec 43 368BS. MIA 25 Feb 44. F/O James R Coleman.

42-31246 To 384BG 27 Nov 43 547BS. MIA 14 Jan 44. 2nd Lt Neill L Britt.

42-31248 To 92BG 30 Nov 43 325BS. Ass 31 Mar 44.

When returning from the mission of 22nd February 1944, 42-31322 of 305th Bomb Group crashed in Endcliffe Park, Sheffield, killing all ten members of the crew. Today a Memorial Stone marks the spot. Photo shows the memorial's dedication with the Bishop of Sheffield, the Mayor of Sheffield, the Chairman of the Sheffield branch of the Royal Air Forces Association and Commander of the US 3rd Air Force in Britain in attendance. *Stan Bishop*

42-31250 To 92BG 2 Dec 43 327BS-B. Ass 31 Mar 44.

42-31255 To 305BG 3 Dec 43 422BS-F. Ass 31 Mar 44.

42-31274 To 384BG 22 Nov 43 544BS 'SAG HAG'. MIA 30 Dec 43. Lt Randolph G E Jacobs. Ditched 50° 42'N, 00° 31'E at 1125hrs. 9 crew picked up by ASR. 1 lost. Act was on way to target.

42-31277 To 92BG 21 Jan 44 327BS-P. Ass but not on hand 31 Mar 44. (At Wormingford).

42-31278 To 381BG 20 Dec 43. Cr at Blooms Farm, Sible Hedingham 4 Jan 44 after TO from Ridgewell for Op Miss. Jettisoned bombs in field just before hitting a wood. Burned and dest. All 10 crew kld. 1st Lt Cecil M Clore.

42-31291 To 381BG 11 Dec 43. Ass 31 Mar 44.

42-31308 To 305BG 23 Nov 43 364BS. MIA 24 Feb 44. 1st Lt Harry A Patterson.

42-31314 To 303BG 18 Nov 43 359BS-E 'SCORCHY'. Cr Ld at Shoreham on ret from Op Miss 11 Feb 44. 1st Lt H Dahleen. 3 crew inj. (13 Feb 44).

42-31315 To 401BG 23 Dec 43 614BS-C 'LIBERTY RUN'. Ass 31 Mar 44.

42-31322 To 305BG 30 Jan 44. Cr at Sheffield on ret from Op Miss 22 Feb 44. All 10 crew kld. Act dest. 2nd Lt John G Krieghauser. (25 Feb 44).

42-31326 To 92BG 30 Jan 44 327BS-W. Ass 31 Mar 44.

42-31327 To 306BG 12 Dec 43 367BS. Cr between Cromer and Walkern on ret from Op Miss 31 Dec 43. 1st Lt Charles B Smith Jnr.

42-31328 To 305BG 22 Dec 43 366BS. MIA 25 Feb 44. Lt Theodore S Czarnocki.

42-31333 To 91BG 20 Dec 43 322BS-W 'WEE WILLIE'. Ass 31 Mar 44.

42-31340 To 303BG 22 Dec 43 360BS-D 'MISS LIBERTY'. Ass 31 Mar 44.

42-31342 To 305BG 3 Dec 43 'BOEING'S BEST'. Ass 31 Mar 44.

42-31346 To 384BG 20 Jan 44 544BS-Q 'SHACK RABBIT'. Ass 31 Mar 44.

42-31353 To 91BG 20 Dec 43 323BS 'QUEENIE' (later to 322BS). Ass 31 Mar 44.

42-31357 To 381BG 13 Dec 43 'OUR DESIRE'. Ass 31 Mar 44.

42-31362 To 92BG 30 Dec 43 326BS. Ass 31 Mar 44.

42-31363 To 306BG 19 Dec 43 368BS. MIA 27 Mar 44. 1st Lt Rene C Fix.

42-31364 To 384BG 10 Jan 44 544BS-D 'NUTTALL'S NUT HOUSE'. Ass 31 Mar 44.

42-31365 To 305BG 3 Jan 44. Ass 31 Mar 44.

42-31367 To 91BG 25 Jan 44 322BS-R 'CHOW HOUND'. Ass 31 Mar 44.

42-31363, assigned to the 306th Bomb Group on 19th December 1943 and Missing in Action on 27th March 1944. Some time between these dates the aircraft was involved in an unknown incident which caused the damage seen here to the right hand wingtip. *Gordon Richards*

A nice early 1944 306th Bomb Group formation. Nearest aircraft is 42-31454 which joined the Group on 27th December 1943 and survived the early 1944 heavy loss period eventually being retired as War Weary. *Gordon Richards*

42-31369 To 401BG 14 Jan 44 614BS-K '**ROUND TRIPPER**'. Ass 31 Mar 44.

42-31372 To 91BG 20 Dec 43 323BS '**MALAYAN LADY**'. MIA 11 Jan 44. 1st Lt Edwin R Reid. (4 Miss).

42-31374 To 401BG 14 Jan 44 613BS-B. MIA 13 Mar 44. 2nd Lt George J Hellmuth.

42-31375 To 384BG 21 Jan 44 546BS-S. Ass 31 Mar 44.

42-31377 To 92BG 27 Dec 43 327BS. During TO for Op Miss 5 Jan 44, right wing hit tail of 42-30580 which had ground looped on runway, causing 580 to be sal. This Act was stopped on runway with dam right wing which was soon rep. 1st Lt Frederick P Wenger. MIA 22 Feb 44. 1st Lt William R Lavies.

42-31381 To 381BG 22 Jan 44 535BS '**JAYNEE B**'. MIA 20 Mar 44. 1st Lt George B McIntoah.

42-31384 To 351BG 20 Jan 44 509BS-T '**BUCKEYE BABY**'. Ass 31 Mar 44.

42-31385 To 306BG 4 Jan 44. Ass 31 Mar 44.

42-31386 To 303BG 18 Jan 44. Ass 31 Mar 44.

42-31387 To 92BG 4 Jan 44 326BS. MIA 8 Feb 44. 1st Lt Warren E McMurray.

42-31388 To 306BG 21 Dec 43. MIA 11 Feb 44. 1st Lt Geno. D Betta.

42-31394 To 379BG 20 Jan 44. Ass 31 Mar 44.

42-31399 To 303BG 27 Dec 43 360BS. MIA 22 Feb 44. 1st Lt Charles D Crook.

42-31402 To 305BG 22 Dec 43. Ass 31 Mar 44.

42-31405 To 303BG 14 Jan 44 359BS '**WALLEROE MK II**'. Ass 31 Mar 44.

42-31406 To 306BG 21 Jan 44. MIA 22 Feb 44. 1st Lt Thomas W Symons III.

42-31408 To 92BG 27 Dec 43 407BS-Z. Ass 31 Mar 44.

42-31409 To 305BG 22 Jan 44 364BS. MIA 22 Feb 44. 1st Lt Charles O Barnes.

42-31411 To 92BG 2 Dec 43 327BS. MIA 21 Feb 44. 2nd Lt James A McEvoy.

42-31414 To 401BG 14 Jan 44 615BS-J. Dam beyond rep after Ld at Deenethorpe 27 Jan 44. LG was raised instead of flaps. (30 Jan 44).

42-31415 To 384BG 8 Jan 44 545BS '**HAM ON RYE**'. Cr Ld at Grafton Underwood on ret from Op Miss 30 Jan 44. (2 Feb 44).

42-31417 To 381BG 11 Dec 43 533BS. MIA 11 Jan 44. 1st Lt Ernest M Klein.

42-31418 To 306BG 27 Dec 43 423BS. Ass 31 Mar 44. (Over 100 Miss by end of war).

42-31423 To 303BG 18 Jan 44 427BS-M '**JIGGER ROUCHE**'. Ass 31 Mar 44.

42-31427 To 305BG 21 Feb 44. Ass 31 Mar 44.

42-31428 To 306BG 21 Jan 44 367BS. MIA 22 Feb 44. 2nd Lt Carey K Olivier.

42-31430 To 305BG 6 Jan 44 366BS. MIA 20 Feb 44. Lt John J Stahl Jr.

42-31432 To 303BG 18 Jan 44 360BS '**OLD GLORY**'. Ass 31 Mar 44.

42-31433 To 384BG 8 Jan 44 547BS-V '**RUM POT**'. Ass 31 Mar 44.

42-31435 To 384BG 2 Mar 44 544BS-S '**WEST'S END**'. Ass 31 Mar 44.

42-31440 To 306BG 4 Jan 44. MIA 4 Feb 44. 2nd Lt Henry L Ware.

42-31441 To 303BG 1 Jan 44. Cr at Catworth 5 Jan 44 after mid air coll with 42-37887 of 379BG while forming for Op Miss. Dest. 2nd Lt H G Burkitt. All crew kld.

42-31443 To 381BG 6 Jan 44 532BS-M '**FRIDAY THE 13TH**'. MIA 22 Feb 44. 1st Lt Francis J Flaherty.

42-31444 To 306BG 8 Jan 44. Ass 31 Mar 44.

42-31445 To 306BG 21 Jan 44. Ass 31 Mar 44.

42-31448 To 381BG 23 Jan 44 532BS '**HALF BREED**'. MIA 6 Mar 44. 2nd Lt Milton A Fastrup.

42-31451 To 306BG 30 Dec 43 368BS. MIA 11 Jan 44. 2nd Lt Ross A McCollum.

42-31454 To 306BG 27 Dec 43. Ass 31 Mar 44.

42-31455 To 92BG 23 Jan 44 326BS. MIA 23 Mar 44. 2nd Lt Clifford L Robbins.

42-31461 To 305BG 28 Dec 43. MIA 30 Jan 44. 2nd Lt Charles A Scott.

42-31467 To 401BG 6 Jan 44 613BS-J 'SAC HOUND'. MIA 2 Mar 44. 2nd Lt William C Sheahan.

42-31469 To 306BG 27 Dec 43. Dam on Op Miss 11 Jan 44. Ld at Foulsham on ret. Out for rep till 31 Jan 44. Ass 31 Mar 44.

42-31471 To 303BG 1 Jan 44 360BS 'DOOLITTLE'S DESTROYERS'. MIA 8 Mar 44. 2nd Lt Leo Mcgrath.

42-31475 To 305BG 28 Dec 43. Ass 31 Mar 44.

42-31480 To 305BG 22 Dec 43 365BS 'REICH'S RUIN'. Ass 31 Mar 44.

42-31481 To 351BG 2 Jan 44 510BS-B. MIA 11 Jan 44. 1st Lt Richard J Case.

42-31483 To 303BG 1 Jan 44 359BS-P 'BONNIE B'. Ass 31 Mar 44.

42-31484 To 384BG 20 Jan 44 545BS-F. To 546BS-F. Ass 31 Mar 44.

42-31485 To 401BG 6 Jan 44 615BS-X 'OLD IRONSIDES'. Ass 31 Mar 44.

42-32486 To 401BG 14 Jan 44 612BS-Y. MIA 29 Jan 44. 2nd Lt John Tannahill.

42-31488 To 401BG 2 Jan 44 614BS-D 'SHADE RUFF'. MIA 8 Mar 44. 2nd Lt Dale A Peterson.

42-31490 To 381BG 10 Nov 44. MIA 24 Mar 44. 2nd Lt John A Rickerson. Coll in mid air with 42-40008.

42-31494 To 92BG 31 Dec 43 407BS. Cr Ld at Matching on ret from Op Miss 4 Feb 44. 2nd Lt William C Reid. 6 crew kld. (6 Feb 44).

42-31495 To 384BG 21 Jan 44 544BS-R 'WABBIT TWACKS'. Ass 31 Mar 44.

42-31496 To 401BG 1 Feb 44 612BS-O. Ass 31 Mar 44.

42-31497 To 381BG 22 Jan 44. Ass 31 Mar 44.

42-31499 To 306BG 21 Jan 44. MIA 8 Feb 44. 1st Lt Howard J Snyder.

42-31500 To 306BG 4 Jan 44 367BS. MIA 22 Feb 44. 2nd Lt Francis W Macomber.

42-31501 To 305BG 24 Dec 43 366BS-R 'OLE MISS DESTRY'. Ass 31 Mar 44. (Completed 138 Miss by end of war).

42-31503 To 92BG 30 Dec 43 325BS. MIA 6 Mar 44. 1st Frank Krizan.

42-31505 Orig of 457BG 'MISS CUE'. Ass 31 Mar 44.

42-31508 To 401BG 22 Jan 44 613BS-Q 'COMMAND PERFORMANCE'. Ass 31 Mar 44.

42-31509 To 351BG 14 Jan 44 510BS-V 'TWINKLE TOES'. Ass 31 Mar 44.

42-31510 To 379BG 9 Jan 44 524BS. MIA 22 Feb 44. 1st Lt Donald P McCall.

42-31511 To 401BG 1 Jan 44 612BS-D 'FOOLS LUCK III'. Ass 31 Mar 44.

42-31513 To 91BG 24 Feb 44 323BS. Ass 31 Mar 44.

42-31515 To 91BG 21 Jan 44 'WILD HARE'. Ass 31 Mar 44.

42-31516 To 384BG 18 Feb 44 546BS. Cr at Irthlingborough 22 Feb 44 after mid air coll with 42-38041 of 303BG during assembly for Op Miss. 1st Lt Sydney R Jeter. (23 Feb 44).

42-31517 Orig of 457BG. MIA 25 Feb 44. 2nd Lt James R Chinn.

42-31518 To 401BG 14 Jan 44 615BS-G 'DOOLITTLES DOUGH-BOYS'. MIA 20 Feb 44. 2nd Lt Edward T Gardner.

42-31520 Orig of 457BG. Ass 31 Mar 44.

42-31521 To 401BG 1 Feb 44 615BS-M 'BADLAND BAT'. Ass 31 Mar 44.

42-31524 To 306BG 21 Jan 44. Cr Ld at Horsey on ret from Op Miss 22 Mar 44. Lt Ragnar L Carlson. 5 crew baled out over enemy territory. (23 Mar 44).

42-31526 To 303BG 1 Jan 44 427BS. MIA 4 Jan 44. 1st Lt Fred C Humphreys.

42-31528 To 305BG 28 Dec 43. Cr near Oxford on ret from Op Miss 31 Dec 43. 2nd Lt J J Quillman. (3 Jan 44).

42-31529 To 92BG 23 Jan 44 407BS. Ass but not on hand 31 Mar 44. (At Boreham).

42-31531 Orig of 457BG. MIA 29 Mar 44. 2nd Lt Lewis W Lenartson.

42-31532 To 92BG 4 Jan 44 326BS. MIA 23 Mar 44. 2nd Lt Henry W Murdock.

42-31533 To 381BG 5 Jan 44 535BS. MIA 22 Feb 44. 2nd Lt Charles H Downey.

42-31535 To 379BG 24 Jan 44 527BS. MIA 30 Jan 44. 1st Lt Kenneth D Adams.

42-31536 To 92BG 27 Jan 44 326BS-O. Ass 31 Mar 44.

42-31538 To 306BG 4 Jan 44. MIA 11 Jan 44. 2nd Lt Perry Cavos.

42-31539 To 306BG 4 Jan 44. Ass 31 Mar 44.

42-31542 Orig of 457BG. To 91BG 12 Mar 44. 323BS 'MUNKY'. Ass 31 Mar 44.

42-31544 To 305BG 21 Jan 44 366BS. MIA 24 Mar 44. Lt Harry L Cornell.

42-31545 Orig of 457BG. Ass 31 Mar 44.

42-31548 Orig of 457BG. To 92BG 11 Mar 44 325 BS. Ass 31 Mar 44.

42-31550 To 381BG 13 Jan 44 534BS-G 'GREEN HORNET II'. Ass 31 Mar 44.

42-31551 Orig of 457BG. Ass 31 Mar 44.

42-31552 Orig of 457BG. Ass 31 Mar 44.

42-31553 To 381BG 19 Feb 44 534BS. MIA 6 Mar 44. 1st Lt Edward E Naushalter.

42-31555 To 379BG 31 Jan 44 527BS. MIA 6 Mar 44. 1st Lt William C Hendrickson.

42-31556 To 306BG 4 Jan 44. Ass 31 Mar 44.

42-31557 To 401BG 21 Jan 44 613BS-R. Ass 31 Mar 44.

42-31558 To 306BG 21 Jan 44. Ass 31 Mar 44.

42-31560 To 351BG 25 Feb 44 510BS-A. Ass 31 Mar 44.

42-31562 To 303BG 13 Jan 44 358BS. MIA 24 Feb 44. 1st Lt John F Henderson.

42-31564 To 92BG 30 Dec 43 325BS. MIA 9 Mar 44. Ld in Sweden.

42-31568 Orig of 457BG. Ass 31 Mar 44.

42-31569 To 381BG 19 Feb 44. Ass 31 Mar 44.

42-31570 To 381BG 2 Feb 44 533BS-W 'LUCKY ME'. Ass 31 Mar 44.

42-31572 Orig of 457BG. To 91BG 23 Jan 44 401BS 'MY BELOVED TOO'. MIA 21 Feb 44. 2nd Lt Irwin Piacentine.

42-31574 To 303BG 13 Jan 44 358BS-G 'OLE GEORGE'. Ass 31 Mar 44.

42-31575 To 381BG 20 Feb 44 'MIZPAH'. Ass 31 Mar 44.

42-31578 To 91BG 29 Dec 43 401BS 'LITTLE PATCHES'. MIA 6 Mar 44. 1st Lt Bob Tibbets Jr.

42-31579 To 91BG 1 Feb 44. Ass 31 Mar 44.

A formation of olive drab B-17Gs from the 457th Bomb Group taken soon after the Group's arrival in England. Nearest aircraft is 42-31587 with 42-31635 and 42-31613 in middle centre. All three were originals which had been assigned to the Group in the USA and all three were to be transferred to the 92nd Bomb Group on 11th March as part of the policy of equipping the 457th with all natural metal finish aircraft. *USAF*

42-31580 To 91BG 29 Jan 44 323BS. Ass 31 Mar 44.

42-31583 To 303BG 13 Jan 44 358BS 'CLOVER LEAF' and 'LITTLE PRINCESS'. Ass 31 Mar 44.

42-31585 To 91BG 1 Feb 44 323BS-B 'MOUNT 'N RIDE'. MIA 16 Mar 44. 1st Lt Doyle E Bradford. Ld in Switzerland. (6 Miss).

42-31587 Orig of 457BG. To 92BG 11 Mar 44. 325BS. Ass 31 Mar 44.

42-31588 Orig of 457BG. Severely dam on Groups first Miss 21 Feb 44. Lt Edward B Dozier. Sal on ret. (25 Feb 44).

42-31591 Orig of 457BG. To 401BG 11 Mar 44 613BS-J 'HOMESICK ANGEL'. Ass 31 Mar 44.

42-31592 Orig of 457BG. To 379BG 18 Mar 44. Ass but not on hand 31 Mar 44. (At Mildenhall).

42-31593 To 401BG 1 Feb 44 613BS-L. Ass 31 Mar 44.

42-31594 Orig of 457BG. Ass 31 Mar 44.

42-31595 Orig of 457BG. MIA 6 Mar 44. 2nd Lt Roy E Graves. Wreckage from 42-31627 fell on this Act causing its loss.

42-31596 Orig of 457BG. MIA 21 Feb 44. 2nd Lt Llewellyn G Bredeson. First 457BG Act MIA.

42-31597 To 379BG 31 Jan 44. Ass 31 Mar 44.

42-31602 To 305BG 22 Feb 44 364BS. MIA 23 Mar 44. Lt Edmund C Forrest.

42-31606 To 384BG 6 Jan 44 544BS-O. MIA 4 Mar 44. Lt Hollie R Lovvorn.

42-31607 Orig of 457BG. Ass 31 Mar 44.

42-31610 To 91BG 1 Feb 44 322BS 'LIBERTY BELL'. Ass 31 Mar 44.

42-31611 To 305BG 29 Jan 44. Ass 31 Mar 44. Group erroneously reported this Act MIA on 29 Mar 44 instead of 42-97466. This was corrected on 2 Apr 44.

42-31612 To 351BG 30 Jan 44 510BS-B. MIA 22 Feb 44. 2nd Lt William H Ritzema.

42-31613 Orig of 457BG. To 92BG 11 Mar 44 325BS. Ass 31 Mar 44.

42-31614 To 381BG 22 Jan 44 533BS-L 'MINNIE THE MERMAID'. Ass 31 Mar 44.

42-31615 Orig of 457BG. Ass 31 Mar 44.

42-31616 To 303BG 14 Jan 44 427BS 'THE SPIRIT OF FLAK WOLF'. Ass 31 Mar 44.

42-31618 Orig of 457BG. Ass but not on hand 31 Mar 44. (At Alconbury).

42-31619 To 401BG 31 Mar 44 615BS-L. Ass 31 Mar 44.

42-31620 Orig of 457BG. Ass 31 Mar 44.

42-31627 Orig of 457BG. MIA 6 Mar 44. 2nd Lt Eugene H Whelan.

42-31629 Orig of 457BG. Ass 31 Mar 44.

42-31630 Orig of 457BG. Ass 31 Mar 44.

42-31633 Orig of 457BG. Ass 31 Mar 44.

42-31634 To 91BG 23 Jan 44. Ass 31 Mar 44.

42-31635 Orig of 457BG. To 92BG 11 Mar 44 327BS-Y. Ass 31 Mar 44.

42-31636 Orig of 457BG. To 91BG 12 Mar 44 323BS-N 'OUTHOUSE MOUSE'. Ass 31 Mar 44.

42-31643 To 379BG 24 Jan 44 527BS. MIA 30 Jan 44. 1st Lt Donald E Winter.

42-31648 To 379BG 17 Feb 44. Ass 31 Mar 44.

42-31656 To 457BG 3 Feb 44. Ass 31 Mar 44.

42-31662 To 401BG 31 Jan 44 612BS-B 'FANCY NANCY IV'. Ass 31 Mar 44. Did 134 Miss by end of war.

42-31663 To 379BG 2 Feb 44 524BS-C. Ass 31 Mar 44.

42-31669 To 303BG 15 Feb 44 'SHOO SHOO BABY'. Ass 31 Mar 44.

42-31670 To 306BG 14 Jan 44 367BS. MIA 22 Feb 44. 1st Lt Fred J Rector.

42-31672 To 91BG 23 Jan 44 401BS. MIA 20 Mar 44. 1st Lt Frank D Turk.

42-31673 To 91BG 27 Jan 44 'LASSIE COME HOME'. Ass 31 Mar 44.

42-31678 To 91BG 27 Jan 44. Ass 31 Mar 44.

42-31680 To 92BG 7 Feb 44. MIA 6 Mar 44. 1st Lt Elmyran R Cooper.

42-31687 To 92BG 28 Jan 44 407BS-M. Ass 31 Mar 44.

42-31690 To 306BG (date in unknown) 'BELLE OF THE BRAWL'. Ass 31 Mar 44.

42-31692 To 379BG 24 Jan 44. MIA 30 Jan 44. 1st Lt Frank E Upson.

42-31694 To 351BG 30 Jan 44 511BS-V. Cr and burned at Southend on ret from Op Miss 11 Feb 44. 2nd Lt Frank W Turboyne. (13 Feb 44).

Another olive drab original of the 457th Bomb Group. 42-31618 landed back at Warboys following the Berlin mission of 9th March 1944. It spent much of the latter part of March 1944 at Alconbury and was not on hand at Glatton at the end of the month. *Bernard Baines*

42-31695 To 306BG 29 Jan 44. MIA 22 Feb 44. 1st Lt William C Quaintance.

42-31696 To 381BG 20 Feb 44 535BS. MIA 22 Feb 44. 2nd Lt Henry Hustedt.

42-31698 To 381BG 23 Feb 44. Ass 31 Mar 44.

42-31700 To 306BG 29 Jan 44. Cr Ld Thurleigh on ret from Op Miss 26 Mar 44. (27 Mar 44).

42-31702 To 351BG 30 Jan 44 508BS-A. Ass but not on hand 31 Mar 44. (At Boxted for rep).

42-31706 To 457BG 14 Feb 44 'SLOW BUT SURE'. Ass 31 Mar 44.

42-31711 To 351BG 30 Jan 44 508BS-F. Ass 31 Mar 44.

42-31713 To 92BG 11 Feb 44 327BS-T. Ass 31 Mar 44.

42-31714 To 351BG 29 Jan 44 511BS-R. To 510BS-R 'SKYBALL'. Ass 31 Mar 44.

42-31715 To 306BG 29 Jan 44. Cr on TO at Drem 4 Feb 44. A three engine TO was made on a short grass runway. Hit house and burned, dest, 6 kld. Lt Michael Roskovitch who had been the first enlisted man in the 8AF to complete a 25 Miss tour was kld on this Act. (5 Feb 44).

42-31720 To 379BG 27 Jan 44 524BS-H. Ass 31 Mar 44.

42-31721 To 351BG 20 Jan 44 510BS-S 'BLACK MAGIC'. Ass 31 Mar 44.

42-31725 To 351BG 30 Jan 44 509BS-L 'CASA DE EMBRIAGOS'. Ass 31 Mar 44.

42-31726 To 306BG (date in unknown). Ass 31 Mar 44.

42-31730 To 401BG 31 Jan 44 615BS-B. To 613BS-O 'MORNING STAR'. Ass 31 Mar 44.

42-31737 To 306BG 27 Feb 44. Ass 31 Mar 44.

42-31739 To 303BG 15 Feb 44 358BS-P 'PUGNACIOUS PETER'. Ass 31 Mar 44.

42-31740 To 384BG 1 Mar 44 546BS-T. Ass 31 Mar 44.

42-31748 To 351BG 19 Feb 44 511BS-V. Ass 31 Mar 44.

42-31754 To 303BG 28 Feb 44 427BS-L. Ass 31 Mar 44.

42-31756 To 303BG 1 Mar 44 360BS-M. Flew a local transition flight on 12 Mar 44. After Ld at Molesworth and on turning to the left off the rwy, the LG coll. No inj to crew. 2nd Lt David F Hicks. (13 Mar 44).

42-31757 To 351BG 25 Feb 44 508BS-G. Ass 31 Mar 44.

42-31758 To 306BG 3 Mar 44. Ass 31 Mar 44.

42-31761 To 381BG 31 Jan 44 533BS-O 'ROTHERHITHES REVENGE'. Ass 31 Mar 44.

Four missions, including two to Berlin, was 42-31756's contribution to the war effort during its 11 day assignment to the 303rd Bomb Group. It had a different crew for each of the four missions. It is shown here after the landing gear collapsed when it was turning off the runway following a transition flight on 12th March 1944. *US Air Force*

42-31763 To 351BG 30 Jan 44 510BS-A 'TEN HORSEPOWER'. Cr near Glatton 20 Feb 44 on ret from Op Miss. Lt Walter Truemper and Sgt Archie Mathies awarded Medals of Honour for their actions in this Act this day. 2nd Lt Clarence R Nelson. (21 Feb 44).

42-31765 To 92BG 2 Mar 44 407BS-L. Ass 31 Mar 44.

42-31768 To 306BG (date in unknown). Out at Abbots Ripton 4–24 Mar 44. Ass 31 Mar 44.

42-31771 To 92BG 2 Mar 44 327BS-R. Ass 31 Mar 44.

42-31772 To 92BG 11 Feb 44 407BS. MIA 9 Mar 44. 2nd Lt Walter E Payne.

42-31776 To 351BG 25 Feb 44 508BS-H 'MAGGIES DRAWERS'. MIA 2 Mar 44. 1st Lt Robert A Seaman.

42-31779 To 379BG 6 Feb 44 524BS-J. Ass 31 Mar 44.

42-31783 To 92BG 5 Feb 44 407BS-T. Ass 31 Mar 44.

42-31794 To 305BG 22 Feb 44 365BS 'BETSY'. Ass 31 Mar 44.

42-31799 To 379BG 7 Feb 44 527BS. MIA 2 Mar 44. 2nd Lt Glen R Hufnail.

42-31801 To 482BG (H2X) 10 Feb 44. To 305BG 422BS-R 20 Mar 44. Ass 31 Mar 44.

42-31812 To 91BG 20 Feb 44 401BS 'DESTINY'S CHILD'. Ass 31 Mar 44.

42-31816 To 305BG 15 Feb 44. Ass 31 Mar 44.

42-31820 To 305BG 22 Feb 44 364BS. MIA 25 Feb 44. Lt Foster Perry.

42-31828 To 92BG 2 Mar 44 407BS-Q. Ass 31 Mar 44.

42-31830 To 303BG 20 Feb 44 359BS-N 'MARIE'. Ass 31 Mar 44.

42-31860 To 92BG 5 Feb 44. MIA 21 Feb 44. 2nd Lt Ralph K Skoubo.

42-31863 To 401BG 6 Feb 44 614BS-X 'MISS B HAVEN'. Ass 31 Mar 44.

42-31869 To 91BG 25 Feb 44 401BS 'HELL AND HIGHWATER'. MIA 6 Mar 44. 1st Lt Clyde V Mason.

42-31871 To 384BG 21 Feb 44 547BS-T. MIA 18 Mar 44. Lt William Laseur. Ld in Switzerland.

42-31875 To 351BG 25 Feb 44 511BS-P. Ass 31 Mar 44.

42-31878 To 381BG 20 Feb 44 'SPAM CAN'. Ass 31 Mar 44.

42-31879 To 351BG 22 Feb 44 508BS-Q 'THE SHARK'. Ass 31 Mar 44.

42-31882 To 351BG 17 Feb 44 511BS-F. Abandoned over England on ret from Op Miss 22 Feb 44. Cr in sea off Cromer. 1st Lt George W Mears. (This Act was not classed as MIA).

42-31883 To 91BG 22 Mar 44 324BS-Y 'JUB JUB BIRD'. Ass 31 Mar 44.

42-31888 To 92BG 19 Feb 44 326BS. MIA 23 Mar 44. 2nd Lt Edward R Larrivee.

42-31891 To 401BG 18 Feb 44 612BS-P. Ass 31 Mar 44.

42-31894 To 306BG 27 Feb 44. Cr Ld at Thurleigh 26 Mar 44. (27 Mar 44).

42-31897 To 306BG 25 Feb 44. Ass 31 Mar 44.

42-31898 To 92BG 2 Mar 44 326BS-A. Ass 31 Mar 44.

42-31899 To 351BG 29 Feb 44 510BS-B 'CHATTERBOX'. Ass 31 Mar 44.

42-31901 To 306BG 25 Feb 44. Ass 31 Mar 44.

42-31907 To 92BG 19 Feb 44 326BS-J. Ass 31 Mar 44.

42-31909 To 91BG 24 Feb 44 323BS-R 'NINE O NINE'. Ass 31 Mar 44. Went on to complete 140 Miss by end of war. Most for any B-17 in 8AF.

42-31911 To 91BG 24 Feb 44 323BS. MIA 6 Mar 44. 1st Lt Douglas Harding. (4 Miss).

42-31914 To 92BG 11 Feb 44 326BS-S. Ass 31 Mar 44.

42-31915 To 379BG 6 Feb 44. Ass 31 Mar 44.

42-31921 To 92BG 5 Feb 44 407BS. Ass 31 Mar 44.

42-31923 To 457BG 23 Mar 44 'PROP WASH'. Ass 31 Mar 44.

42-31926 To 384BG 19 Feb 44 545BS-G 'LOVELLS' HOVEL'. MIA 19 Mar 44. Lt James M Lovell.

42-31927 To 379BG 8 Feb 44. Ass but not on hand 31 Mar 44. (At Lympne).

42-31929 To 303BG 1 Mar 44 427BS. MIA 26 Mar 44. 2nd Lt Mars.

42-31930 To 401BG 7 Feb 44 613BS-M. MIA 22 Feb 44. 2nd Lt Roy M Shanks.

NATURAL METAL FINISH AIRCRAFT

42-31955 To 351BG 29 Feb 44 508BS-K. Ass 31 Mar 44.

42-31966 To 351BG 29 Feb 44 511BS-X. MIA 18 Mar 44. 2nd Lt Paul Martin.

42-31969 To 306BG 22 Feb 44. Ass but not on hand 31 Mar 44. (At Woodbridge).

42-31972 To 379BG 22 Feb 44. Ass 31 Mar 44.

42-31975 To 351BG 22 Feb 44 510BS-O 'QUEEN OF THE AIR'. Ass 31 Mar 44.

42-31978 To 92BG 2 Mar 44 325BS-Q. Ass 31 Mar 44.

42-31979 To 306BG 22 Feb 44. MIA 25 Feb 44. 1st Lt Charles M Bayless. First NMF Act MIA in First BD.

42-31982 To 91BG 24 Feb 44 322BS 'SUPERSTITIOUS ALOUITIOUS'. Ass 31 Mar 44.

42-31983 To 401BG 7 Mar 44 613BS-G 'MARY ALICE'. Ass 31 Mar 44.

42-31984 To 92BG 2 Mar 44 407BS-U. Ass 31 Mar 44.

42-31988 To 351BG 30 Mar 44. Ass 31 Mar 44.

42-31995 To 92BG 23 Mar 44 327BS-M. Ass 31 Mar 44.

42-31997 To 303BG 27 Feb 44 360BS. Ld East Church 2 Mar 44. Ass but not on hand 31 Mar 44. (At East Church).

42-32000 To 379BG 21 Mar 44 524BS. Ass 31 Mar 44.

42-32005 To 401BG 6 Mar 44 613BS-M. Ass 31 Mar 44.

42-32007 To 384BG 1 Mar 44. MIA 4 Mar 44. 1st Lt George Cosentino.

42-32012 To 401BG 5 Mar 44 614BS-P. Ass 31 Mar 44.

42-32024 To 379BG 20 Feb 44 524BS-L. Ass 31 Mar 44.

42-32025 To 381BG 25 Feb 44 533BS-P 'DREAM BABY'. Ass 31 Mar 44.

42-32027 To 303BG 1 Mar 44 427BS-E 'BETTY JANE'. Ass 31 Mar 44.

42-32034 From Stansted to 92BG 20 Feb 44. MIA 24 Feb 44. 2nd Lt John W Rapp Jr.

One of the silver aircraft which was re-assigned to the 457th Bomb Group in early March 1944 and then when plans changed was found to be surplus was 42-32113. It came from Great Ashfield on the 3rd and went to the 306th on the 12th. *Gordon Richards*

42-32037 To 303BG 28 Feb 44. Ass 31 Mar 44.

42-32051 To 457BG 27 Feb 44 **'LADY LUCK'**. Ass 31 Mar 44.

42-32072 To 91BG 31 Mar 44 401BS **'MARY'**. Ass 31 Mar 44.

42-32076 To 91BG 23 Mar 44 401BS-E **'SHOO SHOO SHOO BABY'**. Ass 31 Mar 44.

42-32079 To 457BG 9 Mar 44 **'DELAYED LADY II'**. Ass 31 Mar 44.

42-32084 To 457BG 3 Mar 44 **'L'IL SATIN'**. Ass 31 Mar 44.

42-32086 To 401BG 3 Mar 44. To 457BG 5 Mar 44 **'YOU NEVER KNOW'**. Ass 31 Mar 44.

42-32091 To 379BG 30 Mar 44. Ass 31 Mar 44.

42-32095 To 457BG 14 Mar 44. To 91BG 16 Mar 44 322BS-L. Ass 31 Mar 44.

42-32098 To 457BG 4 Mar 44 **'GI VIRGIN II'**. Ass 31 Mar 44.

42-32099 From Framlingham to 457BG 4 Mar 44. To 306BG 12 Mar 44. Ass 31 Mar 44.

42-32101 To 457BG 6 Mar 44 **'EL LOBO'**. Ass 31 Mar 44.

42-32102 To 381BG 25 Mar 44 535BS-O **'JULIE LINDA'**. Ass 31 Mar 44.

42-32106 To 384BG 24 Mar 44 545BS-R **'SNUFFY'**. Ass 31 Mar 44. Over 100 Miss by end of war.

42-32113 From Great Ashfield to 457BG 3 Mar 44. To 306BG 12 Mar 44. Ass 31 Mar 44.

42-32116 From Deopham Green to 457BG 11 Mar 44. To 91BG 16 Mar 44. Ass 31 Mar 44.

B-17G DOUGLAS

42-37714 Orig of 401BG. To 351BG 18 Nov 43 510BS-T **'RONCHI'**. Ass 31 Mar 44.

42-37717 To 305BG 20 Dec 44. Ass 31 Mar 44.

42-37718 To 306BG 19 Sep 43 368BS. MIA 9 Oct 43. Lt Roy C Ranck Jr. First 306BG B-17G MIA.

42-37719 To 381BG 1 Oct 43 535BS **'DINAH MIGHT'**. MIA 11 Jan 44. 2nd Lt Donald E Nason.

42-37720 To 306BG 18 Sep 43 367BS. MIA 14 Oct 43. 1st Lt Douglas H White.

42-37721 To 381BG 1 Oct 43 534BS-L **'SUGAR'**. Ass 31 Mar 44.

42-37722 To 401BG 21 Jan 44. Caught fire on Ld at Deenethorpe 28 Jan 44. On non Op Flight. (30 Jan 44).

42-37724 To 306BG 20 Sep 43. Ass 31 Mar 44.

42-37725 To 384BG 19 Dec 43 546BS. MIA 31 Dec 43. 2nd Lt John Rich Jr. Abandoned by crew over Sussex on ret from Op Miss. Crew safe. Act cr in sea. The loss of this Act caused some confusion on its Gps records. First reported MIA on 31 Dec 43. Then, on 3 Jan 44 it was gained from MIA and reported as on hand with 2SAD. Finally on 5 Jan 44 it was ret from 2SAD and placed as MIA 31 Dec 43.

42-37726 To 305BG 1 Oct 43 366BS-N. Ass 31 Mar 44.

42-37727 To 303BG 18 Oct 43. To BAD for mod 23 Oct 43. Then to 384BG 2 Nov 43 545BS-Z. MIA 31 Jan 44. 1st Lt Comus R Penney.

42-37728 To 379BG 3 Oct 43 525BS. MIA 9 Oct 43. 2nd Lt James K Lash. First 379BG B-17G MIA.

42-37730 To 381BG 20 Sep 43 533BS-A. MIA 11 Jan 44. 1st Lt Gordon W Crozier.

42-37731 To 351BG 22 Sep 43 510BS-A. MIA 31 Dec 43. Maj John R Blaylock. Was lead Act this day. Col Hatcher CO of 351BG was on board.

42-37732 To 379BG 19 Oct 43 526BS. MIA 25 Feb 44. 1st Lt Joseph S Bochne.

42-37733 To 482BG 3 Nov 43 813BS (SO). To 9AF Stansted 9 Feb 44. Then to 381BG 22 Feb 44 535BS-M **'PATCHES AND PRAYERS'**. Ass 31 Mar 44.

Four new B-17Gs; all equipped to drop Glide Bombs were assigned to the 379th Bomb Group on 21st October 1943. By early March 1944, the sole survivor of the four was 42-37764. The mission to Berlin on the 6th was its last. Badly damaged in the left wing root, it is shown here after arrival back at Kimbolton where it was salvaged. *Roger Freeman*

42-37735 To 482BG 23 Oct 43 813BS-X (SO). To 9AF Stansted 5 Feb 44. Then to 92BG 20 Feb 44 326BS. Ass 31 Mar 44.

42-37736 To 91BG 24 Sep 43 324BS-G. Ass 31 Mar 44.

42-37737 To 91BG 26 Sep 43 401BS-K. MIA 10 Oct 43. 2nd Lt Earl R Verrill. First 91BG B-17G MIA.

42-37738 To 91BG 24 Sep 43 322BS-T. MIA 22 Dec 43. 2nd Lt Edward H Steel Jr.

42-37740 To 305BG 15 Sep 43 365BS-E. MIA 14 Oct 43. Lt Raymond P Bullock.

42-37741 To 305BG 18 Sep 43. MIA 4 Oct 43. First B-17G MIA in 1BD.

42-37742 To 91BG 22 Sep 43 401BS-J. MIA 3 Nov 43. 2nd Lt William B McAdams.

42-37745 To 482BG 2 Oct 43 812BS-M (H2X). Ass 14 Feb 44.

42-37746 Orig of 401BG. To 91BG 20 Nov 43 323BS 'PAPER DOLLY'. MIA 22 Feb 44. 1st Lt Frank R Kolts. 18 Miss.

42-37750 To 305BG 18 Sep 43 366BS-M. MIA 14 Oct 43. 2nd Lt Robert S Lang.

42-37751 To 305BG 16 Sep 43 365BS-P. MIA 8 Oct 43. Lt Wallace E Emmert.

42-37753 To 482BG 20 Oct 43 813BS-O (SO). To 9AF Stansted 5 Feb 44. Then to 92BG 21 Feb 44 326BS. Ass 31 Mar 44.

42-37754 To 381BG 20 Sep 43. Badly dam on Op Miss 28 Mar 44. Abandoned by crew over England on ret. Act headed out to sea. 1st Lt Daniel C Henry.

42-37755 To 92BG 15 Sep 43 325BS-A. MIA 25 Feb 44. 2nd Lt Clifford P Beach. Belly Ld in Switzerland.

42-37757 To 303BG 18 Oct 43 360BS-N. Flew Op Miss on 1 Dec 43 Piloted by Lt W C Osborn and ret to Molesworth. Reported to Lt Stn for rep, 9 Dec 43. Dropped from 303BG 11 Dec 43. Sal 13 Dec 43. Reason for sal unknown, but possibly cr Ld at Lt Stn.

42-37758 To 384BG 3 Oct 43 545BS-W 'KENTUCKY KERNEL'. Ass 31 Mar 44.

42-37759 To 306BG 19 Sep 43. Cr Ld at Thurleigh on ret from Op Miss 9 Oct 43. Hit 42-30730. 730 was rep but 759 was sal. Was first B-17G to be sal in 1BD.

42-37760 To 381BG 20 Sep 43. Ass 31 Mar 44.

42-37761 To 91BG 4 Oct 43 323BS-L 'BLUE DREAMS'. Made wheels up Ld on Steeple Morden afd 6 Mar 44, soon after TO for Op Miss. 2nd Lt Walter E Wilkinson. 29 Miss. (8 Mar 44).

42-37762 To 303BG 22 Oct 43. To BAD for Mod 30 Oct 43. Then to 384BG 2 Nov 43 545BS. MIA 26 Nov 43. 2nd Lt Charles A Zitnik.

42-37764 To 379BG 21 Oct 43. Dam beyond rep on Op Miss 6 Mar 44. (8 Mar 44).

42-37765 To 306BG 14 Dec 43. Ass 31 Mar 44.

42-37767 To 91BG 8 Nov 43 401BS-D. Made wheels up Ld on Cambridge Airport on ret from Op Miss 20 Dec 43. 2nd Lt Howard F Weber. (21 Dec 43).

42-37768 To 379BG 19 Oct 43 527BS. MIA 11 Jan 44. 2nd Lt F A Waggoner Jr.

42-37770 Orig of 401BG 614BS-A 'FLAK RAT'. MIA 31 Dec 43. 2nd Lt Homer R McDanal.

42-37771 To 305BG 18 Oct 43 366BS-M. Ass 31 Mar 44.

42-37774 Orig of 401BG. To 351BG 21 Nov 43 508BS-N. Cr Whitwell on ret from Op Miss 31 Dec 43. 1st Lt Edward B Apperson. All baled out safely. (1 Jan 44).

42-37776 To 303BG 18 Oct 43. To BAD for mod 23 Oct 43. Then to 384BG 2 Nov 43 546BS-R 'LADY DREW'. Ass 31 Mar 44.

42-37778 To 305BG 30 Nov 43. Ass 31 Mar 44.

42-37779 Orig of 401BG. To 91BG 20 Nov 43 'PIST'L PACKIN MAMA'. Ass 31 Mar 44.

42-37780 Orig of 401BG. To 351BG 18 Nov 43 511BS-G. Ass 31 Mar 44.

42-37781 To 303BG 19 Oct 43. To BAD for mod 23 Oct 43. Then to 384BG 2 Nov 43 546BS-U 'SILVER DOLLAR'. MIA 9 Mar 44. Lt Merlin H Reed.

The 303rd Bomb Group's losses were not as heavy as some of the other groups during the great air battles of October 1943. The Group did however, receive the majority of the replacements which came in on 18th and 19th October. Many of these were sent to BAD a few days later and were then re-assigned to other groups. Many were GB aircraft (equipped for Glide Bombing). Shown here is 42-37781 which was assigned to the 303rd for four days, and then was one of 17 B-17Gs assigned to the 384th Bomb Group on 2nd November. It was named 'SILVER DOLLAR' and survived till 9th March 1944. *Mike Gibson*

42-37784 To 379BG 19 Oct 43. Ass 31 Mar 44.

42-37785 To 303BG 18 Oct 43. To BAD for mod 23 Oct 43. Then to 384BG 2 Nov 43 544BS-N 'LITTLE BARNEY'. Ass 31 Mar 44.

42-37786 Orig of 401BG. To 381BG 21 Nov 43 532BS MIA 25 Feb 43. 2nd Lt Donald G Henderson.

42-37787 To 303BG 19 Oct 43. To BAD for mod 23 Oct 43. Then to 384BG 2 Nov 43 544BS. To 379BG 11 Nov 43 526BS-C. MIA 26 Nov 43. 2nd Lt Samuel H Bender.

42-37788 To 384BG 7 Nov 43 544BS. To 547BS-N **'HELLS MESSENGER'**. Ass 31 Mar 44.

42-37789 To 303BG 18 Oct 43. To BAD for mod 23 Oct 43. Then to 384BG 2 Nov 43 544BS-H. Ass 31 Mar 44.

42-37791 To 303BG 19 Oct 43. To BAD 23 Oct 43. Then to 384BG 2 Nov 43 546BS. To 379BG 7 Nov 43. Ass 31 Mar 44.

42-37792 To 384BG 2 Nov 43 545BS-B **'BERMONDSEY'**. Ass 31 Mar 44.

42-37793 To 305BG 23 Nov 43. To 384BG 2 Dec 43 547BS-X **'WINSOME WINN II'**. Ld at Brighton on ret from Op Miss 8 Feb 44. 2nd Lt Norman DeFrees. Ret to Gp 11 Mar 44. MIA 18 Mar 44. Lt Roger E Smith. Ld in Switzerland.

42-37799 To 92BG 21 Oct 43 326BS. Overshot rwy at Podington and nosed over 15 Feb 44. On non Op flight. (17 Feb 44).

42-37081 To 384BG 25 Nov 43 547BS-G **'DYNAMITE EXPRESS'**. MIA 16 Mar 44. 2nd Lt Edwin D Ledbetter.

42-37805 To 379BG 2 Dec 43 **'CAROL DAWN'**. Ass 31 Mar 44.

42-37809 Orig of 401BG 615BS-G **'CAROLINA QUEEN'**. MIA 11 Jan 44. 1st Lt Harold J Chapman.

42-37816 To 384BG 18 Oct 43 545BS-S **'BIG STUPE'**. Ass 31 Mar 44.

42-37817 To 351BG 24 Oct 43 510BS-A **'ARISTOCRAP'**. MIA 26 Nov 43. 2nd Lt Orville L Castle. First 351BG B-17G MIA.

42-37825 To 379BG 19 Oct 43. To 351BG 21 Oct 43 511BS-Q **'SUPERBALL'**. MIA 18 Mar 44. 1st Lt George W Mears. Ld at Dubendorf, Switzerland.

42-37827 To 351BG 27 Oct 43 508BS-J. Ass 31 Mar 44.

42-37828 To 384BG 18 Oct 43 544BS. A truck ran into the tail of this Act at Grafton Underwood on 29 Nov 43. It was trans to MRU on 1 Dec 43 as "Ass but not on hand". It was ret to "on hand" on 4 Dec. On 3 Jan 44 it was turned over to 2SAD for sal. It is not known if this sal was due to the truck incident in Nov 43 or if the dam caused by this incident was rep and the sal was due to another cause.

42-37832 To 351BG 24 Oct 43 509BS-B. MIA 18 Mar 44. 1st Lt Walter R Illies.

42-37833 Orig of 401BG 615BS-F **'OMAR THE DENT MAKER'**. MIA 26 Mar 44. Capt William M Rumsey.

42-37835 Orig of 401BG 612BS-J **'CHANNEL EXPRESS'**. Crew baled out on ret from Op Miss 22 Dec 43. Cr at Washingley. Lt Stuart E Smith.

42-37836 To 306BG 31 Dec 43. Ld at Leiston on ret from Op Miss 22 Mar 44. Overshot. Ass but not on hand 31 Mar 44. (At Leiston).

42-37838 Orig of 401BG 612BS-F **'FANCY NANCY'**. When on Gps first Miss 26 Nov 43 it coll with B-17 of 388BG. Ld at Detling and sal. 1st Lt Scribner Dailey. First 401BG B-17 sal in UK. (9 Dec 43).

42-37840 To 457BG 20 Feb 44. To 306BG 12 Mar 44. Ass 31 Mar 44.

42-37841 To 303BG 18 Nov 43 360BS-P **'BANSHEE'**. Ass 31 Mar 44.

42-37843 Orig of 401BG 615BS-H **'DRY RUN'**. Ass 31 Mar 43.

42-37845 To 351BG 25 Nov 43 509BS-F **'WILDFIRE'**. Ass 31 Mar 44.

42-37847 To 351BG 24 Oct 43 511BS-R. MIA 1 Dec 43. Lt James J Plant.

42-37848 To 384BG 18 Oct 43 546BS-E **'SISSY'**. MIA 16 Mar 44. Lt George W Stier.

42-37851 To 379BG 13 Mar 43 527BS. MIA 20 Dec 43. 2nd Lt Walter H Reichold.

42-37856 To 401BG 23 Dec 43 612BS-B **'FANCY NANCY III'**. MIA 30 Jan 44. 2nd Lt Ronald R Rohner.

42-37870 To 305BG 23 Nov 43 364BS-F **'PALMA II'**. Ass 31 Mar 44.

42-37875 To 303BG 18 Nov 43 427BS-A **'FLYING BISON'** also **'EMPRESS OF D STREET'**. Ass 31 Mar 44.

42-37877 To 92BG 20 Jan 44 325BS-K. Ass 31 Mar 44.

42-37881 To 305BG 23 Nov 43. Ass 31 Mar 44.

42-37884 To 381BG 20 Dec 43. MIA 29 Jan 44. 1st Lt Laurence W Mickow.

42-37885 To 384BG 22 Nov 43 544BS-L. To 545BS-D. Ass 31 Mar 44.

42-37887 To 379BG 22 Nov 43 527BS-S. In mid air coll with 42-31441 of 303BG while forming for Op Miss on 5 Jan 44. Cr at Covington and dest. F/O Wayne P Maresh. 7 kld.

42-37888 To 379BG 6 Dec 43 527BS-J. Ass but not on hand 31 Mar 44. (At 2SAD).

42-37893 To 303BG 18 Nov 43 538BS-O. Ass 31 Mar 44.

42-37896 To 303BG 27 Dec 43 360BS. MIA 11 Jan 44. 2nd Lt Robert H Haliden.

42-37911 To 91BG 10 Jan 44 **'HEATS ON'**. Ass 31 Mar 44.

42-37924 To 384BG 2 Dec 43 547BS. Cr Ld at Lt Stn when right main LG would not lower 9 Jan 44. Was on training flight from Grafton Underwood. 2nd Lt Norman F DeFrees. No injs. (16 Jan 44).

42-37927 To 303BG 18 Nov 43 358BS. MIA 3 Feb 44. Capt Gerald A White.

42-37928 To 92BG 1 Dec 43 407BS. Out of Gp to sal, 6 Jan 44. Reason unknown but probably due to battle dam on one of the late Dec 43 or early Jan 44 Op Miss's.

42-37930 To 305BG 3 Dec 43. MIA 20 Dec 43. Lt Howard D Hunter.

42-37931 To 305BG 5 Jan 44 422BS-D. Ass 31 Mar 44.

42-37933 To 381BG 20 Dec 43. Dam on Op Miss 28 Mar 44. Crew baled out over England on ret. Lt J R Liddle. Act cr in Kent, location not known.

42-37934 To 92BG 30 Nov 43 325BS-E. Ass 31 Mar 44.

42-37938 To 91BG 30 Mar 44. Ass 31 Mar 44.

42-37939 To 91BG 20 Dec 43 323BS **'SUGAR BLUES'**. MIA 22 Feb 44. 1st Lt Roman V Maziara. 15 Miss. Ditched, all crew rescued.

42-37940 To 91BG 13 Dec 43 322BS **'THE SPIRIT OF 44'**. Badly dam on Op Miss 11 Jan 44. Ld at Deopham Green on ret and sal. (13 Jan 44).

42-37942 To 306BG 19 Dec 43. Ass but not on hand 31 Mar 44. (At Beccles).

42-37943 To 306BG 12 Dec 43. Ass 31 Mar 44.

42-37944 To 305BG 12 Dec 43. Ass 31 Mar 44.

42-37945 To 305BG 21 Dec 43. Ass 31 Mar 44.

42-37953 To 306BG 27 Dec 43. MIA 29 Mar 44. 1st Lt Alvin G Schuering.

42-37957 To 305BG 12 Dec 43 366BS. MIA 22 Mar 44. 1st Lt Eldred F Whipple.

42-37958 To 91BG 20 Dec 43 401BS **'OLD FAITHFULL'**. Ass 31 Mar 44.

42-37961 To 92BG 30 Dec 43 327BS. Cr Ld at Lt Stn 23 Jan 44 when LG would not lower. Was on ferry flight. 2nd Lt James B Robinson. No inj to crew. (25 Jan 44).

42-37961 of 92nd Bomb Group crash landed at Little Staughton, 23rd January 1944, when the landing gear would not lower during a ferry flight. *US Air Force*

42-37962 To 381BG 20 Dec 43 532BS. MIA 11 Jan 44. 2nd Lt Robert V Saur.

42-37965 To 91BG 20 Dec 43 323BS **'MY DESIRE'**. MIA 3 Mar 44. 2nd Lt Walter M Pickard. 11 Miss.

42-37969 To 381BG 23 Dec 43 532BS-LO **'OLD IRON GUT'**. At 2SAD for prolonged maintenance 12 Jan 44 to 15 Mar 44. Not Ass to Gp between these dates. Ass 31 Mar 44.

42-37974 To 384BG 21 Jan 44 545BS-O to 544BS-M **'SECTION 8'**. Ass 31 Mar 44.

42-37976 To 92BG 8 Jan 44 407BS-Y. Ass 31 Mar 44.

42-37978 To 305BG 5 Jan 44 422BS-C. Ass 31 Mar 44.

42-37979 To 305BG 5 Jan 44. Ass 31 Mar 44.

42-37982 To 384BG 21 Jan 44 544BS-K **'TREMBLIN GREMLIN'**. Ass 31 Mar 44.

42-37983 To 381BG 22 Jan 44. Ld in sea just off Foreness Point on ret from Op Miss 6 Mar 44. Lt R T Cahill. (Not listed as MIA).

42-37984 To 92BG 6 Jan 44 326BS. MIA 8 Feb 44. 1st Lt Milton V Shevchik.

42-37986 To 381BG 15 Jan 44. MIA 3 Mar 44. 2nd Lt Robert H Rogers.

42-37987 To 91BG 21 Jan 44 322BS **'MAN O'WAR'**. Cr Ld at Bredgar on ret from Op Miss 29 Jan 44. 2nd Lt William S Burtt. (30 Jan 44).

42-37999 To 482BG 6 Dec 43. To 305BG 10 Dec 43. 422BS-E. Sal 6 Mar 44. Reason unknown.

42-38002 To 401BG 21 Jan 44 614BS-Q. MIA 22 Feb 44. 2nd Lt Vernon A Arneson.

42-38004 To 381BG 6 Jan 44. Ass 31 Mar 44.

42-38005 To 351BG 4 Jan 44 509BS-G **'STORMY WEATHER'**. Ass 31 Mar 44.

42-38006 To 91BG 8 Jan 44 324BS **'HOOSIER HOT SHOT'**. Ass 31 Mar 44.

42-38008 To 306BG 21 Jan 44. Went to 2SAD on 4 Mar 44 did not ret to Gp till after 31 Mar 44. Was not Ass during this period.

42-38009 To 381BG 6 Jan 44. Ass but not on hand 31 Mar 44. (At Exeter for rep).

42-38010 To 381BG 13 Jan 44. Ass 31 Mar 44.

42-38012 To 401BG 21 Jan 44 615BS-M. MIA 29 Jan 44. 2nd Lt Leon G Van Syckle.

42-38013 To 384BG 20 Jan 44 547BS-C **'NEVADA AVENGER'**. Ass 31 Mar 44.

42-38014 To 384BG 6 Jan 44 546BS-G. Ass 31 Mar 44.

42-38019 To 306BG 21 Jan 44. Ass 31 Mar 44.

42-38020 To 303BG 20 Jan 44 427BS **'V PACKET'**. Ass 31 Mar 44.

42-38021 Orig of 457BG **'MISSION MAID'**. Ass 31 Mar 44.

42-38023 To 351BG 1 Jan 44 508BS-H. Cr Ld at Framlingham 22 Feb 44 on ret from Op Miss. 2nd Lt Dester E Watson. (24 Feb 44).

42-38025 To 92BG 4 Jan 44 327BS-Q. Ass 31 Mar 44.

42-38026 To 401BG 2 Feb 44 612BS-N **'MY DAY'**. Ass 31 Mar 44.

42-38026 of 401st Bomb Group ran off the runway, 11th February 1944. Only minor damage resulted and it was soon repaired and back in service. *Vic Maslen*

Another victim of landing gear failure. 379th's 42-38036 ended up like this after landing from a practice flight, 2nd February 1944. *US Air Force*

42-38027 To 91BG 10 Jan 44 322BS 'HEAVENLY BODY'. Ass 31 Mar 44.

42-38028 To 351BG 1 Jan 44 510BS-Q 'PAPPYS PRIDE'. Ass 31 Mar 44.

42-38029 To 381BG from Stansted 1 Mar 44. MIA 8 Mar 44. 2nd Lt Thomas A Pintle.

42-38032 To 351BG 14 Jan 44 509BS-X. MIA 18 Mar 44. 1st Lt Raymond E Neuberg.

42-38033 To 401BG 6 Jan 44 612BS-M. MIA 20 Mar 44. 2nd Lt John A Dunaway.

42-38036 To 379BG 21 Jan 44 525BS-T. LG collapsed when ret to Kimbolton after practice formation flight 2 Feb 44. Capt Lester A Gibson. No inj to crew. (4 Feb 44).

42-38037 To 305BG 22 Jan 44 364BS-T later 422BS-M 'LIBERTY RUN'. Ass 31 Mar 44.

42-38038 To 351BG 14 Jan 44 510BS-R later 'P' 'APRIL GIRL II'. Ass 31 Mar 44.

42-38041 To 303 BG 18 Jan 44 'HELLS ANGELS II'. Cr Irthlingborough 22 Feb 44 after mid air coll with 42-31516 of 384BG while forming for Op Miss. Lt Stourner. (24 Feb 44).

42-38042 To 306BG 9 Jan 44. Ass 31 Mar 44.

42-38045 To 381BG 22 Jan 44. MIA 29 Jan 44. 2nd Lt Robert W Monnacky.

42-38050 To 303BG 18 Jan 44 359BS-U 'THUNDERBIRD'. Ass 31 Mar 44.

42-38051 To 303BG 13 Jan 44 427BS 'MY YORKSHIRE DREAM'. Ass 31 Mar 44.

42-38055 Orig of 457BG. Ass 31 Mar 44.

42-38057 Orig of 457BG. To 379BG 18 Mar 44. Ass 31 Mar 44.

42-38058 Orig of 457BG. To 379BG 18 Mar 44. Ass 31 Mar 44.

42-38060 Orig of 457BG. MIA 24 Feb 44. 2nd Lt Max R Morrow.

42-38061 To 381BG 2 Feb 44 535BS-P 'GEORGIA REBEL II'. Ass 31 Mar 44.

42-38063 Orig of 457BG 'THE GI VIRGIN'. Ass 31 Mar 44.

42-38064 Orig of 457BG 'HALF N' HALF'. Ass 31 Mar 44.

42-38073 Orig of 457BG 'LUCK OF JUDY ANN'. Ass 31 Mar 44.

42-38074 To 306BG 23 Jan 44. MIA 24 Feb 44. 2nd Lt Loren E Page.

42-38079 To 381BG from Stansted 20 Feb 44. Ass but not on hand 31 Mar 44. (At Leiston for rep).

42-38082 To 379BG 29 Jan 44. Ass but not on hand 31 Mar 44. (At Gatwick).

42-38083 To 91BG 1 Feb 44 322BS-V 'MAN O' WAR'. Ass 31 Mar 44.

42-38093 To 306BG 28 Feb 44. Ass 31 Mar 44.

42-38098 To 305BG 22 Feb 44. Ass 31 Mar 44.

42-38101 To 92BG 20 Feb 44 327BS-O. Ass 31 Mar 44.

42-38102 Orig of 457BG. To 381BG 12 Mar 44 532BS. Cr 24 Mar 44 soon after TO from Ridgewell on an Op Miss. Came down at Bailey Hill Farm, Birdbrook, exploded and burned. Crew of 10 kld. 2nd Lt Kenneth T Haynes Jr.

42-38103 Orig of 457BG. To 381BG 12 Mar 44. Ass 31 Mar 44.

42-38104 Orig of 457BG to 92BG 11 Mar 44. MIA 23 Mar 44. 1st Lt Douglas Macdonald.

42-38106 To 305BG 16 Feb 44 366BS. MIA 29 Mar 44. 2nd Lt William D Wayenberg.

42-38108 To 305BG 16 Feb 44 366BS. MIA 29 Mar 44. 1st Lt Raymond E Taylor.

42-38109 To 305BG from Stansted 10 Feb 44. Cr Ld at Redhill on ret from Op Miss 20 Feb 44. Lt Lawley won Medal of Honour on this Act this day. 1st Lt William R Lawley. (23 Feb 44).

42-38110 Orig of 457BG. To 92BG 11 Mar 44 407BS-H. Ass 31 Mar 44.

42-38111 To 379BG 12 Feb 44. Ass but not on hand 31 Mar 44. (At Oakington).

42-38112 To 384BG 10 Feb 44 545BS-J. Ass 31 Mar 44.

42-38113 Orig of 457BG 'RENE III'. Ass 31 Mar 44. 1000th B-17 built by Douglas.

42-38117 To 381BG 26 Feb 44 535BS-T 'TOUCH THE BUTTON NELL II'. Ass 31 Mar 44.

42-38118 To 91BG 25 Feb 44 323BS. MIA 6 Mar 44. 2nd Lt Ben Fourmy. (3 Miss).

42-38128 To 91BG 25 Feb 44. Ass 31 Mar 44.

42-38129 To 306BG 25 Feb 44. Ass 31 Mar 44.

42-38136 To 401BG 23 Feb 44 615BS-G. MIA 6 Mar 44. 2nd Lt Claude M Kolb.

42-38141 To 379BG 28 Feb 44. Ass 31 Mar 44.

42-38144 To 91BG 28 Feb 44. Ass 31 Mar 44.

42-38146 To 351BG 29 Feb 44 508BS-D. Ass 31 Mar 44.

42-38149 To 305BG 22 Feb 44. Ass 31 Mar 44.

42-38113. The 1,000th B-17 built by Douglas, stands outside the factory at Long Beach. It was delivered to the USAAF on 16th December 1943 and assigned as an original to the 457th Bomb Group. *Douglas*

42-38153 To 351BG 25 Feb 44 511BS-F **'BEDLAM BALL'**. Ass 31 Mar 44.

42-38154 To 303BG 18 Feb 44. Ass 31 Mar 44.

42-38155 To 306BG 25 Feb 44. Ass 31 Mar 44.

42-38156 To 92BG 23 Mar 44 326BS-E. Ass 31 Mar 44.

42-38158 To 384BG 1 Mar 44 547BS-L. Ass 31 Mar 44.

42-38159 To 381BG 21 Feb 44. Ass 31 Mar 44.

42-38161 To 379BG 19 Feb 44. Ass 31 Mar 44.

42-38162 To 401BG 22 Mar 44 614BS-R. Ass 31 Mar 44.

42-38163 To 306BG 29 Feb 44. Ass 31 Mar 44.

42-38167 To 305BG 22 Feb 44. Ass 31 Mar 44.

42-38168 To 303BG 22 Feb 44 359BS **'DEAR MOM'**. Ass 31 Mar 44.

42-38176 To 305BG 16 Feb 44. Ass 31 Mar 44.

42-38183 To 379BG 19 Feb 44 525BS-C **'THE LOST ANGEL'**. Ass 31 Mar 44.

42-38185 To 379BG 22 Feb 44. Ass 31 Mar 44.

42-38192 To 379BG 1 Mar 44 524BS-C. Ass 31 Mar 44.

42-38194 To 381BG 25 Mar 44. Ass 31 Mar 44.

42-38204 To 303BG 29 Mar 44. Ass 31 Mar 44.

42-38206 To 305BG 1 Mar 44. Ass 31 Mar 44.

42-38208 To 384BG 1 Mar 44 547BS-A to 'R' **'LILLY BELLE'**. Ass 31 Mar 44.

B-17G VEGA

42-39758 To 92BG 2 Dec 43 325BS. MIA 11 Jan 44. 2nd Lt Joseph A Tryens.

42-39760 Orig of 401BG. To 351BG 25 Nov 43 509BS-M. Ass 31 Mar 44.

42-39761 Orig of 401BG. To 351BG 18 Nov 43 511BS-D **'FIREBALL II'**. MIA 11 Jan 44. 2nd Lt Thompson E White.

42-39762 To 379BG 21 Oct 43. Ld at Rattlesden on ret from Op Miss 31 Dec 43 and sal there. (8 Jan 44).

42-39764 To 303BG 18 Oct 43 427BS. MIA 20 Dec 43. 2nd Lt Alexander Alex.

42-39765 Orig of 401BG 612BS-A **'BABY LOU III'**. Ass 31 Mar 44.

42-39766 To 482BG 30 Jan 43 (H2X). To 305BG 25 Mar 44 422BS. Ass 31 Mar 44.

42-39768 To 306BG 21 Oct 43 367BS. MIA 13 Dec 43. 2nd Lt Wesley B Brinkley.

42-39769 To 303BG 18 Oct 43 359BS. LG collapsed after Ld at Molesworth from a local formation flight 19 Dec 43. 2nd Lt Donald W Stouilil. (22 Dec 43).

Final assembly line at Douglas, Long Beach, December 1943. The aircraft are moving backwards away from the camera. At far end of line is 42-38140 which served in Eighth Air Force's Third Bomb Division. Next is 42-38141, assigned to the 379th Bomb Group on 28th February 1944 and still assigned on 31st March 1944. Then comes 42-38142 assigned in USA as an original to the 463rd Bomb Group, Fifteenth Air Force and wrecked before leaving the USA. Next is 42-38143 which survived just over one month in the Fifteenth Air Force, and then 42-38144 which joined the 91st Bomb Group on 28th February 1944. 42-38145 is next and this aircraft served in Eighth Air Force's Third Bomb Division and lost its tail in a mid air collision over Norfolk. Finally with just the left tailplane and fin visible is 42-38146 which joined the 351st Bomb Group on 29th February 1944. All these aircraft were delivered on 28th December 1943. *Douglas*

'THRO HELL AND HI WATER', 42-39785 of 303rd Bomb Group. This is the plane that Lt Jack Watson was flying when he 'buzzed' the Yankee Stadium in New York during the world series. *Mike Bailey*

42-39770 Left Gander 30 Oct 43 and ran into severe icing and turbulence. It took both pilots to handle the controls and at one time 5000ft was lost in a violent dive. Act turned back to Gander where it was found that the rear Gunner was missing. No one saw him leave the Act and it was not known if he baled out thinking the Act was crashing or if he was thrown against the door so that it opened and he fell out. His parachute and life preserver were also missing. To 92BG 25 Dec 43 326BS. MIA 20 Feb 44. 2nd Lt Harvey H Jessen.

42-39771 Orig of 401BG. To 91BG 20 Nov 43 401BS. MIA 4 Feb 44. 2nd Lt James P Lutz.

42-39774 To 91BG 18 Oct 43 323BS-R. Ass 31 Mar 44.

42-39776 To 306BG 6 Nov 43 368BS. Ass 31 Mar 44.

42-39778 Orig of 401BG. To 351BG 18 Nov 43 511BS-A **'LUCKY BALL'**. MIA 22 Dec 43. Lt Lewis J Maginn.

42-39779 To 379BG 21 Oct 43 526BS. MIA 29 Nov 43. 2nd Lt Eldon W Planalp.

42-39780 Orig of 401BG. To 351BG 18 Nov 43 510BS-S **'LITTLE TWINK'**. Cr Ld near Hawkinge on ret from Op Miss 30 Dec 43. Lt Joseph R Adamiak. (2 Jan 44).

42-39781 To 303BG 18 Oct 43 360BS. MIA 1 Dec 43. 2nd Lt George W Luke Jr. First 303BG B-17G MIA.

42-39782 To 379BG 21 Oct 43 526BS-M **'PISTOL PACKIN' MAMA'**. MIA 8 Feb 44. 2nd Lt Herbert D Rossberg.

42-39783 To 303BG 19 Oct 43. To BAD for mod 23 Oct 43. Then to 384BG 2 Nov 43 545BS. To 379BG 11 Nov 43. Ass 31 Mar 44.

42-39784 To 384BG 2 Nov 43 544BS-J **'CABIN IN THE SKY'**. MIA 8 Feb 44. Lt Royston T Covington.

42-39785 To 303BG 18 Oct 43 **'THRO HELL AND HI WATER'**. Ass 31 Mar 44.

42-39786 To 303BG 18 Oct 43 427BS. MIA 29 Jan 44. 2nd Lt James F Fowler.

42-39787 To 303BG 18 Oct 43 358BS **'WANTON WOMAN'**. Ass 31 Mar 44.

42-39789 To 379BG 19 Oct 43 527BS-P. Ass 31 Mar 44.

42-39790 To 305BG 18 Oct 43 365BS-F. Ass 31 Mar 44.

42-39794 To 303BG 18 Oct 43 358BS. MIA 11 Jan 44. 2nd Lt William C Dashiell.

42-39795 To 303BG 18 Oct 43 360BS. MIA 30 Dec 43. 1st Lt William C Osborn.

42-39796 To 303BG 21 Oct 43. To BAD for mod 23 Oct 43. Then to 384BG 2 Nov 43 546BS. MIA 1 Dec 43. Maj Maurice S Dillingham.

42-39797 To 384BG 2 Nov 43 547BS. Until 24 Dec 43. Possibly never on hand with 384BG. To 381BG 22 Jan 44. It is almost certain that this is the aircraft piloted by 2nd Lt Milton A Fastrup which suffered LG collapse at Ridgewell during the Op Miss of 4 Feb 44 when the Co-Pilot hit the LG switch instead of the Flap switch. (12 Feb 44).

42-39798 To 381BG 24 Jan 44 535BS-L **'BUCKET O' BOLTS'**. Ass 31 Mar 44.

42-39800 To 303BG 18 Oct 43. To BAD for mod 23 Oct 43. Then to 384BG 2 Nov 43 547BS. To 379BG 7 Nov 43. Ass 31 Mar 44.

42-39802 To 91BG 7 Oct 43 401BS. MIA 3 Nov 43. 1st Lt Kenneth B Rutledge.

42-39803 To 91BG 7 Oct 43 324BS-N **'THE WOLF'**. MIA 4 Feb 44. 1st Lt Fewer E McGee. 16 Miss.

42-39807 To 303BG 19 Nov 43. Ass 31 Mar 44.

42-39808 To 381BG 19 Oct 43. Cr at Allhallows on ret from Op Miss 1 Dec 43. 1st Lt Harold R Hytinen. (2 Dec 43).

42-39809 To 384BG 6 Jan 44 547BS-M. MIA 22 Feb 44. 2nd Lt Raymond L Macdonald.

42-39810 To 303BG 18 Oct 43 358BS-E **'BIG A BIRD'**. Cr Ld at West Malling on ret from Op Miss 11 Feb 44. 1st Lt Joe R Worthley. (14 Feb 44).

42-39811 To 305BG 19 Oct 43 365BS-C. Ass 31 Mar 44.

42-39815 To 91BG 16 Oct 43 323BS **'EMEIGH'**. MIA 22 Feb 44. 1st Lt Kenneth Sutherland. 22 Miss.

42-39818 To 305BG 19 Oct 43 364BS-H. Ass 31 Mar 44.

42-39820 Orig of 401BG 614BS-J **'ALSO RAN - STILL RUNNING'**. Ass 31 Mar 44.

42-39823 Orig of 401BG. To 351BG 18 Nov 43 510BS-O **'IRON ASS'**. MIA 31 Dec 43. 1st Lt Marvin H Bender.

42-39825 Orig of 401BG 613BS-M **'ZENOBIA EL ELEPHANTE'**. Cr on TO for Op Miss at Deenethorpe 5 Dec 43. Dest. Lt Walter B Keith Jr. All crew safe.

42-39826 Orig of 401BG 612BS-H **'STUBBORN JEAN'**. MIA 30 Dec 43. 2nd Lt Traian Neag.

42-39827 To 306BG 24 Nov 43. Ass 31 Mar 44.

42-39828 To 379BG 19 Nov 43. Ass 31 Mar 44.

42-39829 To 305BG 19 Oct 43 366BS-J. Ass 31 Mar 44.

42-39831 To 92BG 21 Oct 43. MIA 5 Nov 43. Capt John O Booker and Maj Wilson P Todd. Lead Act.

42-39832 To 305BG 18 Oct 43 364BS-A. To 422BS-B Jan 44 'HITLERS HEADACHE'. Ass 31 Mar 44.

42-39833 A mystery Act. Ass as an orig to 401BG in USA. No record can be found of it joining the Gp in England. It was reported as Ld at Wendling following Miss of 11 Jan 44. Not with Gp at 31 Mar 44 but no record of it leaving the Gp can be found. Possible confusion of serial numbers.

42-39834 Orig of 401BG. To 351BG 18 Nov 43 511BS-F 'CANNON BALL'. Cr Ld Polebrook on ret from Op Miss 30 Jan 44. 1st Lt George W Mears. (5 Feb 43).

42-39835 Orig of 401BG. To 351BG 18 Nov 43 510BS-N 'WANNA SPAR'. Ass 31 Mar 44.

42-39836 Orig of 401BG. To 91BG 20 Nov 43. MIA 1 Dec 43. 2nd Lt Charles L Early.

42-39837 Orig of 401BG 612BS-L 'REDS ROGUES'. Ass but not on hand 31 Mar 44. (At Nuthampstead).

42-39839 Orig of 401BG. To 351BG 18 Nov 43 511BS-D. Cr Ld at Marham on ret from Op Miss 26 Nov 43. Lt Clarence P Lemley. (28 Nov 43).

42-39840 Orig of 401BG 613BS-A 'THE LOPIN LOBO'. Ass 31 Mar 44.

42-39843 To 305BG 16 Oct 43 364BS-G 'DAILEY'S MAIL'. Ass 31 Mar 44.

42-39846 Orig of 401BG 614BS-M 'WIDDLE TWINKLE'. Ass 31 Mar 44.

42-39847 Orig of 401BG 614BS-G 'BATTLIN BETTY'. Ass 31 Mar 44.

42-39848 Orig of 401BG. To 351BG 18 Nov 43 511BS-C 'ARCHI BALL'. Ass 31 Mar 44.

42-39849 Orig of 401BG. To 351BG 18 Nov 43 508BS-K. MIA 22 Mar 44. 2nd Lt Wyman C Slossen.

42-39850 To 306BG 22 Oct 43 423BS. Ass 31 Mar 44.

42-39851 To 92BG 2 Dec 43 325BS-J. Ass 31 Mar 44.

42-39853 Orig of 401BG. To 351BG 18 Nov 43 510BS-P 'PAPAS' PASSION'. Ass 31 Mar 44.

42-39857 Orig of 401BG. To 351BG 18 Nov 43 511BS-H 'BELLE OF THE BALL'. MIA 22 Feb 44. 2nd Lt John Pugh.

42-39863 To 91BG 22 Dec 43 401BS. Cr Ld at Steeple Morden, soon after TO from Bassingbourn on an Op Miss 30 Dec 43. 2nd Lt Frank C Ammann. (31 Dec 43).

42-39873 Orig of 401BG 615BS-Q 'STORMY WEATHER'. Ass 31 Mar 44.

42-39875 To 303BG 14 Jan 44. Ass 31 Mar 44.

42-39878 To 305BG 3 Jan 44. Ass 31 Mar 44.

42-39880 To 482BG 30 Dec 43 (H2X). Ass 14 Feb 44.

42-39881 To 401BG 13 Dec 43 614BS-F 'GLORIA J'. Ass 31 Mar 44.

42-39885 To 303BG 31 Dec 43 427BS-Z 'SWEET ROSIE O' GRADY'. Ass 31 Mar 44.

42-39888 To 384BG 23 Nov 43 544BS-B 'HOTNUTS'. Ass 31 Mar 44.

42-39889 To 379BG 22 Nov 43 527BS. Dam by 20mm cannon on Op Miss 30 Jan 44. Sal on ret. (1 Feb 44).

42-39890 To 381BG 20 Dec 43 535BS 'RETURN TICKET'. Ass 31 Mar 44.

42-39891 To 381BG 13 Jan 44. MIA 2 Mar 44. 1st Lt Eugene Shultz.

42-39892 To 91BG 13 Dec 43 401BS. MIA 8 Mar 44. 2nd Lt Claude M Williams.

42-39893 To 401BG 2 Jan 44 615BS-J. MIA 11 Jan 44. 2nd Lt Donald C Sprecher.

42-39895 To 381BG 22 Dec 43 'BERMONDSEY BATTLER'. MIA 22 Feb 44. 1st Lt Leo W Smith.

42-39898 To 91BG 13 Dec 43 322BS-L. MIA 22 Feb 44. 2nd Lt William D Wood.

42-39904 To 401BG 19 Dec 43 615BS-C 'BAD PENNY'. Ass 31 Mar 44.

42-39905 To 351BG 2 Jan 44 508BS-C. MIA 11 Jan 44. 1st Lt Thomas D Garner.

42-39906 To 381BG 20 Dec 43 'SQUAT AND DROPIT'. Ass 31 Mar 44.

42-39910 To 381BG 20 Dec 43 535BS. MIA 31 Dec 43. 2nd Lt Earl B Duarte.

42-39914 To 351BG 20 Jan 44 509BS-S 'LUCKY STRIKE' later 'THE BLACK BITCH'. Ass 31 Mar 44.

42-39915 To 482BG 29 Dec 43. Ass 14 Feb 44.

42-39929 To 91BG 20 Dec 43 401BS 'LACKIN SHAKIN'. Ass 31 Mar 44.

Ground crew of 'BATTLIN BETTY' 42-39847 of 401st Bomb Group. *Vic Maslen*

42-39932 To 401BG 2 Jan 44 613BS-H. Ass 31 Mar 44.

42-39935 To 306BG 6 Jan 44 369BS. MIA 22 Feb 44. 1st Lt Rudolph Horst III.

42-39943 To 401BG 2 Jan 44 612BS-F. Ass 31 Mar 44.

42-39944 To 305BG 3 Dec 43 366BS. MIA 2 Mar 44. Lt Wayne C Keysar.

42-39945 To 306BG 12 Dec 43 423BS. MIA 22 Feb 44. 1st Lt J P Toombs Jr.

42-39946 To 381BG 22 Jan 44 533BS. MIA 22 Feb 44. 1st Lt Hal E Rolling.

42-39947 To 305BG 12 Dec 43 364BS 'CHIQUITA'. Ass 31 Mar 44.

42-39948 To 305BG 3 Dec 43 364BS-M 'LEADING LADY'. Ass 31 Mar 44.

42-39949 To 305BG 30 Nov 43. Ass but not on hand 31 Mar 44. (At Woolaston).

42-39950 To 306BG 28 Dec 43. MIA 29 Mar 44. 1st Lt Nelson W Hardin.

42-39957 To 305BG 12 Dec 43. Coll with another Act when on Op Miss 11 Jan 44. Ret to base and sal. 2nd Lt John W Raedeke. (16 Jan 44).

42-39958 To 92BG 27 Dec 43 326BS-K. Ass 31 Mar 44.

42-39960 To 92BG 23 Jan 44 325BS. MIA 2 Mar 44. 1st Lt Floyd H Chesmore.

42-39962 To 384BG 21 Jan 44 547BS. MIA 11 Feb 44. Lt Widener.

42-39963 To 306BG 30 Dec 43. Ass 31 Mar 44.

42-39965 To 306BG 19 Dec 43 369BS. Dam on Op Miss 11 Jan 44. Ld at Foulsham on ret. Out for rep. Dropped from Ass 12 Jan 44 to 6 Feb 44. Ret to Gp 29 Feb 44. MIA 29 Mar 44. 1st Lt Gerald R Haywood.

42-39966 To 305BG 5 Jan 44. Ass 31 Mar 44.

42-39967 To 91BG 25 Jan 44 324BS 'MARY K'. MIA 18 Mar 44. 1st Lt Henry L Theophilus. 18 Miss.

42-39969 To 401BG 2 Jan 44 614BS-K. MIA 11 Jan 44. Capt James B Foster.

42-39975 To 91BG 10 Jan 44 323BS 'JUST PLAIN LONESOME'. Ass 31 Mar 44.

42-39979 To 401BG 5 Jan 44 612BS-H. Ass 31 Mar 44.

42-39980 To 379BG 14 Jan 44 526BS. MIA 3 Mar 44. 2nd Lt Thomas Soso.

42-39987 To 351BG 30 Jan 44 511BS-D 'PIN BALL'. Ass 31 Mar 44.

42-39991 To 384BG 8 Jan 44 546BS-V. MIA 4 Mar 44. 1st Lt Walter R Carpenter.

42-39992 To 305BG 21 Jan 44. Ass 31 Mar 44.

42-39993 To 401BG 1 Jan 44 612BS-C 'HELLS ANGELS OUT OF CHUTE 13'. Ass 31 Mar 44.

42-39996 To 91BG 14 Jan 44. Ass 31 Mar 44.

42-39997 To 381BG 13 Jan 44 533BS-T 'FRENCHIES FOLLY'. Ass 31 Mar 44.

42-40000 To 91BG 4 Jan 44 324BS-F 'JUST NOTHING'. Ass 31 Mar 44.

42-40001 To 401BG 5 Jan 44 614BS-L 'PARIS EXPRESS'. Ass 31 Mar 44.

42-40002 To 401BG 29 Dec 43 615BS-D 'BREEZING HOME'. Ass 31 Mar 44.

42-40003 To 379BG 20 Jan 44 524BS-H 'OL GAPPY'. Ass 31 Mar 44.

42-40005 To 384BG 6 Jan 44 546BS-A 'SALVAGE QUEEN'. MIA 11 Feb 44. Lt Clifford O Moore.

42-40006 To 306BG 8 Jan 44. MIA 6 Mar 44. 1st Lt Charles W Smith. Ld in Sweden.

42-40007 To 381BG 22 Jan 44 'HONEY'. Ass 31 Mar 44.

42-40008 To 381BG 8 Jan 44 532BS. MIA 24 Mar 44. 1st Lt Thomas P Thompson. Coll with 42-31490

42-40009 To 91BG 21 Jan 44 324BS-K. Cr 24 Jan 44 at Ikleton Abbey while forming for Op Miss. 1st Lt Marco Demara. 4 kld, 6 parachuted to safety. Act on first Miss.

42-40011 To 381BG 6 Jan 44. Ass 31 Mar 44.

42-40014 To 92BG 6 Jan 44 325BS. MIA 3 Mar 44. 1st Lt Walter C Lansford.

42-40017 To 381BG 5 Jan 44 'ME AND MY GAL'. Ass 31 Mar 44.

42-40018 To 482BG 9 Feb 44 (H2X). Ass 14 Feb 44. To 305BG 20 Mar 44. 422BS-U. Ass 31 Mar 44.

42-40020 To 305BG 22 Jan 44. MIA 8 Feb 44. 2nd Lt Phillip D Stuckey.

42-40025 To 381BG 6 Jan 44 535BS 'TOUCH THE BUTTON NELL'. Dam on Op Miss 6 Feb 44. Ld at Dunkeswell on ret and sal. 2nd Lt Henry Putek. (8 Feb 44).

42-40032 To 92BG 27 Jan 44. MIA 8 Feb 44. 2nd Lt Robert D Lehner.

42-40047 To 92BG 31 Dec 43 407BS. MIA 24 Feb 44. 2nd Lt Melvin B Scarborough.

42-40050 To 401BG 1 Jan 44 612BS-J 'CHANNEL EXPRESS III'. Ass 31 Mar 44.

42-40052 To 92BG 30 Dec 43 407BS. MIA 6 Mar 44. 1st Lt Wallace C Upson.

42-40053 To 306BG 27 Dec 43. Ass 31 Mar 44.

42-40057 To 401BG 5 Jan 44 615BS-N. MIA 29 Jan 44. 2nd Lt Donald T Nicklawsky.

B-17G BOEING

42-97058 To 303BG 27 Mar 44 359BS-V 'SCORCHY II'. Ass 31 Mar 44.

42-97059 To 457BG 20 Feb 44. To 381BG 15 Mar 44. Ass 31 Mar 44.

42-97060 To 457BG 4 Mar 44. Ass but not on hand 31 Mar 44. (At Abbots Ripton).

42-97061 To 457BG 13 Mar 44. To 91BG 16 Mar 44 401BS-B 'GENERAL IKE'. Ass 31 Mar 44.

42-97062 To 457BG 15 Mar 44. Ass 31 Mar 44.

42-97063 To 351BG 29 Feb 44. To 457BG 1 Mar 44. MIA 16 Mar 44. 2nd Lt Lewis W Lenartson.

42-97066 To 351BG 26 Feb 44 508BS-O Ass 31 Mar 44.

42-97067 94BG to 457BG 4 Mar 44 'BLACK PUFF POLLY, GEORGIA PEACH'. Ass 31 Mar 44.

42-97070 To 457BG 15 Mar 44. Ass 31 Mar 44.

42-97072 To 384BG 24 Mar 44 547BS-H later 544BS-A. Ass 31 Mar 44.

Settling down gracefully at Glatton, but not resident long enough to get really at home, is 42-97063. It had the distinction of being assigned for one day to the 351st Bomb Group before being transferred to the 457th where it lasted just 15 days before being ditched 15 miles from the enemy coast on return from the mission to Augsburg, 16th March 1944. All ten crew were rescued in this the 457th's first ditching. *Alan Dann*

42-97073 To 401BG 23 Mar 44 614BS-N. Ass 31 Mar 44.

42-97075 To 457BG 7 Mar 44 **'FLAK DODGER'**. Ass 31 Mar 44.

42-97076 To 457BG 8 Mar 44. To 881BG 15 Mar 44 **'DEE MARIE'**. Ass 31 Mar 44.

42-97077 To 305BG 31 Mar 44.

42-97081 To 457BG 11 Mar 44. To 384BG 12 Mar 44 546BS-K. Ass 31 Mar 44.

42-97087 To 379BG 1 Mar 44. To 457BG 2 Mar 44 **'TUJUNGA I'**. Ass 31 Mar 44.

42-97088 To 457BG 9 Mar 44. Ass 31 Mar 44.

42-97097 To 305BG 31 Mar 44. Ass 31 Mar 44.

42-97122 To 457BG 17 Mar 44. Ass 31 Mar 44.

42-97123 To 457BG 8 Mar 44. Ass 31 Mar 44.

42-97124 To 457BG 11 Mar 44. To 384BG 12 Mar 44 545BS-M. Ass 31 Mar 44.

42-97125 To 457BG 13 Mar 44. To 91BG 16 Mar 44 401BS. MIA 22 Mar 44. Capt Charles R Phillips.

42-97128 To 379BG 23 Mar 44. Ass 31 Mar 44.

42-97131 To 457BG 8 Mar 44 **'HOME JAMES'**. Ass but not on hand 31 Mar 44. (At Alconbury).

42-97133 To 306BG 26 Mar 44 367BS **'PRETTY BABY'**. Ass 31 Mar 44.

42-97136 To 457BG 11 Jan 44. To 384BG 12 Mar 44 547BS-J. Ass 31 Mar 44.

42-97137 To 457BG 9 Mar 44. Ass 31 Mar 44.

42-97139 To 457BG 11 Mar 44. To 384BG 12 Mar 44 546BS-M. Ass 31 Mar 44.

42-97141 To 92BG 22 Mar 44 325BS. Ass 31 Mar 44.

42-97142 To 457BG 11 Mar 44. To 384BG 12 Mar 44 546BS-N **'DANIEL WEBSTER'**. Ass 31 Mar 44.

42-97144 To 351BG 26 Mar 44 509BS-R. Ass 31 Mar 44.

42-97146 To 306BG 24 Mar 44. Ass 31 Mar 44.

42-97149 To 351BG 26 Mar 44 509BS-X. Ass 31 Mar 44.

42-97150 To 384BG 12 Mar 44 547BS-F **'SILVER QUEEN'**. Ass 31 Mar 44.

42-97151 To 91BG 22 Mar 44. Ass 31 Mar 44.

42-97157 To 351BG 24 Mar 44 508BS-N. Ass 31 Mar 44.

42-97162 To 457BG 8 Mar 44. Ass but not on hand 31 Mar 44. (At Alconbury).

42-97164 To 457BG 15 Mar 44 **'MISS YU II'**. Ass 31 Mar 44.

42-97169 To 351BG 24 Mar 44 509BS-N **'MY GAL II'**. Ass 31 Mar 44.

42-97170 To 379BG 30 Mar 44. Ass 31 Mar 44.

42-97185 To 306BG 31 Mar 44. Ass 31 Mar 44.

42-97187 To 303BG 26 Mar 44 360BS-I **'MISS UMBRIAGO'**. Ass 31 Mar 44.

42-97190 To 457BG 24 Mar 44. Ass 31 Mar 44.

42-97191 To 351BG 25 Mar 44 511BS-X **'SILVER BALL'**. Ass 31 Mar 44.

42-97193 To 351BG 24 Mar 44 509BS-P later 'L' **'STAR DUSTER'**. Ass 31 Mar 44.

42-97196 To 351BG 24 Mar 44 510BS-M **'BOBBIE ANNE'**. Ass 31 Mar 44.

42-97201 To 384BG 31 Mar 44 547BS-J **'JAMAICA MARY'**. Ass 31 Mar 44.

42-97203 To 92BG 23 Mar 44 407BS-P. Ass 31 Mar 44.

42-97204 To 384BG 30 Mar 44 547BS-K **'SKYLARK'**. Ass 31 Mar 44.

42-97214 To 381BG 25 Mar 44. Ass 31 Mar 44.

42-97217 To 92BG 23 Mar 44 326BS-L. Ass 31 Mar 44.

42-97218 To 92BG 24 Mar 44 326BS. Ass 31 Mar 44.

42-97246. Gleaming in its natural metal finish while out on test flight near Seattle. If only those who had built it and flown it could foresee its fate. Just four days after assignment to the 91st Bomb Group there was another empty hardstand at Bassingbourn and a bewildered ground crew wondering what had happened to the new silver bird that had so recently been charged to their care. *Boeing Archives*

42-97227 To 92BG 27 Mar 44 326BS-P. Ass 31 Mar 44.

42-97228 To 384BG 31 Mar 44 545BS-G.

42-97229 To 379BG 23 Mar 44. Ass 31 Mar 44.

42-97231 To 384BG 24 Mar 44 547BS-D. Ass 31 Mar 44.

42-97236 To 457BG 31 Mar 43. Ass 31 Mar 44.

42-97237 To 384BG 24 Mar 44 547BS-G. Ass 31 Mar 44.

42-97243 To 92BG 23 Mar 44 325BS. Ass 31 Mar 44.

42-97246 To 91BG 25 Mar 44 401BS. MIA 29 Mar 44. 1st Lt Julius D C Anderson.

42-97251 To 384BG 24 Mar 44 546BS-O. Ass 31 Mar 44.

42-97254 To 303BG 26 Mar 44 360BS 'IZA-VAILABLE TOO'. Ass 31 Mar 44.

42-97258 To 351BG 24 Mar 44 508BS-P. Ass 31 Mar 44.

42-97260 To 303BG 23 Mar 44 360BS 'BOW-ER-NECK-STEVENS'. Ass 31 Mar 44.

42-97321 To 305BG 31 Mar 44. Ass 31 Mar 44.

42-97327 To 306BG 31 Mar 44. Ass 31 Mar 44.

B-17G VEGA

42-97440 To 401BG 1 Jan 44 614BS-A 'FLAK RAT II'. Ass 31 Mar 44.

42-97441 To 92BG 10 Jan 44. MIA 30 Jan 44. 2nd Lt David C Russell. Coll with 42-30008 of 92BG.

42-97442 To 381BG 21 Feb 44. Ass 31 Mar 44.

42-97448 To 401BG 1 Jan 44 614BS-H. Ass 31 Mar 44.

42-97449 To 384BG 21 Jan 44 547BS-B. Ass 31 Mar 44.

42-97450 Orig of 457BG. To 384BG 20 Feb 44. MIA 22 Feb 44. 1st Lt Henry V Markow. Ass to Gp two days before being lost.

42-97451 Orig of 457BG 'NANCY B'. Ass 31 Mar 44.

42-97452 Orig of 457BG. Ass 31 Mar 44.

42-97454 To 381BG 13 Jan 44. Ass 31 Mar 44.

42-97455 Orig of 457BG. To 91BG 12 Mar 44 401BS 'KEYSTONE MAMA'. Ass 31 Mar 44.

42-97456 Orig of 457BG 'MIGHTY LITTLE JOHN'. Ass 31 Mar 44.

42-97457 Orig of 457BG. MIA 25 Feb 44. 2nd Lt Archie F Bower Jr.

42-97458 Orig of 457BG dam on Op Miss 25 Feb 44. Ld at Headcorn on ret and sal. 2nd Lt Green B Poore. (29 Feb 44).

42-97460 Orig of 457BG 'DELAYED LADY'. Ass 31 Mar 44.

42-97462 To 379BG 9 Jan 44. Ass 31 Mar 44.

42-97463 To 306BG 27 Jan 44 423BS. MIA 20 Feb 44. 1st Lt Harold G Richard.

42-97464 Orig of 457BG. To 401BG 11 Mar 44 614BS-D. Ass 31 Mar 44.

42-97465 Orig of 457BG. Ass but not on hand 31 Mar 44. (At Burton-wood).

42-97466 Orig of 457BG. To 305BG 8 Feb 44 366BS. MIA 29 Mar 44. Lt Arvid W Engel. This Act was not reported MIA by 305BG until 2 April 44. 42-31611 was erroneously reported MIA instead.

42-97467 Orig of 457BG. To 91BG 12 Mar 44. Ass 31 Mar 44.

42-97468 Orig of 457BG 'TUNJUNGA' 'TUJUNGA III'. Ass 31 Mar 44.

42-97469 Orig of 457BG. To 379BG 18 Mar 44. Ass 31 Mar 44.

42-97470 Orig of 457BG. Ass 31 Mar 44.

42-97471 Orig of 457BG. To 381BG 12 Mar 44 532BS. LG collapsed on Ld at Ridgewell on ret from Op Miss 20 Mar 44. Capt Douglas L Winter. (21 Mar 44).

42-97472 To 351BG 25 Feb 44 511BS-H 'SLOW BALL'. Ass 31 Mar 44.

42-97474 To 381BG 15 Jan 44. MIA 22 Feb 44. 1st Lt Francis N Fridgen.

42-97475 To 482BG 29 Jan 44 (SO Mk 2). To 9AF Stansted 5 Feb 44. Then to 305BG 11 Feb 44. Ass 31 Mar 44.

42-97477 Orig of 457BG. To 384BG 20 Jan 44 545BS-A 'PORKY'S PIG'. Ass 31 Mar 44.

42-97478 Orig of 457BG. To 401BG 11 Mar 44 614BS-Q 'SHADE RUFF'. Ass 31 Mar 44.

42-97479 To 92BG 27 Jan 44 327BS-L. Ass 31 Mar 44.

42-97481 Orig of 457BG. Ass 31 Mar 44.

42-97483 To 91BG 24 Feb 44 322BS. MIA 6 Mar 44. 2nd Lt Bryce S Everston.

42-97485 To 379BG 29 Jan 44 526BS. MIA 26 Mar 44. 1st Lt Stanley L Bielawski.

42-97487 To 401BG 12 Jan 44 612BS-O 'HANGOVER HAVEN'. Ass 31 Mar 44.

42-97488 Orig of 457BG. To 384BG 19 Feb 44 547BS. MIA 22 Feb 44. 2nd Lt Norman F Defrees.

42-97489 To 92BG 23 Jan 44 326BS-F. Ass 31 Mar 44.

42-97492 To 351BG 14 Jan 44 511BS-R. Ass 31 Mar 44.

42-97494 To 92BG 20 Jan 44 325BS. MIA 22 Feb 44. 2nd Lt Robert Wolf.

42-97496 To 401BG 31 Jan 44 615BS-J. Ass 31 Mar 44.

42-97498 To 303BG 14 Jan 44 358BS. MIA 6 Feb 44. 1st Lt Julius E Bass.

42-97500 To 305BG 22 Jan 44 364BS. MIA 20 Feb 44. Lt William G Lindley.

42-97502 To 379BG 18 Feb 44. Ass 31 Mar 44.

42-97503 To 381BG 13 Mar 44 533BS-X 'PRINCESS PAT'. Ass 31 Mar 44.

42-97504 To 91BG 23 Jan 44 'MARY LOU'. Ass 31 Mar 44.

42-97505 To 306BG 423BS 'DINGLEBURY KIDS'. Ass 31 Mar 44.

42-97509 To 303BG 28 Feb 44 358BS 'OLD HICKORY'. MIA 2 Mar 44. 2nd Lt David C Elder.

42-97510 To 384BG 18 Feb 44 546BS-A 'SATANS PLAYMATES'. Ass 31 Mar 44.

42-97511 To 381BG 22 Feb 44 535BS-K 'EGG HAID'. Ass 31 Mar 44.

42-97514 To 482BG 6 Feb 44 (H2X). To 305BG 20 Mar 44 422BS-H. Ass 31 Mar 44.

42-97515 To 92BG 28 Jan 44 325VBS. MIA 18 Mar 44. 1st Lt Gordon L Capp. Ld in Switzerland.

42-97519 To 91BG 12 Feb 44 401BS 'SPIRIT OF BILLY MITCHELL'. Ass 31 Mar 44.

42-97520 To 379BG 8 Feb 44. MIA 22 Feb 44. 1st Lt Sanderson Sloane.

42-97521 To 384BG 10 Feb 44 545BS-H 'THE SAINT'. Ass 31 Mar 44.

42-97523 To 482BG 6 Feb 44 (H2X). To 305BG 20 Mar 44 422BS. MIA 22 Mar 44. 2nd Lt Hugh Burnett.

42-97527 To 92BG 5 Feb 44. MIA 6 Mar 44. 1st Lt Rex M Townsend.

42-97532 To 482BG 8 Feb 44. Ass 31 Mar 44.

42-97533 To 482BG (H2X). To 305BG 20 Mar 44 422BS-E. Ass 31 Mar 44.

One of the olive drab aircraft transferred out of the 457th Bomb Group in early March 1944, was 42-97471. It went to the 381st Bomb Group and lasted just eight days. Photo shows it on its belly at Ridgewell after the landing gear collapsed when the aircraft returned from the Frankfurt mission of 20th March. *US Air Force*

'**VIRGIN MARY**', 42-97590, the fourth silver plane to be assigned to the 457th Bomb Group, on finals at Glatton. When policy concerning the assignment of silver planes changed, it became surplus and was re-assigned to the 303rd Bomb Group on 14th March 1944. *Alan Dann*

42-97534 To 482BG 6 Feb 44 (H2X). Ass 31 Mar 44.

42-97535 To 384BG 10 Feb 44. To 457BG 19 Feb 44. Ass 31 Mar 44.

42-97537 To 457BG 25 Feb 44. Ass 31 Mar 44.

42-97542 To 482BG 6 Feb 44 (H2X). Ass 14 Feb 44.

42-97543 To 482BG (H2X). To 305BG 20 Mar 44 422BS. Ass 31 Mar 44.

42-97545 To 482BG 7 Feb 44 (H2X). Ass 14 Feb 44.

42-97546 To 92BG 11 Feb 44. To 457BG 24 Feb 44. To 303BG 13 Mar 44 360BS-E '**IDALIZA**'. Ass 31 Mar 44.

42-97552 To 351BG 25 Feb 44. To 457BG 1 Mar 44. To 303BG 12 Mar 44. Ass 31 Mar 44.

42-97554 To 482BG 7 Feb 44 (H2X). Ass 14 Feb 44.

42-97555 To 482BG 10 Feb 44 (H2X). Ass 14 Feb 44.

42-97556 To 482BG 7 Feb 44 (H2X). Ass 14 Feb 44.

42-97557 To 482BG (H2X). To 305BG 20 Mar 44 422BS-S. Ass 31 Mar 44.

42-97558 To 457BG 15 Feb 44 '**TIS ME SUGAR**'. Ass 31 Mar 44.

42-97563 To 457BG 13 Mar 44. To 91BG 16 Mar 44. Ass 31 Mar 44.

42-97563 To 482BG 8 Feb 44 (H2X). Ass 14 Feb 44.

42-97567 To 482BG 6 Feb 44 (H2X). Ass 14 Feb 44.

42-97571 To 457BG 24 Feb 44. Ass 31 Mar 44.

42-97574 482BG (H2X). To 305BG 20 Mar 44 422BS-A. Ass 31 Mar 44.

42-97578 482BG (H2X). To 305BG 20 Mar 44 422BS. Cr on TO at Chelveston 24 Mar 44. Was positioning to Deenethorpe from where it was to lead Op Miss. 1st Lt William D Sellers. 11 crew kld plus 8 in barrack and 2 children in bungalow.

42-97579 To 457BG 23 Feb 44 '**LOCAL MISSION**'. Ass 31 Mar 44.

42-97587 To 457BG. Date in not known. Ass 31 Mar 44.

42-97588 To 457BG 7 Mar 44. To 306BG 13 Mar 44. Ass but not on hand 31 Mar 44. (At Tibenham).

42-97590 To 457BG 22 Feb 44 '**VIRGIN MARY**'. To 303BG 13 Mar 44 360BS. Ass 31 Mar 44.

42-97591 To 457BG 2 Mar 44. Ass 31 Mar 44.

42-97592 482BG (H2X). To 305BG 20 Mar 44 422BS-T. Ass 31 Mar 44.

42-97617 To 303BG 23 Feb 44 358BS. Ass 31 Mar 44.

42-97622 To 303BG 1 Mar 44 358BS-K '**PAPER DOLLIE**'. Ass 31 Mar 44.

42-97624 To 457BG 21 Feb 44. Ass but not on hand 23 Feb 44. No further record with Gp. Later went to 447BG. (Possible error on records here confusing 447 with 457BGs).

42-97662 To 457BG 3 Mar 44. Ass 31 Mar 44.

42-97663 From Deopham Green to 457BG 4 Mar 44. To 306BG 12 Mar 44 369BS. MIA 26 Mar 44. 2nd Lt Barney R Price.

B-17G DOUGLAS — NATURAL METAL FINISH

42-106985 To 379BG 1 Mar 44. To 457BG 2 Mar 44. Ass 31 Mar 44.

42-106998 To 379BG 28 Feb 44. To 457BG 2 Mar 44. Ass 31 Mar 44.

42-107001 To 457BG 4 Mar 44. Ass 31 Mar 44.

42-107002 To 303BG 24 Mar 44 358BS. Ass 31 Mar 44.

42-107004 To 379BG 23 Mar 44. Ass 31 Mar 44.

42-107005 To 351BG 24 Mar 44. Ass 31 Mar 44.

42-107009 To 401BG 23 Mar 44 613BS-E '**LADY JANE**'. Ass 31 Mar 44.

42-107012 To 92BG 22 Mar 44 407BS. Ass 31 Mar 44.

42-107013 To 306BG 24 Mar 44 423BS. Aborted Miss on 28 Mar 44. Ret to Thurleigh, LG collapsed on Ld. Had twelve 500lb bombs and nearly 15,000lb of fuel on board. No inj. 2nd Lt John O Baldwin. First Douglas NMF Act lost in 1BD. (29 Mar 44).

42-107014 To 379BG 30 Mar 44. Ass 31 Mar 44.

42-107015 To 457BG 3 Mar 44. Ass 31 Mar 44.

42-107018 To 381BG 25 Mar 44. 'LOS ANGELES CITY LIMITS'. Ass 31 Mar 44.

42-107023 To 381BG 25 Mar 44. Ass 31 Mar 44.

42-107026 From Framlingham to 457BG 4 Mar 44 'HAM TRAMACK MAMA'. Ass 31 Mar 44.

42-107030 To 91BG 26 Mar 44. Ass 31 Mar 44.

42-107033 To 91BG 24 Mar 44. Ass 31 Mar 44.

42-107039 To 401BG 23 Mar 44 612BS-M. Ass 31 Mar 44.

42-107043 To 401BG 23 Mar 44 613BS-B 'FITCHES BANDWAGON'. Ass 31 Mar 44.

42-107044 To 92BG 25 Mar 44 325BS. Ass 31 Mar 44.

42-107046 To 351BG 26 Mar 44 511BS-Z. 'SCREW BALL'. Ass 31 Mar 44.

42-107048 To 303BG 23 Mar 44 360BS-. Ass 31 Mar 44.

42-107075 To 91BG 22 Mar 44. Ass 31 Mar 44.

42-107082 To 379BG 23 Mar 44. Ass 31 Mar 44.

42-107092 To 401BG 23 Mar 44 615BS-E. Ass 31 Mar 44.

No Douglas-built silver aircraft were Missing in Action up to 31st March 1944. Of the 24 assigned the only one to be removed from assignment was the 306th aircraft which aborted the mission of 28th March and crash landed back at Thurleigh.

42-107015 lands at Glatton. One of five silver Douglas-built aircraft serving with the 457th at the end of March 1944. It would be interned in Sweden for nearly a year before being returned to the USA at the end of the war. *Bernard Bains*

B-24D CONSOLIDATED

41-23658 Orig of 93BG 329BS. To 2BW Dec 42.

41-23665 Orig of 93BG 330BS. To 2BW Dec 42.

41-23666 Orig of 93BG 330BS. To 2BW Dec 42.

41-23667 Orig of 93BG 328BS-H 'BALL OF FIRE'. To 2BW Dec 42.

41-23672 Orig of 93BG 328BS 'DOUBLE TROUBLE'. To 2BW Dec 42.

41-23674 Orig of 93BG 329BS. To 2BW Dec 42. Ret to 1BD 20 Dec 43 when it was Ass to 482BG. Classified as B-24DSA. Ass 14 Feb 44.

41-23675 Orig of 93BG 330BS 'CELHALOPOOS'. To 2BW Dec 42.

41-23678 Orig of 93BG 330BS. MIA 9 Oct 42. Capt Alexander Simpson. Only B-24 MIA while Ass to 1BW/BD.

41-23682 Orig of 93BG 329BS-Q 'BLASTED EVENT'. To 2BW Dec 42.

41-23683 Orig of 93BG 329BS-V. To 2BW Dec 42.

41-23686 Orig of 93BG 329BS. To 2BW Dec 42.

41-23689 Orig of 93BG 329BS. To 2BW Dec 42.

41-23692 Orig of 93BG 330BS-D 'EL LOBO'. To 2BW Dec 42.

41-23707 Orig of 93BG. To 2BW Dec 42. Cr into mountain near Tafaraoui, North Africa. 7 Dec 42. Lt Johnson. 14 on board, all kld.

41-23710 Orig of 93BG 329BS 'HARES'S TO YA'. Cr Exeter 7 Nov 42 on ret from Op Miss. Capt Ralph J McBride.

41-23711 Orig of 93BG 328BS-B 'JERKS NATURAL'. To 2BW Dec 42.

41-23712 Orig of 93BG 330BS. Cr Porlock 29 Oct 42. Capt William F Williams II. 11 kld.

41-23717 Orig of 93BG 329BS-H 'EXTERMINATOR'. To 2BW Dec 42.

41-23721 Orig of 93BG 330BS. To 2BW Dec 42.

41-23722 Orig of 93BG 328BS 'BOMERANG'. To 2BW Dec 42.

41-23723 Orig of 93BG 329BS 'HELLS A DROPPIN'. Cr Exeter 8 Nov 42. Lt Harvey.

41-23724 Orig of 93BG 409BS. To 2BW Dec 42.

41-23728 Orig of 93BG 330BS 'HOT STUFF'. To 2BW 6 Dec 42. (This Act cr in Iceland 3 May 43 killing Gen Andrews).

41-23729 Orig of 93BG 328BS-D 'SHOOT LUKE'. To 2BW Dec 42.

Two of the B-24Ds assigned to the 93rd Bomb Group at Grenier Field and flown to Alconbury in September 1942. Above is 41-23711 'JERKS NATURAL', and below is 41-23729 'SHOOT LUKE'. Both survived the 93rd's stay in the First Bombardment Wing and were transferred to the Second Bombardment Wing in December 1942. *Mike Bailey*

41-23732 Orig of 93BG 409BS. To 2BW Dec 42.

41-23734 Orig of 93BG 409BS. To 2BW Dec 42.

41-23737 Orig of 93BG 328BS-E 'EAGER BEAVER'. To 2BW Dec 42.

41-23738 Orig of 93BG 409BS 'WHAM BAM'. To 2BW Dec 42.

41-23740 Orig of 93BG 409BS. To 2BW Dec 42.

41-23742 Orig of 93BG 409BS-H 'LIBERTY LAD'. To 2BW Dec 42.

41-23744 Orig of 93BG 409BS 'GERONIMO'. To 2BW Dec 42.

41-23745 Orig of 93BG 328BS 'KATY BUG'. Cr at Alconbury on ret from Op Miss 18 Nov 42. 2nd Lt Alfred Asch.

41-23748 Orig of 93BG 409BS. To 2BW Dec 42.

41-23754 Orig of 93BG 409BS-U 'TEGGIE ANN'. To 2BW Dec 42.

B-24H DOUGLAS

41-28617 From Warton to 482BG (SO) 24 Jan 44 814BS. To 9AF Stansted 7 Feb 44. Then unknown.

41-28636 From USA to 482BG (SO) 31 Jan 44 814BS. To 9AF Stansted 7 Feb 44. Then unknown.

41-28639 From USA to 482BG 12 Feb 44 814BS. Ass 14 Feb 44.

41-28648 From Warton to 482BG (SO) 29 Jan 43 814BS. To 9AF Stansted 7 Feb 44. Then unknown.

41-28651 From Warton to 482BG (SO) 26 Jan 44 814BS. To 9AF Stansted 7 Feb 44. Then unknown.

41-28652 From Warton to 482BG (SO) 26 Jan 44 814BS. To 9AF Stansted 7 Feb 44. Then unknown.

41-28653 From USA to 482BG 7 Feb 44 814BS. Ass 14 Feb 44.

41-28676 From USA to 482BG 9 Feb 44 814BS. Ass 14 Feb 44.

41-28690 From USA to 482BG 9 Feb 44 814BS. Ass 14 Feb 44.

41-28700 From USA to 482BG 9 Feb 44 814BS. Ass 14 Feb 44.

B-24H CONSOLIDATED

41-29120 From BAD to 482BG (SH) 20 Dec 43 814BS. Ass 14 Feb 44.

41-29163 From BAD to 482BG (SH) 15 Dec 43 814BS. Ass 14 Feb 44.

41-29177 From BAD to 482BG (SH) 15 Dec 43 814BS. Ass 14 Feb 44.

41-29183 From USA to 482BG 12 Feb 44 814BS. Ass 14 Feb 44.

B-24H FORD

42-7499 To 482BG (SO) 8 Oct 43 814BS. To 93BG 31 Dec 43.

42-7629 To 482BG 8 Oct 43 814BS. To 93BG 12 Nov 43.

42-7644 From BAD to 482BG (SH) 20 Dec 43 814BS. Ass 14 Feb 44.

42-7645 From BAD to 482BG (SH) 4 Jan 44 814BS. Ass 14 Feb 44.

42-7646 From BAD to 482BG (SH) 21 Dec 43 814BS. Ass 14 Feb 44.

42-7669 From BAD to 482BG (SH) 26 Dec 43 814BS. In mid air coll with B-24J 42-100005 of 392BG while forming for Op Miss 29 Jan 44. Cr at Gissing. 1st Lt James N Taylor.

42-7672 From BAD to 482BG (SH) 29 Dec 43 814BS. Cr at Shingay 23 Jan 44 while on night training flight. 6 kld. Capt Joseph Avendano Jr. (25 Jan 44).

B-24D CONSOLIDATED

42-40362 From BAD to 482BG (SA) 28 Jan 44 814BS. Ass 14 Feb 44.

42-40474 From BAD to 482BG 25 Dec 43 814BS. Cr at Hamel Down five miles SW of Moretonhampstead 27 Dec 43. 8 kld. Capt Robert L Williams. (28 Dec 43).

42-40478 From BAD to 482BG (SA) 4 Jan 44 813BS. Ass 14 Feb 44.

42-40501 From BAD to 482BG (SA) 30 Dec 43 814BS. Ass 14 Feb 44.

42-40530 From BAD to 482BG (SA) 17 Dec 43 814BS. Ass 14 Feb 44.

42-40538 From BAD to 482BG (SA) 28 Jan 44 814BS. Ass 14 Feb 44.

42-40549 From BAD to 482BG (SA) 17 Nov 43 814BS. Ass 14 Feb 44.

42-40550 From BAD to 482BG (SA) 5 Dec 43 814BS. Ass 14 Feb 44.

42-40618 From BAD to 482BG (SA) 30 Dec 43 814BS. Ass 14 Feb 44.

42-40713 From BAD to 482BG (SA) 5 Dec 43 814BS. Ass 14 Feb 44.

42-40748 From Hethal on loan to 303BG 6 Feb 44. Ass to 303BG from 14 Mar 44. Ass 31 Mar 44.

42-40840 From 479 Anti Sub Gp to 482BG (AS) 31 Oct 43 814BS. To BAD 24 Nov 43.

42-40859 From 479 Anti Sub Gp to 482BG (AS) 6 Nov 43 814BS. To BAD 3 Dec 43.

42-40919 From 479 Anti Sub Gp to 482BG (AS) 31 Oct 43 814BS. To BAD 24 Nov 43.

42-40921 From 479 Anti Sub Gp to 482BG (AS) 31 Oct 43. To Bwd 18 Nov 43.

42-40925 From 479 Anti Sub Gp to 482BG (AS) 3 Nov 43 814BS. To BAD 24 Nov 43.

42-40926 From 479 Anti Sub Gp to 482BG (AS) 6 Nov 43 814BS. To BAD 1 Dec 43.

42-40931 From 479 Anti Sub Gp to 482BG 8 Nov 43 814BS. To Bwd 18 Nov 43.

42-40937 From 479 Anti Sub Gp to 482BG (AS) 31 Oct 43 814BS. To BAD 24 Nov 43.

42-40939 From 479 Anti Sub Gp to 482BG (AS) 3 Nov 43 814BS. To Bwd 18 Nov 43.

42-40944 From 479 Anti Sub Gp to 482BG (AS) 31 Oct 43 814BS. To Bwd 20 Nov 43.

42-40959 From 479 Anti Sub Gp to 482BG (AS) 3 Nov 43 814BS. To BAD 24 Nov 43.

42-40987 From Bwd to 482BG (SH) 28 Sep 43 814BS. Ass 14 Feb 44. First B-24 Ass to 482BG.

B-24D FORD

42-63773 From BAD to 482BG (SA) 20 Dec 43 814BS. Ass 14 Feb 44.

42-63775 From BAD to 482BG 28 Jan 44 814BS. Ass 14 Feb 44.

42-63776 From BAD to 482BG (SA) 20 Dec 43 814BS. Ass 14 Feb 44.

42-63781 To 482BG 814BS. Ass 14 Feb 44.

42-63784 From Bwd to 482BG (SA) 20 Nov 43 814BS. Ass 14 Feb 44.

42-63786 From BAD to 482BG (SA) 30 Dec 43 814BS. Ass 14 Feb 44.

42-63787 Recorded as Ass to 482BG on 8 Oct 43 but no further record can be found.

42-63788 From BAD to 482BG (SA) 29 Jan 44 814BS. Ass 14 Feb 44.

42-63789 From Bwd to 482BG (SA) 17 Nov 43 814BS. Ass 14 Feb 44.

42-63792 From BAD to 482BG (SA) 5 Jan 44 814BS. Ass 14 Feb 44.

42-63798 From BAD to 482BG (SA) 3 Jan 44 814BS. Ass 14 Feb 44.

42-63801 From BAD to 482BG (SA) 3 Jan 44 814BS. Ass 14 Feb 44.

B-24D CONSOLIDATED

42-72863 From 479 Anti Sub Gp to 482BG (SA) 8 Nov 43 814BS. Ass 14 Feb 44.

DOUGLAS DB-7B

AL268 15BS(L). Cr while taxiing 2 July 42. Crew not inj. Probably RAF Act on loan, never Ass to 1BW.

AL372 To 15BS(L). To 12AF, dep 15 Nov 42.

AL381 To 15BS(L). Hit high tension cable 6 Aug 42. Probably RAF Act on loan, never Ass to 1BW.

AL397 To 15BS(L). To 91BG 17 Apr 43. Ass 31 Mar 44.

AL409 To 92BG (before 1 Mar 43). To 305BG 13 Oct 43. To 306BG 28 Jan 44. Ass 31 Mar 44.

AL429 To 15BS(L). To 12AF. Dep 15 Nov 42.

AL436 To 15BS(L). To 12AF. Dep 15 Nov 42.

AL441 To 15BS(L). To 91BG (before 1 Mar 43). Wrecked in taxiing Acc at Bassingbourn 4 Mar 43 when LG raised instead of flaps. Lt Col Baskin R Lawrence Jr. To AFSC 4 Mar 43.

AL442 To 15BS(L). To 12AF. Dep 15 Nov 42.

AL445 To 15BS(L). To 12AF. Dep 15 Nov 42.

AL451 No information.

AL452 From 93BG to 482BG 5 Oct 43. To 1BD flight section. Trans to Kimbolton 27 Mar 44. Ass 31 Mar 44.

AL455 To 15BS(L). Flew Miss of 5 Sep 42. Then no record.

AL486 To 15BS(L). To 12AF. Dep 15 Nov 42.

AL489 To 15BS(L). To 12AF. Dep 15 Nov 42.

AL490 To 15BS(L). To 306BG (before 1 Mar 43). To AFSC 14 May 43.

AL491 To 15BS(L). To 303BG (before 1 Mar 43). Ass 31 Mar 44.

AL492 To 15BS(L). To 12AF. Dep 15 Nov 42.

AL493 To 15BS(L). Flew Miss of 5 Sep 42. Then no record.

AL494 To 15BS(L). To 12AF. Dep 15 Nov 42.

AL397 served originally in the 15th Bomb Squadron (Light) but was not one of the DB-7Bs this squadron flew to North Africa in November 1942. It was assigned to the 91st Bomb Group on 17th April 1943 to replace AL441 which had been wrecked in a taxiing accident on 4th March. Top photo shows the aircraft in its original camouflage finish and the lower later in 1944 after the camouflage had been removed. *Stan Bishop*

AL495	To 15BS(L). To 12AF. Dep 15 Nov 42.
AL496	To 305BG (before 1 Mar 43). To 92BG 31 Mar 43. To 384BG 14 June 43 out on 23 Sep 43.
AL497	To 15BS(L). To 12AF. Dep 15 Nov 42.
AL498	To 15BS(L). To 12AF. Dep 15 Nov 42.
AL 499	To 15BS(L). To 12AF. Dep 15 Nov 42.
AL672	No information.
Z2200	To 15BS(L). Cr 1 July 42. Capt S F Stacker and Lt C R Mente kld. Probably RAF Act on loan. Never Ass to 1BW.

NON OPERATIONAL AIRCRAFT

CESSNA C-78 BOBCAT

42-58434 To 92BG 5 June 43. To 482BG 27 Aug 43. To 1BD flight section, transferred to Kimbolton 27 Mar 44.

42-58511 Alconbury to 306BG 28 Feb 44. Ass 31 Mar 44.

PIPER L-4B-PI CUB

43-648 To 92BG 8 Apr 43. To 381BG 10 July 43. To 91BG 26 Oct 43. Ass 31 Mar 44.

43-657	To 92BG 8 Apr 43. To 482BG 27 Aug 43. To 2 SAD 31 Dec 43.
43-693	Ferry Command to 306BG 19 Oct 43. To AFSC for rep 6 Nov 43.
43-702	Bovingdon to 303BG 18 Oct 43. Ass 31 Mar 44.
43-713	To 92BG 19 May 43. To 482BG 27 Aug 43. Ass 14 Feb 44 when 482BG transferred to Composite Command.
43-714	To 92BG 19 May 43. To 95BG 20 May 43.

STINSON L-5/VW SENTINEL

42-98593 15th Tac Recon Sqdn to 482BG 9 Feb 44. Probably went with 482BG to Composite Command 14 Feb 44.

REPUBLIC P-47D THUNDERBOLT

42-7882 ASFC to 482BG 6 Feb 44. To 1BD flight section. Transferred to Kimbolton 27 Mar 44. Ass 31 Mar 44. (Formerly 78th FG).

FAIRCHILD UC-61A-FA ARGUS

43-14419 Alconbury to 306BG 2 Mar 44. To Abbots Ripton 9 Mar 44.

43-14468 Alconbury to 306BG 9 Mar 44. Ass 31 Mar 44.

43-14469 Bovingdon to 482BG 11 Oct 43. To Composite Command 14 Feb 44.

Fairchild Argus 43-14468 which was assigned to the 306th Bomb Group on 9th March 1944. *RAF Museum*

43-14484 Bovingdon to 482BG 9 Feb 44. To Watton 17 Feb 44. (Out of 1BD 14 Feb 44 when 482BG transferred to Composite Command).

43-14499 479 Anti Sub Grp to 482BG 11 Dec 43. To Composite Command 14 Feb 44.

WESTLAND LYSANDER III

V9778 To 92BG 26 June 43. Out on 27 June 43.

MILES MASTER II

DL899 To 92BG 5 Aug 43. To 482BG 27 Aug 43. To 1BD flight section. Transferred to Kimbolton 27 Mar 44. Ass 31 Mar 44.

AIRSPEED OXFORD

DF299 To 91BG 16 May 43. To 303BG 12 June 43. Ass 31 Mar 44.

DF331 To 91BG 16 May 43. To 1BD 21 Oct 43. To 482BG 22 Oct 43. To 1BD flight section, transferred to Kimbolton 27 Mar 44.

DF335 To 91BG 16 May 43. Ass 31 Mar 44.

DF399 To 91BG 16 May 43. To 351BG 10 Dec 43. Ass 31 Mar 44.

LB513 To 92BG 27 June 43. To 482BG 27 Aug 43. To Honington 17 Dec 43.

LB522 To 92BG 25 June 43. To 305BG 1 Aug 43. To 482BG 25 Dec 43. To 1BD flight section. Transferred to Kimbolton 27 Mar 44.

W-6588 To 92BG 5 June 43. To 306BG 15 June 43. (May have gone via 91BG). To RAF Cambridge 7 Oct 43.

X-7176 To 92BG 5 June 43. To 482BG 27 Aug 43. To Composite Command 14 Feb 44.

V-3559 To 306BG from Podington 9 Jan 44. Ass 31 Mar 44.

SUPERMARINE SPITFIRE

7147 Ass from Alconbury to 1BD flight section at Kimbolton. Not on hand until April 44.

DE HAVILAND TIGER MOTH

T6369 To 303BG 12 June 43. Sal at RAF Polebrook 17 June 43. Rep completed by 54MU 2 Oct 43. To Alconbury 8 Oct 43. Ass to 482BG then to 1BD flight section. Transferred to Kimbolton 27 Mar 43. Ass 31 Mar 44.

VISITORS TO FIRST DIVISION BASES

Recorded as on hand but not Assigned

Serial No	Type	Details
41-24380	B-17F	5th Photo Group of 12AF. At Kimbolton for rep from 21 Jan 44 to 28 Jan 44.
41-36963	YB-29-BW	The first B-29 Superfortress to visit the United Kingdom. Arr at St Mawgan on 7 Mar 44. Arr at Glatton 12 Mar 44 and dep for Horsham St Faith on 13 Mar 44. Should also have visited Bassingbourn and was reported there on 9 Mar 44, this has not been confirmed.
42-3134	B-17F	After service with 92BG this Act was Ass to 8th Fighter Command. Based at Ridgewell from 6 Mar 44 and still there on 31 Mar 44.
42-5905	B-17F	Ass to 388BG of 3BD this Act developed trouble while forming for Op Miss 30 Nov 43 and Ld at Polebrook. Nature of trouble is not known but it was at Polebrook until 10 Jan 44 so must have involved major rep.
42-40748	B-24D	Loaned to 303BG from Hethal 6 Feb 44. Carried as on hand but not Ass until 13 Mar 44 from which date it was Ass to 303BG.
43-666	L-4B Cub	Ass to 56th FG at Halesworth. Made an emergency Ld at Ridgewell on 25 Nov 43, ret to Halesworth on 3 Dec 43.

First Bombardment Division planes often landed at Third Bombardment Division bases in Suffolk or Norfolk when returning from missions. Third Division planes on First Division bases were a much rarer sight. The 388th Bomb Group's 'JUST AG' 42-5905 got into difficulties when forming for the mission of 30th November 1943 and landed at Polebrook. It was there until 10th January 1944.
Ed Huntzinger

AIRCRAFT ASSIGNED TO 8TH AIR FORCE
or units destined for the 8th Air Force, but were lost (a) before departing from the USA, (b) during the Ferry Flight, or (c) on arrival in the United Kingdom

This list includes aircraft lost up to May 1943 which would most likely have been assigned to First Bombardment Wing Units on their arrival in England. After May 1943, only those aircraft assigned to units intended for the First Bombardment Wing/Division are included. These aircraft are included on the Group Aircraft Assigned Charts but are not included in the Aircraft Statistics Listing.

B-17E

41-2588 To 97BG 340BS. Ground looped on rwy at Presque Isle, when Ld after flight from Houlton, 28 June 42. 1st Lt C D Lee. Dam beyond rep. Parts used to rep 41-9022.

41-9032 To 97BG 342BS 'MY GAL SAL'. Forced down on coast of Greenland on flight from Goose Bay to BW1 26 June 42. Lt Ralph H Stinson.

The Piper Cub from the 56th Fighter Group which made an emergency landing at Ridgewell on 25th November 1943. Photo taken later at RAF Digby.
RAF Museum

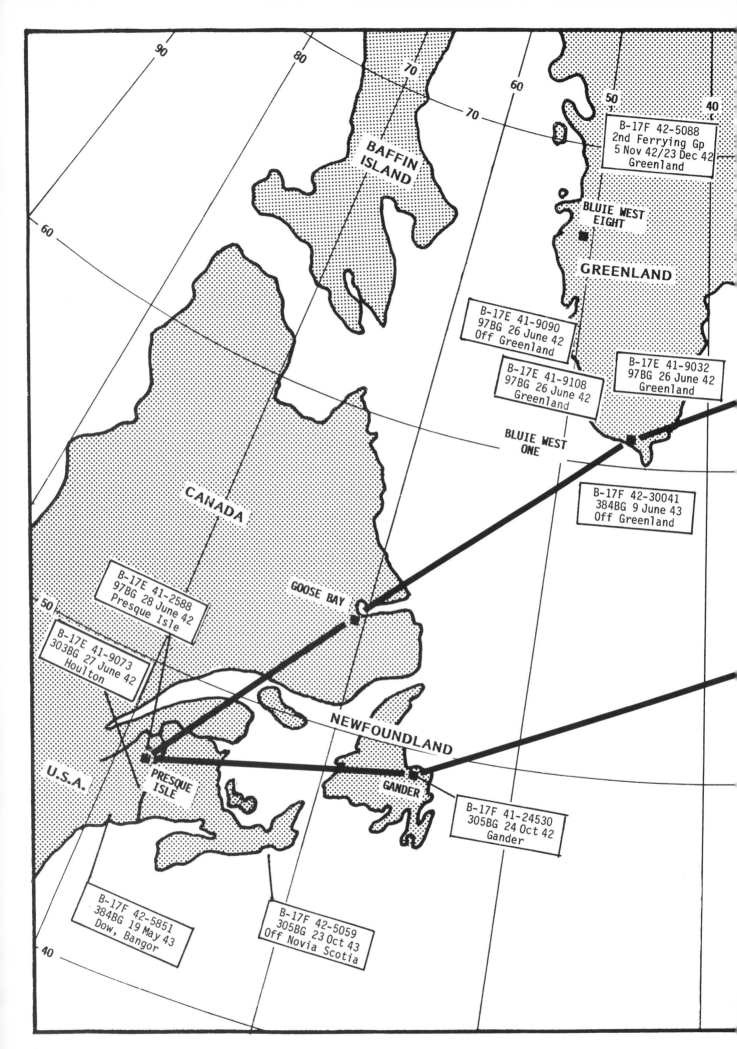

B-17F 42-5088
2nd Ferrying Gp
5 Nov 42/23 Dec 42
Greenland

BLUIE WEST
EIGHT

GREENLAND

BAFFIN
ISLAND

B-17E 41-9090
97BG 26 June 42
Off Greenland

B-17E 41-9108
97BG 26 June 42
Greenland

B-17E 41-9032
97BG 26 June 42
Greenland

BLUIE WEST
ONE

B-17F 42-30041
384BG 9 June 43
Off Greenland

CANADA

GOOSE BAY

B-17E 41-2588
97BG 28 June 42
Presque Isle

B-17E 41-9073
303BG 27 June 42
Houlton

NEWFOUNDLAND

U.S.A.

PRESQUE
ISLE

GANDER

B-17F 41-24530
305BG 24 Oct 42
Gander

B-17F 42-5851
384BG 19 May 43
Dow, Bangor

B-17F 42-5059
305BG 23 Oct 43
Off Novia Scotia

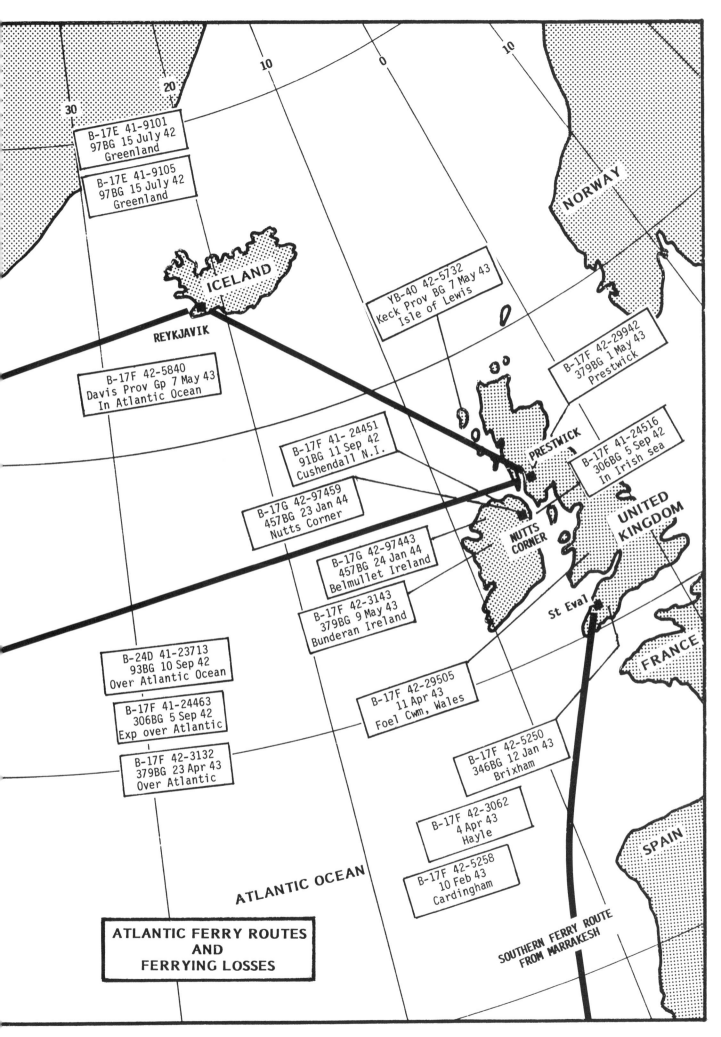

ATLANTIC FERRY ROUTES
AND
FERRYING LOSSES

B-17E 41-9101
97BG 15 July 42
Greenland

B-17E 41-9105
97BG 15 July 42
Greenland

YB-40 42-5732
Keck Prov BG 7 May 43
Isle of Lewis

B-17F 42-29942
379BG 1 May 43
Prestwick

B-17F 42-5840
Davis Prov Gp 7 May 43
In Atlantic Ocean

B-17F 41-24451
91BG 11 Sep 42
Cushendall N.I.

B-17F 41-24516
306BG 5 Sep 42
In Irish sea

B-17G 42-97459
457BG 23 Jan 44
Nutts Corner

B-17G 42-97443
457BG 24 Jan 44
Belmullet Ireland

B-17F 42-3143
379BG 9 May 43
Bunderan Ireland

B-24D 41-23713
93BG 10 Sep 42
Over Atlantic Ocean

B-17F 41-24463
306BG 5 Sep 42
Exp over Atlantic

B-17F 42-3132
379BG 23 Apr 43
Over Atlantic

B-17F 42-29505
11 Apr 43
Foel Cwm, Wales

B-17F 42-5250
346BG 12 Jan 43
Brixham

B-17F 42-3062
4 Apr 43
Hayle

B-17F 42-5258
10 Feb 43
Cardingham

REYKJAVIK

ICELAND

NORWAY

PRESTWICK

NUTTS
CORNER

UNITED
KINGDOM

St Eval

FRANCE

SPAIN

ATLANTIC OCEAN

SOUTHERN FERRY ROUTE
FROM MARRAKESH

One of the 49 B-17Es scheduled to make the BOLERO crossing to England. This is 41-9073 after the landing gear had retracted at Houlton. *US Air Force*

41-9073 To 303BG 359BS. On 27 June, 1st Lt Donald E Sheeler and his crew taxied for TO at Houlton, Maine. After completion of engine run ups, the LG retracted allowing the Act to be lowered on to the ramp. The propellers made contact briefly with the ramp surface, then all was quiet. The crew were uninjured. Act sal.

41-9090 To 97BG 342BS. Force Ld in fiord 35 miles SW of BW1 Greenland after flight from Goose Bay 26 June 42. Lt Nicols.

41-9101 To 97BG 341BS 'BIG STOOP'. Made wheels up Ld on Greenland icecap between BW8 and Iceland 15 July 42. Lt Hanna.

41-9105 To 97BG 341BS 'DO DO'. Made wheels up Ld on Greenland icecap between BW8 and Iceland 15 July 42. Lt Staples.

(41-9101 and 9105 were escorting six P-38s of the 94th Fighter Sqdn which also Ld on the icecap. They were 41-7560, 7583, 7616, 7623, 7626 and 7630).

41-9108 To 97BG 342BS. Forced down on coast of Greenland on flight from Goose Bay to BW1 26 June 42. Lt J H Holmes. Crew uninjured.

41-9127 To 301BG 419BS. Overshot rwy when Ld at Houlton, Maine 26 June 42. Lt Wilson. Subsequently rep but spent rest of its service in USA.

B-17F

41-24380 Orig of 92BG. In Acc at Bangor Maine 26 July 42. Did not proceed to UK. Later served in 12AF.

41-24436 Allocated to 8AF in USA. Probably had Acc which prevented Act from proceeding to UK.

41-24451 Orig of 91BG 401BS. Cr at Cushendall Northern Ireland, on flight Gander to Prestwick 11 Sep 42. Capt Dale Lasalle.

41-24462 Orig of 306BG 369BS. Tailwheel collapsed in USA and Act did not proceed to England with the Group.

41-24463 Orig of 306BG 423BS. Exploded in mid air over Atlantic on flight from Gander to Prestwick 5 Sep 42. 1st Lt John T Leahy. All crew lost.

41-24516 Orig of 306BG 368BS. Ditched in Irish Sea on flight from Gander to Prestwick 5 Sep 42. Capt William C Melton Jr. All crew saved.

41-24530 Orig of 305BG 366BS. Cr while TO at night from Gander on flight to Prestwick 24 Oct 42. Act deviated to left on TO run and collided with a pill box. Slid to a stop on its belly on an adjacent rwy. Badly dam. 2 crew inj. 1st Lt Lyle M Adams.

42-24571 Orig of 91BG. Ass in USA but did not fly to England with the group. Reason unknown. Later served in 15AF.

42-2971 Allocated to 8AF in Oct 42. No details.

42-3062 Cr at Hayle Cornwall 4 Apr 43 at end of ferry flight from North Africa.

42-3132 Orig of 379BG 526BS. Lost in Atlantic on flight from Gander to Prestwick 23 Apr 43. All on board lost. Capt Lawrence M Elstead.

42-3143 Orig of 379BG 524BS. Cr Ld at Bunderan Ireland 9 May 43 on flight Gander to Prestwick.

42-3219 Orig of 381BG 534BS. Probably not to UK with 381BG. Later served in 94BG.

42-5059 Orig of 305BG 366BS 'HELLS ANGELS'. Came down in sea off Nova Scotia while on flight to England 23 Oct 42. Charles D Clark. All crew safe.

42-5079 Allocated to 8AF Oct 42. No details of any presence in UK.

42-5088 Cr on Greenland icecap while on ferry flight to England between 5 Nov 42 and 23 Dec 42. (2nd Ferrying Group).

42-5250 By Sth Fy Rt dep Mrk 12 Jan 43. Cr Ld out of fuel 1½ miles NE of Brixham on arrival in UK. Had been airborne approx 12 hrs. 1st Lt A F Burch. No inj to crew. Act sal. Reported as 346BG(H) controlled and routed by ATC.

305th Bomb Group's 41-24530 on its belly at Gander after an abortive take off attempt for the Atlantic crossing on the night of 24th October 1942. *US Air Force*

42-5258   By Sth Fy Rt dep Mrk 10 Feb 43. Cr Ld in field at Treswithick Farm, Cardingham on arrival in UK at St Eval and Chivenor closed in by weather. Lt Edwin G Pipp. Crew uninjured. Act sal.

YB-40

42-5732   Got lost on ferry flight to UK 7 May 43. Belly Ld near Brenish on Isle of Lewis. Was dismantled and taken to Stornoway Airfield (about 40 miles). History after this is not clear, most likely assembled and flown out of Stornoway but possibly taken out by sea. Ret to USA Feb 44. No record of this Act serving in 8AF. If this Act was dismantled and moved from the site of its forced Ld and then re-assembled and flown again, then it is the only recorded case where a B-17 was rebuilt and flown after having been so dismantled and moved in the 8AF.

B-17F

42-5840   Cr in sea en-route Goose Bay to Iceland 7 May 43. Davis Provisional Group came down near convoy due to lack of fuel. 8 saved 2 lost. Had been in air for 11 hrs.

42-5851   Orig of 384BG 547BS. Cr while Ld at Dow, Maine, when on ferry flight to UK 19 May 43.

42-29505   Cr in Prescelly Mountains, Wales, 11 Apr 43, at end of ferry flight from North Africa.

42-29829   Orig of 379BG. Wrecked at Kearney, Nebraska about 9 Apr 43. Not to UK with Group.

42-29942   Orig of 379BG 527BS. LG collapsed after Ld at Prestwick after ferry flight from USA 1 May 43. No inj to crew. Maj Carlson.

42-30025   Orig of 381BG. Not to UK with Group. Reason unknown.

42-30041   Orig of 384BG 544BS. Cr at sea 185 miles off coast of Greenland while on ferry flight to UK 9 June 43.

42-30074   Orig of 384BG. Wrecked in USA about 1 May 43, not to UK.

B-17G

42-31541   Orig of 457BG. Cr and sal in USA about 24 Dec 43. No further details.

42-31547   Orig of 457BG. Cr and sal in USA about 5 Jan 44. No further details.

42-31586   Orig of 457BG. Had Acc in USA about 11 Dec 44. Rep and later served in 15AF.

42-38056   Orig of 457BG. Probably trans out on Arr in UK. No record in First Bomb Div.

42-38065   Orig of 457BG. Probably trans out on Arr in UK. No record in First Bomb Div.

42-38066   Orig of 457BG. Probably trans out on Arr in UK. No record in First Bomb Div.

42-97443   Orig of 457BG 749BS. Force Ld at Belmullet, Ireland at end of ferry flight from Goose Bay to Nutts Corner 24 Jan 44. Crew uninjured. 2nd Lt Donald G Karr.

42-97459   Orig of 457BG 750BS. Over-ran rwy 22 at Nutts Corner on Ld at end of ferry flight from Goose Bay 23 Jan 44. 2nd Lt Tracy E Geiger Jr. 8 uninjured 1 minor and 1 maj inj. Act severely dam.

42-97473   Orig of 457BG. Probably trans out on Arr in UK. Later served in 390BG of 3BD.

B-24D

41-23679   Orig of 93BG. Was left at Grenier by the Group, stripped of many parts. Details not known.

41-23713   Orig of 93BG 328BS. Disappeared on ferry flight between Gander and Prestwick 10 Sep 42. All crew lost. Lt Henshaw.

The 457th Bomb Group lost two brand new B-17Gs at the end of the ferry flight from Goose Bay to Nutts Corner. One crash landed at Belmullet in Ireland and the other 42-97459 overshot on landing at Nutts Corner. Photograph shows this aircraft broken backed and wrecked after running into a ditch. *US Air Force*

'HELNO GAL' 42-3085. A Bassingbourn based B-17F of the 94th Bomb Group crash landed at North Weald on return from the mission of 21st May 1943. An inspector from Service Command estimated it would take three weeks to return the plane to service. However, later the Command reported that due to negligent removal of parts by the Holding Group it was rendered un-repairable. *Mike Gibson*

B-17Fs which arrived in the United Kingdom late in 1942 and were assigned direct to the 12th Air Force without serving in the First Bombardment Wing

41-24433
41-24434
41-24438
41-24440
These four aircraft were assigned to the 15th Mapping Squadron in the USA. They were modified at Fairfield Air Depot and then went to Westover. Arr in UK 1 Oct 42. Dep Hurn for 12AF 19 Nov 42.

41-24618 Left Gander for UK on 27 Oct 42. Ass to 301BG on Arr in England. Dep Hurn for 12AF 24 Nov 42.

42-5082 To UK Oct 42. To 301BG 7 Nov 42. Dep Hurn for 12AF 28 Nov 42.

42-5085 To UK Oct 42. To 301BG 7 Nov 42. Dep Hurn for 12AF 24 Nov 42.

42-5087 To UK Nov 42. To 97BG 340BS. Dep Predannack for 12AF 10 Nov 42.

42-5090 Dep Gander for UK 26 Oct 42. Took off with only 500ft visibility and Ld at Prestwick 11hrs 32mins later. To 97BG 414BS. Dep Hurn for 12AF 20 Nov 42.

42-5715 Dep Gander 27 Oct 42. To 97BG 342BS. Dep Hurn for 12AF 20 Nov 43.

It is possible that some of the above aircraft were flown to England by crews of the 305BG, the 305th had lost two aircraft early in the ferry flight and the crews of these are reported as being allocated new aircraft to ferry to England.

B-17Fs ASSIGNED TO THE 94th, 95th and 96th BOMBARDMENT GROUPS OF THE FOURTH BOMBARDMENT WING, BASED ON FIRST BOMBARDMENT WING AIRFIELDS, APRIL—MAY 1943

94th BG was at Bassingbourn (B) and Thurleigh (T)
95th BG was at Alconbury
96th BG was at Grafton Underwood

The dates quoted are the dates on which the aircraft were recorded in on the First Wing Base.
Many of these aircraft were later transferred to the First Bombardment Wing
Where this is indicated, the aircrafts history in the First Bombardment Wing will be found in the First Wing's Serial Number Listing

DOUGLAS

42-3042 96BG 26 Apr 43.

42-3061 95BG 13 May 43. Later to 1BW.

42-3063 94BG.

42-3069 94BG later to 1BW.

42-3071 94BG.

42-3072 96BG 2 May 43. Later to 1BW.

42-3073 94BG later to 1BW.

42-3074 94BG later to 1BW.

42-3075 94BG 18 Apr 43 (B). Later to 1BW.

42-3079 95BG 10 Apr 43. Later to 1BW.

42-3082 94BG 'DOUBLE TROUBLE'.

42-3085 94BG 28 Apr 43 (B). Cr Ld at North Weald on ret from Op Miss 21 May 43.

42-3088 94BG later to 1BW.

42-3091 95BG 13 May 43. Later to 1BW.

42-3095 94BG.

42-3104 94BG later to 1BW.

42-3107 96BG 26 May 43.

42-3110 95BG 15 Apr 43. MIA 21 May 43.

42-3115 95BG 10 Apr 43. MIA 14 May 43.

42-3123 96BG 2 May 43. Later 1BW.

42-3162 94BG 18 Apr 43 (B). Later 1BW.

42-3171 95BG 20 Apr 43. Later to 1BW.

42-3175 95BG 20 Apr 43. Later to 1BW.

42-3176 95BG 19 May 43. Later to 1BW.

42-3177 96BG 26 Apr 43. Later to 1BW.

42-3180 96BG 26 May 43. Later to 1BW.

42-3183 96BG 26 May 43. Later to 1BW.

42-3202 92BG to 95BG 15 May 43.

42-3207 94BG later to 1BW.

42-3212 92BG to 95BG 19 May 43. Later to 1BW.

42-3259 94BG 10 May 43. Later to 1BW.

VEGA

42-5791 95BG 18 Apr 43.

42-5795 95BG 10 Apr 43. Later to 1BW.

42-5081 94BG 29 Apr 43 (T). Later to 1BW.

42-5803 94BG.

42-5805 96BG 28 Apr 43.

42-5858 95BG 26 May 43. MIA 29 May 43.

42-5879 96BG 26 May 43.

42-5883 96BG 23 May 43. Later to 1BW.

BOEING

42-29476 94BG.

42-29627 94BG 26 Apr 43 (T) **'MIDNIGHT'**. MIA 17 May 43. First 94BG MIA.

42-29670 94BG 25 Apr 43 (T). Later to 1BW.

42-29675 95BG 20 Apr 43.

42-29679 95BG 18 Apr 43. Later to 1BW.

42-29680 95BG 21 Apr 43.

42-29682 94BG 2 May 43 (T) **'EASY ACES'**. MIA 21 May 43.

42-29685 95BG 18 May 43. Exploded at Alconbury 27 May 43.

42-29686 94BG 18 Apr 43 (B). Later to 1BW.

42-29689 95BG 13 Apr 43. MIA 29 May 43.

42-29690 94BG 25 Apr 43 (B). To 1BW.

42-29692 94BG.

42-29693 95BG 10 Apr 43.

42-29698 94BG later to 1BW.

42-29699 94BG (B) **'FI FI'**. Later to 1BW.

42-29700 94BG later to 1BW.

42-29702 95BG 28 Apr 43.

42-29703 95BG 10 Apr 43. Later to 1BW.

42-29704 95BG 28 Apr 43. Dam on Op Miss 17 May 43. Ld at Exeter on ret and sal.

42-29706 95BG 7 May 43. Dam by explosion of 42-29685 and sal.

42-29709 95BG 13 Apr 43. Later to 1BW.

42-29710 94BG.

42-29711 94BG 18 Apr 43 (B). Later to 1BW.

42-29713 94BG 25 Apr 43 (T). Later to 1BW.

42-29715 94BG.

42-29716 95BG 28 Apr 43. Later to 1BW.

42-29717 94BG 18 Apr 43 (B). Later to 1BW.

42-29718 94BG 25 Apr 43 (T). Later to 1BW.

42-29723 94BG later to 1BW.

42-29724 94BG later to 1BW.

42-29725 94BG later to 1BW.

42-29726 96BG 16 May 43. Later to 1BW.

42-29727 94BG (B) **'IN DER FUHRERS FACE'**. MIA 21 May 43.

42-29728 94BG 25 Apr 43 (B). Later 1BW.

42-29733 94BG 18 Apr 43 (B). Later to 1BW.

42-29734 96BG 4 May 43. MIA 21 May 43.

42-29737 95BG 10 Apr 43.

42-29738 95BG 10 Apr 43. Later to 1BW.

Two B-17Fs of 331st Bomb Squadron 94th Bomb Group at Grafton Underwood after transfer to the 384th Bomb Group, 12th July 1943. Nearest is 42-29700 which lasted 17 days before going Missing in Action. The second aircraft is 42-3074 which later went to the 306th Bomb Group and finally to Cheddington in February 1944. Note: this is the first Douglas-built B-17F generally listed as having the Tokyo tanks fitted. It is here being transferred out of the Fourth Bombardment Wing because it supposedly has not got them fitted. *Mike Gibson*

A B-17F of 332nd Bomb Squadron 94th Bomb Group at Bassingbourn, 10th July 1943. Two days later it was transferred to the 384th Bomb Group. It crash landed at Grafton Underwood on return from the Schweinfurt mission on 17th August 1943. *US Air Force – National Air and Space Museum*

42-29740 95BG 13 Apr 43. Later to 1BW.

42-29748 96BG 26 Apr 43.

42-29751 96BG 25 Apr 43. Later to 1BW.

42-29752 96BG 25 Apr 43. MIA 13 May 43. First 96BG MIA.

42-29754 95BG 13 Apr 43. Later to 1BW.

42-29755 96BG 21 Apr 43. Later to 1BW.

42-29756 96BG 25 Apr 43.

42-29759 96BG 25 Apr 43. Later to 1BW.

42-29767 96BG MIA 17 May 43.

42-29768 95BG 21 Apr 43. Later to 1BW.

42-29778 96BG 28 Apr 43. Later to 1BW.

42-29780 95BG 18 Apr 43. Later to 1BW.

42-29787 95BG 18 Apr 43. Later to 1BW.

42-29791 95BG 18 Apr 43. Later to 1BW.

42-29800 95BG later to 1BW.

42-29803 95BG 18 Apr 43. Later to 1BW.

42-29807 95BG 18 Apr 43. Later to 1BW.

42-29808 95BG 18 Apr 43. Dam by exploding 42-29685 27 May 43 and sal.

42-29811 95BG 28 Apr 43.

42-29822 94BG 18 Apr 43 (B).

42-29827 95BG 28 Apr 43.

42-29828 96BG later to 1BW.

42-29833 95BG 26 Apr 43.

42-29834 94BG 20 May 43 (B).

42-29914 96BG 28 Apr 43. Later to 1BW.

42-29919 95BG 28 May 43.

42-29927 96BG 26 Apr 43. Later to 1BW.

42-29935 96BG 26 Apr 43. Later to 1BW.

42-29938 96BG 26 Apr 43. To AFSC for sal 22 May 43. Reason unknown.

42-29939 96BG 23 May 43.

42-29941 96BG 26 Apr 43. Later to 1BW.

42-29952 96BG 23 May 43. Later to 1BW.

42-29957 94BG.

42-29967 95BG 28 May 43. Later to 1BW.

42-29981 96BG 26 Apr 43. Later to 1BW.

42-29983 96BG 2 May 43. Later to 1BW.

42-29997 94BG 25 May 43 (T). Later to 1BW.

42-30144 95BG 25 May 43.

42-30153 96BG 26 May 43. Later to 1BW.

42-30164 95BG 28 May 43.

There were at least four **'MAN O' WAR'**s among the aircraft listed in this book. Two were B-17Gs. It is believed the B-17F shown having the finishing touches applied to its nose art is 41-24486 of 306th Bomb Group. This aircraft was one of three the 306th lost on 9th November 1942. *USAF*

RUTLAND

LEICESTERSHIRE

PETERBOROUGH

DEENETHORPE STA 128
401BG from 3 Nov 43

POLEBROOK STA 110
97BG 13 June 42 to Nov 42
351BG from 15 Apr 43

GLATTON STA 130
457BG from 22 Jan 44

HUNTINGDONSHIRE

GRAFTON UNDERWOOD STA 106
15BS(L) 14 May 42 to 9 June 42
97BG (2 Sqdns) 13 June 42 to 8 Sep 42
305BG Sep to 26 Nov 42
384BG from 26 May 43

KETTERING

THRAPSTON

ALCONBURY STA 102
93BG Sep 42 to Dec 42
92BG 6 Jan 43 to 15 Sep 43
482BG 20 Aug 43 to 14 Feb 44

HUNTINGDON

MOLESWORTH STA 107
15BS(L) 9 June 42 to 13 sep 42
303BG from 12 Sep 42

NORTHAMPTONSHIRE

CHELVESTON STA 105
301BG 9 Aug 42 to Nov 42
305BG from 26 Nov 42

BRAMPTON GRANGE
STA 103
HEADQUARTERS
FIRST BOMBARDMENT
WING/DIVISION

WELLINGBOROUGH

RUSHDEN

KIMBOLTON
STA 117
91BG
1 Oct 42 to 14 Oct 42
379 BG from May 43

NORTHAMPTON

PODINGTON STA 109
301BG (2 Sqdns) 20 Aug to 7 Sep 42
15BS(L) 13 Sep to Nov 42
92BG from 15 Sep 43

THURLEIGH STA 111
306BG from 7 Sep 42

LITTLE STAUGHTON
STA 127
Ass to First BW
Sep to Dec 1942
But not used

BEDFORD

BUCKINGHAMSHIRE

BEDFORDSHIRE

AIRFIELDS ASSIGNED TO THE FIRST BOMBARDMENT WING/DIVISION

UP TO 31st MARCH 1944

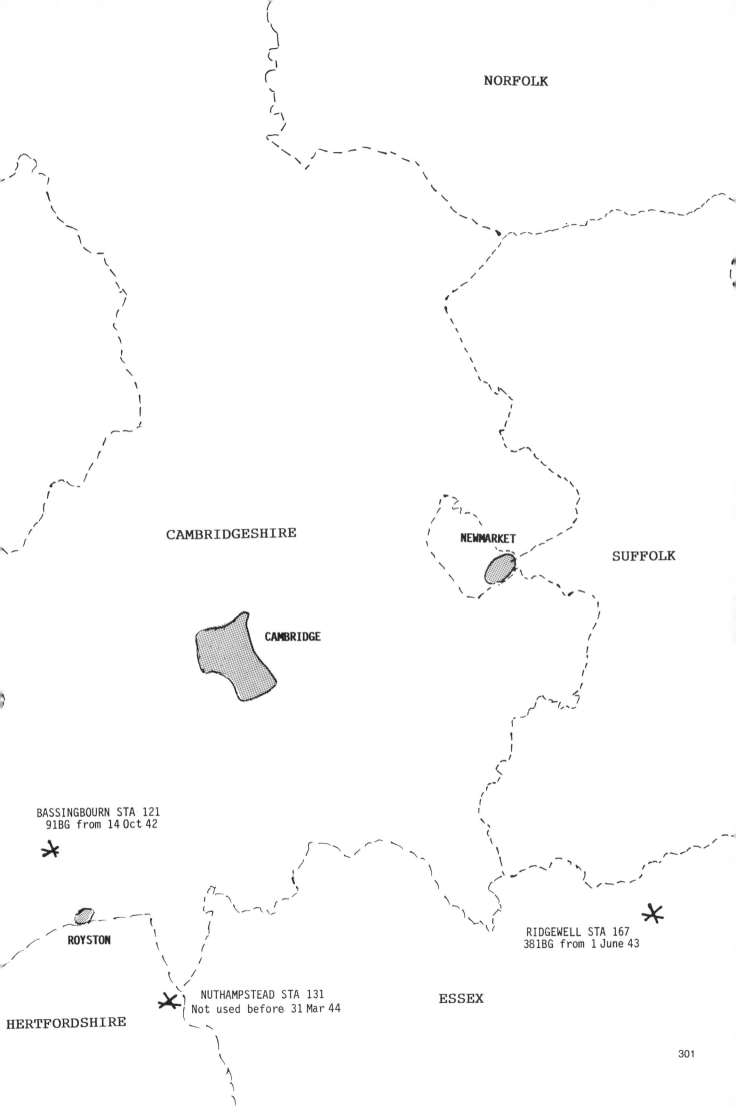

NORFOLK

CAMBRIDGESHIRE

NEWMARKET

SUFFOLK

CAMBRIDGE

BASSINGBOURN STA 121
91BG from 14 Oct 42

RIDGEWELL STA 167
381BG from 1 June 43

ROYSTON

NUTHAMPSTEAD STA 131
Not used before 31 Mar 44

ESSEX

HERTFORDSHIRE

It was unusual for all the aircraft assigned to a Group to be on hand at the Group's station at the same time. Some aircraft would normally be away having scheduled maintenance or modifications carried out at a depot. Others could be located at other USAAF or RAF stations where they had force landed due to battle damage and were undergoing repair by mobile units. These aircraft were often away for several weeks. Diversions due to bad weather at home bases when returning from operational missions were also a cause for many aircraft being away, but these were normally of short duration.

Below is a listing of all aircraft known to have been away from their home stations during March 1944. This list is not regarded as being complete. Note also that the dates given are not necessarily the true dates on which the aircraft arrived or departed from the given station. Unit reports were made up at 2000 hrs each day so an aircraft returning after this time would not be reported until next day. On the other hand, an aircraft landing at another station to refuel when returning from a mission and then proceeding on to its own station and arriving before 2000 hrs would not be reported at all.

**** Aircraft away on the First of the month.   ++++ Still away at the end of the month.

Serial No	Group	Location	Date in	Date out
41-24639	91st	2 SAD	17th	+++
42-31187	91st	Deopham Green	*** *	4th
42-3385	92nd	Hardwick	3rd	16th
42-29975	92nd	Bassingbourn	21st	23rd
42-30644	92nd	Witchford	29th	++++
42-31248	92nd	Friston	15th	30th
42-31250	92nd	Honington	29th	30th
42-31277	92nd	Wormingford	23rd	++++
42-31326	92nd	Halesworth	****	15th
42-31529	92nd	Boreham	26th	++++
42-31687	92nd	Bassingbourn	29th	30th
42-31713	92nd	Sudbury	29th	30th
42-31921	92nd	Mepal	29th	30th
42-37735	92nd	Horham	21st	30th
42-37873	92nd	Rattlesden	7th	9th
42-37877	92nd	Friston	15th	30th
42-37939	92nd	Portreath	2nd	3rd
42-38110	92nd	Deopham Green	29th	30th
42-39851	92nd	Mendlesham	5th	7th
42-39851	92nd	Wratting Common	29th	30th
42-3064	303rd	Abbots Ripton	10th	26th
42-5081	303rd	Metheringham	25th	25th
42-5264	303rd	Watton	***	5th
42-5393	303rd	Abbots Ripton	10th	++++
42-29795	303rd	Shoreham	****	14th
42-31055	303rd	Abbots Ripton	6th	++++
42-31177	303rd	Shoreham	****	11th
42-31213	303rd	Abbots Ripton	6th	21st
42-31405	303rd	Kimbolton	29th	30th
42-31423	303rd	Abbots Ripton	****	17th
42-31574	303rd	Wyton	29th	30th
42-31583	303rd	Abbots Ripton	****	11th
42-31830	303rd	Polebrook	29th	30th
42-31997	303rd	Eastchurch	****	++++
42-32037	303rd	Framlingham	29th	30th
42-37841	303rd	Abbots Ripton	****	13th
42-37168	303rd	Polebrook	29th	30th
42-39807	303rd	Chipping Ongar	****	11th
42-97617	303rd	Abbots Ripton	****	10th
42-24616	305th	Bungay	****	6th
42-31255	305th	2 SAD	16th	27th
42-39949	305th	Woolaston	21st	++++
42-31065	306th	Manston	26th	++++
42-31158	306th	Leiston	****	23rd

Serial No	Group	Location	Date in	Date Out
42-31726	306th	Podington	29th	30th
42-31768	306th	Honington	29th	30th
42-31901	306th	Podington	29th	30th
42-31969	306th	Woodbridge	26th	++++
42-37836	306th	Leiston	21st	++++
42-37840	306th	Eye	29th	30th
42-37942	306th	Beccles	29th	++++
42-39827	306th	Podington	29th	30th
42-39965	306th	Woodhall Spa	24th	26th
42-97588	306th	Tibenham	29th	++++
41-9121	351st	Cluntoe	****	11th
42-3120	351st	New Romney	19th	++++
42-6151	351st	Sculthorpe	****	12th
42-30994	351st	Ludham	10th	16th
42-30994	351st	Alconbury	16th	++++
42-31702	351st	Boxted	4th	31st
42-31827	351st	Hornchurch	****	11th
41-9100	379th	Cluntoe	****	22nd
42-30298	379th	2 SAD	4th	30th
42-31043	379th	Ridgewell	****	3rd
42-31083	379th	Sudbury	29th	30th
42-31228	379th	Manston	****	22nd
42-31228	379th	Molesworth	29th	30th
42-31592	379th	Mildenhall	29th	++++
42-31663	379th	Wratting Common	29th	30th
42-31927	379th	2 SAD	13th	++++
42-37791	379th	Sudbury	29th	30th
42-37888	379th	2 SAD	17th	++++
42-38082	379th	Gatwick	20th	++++
42-38111	379th	Oakington	23rd	++++
42-38161	379th	2SAD	****	11th
42-97128	379th	Framlingham	29th	30th
42-97462	379th	Molesworth	29th	30th
42-5725	381st	Andrews Field	29th	++++
42-31067	381st	Predannack	21st	++++
42-38009	381st	Exeter	21st	++++
42-38079	381st	Leiston	****	++++
42-3051	384th	Abbots Ripton	****	17th
42-29636	384th	Woodbridge	****	7th
42-29651	384th	Metfield	****	9th
42-29703	384th	Rattlesden	****	22nd
42-37758	384th	Nuthampstead	****	3rd
42-37793	384th	Brighton	****	12th
42-38013	384th	2 SAD	****	12th

TABLE ONE

Serial No	Group	Location	Date In	Date Out	Serial No	Group	Location	Date in	Date Out
42-31315	401st	Polebrook	9th	11th	42-32051	457th	Alconbury	21st	31st
42-31508	401st	Wing	16th	17th	42-32098	457th	Burtonwood	15th	21st
42-31591	401st	Alconbury	14th	25th	42-32101	457th	Burtonwood	15th	22nd
42-31593	401st	Great Ashfield	****	17th	42-38102	457th	Alconbury	4th	6th
42-31662	401st	Graveley	29th	30th	42-38113	457th	Alconbury	8th	23rd
42-31730	401st	Horsham St Faith	6th	29th	42-97060	457th	Abbots Ripton	24th	++++
42-37833	401st	Friston	16th	17th	42-97075	457th	Tibenham	29th	30th
42-39837	401st	Nuthampstead	29th	++++	42-97131	457th	Alconbury	20th	++++
42-39873	401st	Friston	18th	20th	42-97137	457th	Burtonwood	21st	28th
42-39881	401st	Woodbridge	****	26th	42-97162	457th	Alconbury	21st	++++
42-39904	401st	Alconbury	7th	8th	42-97452	457th	Warboys	29th	30th
42-40001	401st	Alconbury	7th	8th	42-97456	457th	Leiston	8th	28th
42-40002	401st	Bury St Edmunds	29th	30th	42-97465	457th	Burtonwood	30th	++++
42-97073	401st	Sudbury	29th	30th	42-97468	457th	Chailey	****	13th
42-97464	401st	Alconbury	15th	30th	42-97468	457th	Wyton	19th	20th
42-97487	401st	Knettishall	29th	30th	42-97469	457th	Deenethorpe	****	11th
42-97496	401st	Lakenheath	29th	30th	42-97481	457th	Beccles	****	3rd
					42-97535	457th	Thorpe Abbotts	18th	19th
42-31154	457th	Burtonwood	****	++++	42-97591	457th	Alconbury	4th	8th
42-31531	457th	Martlesham Heath	8th	9th	42-106985	457th	Burtonwood	15th	21st
42-31597	457th	Alconbury	6th	9th	42-106998	457th	Alconbury	8th	10th
42-31618	457th	Alconbury	21st	++++					
42-32051	457th	Alconbury	6th	8th					

Cloud conditions, such as seen below B-17Fs and Gs of 306th Bomb Group proved to be the biggest obstacle to daylight precision bombing, especially in the early days before the introduction of Blind Bombing techniques. *US Air Force*

GROUP	B-17E	B-17F	B-17G	YB-40	TOTAL B-17	B-24D	B-24H	OTHER TYPES
91st	3	137	84	3	227	–	–	8
92nd	37	132	89	12	270	–	–	13
93rd	–	–	–	–	–	35	–	–
97th	35	43	–	–	78	–	–	–
301st	–	41	–	–	41	–	–	–
303rd	1	117	86	3	207	1	–	4
305th	6	140	87	–	233	–	–	3
306th	1	166	91	–	258	–	–	8
351st	1	75	80	–	156	–	–	1
379th	1	100	76	1	178	–	–	–
381st	2	91	86	–	179	–	–	1
384th	1	113	84	1	199	–	–	1
401st	1	4	121	–	126	–	–	–
457th	1	–	123	–	124	–	–	–
482nd	4	21	37	–	62	36	21	16

Table title: AIRCRAFT ASSIGNED BY GROUP.

A mixed formation of olive drab and silver B-17s of the 306th Bomb Group. *USAF*

| AIRCRAFT LOST: BY GROUP | | | | | | | | |
| | MISSING IN ACTION | | | | SALVAGED | | | |
GROUP	B-17E	B-17F	B-17G	YB-40	TOTAL	B-17E	B-17F	B-17G	TOTAL
91st	0	90	29	0	119	0	15	8	23
92nd	2	47	33	1	83	3	12	5	20
97th	0	4	0	0	4	4	2	0	6
301st	0	1	0	0	1	0	3	0	3
303rd	0	64	17	0	81	0	15	7	22
305th	0	66	24	0	90	0	1	6	17
306th	0	81	30	0	111	0	23	10	33
351st	0	36	23	0	59	0	12	9	21
379th	0	61	19	0	80	0	12	6	18
381st	0	51	31	0	82	0	12	10	22
384th	0	62	24	0	86	0	13	7	20
401st	0	0	23	0	23	0	0	10	10
457th	0	0	8	0	8	0	0	2	2
482nd	0	2	2	0	4	1	1	0	2
	2	565	263	1	831	8	131	80	219

TABLE THREE

Back from Stuttgart on three engines. This 303rd Bomb Group B-17F just touching down at Molesworth is believed to be 42-29571 'CHARLEY HORSE'. *USAF*

HEADQUARTERS VIII BOMBER COMMAND OUTGOING MESSAGE

<table>
<tr><td rowspan="2">TO;</td><td colspan="4">CLASSIFICATION</td><td>MESSAGE CENTRE USE ONLY</td></tr>
<tr><td>PRIORITY</td><td></td><td>SECRET</td><td></td><td>ORIG. NO. 8BC F301F</td></tr>
<tr><td>FROM</td><td>ROUTINE</td><td></td><td>CONF.</td><td></td><td>SERIES NO. 52</td></tr>
<tr><td>DATE 4-2-44 TIME 1300 SECT A-4</td><td>DEFERRED</td><td></td><td>REST</td><td>X</td><td>RECEIVED 1355
CLEARED</td></tr>
<tr><td>SIGNATURE</td><td colspan="5">APPROVED</td></tr>
</table>

THE FOLLOWING B-17AND B-24 AIRCRAFT ARE TO BE TRANSFERRED TO AAF STATION 169 WHERE SPECIAL RADIO EQUIPMENT WILL BE REMOVED FOR THE USE OF NINTH AIR FORCE PD DIRECT CONTACT IS AUTHORISED BETWEEN COMMANDING OFFICER CMA AAF STATION 102 CMA AND COMMANDING OFFICER CMA STATION 169 CMA WITH REGARD TO THE FERRYING OF AIRCRAFT TO AND FROM AAF STATION 169 PD SIX AIRCRAFT WILL BE DISPATCHED IMMEDIATELY CMA WEATHER PERMITTING FD ADDITIONAL AIRCRAFT WILL BE DISPATCHED AS DIRECTED BY COMMANDING OFFICER CMA AAF STATION 169 PD COMMANDING OFFICER CMA AAF STATION 102 CMA WILL DO ALL NECESSARY FERRYING OF AIRCRAFT TO AND FROM AAF STATION 169 PD IT IS REQUESTED THAT THE NINTH AIR FORCE SUBMIT A RECEIPT TO HQ EIGHTH AIR FORCE FOR ALL TEST AND SPECIAL RADIO EQUIPMENT RECEIVED PD AFTER REMOVAL OF THIS EQUIPMENT THE AIRCRAFT WILL RETURN TO AAF STATION 102 FOR REASSIGNMENT TO 1st BOMBARDMENT DIVISION STATIONS PD AS ADDITIONAL AIRCRAFT ARRIVE FROM UNITED STATES WITH SIMILAR SPECIAL RADIO EQUIPMENT THE AIRCRAFT WILL BE FERRIED TO AAF STATION 102 AND THEN TO AAF STATION 169 WHERE SPECIAL RADIO AND TEST EQUIPMENT WILL BE REMOVED AND RECEIPT OBTAINED IN SAME MANNER AS THE ABOVE AIRCRAFT TO BE TRANSFERRED COLON

SINGLE INSTALLATION	DUAL INSTALLATION
B-17's	B-17's
42-30328	42-3325
42-23385	42-31166
42-3521	42-97475
42-3527	B-24s
42-30613	42-28636
42-3382	42-28617
42-37753	42-28651
42-3536	42-28652
42-37735	42-28648
42-37733	

DOOLITTLE

THE ORDER TO TRANSFER B-17s and B-24s of 482nd BOMB GROUP FROM ALCONBURY (STA 102) TO THE NINTH AIR FORCE AT STANSTED (STA 169) FOR REMOVAL OF OBOE EQUIPMENT IN FEBRUARY 1944.

TABLE FOUR

HEADQUARTERS
AIR FORCES FIRST CONCENTRATION COMMAND
Union Central Life Insurance Annex
309 Vine Street
Cincinnati, Ohio

353.02 (Bolero)
(9-1-42

Auth: CG, AFFCC
Init:
Date
September 1, 1942

Airplane Loading list
Annex No 3 to Bolero Training Directive.

1. C-47 and C-53.

2. B-17F

Airplane Weight Empty (including armor plate)	35,225		
Gasoline - 2552 gals	15,312		
Oil - 144 gals	1,080		
		51,617	
Crew and Passengers (10)			
1 Pilot / 1 Asst Engineer			
1 Co-pilot / 1 Radio Operator			
1 Navigator / 1 Ass Radio Operator			
1 Bombardier / 1 Gunner			
1 Engineer / 1 Passenger			
Crew weight includes bail-out rations, parachute, steel helmet and 100lbs of baggage per man and personal armament, each officer having a .45 cal pistol weighing 3lbs, and all but one enlisted man having a 10lb .3 cal rifle or .30 M-1 Carbine. The other enlisted man is assigned the sub-machine gun listed below.		3,000	
Emergency Equipment			
2 off Liferafts (5 Man) W/O.W. Kit	316		
30 days emergency ration "E"	115		
45 Flares	33		
4 Thermos Jugs (Water)	56		
1 Bombay Fuel system	500		
		1,026	
Airplane Equipment			
1 .45 Cal Thompson sub-machine gun w/100 rds	21		
11 guns cal .50	869		
1 gun cal .30	32		
Ammunition, cal, .50 200 rds per gun	660		
Ammunition, cal, .30 - 200 rds per gun	13		
1 off kit Navigators	79		
Bomb Shackles, External B-9	60		
Bomb Slings	26		
Maintenance Equipment	300		
VHF, IFF radio equipment	74		
		2,134	
Total Weight			57,771
Max Gross take-off Weight			57,771
Max Gross Landing Weight			45,415

EQUIPMENT LIST AND WEIGHTS FOR B-17Fs DEPARTING OVER NORTH ATLANTIC 1942.

TABLE FIVE

APPROXIMATE MONTHLY B-17 PRODUCTION: JAN 1942 To MARCH 1944								
	B-17E	B-17F			B-17G			
1942	BOEING	BOEING	DOUGLAS	VEGA	BOEING	DOUGLAS	VEGA	TOTAL
JAN	74							74
FEB	75							75
MAR	88							88
APR	90							90
MAY	86	4						90
JUNE		95	2	2				99
JULY		100	4	3				107
AUG		110	6	5				121
SEP		120	8	9				137
OCT		130	8	12				150
NOV		130	18	15				163
DEC		160	39	22				221
1943 JAN		124	51	25				200
FEB		176	55	32				263
MAR		180	66	38				284
APR		190	85	52				327
MAY		201	79	65				345
JUNE		190	86	57				333
JULY		199	12	88		76		375
AUG		190		75		94	34	393
SEP		1			199	80	110	390
OCT					210	90	117	417
NOV					219	87	107	413
DEC					243	95	103	441
1944 JAN					265	99	105	469
FEB					299	110	99	508
MAR					375	104	107	586
	413	2,300	519	500	1,810	835	782	7,159

TABLE SIX

Notes to the INDEX
Information on the aircraft assigned charts in Part Two is not included in the index listings.
Groups assigned to the First Bombardment Wing/Division are not included in the index.
The airfields listed in Table One are not included in the airfield index on page 317.

Individual Aircraft Names

Name, Serial Number, Group, Page. All entries are B-17s unless stated otherwise.

ADORABLE, 41-24476, 306BG 233
AINT IT GRUESOME, 42-29863, 351BG 255
ALABAMA EXTERMINATOR, 41-9022, 97BG 229
ALABAMA WHIRLWING, 42-3259, 384BG 242
ALI QUIPPA, 42-3184, 92BG 240
ALOHA, 42-31055, 303BG 264
ALSO RAN-STILL RUNNING, 42-39820, 401BG 279
AMOTOL, 42-29848, 351BG 254
ANNIE FREEZE, 41-24500, 381BG 234
ANNIHILATOR; THE, 42-29859, 351BG 254
ANY TIME ANNIE, 42-30422, 305BG 260
A.O.G. NOT IN STOCK, 42-5788, 303BG 247
APRIL GIRL, 42-3523, 351BG 244
APRIL GIRL II, 42-38038, 351BG 276
APRILS FOOL, 42-3122, 384BG 63, 240
ARCHI BALL, 42-39848, 351BG 280
ARGONAUT, 42-29817, 351BG 254
ARGONAUT I, 42-29821, 351BG 254
ARGONAUT III, 42-29851, 351BG 84, 254
ARISTOCRAP, 42-37817, 351BG 274
ARKY, 42-29553, 305BG 250
AUGERHEAD, 42-29635, 303BG 250

BABS BEST, 42-29779 253
BABY LU III, 42-39765, 401BG 277
BACTA-TH'SAC, 42-3540, 381BG 244
BAD CHECK, 41-24587, 303BG 105, 159, 166, 236
BAD EGG, 41-24484, 91BG 166, 233
BADLAND BAT, 42-31521, 401BG 268
BAD PENNY, 41-24480, 91BG 29, 233
BAD PENNY, 42-39904, 401BG 280
BAD PENNY; THE, 42-31200, 303BG 265
BALLS OF FIRE, B-24, 41-23667, 93BG 286
BANSHEE, 42-37841, 303BG 274
BANSHEE II, 41-24488, 306BG 174, 234
BARREL HOUSE BESSIE, 42-5051, 384BG 244
BAREL HOUSE BESSIE, 42-29985, 384BG 257
BATTLE WAGON, 42-30026, 384BG 206, 258
BATTLIN BETTY, 42-39847, 401BG 280
BATTLIN BOMB SPRAYER, 42-29958, 381BG 257
BATTLIN B, 42-29677, 306BG 251
BEARDED BEAUTY; THE, 41-24453, 91BG 233
BEATS ME, 41-24567, 303BG 236
BEDLAM BALL, 42-38153, 351BG 187, 277
BELLE OF SAN JOAQUIN, 42-5054, 303BG 244
BELLE OF THE BAYOUS, 42-29749, 351BG 252
BELLE OF THE BRAWL, 42-31690, 306BG 269
BELL OF THE BALL, 42-39857, 351BG 280
BERLIN SLEEPER, 41-24370, 97BG 232
BERMONDSEY, 42-37792, 384BG 274
BERMONDSEY BATTLER, 42-39895, 381BG 280
BETSY, 42-31794, 305BG 271
BEFTTY J, 42-31072, 401BG 264
BETTY JANE, 42-32027, 303BG 271
BIG A BIRD, 42-39810, 303BG 279
BIG BITCH; THE, 41-9121, 97BG/351BG 231
BIG MOOSE, 42-29870, 305BG 255
BIG PUNK, 41-9030, 97BG 229

BIG STOOP, 41-9101, 97BG 294
BIG STUPE, 42-37816, 384BG 274
BIG TIME OPERATOR, 42-29789, 381BG 253
BILLIE KAY, 42-5787, 91BG 247
BIRMINGHAM BLITZKREIG, 41-9100, 97BG 230
BLACK BITCH; THE, 42-39914, 351BG 280
BLACK DIAMOND EXPRESS, 41-24416, 303BG 232
BLACK GHOST, 42-5843, 384BG 248
BLACK MAGIC, 42-31721, 351BG 270
BLACK PUFF POLLY, GEORGIA PEACH, 42-97067, 457BG 281
BLACK SWAN, 42-29895, 91BG 255
BLACK SWAN, 42-29641, 305BG 251
BLASTED EVENT, B-24, 41-23682, 93BG 286
BLOND BOMBER, 42-3057, 91BG 239
BLOWIN BESSIE, 42-30852 262
BLUE DREAMS, 42-37761, 91BG 273
BOBBIE ANNE, 42-97196, 351BG 282
BOBBY T, 42-30722, 381BG 261
BOCH BUSTER, 42-31087, 401BG 264
BOEING'S BEST, 42-31342, 305BG 266
BOLEVICH; THE, 42-30191, 379BG 259
BOMBOOGIE, 42-5763, 91BG 247
BOMERANG, B-24D, 41-23722, 93BG 286
BONNIE B, 42-31483, 303BG 268
BONNIE DONNIE, 42-31034, 401BG 263
BOOMERANG, 41-9148, 997BG 231
BOOMERANG, 41-24377, 97BG 31, 33, 233
BOOMERANG, 41-24611, 305BG 39, 237
BOSTON TEA PARTY, 42-5738, 92BG 246
BOW UR NECK STEVE'S, 42-97260, 303BG 283
BREEZING HOME, 42-40002, 401BG 281
BROADWAY ROSE, 42-3440, 384BG 243
BUCKET O'BOLTS, 42-39798, 381BG 279
BUCKEYE BABY, 42-31384, 351BG 267
BUCK SHOT, 42-29861, 351BG 254
BUNDLES FOR BERLIN, 92BG 149
BUTCHER SHOP, 41-2578, 97BG 229
BUZZING BRONCO, 42-29944, 303BG 256

CABIN IN THE SKY, 42-39784, 384BG 279
CALAMITY JANE, 241
CANNON BALL, 42-5812, 351BG 248
CANNON BAL, 42-39834, 351BG 280
CAPTAIN BILL, 42-3272, 351BG 242
CAREFULL VIRGIN, 41-24639, 91BG 59, 140, 238
CAROL DAWN, 42-37805, 379BG 274
CAROLINA QUEEN, 42-378090, 401BG 274
CAROLYNE, 42-31089, 401BG 264
CASA DE EMBRIAGOS, 42-31725, 351BG 270
CASED ACE, 42-29632, 384BG 250
CAT O'NINE TAILS, 42-5482, 303BG 246
CAVALIER, 42-3301, 306BG 242
CAWN'T MISS, 42-31116, 401BG 264
CELHALOPOOS, B-24D, 41-23675, 93BG 286

CENSORED, 42-29858, 351BG 254
CENTAUR, 42-29555, 305BG 74, 250
CHANNEL EXPRESS, 42-37835, 401BG 95, 274
CHANNEL EXPRESS III, 42-40050, 401BG 281
CHAPS FLYING CIRCUS, 42-30029, 381BG 200, 258
CHARLEY HORSE, 42-29571, 303BG 250
CHATTERBOX, 42-31899, 351BG 271
CHENNAULTS PAPPY, 41-24496, 306BG 234
CHENNAULTS PAPPY, 42-3172, 91BG 240
CHEROKEE GIRL, 42-29839, 351BG 254
CHICAGO, 42-5741, 92BG 247
CHIEF SLY, 41-24439, 91BG 36, 233
CHIEF SLY II, 42-5139, 91BG 245
CHIEF SLY'S SON, 42-31076, 91BG 264
CHIQUITA, 42-39947, 305BG 281
CHOW HOUND, 42-31367, 91BG 266
CHUG A LUG, 42-30765, 381BG 95, 261, 262
CHUG-A-LUG-LULU, 42-3225, 381BG 241
CLOVER LEAF, 42-31583, 303BG 269
COMMAND PERFORMANCE, 42-31508, 401BG 268
CONCHO CLIPPER; THE, 42-29838, 351BG 254
CONNECTICUT YANKEE, 42-2970, 91BG 238
COUP DE GRACE, 42-29762, 351BG 252
CUE BALL, 42-30790, 351BG 262

DAILEY'S MAIL, 42-39843, 305BG 280
DAKOTA DEMON, 42-5737, 92BG 246
DALLAS REBEL, 42-29814, 384BG 254
DAME SATAN, 42-2990, 91BG 238
DAMFINO, 42-3220, 381BG 241, 242
DAMN YANKEE, 41-24557, 384BG 235
DAMN YANKEE II, 42-29809, 384BG 253
DANELIEN, 41-24432, 91BG 233
DANGEROUS DAN, 42-29891, 379BG 255
DANIEL WEBSTER, 42-97142, 384BG 282
DEARLY BELOVED, 42-29666, 306BG 251
DEAR MOM, 42-38168, 303BG 277
DEE MARIE, 42-97076, 457BG 282
DELAYED LADY, 42-97460, 457BG 282
DELAYED LADY II, 42-32079, 457BG 272
DELTA REBEL No 2, 42-5077, 91BG 33, 244
DESTINY'S CHILD, 42-31812, 91BG 271
DUECES WILD, 42-3222, 384BG 70, 241
DEVIL'S ANGEL, 42-29954, 381BG 256
DEVILS BALL, 42-31238, 351BG 265
DEVILS PLAYMATE, 42-5056, 305BG 244
DINAH MITE, 42-30704, 305BG 261
DIHAN MITE, 42-37719, 381BG 272
DINGLEBERRY KIDS, 42-97505, 306BG 284
DIXIE DEMO, 41-9103, 97BG 230
DO DO, 41-9105, 97BG 294
DOLIE MADISON, 42-5744, 92BG 69, 247
DOOLITTLE'S DESTROYERS, 42-31471, 303BG 268
DOOLITTLES DOUGHBOYS, 42-31518, 401BG 268
DORIS MAE, 42-3218, 384BG 206, 241

313

Place Names: Airfields in United Kingdom

Place Names: United Kingdom (except airfields)

Place Names: USA

Place Names: Germany and German Occupied Europe

Other Place Names